BUSCH, Briton Cooper. Mudros to Lausanne: Britain's frontier in West Asia, 1918–1923. State University of New York, 1976. 430p map bibl index 76-21641. 30.00 ISBN 0-87395-265-0. C.I.P.

With this book Busch completes a series of three volumes, which includes *Britain and the Persian Gulf, 1894–1914* (CHOICE, Mar. 1969) and *Britain, India, and the Arabs, 1914–1921* (CHOICE, Mar. 1972). He deals authoritatively with British diplomacy in Asia from the Straits to Afghanistan, using a wide range of manuscript collections, both public and private, most notably, perhaps, papers from the India Office. Although he largely ignores the domestic dimensions of foreign-policy making, Busch provides a mass of detail on the official side of British policy in western Asia. He offers a mine of information to scholars and advanced students interested in postwar Russia, Turkey, and the Mid-East, and in British diplomacy in regard to those areas. *Mudros to Lausanne* is a useful supplement to such diverse works as Harold Nicolson's *Curzon: the last phase* (1934) and R. H. Ullman's three-volume *Anglo-Soviet relations, 1917–1921* (v.2 and 3, CHOICE, Nov. 1968 and Nov. 1973). The book has an extensive bibliography and good index. The notes are where they should be in a scholarly work: at the bottom of the page.

MUDROS TO LAUSANNE: BRITAIN'S FRONTIER IN WEST ASIA, 1918-1923

Briton Cooper Busch

State University of New York Press, Albany, New York
1976

First published in 1976 by
State University of New York Press
99 Washington Avenue, Albany, New York 12210

Printed in the United States of America

Library of Congress Cataloging in Publication Data

Busch, Briton Cooper.
Mudros to Lausanne.

Bibliography: p.
Includes index.
1. Great Britain—Foreign relations—Near East.
2. Near East—Foreign relations—Great Britain.
3. Near East—History—20th century.
I. Title.
DS63.2.G7B86   327.41'056   76-21641
ISBN 0-87395-265-0

For
two friends and teachers
there at the beginning
but not the end
CHRISTINA PHELPS HARRIS
RAYMOND JAMES SONTAG

Contents

Maps

MAPS

Following
Page

Preface

"An examination of the years from 1918 to 1922 gives the impression of a journey through chaos," L.C.B. Seaman has written of post war Britain.[1] It is an apt characterization, for Britain was even less prepared for peace than for the devastating war which preceded it. One of the more striking changes which that peace brought in its wake was the sudden expansion of the British Empire in Asia. The Ottoman Empire lay defeated in war and torn by the revolt of the subject nationalities; the long-standing rivalry with Tsarist Russia, temporarily set aside through prewar agreements, was still in abeyance as Russia struggled through revolution and civil war. It was Britain which stood now as master in western Asia, limited only by certain pledges to her allies and to her friends.

Ironically, only vague or contradictory plans existed for utilizing this unexpected opportunity to establish a satisfactory new order in the Middle East. British policy was therefore often pragmatic and reactive, its influence flowing out to fill an apparent vacuum, retreating in the face of unforeseen new hostilities and dwindling resources. It is the ebb and flow of Britain's "frontier" in Asia, reaching physically from the Dardanelles to the Khyber and chronologically from the armistices of 1918 to the belated recognition of a new world in the Treaty of Lausanne in 1923, that is the principal subject of this book.

This work is also the final volume of a series. The first volume, *Britain and the Persian Gulf, 1894-1914,* dealt with the empire in its heyday when Britain achieved firm control over an area of considerable importance. The second, *Britain, India, and the Arabs, 1914-1921,* treated the growth of British influence and power in the Arab world immediately following World War I. In the present volume, I have been concerned with the non-Arab Middle East, and with the post-

1. Seaman, L. C. B., *Post-Victorian Britain, 1902-1951* (London, 1967), p. 107.

war era only. In each case, however, I have been anxious to explore the considerable contribution of India to policy making, both directly and through the India Office in London. India at the turn of the century had been imperial and imperious, urging the defense of India's approaches. Directly concerned through the Mesopotamian campaign, wartime India had suggestions for the future Middle East which differed substantially from those of Cairo or London—at least until India's share of responsibility for the area was largely reduced. In the postwar era, however, India responded in still another way. In a declining ratio directly related to distance from Indian frontiers, the intervention of India now helped shape policy throughout western Asia, but less as administrator than advisor. At times it was the secretary of state for India in London, not the government in India itself, which exerted this influence—but only the existence of the Indian empire made such intervention possible. When Afghanistan invaded India, when Soviet troops cut off a garrison in Enzeli, when a serious revolt took place in Iraq, or a disaster at Smyrna, or a confrontation with Kemalist forces at Chanak—on each occasion, India and the India Office at least had its opinion to offer.

Less startling than the fact of this influence is its nature. The defense of India was often assumed to be the justification for sending the Royal Navy to the Caspian or Indian troops to Merv, but it was, paradoxically, India which was least inclined to argue on behalf of this viewpoint. India was far more concerned with internal Indian problems, which in this era took the rare form of Hindu-Muslim nationalist collaboration. India (used throughout to mean the British government in India) was therefore more eager to argue against imperial ventures and for realistic concessions to nationalist forces so that policy in the Middle East could no longer provide Indian nationalists with a basis for attacking Britain. It was some time before the government of Lloyd George (in power for nearly the entire period covered in this work) was as willing to face up to the realistic relationship between Asian nationalism and British imperial strength. To that extent, this book, and this series, is about an awakening, beginning slowly at first in Britain, but developing with surprising suddenness in India, to the point where India assumed the leadership in pressing the new policy. It was only at Lausanne that the two divergent views were at last brought into harmony.

This work is based, like the two preceding volumes, primarily upon British archives, public and private, and above all those in the holdings of the Public Record Office and the India Office Library in London. A number of other sources have provided unpublished source material, and they are listed in the bibliography; in particular I have found the National Archives of India (New Delhi) to be of great use on internal events in India. Some of the raw material upon which the policy of the Foreign Office (but not necessarily that of other departments) was based has been published in the series *Documents on British Foreign Policy, 1919-1939.* For the sake of convenience, I have listed such documents when they have been published; in each case, however, I have consulted the original document files. In discussing internal events I have relied heavily on the excellent works recently produced by scholars of various areas, and my debt to these scholars (and apologies for interloping in their respective areas of expertise when I have felt that the subject might be treated differently) will be evident from the notes.

In a decade's research and writing, I have incurred a vast number of obligations. The interest and tolerance of my colleagues in the History Department of Colgate University have been unflagging. Without the support of the Colgate Research Council and the Humanities Faculty Development Fund administered by Colgate University the work would not have been possible. Research in India, in addition, was performed under an earlier grant from the Joint Committee on the Near and Middle East of the Social Science Research Council. The assistance received in a number of libraries was invaluable; special thanks in this respect are due Dr. R.J. Bingle and Mr. M.I. Moir of the India Office Records for their constant help over many years. I also thank Sir Philip Magnus-Allcroft, C.B.E., for making the Curzon Papers available; Capt. S.W. Roskill, for permitting me to examine the de Robeck Papers; Major Leonard Ridgway, M.B.E., for sharing his memories of postwar Constantinople; Ronald Herbst and Steven Silver, for various research tasks; Dean Wise for the maps; and my Colgate colleague, Professor John E. Rexine, for taking time from his busy schedule as associate dean of faculty to read and comment upon the manuscript. To my wife, who exhausted her own hard-earned vacation typing and editing the manuscript, for the third time, thanks.

comes from the Public Record Office, by permission of the controller
of H.M. Stationery Office; and the Lloyd George Papers by permission
of the director of the Beaverbrook Library, London.

Hamilton, New York   B.C.B.
June, 1975

I

War's End, 1918

On the 30th of October 1918, on board the British battleship *Agamemnon* anchored in Mudros harbor on the Aegean island of Lemnos, Vice-Admiral the Honourable Sir Somerset Gough-Calthorpe, British commander-in-chief of the Mediterranean Station, "acting under authority from the British Government, in agreement with their Allies," signed an armistice with accredited representatives of the Ottoman government.[1] Hostilities ceased at noon on the 31st. The next day a force of several dozen mine-sweepers, trawlers, drifters, and motor launches began the slow process of sweeping the mines, both Allied and Turkish, from the Dardanelles and its approaches; more than one ship was lost in this dangerous operation. On the morning of 7 November, Lieutenant-Colonel C.C.R. Murphy, deputized as advance Allied representative and sent up the Straits to board the Turkish destroyer *Basra* at Chanak, arrived at Galata Bridge wharf in Constantinople. His job was to begin arrangements for the repatriation of British prisoners-of-war, Turkish demobilization, and other steps necessary to fulfill the armistice.

By the 10th, the Straits were clear enough for British troops from the 28th Division (Salonika Force) to be landed to occupy the Dardanelles forts; on the 12th, an impressive Allied flotilla led by the British battleships H.M.S. *Superb, Temeraire, Lord Nelson,* and *Agamemnon,* preceded by cruisers and destroyers and followed at half-hour intervals by French, Italian, and Greek units, passed through the Dardanelles. The next day the lengthy line of ships rounded Seraglio Point in the early morning and steamed slowly and in silence to the Bosporus, each fleet going to its assigned anchorage while four large British destroyers

---

[1] Great Britain, Parliamentary Papers, Cmd. 53 (1919). "Terms of the Armistices Concluded between the Allied Governments and the Governments of Germany, Austria-Hungary, and Turkey."

patrolled the Bosporus itself. On the 14th, formal entry was made by the third battalion, the Middlesex Regiment; on the 13th, the first French troops had already disembarked, to be followed in the coming weeks and months by Italians, Greeks, and Serbs. The Turkish war was over.[2]

Constantinople was not under formal occupation: the armistice had provided for the opening of the Straits, but negotiations had bogged down on occupation; Turkish complaints of the size of the Allied force were answered with the bald statement that only a headquarters detachment had been landed. Article Seven of the armistice, moreover, conferred "the right to occupy any strategic points in the event of a situation arising which threatens the security of the Allies"—sufficiently vague wording to allow occupation of any part of Turkey. This article was soon invoked by Lieutenant-General Sir William Marshall, General Officer Commanding British Forces, Mesopotamia, who ordered his forward units to push on at once to Mosul, although his troops were more than ten miles south of that important provincial capital when news of the armistice reached his Baghdad headquarters on the evening of 1 November. The commander of the Turkish VI Army at Mosul

[2] Based upon Gwynne Dyer, "The Turkish Armistice of 1918," *Middle East Studies,* 8 (1972): 143-78, 316-48; Lt.-Col. C.C.R. Murphy, *Soldiers of the Prophet* (London, 1921), pp. 222-25; E. Keble Chatterton, *Seas of Adventures: The Story of the Naval Operations in the Mediterranean and Aegean* (London, 1936), pp. 312-13; Sir Frederick Maurice, *The Armistices of 1918* (London, 1943), p. 23; Caleb Gates, *Not to Me Only* (Princeton, N.J., 1940), p. 245; Col. D.I. Shuttleworth, "Turkey from the Armistice to the Peace," *Journal of the Central Asian Society* 11 (1924): 51-67; Brig.-Gen. Sir James E. Edmonds, "The Occupation of Constantinople 1918-1923," Memorandum for Historical Section, War Cabinet Secretariat, 27 September 1944, War Office files, Public Record Office, London, series 161 (miscellaneous unregistered files), volume 85 [hereafter *WO* 161/85]; and Commander-in-Chief, [British Naval Forces in the] Mediterranean [CinC Med] to Secretary of the Admiralty, 10 December 1918, Foreign Office files, series 371, volume 4166 [hereafter *FO* 371/4166]. Documents are normally filed chronologically by volume in this series, with the entire volume devoted to the same subject; for this reason, the registry numbers assigned to each individual document will be given in these notes only where some difficulty might otherwise be encountered in tracing the document; where document numbers are included, the initial letter (identifying the department) and final number (identifying the country) have been omitted as redundant, since the *FO* volume number is always given.

withdrew only under protest. The town was occupied on the 3rd, but the last Turkish soldiers were not withdrawn until the 15th. Both civil and military British authorities in Baghdad had urged that Mosul would be an essential, constituent part of British-administered Iraq, but Marshall had been given no orders to this effect, and, according to his own later account, was never quite certain that his action might not be disowned. The problem, as he was well aware, was not Turkish recalcitrance but allied susceptibilities, for in the famous Sykes-Picot Agreement with France of 1916 the bulk of the Mosul vilayet (province) had been assigned to the French sphere. Still, inter-allied division of the spoils could be made later; the important thing was to push the Turks back.[3]

The sudden collapse of Turkey had come as something of a shock, and the Allies could take great satisfaction in the fact that the Straits were open, the capital of the once-great Ottoman Empire occupied, and Turkish forces in Palestine and Iraq defeated and driven back to the very gates of Anatolia. All that was now necessary was to make a

[3] In addition to the source listed in note 1, chapter 1, the text of the armistice (but not of the preamble) is given in J.C. Hurewitz, *Diplomacy in the Near and Middle East: A Documentary Record* (Princeton, N.J., 1956), II, pp. 36-37. On the last stages of the Mesopotamian campaign, see Great Britain, Committee of Imperial Defence, *The Campaign in Mesopotamia, 1914-1918,* compiled by Brig.-Gen. F.J. Moberley, IV (London, 1927); Lt.-Col. A.H. Burne, *Mesopotamia, the Last Phase* (Aldershot, 1936); and Lt.-Gen. Sir William Marshall, *Memories of Four Fronts* (London, 1929), pp. 324-25; Marshall was franker in his letters to his brother, particularly that of 4 November 1918, *Marshall Papers,* Centre for Military Archives, King's College, London. The possible role of oil in the occupation of Mosul is discussed in Helmut Mejcher, "Oil and British Policy towards Mesopotamia, 1914-18," *Middle East Studies,* 8 (1972): 377-92. Details of the last movements are in India Office [IO] to Foreign Office [FO], 29 October, enclosing Commissioner, Baghdad, telegrams to Secretary of State for India [SSI] with reply of 2 November and FO minutes, *FO* 371/3384; and CinC Med telegram to Admiralty, 4 November, and Admiralty telegram to CinC Med, 5 November 1918, *FO* 371/3416. For an interesting much later exchange on the details of the Mosul armistice, see Curzon telegram to FO, 20 January 1923, and other documents in file 832/1, *FO* 371/9060.

On the Sykes-Picot agreement, see Briton Cooper Busch, *Britain, India, and the Arabs, 1914-1921* (Berkeley, 1971), Ch. II and IV, for further references. The text itself is in Hurewitz, *Diplomacy,* II, pp. 18-22, and Dyer, "Turkish Armistice," 340-41.

satisfactory peace. A momentary euphoria gripped those who shared in this great victory, particularly those who had the capacity to conjure up visions of crusading knights, Cross against Crescent, and the age-old Christian European dream of expelling the Turkish interloper. That euphoria turned to bitterness as peace—other than on paper—proved impossible of achievement for five long and difficult years. When it came, moreover, it in no way resembled the vision of the policymakers of 1918. The reasons for that delay, so interminable to those who experienced it, are complex and numerous, but more than one strand of the complicated knot is to be found in the history and terms of the armistice of Mudros itself.

MUDROS

Although several attempts were made during the war to lure the Turks away from the Central Powers through negotiation or bribery, it was not until the collapse of Bulgaria in late September 1918 that there seemed any serious possibility of Ottoman surrender.[4] Events had gone badly for the Turks in Palestine and Iraq for some time; but the Caucasus provided a different story following the breakdown of Russian military efforts, and the heartland of Antolia itself had not been directly touched by the fighting. While the prospect of carrying the war to Turkey proper had been dismal, that of freeing resources for use against Germany and Austria-Hungary (particularly if this would shore up the cracking Russian front) was so brilliant that any Turkish overtures had to be considered. The first gestures, vague and unau-

[4] For earlier negotiations, see David Lloyd George, *War Memoirs* (London, [1938]), I, p. 1490; Arthur J. Marder, *From the Dreadnought to Scapa Flow* (London, 1965), II, p. 217n.; Lord Beaverbrook, *Men and Power, 1917-1918* (N.Y., 1956), pp. 193f.; Frank G. Weber, *Eagles on the Crescent: Germany, Austria, and the Diplomacy of the Turkish Alliance, 1914-1918* (Ithaca, N.Y., 1970), pp. 133-34; Stephen Roskill, *Hankey, Man of Secrets* (London, 1970), I, pp. 159, 237, 417, 466-67; M.S. Anderson, *The Eastern Question, 1774-1923: A Study in International Relations* (N.Y., 1966), p. 348; Admiral Sir William James, *The Eyes of the Navy: A Biographical Study of Admiral Sir Reginald Hall* (London, 1955), pp. 61-64.

thorized, came in early October 1918 and required some sort of answer to anticipate a formal and official approach.[5]

The most urgent question was whether the Turks should be offered an immediate peace treaty or simply a military armistice. The War Cabinet in London, many of whom knew how complex inter-allied relations on the Ottoman question were, chose to accept the happy precedent Bulgaria offered and conclude a military armistice, leaving all other issues for the future. The War Office, in collaboration with the Admiralty, was already drafting a Turkish armistice which concentrated on opening the Straits, controlling their defenses, and securing the strategic Turkish railway system (particularly the Taurus tunnels).[6]

Some members of the Foreign Office, however, realized that a simple military armistice was inevitably also a political document, even though it did no more than specify areas of occupation. Arnold Toynbee, then a junior Foreign Office clerk, pointed out several issues, including the long-standing problem of Armenia. The Armenian minority in Turkey had suffered disastrously in the war, but only with the war's end could anything be done for that oppressed people. To forego mention of the problem of the six vilayets of Bitlis, Erzerum, Diarbekir, Kharput, Sivas, and Van in eastern Turkey where Armenians were to be found (or, more properly, had been found before decimation and dispersal) would be morally undesirable and would bring a storm of hostile world criticism.[7] Armenia was overshadowed, however, by the more general question of how the Allies would dispose of the Ottoman Empire as a whole. Since possession of Constantinople and the other important ports and military centers would play a major role, their occupation was more than a military matter. Sir Eyre Crowe, assistant undersecretary

[5] Rumbold (Berne) telegram to FO, 1 October, FO telegram to Rumbold, 3 October 1918, and other documents in file 165564, *FO* 371/3448.

[6] War Cabinet 481A, 2 October 1918, Cabinet Records, Public Record Office, series 23, volume 14 [hereafter *CAB* 23/14].

[7] Arnold Toynbee minute on draft terms, 3 October 1918, 166382/ 165564, *FO* 371/3448; on the background of Armenia, see the works of Richard G. Hovannisian, particularly "The Allies and Armenia, 1915-18," *Journal of Contemporary History* 3 (Jan. 1968): 145-68; and *Armenia on the Road to Independence, 1918* (Berkeley, 1967). Definitions of "Armenia" may be found particularly in Hovannisian's *The Republic of Armenia* (Berkeley, 1971), I, p. 8, and Great Britain, Foreign Office, Historical Section, *Peace Handbooks,* no. 62 ("Armenia and Kurdistan") (London, 1920), p. 1.

with an influential voice in Foreign Office policymaking, represented an important strand of opinion when he noted that the occupation of Constantinople would be an excellent beginning, "if, as I understand, our policy is to get rid of the Turk once for all out of Europe."[8]

Nor was such discussion left to Foreign Office officials. Prime Minister David Lloyd George, in a Cabinet meeting on 3 October, expressed the view that a quick peace would settle the problem of Mesopotamia. His colleagues, however, reminded him that he had already stated that the future of such areas would be settled by the inevitable peace conference, and that any quick solution of the future of Mesopotamia would initiate a major dispute over the Sykes-Picot agreement. That very day the French ambassador in London had insisted on the validity of this agreement despite British attempts to modify or eliminate it. The Cabinet had no choice but to approve the War Office-Admiralty armistice draft as amended by the Foreign Office.[9]

So far the British seemed to be keeping in close communication with France, and the chance that one ally would cut and run for his own advantage in the last days of the war seemed remote. No disagreement was evident even when Lloyd George tried out his idea of a quick peace on the French and Italian premiers (Clemenceau and Orlando) and foreign ministers (Pichon and Sonnino) at an inter-Allied conference at Paris on 6 October. These leaders soon impressed upon Lloyd George that wartime inter-Allied pledges and agreements, particularly the Constantinople Agreement of 1915 (which gave Constantinople and the Straits to Russia) and the agreement of Saint-Jean de Maurienne of 1917 (which promised Italy a share of the spoils in western Turkey under certain conditions), would have to be reconciled and harmonized. Sonnino went even further, raising the specter of President Wilson, who, he implied, would want a voice in the future Turkish settlement (the point had not escaped Lloyd George). The alternative, then, was armistice, and the British draft, which Lloyd George had on hand, was approved with only minor changes. There was no reference to Armenia, but the next day an article (Article Twenty-Four in the final version) was added which reserved to the Allies the right to occupy the six eastern vilayets in case of disorder and stipulated that the Allies would

---

[8] Crowe minute, 4 October 1918, 166382/165564, *FO* 371/3448.
[9] War Cabinet 482A, 3 October, and appendix, *CAB* 23/14; Roskill, *Hankey,* I, p. 606; Cecil note for Balfour, 3 October 1918, *FO* 371/3448.

also occupy the four Cilician towns of Sis, Hanjam, Zeitun, and Aintab in southwestern Anatolia. Cilicia too was an area of Armenian settlement and aspirations. After final approval the terms were telegraphed to General Allenby in Palestine, for he was expected to receive the initial Turkish overtures.[10]

The Turks preferred a less orthodox method of contacting the enemy. Perhaps because he was near at hand, perhaps because his use left no chance for intervention by Turkish field commanders, perhaps because they hoped for better terms, the Turkish authorities turned to their highest ranking prisoner-of-war, Major-General Sir Charles Townshend, who had been taken at the surrender of Kut al-Amara in Iraq in 1916 and was held on Prinkipo Island in the Sea of Marmora—in better times, a holiday resort. On 17 October, Townshend was brought to Constantinople and asked by Ahmed Izzet Pasha, grand vizier and head of a newly constituted (14 October) Turkish government, if he would help in arranging terms. Townshend, eager to get back under the British flag, and with an exalted estimate of his own abilities, accepted, a decision which placed him in a very invidious position and subsequently finished any military career which he might have had. By the 20th he had appeared at Mitilini on Lesbos, and news of the Turkish overture was cabled out. Townshend, moving on to Mudros, urged the need for speed, but the Ottoman authorities were told there could be no negotiation without authorized representatives. On the 26th, the Turks managed to produce at Mudros a three-man delegation headed by Rauf Bey [Hüseyin Rauf Orbay], minister of marine, and accredited to Admiral Gough-Calthorpe only. Whether by design or not, such disregard of the French was well calculated to upset the delicate balance of Anglo-French relations in that part of the world.[11]

[10] Allied Conferences IC 77 and 79, 6 and 7 October, *CAB* 28/5; Chief of the Imperial General Staff [CIGS] telegram to Allenby, 8 October 1918, *FO* 371/3448; Hovannisian, *Republic,* I, pp. 55-58. For text of the Constantinople and Saint-Jean de Maurienne agreements, Hurewitz, *Diplomacy,* II, pp. 7-11, 23-25.

[11] On Townshend and his role, see the not entirely satisfactory biography by A.J. Barker, *Townshend of Kut: A Biography . . .* (London, 1967); Maj.-Gen. Sir Charles Townshend, "Great Britain and the Turks," *Asia* (N.Y.) 12 (Dec. 1922): 949-55; and Lt.-Col. C. à Court Reprington, *The First World War, 1914-1918: Personal Experiences of . . .* (London, 1920), II, p. 476, Mitilini telegram to War Office [WO], 20 October 1918, *WO* 106/1433; WO to FO, 21 November 1921, *FO* 371/6478.

When news of the new Turkish approach reached the Cabinet, Lloyd George quickly seized upon the advantages a separate Anglo-Turkish agreement would offer for future British power and prestige in the Middle East. In a Cabinet meeting on the 21st, he urged that the French had similar designs, as shown by their persistent claims of superior authority for General Louis Franchet d'Espérey, Allied commander of the Salonika Force, and their reluctance to agree that British forces would spearhead the land march on Constantinople which still had appeared to be necessary in the negotiations at Paris two weeks before. There were other valid reasons for a quick end to the Turkish war, however unusual the Turkish approach, or, as Foreign Secretary Balfour put it, however badly Townshend had acted. Access to the Straits was the essential benefit to be gained; above all, as Lieutenant-General Sir Henry Wilson, Chief of the Imperial General Staff, had urged in a memorandum, there now glittered the glorious prospect of opened Straits, command of the Black Sea, operations on the Danube, renewed Rumanian participation in the war, and the collapse of Austria-Hungary.[12] For these reasons Admiral Gough-Calthorpe was told to go ahead with negotiations on the basis of the terms agreed to at Paris; on the 22nd he received a list of twenty-four articles in order of precedence with flexibility to discard the last twenty if essential to achieve the first four: opening and clearing of the Straits and Straits fortifications (Articles One, Two, and Three) and release of prisoners-of-war (Article Four). So important was control of the Straits, in other words, that Turkish demobilization, intervention in Armenia or the Caucasus, and Turkish withdrawal from Persia would all be thrown overboard if necessary to achieve it.[13]

This decision was not arrived at without a struggle; four Cabinet meetings gave priority of discussion to the several dangers inherent in the orders. Lord Curzon (lord President of the Council) was especially

[12] War Cabinet, 489A, 21 October, *CAB* 23/14; CIGS memorandum, 21 October 1918, *WO* 106/1433; Maj.-Gen. Sir C.E. Callwell, *Field-Marshal Sir Henry Wilson . . .* (London, 1927), II pp. 139-41; Wilson was Lt.-Gen. until his promotion to Field-Marshal in July 1919 (p. 206). On Salonika and Franchet d'Espérey, see Alan Palmer, *The Gardeners of Salonika* (London, 1965), and Général Paul Azan, *Franchet d'Espérey* (Paris, 1949).

[13] Admiralty telegram to CinC Med, 22 October, *FO* 371/3448; War Cabinet 489B, 22 October 1918, *CAB* 23/14.

concerned lest the advantages of complete victory be dissipated in order to achieve immediate passage of the Straits. Significantly, he saw four items of importance: first, if the Turks were not forced by the armistice terms to evacuate Arab areas, particularly northern Syria, it would be most difficult to dislodge them subsequently as required by pledges made to the Arabs; second, the same considerations applied to Turkish forces in occupation of the Caucasus and northwest Persia (Azerbaijan); third, opinion in India, already of some importance in the Middle Eastern war and soon to play an even greater role, would be gravely disappointed; finally, there was still Armenia to be considered. To these arguments there could be no real answer except that open Straits meant new pressures on Austria and Germany. The Allied presence in Constantinople would be quite enough, said Lloyd George, to ensure that the Turks would do what the Allies wanted in Armenia—a viewpoint which Balfour shared. Curzon's suggestion that Gough-Calthorpe be told to do his best to secure all the terms was turned down in the meeting of the 26th.[14]

There was another problem which had also been brushed aside: on the 23rd, Lord Derby, British ambassador in Paris, reported that in the French view Gough-Calthorpe's instructions amounted to a revision of the terms agreed upon. The next day, a formal French note went on to point out that Gough-Calthorpe was not Allied commander-in-chief in that area and was not empowered to undertake direct negotiations with the Turks. Even if he had that authority, prior Allied agreement would be essential.[15] The problem of command was actually rather complicated—and very sensitive. Franchet d'Espérey was field commander in the Balkans, but General Sir George Milne was designated commander of the force moving on Constantinople. Allenby was Allied commander in Palestine, and there was no formal Salonika-Palestine demarcation line (none was required until the armistice issue arose). But the Turks had approached Gough-Calthorpe, British commander-in-chief in the Mediterranean. In fact, Gough-Calthorpe was subordinate to French Vice-Admiral D.M. Gauchet, Allied naval commander

[14] War Cabinet 489A, 490A, 491A, 491B, 21, 24, 25, and 26 October 1918, *CAB* 23/14.

[15] Derby telegram to FO, 24 October, *FO* 371/3448, and Derby private to Balfour, 23 October 1918, *Balfour Papers* (British Museum), Add. Mss. 49744.

for the Mediterranean, according to a prewar agreement which gave to Britain commander over the North Sea and to France the Mediterranean.[16]

Nevertheless, when the Turkish delegates had arrived at Mudros, Gough-Calthorpe had assumed charge of five days of hard negotiations. The Turks were concerned primarily to see as little of their country as possible occupied—a natural enough desire—and, above all, none by Greeks or Italians. They hoped to avoid the occupation of Constantinople in particular, recognizing the psychological and political effects of such an occupation. Armenia, of course, should not be given any special treatment. To these objections, Gough-Calthorpe made what he considered to be minor concessions. He was willing, for example, to assure the delegates that only British and French troops would occupy the Dardanelles forts, although no further assurances could be given about Greek and Italian occupation elsewhere. Constantinople was not specified for occupation; on the other hand, it could be occupied under any of several terms, such as Article Seven. With regard to Armenia, the Turkish suggestion of a British commission to study the situation on the spot was refused; but while Article Twenty-Four gave Britain the right to occupy the six vilayets "in case of further disorder," the reference to the four specific Cilician towns was removed, thereby reducing, at least in Armenian eyes, the chances of including Cilicia in any future Armenia.[17]

Gough-Calthorpe had done well, considering the strong British desire to see an armistice concluded at once, for the Cabinet was willing to give up much more than he had surrendered. It should be added that he was at the same time fending off a French assult to share in the negotiations and signature with the argument that the Turks were only accredited to himself. The British Admiral was understandably worried,

[16] Undated memorandum (December, 1918), Director of Military Intelligence [DMI], *WO* 106/1389; see also Hovannisian, *Republic,* I, p. 57. Problems of Mediterranean command are discussed in Marder, *From the Dreadnought,* V, pp. 20-30.

[17] CinC Med (Mudros) telegram to Admiralty, 25 October, Admiralty Records, Public Record Office, series 1, volume 8541 [hereafter *ADM* 1/ 8541]; and telegrams of 28 and 31 October, and letter to Rauf Bey, 31 October 1918, *FO* 371/3449; Hovannisian, *Road,* pp. 238-40.

since the local French commander told him that everything would have to be referred to Paris in any case.[18]

The French were not pleased, but Lloyd George pointed out that they had not asked the British commander about the Bulgarian armistice; hardly a parallel, responded Clemenceau, for Franchet d'Espérey was in command of the theater involved. Lloyd George, at his best in this sort of exchange, flashed back that the French did not rush in when it was a question of fighting Turks, only when it was a matter of signing an armistice. If it was going to be a question of the Allies all having to participate in negotiations on every front, Britain would require its say in France, in Italy, in the Balkans. Pichon, with Gallic logic, insisted that each commander-in-chief would have to end the fighting on his respective front. Balfour managed to save French face—for Lloyd George was not going to give on this matter—by the specious argument that the armistice really referred to the Straits, the Black Sea, and Turkey, and not at all to the Mediterranean. The *fait accompli* was accepted, but it was by no means the end of the command problem, which was again to fray tempers as symbolic of the respective positions of the powers involved.[19]

The team of Lloyd George and Gough-Calthorpe had emerged victorious. There might be grumbles from the military, or the Italians, or the Greeks, and alarm among Armenian leaders, but in the Cabinet and the world at large there was jubilation at the surrender of yet another enemy. Curzon could not conceal his great relief at terms much better than he had anticipated.[20] With the Straits clear and British troops in

[18] Admiralty to FO, 1 December 1919, enclosing Gough-Calthorpe to Admiralty, 3 November 1918, enclosing in turn Amet to Gough-Calthorpe and Gough-Calthorpe to Amet, both 28 October 1918, 157330/136945, *FO* 371/4237; Roskill, *Hankey,* I, p. 622. David Walder, *The Chanak Affair* (London, 1969), p. 55, is in error in noting that the French lack of signature was simply an oversight by Gough-Calthorpe.

[19] Allied conference IC 84, 30 October 1918, *CAB* 28/5. This account is also based on Great Britain, Committee of Imperial Defence, Historical Section, *Naval Operations,* compiled by Sir Julian S. Corbett, VI [1927], pp. 351-56; Harry R. Rudin, *Armistice 1918* (New Haven, Conn., 1944), pp. 191-92, 410-11; Maurice, *Armistices,* pp. 17-21; Lloyd George, *War Memoirs,* II, pp. 1974-77; Augusté Gauvain, "Five Years of French Policy in the Near East," *Foreign Affairs* 3 (1924): 277-92. The text of the Mudros armistice is in Hurewitz, *Diplomacy,* pp. 36-37.

[20] War Cabinet 494A, 31 October 1918, *CAB* 23/14.

Constantinople, a new day had dawned. As if the poisition were not safe enough, Gough-Calthorpe's terms set the stage for Turkish withdrawal from the Allied occupation of the Caucasus. Once again it was time to consider the situation in that corner of the world, which, however remote, had already seriously concerned the Allied war planners.

THE CAUCASUS

The first Russian Revolution of 1917 brought hope that a liberal and progressive regime might instill new energy into the flagging Russian military operations. The second, November, revolution brought despair as the Bolsheviks assumed control where they could and proceeded to close down an already languishing war effort. Disorganization at the center both caused and justified the powerful centrifugal forces that came into play as competing national and political elements fought first for control and then for survival. Collapsing Russian lines presented the prospect that Germany might gain control of the rich provinces of southern Russia; possession of the Ukraine would at the least negate all the energy expended in the close blockade of the Central Powers. It was for this reason, initially, that the Allies intervened in Russia. Other motives were to come, but the pioneering work of recent scholars has demonstrated that at first intervention had little to do with hostility to the revolutionary regime.[21]

The collapse of Russian government made it appear that any policy which continued to treat Russia as a functioning monolith would fail to achieve the continuance of the war. British policymakers were convinced that war efforts and empire alike might be jeopardized by the new situation, particularly in the light of events in the Caucasus. After a Turkish advance in 1915, Russian armies had swept into Turkish territory early the following year, capturing Erzerum (February), Trebizond (April), and Erzincan (July). The Turks countered with an offensive against the Russian presence in Persia; in June-July 1916 they took Khanikin, Kermanshah, and Hamadan. The Russians recaptured the

[21] A number of works referring to Russian intervention and the civil war will be found in the bibliography. I have found most useful the three volumes by Richard H. Ullman, *Anglo-Soviet Relations, 1917-1921* (Princeton, N.J., 1961-72), and George A. Brinkley, *The Volunteer Army and Allied Intervention in South Russia, 1917-1921 . . .* (Notre Dame, Ind., 1966).

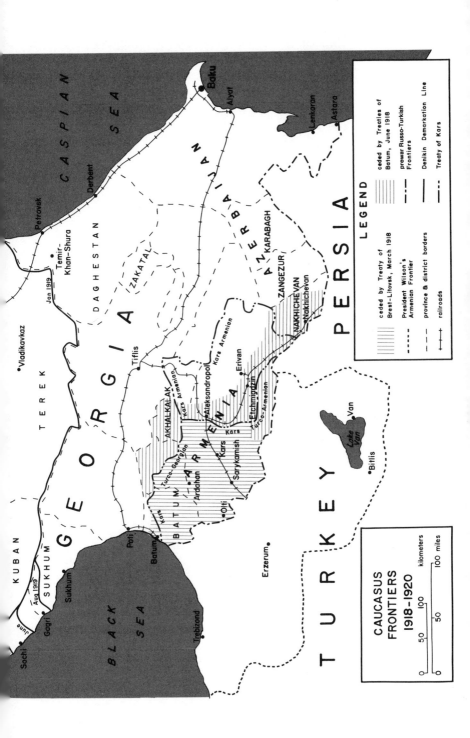

LEGEND

▨ ceded by Treaty of Brest-Litovsk, March 1918	▦ ceded by Treaties of Batum, June 1918
----- President Wilson's Armenian Frontier	┼┼┼ prewar Russo-Turkish Frontiers
— — province & district borders	━━━ Denikin Demarkation Line
✛✛✛ railroads	─··─ Treaty of Kars

CAUCASUS FRONTIERS 1918-1920

kilometers
0 50 100

0 50 100 miles

towns in March 1917, but in July one of the first effects of the Revolution was the withdrawal of Russian forces in western Persia toward the Persian port of Enzeli on the Caspian. The situation in the next half year was confused. The Turks had their hands full in Mesopotamia and Palestine, and events in the Caucasus tended in general to wait upon events in Russia, where the provisional government attempted to fight on through the summer and fall, until the second revolution of early November and the opening of the Russo-German peace conference at Brest-Litovsk in December. Not until March of 1918 was a settlement actually reached, but by this treaty Russia forfeited the Ukraine, and by May the Germans had occupied Kiev, Odessa, and Sebastapol.[22]

Russia was also made to sacrifice the districts of Ardahan, Kars, and Batum in the Caucasus and to withdraw its troops from Anatolia and Persia; but even before the treaty of Brest-Litovsk the Transcaucasian Commissariat ("Zavkom," established in November 1917), in the absence of clear-cut central authority, had taken the first step toward separatism by negotiating a local armistice with the Turks which lasted from mid-December 1917 to mid-February 1918. In April, urged on by Turkish refusal to deal with other than a locally independent (from Russia) regime and by the need to escape the effects of Brest-Litovsk on the Causasus, the *de facto* government of the Commissariat was transformed into an independent Transcaucasian Federal Republic. So loose was this structure, however, and so disparate the three principal peoples (Georgian, Armenian, and Azerbaijani), that independence, originally proclaimed only reluctantly (for separatism was not a dominant feature of the pre-1917 Caucasian situation) became more and more desirable, as each area looked to itself for salvation under whatever local nationalist party was the strongest. Only expediency held the Republic together, and it was inadequate cement; after only a month the union broke into its three constituent parts, each of which now claimed independent status.[23]

[22] John W. Wheeler-Bennett, *Brest-Litovsk: The Forgotten Peace, March 1918* (London, 1938) is still the standard source for this treaty; for the general struggle in the Caucasus, see W.E.D. Allen and Paul Muratoff, *Caucasian Battlefields: A History of the Wars on the Turco-Caucasian Border,* 1828-1921 (Cambridge, 1953).

[23] Brinkley, *Volunteer Army,* pp. 38-40; Allen and Muratoff, *Caucasian Battlefields,* Ch. XLI; Firuz Kazemzadeh, *The Struggle for Transcaucasia*

A further complication, which had contributed to the collapse, was
the growing German-Turkish rivalry for Caucasian influence and resources, notably the oilfields at Baku on the Caspian and the associated
rail and pipeline connection to Batum on the Black Sea (which port
was not held by the Turks). Christian Georgia, more concerned with
Turkish ambitions than any German danger and fearing, with some
justification, for Georgian national existence, requested German protection. In late May a German-Georgian treaty was signed and 3000
German troops landed at the Georgian port of Poti to lend material
support to Georgian independence. For the moment, German protection saved Georgia. Armenia, about which the Georgians cared little,
was caught squarely in the middle.[24] The Turks had already been advancing in this direction since the collapse of the local armistice in
February, and by the end of May had reoccupied Van, Batum, and Kars.
In early June Armenia capitulated, signing treaties with both Germany
and Turkey; with both Georgia and Armenia out of the way, the Turks
advanced on into Azerbaijan.

If Caucasian politics were complex, those of Azerbaijan were doubly
so. The majority of the population, generally referred to at the time as
Tatars, were Muslims, speaking a Turkic language (Azerbaijani).
The capital city of Baku contained important Christian (particularly
Armenian) and Russian elements, and the substantial working force
and garrison provided sufficient support after March 1917 for a non-
Muslim revolutionary government to control Baku and its environs.
Internal rivalry among political groups was vicious, however, and af-

(1917-1921) (N.Y., 1951), Ch. III-IV; David Marshall Lang, A Modern
History of Georgia (London, 1962), Ch. IX; Peter Kenez, Civil War in
South Russia, 1918: The First Year of the Volunteer Army (Berkeley,
1971), Ch. VIII; Serge A. Zenkovsky, Pan-Turkism and Islam in Russia
(Cambridge, Mass., 1960), pp. 257-62; and Ronald Grigor Suny, The Baku
Commune, 1917-1918 . . . (Princeton, N.J., 1972), pp. 261-64.

[24] The problem of German-Turkish relations is treated in Weber, Eagles
on the Crescent; Ulrich Trumpener, Germany and the Ottoman Empire,
1914-1918 (Princeton, N.J., 1968); and, in relation to Georgia, in Lang,
Georgia; Suny, Baku Commune; Allen and Muratoff, Caucasian Battlefields, Ch. XLI; and Kazemzadeh, Struggle, pp. 113-24, 147-62. The following general works on Turkey and the war should also be consulted:
Commandant M. Larcher, La guerre turque dans la guerre mondiale (Paris,
1926); Ahmad Emin [Yalman], Turkey in the World War (New Haven,
Conn., 1930).

fected by events in the rest of Russia. Following bloody fighting in March-April of 1918 (as much the product of racial as political animosities), the Bolsheviks dominated the Baku government; among other measures they nationalized the oil industry. In late July, this government was overthrown by a Social Revolutionary-Armenian coalition (soon calling itself the Centro-Caspian Dictatorship) just as the Turkish armies, already in possession of Tabriz in Persian Azerbaijan to the south, moved on Baku. The change of government was important, for it permitted Britain at last to provide the aid which for some time had been under consideration for the Caucasian front.[25]

That Britain, of all the Allies, should furnish this aid was not surprising, considering the proximity of British forces in Persia and Mesopotamia. An inter-Allied agreement of December 1917 had confirmed that there was no justification for competing Allied delegations to work at cross purposes with the various local Russian political groups and statelets emerging since the collapse of the provisional government. It assigned to France responsibility for the Ukraine and south Russia, for supporting the Rumanians, and for commanding in the nearest theater of war in Salonika. Britain's area was defined as Mesopotamia, the Caucasus, and (more vaguely) the Cossack area.[26] The agreement only recognized a natural division of effort; the War Cabinet had in fact already approved the expenditure of funds through local British representatives to aid the progress of the war in Persia and among the national armies of the Georgians and Armenians. The war effort was the main incentive; where the Bolsheviks were antiwar, then so far was serving the war an anti-Bolshevik cause.[27]

The war had to be viewed on a larger scale than even Europe with

[25] The best work on wartime events in Azerbaijan is Suny, *Baku Commune;* see also Hovannisian, *Road,* pp. 189-99; Zenkovsky, *Pan-Turkism,* pp. 258-61; Brinkley, *Volunteer Army,* pp. 62-63; Kazemzadeh, *Struggle,* pp. 69-78, 83-105; GHQ Diary, Constantinople, summary on Caucasus events, February, 1918, to September, 1919, 7 November 1919, *CAB* 45/105.

[26] Allied conference, Quai d'Orsay, IC 37, 23 December 1917, *CAB* 23/3; Arno J. Mayer, *Politics and Diplomacy of Peacemaking: Containment and Counterrevolution at Versailles, 1918-1919* (N.Y., 1967), p. 297. p. 297.

[27] War Cabinet 289, 3 December, 294, 7 December, Balfour note, 9 December, annexed to War Cabinet 295; War Cabinet 298, 14 December, and 302, 19 December 1917, *CAB* 23/4.

its Caucasian appendage. Particularly to those with a professional interest in the Muslim world and the defense of India, Turkish acquisition of Russian and Persian Azerbaijan presented the horrifying possibility of a hostile Muslim coalition. At the least Turkey might attempt to play upon the theme of kinship by blood and language in the widest sense, pan-Turanism, as distinguished from the narrower, Anatolian pan-Turkism or the wider but more diffuse pan-Islam. Linking Transcaspian and Transcaucasian peoples and extending "from Constantinople to China," pan-Turanism could provide—in skillful German hands—a weapon "of even greater danger to the peace of the world than the control of the Bagdad Railway" (a prewar German project which had attracted more than a little attention).[28]

Bolstering the Caucasus, therefore, gave some hope not only of continuing the war effort and, by supporting stable elements with anti-Bolshevik proclivities, incidentally undermining Bolshevik strength in Russia, but also, by containing the Turkish danger, both direct and indirect, "of protecting our own interests to the south of the Caucasus, which are of great importance not only to us but to the Allies as a whole," as Lord Hardinge, permanent under-secretary in the Foreign Office, put it. So long as the Bolshevik movement continued to represent "the very negation of liberty," said Hardinge, so long would he oppose it, although British policy could change if the Bolshevik movement changed.[29] Hardinge here touched upon the principal confusion of early postrevolutionary policy toward Russia: the Allies advocated noninterference and continuing negotiations with the Bolshevik government on the one hand and, on the other, supported autonomous or independent Caucasus and other fringe areas, in a policy which was naturally viewed as interference by all Russian governments save those claiming independence. That this understandable but contradictory policy was formally accepted by the French in the same December 1917

[28] A.J. Toynbee report on the Pan-Turanian movement, October 1917, Supreme War Council files, *CAB* 25/42; War Cabinet 306, 26 December 1917 (quoted), *CAB* 23/4; Balfour telegram to Spring Rice (Washington), 25 October 1917, *FO* 371/3016. On the general problem of ideology see Zenkovsky, *Pan-Turkism;* Zarevand [Zaven and Vartouhie Nalbandian], *United and Independent Turania . . .* (Leiden, 1971); Bernard Lewis, *The Emergence of Modern Turkey,* 2nd ed., (London, 1968), especially Ch. X; Ziya Gokalp, *The Principles of Turkism* (Leiden, 1958).

[29] Hardinge minute, 15 December 1917, 238606/224839, *FO* 371/3018.

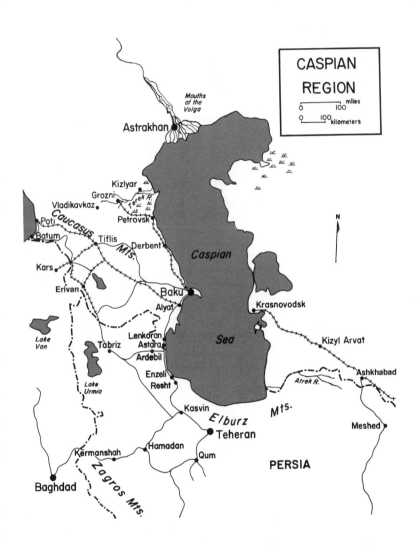

CASPIAN
REGION

0   100 miles

0   100 kilometers

Mouths
of the
Volga

Astrakhan

Kizlyar

Grozni

Vladikavkaz

Caucasus

Poti

Batum

Tiflis

Kars

Erivan

Terek R.

Petrovsk

Derbent

Caspian

N

Baku

Alyat

Krasnovodsk

Lenkoran
Astara

Tabriz

Ardebil

Sea

Kizyl Arvat

Lake
Van

Lake
Urmia

Enzeli

Resht

Kasvin

Atrek R.

Ashkhabad

Mts.

Elburz   Mts.

Meshed

Kermanshah

Hamadan

Teheran

Qum

PERSIA

Baghdad

Zagros   Mts.

agreement which divided Russia into spheres made it all the more difficult to alter and in the final analysis allowed each power the freedom to do whatever it pleased in its area.[30]

General questions of Russian and Middle Eastern policy aside, there was always a chance that a small British force, or even selected officers, might provide the leadership necessary to galvanize existing and potential forces in the Caucasus into delaying or halting a Turkish advance. This was far easier said than done, for as has been seen, the Caucasian situation was desperately confused. Although a British mission had been with the Russian command on the Turkish front for some time, Brigadier-General Offley Shore, its chief officer, had neither the facilities nor the manpower to control local activities from his headquarters in Tiflis; worse, he reported that the Transcaucasian Commissariat was little more than a dozen locally elected commissars, not really separatists at all. Captain E.W.C. Noel, sent from Persia as liaison officer, found Offley Shore insufficiently enthusiastic on the question of supporting the Commissariat (a natural attitude, since the general was attached to Russian headquarters). Noel reported that Offley Shore insisted upon dealing directly with his superiors in the War Office rather than with the British minister in Teheran, already designated the main dispenser of aid funds. Noel advised that some central authority, which Georgians, Tatars, and Armenians could all recognize, would be essential; the best rallying point would be a British unit of a thousand men on the scene.[31]

Noel differed with Offley Shore on another matter, too: Noel had concluded that too much weight was being given to the Armenians and their anti-Turkish resistance and not enough to the possibility of winning over the Muslim Azerbaijanis to the British cause. A Tatar

[30] Milner-Cecil memorandum on Russia, accepted by Clemenceau and Pichon on 23 December, appendix to War Cabinet 306, 26 December 1917, *CAB* 23/4.

[31] Cox telegram to SSI, 23 December, Offley Shore telegram to DMI, 24 December 1917, 243239, 244369/229217, *FO* 371/3019. General Offley Shore had come from India; Hardinge thought little of him (minute, ca. 18 January 1918, 8392/2, *FO* 371/3283), but he was well regarded by Lt.-Gen. Sir George MacMunn (see his *Behind the Scenes in Many Wars* [London, 1930], p. 270). Noel's mission is discussed in Ranald McDonell, *". . . and Nothing Long"* (London, 1938), p. 187; McDonell was sometime British representative in Baku.

national movement was inevitable; the only question was whether or not it would grow under British auspices. Viewed in isolation, friendship with a future Azerbaijani state was desirable, but in the context of Caucasian politics, to aid one party was to attack that party's neighbor. Azerbaijanis were more interested in cutting down Armenians than anything else, and since British aid to Armenia could hardly be abandoned, British policy had the unfortunate but predictable effect of exacerbating precisely the inter-Caucasian conflicts it hoped to avoid. Sir Charles Marling, the minister in Teheran, was aware of this but could see no alternatives short of the impossible one—abandoning the area to the Turks.[32]

The situation was most confused. The India Office, for example, involved because of long-standing interest in Persia and Mesopotamia, was unable even to determine whether the Foreign Office or the War Office was responsible for policy administration in the Caucasus.[33] Still, the area offered a possible focus for pragmatic action lacking in Russia as a whole; something could be done here using local troops with only a stiffening of British forces which would stop the Turks and their pan-Turanian aspirations. Solution of inter-Caucasian squabbles would have to take care of itself. At the least, as one War Office document circulated to the Supreme Allied War Council at Versailles put it, the route from Baghdad to Enzeli (via Kermanshah and Kasvin) could be secured and use made of such Russian military units still in contact with British forces in Mesopotamia as were willing to continue the war effort.[34]

The Cabinet, in fact, had already decided upon the principle of aid to the Caucasian forces; the actual form of the new military mission urged from all sides was a War Office decision. A small force (initially just over 100 men in forty vehicles) set out from Baghdad on the long road to the Caspian and, hopefully, Tiflis, under Major-General L.C. Dunsterville, a colorful and courageous officer well known in some circles as the model for Kipling's *Stalky & Co.* Dunsterville's orders

[32] Viceroy telegram to SSI, 1 January, Cox telegram to SSI, 3 January, and demiofficial telegram to SSI, 25 January, and Marling telegram to FO, 30 January 1918, *FO* 371/3300.

[33] Shuckburgh to Graham, 24 December, 243239/229217, *FO* 371/3019; also interdepartmental conference, 19 December 1917, and G.R. Clerk minute, 4 January 1918, 4022/2, *FO* 371/3283.

[34] Note by Lt.-Col. A.P. Wavell, 13 January 1918, *CAB* 25/43.

appointed him British representative in Tiflis and chief of the British mission to the Caucasus. All Russian and Turkish Caucasian territory south of the main Caucasus mountains was his responsibility; his objective was to prevent the realization of pan-Turanian ideals, at the same time holding as many of the enemy as possible in the Causasus as a way of relieving pressure upon General Marshall in Mesopotamia. His orders entailed vast responsibility, and Dunsterville understood his mission as a vital link in an unbroken Allied chain reaching through the Caucasus and the French in the Ukraine (with whom he was to keep in touch) to Rumania.[35]

After much effort, Dunsterville's force reached Enzeli on 17 February, but here he found himself in an untenable position. His small force was no match for several thousand Russian troops with Bolshevik proclivities—at least, they appeared loyal to Petrograd's orders—nor indeed for a local, antigovernment movement, headed by one Mirza Kuchuk Khan, known as the Jangalis, whose friendship seemed dubious at best. The Jangalis appeared to control the countryside and were vying for control of Enzeli with the "Military Revolutionary Committee of the East Persian Circle of the Caucasus Front." By the 24th, Dunsterville had retreated back down the road toward Hamadan.

The question at that point was whether Dunsterville should pull back to Mesopotamia or remain to establish a *cordon sanitaire* in west Persia. Two arguments stood in the way of remaining: one, primarily political, came from British officials in India who were worried about possible adverse effects upon Persian opinion—for, like Turkish and Russian military operations earlier, British maneuvers on the Hamadan road had been initiated without asking the technically neutral Persian government. Against this Marling in Teheran could argue that a policy of complete conciliation and its concomitant withdrawal would open the area to enemy advance, while remaining in strength would not

---

[35] Account of Dunsterforce based on War Diary of General Staff, Army Headquarters, India, India Office Records, London [hereafter *War Diary*], Dunsterforce and Persia, volumes 37-41; Maj.-Gen. L.D. Dunsterville, *The Adventures of Dunsterforce* (N.Y., 1920), *Stalky's Reminiscences* (London, 1928), and "Military Mission to North-West Persia, 1918," *Journal of the Central Asian Society* 8 (1921): 79-98; Maj. M.H. Donohoe, *With the Persian Expedition* (London, 1919); Brinkley, *Volunteer Army,* pp. 60-63; Kazemzadeh, *Struggle,* pp. 139-42; McDonell, *". . . And Nothing Long",* pp. 223ff.; and Suny, *Baku Commune,* Ch. 11.

only help to avoid this danger but would also support the central Iranian government by helping to end the Jangali problem. The second issue was military; Dunsterville's force was simply too small, even with such levies as he might organize, to stop any substantial enemy attack in his direction, while the drain upon the resources of the Mesopotamian forces was out of all proportion to the smallness of his force. There were 600 long miles of difficult road from the Mesopotamian railhead northeast of Baghdad to the Caspian, and Baghdad was already at the end of a long line of communications. It could even be argued that serious resistance to the Turks in the Caucasus would be disadvantageous in any case, for a setback there might motivate them to turn back to Palestine and Iraq.[36]

Thus Dunsterville's mission had little justification once he turned back from Enzeli, but for the moment he was told to stay on. The fact that his presence on the Caspian road coincided with the treaty of Brest-Litovsk explains this decision. With a hold on the Ukraine, argued a General Staff paper of late March, the Germans need advance no further in Russia proper but would now doubtless look to Baku, the Caspian, and Central Asia to create trouble for Britain in an area with much potential for trouble. The British section of the Supreme War Council could only envisage a series of holding points (Mosul, Hamadan, Resht, Tabriz), a rapprochement if possible with the Persian authorities, involvement of a friendly Afghanistan, and so on to Japanese intervention in Siberia.[37]

Dunsterville remained in Hamadan, with an eye not only on the situation to the northwest but also on his supplementary instructions to watch for an opportunity to slip through with a few men to the Caucasus. The Cabinet, however, turning to Marling's plan for concentration on northwest Persia as a preferred alternative, tended to forget Dunsterville's original orders. In fact, when in May Dunsterville proposed to go to Tabriz with a dozen men to work up the local population, Marling opposed the suggestion as a dispersal of effort from the Hama-

[36] Viceroy telegram to SSI, 22 February, Marling (Teheran) telegram to FO, 24 February, *War Diary,* Persia, 39; Marshall to brother, 25 May and 13 September 1918, *Marshall Papers;* Edmund Dane, *British Campaigns in the Nearer East, 1914-1918 . . .* (London, 1919), II, pp. 214-15.

[37] Lt.-Col. A.H. Ollivant (GS) memorandum, 23 March 1918, *CAB* 25/72.

dan road.[38] The controversy was too specific to be resolved at Cabinet level and was delegated to the interdepartmental Eastern Committee, an amalgamation of previous committees dealing with the Middle East. Lord Curzon chaired the group with a strong hand, and this decision gave the acknowledged expert a considerable voice in Caucasian affairs as well as other Middle Eastern areas already in the committee's purview.[39]

The first major consideration of Dunsterville's mission took place on 31 May, and the committee could hardly fail to be puzzled by conflicting advice. The German landing in Georgia and the Turkish advances on Baku made it imperative to protect the latter city, yet Marling was convinced that any such effort would only be wasted and urged that the cordon be limited to west Persia. But Dunsterville, on the strength of his own intelligence information, now saw a chance of getting to Baku, and Baku was tempting. No cordon would be worthwhile without the Caspian, and the Caspian could not be held without Baku. The War Office was sympathetic but could make no new commitments. Dunsterville could go to Baku only if his force would not thereby be reduced— i.e., without any substantial escort.[40]

Dunsterville's hopes were kept alive by the presence of friendly pockets of resistance in Armenia and among the Assyrian Christian minority near Lake Urmia. There was also Colonel Lazar Bicherakov, an Ossietin Cossack from the Russian forces in Persia who was inclined to work with the Allies and against the Bolsheviks. Giving nominal allegiance to the Soviet regime, Bicherakov moved to Russian Azerbaijan with 1500 men in early July and took up a position in the lines against the Turks, but his relationship with the Baku Bolshevik government was seriously strained, and for the time being he preferred to move northward to join an anti-Bolshevik army in Daghestan. The col-

[38] *War Diary,* Dunsterforce, 1 April; War Cabinet 354, 26 February, and 369, 21 March 1918, *CAB* 23/5; War Cabinet 408, 10 May 1918, *CAB* 23/6.

[39] Eastern Committee, 5 April 1918, India Office Records, Political and Secret, series 10, volume 807 [hereafter *L/P&S*/10/807]; the history of the Eastern Committee may be traced in Busch, *Britain, India and the Arabs,* pp. 154ff., 207f.

[40] Eastern Committee, 31 May, *L/P&S*/10/807; GOC Baghdad telegram to Teheran, 25 May, WO telegram to GOC Baghdad, 27 May 1918, *War Diary,* Persia, 42.

lapse of the Bolshevik regime in Baku and the establishment of the Centro-Caspian Dictatorship allowed Bicherakov's return; his influence—and that of the Turkish shells landing in the town—was sufficient to inspire an appeal for British aid from the Dictatorship.[41]

Dunsterville had been convinced for some time that with sufficient force (an armored car squadron, a field artillery battery, a British infantry battalion) he could hold Baku. The War Office's misgivings were overridden by the advantages to be gained from possession of Baku port and the oilfields, the lack of alternatives, and Dunsterville's own estimate of the situation. General Marshall in Baghdad, who had control over Dunsterville's operations, remained to be convinced, but London urged him to make full use of the available opportunity. Meanwhile, Dunsterville himself had managed to reach a truce of sorts with the Jangalis, and he was able to respond quickly to the fall of the Soviet and the appeal for aid; within a week, his advance parties were in the town, and he arrived on 17 August with such forces as could be spared from guarding the lengthy line of communications. Nearly 1000 British and Indian troops cooperated against the Turks with a larger Russian force under Bicherakov and local Armenian troops, but it was still a case of too little, too late. Even at that, Marshall felt that Dunsterville had exceeded his authority in pulling so substantial a section of the Persian force to Baku in such uncertain circumstances.[42]

On 14 September, Dunsterville successfully evacuated Baku and returned to Enzeli; his force (without Dunsterville in command, for Marshall had ordered him to Baghdad) remained at Enzeli and on the Hamadan road. Bicherakov and those of his forces who escaped after the fall of Baku went north to Petrovsk, where the Centro-Caspian Dictatorship continued to hold out against the Turkish forces. Gratitude toward Britain's token support and precipitous withdrawal was not noticeably in evidence.[43] However, something of the complexities

[41] *War Diary,* Persia, 43-45; Brinkley, *Volunteer Army,* p. 61; Kazemzadeh, *Struggle,* Ch. VIII; Dunsterville, *Dunsterforce,* pp. 21, 159, 167; Suny, *Baku Commune,* Ch. X-XI.

[42] GOC, Baghdad, telegrams to WO, 9 June, and to Army Headquarters, Simla, 10 and 17 June and 4 July; WO telegrams to GOC, Baghdad, 13 and 29 June and 6 July 1918; *War Diary,* Persia, 43-44; Marshall, *Four Fronts,* p. 311; Burne, *Last Phase,* pp. 88-90; Kazemzadeh, *Struggle,* pp. 133-40.

[43] In addition to the sources cited above, Eastern Committee minutes, 11 and 18 September, *L/P&S/*10/807; War Cabinet 466, 30 August,

of the Caucasus had been learned and a precedent set for British intervention—but for the moment, until the Turkish armistice in late October, activities would have to be focused on Persia, the Caspian, and
Central Asia.

CENTRAL ASIA

The same Russian collapse and pan-Turanian ambitions which jeopardized Allied Caucasian interests created dangers further east; there
was no reason why, having once seized upon Baku and the Caspian, the
German-Turkish alliance would not work to disrupt a situation in Central Asia and Afghanistan which up to 1917 had not presented any
real worry to India. Afghanistan, it was true, had been carefully watched
as a place where Indian dissidents took refuge and as the object of small
enemy missions, but the ruler, Habibullah, remained faithful to his
British commitments.[44] Only in late 1917, when the Caucasus seemed
on the point of falling, and when separatist regimes were being established in the half-dozen provinces of the Turkistan governor-generalship as well as in the autonomous khanates of Khiva and Bukhara,
was it deemed necessary to mount a small mission, analogous to that of
Dunsterville, in the direction of Central Asia. The worries were, once
again, possible enemy activity, useful resources (cotton in particular),
and the added feature of many thousands of German and Austro-Hun-
garian prisoners-of-war taken in various Russian campaigns (although

---

and 468, 3 September 1918, *CAB* 23/7. The *War Diary* volume (Persia,
volume 46) for September, 1918, cannot be found in the India Office Library; it is the only missing volume from this series. These volumes had
not previously been used by any nonofficial historian, and the absence is
highly unfortunate, to say the least—for September, 1918, was the month
of the "affair of the twenty-six commissars" (see p. 44), and this volume
might possibly have shed new light on that incident. The author wishes to
express his thanks to the staff of the India Office Records, however, for
the very thorough search carried out for the missing volume among these
uncatalogued materials (a search in which the author participated).

[44] *L/P&S/*10/581 and 633. For general background on Afghanistan,
see Ludwig W. Adamec, *Afghanistan 1900-1923: A Diplomatic History*
(Berkeley, 1967), and Vartan Gregorian, *The Emergence of Modern
Afghanistan* . . . (Stanford, 1969). Political Intelligence Department, FO,
memorandum, 25 June 1918, *FO* 371/3304.

how numerous, and where, were moot points).[45] Already, before the year was out, the British had decided to replace the Russian element (now evacuating) in the Anglo-Russian cordon in eastern Persia, which ran from Robat in Seistan province near the Indian frontier through Birjand, where the Russian Cossack force of some 400 men assumed responsibility for the cordon, on through Qain, Turbat-i-Haidari, and Meshed to the Russian frontier south of Ashkhabad. At the same time, the Indian railway was carried on to Duzdab (Zahidan) in Persia (thirty miles south of the junction of Persia, India, and Afghanistan).[46]

Extension of British responsibilities in eastern Persia, however, did not ensure Central Asian intelligence, let alone security, and in early January India, which had primary responsibility for Persian operations (excluding those based upon Mesopotamia) was asked if the establishment of a British organization in Turkistan to support the anti-Bolsheviks was possible; insufficient information was available at home upon which to make such a decision. Authorities in India were not favorably disposed to the idea (which emanated from the War Office, anx-

[45] Wilson note, 24 June 1918, appended to Eastern Committee 16th Minute, *L/P&S/*10/807; C.H. Ellis, *The British 'Intervention' in Transcaspia, 1918-1919* (Berkeley, 1963), pp. 18 and 50. Arthur Swinson, *Beyond the Frontiers: The Biography of Colonel F.M. Bailey . . .* (London, 1971), perpetuates this report but gives the figure (p. 145) of 180,000 prisoners. Col. P.J. Etherton, *In the Heart of Asia* (London, 1925), p. 155, says there had been 106,000, now reduced to 38,000. The background may be found in Richard A. Pierce, *Russian Central Asia, 1867-1917: A Study in Colonial Rule* (Berkeley, 1960); Alexander G. Park, *Bolshevism in Turkestan, 1917-1927* (N.Y., 1957); Hélène Carrère d'Encausse, "The Fall of the Czarist Empire," and "Civil War and New Governments," in E. Allworth, ed., *Central Asia: A Century of Russian Rule* (N.Y., 1967), 207-253; R. Vaidyanath, *The Formation of the Soviet Central Asian Republics* (New Delhi, 1967); Manuel Sarkisyanz, "Russian Conquest in Central Asia . . .," in Wayne S. Vucinich, ed., *Russia and Asia* (Stanford, Calif., 1972), 248-88; Capt. A.H. Brun, *Troublous Times: Experiences in Bolshevik Russia and Turkestan* (London, 1931); and P.-G. La Chesnais, *Les Peuples de Transcaucasie pendant la guerre et devant la paix* (Paris, 1921).

[46] Military Department, IO, note, 25 December 1917, *L/P&S/*10/725; Political Department, IO, memorandum, 23 April 1917, 73940/3172, FO 371/3303; B.J. Gould, *The Jewel in the Lotus: Recollections of an Indian Political* (London, 1957), Ch. V (Gould served in East Persia, 1918-25); and Brig.-Gen. W.E.R. Dickson, *East Persia: A Backwater of the Great War* (London, 1924) (Dickson was Inspector-General of the cordon and later head of the British military mission to Persia).

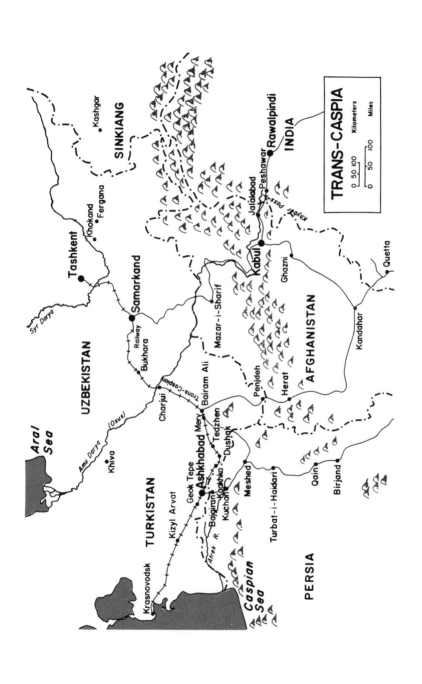

ious to find out what was happening in Turkistan), replying that aside from the obvious problem of supply of such a mission, there appeared to be no sort of government in existence in Central Asia to which a mission would be helpful and which would in turn be useful to Britain, although doubtless it was a good idea to make preparations in case conditions changed.[47] Only substantial pressure from London and the news reported by the British consul in Meshed that a non-Bolshevik, Muslim government in Khokand had declared for Turkistani autonomy and wished to establish relations with Cossack and Caucasian elements with a view to concerted action persuaded India to provide a positive plan of action.[48]

Two centers, India suggested, should be established for information-gathering and other activities: Meshed, already in the British cordon and the base of a consul-general and a military intelligence officer (Lieutenant-Colonel E.A.F. Redl at that time), could be the center of operations for the area west of the Oxus and Bukhara. Kashgar in Sinkiang, with its well-established British consulate, could serve for Fergana and Samarkand. If one post were disrupted, the other could continue to operate. But before the final decision was taken, India urged, the whole question should be reconsidered: the objects of the mission, as specified so far, were so "hopelessly vague" that its chances of success were very slim. Worse, emissaries to Russian Turkistan would arouse strong suspicions in the amir of Afghanistan; at that very moment India was awaiting a reply to its letter warning the amir of the Bolshevik danger.[49]

India was able to get no more than a temporary delay. In fact, the objectives of the mission tended to grow as time passed to include the extension of activities in the Kashgar area with an eye to building Chinese (as opposed to Russian) authority in that nominally Chinese province. Another scheme, a product of fertile minds in India think-

[47] SSI telegram to viceroy, 29 October, Col. Browning (WO) to Shuckburgh (IO), 22 November, Shuckburgh note, 13 December 1917; SSI telegram to viceroy, 4 January, viceroy telegram to SSI, 8 January 1918, *L/P&S*/10/721.

[48] SSI telegram to viceroy, 5 January, *L/P&S*/10/725; WO to IO, 18 January, SSI telegram to viceroy, 25 January, *L/P&S*/10/721; consul-general, Meshed, telegram to FO, 10 January 1918, *FO* 371/3303.

[49] Viceroy to amir, 10 January, and telegrams to SSI, 2 and 12 February, IO to FO, 16 February 1918, *FO* 371/3303.

ing mainly about the Indian frontier, was to encourage the amir of Afghanistan to pursue his ambitions toward the north, particularly the Russian frontier area of Penjdeh (scene of an important clash in the 1880's)—a delightful plan, since it would turn Afghanistan away from Indian ambitions and at the same time remove this Muslim state from Turanian dreams of Asian Muslim solidarity. Even the War Office balked at this proposed violation of Britain's own responsibility for the Afghan-Russian border settlement of 1885-87; far more important, the possible repercussions of such intervention were not at all clear. The amir must be left to decide upon any such ambitions on his own initiative.[50]

But the amir's response was not immediately forthcoming, and the missions departed for their bases. Captain L.W. Blacker and Lieutenant-Colonel F.M. Bailey were ordered to Kashgar with Colonel P.T. Etherton, who was to be the new consul-general there, while Redl in Meshed was to be reinforced by two officers who would be under his command. Their objectives, then as later, were unclear. While the designated officers proceeded to their starting positions, the debate continued. Redl's group in particular had been told only to obtain all possible information on Turkistan and to open communication with possibly helpful local notables; the War Office urged that at least the officers be allowed to cross into Turkistan and begin active propaganda. By mid-April 1918 it added the idea of a mission to the amir of Bukhara (semi-independent in name if not in fact). This proposal evolved as a response to news of serious fighting between the Khokand Muslim authority and local Bolshevik units based on Tashkent, where a Soviet appeared to be in control.[51]

Activities across the Russian frontier would be skating upon thin ice, warned the India Office's Sir John Shuckburgh, apparently the only

[50] IO to FO, 16 February, and WO to IO, 23 February, *FO* 371/3303, and IO to FO, 16 February 1918, *L/P&S*/10/721.

[51] Viceroy telegrams to SSI, 21 March and 9 April 1918, *L/P&S*/10/721. All the participants in the Kashgar/Tashkent mission have left their own accounts: Lt.-Col. F.M. Bailey, *Mission to Tashkent* (London, 1946); Capt. L.V.S. Blacker, *On Secret Patrol in High Asia* (London, 1922); and Etherton, *In the Heart of Asia.* See also a memordandum by Etherton (then a major), IO Memorandum C. 181, May 1918, on the pan-Turanian movement, 122038/3828, *FO* 371/3391. Swinson, *Beyond the Frontiers,* is a recent biography of Bailey, full of errors and of little value.

official concerned who knew or remembered that other British agents
were at that time negotiating some sort of modus vivendi in Petrograd
with the Bolshevik authorities. If the policy which emerged proved to
be alliance with Petrograd, Britain could hardly encourage anti-
Bolshevik movements in Central Asia. And how awkward it might be
if a Bolshevik-Afghan coalition developed while Britain was making
impossible commitments to the Bukharan amir.[52] With these opinions
the civilian experts of the Eastern Committee agreed: the plan had not
been well thought out. The Meshed mission's orders remained un-
changed; they were not to cross the frontier without orders to that
effect. At the same time, the door was kept open for future extension
of activities in the north or northeast of Meshed with the objective of
controlling or cutting the Transcaspian railway between Krasnovodsk
on the Caspian and Samarkand—a vital line of approach for any power
hostile to British interests in Asia.[53]

Redl was simply told that any parties willing to work against the
German-Turk alliance should be aided in turn; the current policy toward
the Bolsheviks was to treat them as if they were acting in good faith until
proven otherwise, but this was not considered inconsistent with support
of any non-Bolshevik elements willing to stand up against the main
enemy. In any case, the mission's work could not be laid down in detail
until the Turkistan situation was considerably clearer; meanwhile,
he was to extend his intelligence organization to the Caspian railway.
Decisions would have to be taken on the spot. To this end, a higher
officer with considerable experience in intelligence, but little in field
command, Major-General Wilfrid Malleson, had been selected by India
to take charge of the Meshed mission.[54]

[52] Shuckburgh minute, 18 April, and note for under-secretary (IO),
22 April, *L/P&S/*10/721, documents at registry numbers 1556 and 1617
of 1918 [1556/18 and 1617/18]; Sir John Evelyn Shuckburgh was secretary of the Political Department of the IO (1917-21), later joining the
Colonial Office as assistant under-secretary when that department took
over responsibility for the Middle East.

[53] Eastern Committee minutes, 22 April, *L/P&S/*10/807; CinC India
telegram to WO, 2 May, FO telegram to Marling, 6 May, and SSI telegram
to Viceroy, 8 May 1918, *FO* 371/3303.

[54] DMI telegrams to CinC India, 15 and 29 April and 7 May, chief of
staff, India [CGSI] telegram to Redl, 23 April 1918, *War Diary,* Persia,
41-42. On Malleson's background see Ellis, *British Intervention,* p. 25;
see also Malleson's own brief account, "The British Military Mission to

Redl's reactions to this appointment are unrecorded, but India objected strenuously to this escalation of the mission's aim and scope. Afghani suspicions were already aroused by Bolshevik activities to the north of their frontier; enlargement of the mission would not help. Nor would it be easy to find the means to aid cooperative local elements, even if they could be found, and they would in any case have to be acceptable to the Afghanis as well as to the British.[55] But the War Office knew that a representative of anti-Bolshevik elements in Turkistan had recently reached the British military agent in the Caucasus, Colonel G.D. Pike, temporarily at Tiflis. This representative proposed the establishment of an autonomous governor-generalship in the area Orenburg-Semiretchia-Krasnovodsk, and he asked British support for this. Pike, about to retreat with his mission to Vladikavkaz (where he was killed in August), had time to give much advice, 20,000 rubles, and promises of moral and material support, with the object in mind of immediate purchase of the Caspian merchant fleet, close control of Krasnovodsk, and expansion of military forces to the 10,000 deemed necessary for such operations.[56]

Moreover, the approaching fall of Baku to the Turks made it seem likely that the Bolsheviks of Central Asia would be more cooperative against the common enemy. So, at least, Redl thought, and he anticipated permission to cross the frontier by sending Captain (subsequently Major) R.F. Teague Jones to Kuchan, just short of the frontier.[57]

Turkestan, 1918-1920," *Journal of the Central Asian Society* 9 (1922): 95-110, and, for general background, Col. J.K. Tod, "The Malleson Mission to Transcaspia in 1918," *Journal of the Central Asian Society* 27 (1940): 45-67, and "Operations in Trans-Caspia, 1918-1919," *Army Quarterly* 16 (1928): 280-303; and "Anglo-Indian Troops in Persia, Transcaucasia, and Turkestan, 1914-20," *Central Asian Review* 8 (1960): 296-99.

[55] CinC India telegram to WO, 2 May, viceroy telegrams to SSI, 15 May and 3 June 1918, *FO* 371/3303.

[56] Military agent, Caucasus, telegrams to DMI, 20 May, and to Redl, undated (attached to telegram to DMI, 8 July 1918), *WO* 106/60. On Pike, see an interesting report by his successor: Maj. G.M. Goldsmith (Intelligence Corps), acting British military agent, Caucasus, to DMI, 1 July 1919, *WO* 95/4960 (86 pp. plus documents); Goldsmith took over when Pike was killed in mid-August but was himself taken prisoner by the Soviet troops, to be released only in May of the following year.

[57] Meshed telegram to Foreign Secretary, India [FSI], 4 June, Redl

India continued to insist that nothing be done until Malleson arrived, but even India was becoming anxious about the railway and Turko-German efforts if Baku fell. The situation on the east of the Caspian was unclear (". . . we are so much in the dark that it is always doubtful whether a success won by one of these parties over the other is a subject of rejoicing or the reverse," wrote Shuckburgh), but news of a successful revolt against the Tashkent Soviet by Mensheviks and Social Revolutionaries in the important rail town of Ashkhabad (a new Ashkhabad Executive Committee was established on 14 July) and of hasty Bolshevik withdrawals from Samarkand, Merv, and Tashkent, only spurred on the process of intervention: clearly there were friends in the area if only the British would make an appearance.[58]

On 24 June, General Wilson attended an important Eastern Committee meeting to urge that an active policy be pursued in both Central Asia and Afghanistan. The Afghani amir had at last answered India's letter with a wary request for substantial aid in arms; while his demands could not be met in full, his attention could at least be directed northward. Only the Afghan army, really, was available to stop the enemy in that area, and the amir should be brought in on the British side while the British star was still high; surely no loyal Russian would begrudge the amir the territorial compensation from Russia necessary for his assistance (Wilson was still not very aware of Russian realities). Malleson's mission, "Malmiss" in telegraphic jargon, must of course be allowed into Turkistan.

Civilian members—notably Curzon—were still concerned about the possible effects of the War Office's policy: Balfour, as foreign minister perhaps more conscious of his responsibilities for Russian policy as a whole, opposed encouraging Russian separatist movements, especially since Britain was castigating the Germans for just that policy. Curzon's

---

telegram to CGSI, 8 June, DMI telegram to CinC India, 17 June 1918, *War Diary,* Persia, 43.

[58] IO to WO, 10 June, viceroy telegram to SSI, 17 June, with Shuckburgh minute (quoted), 19 June, and WO telegram to CinC India, 17 June, *L/P&S/*10/721; Redl telegrams to CGSI, 20 and 24 (2 of date) June 1918, *War Diary,* Persia, 43; Ellis, *British Intervention,* Ch. II, and "Operations in Transcaspia 1918-1919 and the 26 Commissars Case," in *St. Antony's Papers,* No. 6 (Soviet Affairs, No. 2), ed. by David Footman (London, 1959), 134-38. Malleson, "Mission," differs substantially from the account given here.

vision was rather different: a "Moslem nexus of states" was the best way to halt the enemy advance—and anyway, was it wrong to encourage the Afghanis to recover territory which had been filched from them years ago? Curzon, of course, had written the standard text on the subject, and Balfour could only answer that the whole question of Russian policy would have to be studied anew, a conclusion which was to be heard rather often in days to come.[59]

Meanwhile, the results of the meeting were cabled out to India: London suggested that the embargo on Malleson's and Bailey's missions entering Russian should be lifted and that Afghan policy should be completely revised, specifically advocating negotiation of a treaty of alliance and the discard of the policy of keeping Afghanistan neutral which had been followed throughout the war. Indian authorities were willing to yield on the point of intervention in Russia, and the two missions were given discretion to cross the frontier if it appeared desirable. But Persia and Afghanistan were very much in India's wider sphere of concern, and India very much disliked the idea of approaching Habibullah for an alliance. Since, practically speaking, he was an ally already, the Afghanis would interpret such a request as a confession of weakness and would see any suggestion that they move on Penjdeh as a crude attempt to involve them with the Russians. The Indian response was hardly encouraging, but the Eastern Committee—a body which included two former viceroys (Curzon and Hardinge) as well as the secretary of state for India (Edwin Montagu)—knew very well that it was an exceedingly grave step even to contemplate overruling the government of India from London on Afghan affairs.[60]

On 16 July, Malleson arrived in Meshed, eager to make a success of his mission. He must have been a bit surprised to find that a small mission from Dunsterville (at that time still in Enzeli) had been authorized to proceed to Krasnovodsk, on the eastern coast of the Caspian, and India intervened to suggest that this unit be placed, when it arrived, under Malleson's authority. Jurisdictional problems of this sort bedeviled the whole of Britain's Asian operations, but in this case Malle-

[59] Eastern Committee, 24 June; Wilson views in CIGS memorandum, 21 June 1918, appended to E.C. minutes, *L/P&S/*10/807.

[60] SSI telegrams to viceroy, 25 (3 of date) June, viceroy telegrams to SSI, 1 (2 of date) July, *L/P&S/*10/721 (FO copies in *FO* 371/3303); FSI telegram to consul-general, Kashgar, 1 July, *War Diary,* Persia, 44; Eastern Committee, 4 July 1918, *L/P&S/*10/807.

son was given control of all forces east of the Caspian, while the Caspian itself was under the authority of Baghdad. Malleson personally was more interested in affairs in the direction of Central Asia and soon moved off to the Russian frontier with a force of roughly 200 men. His goal was "generally to form rallying point for pro-Entente parties in Russian territories and give them all possible assistance and support."[61]

How much this action had been approved in India was unclear to London, but the very appointment of the higher officer to the command and the advance preparation of his force would indicate that Malleson's procedure came as no surprise to Indian military authorities. In any case, Malleson had no hesitation in sniffing out just such "pro-Entente" groups as he was looking for—in particular, the Ashkhabad Executive Committee. His first reports indicated that the Bolsheviks had indeed been defeated in fighting near Ashkhabad and Kizyl Arvat, and now was the time to give aid to their enemies (apparently, in his mind at least, "pro-Entente" meant "anti-Bolshevik"). Teague Jones, sent on ahead, reported Krasnovodsk quiet and the railway functioning normally, as was steamer traffic to Baku (although all bigger ships had been taken north to the mouth of the Volga). While the situation in Baku was increasingly desperate, there were as yet no major obstacles to British operations on the eastern side of the Caspian. The Ashkhabad Executive Committee, apparently composed mainly of railwaymen, military cadets, and officers, appealed for aid, notably heavy guns with which to protect Krasnovodsk from the sea (the main danger was Bolshevik ships from the Volga, not an attack down the railway).[62]

Malleson had reportedly given financial aid to this group and favored a firm commitment to do so. He recognized that Britain might be siding with the loser in this gamble, but the Turkomans were coming more

---

[61] Meshed telegram to CGSI, 16 July, *War Diary,* Persia, 44; WO telegram to GOC Baghdad, 2 July, viceroy telegrams to SSI, 2 and 20 July, SSI telegrams to viceroy, 15 (quoted) and 16 July, *L/P&S/*10/721 (*FO* 371/3304); MI 2d note, 14 July, CinC India telegram to WO, 8 July, *WO* 106/60; CGSI instructions to Malleson, 27 June 1918, *War Diary,* Persia, 47; Ellis, *British Intervention,* p. 30.

[62] MI 2d note, 14 July, CinC India telegram to WO, 13 July, *WO* 106/60; Malleson telegrams to CGSI, 17 and 19 July 1918, *War Diary,* Persia, 44. Teague Jones's report (dated 26 January 1919) is in *WO* 106/61; Ellis, *British Intervention,* p. 31.

and more into the field in support of the Committee as the forces of the Turkistan Soviet receded. London, convinced by Malleson's optimistic reports, agreed; Krasnovodsk would get its guns and the Committee its aid. In August, a British force of several hundred men (1/4 Hampshire Regiment) arrived in Krasnovodsk; Malleson at the same time was authorized to provide several machine guns and crews for frontline operations of the Committee against the Bolsheviks. This small commitment had considerable political importance: when the British unit later came into action against the Bolsheviks, any chance of Anglo-Soviet cooperation in this part of the world, however remote, was at an end.[63]

Unfortunately for the Kashgar mission, while it was told of the aid for the Ashkhabad Committee, it could not be told of the military commitment, for Bailey and Blacker had departed for Tashkent in the last week of July with Bolshevik-provided passports. On their arrival in Tashkent in mid-August they were rather surprised to be treated with grave suspicions by the Bolsheviks, who were aware that Soviet and British troops were already shooting at each other. The participants tended later in life to blame their superiors for this awkward situation— but the Bolsheviks were most courteous and allowed the mission to return across the frontier (aside from Bailey, who in the traditional "Great Game" approach to intelligence operations remained on in hiding, in the hope that he would be in a useful position if the Soviet collapsed).[64]

[63] Malleson telegrams to CGSI, 1 (2 of date), 3, 7, and 18 August, SSI telegram to Viceroy, 3 August, CGSI telegram to Malleson, 5 August, WO telegram to GOC Baghdad, 3 August, *War Diary,* Persia, 45; H.V. Cox, Military Advisor, IO, note for DMI, 10 August, *WO* 106/60; FSI telegram to Kashgar, 22 July 1918, *War Diary,* Persia, 44, says Malleson had given financial aid.

[64] FSI telegram to Kashgar, 22 July 1918, *War Diary,* Persia, 44, informs of cooperation with the "Executive Committee," and CGSI telegram to Malleson, 12 August 1918, *War Diary,* Persia, 45, informs of Bailey's departure. The often-made assertion that Malleson and Bailey were uninformed of each other's progress is simply not accurate. That of Ellis (*British Intervention,* p. 72), in particular, blames the Indian authorities for not passing information of the Ashkhabad revolt to Kashgar in time for Bailey to receive it; in fact, Kashgar was informed, but it could not be told of Malleson's formal commitment of early August before Bailey departed (and was thus out of communication) on 24 July. A further mistaken ac-

It simply had not been possible to communicate the most recent developments to Bailey's mission, always the more minor operation of the two. In addition, a certain lack of harmony resulted from the fact that Malleson's mission, as a military one, continued to be dealt with by army headquarters in India, which in turn had direct communication with the War Office. Bailey and Blacker, based upon a consulate-general, were regarded as political officials and therefore came under the Foreign and Political Department, whose normal chain of communication with Britain was by telegram to the India Office and from there to the Cabinet or Foreign Office.[65] The difference was important, for the Foreign Department of India more than once found itself criticizing a policy which flowed from the larger implications of military decisions on which it had had little or no chance to offer advice.

Even more unfortunately, the apparent sacrifice of poor Bailey seemed wasted, for things began to go badly for the Ashkhabad Executive Committee. Alarmed at the British delay in reinforcing Krasnovodsk and the Merv front and in providing financial aid, by mid-August the Committee had been forced to give up Merv. The War Office had to trust the man on the spot (although all were agreed on the need to hold Krasnovodsk), and Malleson was authorized to dispatch his larger force across the frontier (so far only officers and the machine-gun units had gone). On the 18th, the machine-gunners were involved in heavy fighting at Bairam Ali on the eastern outskirts of Merv; on the next day, the frontier force was dispatched to Tedzhen on the railway. Malleson advised the Committee that if they stood firm Britain would similarly stand behind them with military and financial aid: indeed, he was willing that very day to sign an agreement or "protocol" to this end with "the representative of the existing Government of Trans-Caspia." Britain—through Malleson—undertook to defend Baku, garrison Krasnovodsk (against attacks "either by Turco-German or Bolshevik forces"), and supply to its utmost power "British troops, guns, machine guns, aeroplanes, rifles, ammunition and explosives," aside

---

count is in Swinson, *Beyond the Frontiers,* p. 145. Bailey's later career may be traced in Swinson and, in the official sources, in *L/P&S/*10/722 (parts 2-3). He did not emerge until January 1920; see particularly in this file Bailey to deputy FSI, 19 May 1920. In general, see Gerald Morgan, "Myth and Reality in the Great Game," *Asian Affairs* 60 (1973): 55-65.

[65] Viceroy telegram to SSI, 31 July 1918, *FO* 371/3304.

from financial aid, in return for free access to Caspian shipping, Krasnovodsk, and the railway. The final paragraph pledged such aid so long
as the Committee remained in power "and has as the main plank in its
political platform the restoration of order and the suppression of all
Bolshevik or Turco-German intrigues or projects for invasion."[66]

There was little immediate reaction to this commitment, which
surely went beyond Malleson's authority. Attention was focused at
the moment on Dunsterville's trials in Baku, and it soon seemed as
if the Ashkhabad government would expire before the promised aid
could materialize in any case; but the implications for Russian policy
as a whole must have disturbed some, at least, of the handful of individuals who were doing their best to follow the rapid sequence of
events in that part of the world. On 20 August, Malleson's frontier
detachment joined the front, but it was little more than a morale-
boosting gesture. His local allies found it impossible to make a determined and successful stand, although serious fighting occurred more
than once as the struggle pushed down the railway. Malleson's reports
moved from euphoria to mild optimism to stark pessimism; plans to
develop communication lines and railway links on the long road south-
ward to India (Malleson, unlike Dunsterville, was supplied up the East
Persia Cordon line) were dropped, and Malleson warned his superiors
that he could not take on responsibility for Krasnovodsk; if Ashkhabad,
his main base on the railway and his link to the south, should be captured, he would have to fall back on his line of communication and thus
would be cut off from Krasnovodsk. As Montagu wrote privately to
Lord Chelmsford, the viceroy, ". . . a few days ago it looked as if the
position in Baku was irretrievable and the position in Trans-Caspia
promising. It now looks as if the position in Trans-Caspia was irretrievable, and the position in Baku promising!"[67]

On the latter point, however, he was misinformed, for Dunsterville

[66] Malleson telegrams to CGSI, 11, 15, 16, 18, 19 (2 of date), 20 (2)
August, CGSI telegram to Malleson, 18 August 1918, *War Diary,* Persia,
45; a copy of the agreement (quoted), IO Memorandum C. 187, may be
found at 2269/2269, *FO* 371/4106; see also Ellis, *British Intervention,*
Ch. IV.

[67] CGSI telegram to WO, 21 August, Malleson telegrams to CGSI,
21, 22, 28, and 29 August, *War Diary,* Persia, 45; Montagu private to
Chelmsford (quoted), 22 August 1918, *Montagu Papers,* IO Library, European Manuscript series D. 523, volume 2 [D. 523/2].

evacuated Baku in mid-September. The Committee managed to hold on in Ashkhabad through September and October, and while Dunsterville fell back on Enzeli and Bicherakov moved northward to Petrovsk, Krasnovodsk remained in Allied hands and began to assume considerable practical importance in the anti-Turko-German cordon (to say nothing of anti-Bolshevik operations). In an episode which has never been satisfactorily explained, more than two dozen Bolshevik officials who left Baku before its capture by the Turks passed through Ashkhabad, into the hands of the Ashkhabad Executive Committee for summary execution. Bolshevik commentators placed the blame squarely on Teague Jones, who was in Ashkhabad at the time, for connivance in, if not instigation of, this deed, although Teague Jones heatedly denied any responsibility for an act committed by the Ashkhabad authorities. The consensus seems to be that British representatives could have stopped the execution but did not.[68]

Investigation of this incident would have to await a calmer day. For the time being, it was much more pressing to halt the enemy's next likely step now that Baku was in their hands. Ashkhabad was no more than holding its own; India was unenthusiastic about recruiting Afhgani or Bukharan support. The best step, therefore, was to focus on the Caspian itself and control of its remaining fleet and ports. The Eastern Committee was by now convinced that only its members saw the dangers if the Caspian was lost. General Smuts, an occasional member of the committee, advocated ending the disabilities imposed by responsibility divided among Baghdad-Enzeli-Krasnovodsk-Meshed-Delhi. General Monro, Indian commander-in-chief, should, he proposed, be in charge of all Caucasian-Caspian-Central Asian operations—but in Baghdad, and under War Office control. The Indian authorities, who had actually initiated this plan—but never suggested a move to Baghdad—

[68] The twenty-six commissars are discussed in Ellis, "26 Commissars" and *British Intervention*, pp. 58-65; MacDonell, *". . . And Nothing Long",* pp. 258-59; Kazemzadeh, *Struggle,* pp. 144-46 (including references to Russian comment); Suny, *Baku Commune,* pp. 337-41.

The *War Diary* for September cannot be traced (see note 43, chapter 1). When Soviet accusations in this matter were made public, Teague Jones's defense was similarly published: Great Britain, Parliamentary Papers, Cmd. 1846 (Russia, No. 1, 1923): "Correspondence between His Majesty's Government and the Soviet Government respecting the Murder of Mr. C.F. Davison in January 1920."

recoiled in horror. No real solution in fact could be found to the need for "a sort of Eastern Foch," to use Montagu's phrase, and discussion of the idea turned largely into a comparison of the respective virtues, and faults, of Marshall in Baghdad and Monro in India. As Wilson, the commander of the Imperial General Staff, put it, all the changes in the world in the command structure would not put more Ford cars on the long road from Baghdad to Enzeli.[69]

Fortunately for all concerned, a new department now entered the fray. Regardless of distance from the open seas, Caspian operations were naval operations—and it was the only sea where the Royal Navy had never sailed. As early as June the Eastern Committee had agreed to consult with the body most knowledgeable on naval affairs. The Admiralty was not over-optimistic about seizing a fleet which was in Russian—and presumably hostile—hands, but the attempt could be made, and a hundred or so officers and men under Commander David T. Norris (Commodore, Persian Gulf and Mesopotamia) with a dozen 4" and 4.7" guns lifted from idle ships in Bombay harbor made the long trip to Baghdad and Enzeli. By August Norris was on the Caspian, trying to arm and equip a flotilla, although he found the going most difficult. Bicherakov, still in Baku and nominally in command there, was friendly, but the Russian sailors were much less so; the ships in Baku harbor were under the control of their several soviets, which had to pass on each order. Moreover, Norris found even the most ardent anti-Bolshevik Russians suspicious of British designs on what had been, after all, a Russian lake, and several generations of Anglo-Russian rivalry for Middle Eastern influence were not forgotten so easily. In fact, the more "White" the Russian, the more likely he was to uphold Tsarist claims to every last corner of the empire and all possible influence beyond, whether Caucasus, Caspian, or, as will be seen, Persia. In this case, for example, Russian authorities at Baku refused permission to fly the British white (naval) ensign.[70]

---

[69] Viceroy telegram to SSI, 26 August, *FO* 371/3304; CGSI telegram to Malleson, 7 October, *War Diary,* Persia, 47; Eastern Committee minutes, 17 and 18 (quoted) September, with documents appended: CinC India telegram to CIGS, 21 August, Smuts memorandum, 16 September, and Cecil private to Balfour, 15 September 1918, *L/P&S/*10/807.

[70] Secretary, Eastern Committee, to Admiralty, 5 June, Admiralty Plans Division note, 9 July, Admiralty Records, Public Record Office, series 137, volume 1736 [*ADM* 137/1736] ; senior naval officer, Baghdad, tele-

Even in the desperate days of late August and early September at
Baku, with the government of that city nominally friendly, Bolshevik-
dominated ships proved the opposite and, seizing guns and munitions
in the town, tried to escape to some point further up the coast. On 21
August, Norris and Dunsterville were fired upon near Derbent while
on a tour of inspection; for the second time British forces were in action
against the Bolsheviks in the Caspian area. The fall of Baku did not alter the situation, for the fleet retreated temporarily to Petrovsk with
Bicherakov. Norris was willing to continue operations from Enzeli,
and he had the Admiralty's full support. General Marshall in Baghdad,
however, was of a different opinion. Baku was in Turkish hands, Malleson was unwilling to reinforce Krasnovodsk, and there was little remaining prospect of controlling the Caspian fleet (it would probably
be worthless without Baku's oil in any case). The narrow escape of
Dunsterville should be a lesson well learned, not one requiring repetition at Krasnovodsk.[71]

Marshall's advice appeared to be sensible, particularly in the light
of Bicherakov's defeat at Vladikavkaz far to the north, where his "front"
could be said to operate. Cossack forces here suffered at Bolshevik
hands, and the death of the chief British military agent, Colonel Pike,
had hardly helped communications or intelligence.[72] In Ashkhabad on
the other side of the Caspian, Malleson's allies were in serious trouble;
Malleson was now reporting that the mobs of Turkoman tribesmen
who had taken to the field might well make a bid for power themselves.
The only defense against this, he pleaded, was massive aid for the Ash-

---

gram to Admiralty, 14 August 1918, *ADM* 137/1739 and other documents in file; Admiralty Naval Staff, Operations Division, memorandum,
ca. 28 March 1919, *ADM* 116/1862. See Capt. David Norris, "Caspian
Naval Expedition, 1918-1919," *Journal of the Central Asian Society* 10
(1923): 216-40; and Brig.-Gen. Sir Percy Sykes, "The British Flag on the
Caspian: A Side-Show of the Great War," *Foreign Affairs* 2 (1923): 282-94.

[71] Norris to CinC, East Indies Station, 28 August and 16 September,
Norris Papers, NOS/4, National Maritime Museum, Greenwich; Eastern
Committee, 26 September, *L/P&S/*10/807; GOC Baghdad telegram to
WO, 17 September, *WO* 106/60; Malleson telegram to Dunsterville (Enzeli), 7 October 1918, *War Diary,* Persia, 47. Ullman, *Anglo-Soviet Relations,* I, p. 310, is strictly accurate, however, in noting that there was no
fighting against the Bolsheviks.

[72] "Norpers," Kasvin, telegrams to DMI, 4 and 6 October 1918, *War
Diary,* Persia, 47.

khabad authorities—aid which had been pledged to them. He referred, of course, to his own unauthorized pledge, but London recognized that while it would not attempt large-scale aid to prop up a tumbling structure, it must do something for reputation's sake. Malleson now had 570 British and Indian troops (with two guns) operating with Ashkhabad's force at Dushak, where the front was now located, halfway from Ashkhabad to Merv on the railway. Fortunately, after heavy fighting in mid-October, the Bolshevik forces retreated, and by the end of the month Malleson's allies occupied Merv.[73]

The danger was not over, however. Although the Turks were crumbling in Palestine, which the War Office thought made assistance to Ashkhabad less imperative, the force at Krasnovodsk (by then 270 men) faced an estimated 7000 Bolsheviks headed down the railway in their direction and another 30-40,000 German and Austrian prisoners (or so estimates went) who might be brought into the fray. All that stood in their way was Malleson's main force and the uncertain Ashkhabad units. To London the Caspian was still essential, and for the Caspian, Krasnovodsk, and for Krasnovodsk, local allies—and only the Ashkhabad Executive Committee fit that category. The Eastern Committee, moreover, now not only thought to keep the Caspian and Central Asian railway secure, but also to protect Persia and Afghanistan from Bolshevik penetration, new goals which the military representative raised as the war came nearer to a close.[74]

The Turkish armistice in late October naturally eased fears of Turkish penetration beyond the Persian-Caspian cordon so tenuously constructed between Baghdad and Krasnovodsk. But that cordon availed little on the Caspian or in Central Asia, and in both areas the first serious Anglo-Soviet clashes had taken place. Just how Malleson had become so heavily committed to an anti-Bolshevik policy was hard to explain, nor did Malleson appear to consider any connection between his operations and those further west—let alone the entire issue of Russian policy. The postarmistice fall of the remaining Daghestan area to the

[73] Malleson telegrams to CGSI, 16, 17, and 18 October, SSI telegram to Viceroy, 17 October, CGSI telegram to Malleson, 19 October 1918, *War Diary,* Persia, 47; Ellis, *British Intervention,* Ch. IX.

[74] Eastern Committee, 16 and 24 October; viceroy telegram to SSI, 23 October, appended to Eastern Committee minutes for 21 November, *L/P&S/*10/807; G.O.C. Baghdad telegram to WO, 21 October 1918, *War Diary,* Persia, 47.

still-advancing Turkish forces, for example, left Bicherakov again without a base of operations; but Malleson saw to it that the "Caspian-Caucasus" state (for such was the new name of Bicherakov's structure) would not fall back on Krasnovodsk on the edge of his own sphere, fearing, he reported, that fresh hordes of undisciplined troops might be used by the Ashkhabad authorities against the local Turkomans in a small civil war. It was indicative of Malleson's attitude that in his telegrams to Simla headquarters on the subject he added that Bicherakov's appearance and the reemergence of a Russian presence at Krasnovodsk could well reduce British prestige in the area.[75] Here he probably was in unknowing agreement with Bicherakov himself, to whom preservation of Russian integrity was as important an objective as anti-Bolshevism or anti-Turkism, and his superiors were sufficiently sympathetic to this argument (or convinced that the man on the spot must be supported) that he was not overruled. The refusal to permit Bicherakov and the Petrovsk forces to operate from Krasnovodsk did not make Norris's job any easier, however, for it hardly reduced Russian suspicions. In the larger sense, in fact, the decision tended to contradict Malleson's own mission, since it severed, rather than preserved, connections between his operations on the one hand and those of the Caspian and Caucasus on the other.

Eastward of Malleson's front, the attempt to penetrate Turkistan from Kashgar had failed (although Etherton still provided valuable information from Kashgar, where he was now consul-general). Bailey remained in hiding, his very existence hampering Anglo-Soviet relations, since Malleson, with government approval, went out of his way to take hostages pending Bailey's safe return.[76] Only Afghanistan

[75] Malleson telegram to CGSI, 2 November 1918, *War Diary,* Persia, 48. Ellis, *British Intervention,* notes that Malleson was uncertain of Bicherakov's aims (pp. 113-34) but adds that the Ashkhabad Committee was able to come to terms with him sufficiently to bring some Daghestani cavalry across (pp. 128-29). The Ashkhabad Committee took the name Trans-Caspian Provisional Government in November and was briefly associated with Bicherakov's Centro-Caspian group before its demise in December; see Teague Jones report, note 62 chapter 1. On the Daghestan fighting, see W.E.D. Allen, "Military Operations in Dagestan, 1917-21," *Army Quarterly* 19 (1934): 39-53, 246-60, and Allen and Muratoff, *Caucasian Battlefields,* pp. 497-527.

[76] FO to IO, 31 October 1918, *L/P&S/*10/722 and other documents in

appeared untouched by these events; the British policy of preserving a
neutral and guaranteed Afghanistan seemed to be working. Even here
echoes from the north were having an effect, but it would be some
months before their impact would be felt. Afghanistan could be left
to its own devices at the moment, for the direct pan-Turanian or pan-
Islamic danger was deemed to have receded significantly after the
armistice.

The area could in no way be abandoned, however, because of the
Bolshevik problem. There appeared to be no coherent policy toward
Russia—what the policy was mattered less to India than that there be
one—and by default Britain had been pushed into an anti-Bolshevik
position in its operations between Krasnovodsk and Merv. Indian authorities found that every request to the Foreign Office or War Office
for a description of policy met with delay; pending decision by the Cabinet, they were told, the position should be held—if only because several
of the Turkish leaders such as Enver, Taalat, and Djemal Pashas had
disappeared, and if at all possible a Bolshevik-Turkish connection should
be prevented (on the theory, presumably, that all British enemies would
necessarily unite on that principle).[77] Anti-Turkish, like anti-German,
efforts were rapidly becoming anti-Bolshevik operations. For this reason, Britain would presumably stay on. But just as the position in the
Caucasus and Ukraine required that the Turkish Straits be open, operations in Central Asia and Trans-Caspia depended upon free operation
in Persia. This would be even more important if hostile forces came to
dominate the Caspian and the railway beyond. If Afghanistan was largely unaffected by the war, the same safe generalization was not at all
true for Persia.

PERSIA

At first glance, the Qajar monarchy of Persia had escaped the suicidal
fate of the Hohenzollern, Hapsburg, and Ottoman dynastic structures
by remaining neutral in the war. But the Qajars lasted very few years
longer than their Ottoman neighbors, and the war had as much to do
with their collapse. So weak was the Persian state when the war began

file; Ellis, *British Intervention*, p. 123.
[77] Viceroy telegram to SSI, 6 November, IO to FO, 14 November, with
minutes, FO to IO, 23 November 1918, *FO* 371/3304.

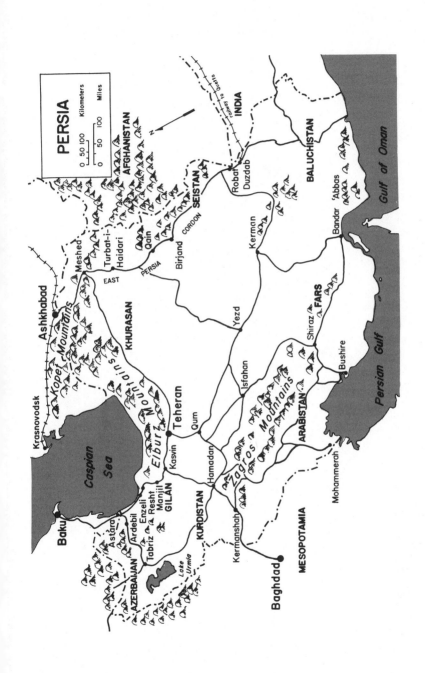

that it could not effectively deter any Persian adventure, whether by the British in the southern oilfields, the Turks or Russians in Kurdistan and Azerbaijan, or the tribes whose upheavals, so common in times of Persian monarchical weakness, were now spurred on by German agents. This weakness was no new phenomenon. A nationalist movement of prewar years, deceptively similar to the Young Turks, had looked to Britain for support, but despite gains, including a constitution, it was to a considerable extent undermined when the Anglo-Russian Accord of 1907 removed the possibility of playing Britain off against Russia. The agreement was seen by Persian nationalists as a betrayal, but it resolved the long-standing Anglo-Russian rivalry in Persia (in the interests of Anglo-Russian cooperation against Wilhelmian Germany) by dividing all Persia into three parts, the middle ground being neutral for concession-hunting. The war and inter-Allied negotiations of 1914-15 gave Britain a chance to trade recognition of Russian claims to Constantinople and the Straits for the neutral sphere of Persia. The Russian Revolution and renunciation of such treaties nullified the 1907 pact, and Tsarist Russian agents on the spot had often conducted themselves as if it did not exist, but at least the groundwork for official wartime Anglo-Russian association (and hostility to Persian nationalists) had been laid.[78]

Turkish-German activity in Persia and Afghanistan, real or anticipated, had to be forestalled, regardless of official Persian government desires. For this reason, Britain established a force of tribal levies known

[78] On the Persian background, see Peter Avery, *Modern Iran* (N.Y., 1965), and Brig.-Gen. Sir Percy Sykes, *A History of Persia*, 3rd ed., (London, 1930), vol. II. The Anglo-Russian rivalry is discussed in Firuz Kazemzadeh, *Russia and Britain in Persia, 1864-1914 . . .* (New Haven, Conn., 1968), and Briton Cooper Busch, *Britain and the Persian Gulf, 1894-1914* (Berkeley, 1967); Nasrollah Saifpour Fatemi, *Diplomatic History of Persia, 1917-1923* (N.Y., 1952) predates the opening of official documents. On wartime activities, Christopher Sykes, *Wassmuss, "The German Lawrence"* (London, 1936); Dickson, *East Persia;* Sir Clarmont Skrine, *World War in Iran* (London, 1962); Ulrich Gehrke, *Persian in der deutschen Orientpolitik während des Ersten Weltkrieges,* 2 volumes, (Stuttgart, [1961]); F.A.C. Forbes-Leith, *Checkmate: Fighting Tradition in Central Persia* (London, 1927); Maj.-Gen. J.A. Douglas, "The Bushire-Shiraz Road, 1918-1919," *Journal of the Central Asian Society* 10 (1923): 104-22; and, from the Soviet viewpoint, L.I. Miroshnikov, *Iran in World War I* (Moscow, 1963).

as the South Persian Rifles to combat the efforts of Wassmuss, "The German Lawrence," the former German consul at Bushire who was doing an admirable job of disrupting the province of Fars in the area of Shiraz. The East Persian Cordon was established on the other side of the country, and other minor operations—known only to devotees of gallant but unknown British military campaigns—involved the Baluch Camelry of some 400 men, the Meshed Hazara Contingent of 200, and the Seistan Levy Corps, established in 1915, which eventually reached 2500 men in 1919 and was closed down only in 1920.[79]

Such operations would have had a more popular following, perhaps, had they been regularized by formal recognition from the Persian government. In 1916 an opportunity for such a settlement was provided when a friendly grand vizier went so far as to propose an open alliance to British and Russian ministers in Teheran, but the cost was too high for Allied acquiescence: the Persians asked among other things recognition of Persian sovereignty over the Persian Gulf islands, tariff revision, military aid, and pledges respecting Persian independence. Yet it was agreed in India that a treaty on moderate terms, which shared responsibility for Persian expenses and hence, to some extent, policy, was very desirable, and would help conciliate Shiah Muslim opinion in Iraq and Muslim opinion in India—an aspect of Indian politics with which the Indian government was then closely concerned.[80]

Negotiations continued throughout 1916, but Russian unwillingness to make concessions sufficiently acceptable to the Persians limited agreement to the establishment of the Mixed Financial Commission of British, Russian, and Persian representatives. This would supervise expenditure of sums advanced to Persia under a procedure nominally related to outstanding Persian debts but actually amounting to an Allied subsidy. In return Persia would legitimize British and Russian operations by artfully disguising them as Persian forces under the headings, respectively, of South Persian Rifles and Persian Cossack Brigade. The financial aspect was complicated to an extent beloved by dealers in prewar Middle Eastern finance, but the details are unimpor-

[79] Consul, Seistan, to FSI, 7 October 1920, *L/P&S/*10/748. Various operations are discussed in Dickson, *East Persia;* Skrine, *World War in Iran;* Gould, *Jewel in the Lotus;* Sykes, *History of Persia,* II; Brig.-Gen. R.E.H. Dyer, *The Raiders of the Sarhad . . .* (London, 1921).

[80] The relations of India and Mesopotamia in wartime are discussed in Busch, *Britain, India, and the Arabs.*

tant since the Persian government never ratified the agreement and the Russian Revolution obviated formal Anglo-Russian cooperation.[81]

The revolution did not encourage a false feeling of British security in Persia, however. Quite the contrary: since Britain had come down on the side of agreement with Russia and not with the nationalists, the overthrow of the Tsarist government was an incentive to Persian nationalist sentiments. By June of 1917, even before the Bolshevik seizure of power, India was advising London that the formation of a hostile, pro-German government in Teheran—a real possibility at the time—would bring the collapse of the South Persian Rifles and an open road for the Turks to Afghanistan. Special measures would be required for the defense of the Persian Gulf ports and the Persian oilfields. The answer, as viewed from India, was conciliation of the nationalists, even if this meant scrapping the 1907 agreement. "It is obvious," telegraphed the viceroy, "that any attempt to continue old reactionary policy is doomed to failure in Persia and can only discredit us deeply elsewhere."[82]

It was an unpopular suggestion in the British Legation in Teheran. Marling advised the Foreign Office that India exaggerated the possible adverse repercussions of a democratic government which was only displaying a little predictable xenophobia. London agreed, not unnaturally, for India was asking the death of a basic principle of Middle Eastern policy for the last decade. As Shuckburgh noted in the India Office, the needs in Persia were based on protection of the Indian flank, and they took the form of defense against external aggression and internal anarchy. For the former, the 1907 agreement had been designed; for the latter, Britain had gradually been drawn by a process of trial and error to the conclusion that she had to assume responsibility for prevention of this herself, i.e., through the South Persian Rifles. Whatever the future had in store, it did not include the death of these needs. "What we cannot afford to do is to sacrifice essentials, or to assume that the Persian Gov[ernmen]t, however reconstituted or rehabilitated,

[81] Marling telegram to FO and viceroy telegram to SSI, 16 January, and Marling to Sir Edward Grey, 26 August 1916, *L/P&S*/10/584 and other documents in this volume; Shuckburgh note, 17 January 1917, 4546/ 17, *L/P&S*/10/550. See also Harish Kapur, *Soviet Russia and Asia, 1917-1927 . . .* (London, 1966), Ch. VI.

[82] Viceroy telegram to SSI, 25 June 1917, *L/P&S*/10/712.

will ever do for us what bitter experience has taught us that we must do for ourselves."[83]

This important policy debate continued throughout the summer of 1917. The principal contenders were Marling, who at best would make moderate concessions to undermine nationalist xenophobia, and the Indian Government, which saw full-fledged support for the democratic nationalists and their reform programs as the cheapest and most logical policy to achieve the aim of a friendly Persia. But to Marling, encouragement of reform was simply a different form of interference and would only reap further anti-British hostility with no consequent gains—for in his eyes the nationalist movement had proven itself incapable of real reform achievements.[84]

Marling's policy appealed to those who recalled the heavy diplomatic cost paid to achieve the 1907 accord in the first place. It also had the virtue of continuity with previous policy. Marling was unable to get the 1916 financial agreement ratified, but he did win recognition, of a sort, for the South Persian Rifles and its commander, Sir Percy Sykes, from the Persian government of Vossuq ed-Dowleh (July 1916-May 1917), generally regarded at the time as a true rarity since he was considered both capable and friendly to Britain. This was enough to persuade a newly formed (late July 1917) interdepartmental Persian committee (Curzon, chairman once again, Balfour, Hardinge, Montagu, Shuckburgh, and other War Office, Foreign Office, and India Office representatives). In the first meeting, the new committee in effect voted against India by concluding that the time was not opportune for large-scale reconsideration of policy toward Persia.[85]

But the Indian government could be maddeningly persistent, even when it had been overruled. Officials of the Foreign Department in Simla, particularly its secretary, Sir Henry Dobbs, were convinced that both London and Teheran were wrong. In a series of communications,

[83] Marling telegram to FO, 3 July, and Shuckburgh note, 5 July 1917, *L/P&S/*10/712.

[84] Viceroy telegram to SSI, 5 July, Marling telegrams to FO, 7 and 10 July, FO telegram to Marling, 7 July 1917, *L/P&S/*10/712.

[85] Marling letter to R. Cecil, 11 June, interdepartmental conference, 31 July 1917 (1st meeting of Persian Committee), *L/P&S/*10/712. Due to vagueness on chronology, Vossuq ed-Dowleh was generally thought by all concerned to have been the signatory of the 1916 agreement; it was in fact concluded by his predecessor.

India urged that no agreement was workable which did not regularize the position of the Rifles in Persian eyes; Britain had to show, if only to counteract Russian propaganda, that she had no designs on Persia. By mid-October, India's suggestions had become warnings; Britain was creating a costly force in the Rifles, which not only was most unpopular in Persia but which now lacked even the justification of being a counterpoise to a Russian force in the north. "The time has come when we must decide whether we are forcibly, and regardless of Persian opinion, to proceed with undertaking on proposed elaborate lines, or to modify it so as to conform more nearly to Persian opinion." The answer lay in turning over the SPR to Persia to such a degree as to make it tolerable to opinion in that country. Even Marling was willing to accept this concession, but in London neither the Foreign Office nor the India Office saw any advantage to be gained. The most the Persia Committee would authorize was that Marling should work for the restoration of Vossuq ed-Dowleh, now out of office, and that he might indicate a willingness to talk of subsidies and postwar SPR reorganization; no further concessions were to be made without a change in the Persian government and guarantees of security against both Turkish and German intrigues and Persian recognition of the Rifles.[86]

Marling's options were limited, but he asked for no more; as he explained in early December, what might have worked up until the summer of 1917 would now only give Persia an exaggerated idea of her own importance. He was given freedom to offer a subsidy of 250,000 tomans per month (some £8,500), and to this India objected. This meant a government friendly only because it would have been bribed, said Dobbs, and that was hardly a guarantee of permanence or security. The objection was overruled, but Vossuq ed-Dowleh himself raised the terms by asking a further substantial sum to maintain the Cossack force (Russian contributions having run out) and to undertake operations against the Jangalis. He also wanted such diplomatic concessions

[86] Viceroy telegrams to SSI, 18 August, 20 September, 13 October (quoted), Marling telegrams to FO, 4 and 13 (with IO minutes) October, and private telegram to Hardinge, 10 September, Persia Committee, 20 October and 10 November, DMI note, 22 October, FO telegram to Marling, 23 October, Shuckburgh note for Persia Committee, 9 November, *L/P&S/* 10/712; viceroy telegram to SSI, 20 September, with Oliphant (FO) minute, 30 September, FO telegram to Marling, 15 November 1917, *FO* 371/2988.

as immediate cancellation of the 1907 accord and representation in any postwar peace conference. These demands were too extensive, but London never saw the Indian alternative of an accommodation with the "democrats" as acceptable. Perhaps the greatest reason for this was Marling's opinion that such an agreement would only mean that every concession demanded henceforth by the "democrats" would have to be acceded to, and each demand would only bring another on the analogy of the prewar Young Turks in Constantinople; another reason, however, was that India never quite managed to spell out the specific steps by which such an accommodation might be reached.[87]

By the end of 1917, the sense of urgency was increasing. In late November, Vossuq ed-Dowleh had again become a cabinet member, although not prime minister; the chance for reaching terms with him was thus more realistic, but nationalist agitation was also on the increase. Marling's warnings of a possible nationalist coup d'etat, however, only brought "I told you so" comments from India. Nationalist activity, of course, was in direct response to the visible increase of the British presence in the eastern cordon, the South Persia Rifles, the several smaller forces, and the Hamadan road: in fact, on all Persian frontiers save the Caspian coast. With the age-old Russian rival removed, logic concluded that Britain was extending her sway over the whole of Persia; the absence of the Russian rival simply focused all nationalist attention on anti-British activity.[88]

It was not too difficult to see the drift of events from London. As Sir Arthur Hirtzel, influential in the India Office's Political Department, commented, both the Turks and the Russians loudly proclaimed their withdrawal from Persia (or rather, in the Turkish case, that they would withdraw if the British did also). Ironically, concluded Hirtzel, it was too late for concessions, and Britain could only go on with Marling's line. With this sort of thinking in London, it is not surprising that when Marling requested £50,000 for bribes to give Vossuq ed-Dowleh control of the government it was given him. Moreover, he was also given permission to declare that Britain agreed to cancel the 1907

[87] Marling private telegram to Oliphant, 28 November, viceroy telegram to SSI, 3 December, with Shuckburgh note, 5 December, *L/P&S*/10/712; Marling telegrams to FO, 5, 16, and 20 December, Curzon note for Hardinge, 17 December 1917, *FO* 371/2988.

[88] Marling telegram to FO, 22 November, viceroy telegram to SSI, 18 December 1917, *L/P&S*/10/712 (and *FO* 371/2988).

treaty (when Russia, the other signatory, also agreed)—but the South Persia Rifles could not be given up, at least not yet.[89]

On the other hand, Marling's position was made more difficult by the British decision to take over the Russian section of the East Persia Cordon. Active defense measures were simply not compatible with conciliation; the Persia Committee could not accept that the Indian solution—concession, conciliation, and the replacement of "reactionary" Marling—would somehow remove the need for military operations in Persia.[90] "George Curzon says that he understands all about [the Persian situation]," wrote Robert Cecil, committee member and no admirer of the group's chairman,

> . . . but I have my doubts, and I am sure that no one else has even a glimmer of understanding of what is going on there. In these circumstances the only possible course seems to be to let Marling do what he likes, as far as George can be persuaded to allow him to do so, and to try to find money to bribe those Persians whom he thinks worth bribing.[91]

As telegraphed to Marling, however, the policy was represented as a careful reconsideration of Persian policy that had resulted in a willingness to make conciliatory gestures, including the conversion of the South Persia Rifles into a Persian rather than British force (although with British officers until war's end). An afterthought suggested that in return for recognition of the South Persia Rifles and the appointment of British officers for the Cossack force, Britain would remove from central Persia those British army units that had come to the aid of the South Persia Rifles. These proposals go no further than Marling; the Cossack force, he reported, was scattered and unreliable. Nor would

[89] Hirtzel minute, 20 December, on viceroy telegram, 18 December, Marling private telegram to Hardinge, 17 December, Hardinge demi official to Holderness (IO) 18 December, and Holderness to Hardinge, 19 December, FO telegram to Marling, 22 December, *L/P&S/*10/712; FO telegram to Marling, 25 December, *FO* 371/2988; WO memorandum, 31 December 1917 and Marling telegram to FO, 5 January 1918, *FO* 371/3258.

[90] SSI telegram to viceroy, 1 January, Persia Committee, 12 January, IO to FO, 16 January 1918, with Oliphant, Hardinge minutes, *FO* 371/3258.

[91] Cecil private to Balfour, 8 January 1918, *Balfour Papers,* Add. Ms. 49738.

the Persians reach any decision until Britain had demonstrated her strength and clarity of intention by a show of force on the Hamadan road in the suppression of the Jangalis. Concessions now would only show weakness and would make no new friends.[92]

India, as could be expected, opposed Marling again. If force were used, it would have to overawe the country, which would not only discredit British policy completely in Persia and Afghanistan, but would probably turn into an expensive occupation. This could be justified only by the strongest possible political motives, invisible in India, such as the immediate likelihood of a Turko-German thrust into Persia. As for the Hamadan road, an advance in that direction would only bring disorder in Teheran and the provincial capitals; in any case, communication to the Caucasus was a secondary goal, and Dunsterville seemed unlikely to reach Enzeli. The western cordon was mainly to stop agents intended for Afghanistan, but the eastern cordon could do that job. India did not accept the Foreign Office argument that the Persians realized that Hamadan-Enzeli operations were in Persia's own interests.[93]

Unfortunately for Marling's influence, his opinion now appeared to undergo complete reversal. Discouraged when his suggestion for full military occupation of the Kermanshah-Kasvin road was rejected (India had won that point), he now claimed to see no alternative except the conciliation policy he had so consistently opposed, although he still warned that there would be no end to nationalist demands. Disbanding the western cordon, removing a newly landed force from Bushire on the Persian Gulf, shutting down the South Persia Rifles—the result would be the complete removal of Persia from British influence, and Persia was no less important to Britain than the Afghanistan which so preoccupied India.[94]

But as the Foreign Office pointed out, the choices were not so simple. Refusal to send a major force against the Jangalis did not mean abandoning the Hamadan road; Dunsterville was there already. Indeed, if a definitely hostile Persian government came into power, more and

[92] SSI telegram to viceroy, 9 February, Marling telegrams to FO, 3, 5, 12 (2 of date), 14, and 18 February, viceroy telegrams to SSI, 12, 16, and 23 February, FO telegram to Marling, 21 February 1918, *FO* 371/3258.

[93] Viceroy telegram to SSI, 23 February 1918, *FO* 371/3258.

[94] Nicolson (FO) memorandum, 22 February, FO telegram to Marling, 21 February, Marling telegram to FO, 24 February, *FO* 371/3258; IO memorandum, 24 February 1918, *FO* 371/3259.

sizable forces might have to be stationed on the road to keep clear communications with the Caucasus and prevent incursions into Persia. It was possible the enemy might occupy the oilfields, or even Isfahan or Teheran itself, for the more London became aware of the problems in Gilan, the more this main communications route to the Caspian and Caucasus seemed jeopardized. Moreover, bigger plans for the western cordon were in harmony with the steady drift toward intervention in Russia.[95]

In the spring of 1918, the War Office more and more urged extreme measures upon the Persia Committee, particularly the occupation of Isfahan, with or without Persian permission, while the Foreign Office favored caution, warning that a dangerous anarchy might follow upon such an action. Curzon wrote privately to Henry Wilson that the problem was not simply to find jobs for Dunsterville's force because it could not get through to the Caucasus. Even Marling was alarmed at the Isfahan idea, and for the moment the Eastern Committee (a new body which had absorbed the Persia Committee) shelved the plan in favor of pushing forward in the northwest. From that direction events in Teheran could better be influenced than from the more remote Isfahan in any case, and meanwhile the Bakhtiari tribesmen of Arabistan (and the oilfields) could be persuaded to adopt a closer relationship with Britain.[96]

The idea of a special alliance with Persia was still alive, however. While the Eastern Committee and Marling were complaining that the army was not building up the Hamadan road position (a lethargy traceable to General Marshall's complete lack of enthusiasm for the project), Marling continued to urge that a treaty with Vossuq ed-Dowleh was an alternative to a Persian association with an apparently victorious (at least in the Caucasus) Turko-German combination. The fallacy here, countered India, was the assumption that a Persian cabinet—any Persian cabinet—could control the situation in Persia. On the contrary, simply signing such a treaty would inevitably be the death-blow to any

[95] Marling telegram to FO, 26 February, viceroy telegram to SSI and FO telegram to Marling, 27 February, Persia Committee, 1 March, R. Graham memorandum (making the connection with intervention), 28 February 1918, *FO* 371/3258.

[96] FO telegram to Marling, 7 March, Persia Committee, 5, 11, and 22 March, WO to FO, 15 March, Wilson private note to Curzon and Curzon private note to Wilson, 23 March, viceroy telegram to SSI, 25 March, FO 371/3258; Eastern Committee, 28 March 1918, *L/P&S/*10/807.

cabinet. In any case, a treaty would doubtless require British commitment to defend Persia against attack . . . the idea was, in short, absurd.[97]

Not even the South Persia Rifles, on which so much hope was placed, appeared reliable; in June the SPR seemed stymied by a local rising near Shiraz, and if the force could not deal with local enemies, it was hardly going to influence Persian events as a whole. In fact, London saw no alternative to sending Bushire the two battalions of reinforcements for which Sykes asked, despite Montagu's objections in the Eastern Committee. Nor was Marling happy about this. He had argued in support of a greater show of force to rally Vossuq ed-Dowleh's party, but Sykes had rather too much of an independent hand in south Persia for his liking; Marling's relations with Sykes were bad enough to cloud any rational analysis of the situation.[98]

The paradox of Persian policy was that while small doses of force could achieve local objectives, they hardly corresponded with conciliation and persuasion of even the conservative element in Persia, for they appeared as simple dismemberment. By late June 1918 Montagu was a convinced advocate of withdrawal from Persia, although he wanted a secure alliance first, hardly a real possibility. He was willing to trade the South Persia Rifles for such an alliance, but the Eastern Committee was unable to decide which was the less worthless, a paper alliance or a force mired in the Shiraz area. For the complete muddle Marling tended to receive a good deal of blame, particularly when he was assailed by Dobbs in India, Montagu in London, and Sykes around the

[97] Marling telegram to FO, 14 May, *FO* 371/3259; Marling telegram to FO, 20 May, FO telegram to Marling, 23 May, Viceroy telegram to SSI, 24 May, *FO* 371/3260; Montagu note for Eastern Committee, 5 June, *L/P&S*/10/727. Marling did not help his case by urging that Dunsterville was needed in Persia and should not go to the Caucasus, for this appeared— in India, at least—to be a sign of panic; GOC Baghdad telegram to Marling, 25 May, with Indian GHQ minutes, and WO telegram to GOC Baghdad, 27 May 1918, *War Diary,* Persia, 42.

[98] Viceroy telegram to SSI, 6 June, Shuckburgh note, 8 June, *L/P&S*/10/727; Eastern Committee, 11 June, *L/P&S*/10/807; Montagu private to Chelmsford, 31 May, *Montagu Papers,* D. 523/2; Marling telegrams to FO, 13, 15, 19, and 24 June 1918, *FO* 371/3260. Marling's reports on Sykes changed from full support (Marling telegram to FO, 13 June 1917, *L/P&S*/10/727) to requesting the removal of an obstreperous local dictator (Marling private telegram to Hardinge, 31 August 1918, *FO* 371/3262).

corner. Still, the only solution for the moment appeared to be to re-inforce Bushire, thereby committing more troops, and to give Marling a free hand in Teheran concession-making. As a gesture to India, Indian military authorities were given control of all Persian military operations (the Hamadan road had been under Baghdad), a tainted gift to which India took strong exception, since military control was not accompanied by political control.[99]

Marling's free hand resulted in some new activity—although not quite what the Eastern Committee had in mind. Convinced that Ahmed Shah's persistent opposition to appointing Vossuq ed-Dowleh as chief minister stemmed from enemy encouragement as much as personal animosity, and more concerned now with the Persian than the Caucasian situation, Marling concluded that a show of force was necessary. He urged that Dunsterville be reinforced and not allowed to dissipate his energies in the direction of Tabriz. Force on the level Marling advocated, however, was simply impossible, given Marshall's resistance, London's confusion on objectives, and the sheer physical problems of supply of which Marling appeared to India to have absolutely no understanding. The more Marling insisted, the more the Eastern Committee agreed with India that Marling should be removed. A candidate for his appointment came immediately to mind in Sir Percy Cox, long on experience in the Persian Gulf area and already involved as Marshall's chief political officer in Baghdad.[100]

Marling had one more shot in his locker, however. In mid-July his military attache, Lieut.-Colonel C.B. Stokes, organized a demonstration of Vossuq ed-Dowleh's followers in Teheran with the apparent approval of both Vossuq ed-Dowleh and Marling. The matter went further than anticipated and ended farcically with a small armed band occupying a mosque in a Teheran bazaar. Marling packed Stokes off to Dunster-ville's force (the nearest available Siberia), as much for reporting in-

[99] Eastern Committee, 21 and 24 June, *L/P&S/*10/807; FO telegrams to Marling, 29 June and 1 July, *FO* 371/3260; viceroy telegram to SSI, 1 July 1918, *L/P&S/*10/735.

[100] Marling telegrams to FO, 15 and 24 June, FO telegram to Marling, 1 July, *FO* 371/3260; viceroy telegram to SSI, 9 July, *FO* 371/3261; Eastern Committee, 4 July 1918, *L/P&S/*10/807. On Cox, Philip Graves, *The Life of Sir Percy Cox* (London, 1941); further details of his earlier career may be found in Busch, *Britain and the Persian Gulf* and *Britain, India, and the Arabs.*

dependently to the Chief of the Imperial General Staff in London as
for failure. Stokes revealed to London that Marling had paid out
£10,000-£15,000 for the episode and had assured the demonstrators
that the Cossacks would not intervene (after all, Britain was now paying their expenses of £50,000 per month)—only to find that force
putting down the coup. More doubtless would have been heard of this
affair had not Marling's intrigues apparently been successful.

In the first week of August Vossuq ed-Dowleh accepted office, and
Marling began to pay out the subsidy authorized earlier.[101] In any case,
recriminations were unnecessary, for the decision to remove Marling
had been taken even before the demonstration and change of Persian
government. Only Cox's sense of duty made him leave a successful
appointment in Mesopotamia for a dubious honor in Persia. [102]

Cox was not to arrive until mid-September, and in the meantime
India urged that with a new minister and a new Persian cabinet the time
had come to reconsider the whole of Persian policy. The military situation, however, had not improved. Shiraz was now under control, it
was true, but Resht, on the Hamadan road a few miles south of Enzeli,
was attacked in mid-July by the Jangalis; some fierce fighting ensued,
and several British representatives were taken prisoner. Dunsterville
himself soon moved off to Baku, but his lines of communication were
hardly secure; his precipitous return to Enzeli may not have helped
Britain's reputation in Persia, but it did put more British forces on the
Persian road. In any case, all admitted Cox would need time to assess
the situation in Teheran and to guide events toward an agreement of
some sort. But nothing formal had been achieved by the Turkish armistice in October, after which Persian problems became all the more Russian problems and peace settlement problems.[103]

The situation in Persia at the end of the war was thus a complicated

[101] Marling telegrams to FO, 16 July and 5 August, *FO* 371/3261;
Stokes telegram to CGSI, 10 July, Marling telegram to FO, 16 July, and
FO telegram to Marling, 13 July 1918, *L P&S*/10/735.

[102] Chelmsford private to Montagu, 13 and 27 July, Montagu private
to Chelmsford, 7 August, *Montagu Papers,* D. 523/2 and 7; Chelmsford
private telegrams to Montagu, 22 and 25 July and 10 August 1918, *Chelmsford Papers* (IO Library), E. 264/9. In order to modify the public impact of
this change, Cox went as "special commissioner," with minister-level salary,
while Marling technically returned home on leave.

[103] Marling telegram to FO, 23 July, *FO* 371/3261; Cox telegrams to

one. Britain had a legacy of operations conducted in Persia, without Persian permission, to preserve law and order as defined by Britain and to govern Persia's choice of friends or enemies. These operations never overawed Persian opinion completely or frightened the population into compliance, but they were more than enough to engender a new wave of Persian nationalism, now directed solely against Britain. Worse, Russia now appeared ready to forswear all earlier great-power advantages, and even the most conciliation-minded expert in India had not moved that far. Still worse, while a new, presumably wiser and more experienced advisor was in Teheran, he was fairly well committed to a line of action initiated by Marling. Vossuq ed-Dowleh, after all, had been put in power by British efforts and was being kept there by a substantial British subsidy. One final factor existed. By 1918 it was not solely Indian security that depended upon Persian security, but the very existence of a British presence in the Caucasus, the Caspian, and Central Asia. Indian security had depended upon a quiet Afghanistan and a quiet Persia, which in turn depended upon a relatively quiet Russia; but Russia was an unknown quantity now. Nobody was yet willing to admit that its collapse left an all too tempting vacuum (although Montagu was not far from just such a conclusion). By default and by design, Britain's frontier in western Asia had advanced through the Ottoman and Persian Empires to a line which, in October of 1918, could be described as Aegean Sea-Mosul-Enzeli-Krasnovodsk-Ashkhabad-Meshed-Indian frontier. This was a substantial advance over a position which in 1914 had included none of the Ottoman Empire beyond Egypt and a tenuous foothold in Kuwait, and only a third of Persia. Already the British wave lapped at the Turkish Straits, at Baku and Krasnovodsk on the Caspian, and as far as Bukhara and even Tashkent in Central Asia. Persia was dominated more than ever before, and Afghanistan had been kept isolated, pristine and intact. The end of the Turkish war, however, removed one last obstacle by opening up the Black Sea to Allied intervention; the solution to the Eastern Question—British style—was one step closer.

FO, 17 and 23 September, *FO* 371/3262; Hirtzel note, 21 August 1918, *L/P&S/*10/728.

II

Flood Tide: Turkey, 1918-1919

The armistice of Mudros, like other armistices, was designed as a temporary agreement to end hostilities in anticipation of a more permanent peace. The idea of bypassing an armistice and moving directly to a peace treaty had not been adopted, but there remained certain clear-cut Allied needs in whatever settlement the future provided; the irony of the situation was that the Allies, in the process of securing those needs, jeopardized the possibility of quickly establishing the secure and peaceful Turkey on which the position in the Caucasus, Caspian, and south Russian areas heavily depended. The link between Russian and Turkish problems was a fateful one. For example, any Allied presence in Constantinople would be temporary, but the permanent treaty would be expected to permit access to the Black Sea and beyond, for even as the Allied troops settled in Constantinople that city was becoming an important way-station on the route to Russian intervention.

In late December 1918 the leading brigade of the Salonika Force's 27th Division was in Batum. This division, together with the 28th, made up the Army of the Black Sea under General Sir George Milne. Milne was senior British commander and had the perplexing position, familiar in this war, of independent command responsibility under the War Office coupled with technical subordination to a French general: in this case, General Franchet d'Espérey, who remained in command of the Salonika Force. Double lines of authority, the rather fiery and ambitious character of the French general ("desperate Franky" to his critics), and the strong Anglophobia of both that officer and some of his superiors contributed to a situation in which Milne's first concern was as likely to be the French as the Turks.[1]

---

[1] Edmonds memorandum, note 1, chapter 1. The British 22nd and

Milne was not the local British spokesman. Admiral Gough-Cal-thorpe, who had signed the armistice, had that honor; when it became clear that Britain would require a "high commissioner" to act in place of the prewar British ambassador, it was only natural that Gough-Cal-thorpe should be given this position. As the official channel for com-munications between the British and Ottoman governments, he thus had dual responsibility to Admiralty and Foreign Office. Since Gough-Calthorpe remained commander-in-chief of the (British) Mediter-ranean Fleet, with its main base at Malta and a range of problems ex-tending well beyond Turkey, local negotiations often fell to his assistant high commissioner, Rear-Admiral Sir Richard Webb, who remained on shore at Constantinople.[2]

Inevitably, this complicated command structure led to friction and delay, but less than might have been predicted. A common front was required in the face of the Turks and French, and the traditional fric-tion between army and navy was minimal under the circumstances. Fortunately for Allied unity, Franchet d'Espérey did not formally occupy his new headquarters until February 1919, a delay which allowed the various British departments to work out their own relationships; but when the French general did arrive, he communicated with Milne through a liaison officer, Lieutenant-General Sir Tom Bridges. Neither Milne nor Franchet d'Espérey saw the need for this position, and an official historian has argued that Bridges only aggravated an already tense situation, although Bridges himself felt he served an essential function in a setting which was "like having two prima donnas on the stage together." Franchet d'Espérey claimed that Milne's operations fell under his authority; Britain argued that the Salonika sphere ended at the Straits. Early in December 1918 agreement had been reached on the independence of Milne's authority in the Caucasus and on the Asiatic side of the Straits, but, since no formal lines of demarcation were laid out, arguments continued.[3]

26th Divisions, also in the Salonika force, were demobilized.

[2] R. Cecil for Balfour, 6 November, and Balfour-Cecil draft of private letter to Gough-Calthorpe, 9 November 1918, 185243 and 186801/185243, *FO* 371/3415. A discussion of abortive plans to send Allenby, not Gough-Calthorpe, may be found in *Balfour Papers, FO* 800/206.

[3] Edmonds memorandum, note 1, chapter 1; Lt.-Gen. Sir Tom Bridges, *Alarms and Excursions: Reminescences of a Soldier* (London, 1938) p. 258; DMI memorandum, n.d. (but December 1918), *WO* 106/1389.

The most convenient arena of conflict was Constantinople, where the French had landed forces from their 122eme division as part of Allied operations to enforce the armistice terms—operations which included posting units along the Turkish railway network with supervisory control officers at the main provincial centers. Constantinople was naturally the focus of Allied activity. Even without formal occupation of the city, Allied officers had to control Turkish demobilization, armaments stores, and so on. The general malaise of the Turkish administration coupled with the presence of numerous foreigners, official and unofficial, who roamed the city, soon forced the creation of an international police force which, although nominally responsible only for these foreigners, also oversaw the 3200 local police.

The Allied force, headed by a British president of commission, divided the city into areas of responsibility. Britain assumed charge of Pera and Galata, which housed most of the foreign population, while France and Italy respectively watched the quieter Turkish residential areas of Stamboul and Scutari across the Bosporus. Before many months had passed, the force numbered some 400 officers and men, and much of its attention was shifting to the flock of refugees pouring into the city. By the end of 1919 there were roughly 100,000 such homeless individuals in Constantinople, the majority of whom were Russians in flight from turmoil in the Ukraine and the Crimea. Technically the Allied force had no legal powers from the Turkish standpoint (the infamous capitulatory privileges had been abolished early in the war), nor did the special courts which had sprung up by necessity to deal with culprits apprehended by this force. The result was perhaps *"trop de policies, et trop peu de justice . . ."* as one observer put it, but there appeared little alternative at the time.[4]

[4] Conditions in Constantinople are discussed in Clarence R. Johnson, ed., *Constantinople Today . . .* (N.Y., 1922); Sir Telford Waugh, *Turkey Yesterday, To-Day and Tomorrow* (London, 1930); Gates, *Not to Me Only;* Harold Armstrong, *Turkey in Travail* (London 1925); Maurice Pernot, *La question turque* (Paris, 1922), p. 14 (quoted); Edgar Peck, *Les Alliés et la Turquie* (Paris, 1925); Mary Mills Patrick, *A Bosporus Adventure . . .* (Stanford, 1934); Henri Mylès, *La fin de Stamboul* (Paris, 1921); Roy Elston, *The Traveler's Handbook for Constantinople, Gallipoli, and Asia Minor* (London, 1923); Sir Andrew Ryan, *The Last of the Dragomans* (London, 1951), pp. 118-51; John Dos Passos, *Orient Express* (N.Y., 1922); K. Zia Bey Mufty-Zade, *Speaking of the Turks* (N.Y., 1922); Bridges, *Alarms and Excursions;* Lt.-Col. P.R. Butler, "Grief and Glamour

Police and courts and refugee control were soon supplemented by sanitary control, harbor police, censorship (in answer to attacks on the Allies in the local press), a prison commission, and an international requisitions agency (mainly to requisition homes and offices for the Allied forces serving the many commissions). All required staffs, housing, amenities, and complex inter-Allied committees to run their affairs. Usually these commissions included British, French, and Italian representatives, but further complications resulted from a substantial official Greek presence and a very active American relief effort, which from February 1919 was using Constantinople as a base from which to feed most of the Caucasian and Armenian refugees. The result was another foreign colony, largely naval in this case, under the leadership of Rear-Admiral Mark L. Bristol, who pursued a course described by himself as "based upon the American idea of a square deal and clean, open policy." During this unofficial gradual assumption of the governance of Constantinople, relations between the several commanders were often strained. There were few common aims, and fewer common policies; in general, the various high commissioners did little but watch each other jealously.[5]

---

of the Bosporus," *Blackwood's,* 209 (1921): 203-12; Maj. Leonard Ridgway, "A Unique Army Headquarters," unpublished ms. (1971), Imperial War Museum, London (the author is further indebted to Major Ridgway for his personal recollections). Specific responsibilities are studied in WO (MO1) note, 6 December 1918, *WO* 106/1434 (general situation); Harington to WO, 28 October 1921, *FO* 371/6571 (police); Capt. J.C. Thomson, R.M., report, 4 February 1919, 31314/3405, and other documents in file, *FO* 371/4197 (censorship). An essential work on the legal position and capitulations is Nasim Sousa, *The Capitulatory Regime of Turkey . . .* (Baltimore, 1933); wartime abolition is discussed on p. 193. The text of the abolition is in Hurewitz, *Diplomacy,* II, pp. 2-3.

[5] American relief is treated in James L. Barton, *Story of Near East Relief (1915-1930) . . .* (N.Y., 1930); William H. Hall, ed., *Reconstruction in Turkey . . .* (N.Y., 1918); Hovanissian, *Republic,* I, pp. 133-44. On Bristol, and American policy in general, see Thomas A. Bryson, "Mark Lambert Bristol . . .," and "An American Mandate For Armenia . . .," *Armenian Review* 21 (1968): 3-41; James B. Gidney, *A Mandate for Armenia* (Kent, Ohio, 1967) (pp. 200-1 treat Bristol); Marjorie Housepian, *The Smyrna Affair* (N.Y., 1971), a determined critic of Bristol; Roger R. Trask, *The United States Response to Turkish Nationalism and Reform, 1914-1939* (Minneapolis, 1971), Ch. II; Lawrence Evans, *United States Policy and the Partition of Turkey, 1914-1924* (Baltimore, 1965); Joseph

One extremely bitter argument was the prolonged struggle for control of the city's single powerful radio station; another the French issuance of passports to persons Britain considered deserving of arrest or examination. Particularly worrisome was the apparent French attempt to reestablish commercial and mercantile dominance in Turkey by focusing on possession of enemy property and business interests. Before long, reported one British officer in a later account, the French were subsidizing Turkish (European language) newspapers to publish anti-British articles. Franchet d'Espérey's high commissioner, Defrance, proved nearly as troublesome as his master (despite some old British connections), and the various French officers associated with control functions at centers such as Afyonkarahisar and Eskishehir reflected the attitudes of their superiors.[6] These quarrels and conflicts were nothing new. To some extent the First World War had only been a new stage in a historic Anglo-French struggle for influence in the Middle East—a stage which was particularly galling to the French, for, as Lloyd George had the effrontery to persist in repeating, Britain had done the bulk of the fighting in this theater and apparently expected to reap all the rewards.

Constantinople was thus in a peculiar position, occupied but unoccupied, Turkish but Allied, packed with impoverished refugees (with more on the way) and Allied officers and men on temporary duty expecting rewards and entertainments due them as victors and as compensation for lack of demobilization. The city was crowded and ex-

---

L. Grabill, "Missionary Influence on American Relations with the Near East, 1914-1923," *Muslim World* 58 (1968): 43-56, 141-54; Henry P. Beers, *U.S. Naval Detachment in Turkish Waters, 1919-1924* (Washington, D.C., 1943); Robert L. Daniel, "The Armenian Question and American Turkish Relations, 1914-1927," *Mississippi Valley Historical Review* 46 (1959): 252-75; Howard M. Sacher, *The Emergence of the Middle East, 1914-1924* (N.Y., 1969), pp. 336-65. Bristol's self-characterization is from Bristol private to Rear-Admiral H.S. Knapp (Commanding US Naval Forces in Europe), 15 January 1920, *Bristol Papers* (Library of Congress), box 37.

[6] GOC Constantinople telegram to WO, 9 January, and WO telegram to GOC Constantinople, 11 January 1919, *FO* 371/4164, on the radio station; Armstrong, *Turkey in Travail,* pp. 92-93, on passports and newspapers. On Defrance, see Derby (Paris) telegram to FO, 11 January, and memorandum, 12 February 1919, 6363 and 51844/6363, *FO* 371/4201; Derby knew Defrance personally.

pensive, but plenty of opportunities for recreation were available: Constantinople earned a reputation for liveliness not far exceeded even by fabled Paris or Berlin in the early twenties. For many, life was grim indeed, with shortages of essential commodities and soaring prices. Corruption was rife and salaries of Turkish government officials often unpaid. But there was another Constantinople. "Life was gay and wicked and delightful," wrote Harold Armstrong, and he was not referring to the newly installed sports facilities or the pack of hounds kept in the country across the Bosporus.[7] Gypsy violins, motor boats on Marmora, demimondaines, requisitioned Bosporus villas—for unattached young officers, Constantinople was more than bearable. It almost comes as a surprise that along with regard for the passing world at large, and suspicion for the French and Italians, some notice could also be taken of Turkey itself.

WARTIME COMMITMENTS

It was not as if Turkey's future had received no consideration during the war. Quite to the contrary, the plethora of wartime negotiations, agreements, and half-promises squarely blocked any simple peace treaty with Turkey from the very inception of the armistice negotiations.One catalogue of British commitments outstanding in early 1919 lists nineteen pledges by which Britain alone was bound in regard to the future of Turkey and its constituent parts. It includes such memorable documents as the Balfour Declaration (affecting Palestine) and the Hussein-McMahon Correspondence (which made certain promises to the Arabs)—but several commitments, particularly to Russia, were no longer regarded as binding. In the negotiations of 1914-15 Russia had been given Constantinople and southern Thrace to a line from Enos on the Aegean to Midia on the Black Sea, all in addition to Armenia. Had Russia not been convulsed by revolution, and had the Allies felt bound to stand by that pledge, much of the ensuing debate on the future of Constantinople would have been unnecessary, although Russian possession of that city would have hardly ended the Eastern Question.[8]

[7] Armstrong, *Turkey in Travail,* p. 97; Bridges, *Alarm and Excursions* p. 274, notes the pack of hounds.

[8] Memorandum, 8 February 1919, cited and outlined in Zeine N. Zeine, *The Struggle for Arab Independence* (Beirut, 1960) pp. 190-91; the Rus-

Russian demands, inspired by fears that the Gallipoli campaign might be successful, insured Britain's consideration of its own hopes and needs in the Ottoman area. A special committee on "British Desiderata in Turkey in Asia," established under Sir Maurice de Bunsen in 1915, outlined in its often-discussed final report a number of points important to Britain, including maintenance of Persian Gulf influence, commercial importance, strategic communications, a suitable Armenian solution, and a settlement for Muslim holy places which would satisfy these aims and yet—a significant point—be acceptable to Indian Muslim opinion. Several means were available to accomplish these goals, including partition of Turkey, spheres of control, or some sort of federalist or decentralized solution. The last, was judged by the committee to have the edge in terms of convenience.[9] In a sense, however, these discussions were already academic at the time, for the pledge to Russia meant practical partition; Britain had already moved in that direction early in the war by declaring formal annexation of Cyprus and protectorate status for British-occupied Egypt. Moreover, Asquith, as prime minister, had made a very official-sounding pledge that the war tolled the death-knell of the Ottoman Empire, "not only in Europe, but in Asia." The committee, recognizing the problem such commitments created, indicated that if decentralization proved impossible, Britain's special interests lay in Mesopotamia and Palestine, and there her efforts should be centered.[10]

But the Russian negotiations had involved France, and the pledge to Russia had brought indication of French interests in Syria and Lebanon.

---

sian negotiations may be followed in *FO* 371/2481 and C.J. Smith, Jr., "Great Britain and the 1914-1915 Straits Agreement with Russia," *American Historical Review,* 70 (1965): 1015-34, and *The Russian Struggle for Power, 1914-1917* (N. Y., 1956), pp. 210-13, 238-43. For text, see Hurewitz, *Diplomacy,* II, pp. 7-11.

[9] *CAB* 27/1; see Busch, *Britain, India, and the Arabs,* pp. 45ff.

[10] Egypt protectorate declaration: Hurewitz, *Diplomacy,* II, pp. 4-7; Asquith is quoted in Laurence W. Martin, *Peace without Victory . . .* (New Haven, Conn., 1958), p. 27. For further discussion of Middle Eastern war aims, see Jukka Nevakivi, *Britain, France, and the Arab Middle East, 1914-1920* (London, 1969), and "Lord Kitchener and the Partition of the Ottoman Empire, 1915-1916," in K. Bourne and D.C. Watt, eds., *Studies in International History* (Hamden, Conn., 1967) pp. 316-29; and Aaron S. Klieman, "Britains war aims with the Middle East in 1915," *Journal of Contemporary History* 3 (1968): 237-52.

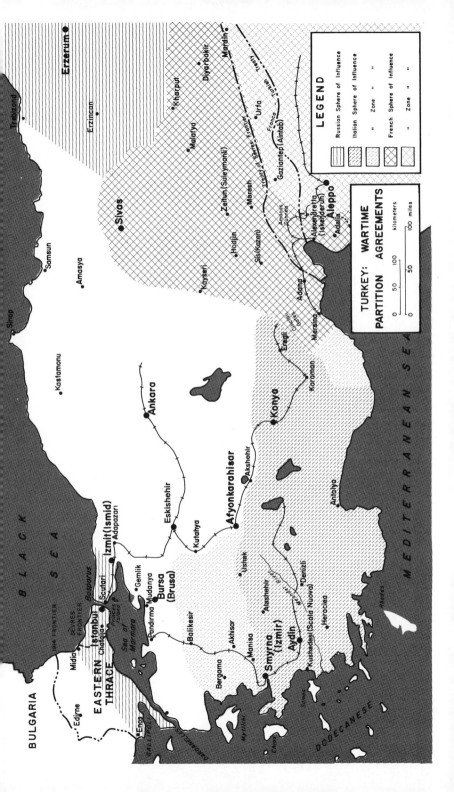

The absence of French, and the success of British, military efforts in this theater aroused French susceptibilities as well as Russian. The Anglo-French Sykes-Picot Agreement of 1916 only temporarily assuaged those suspicions by promising French control of Greater Syria, the vilayet of Mosul, and the area of Cilicia (an ancient name for the vilayets of Seyhan and Marash in southeastern Turkey). Cilicia had important historical associations with Armenia, and it was argued that, taken as a whole, Cilicia still had a Christian majority in 1918. When in late November of that year an Armenian national delegation proclaimed the establishment of an Armenian state, it included with the seven eastern vilayets (those already referred to plus Trebizond on the Black Sea coast) the constituent parts of Cilicia, including Marash, Sis, and Alexandretta. It seemed that Armenian control of this area would become a reality when first the armistice called for Turkish withdrawal from Cilicia and then in December French troops (under French command but in the name of the Allies) moved into Cilicia. They were accompanied by the *Legion d'Orient,* three battalions of Syrian and Armenian volunteers who had fought well under Allenby's command in Palestine. The French were to find occupation of Cilicia a dubious advantage, but it was important in any consideration of the future of Turkey, particularly when the substantial Anglo-French discord associated with jurisdiction over Syria and Lebanon is recalled.[11]

Nor were these obligations only to the French and Russians. Territorial negotiations had played a most important role in Italy's entrance into the war; in April 1915, Italy was promised the Dodecanese Islands, confirmed possession of Libya, and, should there be further partition of the Ottoman Empire, "a just share of the Mediterranean region adjacent to the province of Adalia," as well as that province itself. Since Adalia (modern Antalya) vilayet lies in the southwest corner of Turkey, any "adjacent" area would probably mean, if France kept Adana, "adjacent" to the north in the direction of Smyrna—although the interlying vilayet of Konya was as yet unassigned. The word "adjacent"

[11] On Cilicia, see Hovannisian, *Road* and "Allies and Armenia;" Pierre Redan, *La Cilicie et la problème ottoman* (Paris, 1921); Comte R. de Gontaut-Birion, *Comment la France s'est installée en Syrie (1918-1919)* (Paris, 1922), especially p. 214; and particularly Paul Du Véou, *La passion de la Cilicie, 1919-1922,* 2nd ed., (Paris, 1954), which discusses the Legion, pp. 59ff.

was too vague to satisfy Italian aspirations, and Italian diplomacy centered on clarification of that term.[12]

In 1916 Italy pressed for publication of the agreements and for assurance that the Italian sphere would be equal to that of any other power. These requests—or demands—were all the more urgent when Italy learned of the promises made to France in the Sykes-Picot Agreement. In November 1916 the Italians asked that the "zone d'Adalia" be specifically defined as the vilayets of Aydin, Adalia, and Konya, thus including all of southwestern Turkey. The zone was large, and some hard negotiation followed in an Allied attempt to limit its extent—but none of the Anglo-French leaders apparently was willing to risk cutting Italy out of Turkey altogether. In the inter-Allied meeting at Saint-Jean de Maurienne in April 1917 and in subsequent correspondence, the Allies, again subject to Russian approval, assigned to Italy "Zone C" and the "Green Zone" on the maps which always accompanied these documents ("A" and "B" and "Red" and "Blue" had been respectively the zones of close control and looser influence assigned to France and Britain in the Sykes-Picot Agreement).[13] By this means, Italy was actually granted the larger territory which she claimed in southwestern Turkey plus the important port center of Smyrna (Izmir), but the Russian Revolution ensured that Russian approval was impossible to obtain; Italy could not be certain that its claims would be recognized.

For several reasons, the agreement with Italy was unpopular in British governmental circles. Italian demands had grown steadily as the war progressed, and not everyone agreed that such demands corresponded either to the level of Italy's war effort and its capacity for administration and economic development or to the future of friendly British relations with a Greece which had directly conflicting aspirations in the Smyrna area. Confirmation of its own ambitions was one virtue which the agreement possessed in the eyes of Italian statesmen, for Greece at that time was regarded as part of a Franco-Greek anti-Italian coalition in the Mediterranean. The assurances given in the course of the 1917 negotiations were an improvement, from the Italian view,

[12] London Agreement, 26 April 1915, Hurewitz, *Diplomacy,* II, pp. 11-12; Grey to Sir R. Rodd (Rome), 21 September 1916, and other documents in file 173725, *FO* 371/2780.

[13] Hurewitz, *Diplomacy,* II, pp. 23-25.

over those of the previous year, but the continued insistence on Russian approval as a prerequisite and on greater Italian war efforts was as disquieting as the proviso that if the areas assigned to one or more powers could not be entirely assured, then "in whatever alteration or arrangement of provinces" which would ensue "the maintenance of equilibrium in the Mediterranean" would be given equitable consideration. This vague promise was little more satisfactory; from the British side, the promises made to Italy, taken altogether, did not quiet either fears of Italian absorption of British commercial interests in southwest Turkey or the Admiralty's concern that Franco-Italian control of the southern Turkish coast constituted a serious potential danger. Given the uncertain nature of the agreement, it should have come as no surprise when Italy pressed strongly that its claims not be ignored as the war came to an end. Baron Sonnino, the influential foreign minister (1914-19), saw the issue of the Constantinople occupation forces, for example, as important enough to make a personal appeal that Italian troops be allowed to participate as well.[14]

The conflict of Italian aspirations with those of France in Adana was potentially troublesome, but it was susceptible to at least temporary resolution, given the substantial territories available for division in southwestern Turkey. The same could not be said of the conflicting Italian and Greek claims, for the existence of a substantial Greek minority in the Smyrna vilayet and a Greek (or at least Christian) majority in the town of Smyrna made it unlikely that Greek irredentism could forego these territories even if they were claimed by Italy—or especially if they were claimed by Italy. The Allies felt that substantial obligations were owed to the current Greek government. Eleutherios Venizelos, its leader, was credited with bringing his country almost singlehandedly into the war on the Allied side.

The history of wartime Allied relations with Greece is not a simple one, but its outlines must be grasped if subsequent British policy in Turkey is to be understood.[15] The assassination of King George I

[14] British views may be found in *FO* 371/3043 (see especially Rodd private to Balfour, 19 February 1917); Board of Trade to FO, 22 December, and Admiralty to FO, 28 December 1916, *FO* 371/2780. Italian appeal: Cecil note for Balfour, 23 December, and FO to Marquis Imperiali (Italian Ambassador), 31 December 1918, 211789/200137, *FO* 137/3240. Saint-Jean de Maurienne agreement, quoted, Hurewitz, *Diplomacy*, II, pp. 23-25.

[15] The following remarks are based upon Michael Llewellyn Smith,

of Greece in 1913 had brought King Constantine to the throne; he was a ruler of strong will, imposing presence, and substantial military experience as commander-in-chief in both the Turkish war of the 1890s and the Balkan wars of 1912-13. The First World War put new pressures upon the monarchy as both alliances attempted to lure Greece to their side. Constantine's policy was one of neutrality—designed to aid Germany, said his detractors—and Constantine did his best to keep Greece out of the war. Venizelos, a Cretan of forceful personality and revolutionary background who had become prime minister in 1910 and was reelected in a sweeping victory of 1912, took the opposite view.

In 1915 the Allies, or more specifically British Foreign Secretary Sir Edward Grey, offered to Greece the prospect of compensation in Smyrna and Aydin in return for cession of Greek Macedonian territory to Bulgaria to keep that as yet uncommitted country out of the war; Venizelos and Constantine disagreed sufficiently to cause Venizelos's flight to Salonika. Here he organized a provisional government under Allied auspices when that new front was opened in an Allied (principally French) attempt to alter the balance in the Balkans. Constantine, for all his German family connections and monarchical tendencies to override his constitutional advisors, appears in retrospect to have acted in the long-run interests of his country, but Venizelos had both con-

---

Ionian Vision: Greece in Asia Minor, 1919-1922 (N.Y., 1973); Paxton Hibben, *Constantine I and the Greek People* (N.Y., 1920); A.A. Pallis, *Greece's Anatolian Adventure—and After . . .* (London, 1937); Douglas Dakin, *The Unification of Greece, 1770-1923* (N.Y., 1972); G.F. Abbott, *Greece and the Allies, 1914-1922* (London, 1922); Herbert Adams Gibbons, *Venizelos,* 2nd ed., (Boston, 1923); S. Cosmin [S.P. Phocas Cosmetatos], *Diplomatie et presse dans l'affaire grecque, 1914-1916* (Paris, 1921); George M. Mélas, *Ex-King Constantine and the War* (London, [1920]); J.C. Lawson, *Tales of Aegean Intrigue* (London, 1920); S.P. Chester, *Life of Venizelos* (London, 1921); Doris Alastos, *Venizelos . . .* (London, 1942); Palmer, *Gardners of Salonika*; and, for wartime intelligence activities, Compton Mackenzie, *First Athenian Memories* (London, 1931), *Greek Memories* (London, 1939), and *Aegean Memories* (London, 1940), and Sir Basil Thomson, *The Allied Secret Service in Greece* (London, 1931). French accounts are A.F. Frangulis, *La Grèce et la crise mondiale* (Paris, 1926); Robert David, *Le drame ignoré de l'Armée d'Orient . . .* (Paris, 1927); Capt. F.-J. Deygas, *L'Armée d'Orient dans la guerre mondiale (1915-1919)* (Paris, 1932), and the larger work by Edouard Driault, *Histoire diplomatique de la Grèce de 1821 a nous jours,* U (Paris, 1926).

stitution and Allies on his side. It is difficult, on the other hand, to justify Venizelos's developing concern with Smyrna at the cost of more likely Greek objectives such as Thrace or Constantinople—but Venizelos was aware that Russia would probably acquire this area.

The advantages were all on the side of Venizelos. His conduct contrasted most favorably with that of the ruler in Athens, and his supporters multiplied daily both among the Allies and among those Greeks who favored the Allied cause. Under French leadership, the Allies moved to intervene in the Greek mainland and capital in late 1916. The attempt to occupy Athens by main force, however, was a tragic farce which cost a number of lives. For France, the affair was awkward, because neither Russia (pro-Greek and promonarchy) nor Italy (anti-French and anti-Venizelos as a French puppet) wished to see Constantine overthrown. But war-inspired fears—a German submarine in every Greek cove, for example—temporary Italian appeasement through Saint-Jean de Maurienne, and the removal of Russian interests after the revolution permitted a change of masters in Greece. In mid-1917 Constantine was forced to abdicate, and Venizelos was in supreme power. His victory, it should be pointed out, was of a very limited type; Venizelos was no revolutionary in the social sense, nor were republicans the majority in Greece. The change of government was thus more personal than ideological, and Constantine had only temporarily passed into the wings.

For those who preferred oversimplification, however, the exiled monarch was the personification of enemy evil. "The King was our enemy—Venizelos our friend," as Lloyd George put it in a Cabinet meeting of early 1918.[16] And Venizelos was owed much by the Allies for his constant support of their cause against a strong faction of his countrymen. The location of some subsequent compensation had already been indicated in Thrace (adjoining western Greece), and while Russian collapse again opened the issue of Constantinople, the new prospect did not quiet aspirations already aroused regarding Smyrna. To the contrary, Greek opinion seemed capable of contemplating acquisition of both. Some British advisors suggested immediate conversion of St. Sophia from mosque to church to assuage some of that feeling (the Russians, it was argued, would have done so the moment they took over the city). This sort of demand would become most insistent in the en-

[16] Thomas Jones, *Whitehall Diary*, I (London, 1969), p. 51.

suing months, and the convenient answer was always that the peace conference would first have to pass on the future of the city. But the argument that developed in late 1918 over this issue was indicative of strongly held positions when the India Office, always observant of Muslim opinion, real or potential, urged delay and reconsideration, while Greek sympathizers and old-school, liberal, Gladstonian anti-Turks took the other tack.

British, French, Italians, Greeks—they only began the list of claimants. Armenian sympathizers had much to say on future Turkish arrangements, and even the most ardent anti-Armenian could not deny the extent of world—and especially United States—interest in the recreation of an Armenian state. There were other minorities, too, each with its supporters and spokesmen; similarly, American interests, Russian problems, Caucasian statelets, all had to be considered in writing an acceptable peace treaty with Turkey. Only the most simplistic of observers could afford to place complete faith in Lloyd George's famous speech of 5 January 1918, in which he said:

> Nor are we fighting to destroy Austria-Hungary or to deprive Turkey of its capital, or of the rich and renowned lands of Asia Minor and Thrace, which are predominately Turkish in race . . . While we do not challenge the maintenance of the Turkish Empire in the homelands of the Turkish race with its capital at Constantinople—the passage between the Mediterranean and the Black Sea being internationalized and neutralized—. . .

The same could be said of President Wilson's Fourteen Points, or the Anglo-French Declaration of 1918, which promised or appeared to promise self-determination to the peoples of Turkey. Indeed, it could be said of any one document.[18] So complicated was the situation

[17] Earl Granville (minister, Athens, 1917-21) telegram to FO, 20 November (recommending approval), with Oliphant and Hardinge minutes (disagreeing), FO to Granville, 25 November, IO to FO, 28 November (opposing), and S. Gaselle memorandum, 4 December 1918 (noting interest of Archbishop of Canterbury), *FO* 371/3417. A sample of the literature on the subject is Rev. J.A. Douglas, *The Redemption of Saint Sophia . . .* (London, 1919), arguing that England's duty was to make Constantinople a Christian—not including Catholic or Orthodox—city.

[18] Lloyd George, *War Memoirs,* II, pp. 1510-17; see Martin, *Peace Without Victory,* pp. 157-58, on origins and intentions of this speech. The Anglo-French Declaration is discussed in Busch, *Britain, India, and the Arabs,* Ch. IV.

that the best Britain could do was to try to determine her own views on the optimum Turkish future.

POST-WAR PLANS

The approaching end of the Turkish war had already occasioned serious internal reconsideration of wartime agreements and lists of desiderata. In September of 1918 Toynbee in the Foreign Office advised that the time had arrived for a statement of aims on Turkey, aims which he listed as strong support for an Armenian settlement and internationalization of the Straits. He would include, however, a pledge of British disinterestedness in Constantinople and Anatolia, on the grounds that self-determination should apply to Turks as well as to other peoples, and possible concessions on the capitulatory regime which the Turks had already abrogated unilaterally. Toynbee's memorandum only indicated one line of thought, and it was not until nearly a month had passed that the problem was taken up at high level.[19]

Late in September, Mark Sykes, working under Hankey in the Cabinet Office, focused upon the sort of armistice terms required to enforce the agreed-upon necessity of an Armenia. Occupation of the "Cilician Gates," the Amanus (Alma Dag) tunnels on the Turkish railway, and the towns of Zeitun, Hadjin, and Sis, which together gave road and rail access through the Taurus Mountains, would ensure, since the British held Mosul at the time, that the Armenians could receive assistance and that the Kurdish population of northern Iraq would be severed from the Turkish majority areas and thereby driven to make common, anti-Turk cause with the Arabs, to whom Britain had also made pledges. Such vast schemes were typical of Sykes's fertile mind, but Toynbee, commenting on his memorandum, pointed out that Marash, Van, and Erzerum, all essential to the future Armenian state, would still remain in Turkish hands. Presumably, however, in Sykes's plan British forces would be well enough placed to dictate events in even those remote centers.[20]

Gough-Calthorpe's armistice terms, however, cut out all mention of

[19] Toynbee memorandum, 9 September 1918, 156677/156677, *FO* 371/3411.

[20] Sykes memorandum for Crowe, 30 September, with Crowe and Toynbee minutes, 30 September and 1 October 1918, 167860/155461, *ibid.*

specific Cilician towns to be occupied and only made reference to possible occupation of the eastern vilayets and Turkish withdrawal from (but not necessarily Allied occupation of) Cilicia. Armenian leaders in western Europe were understandably alarmed, but protests were met by the legitimate if unsatisfying argument that the armistice was not yet a peace treaty. As Cecil put it in an annoyed comment, "the policy of H.M.G. has been quite clearly declared & nothing but folly or perversity can read into the Armistice terms any modification of it."[21] It was the assertion of a man who doubts his own position; the Foreign Office instructions for Gough-Calthorpe, drafted by Cecil himself, already noted that the armistice permitted Britain to take action to protect the Armenians only if there were further "disorders," meaning massacres. It should be remembered, however, in defense of Foreign Office reluctance, that Cilicia was an area assigned to French, not British, responsibility. The eastern vilayets had been allotted to Russia, and while Russia was out of the picture, the argument of contiguity would seem to dictate expanding the French role to include this area as well. This line of reasoning was supportable only if it was assumed that France would also control neighboring Mosul, and Britain was already trying to pressure France to yield exactly that area, although without much success.[22] The complications, in short, were many, and the general attitude was that an Armenian solution would have to await the satisfactory general settlement which would doubtless follow Turkish demobilization and Allied ability to dictate policy from their position in Constantinople.

The situation in the capital was more pressing in any case. All knew that Armenia would be established, and only the details remained; the same could be said for separate Arab states, although form of government and boundaries as among Iraq, Syria, and Arabia were different questions. But what of Constantinople and the Straits? Toynbee had to admit that the balance was fairly even whether the Turks should go or stay, but not all were so impartial. Eyre Crowe, for one, although most uncertain as to what was actually happening in Constantinople, let

[21] Rodd telegram to FO, 3 November, including report of Sykes talk with Boghos Nubar in Paris; H.M. [Headlam Morley] note for Sir William Tyrell (FO), 1 November 1918, with R. Cecil undated note (quoted), *FO* 371/3404.

[22] Balfour private to Gough-Calthorpe, 9 November, *FO* 371/3415; Cambon to Balfour, 16 and 18 November, and Balfour to Cambon, 26 November 1918, *FO* 371/3385.

along in remote eastern vilayets, was clear Greek public opinion and just claims should be satisfied at the same time that the Turk was at long last expelled from Europe. The details, he thought, could be left to Venizelos, who would work out a settlement with the Bulgarians, who had so long been interested in this area. Crowe would also give Smyrna to Venizelos, but here Lord Hardinge disagreed, reminding Crowe of the conflicting Italian claims. Since Crowe would also have established a Great Armenia stretching from Mersina and Alexandretta (Iskenderun) on the Mediterranean to the Black Sea coast west of Trebizond, he represented a rather extreme position on the partition of the Ottoman Empire. Crowe had another, more devious point to argue: Armenia would probably be under French influence in the future, and Britain should work to facilitate this association, "on condition that they [the French] agree to leave us free in the Arab region where we are interested . . ."[23]

Once again, Hardinge was more cautious; French ambitions in the Middle East were vast, and it would be much easier for Britain to deal with the Americans—for American interests in Armenia were famous. In any case, the American position at the forthcoming peace conference would probably be that all wartime treaties and conventions were overridden by the Fourteen Points, and, if so, the future of French and Italian claims would be even more uncertain. American responsibility for Constantinople and the Straits was even a possibility, but that solution would put the United States in an extremely important and perhaps undesirable position in European affairs.[24]

The logical body to make some decisions on eastern desiderata was the Eastern Committee, and in preparation for discussion, all concerned

---

[23] Political Intelligence Department, FO, memorandum P.C. 1 (Toynbee), 21 November, *FO* 371/4352; Crowe minutes, 2 December (quoted), on Webb telegram to FO, 30 November, 6 December, on Grahame (Paris) to Balfour 2 December, *FO* 371/3405, and 27 December, on WO to FO, 21 December 1918, *FO* 371/3411.

[24] Granville to Balfour, 17 November, with Toynbee, Crowe, and Hardinge minutes, *FO* 371/3417; Political Intelligence Dept. memorandum PC 9 (Crowe), 7 November 1918, *FO* 371/4352.

The probable American position is discussed in E. Drummond note for Balfour, 5 December, on Cambon to Balfour, 30 November 1918, *FO* 371/3385. Point XII of President Wilson's Fourteen Points (8 January 1918) is important enough to quote here: "The Turkish portions of the present Ottoman Empire should be assured a secure sovereignty, but the

parties did their best to set forth a persuasive case on these complex issues. The extreme positions were represented by Crowe on the one hand ("If we fail this time to cut out this Turkish cancer, we shall be throwing away one of the most important advantages ever obtained by a successful war") and Sir A.H. Grant on the other. Grant was fresh from India, where he had been secretary of the Foreign Department through the war years. His principal aim was to set forth the Indian—and Muslim—point of view. Despite any protestations to the contrary, said Grant, Indian and Muslim opinion would view Turkish loss of Constantinople as a reflection of religious warfare, of Cross versus Crescent, while that some opinion would accept the severance of Arab and Armenian areas without a struggle. The amputation of European Turkey would reawaken pan-Islamic energy and (a major worry to Indian officials) Muslims in India would be driven by anti-British sentiment into the arms of the growing Hindu nationalist movement. On the other hand, Britain owed much to her Muslim soldiers in the war, and if it was plainly stated that the capital would be left to the Turks, ". . . we should regain the trust and confidence of our Moslem subjects to a very large extent." Arguments about Greek claims overlooked the fact that Greece could easily become another European state's puppet; and much the same could be said against internationalization. Nobody talked of depriving Germany of Berlin: "Does Turkey deserve heavier punishment than Germany? And if she gets it, is it not merely because she is weaker?"[25]

Grant's very point told against him. As Sir Arthur Hirtzel, assistant undersecretary in the India Office's Political Department, noted, ". . . if once it is admitted that Indian Moslems can influence the policy of H.M.G. in Europe a very awkward precedent will be created." Crowe, similarly, used Muslim opinion against Grant. Agreeing that Muslims might be disquieted by the ejection of the Turks, in the long run such an action would be a convincing lesson in the total collapse of Turkish power. To the question of who would then administer the capital and the Straits (for the two were not yet regarded as separable), Crowe

---

other nationalities which are now under Turkish rule should be assured an undoubted security of life and an absolutely unmolested opportunity of autonomous development . . .".

[25] Crowe memorandum, 21 December, and Grant memorandum, 20 December 1918, *L/P&S/*10/623.

turned to the United States. But it was precisely such conclusions that worried the General Staff, for no uninvolved or weak power (Greece, for example) could or would hold the Straits against any future Russian revival. Better by far, said the War Office, to establish some sort of international control and leave formal sovereignty to the Turks.[26]

On 23 December, the Eastern Committee met to consider the question,[27] and Curzon opened with a review which borrowed much from Crowe: history, ran his argument, showed that no good purpose was ever served by the presence of the Turks in Constantinople, and it would be far better to leave to Turkey only a homogenous state in Asia Minor. All agreed at least, he concluded, that the Straits should be internationalized, but to whom should be assigned supervision? The Admiralty worried about American seapower here, and Britain could not take on more responsibilities herself—but Curzon objected to leaving the Turks in formal possession. He did not find the Indian argument persuasive; Indian Muslim nationalists sided with the Young Turks in spirit, he thought, not because they were Muslim but because they were anti-British. The allegiance to the caliphate (a historic title conveying a concept of Muslim religious leadership, vague and imprecise by the twentieth century, but not without emotional impact in increasing magnitude as distance from the problems of Ottoman administration increased), a point which Grant had stressed, really was not significant.

To Curzon's statement, Edwin Montagu, secretary of state for India, took the strongest exception. Constantinople was equally part of the Turkish homeland, and if a desirable substitute for Turkish authority there could not be found the logical recourse was to leave it in Turkish hands. Britain had made several declarations of noninterference in Muslim religious affairs during the course of the war, but now Britain planned to remove the caliph from his own capital. Anti-British agitators would find that a marvelous demonstration of Britain's anti-Islamic orientation.

To Balfour and Cecil, also present, the question was not so simple, and they were as uncertain as Curzon, although equally anti-Turkish,

---

[26] Hirtzel minute, 20 December, on Grant note of 20 December, Crowe memorandum, 21 December, and General Staff, WO, memorandum, 22 December 1918, *ibid.*

[27] Eastern Committee, 23 December 1918, Curzon memorandum (IO memorandum B 310A), 2 January, Grant memorandum, 7 January, and Montagu memorandum (B. 306F), 18 January 1919, *ibid.*

as to what future regime should be established. Balfour saw no insurmountable obstacle to leaving the Turks in Constantinople—although he opposed this, he thought there was no satisfactory alternative—while at the same time establishing some international Straits control. This was an essential step forward from the 1915 Constantinople Agreement, which assumed the necessary integrity of capital and Straits administration. Cecil would have much preferred to see American administration and Turkish expulsion. He had not at first favored such a solution, but now he thought a multipower administration would produce difficulties and intrigue. The only conclusion from all this was that some special regime guaranteeing passage of the Straits was essential. The other issues would simply have to await the Paris conference.

All the British discussions did make one assumption: whatever the difficulties of a settlement, in general and in detail that settlement would be made by the Allies alone. The situation at Constantinople gave no reason for thinking otherwise, for Webb and Gough-Calthorpe reported general quiet. Nor was Gough-Calthorpe interfering more than necessary with the Turkish government of Ahmed Tevfik Pasha. Tevfik Pasha, former ambassador in London (1909-14) and well known in British government circles (a reason for making him grand vizier on 11 November after the armistice), was well-meaning but not a man of outstanding ability or force of personality, and no sweeping changes in policy or personnel were made under his administration. The government was therefore still essentially "Young Turk," which might have been construed as hostile, but Gough-Calthorpe was specifically ordered not to encourage opposition to the Committee of Union and Progress (Young Turk) government on the grounds that if such opposition should come to power it "would be followed by internal disintegration and disturbances which could only be to our disadvantage." Changes in the Constantinople situation, however, seemed by their own weight to direct affairs in Britain's favor; by the end of November, Gough-Calthorpe could report that Tevfik Pasha's government was proving legitimately anti-CUP. However, British intelligence knew the Young Turks to be very much alive, and in the interior demobilization and disarmament proved most difficult to accomplish. By the end of the year, a system of control had as yet not been established to cover the whole of Turkey.[28] The signs were perhaps a bit ominous, but as the peace-

[28] Balfour private to Gough-Calthorpe, 9 November (quoted), *FO* 371/

makers headed for Paris the only reason for worry seemed to be the difficult task of reaching inter-Allied agreement on Turkey.

PARIS

When the British delegation reached Paris, it knew only that it did not wish for Britain herself to control Constantinople—nor for any other power to do so with the possible exception of the United States. The future of the Straits, of Smyrna, of Thrace, or Armenia—none was clear, although on some issues there was a vague consensus: there should be an Armenia, there should be a Straits regime. In part the lack of agreement on detail is explained by the fact that a British position on the Arab world, hard enough to hammer out on its own, had first priority. The Foreign Office draft for the whole Ottoman Empire, prepared in early January before the conference opened, was simply a matter of guesswork, since quite obviously the underlying premises were unknown: would Allied wartime agreements prevail or be replaced by "self-determination" for all? But at least the draft proposed, without too much disagreement within the Foreign Office, a special enclave for Greece in Smyrna, the loss (to either Greece or Bulgaria or both) of Thrace, and a special zone for the capital and the Straits with guaranteed free Straits passage in peace and war under international or American control—and, finally, some sort of Armenia.[29]

A Foreign Office memorandum was not British policy without Cabinet approval, however, and at Cabinet level no decision had been reached. When the War Cabinet had discussed Constantinople, it had been only to talk of that city's immediate control. The principal figures were all in Paris (except for Curzon, minding the Foreign Office in London), and it was in Paris that a decision would have to be reached. Balfour was prepared to instruct his subordinates to work up a draft treaty based upon the assumption that the Turks would be expelled

---

3415; Gough-Calthorpe to FO, 23 November, *FO* 371/3416, and 20 November, *FO* 371/3411; Director of Naval Intelligence, Admiralty, to FO, 31 December, *FO* 371/4141, and report by Brig.-Gen. Sir W. Deedes to WO, 15 December 1918, *WO* 106/1435; Deedes was military attaché under Gough-Calthorpe. See John Presland, *Deedes Bey: A Study of Sir William Deedes, 1883-1923* (London 1942), especially pp. 300ff.

[29] Draft outline, 11 January 1919, *FO* 371/4156; plans for the Arab areas are discussed in Busch, *Britain, India, and the Arabs,* Ch. VI.

from Europe. The other issues could not be resolved so long as the War Office advised that at least eastern Thrace, especially Adrianople (or Edirne), should be attached to Constantinople and that the Greeks should not be allowed to take Smyrna. Only at the very end of the month, after two meetings of concerned Foreign Office, India Office, and military advisors assembled under Lord Hardinge's chairmanship, did some formal recommendations emerge.[30]

As usual by now, a safe starting assumption was free passage of the Straits; the issue was how to ensure it. The military advisors proved anti-American on this control, for American presence would afford ". . . opportunity and pretext for basing a strong American fleet in the Mediterranean—a danger which, from a strategical point of view, must at all costs be avoided." Nor would they accept French, Italian, Greek, or Turkish control: since Britain was unwilling to take on the job, that left only some international format, preferably, said the military, in conjunction with preservation of the sultan's formal suzerainty. As for Smyrna, the meeting concluded that better the Greeks there than the Italians, if anybody had to be there at all. Major-General W. Thwaites, director of Military Intelligence, took what in hindsight appears to be a most logical view—perhaps because the War Office understood the limits of Allied control over Turkey itself—that presenting Smyrna to Greece "might give the people of Anatolia just cause for resentment and should not be done except as an unavoidable political expediency." It was agreed that there was no objection to a Greek zone in Smyrna and Aydin, subject to the reservation made on this point by the military; in other words, this group too was unable to agree on the details.[31]

These meetings had, however, set the general policy of approving the transfer of Smyrna to Greece. When considering subsequent attempts to place blame for Britain's contribution to the disasters associated with the Greek venture in Anatolia, this January 1919 position should not be forgotten. Nor, when the conclusions were passed

[30] War Cabinet 516, 15 January, *CAB* 23/9; FO delegation recommendations, Astoria Hotel (Paris) meetings, 30 and 31 January, with Curzon minute, 5 March 1919 (quoted below), *FO* 371/4156; Harold Nicolson, *Peacemaking 1919* (N.Y., 1965), pp. 252-53.

[31] Mallet note, 25 January, Maj.-Gen. W. Thwaites, D.M.I. (on whose appointment see Callwell, *Wilson,* II, p. 123) note, 1 February 1919, *FO* 608/88.

home to the Foreign Office five weeks later (the delay, some would have said, typified the delegation's lack of consideration for officials left in London) was there any strong disagreement. Curzon was angered by the delay, but he had to agree that "by a happy coincidence" his own views were "practically identical" with those reached at the Astoria Hotel in Paris; the exception was Smyrna, but he did not protest at this time.

It was fortunate that there was agreement, however nebulous, on the general lines of a preferred settlement, for in early February the conference turned to Middle Eastern affairs long enough to hear out Venizelos's exposition on behalf of the Greeks—part of that interminable process by which nearly every party with a special interest absorbed the time, if not attention, of the world's leaders. The object, remarked the cynical, was that once they were heard no further attention need be paid to such people. The Council of Ten (premiers and foreign ministers of the five principal powers) had already turned briefly to the Arab and Caucasian world on 30 January, but no decisions had resulted. President Wilson made the rather interesting remark that so far as he could tell, there was nothing the American people would be less likely to want than a burden of military responsibility in Asia, but in a conference atmosphere where no one appeared to know what was happening outside his own special sphere it was very easy to overlook or disregard his words.[32]

On 3 and 4 February, Venizelos presented the Greek case, and his claims proved rather extensive: Aegean islands, Thrace (including Adrianople), the Dardanelles, part of the Marmora coast . . . Venizelos's principle, expounded in the charming and openhearted manner so befitting the representative of a major European power (which, alas for Venizelos, Greece was not), appeared to be that no part of the old Ottoman Empire could be included in the new Turkey unless it contained an absolute majority of ethnic Turks. This was perfectly acceptable, the more so when Venizelos waived his own principle in the case of Constantinople, for he was prepared to leave the capital with its surrounding area to the Turks, provided suitable safeguards were established for non-Turks. Population arguments presented one substantial prob-

---

[32] Council of Ten, 30 January 1919, Department of State, United States, *Papers Relating to the Foreign Relations of the United States: The Paris Peace Conference,* 1919 [hereafter referred to as *FRUS,* Paris Conference], II (Washington, D.C., 1943), p. 807; Gidney, *Mandate,* pp. 92-93.

lem: at no time in the peacemaking process from 1918 to 1923 was there either impartial census of or general agreement upon the population in any of the contested areas. So vast were the problems raised here—and not only population—that the only solution for the time being was to put off decisions by appointing a committee of experts to study the issue of Smyrna and Greek claims. This suggestion was made by Lloyd George, shortly to become the most famous (or infamous, depending upon viewpoint) Philhellene of the Paris peacemakers apart from Venizelos himself.[33]

Lloyd George was facing reality, however, for already there had been inter-Allied disagreements, some considered of rather more intrinsic importance in early 1919 than the future of Constantinople or Smyrna. Moreover, Lloyd George, like the American and French leaders, was trying to solve the problem of growing Italian claims, but putting Greeks into Smyrna did not yet seem the way. Nor, as has been seen, was British official opinion squarely behind the prime minister, although with the exception of the War Office there was less opposition to Philhellenic policies than is often supposed. Montagu in Paris had the not insignificant weight of the Indian government behind him. Montagu had several interests at Paris, not the least of which was the maximum possible Indian representation in general and the maximum voice on Mesopotamia and Arab areas in particular. About Turkey, he argued as he had in the Eastern Committee, for lenience toward the Turks on the grounds that a punishing treaty could produce repercussions in Indian Muslim circles. Although he and his associated representatives, Lord Sinha (parliamentary undersecretary of state for India) and the Maharaja of Bikaner (a military figure primarily representing the Native States), argued at every opportunity that Muslim loyalty must not go unrewarded and Muslim religious fervor aroused, none of these men was Muslim—India had no Muslim delegate at the conference.[34]

[33] Council of Ten, 3 and 4 February, *FRUS,* Paris Conference, III, pp. 859-75; see also pp. 83-84. Nicolson, *Peacemaking,* pp. 129, 249-50, 256-58, 291; Dakin, *Unification of Greece,* p. 223; Arnold J. Toynbee, *The Western Question in Greece and Turkey . . .,* 2nd ed., (London, 1923), pp. 69-71; F.S. Marston, *The Peace Conference of 1919: Organization and Procedure* (London, 1944), pp. 117-19.

[34] Montagu private to Chelmsford, 22 January, 18 February, and 4 March, *Montagu Papers,* D. 523/3; and private telegrams to Chelmsford, 28 and 31 January, *Chelmsford Papers,* E. 264/10; Montagu to C. Jones,

Finally, the growing debate with France over Syrian administration and the application of the Sykes-Picot Agreement had its closely related repercussions in Turkey, where the large number of issues, great and small, were collectively producing something akin to inter-Allied chaos. A French suggestion that an Anglo-French committee be established in Paris to iron out the problems of the Constantinople administration was adamantly opposed by the military advisors, including General Wilson, on the grounds that the French would thereby achieve parity in what should be primarily a British occupation. Britain, after all, had done most of the fighting in this sector, and the French only wanted to be able to apply leverage in Constantinople to move Britain in Syria.[35]

The problem would have been difficult to resolve by committee in any case, for Italian claims were growing insistent. Even before the conference convened, London saw fit to urge Italian leaders to take no precipitate action such as a rumored plan to descend upon Adalia in order to preserve the area from expanding French administration. Since Italy had already occupied Rhodes without awaiting Allied approval, such a coup de main was well within the bounds of probability. The Italian operation was postponed; but British assurances that the French occupation of Cilicia (under Allenby's superior command) was not the

---

assistant secretary, War Cabinet, 1 and 6 February, *CAB* 21/139; War Cabinet 537, 26 February, *CAB* 23/9; Sinha (Lord Sinha, First Baron Jaipur, was parliamentary undersecretary, 1919-20) memorandum, 5 February 1919, *FO* 608/109; British Empire Delegation meeting minutes, no. 1, 2, 7, 9, 16, and 31a, *CAB* 29/28; K.M. Panikkar, *His Highness the Maharaja of Bikaner: A Biography* (Oxford, 1937), pp. 202-6.

Support for the War Office position, it should be pointed out, was somewhat undermined by the fact that the military officials in Constantinople took the opposite view; see Admiral Webb private to Sir R.W. Graham (FO), 11 March, *FO* 371/4165, and telegram to FO, 13 March, *FO* 608/103, and Milne minute, Constantinople, n.d. (received in Paris 11 March 1919), 385/4/2, *FO* 608/118. To some extent the IO position was similarly weakened by the opposition to its views of Col. A.T. Wilson in Baghdad, who urged that the Turks be expelled from Europe: Baghdad telegram to SSI, 23 January 1919, *L/P&S*/10/623, on which Curzon minuted (15839/604, *FO* 371/4162), "I am delighted to find in Col. Wilson so warm an ally, since I do not in the least share the view of the Indian Govt. on the subject of Constantinople."

[35] Pichon private to Balfour, 14 February, with H. Wilson, Hardinge, Balfour, and Col. Gribbon minutes, *FO* 608/108; Inter-Departmental Committee, 22 February 1919, *L/P&S*/10/807.

same thing as French acquisition of the area were not completely convincing. In mid-February, Baron Sonnino again strongly urged that
Italian troops be allowed into Adalia. Balfour, aware that part of the
problem was the approaching Italian parliamentary session, approved
the idea; possibly it would be of use, be concluded in a typical bit
of short-sighted evaluation, by discrediting the Turkish (and doubtless Young Turk) government. Since orders had already gone out over
Balfour's signature to avoid any measures tending to increase anarchy
in Turkey, it was a less-than-skilled bit of diplomacy, but Balfour seldom
appears to have applied the full resources of his considerable intellect
to Turkish problems. A more logical reason for support of this request,
as at least one Foreign Office member realized, was to put Italy here as
a counterpoise to France in Cilicia. But Curzon felt otherwise: once
the Italians had landed, the Greeks would demand Smyrna all the more,
the French would want separate control of Cilicia, Turkey would be
half-partitioned, and the peacemakers would be faced with a *fait accompli* before anyone realized what had happened.[36]

The issue was complicated, of course, by the wartime agreements.
As Crowe pointed out, if a mandatory power were to be assigned—for
mandates were now the rage at Paris—it would probably be Italy. Clearly
Italians could not put in to rule Greeks, and while nobody could state
positively how many Greeks were in Smyrna, however many there
were would not have adequate justice so long as they were administered
by a Turkey considered unfit even to govern Turks. The only safe conclusion, therefore, was to give Smyrna to Greece. All very fine, responded General Thwaites, but the realism demanded by Crowe was
less in Greco-Italian than in Greco-Turk relations. The result of sending Greece to Smyrna would be disaster. "Policy, unless leavened with
understanding, is apt to make an early call on strategy," he advised
in justification of his remarks, but such pointification was unlikely to
win friends in the Foreign Office.[37]

---

[36] Rodd telegram to FO, 31 December 1918; FO telegram to Rodd, 3
January, DMI to FO, 7 January, Balfour (Paris) telegram to FO, 17 Feb-
ruary, with G. Kidston minute, FO telegram to Balfour, 19 February (writ-
ten by Curzon), *FO* 371/4164; Hardinge private to Curzon, 17 February,
Curzon Papers (IO Library), F/2/2; and Curzon private to Hardinge, 26
February 1919, *FO* 800/153.

[37] Webb telegram to FO, 13 March 1919, with Crowe (11 March) and
Thwaites (20 March) minutes, *FO* 608/103.

Somebody's interest was going to have to be sacrificed: a Foreign Office delegation minute of late March settled on both Turks and Italians. The proposal now called for Constantinople to be a League mandate, Anglo-American negotiation to settle the Armenian frontier, and the Greeks to occupy Smyrna. Since the area assigned was estimated to have a slight Greek majority, justice would be served. The Turks would have outlets to both north and south (that is, the Greek area would not be contiguous with the Italian to the south), and Smyrna would be a free port. Greece would also obtain the north shore of the Dardanelles and Marmora, although the boundaries would have to be settled later. The choice of mandatory for Constantinople and the Bosporus (not, in other words, now including the Dardanelles) was the United States, although that power was driving a hard bargain in these incredibly unrealistic negotiations, requesting the Dardanelles as well and thus asking, as Hardinge minuted irritably, for the whole of the Straits in the face of principles of nationality, self-determination, and "sure access to the sea"—principles elaborated, of course, in the president's own Fourteen Points.[38]

These discussions reveal how remote the negotiations had become, in their committees, from the true state of affairs in Turkey or, for that matter, in Rome or Athens, but it must be argued in their defense that only in late March, with the return of President Wilson from a brief trip to the United States and the reconstruction of the Council of Ten into the Council of Four, did serious work again commence. Unfortunately the hazy decisions of the chief leaders, so often taken without regard to the specialists' advice, only complicated the situation. Lloyd George's Philhellenic proclivities and friendship with Venizelos and Balfour's lethargy on Middle Eastern problems would have led the pessimistic to abandon hope. They would have been even more discouraged to learn what Balfour thought about his own prime minister's penchant for private diplomacy. As he wrote privately to Curzon,

> . . . while I entirely agree with what I understand to be his main objects, I am by no means sure that he has thought out the questions as a whole; or that, in more or less informal conversations with this or that Member of the Conference, he may

[38] Mallet and Crowe minutes, 26 March, and Hardinge minute, 30 March 1919, *FO* 608/110.

not give away to one Power what ought to be reserved for
another.[39]

To Balfour the problem of a small Italian force had been magnified
out of proportion. All was well so long as the main lines of the settlement proceeded in their current direction, with the Americans in Constantinople and Armenia (including Cilicia, if the French could be
persuaded to give it up), the Greeks in the west, and Britain in Palestine and Mosul (now yielded by the French in order to ensure eventual
acquisition of Syria). The Italians would be annoyed; but perhaps
they could be tempted to accept the Caucasus instead (of which idea
more later), even if it was not the Mediterranean balance they wanted
above all. It was all most difficult, sighed Balfour, and Italian nasti-
ness was a root cause: "Their main object appears to be to disgust all
their neighbours and all their Allies, and they are accomplishing this
object with extraordinary success." "Madness," replied Curzon—
particularly to send Italy to the Caucasus—and incredible to contemplate
sending French and Greeks to "gallop about all over Asia Minor."
But even as Balfour was writing his appreciation, the Council of Four
was discussing just such a scheme: France in Syria and Cilicia, Britain
in Iraq and Mosul, and Italy in Konya and the Caucasus.[40] No formal
decision was taken, as usual, but this time Italy, increasingly concerned
at the prospect of a general European settlement unfavorable to its
claims and interests, acted on its own in one area where it was convinced justice was on its side and where action was also possible at
short notice. During the last week of March, Italian troops landed in
Adalia, without obtaining the prior approval of the Allied leaders.[41]

[39] Balfour private to Curzon, 20 March, *Curzon Papers,* F/2/2, and
private to Webb, 8 April, *FO* 371/4215. Anglo-French conversation: IC
159, 11 March 1919, *FO* 608/110. Nicolson's diary entry for 27 March
1919 (*Peacemaking,* p. 290) is a typical sample of Balfour's initiative: "Go
round afterwards to see A.J.B. at the Rue Nitot. Explain to him about Turkey. Impossible to extract from him any answer or decision. He merely
lolled and looked bored . . .".

[40] Balfour private to Curzon, note 39, chapter 2, and Curzon private
to Balfour, 25 March, *Curzon Papers,* F/2/2; Council of Four, 20 March
1919, *FRUS,* Paris Conference, V, pp. 1-14.

[41] Paul C. Helmreich, *From Paris to Sèvres: the Partition of the Ottoman
Empire at the Peace Conference of 1919-1920* (Columbus, Ohio, 1974),
p. 74, makes the point that the Italians always reembarked after their early
landings at Adalia in March and April; this fact, however, seems to have

ITALIAN AND GREEK LANDINGS

The official Italian explanation was that a local mutiny and wide-spread brigandage had brought an appeal from local Muslim notables for Italian assistance; following an outbreak of violence in the Christian quarter of Adalia, two companies of Italian seamen had landed to keep order. Although this rationalization was hardly acceptable given the background, no recriminations followed immediately, partly because of the excuse provided and partly because some confusion existed about a previous plan to send Italian troops to Konya as a face-saving gesture (but not as recognition of Italian territorial claims). Curzon in London, for example, assumed that however unpalatable the news the Italians had moved into Turkey "under the encouragement of Paris." Greek nervousness was substantially increased; Greek offers of troops for order-keeping in Smyrna had already been opposed by military advisors, who countered with a suggested Turkish division with British officers—an idea Venizelos vehemently opposed.[42]

Within a few weeks, the Greek representatives were complaining of Italian anti-Greek propaganda in the Smyrna area. London viewed such complaints as a preliminary to a Greek landing in the Italian style, and the Foreign Office urged that Venizelos be warned off from such dangerous proceedings. Athens reported that the general mood there supported no such expedition, and Venizelos, as head of his government, declared the same to Sir Louis Mallet in Paris. Venizelos knew well that the achievement of Greek aspirations would require Allied support; in any case, Italian policy now played directly into Greek hands.[43]

---

escaped the peacemakers. Helmreich's main contribution is the light he throws upon Italian policy through his extensive use of the Sonnino Papers.

[42] Rodd telegram to FO, 3 April, with Curzon note (quoted), DMI to FO, 4 April, Mallet (for Balfour) to Curzon, 7 April, *FO* 371/4165; Gough-Calthorpe telegram to FO, 26 March, FO telegram to Delegation, Astoria, 3 April, Tyrell to Curzon, 12 April, *FO* 371/4166; Mallet memorandum (on private conversation with Venizelos), 9 April 1919, 357/1/3, *FO* 608/89. Sir Louis Mallet, an FO assistant undersecretary, had been ambassador in Constantinople, 1913-14, and was attached to the peace conference delegation in Paris prior to his retirement in 1920.

[43] FO (Cecil) telegram to Balfour, 15 April, Granville (Athens) telegram to FO, 17 April, Balfour telegram to FO, 18 April 1919, *FO* 371/

On 24 April, Italy's delegates left Paris in protest over the conference's failure to yield to Italian demands in the Adriatic. From the standpoint of Italy's Asia Minor position, this maneuver was a serious error, for Venizelos was left in sole possession of the Allied ear at Paris, and the chances that the Allies would eventually approve the Italian presence at Adalia were seriously reduced. Moreover, the Turkish government of Damad Mehmed Ferid Pasha (in office since March), pledged to cooperate with the Allies, protested against the landings as liable to encourage widespread unrest in the interior. Admiral Webb, passing these complaints home, added that he himself had received no warning of the Italian move; like Curzon, Webb assumed that the conference had approved the landings.[44]

The Italian maneuver had at last galvanized the Council of Four (more accurately, the Council of Three, with the Italians absent) into action. The landing at Adalia could be tolerated if need be, but disruption of the conference as a whole could not. At a meeting on 5 May, Lloyd George made it clear that, in his view, the Italian presence at Konya, agreed to earlier, was authorized, but the landing at Adalia was not. Now new reports had arrived of Italian landings along the coast to which they laid claim, including the harbor of Marmaris opposite Rhodes. The whole of Italian policy pointed to some future coup d'etat whereby they would seize control of Anatolia, from which it would be most difficult to expel them. No formal division of Turkey could be made at the moment, for a commission had only just been dispatched to examine the conditions in and desires of the inhabitants of the empire. But pending the report of that commission, the British proposal for redistribution of the occupation forces could be implemented: the

4177; Roskill, *Hankey,* II, pp. 78-79; Lord Hankey, *The Supreme Control at the Paris Peace Conference, 1919* (London, 1963), p. 119.

[44] Webb to Curzon, 3 April, *FO* 371/4156, and telegram to FO, 29 April, FO telegram to Webb, 2 May 1919, *FO* 371/4165. Damad Ferid Pasha (1853-1953) had married into the royal family (hence the honorific "damad," denoting sultan's son-in-law) and had served in various posts at home and abroad in a career noted mainly for anti-Young Turk activities and, after the armistice, friendship toward the Allies. Close to Sultan Mehmed VI, he was rich and cultivated—but he made the cardinal error of assuming that the Allies would support him in order to oppose his (and their) enemies. See Ryan, *Last of the Dragomans,* p. 127, and Feroz Ahmad, *The Young Turks . . .* (Oxford, 1969), p. 169.

Americans would go to the capital and Armenia, the French to Syria, the British to Mesopotamia (but not the Caucasus), and the Greeks could finally occupy Smyrna—and it would be nice to settle the zones of occupation before the Italians returned to Paris, that very day if possible.

President Wilson found such haste most alarming, not because of the Italian absence, but because of the substantial role assigned to American forces in the "redistribution." While General Wilson said that a division would be required for Constantinople, no estimate at all could be made on how many men Armenia would require. The clearly associated question of the Caucasus was also a problem: was Italy to be let into this area to replace Britain? The future of the Caucasus proved too hard a nut to crack at the moment, but Lloyd George made it clear that British troops were pulling back to Constantinople, "in order to have them ready to counter any move by the Italians."[45] That Orlando and Sonnino would be misguided enough to attempt a major descent on Constantinople or western Turkey seems incredible, even had Italy the available resources and manpower. But while Lloyd George may easily be charged with alarmist propaganda in order to put his favored Greeks into western Turkey and thus at once serve the Greeks and "dish" the Italians without having to use British troops in the process, it should be rememberd that Italian appetites at the time were substantial enough for their leaders to have risked the dangers of abandoning the conference. Occupation of Turkey, after all, was not entirely out of the question for a power which was already prepared to assume responsibility for the whole of the Caucasus.

President Wilson was not to be rushed. On the next day he informed Lloyd George and Clemenceau that his advisors had told him that he, although president, had not the authority to send troops to Turkey without a declaration of war (for the United States had never declared war against the Ottoman Empire). Whatever the explanation, America could not be forced to assume the burden of Constantinople and Armenia. But something could still be done to ward off the Italian danger, and Lloyd George had the answer: Venizelos should be allowed to land two or three divisions at Smyrna to protect his fellow countrymen. Clemenceau and Wilson formally assented, both no doubt relieved

[45] Council of Four, 5 and 6 May 1919, *FRUS,* Paris Conference, V, pp. 463-85 (p. 468 quoted).

that their own troops would not be involved. It now remained to work out the details, and this was done that afternoon and the next day. President Wilson had lingering doubts, for he several times asked for reassurance that the Allies had the right to so order troops to Turkey (he had to be disabused of the notion that what the Allies could do collectively, Italy should be able to do unilaterally). Transport to Smyrna was ordered by the evening of the 6th for one division from Macedonia (about 9000 effectives), as an independent command leaving Franchet d'Espérey's authority but not entering Milne's.[46]

One question which remained was the degree of secrecy which should be imposed. The official reason for intervention was to avoid "disorders and massacre of Christians in Smyrna." The larger question, discussed by the Council of Four on the 10th, was whether the Turks or Italians should be given prior information. If the Turks were warned that the Greeks were coming, there could be resistance; if the Italians were told, they might well demand a share in the Allied landings or tell the Turks and encourage their resistance. General Wilson suggested a means of avoiding this: the Turks would be told simply to clear out of the Smyrna defenses in preparation for an Allied occupation. The Turkish government was told at the last minute, by Admiral Webb alone, for his colleagues conveniently had no instructions and thus ensured that Britain took the major share of odium for the Greek landings. Webb had stressed that Ferid Pasha would probably fall in consequence of the Greek invasion, but the Paris peacemakers did not really take this possibility into account. In Athens, the Greek government released the information that the Council of Four had authorized the landings, and thus by implication managed nicely to assign responsibility to Italy as well.[47]

Meanwhile, Italy had returned to the conference. On the 12th, with the landings scheduled for two days later, the Allies attempted to explain to Orlando the reasons for them. Clemenceau's basic argument was simple: the Allies had acceded to a Greek request to land forces. Presi-

[46] Council of Four, 7 May 1919, *ibid.,* pp. 501-4, including appended conclusions of Astoria Hotel conference, 6 May, Venizelos and Allied military commanders. Smith, *Ionian Vision,* pp. 78-9, includes Venizelos' diary account of these decisions.

[47] Balfour telegram to Curzon, 7 May, delegation telegram to FO, 11 May, Webb and Granville telegrams to FO, 14 May, *FO* 371/4217; Council of Four, 10 May 1919, *FRUS,* Paris Conference, V, pp. 553-58.

dent Wilson felt obliged to add that in fact the Allies had suggested it to the Greeks. It remained for Lloyd George to assume the offensive, charging the Italians with unauthorized landings on the Turkish coast and demanding explanations from Orlando. Orlando, after consulting with Sonnino, had no protest to make—but he asked that Italy be represented in the Allied forces which would initially take over the Smyrna forts. This was agreed, although Orlando's subsequent request that the Allied forces remain until the final disposition of the area was not. Italy's willingness not to press for division of all Anatolia brought forth from Lloyd George a diplomatic statement that after all, Italy had done well in the war and had been disappointed in the whole question of the peace—not only in Fiume. Surely Italy could be given, not the whole of Anatolia, but some zone for administrative mandate. This suggestion led to a discussion over maps on the puzzle of how the Americans might fit in Constantinople and Armenia, the French in Cilicia, the Italians here, the Greeks there—as usual, President Wilson could make no commitment, nor did he think that the Turks would appreciate such division.[48]

The decision was not formally taken in favor of this distribution of mandates, but the way was indicated for the future; Lloyd George, with Italy humbled and Greece about to be installed in Smyrna, was willing to be accommodating. By the 14th, the discussion had advanced to the point of considering two Turkeys: a Turkish state in the north under some power's supervision, probably France's, and the rest under various mandatories. Balfour, however, was moved to a rare protest on paper when he learned of this scheme, for neither principle nor expendiency justified such a partition, once again designed only to meet the vexing problem of Italian ambitions. Italy could be bought off with economic concessions, although he himself felt that Italy grossly overestimated their value (they would no doubt soon turn up under German management in any case).[49]

Lloyd George's apparent generosity was soon tempered by information from Venizelos that the Italians had continued to move troops into the coast and were now in possession of the entire littoral from

[48] Council of Four, three meetings of 12 May 1919, *FRUS,* Paris Conference, V, pp. 565-88.
[49] Council of Four, 14 May, Balfour memorandum, 16 May, appended to Council of Four meeting of 17 May 1919, *ibid.,* pp. 614-20, 669-72.

Scala Nuova to Adalia. This behavior, he charged the Italians, would prejudice the future peace settlement. At the same time, continued pressure by various groups interested in keeping the Turks in Constantinople (Lloyd George heard an ardent Indian delegation on the 17th) warned him off the idea of establishing a separate state for the Turks with its capital at Bursa, for example. He therefore favored keeping the caliphate in Constantinople, where it could be controlled, preferably by an impartial American mandate. In defense of his mercurial change of opinion he now informed the French, American, and Italian leaders that he felt bound by the declaration he had made on that very point in January 1918. No one had the courage to ask why he had not felt similarly bound in the earlier discussion, but it was a striking *volte face,* which must be credited to a mixture of Indian pressure and, perhaps, Balfour's warnings.[50]

The prime minister's willingness to give Italy a share was also tempered by the Italian insistence on so large a portion—indeed it was very clear more would willingly be sacrificed for Fiume. Lloyd George as a result turned against spheres altogether, with apologies for his lack of consistency (no matter, said President Wilson graciously, if the decision reached was the right one); Muslim representatives insisted that the Turks would not live under the Italians, and it was a mistake to tear up the purely Turkish areas. After all, the president himself had urged self-determination for the Turkish areas. This remark proved the futility of quoting the Fourteen Points to Wilson who, while regarding them as sacrosanct, appears to have seldom reread them: he admitted to have forgotten that particular point on a sure "sovereignty." The alternatives were unclear, but perhaps a general mandate for the whole with responsibility to advise in certain areas? Perhaps to France? Perhaps, responded Lloyd George, but this would mean reconsideration of the already vexing Middle Eastern mandates. Far better to get Italy out of the way safely by yielding on a problem where Italy was directly con-

---

[50] Council of Four, 17 May, 11 A.M. (without Orlando) and 4:15 P.M. (with Orlando), and Italian Delegation memorandum, 18 May, appended to 19 May 1919 Council of Four meeting, *ibid.,* pp. 668-69, 686-89, and 726; Gidney, *Mandate,* p. 92; Helmreich, *Paris to Sèvres,* p. 118. As Richard M. Watt remarks in *The Kings Depart: The Tragedy of Germany: Versailles and the German Revolution* (N.Y., 1968), p. 444, Lloyd George's mercurial temperament made such reversals easier for him than they might have been for another.

cerned—Yugoslavia—even if it meant that the Allies must swallow their own words. Wilson would not approve; he could not break with his principle of not giving one people into the rule of another without their consent.

The future of Turkey was not being advanced by these discussions. It could even be argued that a definite retrograde step was taken when the same day Baron Sonnino joined the Allied leaders for a session of recriminations and accusations, the opening tone of which was set by his refusal to discuss the problem with Venizelos present in the room. Italy, said Sonnino, had landed some troops to quell local disorders, and the local situation had not allowed time to make reference to the Allies—but Italy had not been consulted about the Greek landings either. Lloyd George's answer, that not a single Greek soldier had been sent before Italy had been consulted, was too twisted an interpretation to calm tempers. He had now come full circle to an intense anti-Italian attitude, and that attitude should be emphasized, for it has too often been overshadowed by his concomitant but differently motivated support for the Greeks: one may, after all, love Greeks without hating Italians.

Lloyd George's main argument, however, was that Greece had the Council's approval, Italy did not; he for one would refuse to discuss the question further until those Italian troops were removed. Sonnino's defense that the area had been assigned to Italy in 1917 was met by references to required Russian approval and Wilsonian self-determination. Sonnino's position was weak, but it was his only position; Italian public opinion was involved, he pleaded—but Lloyd George and Wilson had now the fury of the morally aggrieved.[52]

The Greeks had already landed (the Allies occupied the forts on the 14th and the Greeks disembarked the next evening). News soon filtered back of considerable ill-discipline and looting by the Greek troops. Gough-Calthorpe, on the scene in Smyrna, reported several dead and several dozen sent to prison: just how far, he asked, would the Greeks be allowed to penetrate? The Turks had already protested, although the occupation had been carried out under Article Seven (strategic places); the only result so far had been the arrest of the complaining Vali (gov-

[51] Council of Four, 11:30 A.M., 19 May 1919, *FRUS,* Paris Conference, V, pp. 705-10.
[52] Council of Four, 4 P.M., 19 May 1919, *ibid.,* pp. 716-23.

ernor). On the 20th, Gough-Calthorpe reported that the situation had eased with the replacement of the incompetent Greek colonel originally in charge and the appointment of Aristeidis Stergiadis, Governor-General of Epirus, as political advisor. Stergiadis, a competent civil servant and friend of Venizelos, soon established order. Several Greeks were executed for their crimes on order of their own officers, reported Gough-Calthorpe, and the Greek government explained oficially that a commander's error, compounded by Italian intrigue, Turkish hostility, and uncontrollable enthusiasm of local Greek patriots, had led to the trouble. The Allies could only accept these explanations, for they had sent in the Greeks.[53]

Such incidents could be waved away as undesirable but temporary flare-ups. The wider repercussions of this policy, however, were vast, not only for Greece and Turkey. Italy was hardly encouraged to a more accommodating attitude at Paris by the conference's favor of Greek occupation and its condemnation of Italian occupation.[54] In a still wider sense, the discussions would affect the whole of Britain's Middle Eastern policy and even, in an important way, India. None of this was foreseen, of course, in Paris. Clemenceau was willing to share in anti-Italian action and found Greek cooperation useful in south Russia. Lloyd George delighted in quick decisions which bypassed his ante-diluvian advisors (some of whom, it bears repeating, were whole-heartedly behind him) and cherished his friendship with Venizelos and with future Greek greatness. What, however, of President Wilson? He ". . . wallowed in arrangements as a tourist agent wallows in cross-country connections," said Harold Nicolson, and certainly the president's approval of a maneuver with such extensive ramifications shows little understanding of Turkish realities. But then, Wilson assumed, as did many, that Greece was legitimately entitled to Smyrna, what-

[53]Webb telegram to FO, 17 May, Gough-Calthorpe telegrams to Admiralty, 16 and 20 May, FO 371/4217; Gough-Calthorpe to Admiralty, 20 May, Granville telegram to FO, 24 May, Acting Capt. H.N. Boyle (Senior Naval Officer, Smyrna), report to commodore, Aegean Squadron, 17 May, Turkish GOC, Smyrna, telegram to Turkish Ministry of War, Constantinople, 20 May 1919, FO 371/4218. On Stergiadis, Smith, *Ionian Vision,* pp. 91-101.

[54] Council of Four, 21 and 26 May 1919, *FRUS,* Paris Conference, V, pp. 756-66, VI, pp. 47-50.

ever that term meant in precise boundaries.[55] Repercussions were in the future; for the moment, the task was still to reach a settlement with Turkey, and while Greece would have Smyrna in some form, the remainder still required distribution.

INDIA'S INTEREST

Already in mid-April, the British delegation experts had attempted in their perpetual redrafts to reach some sort of compromise solution. Toynbee and Nicolson together set forth a draft at this time which would expel the Turks from Constantinople (Balfour had issued instructions that drafts be based on this assumption) and give the city and the Straits to the Americans. Smyrna with a limited zone would go to Greece, but Armenia would now run from west of Mersina to the Russian frontier east of Samsun. The authors admitted that this solution—leaving more of Turkey to the Turks—was not really desirable, if only because Constantinople would be too small for viability. Better by far to give Constantinople to Greece and let the Turks keep Smyrna, but this seemed not to be the direction of higher policy. As Crowe pointed out, there was increasing doubt about American intent or ability to assume Turkish responsibilities. He, too, suggested that the Greeks be given the capital district. But where to put Italy? Clearly Italy would not be fobbed off with the Caucasus. The Crowe solution might be feasible without Italy's involvement, for it would leave the Turks with a chance to reform and evolve in a stable direction, a chance rather more remote if Greece were given Smyrna.

The vicious circle continued. No decision could be taken until America's future role was clear and Italian claims resolved; but Italian claims could not be dealt with until it was clear where the Greeks would

---

[55] Nicolson, *Peacemaking,* p. 202. On the landings and reactions to them see: Smith, *Ionian Vision,* Ch. V; Nicolson, *Curzon,* pp. 94-97; Armstrong, *Turkey in Travail,* p. 90; Winston S. Churchill, *The World Crisis,* V: "The Aftermath" (London, 1929) p. 387; Toynbee, *Western Question,* p. 74; Gidney, *Mandate,* pp. 119-20; Helmreich, *Paris to Sèvres,* pp. 98-101, 125. Richard D. Robinson, *The First Turkish Republic . . .* (Cambridge, Mass., 1965), pp. 35-36; Jean Schlincklin, *Angora . . . L'Aube, de la Turquie nouvelle (1919-1922)* (Paris, 1922), pp. 10-11; 'Adalia,' "The Problem of Asia Minor," *Edinburgh Review* 235 (1922): 131-46.

[56] Toynbee-Nicolson memorandum, 14 April 1919, with Crowe, Hardinge, Balfour, Mallet, and again Balfour minutes, *FO* 608/110.

go, and the Greek role depended upon American decisions . . . Only the Turks appeared to have a clear goal: the increase of incidents gave evidence that some, at least, contemplated resistance. Such resistance would not only prejudice Allied ambitions, it would also jeopardize the future of Armenia and might be repeated elsewhere in Asia, for such viruses spread quickly.[57]

Turkish resistance was not the only thing to be feared. The spokesmen for India also knew what they wanted, and in the absence of decision their arguments rang louder and louder. A separate state for the Straits, ran this view, would be unnecessary, artificial, and dangerous. The Turks would hate the Greeks. Muslims the world over would take amiss any change in St. Sophia's status. As Curzon pointed out, delays in reaching a settlement allowed time for Muslim sentiment to coalesce, but Paris responded only with a commission to study opinion—and therefore further delay. Indian nationalist opinion was increasingly turning to the issue of Turkey's future.[58]

Pressures had been building for some time in this direction, for India's very substantial efforts in the war, coupled with prewar promises of gradual reform, had raised expectations of progress in the immediate postwar era. Unwisely, the most prominent initial British reaction to India was the passage of legislation designed to continue wartime restrictions on agitators (the Defense of India Act). This legislation, known by the name of the chairman of the recommending committee as the Rowlatt Bills, seemed to its detractors the decree of a tyrannical government in war, and the war was now over. The actual terms mattered little; what mattered was that the power it gave to the authorities to make arrests and detentions without trial was power in no way seemly for a grateful and liberal government. Even Montagu, as secretary of state, felt that "rebellion," such as it was, could be stamped out by the

[57] An analysis along these lines is in Caleb F. Gates (president of Robert College, Istanbul) to H. Lybyer (American Delegation, Paris), 12 April (passed to British Delegation); also Lt.-Col. Ian M. Smith, area control officer, Smyrna, report, 7 April; Capt. L.H. Hurst, relief officer, Samsun, to high commissioner, 24 March; Lt. J.S. Perring (Samsun area) report, 23 March 1919, are some examples of reported resistance; these and others in similar vein are found in file 521, *FO* 371/4157.

[58] Montagu private to Lloyd George, 28 February, *Lloyd George Papers* (Beaverbrook Library), F/40/2/40; Toynbee memorandum, 30 March, Grant memorandum, 18 April, *FO* 608/111; Curzon memorandum, 18 April 1919, *FO* 608/83.

normal, rather than the new and exceptional, legal processes. Montagu's heart was largely in the reforms he had worked out in 1917-18 with Lord Chelmsford, his viceroy, and they naturally feared that reforms launched in the midst of antigovernment agitation would have a less-than-auspicious beginning.[59]

This is in fact precisely what came to pass; at Delhi on 20 March nonviolence became violent. It was an important event in the escalation of Indian political activity, particularly since both Hindus and Muslims took part. Anti-British activity mounted, and although Gandhi, principal leader of the movement, did all he could to restrict it to "satyagraha" (loosely, "forceful passive resistance") and noncooperation, the movement reached a temporary climax in the terrible tragedy of Amritsar on 13 April, which left something over 1500 killed and wounded by the bullets of British authority. The intentions and actions of those responsible have often been debated, but there is no question that this shocking event was a major turning point in the decline of the British Empire in India. The immediate intention of General Dyer, in command at Amritsar, was achieved: agitation lapsed into stunned silence. The government of India watched the situation with nerves rubbed raw, but no immediate revolution was anticipated.[60]

[59] Montagu private to Chelmsford, 10 October 1918, *Montagu Papers,* D. 523/2. On the Rowlatt Bills (technically, Criminal Law Amendment Bill, No. 1 of 1919, and Criminal Law Emergency Bill, No. 2 of 1919) and Indian agitation generally, see J.H. Bromfield, *Elite Conflict in a Plural Society: Twentieth Century Bengal* (Berkeley, 1968) pp. 118-24; India Home Department, *Histories of the Non-Co-Operation and Khalifat Movements,* by P.C. Bamford (Deputy Director, Intelligence Bureau, Home Department), (New Delhi, 1925); A.C. Niemeijer, *The Khalifat Movement in India 1919-1924* (The Hague, 1972); Sukhbir Choudhary, *Indian People Fight for National Liberation . . . 1920-22* (New Delhi, 1972), V.N. Data, *Jallianwala Bagh* (Ludhiana, 1969), pp. 30-35; Ram Gopal, *Indian Muslims: A Political History (1858-1947)* (N.Y. 1959) pp. 122-34; N.N. Mitra, ed., *Punjab Unrest Before and After* (Calcutta, 1920), which includes many of the relevant documents; S.R. Mehotra, "The Politics behind the Montagu Declaration of 1917, " in C.H. Philips, ed., *Politics and Society in India* (N.Y., 1962), pp. 71-96; H.F. Owen, "Organizing for the Rowlatt Satagraha of 1919," in R. Kumar, ed. *Essays in Gandhian Politics* (London, 1971), pp. 64-91; *C/J&P/6/*1546 [Judicial and Public Department] and 1588; in addition to the better known works on and by Gandhi, etc.

[60] The most comprehensive and detailed scholarly study of Gandhi's

It is understandable, in light of these events, that the government of India and the India Office pressed in every possible way for conciliation of Muslim opinion regarding Turkey. Such a gesture, of course, would cost India nothing, but would show that the Indian government was fighting on behalf of the views of its (Muslim) citizens. Dissatisfaction over the Turkish peace terms, moreover, might well add to the fuel of agitation just that kindling which was to be avoided above all: Hindu-Muslim collaboration.[61]

One limitation to the forcefulness of Indian representations was a certain disagreement within the bureaucracy on specific goals. No problem was presented by Constantinople, Thrace, or Smyrna: all should be Turkish. The caliphate was another matter. While interference in this institution was undesirable (during the war Britain had pledged not to intervene), rehabilitation of the caliph's image and authority would give him in theory a claim of some sort over the world's Muslims, which could complicate the separation of Iraq from Turkey, an operation the India Office favored. Iraq's chain of legal administration, for example, had ended in Constantinople, and the continued existence of such a connection would be rather tedious. In India itself, however, where the problem of Iraq was rather remote after the war, it was thought easier to press for extension of the caliphal authority which had not previously raised problems in prewar India but which seemed of such current importance to Indian Muslim leaders.[62]

role in these events is Judith M. Brown, *Gandhi's Rise to Power: Indian Politics, 1915-1922* (Cambridge, 1972), which should also be consulted on the Khalifat movement generally. Datta, *Jallianwala Bagh,* is the most useful account of Amritsar; see also Arthur Swinson, *Six Minutes to Sunset: the Story of General Dyer and the Amritsar Affair* (London, 1964). N.B. Bonarjee, *Under Two Masters* (Oxford, 1970), aptly remarks (p. 80) that many regretted the tragedy—but it was simply too great a tragedy to be overcome by a handshake and regrets.

[61] Montagu private to Lloyd George, 25 October, *Lloyd George Papers,* F/40/2/17 and private to Bonar Law, 2 December 1918, *Bonar Law Papers* (Beaverbrook Library), 98/5/2; Montagu made a practice of speaking to anyone of influence: for example, Colonel House—Charles Seymour, ed., *The Intimate Papers of Colonel House,* IV (Boston, 1928), p. 467—or Henry Wilson—Callwell, *Wilson,* II, p. 193. Further letters to Lloyd George (15 April and 22 June 1919) are quoted in S.D. Waley, *Edwin Montagu . . .* (N.Y., 1964), pp. 240, 243.

[62] Shuckburgh and Hirtzel notes, 31 December 1918, 5817/18, *L/P&S/*

The most vociferous Muslim leaders, the brothers Mohammad and Shaukat Ali, had emerged from wartime internment to assume the offensive on behalf of the caliphate; they now found that Gandhi's influence brought considerable Hindu support to their movement. Gandhi had given some thought to Hindu-Muslim cooperation and saw in the "Khilafat" movement a chance to further this aim by siding with what to him was a legitimate religious aspiration. It was to prove perhaps the cardinal error of Gandhi's career, for the growth of Muslim religious sentiment ran counter to the nonviolent achievement of unified independence which Gandhi came to symbolize. Gandhi, if he faced the issue at all, convinced himself through the self-deluding process often associated with prophethood that the fruit of cooperation would outweigh the dangers of aroused religious zeal. Not only was this conclusion wrong, but by supporting the Ali brothers Gandhi undermined those moderate Indian Muslims who claimed that Turkish problems were not India's direct concern. Gandhi's defense is worth considering, for he argued that his cooperation with the Ali brothers acted to limit and focus a religious sentiment which was already gaining strength.[63]

Naturally there was growing concern in Indian governmental circles with this ominous Hindu-Muslim cooperation. The provinces reported in alarmed tones to Delhi, and Delhi passed the news on to London, the Indian Office, and Montagu.[64] More than once, India asked that some proof be furnished to Indian opinion that Indian views were actually reaching the peacemakers. When Montagu was not able to give

---

10/852; India and Iraq are discussed in Busch, *Britain, India, and the Arabs,* Ch. III, VI.

[63] Owen, "Organizing for the Rowlatt Satagraha," 67-68; Gandhi, *Autobiography,* p. 442; Penderel Moon, *Gandhi and Modern India* (N.Y., 1969), especially p. 133; Sir Valentine Chirol, *India Old and New* (London, 1921), p. 174. IO to FO, 25 April, *FO* 371/4204; Sir William Marris, home secretary, to all local governments, 3 May, enclosing Ali brothers' letter to viceroy, 24 April 1919, *FO* 371/4231, and *C/J&P/6/*1574 deal with the Ali brothers; Mohamad and Shaukat Ali, *For India and Islam* (Calcutta, 1922), is representative of their views and opinions.

[64] Earl of Ronaldshay (governor of Bengal) private to Montagu, 14 May, *Montagu Papers,* D. 523/30; C.A. Barron (chief commissioner, Delhi) private to Chelmsford, 21 April, Sir Harcourt Butler (lieutenant governor, United Provinces) private to Chelmsford and Sir George Roos-Keppel (commissioner, North-West Frontier Province) private to Chelmsford, 22 April 1919, *Chelmsford Papers,* E. 264/22.

satisfactory reassurances, officials in both the Home and Foreign Departments in India advised that if necessary even the private correspondence through which most such requests had been made should be made public. The most that could be won, however, was approval by Montagu and Lloyd George of a statement that India had strongly pressed its case. Such general statements could have but little result, and Sir C.R. Cleveland, director of Criminal Intelligence in India and as such responsible more than any other single official for watching "agitators," even had doubts about making such general statements unless details were forthcoming on exactly what points had been urged by India's representatives in Paris (none of whom, after all, was Muslim).[65]

While the efforts of Montagu and his associates must be considered within the Indian framework, there is an even wider circle of association which must be kept in mind. Many who concerned themselves with British policies and position in the world tended to connect outbursts of "revolutionism" wherever it appeared, from Irish nationalists to Yorkshire miners to German Spartacists to Russian Bolsheviks to Young Turk leaders (they had after all won power by revolution in 1908, and Mustafa Kemal, their lineal successor, fit aptly into the revolutionary mold) to Gandhi and Tilak and even to Annie Besant, theosophist and home rule leader in India. It was, in fact, seen as a conspiracy which often took the form of a "nationalist movement," but which had as its link what a later generation would call "anti-establishment" tendencies designed to destroy law and order and recognized authority. "Surely," wrote Kidston of the Foreign Office in April 1919, "it is no longer excusable or wise to treat its varying manifestations as if they spring from entirely different zones.[66]

Furthermore, too many disturbances scattered the forces available to deal with them. The military authorities made it quite clear that enforcing partition of Turkey, which they opposed for other reasons,

[65]Chelmsford private telegrams to Montagu, 31 January, 10 and 16 May, Montagu private telegram to Chelmsford, 11 May, with comments of Marris, D. Bray, W.H. Vincent, *Home Department Proceedings,* Political files (National Archives of India, New Delhi), May 1919, 524-32, part A; Montagu private telegram to Chelmsford, 7 April 1919, with minutes (including Cleveland) and other documents in file, *Home Dept. Proc.,* June 1919, 362-76, part A.

[66] Kidston minute, 9 April 1919, 53941/71, *FO* 371/4141.

would not be possible given the problems in India, the new war with Afghanistan, the wave of Egyptian nationalist activity which was reaching "revolution" proportions, and other problems. As disagreement grew over an alternative Constantinople state, concluded Mallet in Paris, the only solution seemed to be leaving the Turks there—if possible with Greece only in Thrace and not Smyrna. Probably it would still be necessary to put Italy into Adalia, but the future of Armenia was most uncertain. Crowe disagreed, but Nicolson was even more at sea than ever: Constantinople to the Greeks, or the Americans? Internationalize the Straits, leaving the rest to the Turks? Unless the major statesmen gave a lead in the solution of these basic questions, no detailed treaty could ever be worked out; all that was certain was that the original British draft was neither accepted nor rejected, and a conference commission on Greek claims had supported Greek possession of Smyrna.[67]

Something approaching a decision was now made by Lloyd George in the context of Italian relations—but on 17 May a major meeting took place between the Council of Four and the Indian representatives led by Montagu. This discussion perhaps directed the prime minister's thinking toward the caliphate and helped dissuade him from the idea of dividing Turkey into Allied spheres.[68] On the 19th, an ad hoc Cabinet meeting was held in Paris. Churchill, secretary of war, and Montagu led the opposition to further British responsibilities in Turkey, and Lloyd George was sufficiently attuned to this pressure and the likely difficulties of working with an Italian mandate in Anatolia that he reported to the Council of Four on the 21st that the British delegation, while wishing to see mandates established for Anatolia and Constantinople under the same mandatory, preferably the United States, realized that the alternative to American control was to leave the Turks there. There could in any case be no division of Anatolia aside from Smyrna and Armenia. The prime minister did not pretend that he personally had been consistent in this matter, but he saw, at last, that no other conclusions were possible.[69]

[67] British Delegation memorandum, 25 April, with FO minutes, *FO* 371/4156; H. Nicolson memorandum, 30 April 1919, with Balfour, Mallet, Crowe minutes, *FO* 608/110.

[68] Council of Four, 17 May 1919, *FRUS,* Paris Conference, V, pp. 690-701.

[69] Gidney, *Mandate,* pp. 111-12; Nicolson, *Peacemaking,* p. 343; Mon-

President Wilson, still alarmed about the American role and even more at this new and dubious proposal from Lloyd George, and Clemenceau, quickly grasping that the French sphere was to be sacrificed as the cost of getting rid of the Italians, could not agree. Neither, however, had an alternative plan. Clemenceau tended to focus irritably on the arrival of Lord Curzon in Paris as the cause of Lloyd George's new Francophobe hostility—an accusation which rather lowered the tone of the discussion. Once again, the decisions had to be postponed while the United States meditated on the British plan and the French waited for a British concession on Syria before conceding anything in Turkey. Montagu, at any rate, returned home encouraged enough about Asia Minor to conclude that there would be no partition, although the Turks might still lose Constantinople. This possibility did, however, lead him to contemplate resignation (neither for the first nor the last time), despite the fact that there would be no interference with India's special concerns—the caliphate, holy places, and religious buildings such as St. Sophia.[70]

There was no further immediate progress except that Ferid Pasha's government was permitted to send a delegation to Paris to put the Turkish case. In late June, the delegation, headed by Tevfik and Ahmed Izzet Pashas, was in Paris arguing for an unrealistic proposal to reorganize and reform the empire—the whole empire. When the delegation returned to Constantinople in late July, they had accomplished very little indeed, although it was clear in London that both Greeks and Italians had used the time to advantage by advancing their lines in Asia Minor.[71]

A fine superior tone was taken to Turkish protestations, but some

---

tagu private to Lord Willingdon (governor of Madras), 21 May, *Willingdon Papers* (IO Library), F. 93/4; Council of Four, 21 May 1919, *FRUS,* Paris Conference, V, pp. 756-66.

[70] Council of Four, 21 May 1919, *FRUS,* Paris Conference, V. pp. 756-66, with Scheme for Settlement appended, pp. 770-71; Roskill, *Hankey,* II. p. 91: Montagu private telegram to Chelmsford, 22 May 1919, *Chelmsford Papers,* E. 264/10.

[71] Gough-Calthorpe telegrams to FO, 3, 5, and 6 June, 22 and 26 July, Turkish Delegation to Clemenceau, 23 and 30 June, British Empire Delegation to Turkish Delegation, 23 June, *FO* 371/4229; Curzon to Balfour, 20 June, *FO* 371/4218; draft answer to Turks, appended to Council of Four, 21 June 1919, *FRUS,* Paris Conference, VI, pp. 577-80; Montagu private to Lloyd George, 22 June 1919, *Lloyd George Papers,* F/40/2/55.

material action was necessary as the end of the conference and the final departure of President Wilson appeared imminent. In the Council of Four on 15 June, Lloyd George argued that something must be done to put the Turks out of their misery: the delay could not continue. Perhaps the portions which were going to be detached could be detached, leaving the final disposition of the remainder until it was quite clear whether the Americans would take a mandate. But, as Clemenceau and Wilson were both quick to point out, this raised the same question of the amputation of Constantinople and Armenia and the Italian area. Once again, all the old arguments were brought forth; in this meeting and the next no agreement could be reached. The only conclusion possible in late June as the conference disbanded was that the Turkish question would have to be held over until the question of American participation was resolved.[72]

The hasty efforts of June thus brought no answer—after all, the Eastern Question had continued for centuries and was not to be ended in weeks. But a problem that seemed difficult in October 1918 had become insoluble by July 1919. Lloyd George had withdrawn troops from the Caucasus in order (or so he claimed) to deal with Italy. It remained to be seen what impact decisions so far made on Turkey would have on Russia and the Caucasus. Events in Paris had, moreover, been influenced by the wave of troubles spreading from Egypt to India and farther Central Asia. Just as problems of Turkish peacemaking had caused some strategists concerned with the Russian civil war, the Caucasus, and the Caspian to focus a bit closer on the Mediterranean, so too were events in Persia and Afghanistan redirecting the attention formerly devoted to Central Asia.

[72] Council of Four, 25 June (with draft of answer for Turkish delegation, 23 June) and 27 June 1919, *FRUS,* Paris Conference, VI, pp. 675-76, 688-90, 729-30; Montagu's views on draft, 26 June 1919, 385/3/5, *FO* 608/118.

III

Flood Tide:
The Eastern Marches,
1918-1919

The armistices of October-November 1918 dramatically altered the Russian situation, for they facilitated Allied intervention, which could ensure German withdrawal and in some way resolve a confused political and still dangerous military situation. Intervention had, of course, already begun. As early as March 1918 Allied troops had landed at Murmansk, and Japanese detachments appeared in Vladivostok in April. In south Russia, however, Anglo-French diplomacy had only achieved assignment of spheres in December 1917 and the provision of financial aid to the "Volunteer Army" of General Alexeiev.[1]

Since the German danger was the motive for intervention, presumably the Allies would not push on once the war was over. But logic did not rule. Gradually, and obscurely, Allied motivation underwent a dramatic metamorphosis from "aiding the Russian ally" to the suppression of the dark forces unleased by the revolution. However damaging such activity was to long-run Allied interests, it is understandable given the general association in Allied minds of "German" and "Bolshevik." The armistice with Germany, moreover, might conceivably break down and fighting resume once more. In such an eventuality, German influence and power in Russia, as epitomized by the Treaty of Brest-Litovsk, was an ominous and all too realistic prospect.

---

[1] In addition to the works of Ullman, Brinkley, Kenez, and Silverlight in chapter 1, the following remarks also make use of Richard Luckett, *The White Generals . . .* (N.Y., 1971), John S. Reshetar, Jr., *The Ukranian Revolution, 1917-1920* (Princeton, 1952), David Footman, "Nestor Makhno," in David Footman, ed., *St. Antony's Papers, No. 6* (London, 1959): 75-127.

It is in this context that events in south Russia and the Caucasus must be viewed. Alexeiev's force—taken over on his death in October 1918 by General A.T. Denikin—had established itself at Ekaterinador in Kuban province and was building an army officered by Russians and manned largely by Don and Kuban Cossacks. In December, an independent Don Cossack organization acceded to Denikin, and this event, coupled with the defeat of local Bolshevik opposition, Germany's surrender, and a pledge of French aid in November 1918 (the so-called Jassy agreement), indicated that Denikin would be the focus of efforts to reestablish order in south Russia. Unfortunately, Denikin was a man of limited vision and overzealous Tsarism, anxious to defend Russia against all enemies, including "separatists," whether Ukranians, Georgians, or the Cossacks who made up so much of his army. In his Kuban campaign of mid-1918, he so alarmed Georgian leaders that they had felt obliged to assume control of Tuapse, an important Black Sea port and rail and pipline terminus. Worse, Denikin was temperamentally unable to make concessions to the "politicians" of competing local governments, who might have provided the administrative and ideological ability which was so sadly lacking in Volunteer Army circles. But Russian political depths were unfathomable in Russia, let alone Paris and London, and Denikin was the logical choice for the British mission which reached him in early December.[2]

Denikin expected such aid as a natural return for the assistance which Russia had given her allies during the war. He also expected that the Allies would provide no aid for the "separatists"—particularly the Georgians—who should be punished for their wartime collaboration with the enemy. Both expectations depended upon Allied agreement and such agreement was long delayed. Official British policy was nonintervention, and unofficial policy leaned toward supporting the independence of the border states emerging in an arc from the Baltic to the Black Sea. Arguments existed on both sides: dissipation of effort, expense, support for self-determination, "giving Russia a chance" to settle her own affairs—there were numerous aspects to be considered, but in effect the policy was one of ". . . letting policy and action drift

[2] WO telegram to Constantinople, 31 January 1919, *FO* 371/3977. The Jassy agreement is discussed in Kenez, *Civil War in South Russia,* pp. 256-58, Luckett, *White Generals,* pp. 194-95, and Mayer, *Politics and Diplomacy,* pp. 296-97.

on with no basis other than that which had in fact evaporated," as one historian has put it. But the "drift" was into, not away from, Russia. By a sort of law of Anglo-Russian relations, from the Straits to Tibet, where one power receded the other advanced, and the sudden collapse of the entire Russian structure had the effect of a broken levee in flood time.[3]

Little consideration was given to justifying the British flood, although there were reasons in plenty. That was part of the difficulty: it was never a case of imperialists (like Milner) or anti-Bolshevik conservatives (like Robert Cecil) only. Interventionists were interventionists by degree; very few supported Churchill's demand for total involvement in the civil war, aware, as he seemed not to be, of the great and unrelenting pressure from a conscript army demanding immediate demobilization. The plain fact was that British opinion would not countenance a British war in Russia, although the Cabinet in general approved intervention. Lloyd George, consistently opposed to Russian entanglement, was long a minority in his own Cabinet. Churchill was his main antagonist; that the positions of the two men were equally far apart on Greco-Turkish affairs was not mere coincidence. But while individuals had positions, there was no policy.

The French view was differently conceived but no more clear-cut. France had promised aid to Denikin in the Ukraine and the Crimea, and in mid-December 1918, shortly after the German evacuation of Odessa, French troops landed there and soon assumed administration of the neighboring area. That this area was not simply handed over to Denikin was the first issue; the French desire to ensure their south Russian interests by agreement with a friendly local government was the second. Denikin proved to be bitterly opposed to the Ukrainian Directory with which the French negotiated. An easy occupation soon turned out to be serious combat against all comers, and the morale of the French army (and navy), tired and weary and infected by leftist political propaganda and agitators, was badly sapped in the fighting. When in March 1919 the French were driven from Kherson by a partisan Cossack band, they had had enough. General Franchet d'Espérey in Constantinople strongly advised evacuation, and by early April they

[3] Brinkley, *Volunteer Army,* p. 76; see also Mayer, *Politics and Diplomacy,* pp. 308-15, and Ullman, *Anglo-Soviet Relations,* II, pp. 13-18, for general policy discussions and British positions.

were gone, leaving Odessa to the Cossacks with the Bolsheviks in hot pursuit. Only Denikin remained in the Donetz Basin, taken badly by surprise by the French move, which exposed his flank and cost him supporters and supplies. While the French had been at fault, this action nevertheless colored Denikin's relations with all the Allies. The French command in Odessa, on the other hand, had found Denikin hard to work with, and for that they tended to blame the British.[4]

The uninspiring story of French intervention in south Russia was yet to evolve when the peacemakers gathered at Paris in January 1919. There was legitimate concern that a European settlement which excluded Russia would be of little utility. Anti-interventionist opinion and the immediate need to reduce military commitments produced an approach to the Bolsheviks to ascertain whether some sort of compromise was possible, and an invitation went out in late January to all Russian governments competing for recognition and power to attend a conference in February at Prinkipo Island in the Sea of Marmora. The effort was half-hearted from the outset; France in particular objected— Clemenceau gave only grudging approval to this proposal initiated by Lloyd George and drafted by President Wilson. The essential condition, cessation of hostilities, proved unrealistic in a bloody civil war, and the White leaders, who had much to lose and nothing to gain by recognition of the Bolsheviks at the bargaining table, rejected the invitation. France is often charged with having encouraged this resistance, but such encouragement seems hardly necessary to explain the White attitude. Recognition of the Bolsheviks, and implicit partition of Russia, was not what the Whites were fighting for.[5]

[4] Ullman, *Anglo-Soviet Relations,* II, pp. 47-48; Brinkley, *Volunteer Army,* Ch. IV; Stephen Roskill, *Naval Policy between the Wars* (N.Y., 1968), I, p. 156; Churchill, *World Crisis,* V, pp. 167-69; John Swettenham, *Allied Intervention in Russia, 1918-1919* (London, 1967), pp. 247-50; Paul Mantoux, ed., *Paris Peace Conference, 1919; Proceedings of the Council of Four (March 24-April 19)* (Geneva, 1964), pp. 6-10; Silverlight, *Victor's Dilemma,* pp. 206-7; Mayer, *Politics and Diplomacy,* pp. 300-1. The French troops, it should be mentioned, were troubled by a serious mutiny; see in addition pamphlets by Andre Marty, *The Epic of the Black Sea* (London, 1940), and Maurice Paz, *Les Révoltes de la Mer noire* (Paris, 1921).

[5] Prinkipo proposal is discussed in Ullman, *Anglo-Soviet Relations,* II, pp. 110-13; Brinkley, *Volunteer Army,* pp. 108-11; Watt, *Kings Depart,* p. 78; Mayer, *Politics and Diplomacy,* pp. 365, 428-32; Luckett, *White*

The failure of Prinkipo left Britain little choice save the "non-policy" already described. In early March the Cabinet decided to withdraw its units in northern Russia when summer came; attention could then be focused on operations in the Caucasus and Denikin's sphere. And, while no comprehensive policy for the whole of Russia seemed capable of being formulated, logic and realism could hopefully be applied here on a smaller scale.

A POLICY FOR THE CAUCASUS

The future of the Caucasus was a Middle Eastern, as well as a Russian, question; after all, it was the combined Turko-German threat which had prompted the Caucasian adventure at the end of the war. In late October 1918 it was necessary to decide, and quickly, whether or not to reoccupy the Caucasus—with British troops, for it was still Britain's sphere. On 29 October the Eastern Committee agreed, with little dissent, that because Enver Pasha (one of the principal Turkish wartime leaders) reportedly planned to establish a pro-Turkish state in Azerbaijan, and because connections with the Whites north of the Caucasus were still needed, occupation in fulfillment of the armistice was desirable and should proceed forthwith.[6]

More was required than a decision on occupation. In a memorandum of 1 November, the Foreign Office Political Intelligence Department (meaning Toynbee in this case) outlined a policy based upon self-determination: recognition of Georgia, Armenia, and Azerbaijan, which would be overseen by some superior power, preferably Britain or the United States. Armenia would be a special problem, given the destruction of that people and such other factors as the need to find an

---

Generals, pp. 244-45; Hovannisian, *Armenian Republic,* I, pp. 389-90; John M. Thompson, *Russia, Bolshevism and the Versailles Peace* (Princeton, N.J., 1966), Ch. IV. Prinkipo had the advantages of adequate housing, sufficient remoteness from Europe (thus not allowing the Bolsheviks to contaminate Paris, for example), nearness to Allied occupation forces in Constantinople, and access by sea, thus requiring the delegates to cross no frontiers. The fact that another of the islands was once used for internment of Constantinople's dogs provided an opportunity for eloquent analogies by Churchill (*World Crisis,* V, p. 172).

[6] Eastern Committee, 29 October, and IO note, 1 November 1918, *L/P&S/*10/807.

equitable arrangement with the Kurdish areas to the south—but the principle was clear. As usual, there were other opinions: Crowe, for example, stressed the provisional nature of any such settlement pending Russian revival. Even where there was a general consensus, such as on recognizing Georgia, it still seemed necessary to leave initiative in the matter to the peace conference.[7]

It was assumed, of course, that once occupation was decided upon detailed plans for the future could await reports from the men on the scene. The presence of British forces, however, was no guarantee of clarity. On 6 November, British naval units reached Bicherakov at Petrovsk to find him engaged in serious fighting against a Turkish force which had moved north after the fall of Baku. Since the Turks were fighting nominally on behalf of Azerbaijan, not Turkey, British forces refused to become involved until it was clear whether the Turkish armistice had actually been violated. This attitude did not smooth relations with Bicherakov, and even in the midst of evacuating Petrovsk he insisted that Commander Norris's ships fly both Russian and British flags; Bicherakov recognized the leadership of Admiral A.V. Kolchak in Omsk and in his name claimed to speak for Russia.[8]

Meanwhile, Major-General W.M. Thompson, commanding the North Persian Forces (or Norperforce), disembarked units of the 39th Infantry Brigade (17th Indian Division) at Baku on 17 November. The city was held by the Azerbaijanis who, with Turkish help, had taken over on Dunsterville's withdrawal. Ordering the disbandment of the Azerbaijani military forces, Thompson assumed charge of the city in cooperation with—but without yielding authority to—the Centro-Caspian government which Bicherakov now brought to Baku from

[7] Political Intelligence Dept., FO, memorandum, 1 November, Crowe memorandum, 7 November, *FO* 371/3301; DMI to FO, 15 November 1918, with Mallet, Hardinge, and Balfour minutes, *FO* 371/3321.

[8] Senior naval officer, Caspian, to GOC Norperforce, 7 November, *Norris Papers,* NOS/4; Maj. Radcliffe Smith, report, 7 November, War Diary, H.Q. 27th Division, Tiflis, *WO* 95/4045 and 4879; Acting Capt. B.G. Washington, flag captain, East India Station, to CinC East Indies Station, 31 December 1918, Admiralty Records, Public Record Office, series 137, volume 1736 [hereafter *ADM* 137/1736] notes that Washington was in acting command for much of the time between October 1918 and February 1919, owing to an injury to Norris. On the fighting north of Baku, report of Brig.-Gen. D. Shuttleworth, 12 January 1920, *WO* 106/1562; Allen and Muratoff, *Caucasian Battlefields,* pp. 497-527.

Petrovsk. Bicherakov could make little complaint, for he had not the forces to control Baku alone, and his enemies were numerous. In addition to the Turks to the north, the Bolsheviks now held some Caspian fleet units and the port of Astrakhan on the Volga. Britain remained in control of Baku, Enzeli in Persia, and Petrovsk, once the Turks were persuaded to withdraw persuant to the armistice, and so for the time being Bicherakov required British friendship for survival.[9]

The possible intention of the Turks to stay on in the Caucasus—the postarmistice operations against Petrovsk were a case in point—and the general situation both there and in Russia were convincing justifications for extension of British occupation. Marshall in Baghdad (still, to his own intense regret, responsible for the Caucasus) reported that the Turks had 25,000 troops in the area and that two divisions would be required to deal with them. For that reason alone, Britain could not shirk her responsibility to put forces into Batum on the Black Sea as soon as through communications were established. On 21 November, the War Cabinet approved the transfer of one division only, the 27th, from Salonika to Batum. With Thompson's brigade in Baku this was enough to clear the Batum-Baku railway by 23 December, and with its headquarters in Tiflis it soon found itself strung out along the railway. The mission of seeing to Turkish withdrawal was soon expanded, however, to that of dealing with many serious local problems.[10]

Every local decision had political repercussions; small units sent to adjudicate or arbitrate disputes in areas such as Nakhichevan, Akhalkalak, or the Kars district were automatically considered increasingly partisan with each decision made. Turkish evacuation was accomplished, and by the end of January 1919 only 6,000 Turks remained in the Caucasus; but little could be done about serious clashes such as that of Denikin with the Georgians or the Georgians with the Ar-

[9] 39th Brigade diary, *WO* 95/4955; Thompson official diary as commander of Norperforce, 17-24 November 1918, with attached appreciation of situation by Thompson, 13 May 1919, *CAB* 45/107 (correspondence of historical section of Cabinet Office); Operations section, Norperforce H.Q., *WO* 95/5045; G.H.Q. diary, Constantinople, *CAB* 45/105.

[10] Marshall private telegram to Gen. H. Wilson, 18 November; Wilson private telegram to Milne, repeated Baghdad and India, 18 November, *War Diary,* Persia, 48; War Cabinet, 21 November, *CAB* 23/8; Eastern Committee, 21 November 1918, *L/P&S*/10/807; diaries of 27th Div. H.Q. (*WO* 95/4879), 39th Brigade, especially 84th Punjabis (*WO* 95/4955), 1/89 Punjabis, 2/4 Gurkhas (*WO* 95/4893).

menians.[11] At the same time, Commander Norris had to drive off the Bolshevik fleet on the Caspian from an attempt to establish a base on Cheleken Island near Krasnovodsk, for a base in the deeper waters of the south Caspian would be most dangerous to British operations. To assist the navy, a squadron of DH9 planes found its way to the Caspian, to be followed by thirty longer-range DH9A's from HMS *Ark Royal* in the Black Sea and a squadron of Short Seaplanes. From bases north of Baku these planes were to wreak havoc on the Bolshevik presence on the Volga, but the energy displayed by pilots and naval ratings alike could not ensure the adoption of some coherent policy which might adequately explain why they were engaged in such operations.[12]

A general decision made before the armistice to support Caucasian separatists relieved the military of having to determine whether local movements were artificially encouraged by Turks and Germans or were honest attempts at self-determination. But the general principle was not enough; even assuming support for Caucasian movements (an assumption persistently challenged by British representatives with Denikin, who tended to adopt his viewpoint), which group would be preferred in case of conflict? The military was blamed for preferring Armenians (long considered allies) to Georgians in one area and for preferring Azerbaijanis to Armenians in another. Since elements from the Baku side tended to favor Azerbaijan, the unjustified charge was leveled that the units from Baghdad and India tended to favor Muslim Azerbaijanis over Christian Armenians. A moment's thought would have pricked that balloon: while India favored concessions on the caliphate, it hardly desired to see the creation of a new and possibly hostile alliance of Muslim states forged from Turkey to Afghanistan.[13]

[11] Hovannisian, *Republic,* I, and Kazemzadeh, *Struggle* (especially Ch. XII) deal in depth with the various territorial disputes; added details may be found in the relevant war diaries for the units involved, cited above.

[12] Norris letters of proceedings to CinC East Indies Station, 1 and 19 December 1918, 21 January, and 6 April 1919, *Norris Papers,* NOS/4; air operations are reported in rear-admiral, Black Sea, letter of proceedings, 28 February 1919, Air Ministry records, Public Record Office, series 1, volume 344 [*AIR* 1/344]; a request for Handley Page bombers, the largest of World War I, was refused owing to problems of supply: R. Groves, Director, Air Division, Admiralty, minute, 18 December 1918, *ADM* 137/1736.

[13] It is not necessary to enter here into a discussion of the justice of this

Clear directives from home would have eased a difficult situation, but there were none, and none was forthcoming from the assembled powers in Paris. It was not for lack of trying on the British side; indeed, the Caucasus and Caspian took more Eastern Committee discussion in December than almost any other subject.[14] There were simply too many problems, too many views: the size of Armenia, the nature and area of the mandatory power, the American role, the French role . . . endless debate seemed to be the only outcome of every meeting on Turkey and the Caucasus. Tentative agreement could be reached only on some sort of Armenia and some sort of barrier, "if it can be done reasonably," as Cecil put it, which would secure the oil and railway (although to Curzon the issue was more preventing some "Asiatic Balkans" and creating a "palisade" against pan-Turanian ambitions).

After a week's discussion, Montagu was still doubtful; each section of the Caucasus appeared to be treated individually, he noted on 9 December, but the net result appeared to be that Britain would stay on in control of everything. Curzon maintained that each temporary oc-

---

or that decision, for their importance was primarily local. It is commonly asserted, however (as in Hovannisian, *Republic,* I, p. 157, or Ullman, *Anglo-Soviet Relations,* II, pp. 223-24) that officers from India tended to favor local non-Christian movements, while those from Salonika or Europe more often favored Christian minorities—and, similarly, that India thought more of local separatism and "westerners" of the Great Russian position. There is little evidence, in fact, for such an assertion, except that this or that particular decision seems to have gone against one or another party. The Armenians were denied Karabagh or Zangezur—but were given all of Kars (although they could not hold it) and, eventually, Nakhichevan provinces. The Georgians, as will be seen, were distrusted even more by the authorities in Constantinople than those in London. Hovannisian offers no evidence in support of his contention (p. 157) that "British strategists" felt that a viable Azerbaijan would be less susceptible to pan-Islamic and pan-Turanian propaganda; while it might have been a consideration, a larger one was the danger of encouraging such ideologies by fostering a Muslim Azerbaijani state. The views of individual officers must not be confused—as unfortunately is the natural tendency—with the views of the government of India or the India Office, whose consistent desire was to withdraw from Caucasian responsibilities. For an example of simplistic generalizations, see MacDonell, *". . . And Nothing Long",* a very partisan account by an anti-Muslim participant; too many such commentators have sought for an explanation of the failure of their favored Armenians or Georgians in Indian attitudes.

[14] Eastern Committee, 2 (quoted), 5, and 9 (quoted) December 1918, discussed at length in Ullman, *Anglo-Soviet Relations,* II, pp. 67-82.

cupation would last only as long as necessary to set the individual state-lets on their feet, but even Cecil found problems with this; the more he reacted to the expression "temporary" and related it to the "temporary occupation" of Egypt, the more he was drawn to Montagu's position. Balfour was also becoming alarmed as the defenses of India moved further and further from the frontiers of that country. But, pleaded Curzon, the Caucasians would tear each other apart; let them, said Balfour. Montagu, encouraged by these desertions from the cause of occupation, now assumed the offensive, but Balfour, eager to be done with this issue, suggested that it all be consigned to the conference: "I do not think," he said in answer to Curzon, "that it is our business to have a policy with regard to these places," in advance of the conference—an attitude, coming from a foreign minister, which drove Curzon to despair.

The only result of further discussion in both Eastern Committee and Cabinet, aside from the usual pious hopes for Armenia (which would be French or American in any case), was an indication the Caucasian states were desirable and that temporary British involvement would be necessary there if no alternative arose. Even this Montagu argued against, as he argued against any sort of involvement in the Caucasus and Trans-Caspian areas. The policy, as prepared for Paris and telegraphed to Milne and his subordinate commanders, was to enforce the armistice, reopen the rail and pipelines (which would probably mean occupation of Batum and Tiflis and as much as necessary of the railway), and support the creation of strong and independent states in Georgia, Azerbaijan, the Daghestan (on the north side of the Caucasus, home of a vigorous and independent-minded—if politically unsophisticated—people). Armenia would have to await a conference decision on boundaries and mandatory supervision. Commitments were to be avoided; but only nonintervention could have avoided commitments, and in late December British troops formed a solid cordon across the Caucasus from Batum to Baku, supported by powerful fleet elements in the Black Sea and a scratch force in the Caspian, with friendly forces in the White army to the north. When in January Denikin's forces destroyed for the moment the claims to existence of the "Soviet Republic of the North Caucasus," it seemed that at least in the Caucasus the Allies had a strong position as the peacemakers moved to Paris.[15]

[15] WO telegram to GOC Constantinople, 11 December, *FO* 371/3361;

THE CAUCASUS AT PARIS

When Paris could consider the Caucasus, however, it was not in isolation, but rather as part of the Russian and Turkish problems. Just
as the future of Smyrna or Constantinople awaited a conference principle on Turkey, the Caucasus awaited a general principle on Russia.
How true this was became clear in January, when Georgia clashed with
Denikin—two parties which both aspired to British friendship. Denikin
was several times warned off—and demarcation lines set for him—but
he could not be pressed too hard.[16] Britain and her allies wanted Denikin's victory in Russia, but the arms supplied him seemed destined
for use against Georgia. "Everything that we *say* is in support of self-
determination; everything that we *do* is in support of those who are
opposed to that principle . . .," complained Professor J. Simpson, attached to the Political Intelligence Department as an area expert; and
certainly it appeared so to the Georgians when their request for recognition was answered by another reference to the conference. Georgia,
unwilling to negotiate with Denikin, had refused to attend Prinkipo,
and Milne and Gough-Calthorpe in Constantinople persistently discouraged relations with a socialist Georgia (the government was under
Menshevik control). So long as only the military were on the spot, remarked the Foreign Office's Kidston, this opinion would prevail; Paris
might recognize the Menshevik authorities only to find that they had
been suppressed locally by Allied forces.

Curzon, writing in the Foreign Office on 2 February, found the situation most disquieting. General Thompson appeared to be establishing a
base at Petrovsk and holding part of the Petrovsk-Vladikavkaz railway.
Foreign Office information was sketchy, but so far as Curzon could
tell, no authorization for this had ever been given; the policy was to

---

WO telegram to GOC Baghdad, 16 December 1918, *War Diary,* Persia,
49; Kenez, *Civil War,* p. 190.

[16] Demarcation is discussed in Brinkley, *Volunteer Army,* pp. 154-65;
Kazemzadeh, *Struggle,* Ch. XVI; Ullman, *Anglo-Soviet Relations,* II,
p. 225; Hovannisian, *Republic,* I, pp. 368-72. The line was discussed,
but not seriously imposed, in January, established in June (but by it Denikin
was denied Daghestan, which he had occupied in May), and altered in
August.

[17] Kidston note, 8 January, GOC Constantinople telegram to DMI,
3 January, with Simpson note (quoted), 17 January 1919, *FO* 371/3661.

hold only Batum, Tiflis, and Baku, and the railway in between. Preserving the peace and assisting local governments against Bolshevik aggression was the objective—but without formal recognition of those governments and without becoming deeply involved in either administrative or military responsibilities. Curzon appears to have sincerely believed that such a temporary policy could be followed and that the military could be in occupation of the area and yet not become deeply involved. If the army persisted in occupying Kars in one direction and Petrovsk in the other, they were exceeding their authority and altering the accepted policy, and Curzon was hardly surprised when they then sent in repeated requests for additional troops to hold the expanded area.[18]

The Foreign Office could not simply wash its hands of the Caucasus, as Curzon knew well. Since the early days of the war, however, this area had been in the War Office's purview, and if the Foreign Office was to influence Caucasian policy it was necessary to have adequate representation in the area. At the moment, that amounted to one elderly consul in Batum trained only for economic duties, and, in other than commercial and consular affairs, ". . . the Foreign Office have literally no Caucasus correspondence upon their registers at all," wrote Kidston in despair. Until this situation could be altered, the Foreign Office would have to rely on the military, and the military was already demanding more troops—not only from Thompson, but also from General Milne in Constantinople.[19]

Milne paid a personal visit to both Trans-Caspia (from which he recommended immediate withdrawal) and the Caucasus in February. His requirements for the latter area alone—assuming no need to support any forces in Trans-Caspia and no change in the Caucasian situation—included two and a half battalions for Batum, where both Georgians and Bolsheviks were a danger; another division for Armenia, ruled by a government "as honest as any collection of Armenians is capable of being," to watch Armenian relations with Georgians and Azerbaijanis; a battalion and some cavalry to keep the Nakhichevan areas quiet, and another brigade in Baku; other units, including a half-battalion to ensure German evacuation from Poti, where the Georgian government,

[18] Curzon memorandum, 2 February 1919, 19030/5890, *FO* 371/3667.
[19] Kidston minute (quoted), 6 February, and DMO note to FO, 12 February 1919, *FO* 371/3667; GOC Baghdad telegram to WO, 17 December 1918, *War Diary,* Persia, 49.

"ultra-Socialistic of the most advanced type," could not be trusted—
the total came to two divisions, every single soldier of which would be
accounted for.[20]

On the larger question of policy, the War Office saw three alternatives. One was withdrawal, which was not desirable at all, for it would
end control of the Caspian and impede operations in north Persia (now
supplied from Constantinople and the Caucasus, in preference to the
more difficult route from Baghdad). The second possibility was so extensive a control it would amount to a virtual protectorate; this obviously would call for even more military commitment than was now
contemplated. The third choice, and the most desirable, was to deny
local requests for intervention, withdraw all unessential units, and concentrate forces on the railway.[21] It sounded superficially like Curzon's
policy, but the difference was substantial: there would be no more
"keeping order in the district" and "putting them on their feet."

The issue could only be resolved at Cabinet level, but the Cabinet
was much more concerned with south Russia generally and the possibility of renewed activity in Odessa—for Venizelos, perhaps drawing
on the model of Cavour in the Crimean War, was willing to commit
substantial forces to the anti-Bolshevik war effort there. There was
also the matter Churchill so strenuously urged of massive infusions
of British aid, mainly financial, to the White Russian allies. Here again,
Caucasus decisions would have to await Russian decisions, and Russian
decisions tended to await direction from the leaders now assembled
at Paris.[22]

The problem was raised, however, at a 13 February meeting of the
Interdepartmental Committee on Eastern Affairs (replacing the now disbanded Eastern Committee), when Curzon stated that among other
things General Forrestier-Walker appeared to have made some sort of financial commitment to the Kars government, thus, like Malleson, involving Britain "in pledges of which we were completely ignorant," and
that Thompson at Baku was printing worthless paper rubles to finance
the continued operation of the railway. Britain seemed to be committed

[20] GOC Constantinople to CIGS, 6 February, appended to IDCE, 6
March 1919, *L/P&S*/10/807.

[21] DMO note, note 19, chapter 3.

[22] War Cabinet 531 and 532A, 12 and 13 February 1919, *CAB* 23/9
and 5.

financially to regimes which it had not yet recognized diplomatically. Curzon did not ask how much his own policy was responsible for this situation, for it could well be questioned how else the largely penniless, embryo Caucasian governments could be encouraged to survive.[23]

Far more alarming was the news, at first quite incredible, and in fact not entirely accurate, that the Paris conference had reached the astonishing decision that Italy was to take over responsibility for the Caucasus. Aside from a passing Eastern Committee reference in December by Smuts (who may have originated the idea of Italian occupation), Curzon's first serious indication of this plan was in the Cabinet from Lloyd George, who told him the decision had been taken in Paris. Curzon was bewildered: what had Italy to do with the Caucasus? Certainly Italy had nothing like the necessary resources for such as task. Montagu, fresh from the conference, could provide explanation, but no justification. The prime minister, opposed to intervention in Russia, had somehow managed to get a committee appointed (Montagu heard of it first from the French Foreign Office) on "trooping of various areas," and this committee had decided that, to spread the burden, French troops would be sent to Syria, the British would stay on in Mesopotamia, and two Italian divisions would take over the Caucasus. Montagu had been as surprised as Curzon; Hirtzel, on reading this report in Paris, was convinced that the word "Italy" was a misprint.[24]

The minutes convey Curzon's dismay: "The whole position was astounding. The Italians had as little to do with the Caucasus as he with the Peak of Teneriffe, and it had never occurred to him that they would come in. No local considerations seem to have counted. It almost looked like a joke, and to his mind it was a chimera . . .". At least, he remarked after pulling himself together, the decision showed one thing: Britain was not to stay on permanently. But, said Admiral G.P. Hope (deputy first sea lord), what then of the Caspian? If the British left Baku, the Bolshevik destroyers and submarines in Astrakhan were enough to

[23] IDCE, 13 February 1919, *L/P&S/*10/807.

[24] *Ibid.* (in which Montagu quotes Hirtzel); Curzon private to Hardinge, 26 February 1919, *FO* 800/153. Ullman, *Anglo-Soviet Relations,* II, pp. 227-31, 271-82, attributes to Smuts the idea of putting Italy in the Caucasus, correctly referring to mention of the possibility by him in an Eastern Committee meeting in December; it is not necessarily proof, however, that the idea originated with Smuts. See also Kazemzadeh, *Struggle,* pp. 227-29, and Hovannisian, *Republic,* I, pp. 306-7.

seize control. Why hold it at all? asked Montagu; the committee was always told that the Batum-Baku line was needed to hold the Hamadan-Enzeli line and the Caspian for the Batum-Baku line, and so on in endless circles. The answer was to evacuate both lines, and then neither position would endanger the other.

This viewpoint, coming from the secretary of state for India, was most alarming to Curzon; he had serious reservations about the Caucasus, but none about the need for troops in Persia to assist the task of the British minister in Teheran (now Sir Percy Cox). And if the Batum-Baku line was important, and he thought it was, then the Caspian flank was also important — just the sort of argument Montagu was criticizing, as it happened. But at least Milne could be told to concentrate on the railway and pull back from outlying areas to avoid unnecessary entanglement in local problems.[25]

Temporary orders of this sort did little to aid the Caucasian situation, which could be neither understood nor governed from London, particularly when London was not adequately informed of the decisions made in Paris. Curzon was at his wit's end attempting to fathom the situation from such scanty information as did filter in; his frustration is exemplified by a minute on a telegram from Admiral Webb that the "North Caucasian" delegation was showing disappointment at having been detained on their way to Paris. Curzon could only ask who these North Caucasians were.[26]

The representatives in Paris were a bit clearer on both the Caucasian situation and British aims, for their sources at least included the myriad delegations, official and unofficial, only too ready to catch the ear of the unwary. The Paris delegation was able, therefore, to take the lead in policy-formation, and in an important paper of mid-February entitled "Statement of British Policy in the Middle East for Submission to the Peace Conference (if Required)" proceeded to outline British desiderata.[27] Armenia was, of course, a necessity, and the paper advocated the larger, fully independent Armenia which would extend to the

[25] IDCE, note 23, chapter 3; WO telegram to Milne, 15 February, *FO* 371/3661; Montagu private to Lloyd George, 14 February 1919, *Lloyd George Papers,* F/40/2/35.

[26] Webb telegram to FO, 23 February, Curzon note, 26 February 1919, with FO minutes, *FO* 371/3661.

[27] 18 February 1919, *FO* 608/83; also Mallet minute, 10 February 1919, *FO* 608/79.

Mediterranean coast, still in the hope that the United States would assume the Armenian mandate. Probably the Americans would wish to include Russian Armenia as well, but the draft left unification to the choice of the inhabitants. That none of the Caucasian states should be barred from some future reunification with Russia was an important principle; but so too was facilitation of independence if that was desired. Russian Armenia would be allowed to unite with Turkish Armenia, and independence of any other Caucasian country should be provisionally recognized by the conference, which would provide a mandatory power to supervise, postponing final acceptance of independence of or reunification with Russia to a later date. Local problems would require treatment also. Georgia would have to give autonomy to the Muslims of Batum and neighboring districts such as Sukhum on the Black Sea coast; Azerbaijan would probably have to conduct a population exchange with Armenia in several districts. Only Daghestan appeared to lack the necessary elements to form a viable state and for that reason perhaps could be policed by whatever mandatory watched over Azerbaijan, failing which it might be left to itself behind a sanitary cordon. The whole was a nice, logical exposition; it made no choices among possible mandatory powers and, while leaning toward Caucasian independence, still gave at least recognition to the fact that Caucasian settlement would always depend ultimately on Russian settlement.

The conference mechanism, so heavily dependent upon the handful of top leaders for directives, was not up to deciding upon Russia or the Caucasus as yet. When this memorandum was ready, the Council of Ten had only just heard the twin Armenian delegations (speaking respectively for Turkish and Russian Armenia). The Interdepartmental Committee in London, still responsible for sending out orders until superseded by Paris, struggled to deal with a situation which Curzon described accurately in a 6 March meeting as more confused than ever.[28] Nobody wanted to replace Britain, not even Italy, but on the scene Britain was more and more distrusted by all parties. The military had to act to keep local disputes from shutting the railway; however, the action was always condemned from all sides as local interference prejudicial to future decisions and equivalent to unwanted and

---

[28] Council of Ten, 26 February 1919, *FRUS,* Paris Conference, IV, pp. 147-56; IDCE, 6 March, *L/P&S*/10/807, following roughly the lines of the FO memorandum of 5 March appended to minutes.

unauthorized British commitments. If Britain withdrew, the states would fall to Denikin or the Bolsheviks, yet Lloyd George was most adamant against Britain staying on.

There appeared no escape, and such discussions had a way of becoming interdepartmental squabbles. The meeting of 6 March was no exception: the army, said Churchill, was only doing what the committee had told it to do, keep order and enforce the armistice and aid the states. The military commanders had only done what was necessary to obey these orders, and there was no question of exceeded instructions. Churchill himself wished to withdraw (for once, he agreed with Lloyd George) to reduce costs and release badly needed troops for elsewhere. All that was necessary, he suggested, was to establish a line beyond which Denikin could not move without forfeiting British aid. That, replied Curzon, grossly overestimated the British hold on Denikin . . . and so it went. There was also the added point, provided by Shuckburgh of the India Office, that India really regarded the Caucasus as remote and therefore had no strong views on the matter of evacuation: a minor point, perhaps, but it further undermined the defense-of-India argument so often used (although not at this meeting) to defend a Caucasian presence.

There was an answer to these arguments; Denikin, Britain's champion in the Russian civil war, could only hurt his own position if he diverted vitally necessary troops, paid for by British funds, to the Caucasus, and he was likely to do so if the temptation was not removed. But India cared little for the civil war; the restoration of Russian authority in the Caucasus would only restore, and not worsen, the prewar status quo. When the navy admitted that it was only in the Caspian to protect British troops in the Caucasus, support was clearly growing for Churchill's position: desirable as the Caucasus and Caspian might be in the abstract, they could not now be held in the face of competing demands on resources, nor be held in the future in the face of inevitable Russian recovery, whichever party won the civil war.

Once more, the answer was to wait for a conference decision, and meanwhile to promise aid (including naval aid on the Caspian) to Denikin on the one hand while setting a new frontier line to his south on the other. Plans for evacuation, starting with Trans-Caspia, would have to be forwarded to Paris. Curzon's last-ditch argument that Russian control of the Caucasus would jeopardize the delicate Persian situation was insufficient to keep British troops on the Batum-Baku railway for long. As presented to the Cabinet the same day, the plan became policy.[29]

The plain truth was that four months after the armistice few wanted to keep expensive forces in the Caucasus and the area beyond. Cecil, himself an early advocate of intervention—if only to protect Baku's oil—indicated that he, for one, had changed, and a careful inquiry should be conducted to decide if there was really any sense in keeping British forces there.

> I know that a certain section of the Government consider that the Caucasus is one of the gates to India, treating, I suppose, the Caspian, Transcaucasia and Afghanistan merely as a kind of private avenue leading up to the actual Indian frontier. Even if this somewhat fantastic theory be accepted, may we not enquire what conceivable hostile Power is likely to attempt to invade India at this stage of the world's history.[30]

Oddly enough, the answer, which Cecil probably would not have believed, was Afghanistan. He was arguing, however, only for withdrawal from the Caucasus; the decision to pull out of Trans-Caspia had already been made.

MALLESON'S MISSION

The end of the war left General Malleson astride the Trans-Caspian railway with a mixed force of 600 British and Indian soldiers and a further 2000 strung out along the East Persian Cordon, his line of communication. His forward positions were at Merv, where 300 of his troops combined with 2700 Turkoman infantry and cavalry to hold off the Bolshevik forces. Malleson's position was precarious, and the Ashkhabad government to which he had made commitments too far-reaching for London's peace of mind was teetering on the brink of collapse. For the moment, no alternative local ally was in sight, for Malleson had ensured that Bicherakov did not establish himself in Krasnovodsk.[31]

Malleson obviously regarded himself as a second, separate cordon

[29] War Cabinet 542, 6 March 1919, *CAB* 23/9.

[30] Cecil private to Lloyd George, 9 March 1919, *Cecil Papers* (British Museum), Add. Mss. 51076.

[31] Malleson telegrams to CGSI, 2, 5, and 6 November 1918, *War Diary, Persia*, 48; Teague Jones report, 26 January 1919, *WO* 106/61.

against any comers—now more likely to be Bolshevik than Turko-German. To the extent that a friendly government in the area was desirable, and that a watch must be kept on Bolshevik moves in the direction of Aghanistan, India agreed with him. Shortly before the armistice, India admitted that Krasnovodsk and the Meshed line of communication should be maintained to facilitate the position on the railway, but no major force could be passed up the line, let alone supplied through it. Even this much cooperation was based on the assumption that London wanted to hold the Caspian: India would participate for reasons of imperial strategy, not for specifically Indian interests.[32]

But India did not want Malleson to continue operations in Merv—let alone advance to Charjui, 150 miles further on to Bukhara and an important bridge crossing of the Oxus (Amu Darya), as the general proposed. Instead, he was ordered to be particularly careful of Muslim (meaning primarily Afghanistan) susceptibilities now that Turkey was out of the war and to tell the Ashkahabad authorities that they would have to hold their own against the Bolsheviks. Malleson thought that without the aid of Ashkhabad all central Asia would have become Bolshevik, and for that reason Britain owed Ashkhabad an obligation. India, disregarding Malleson's proposals, ordered him to remain west of Tedzhen, itself 50 miles west of Merv and 200 miles short of where Malleson thought he should be. As India telegraphed to London, the issues here once again involved Russian policy, and above all, the question whether Bicherakov, representing the Whites, could be kept out.[33]

Kidston in London was uncertain. There was still, he noted, the question of Enver Pasha and other Turkish leaders, even if the war was over; their escape to and cooperation with Bolshevik leaders in Central Asia would be dangerous. Then there was the suspicious pro-Turk Azerbaijani situation. It would be better, the India Office was told, to keep the Caspian under British control and to prevent as much as possible any conceivable Bolshevik-Young Turk connections in Transcaucasia and the Caucasus. It was an interesting conversion of policy; the cordon surrounding Turko-German activities had suddenly become one against "revolutionism." It is significant that Kidston him-

---

[32] Viceroy (Army Dept.) telegram to SSI, 23 October, appended to Eastern Committee, 21 November 1918, *L/P&S/*10/807.

[33] Malleson telegram to CGSI and viceroy telegrams (Foreign Dept. and Army Dept.) to SSI, 6 November 1918, *War Diary,* Persia, 48.

self not only wrote several memoranda which specifically made the connection, but that he was really the first to enunciate the policy on paper in the Foreign Office, without alteration by Curzon or Balfour.[34]

Malleson was as yet unaware of Foreign Office support. At the moment, his task as he saw it was to protest against India's restrictions and even more wounding implications that he had gone too far on his own initiative. Each step he had taken had been approved, he claimed, and all had been anti-Bolshevik steps. If the new orders were to be taken literally, moreover, they meant no aid at all would be given to the Ashkhabad authorities: was this really the policy? Not at all, replied India; limited aid to local groups had been approved, as had several of Malleson's maneuvers, but always for anti-Turkish and anti-German reasons. No authorization had ever been given for anti-Bolshevik operations. Afterthoughts from Indian high command chose to put Malleson's argument the other way around: that without British support, there would have been no Ashkhabad government. Pending orders from London, Malleson was allowed to stay on in Merv, but not to advance beyond it without specific orders.[35]

In London, the India Office could only pass the correspondence to the Foreign Office and ask for a Cabinet decision on definite policy. Meanwhile, "in view of the great importance of keeping the Caspian under British control" (implicitly, importance to London), Krasnovodsk should be held, which required that Malleson "should remain in occupation of such points on the Transcaspian railway as will enable [him] to cut off the Bolshevik forces from access to that port." India would still have to set detailed limits to his movements. For guidance Delhi received only the somewhat contradictory statement that policy was not to embark upon an anti-Bolshevik campaign but that considerations "both of honour and of interest" demanded that Bolsheviks should be kept out of regions east of the Black Sea, particularly by helping local regimes to help themselves, without, however, making large commitments. The Trans-Caspian policy thus paralleled the Caucasian policy:

[34] Viceroy (Foreign Dept.) telegram to SSI, 6 November, Kidston minute, 18 November, and FO to IO, 23 November 1918, *FO* 371/3304.

[35] Malleson telegram to CGSI, 7 November, CGSI telegrams to Malleson, 8 and 12 November 1918, *War Diary,* Persia, 48. The *War Diary* version appears to differ from Malleson, "British Military Mission," which contends that he obtained a reversal of his orders.

keep the Bolsheviks out and stay on, temporarily, in Merv as in Baku.[36]

Malleson was unwilling to let well enough alone, however, and continued to insist that Merv was indefensible; although fighting at the moment was limited to desultory duels between armored trains on the outskirts of Merv, he should be allowed to move to the Oxus. More important, it now proved that he had assured the Ashkhabad authorities that Britain would not evacuate Merv without a fight, a pledge which India regarded as decidedly embarrassing. Permanent occupation of Merv would mean continued problems with Afghanistan; and even continuing operations on the existing scale would require considerable extension of the East Persian railway (the basic feeder line from the Indian system to the base of the East Persian Cordon near the Persian-Indian frontier). Already, the dispatch of six cavalry squadrons from Quetta to Meshed had been stopped for supply and financial reasons.[37]

At last, on 21 November, the Eastern Committee took up the matter. Trans-Caspia was inseparable from Russia, they agreed, but some special problems were involved. The Treasury, for example, seriously questioned the Ashkhabad subsidy, while the India Office representatives could make no strong brief for Malleson, their nominal subordinate. But the main duel resolved into a discussion between Curzon, who desired to preserve a connection which would link anti-Bolshevik forces in Trans-Caspia with those of Admiral Kolchak in Omsk, and Cecil, who maintained that it was one thing to support Denikin, quite another to prop up the rotten structure at Ashkhabad. The ramifications were wide. General H.V. Cox, military secretary at the India Office, speaking for India (although not really with Delhi's arguments), warned that the continued presence of British forces on the line would cause unfavorable reactions in Persia and Afghanistan. Exactly the point he had in mind, said Curzon: the amir of Afghanistan would hold Britain responsible if anything went wrong, and "hordes of triumphant Bolsheviks" must be kept out of Persia. It was decided that Ashkhabad would be paid a lump sum in final fulfillment of Britain's obligations. The policy in general was no clearer, however, for the War Office was still preparing to send General Milne to assist Malleson, whose 734

[36] IO to FO (quoted), 14 November, *FO* 371/3304; SSI telegram to viceroy (Army Dept.), 15 November, appended to Eastern Committee minutes, 21 November 1918, *L/P&S/*10/807.

[37] Malleson telegram to CGSI, CGSI telegram to Malleson, and viceroy (Army Dept.) telegram to SSI, 20 November 1918, *War Diary,* Persia, 48.

men now at Merv could not be expected to hold without reinforcements, as soon as the Batum-Baku-Krasnovodsk supply route was safely open.[38]

Even India had to agree with Malleson that withdrawal from Merv would bring the Bolsheviks down the railway and possibly give them Ashkhabad, but what was the alternative? Without control of the resources at Tashkent—an impossibility at the moment—the Ashkhabad authorities could not conceivably remain financially solvent unless a British subsidy lasted indefinitely. Indian interests would be satisfied if access were maintained to Birjand 250 miles down the Persian corridor from Meshed, for Birjand commanded all the approaches to Khurasan in eastern Persia and to western Afghanistan. Malleson would be secure if he fell back on Meshed, and the continued hold on Enzeli and Krasnovodsk would ensure that no damage would be done to Indian interests. Implicitly, India had no need even for Meshed and the southern Caspian. The India Office agreed, but Malleson would have to stay in Trans-Caspia until larger imperial policy, as yet undecided, had no need for British troops on the railway; and as long as he stayed, he would have to support Ashkhabad.[39]

To India, the India Office's temporizing was the wrong solution. Malleson was now suggesting that if the Ashkhabad government fell he should be given authority to appoint his own provisional government, and this India gave as one more reason for urging his retreat to Meshed. But India's protest was too late; Ashkhabad's government toppled, and a new committee of Public Safety, containing no "troublemakers," was installed with Malleson's approval and with the advice of the local military mission headed by Teague Jones. Malleson, convinced that his actions had saved the day, was now prepared to advance to crush a weak Bolshevik regime in Tashkent. The subsequent possibilities were large, including a pacified area, a viable and loyal govern-

[38] Eastern Committee, 21 November 1918, *L/P&S*/10/807; WO telegram to GOC Salonika [Milne], 28 November 1918, *FO* 371/4106. The financial problems of Malleson in Trans-Caspia, it should be added, were very much complicated by problems of valid and acceptable currencies: he was told to pay Ashkhabad in Persian krans, for example, although this currency was not generally acceptable along the railway.

[39] Malleson telegram to CGSI, 2 December, viceroy (Army Dept.) telegrams to SSI, 7 and 10 December, SSI telegrams to viceroy, 12 and 24 December, *War Diary,* Persia, 49 (also *FO* 371/4106); H.V. Cox note, 20 December 1918 (circulated to Cabinet by Montagu), *Military Secretary Files* (IO Library), uncatalogued.

ment, and Central Asian influence, but the decision went against Malleson's vast scheme.[40]

In the interdepartmental meeting of 7 January 1919 only the War Office stood out against Montagu's strenuous arguments for withdrawal to Meshed. General Thwaites maintained that Malleson was needed to stop Bolshevik penetration into Persia, to protect Krasnovodsk, and to occupy the attention of the estimated 14,000 Bolsheviks opposed to him. But how long, asked Curzon, was this to continue? That depended, said Thwaites, on how long it would be necessary to hold Baku and the Caspian; and the circular arguments continued. For once, however, the positions were clear: Montagu had silenced his own Military Department, and the India Office stood firm with Curzon for withdrawal. A final decision was postponed pending a report from General Milne who had now assumed authority for the whole Caspian-Caucasus area including Krasnovodsk and, from 8 January, for Malleson (but not for the line of communications south of Ashkhabad into Persia). By the end of January, Milne had met Malleson at Krasnovodsk and proceeded up the line; a week later, both London and Delhi had the essence of his report.[41]

The anti-Bolshevik allies working with Malleson, General Milne reported, were a rag-tag band of Russians and Turkomans kept together by fear of Bolshevik retaliation if the "Reds" ever took the area. Only the presence of British troops prevented Bolshevik coups in Merv and Ashkhabad; only British promissory notes kept the railway operating. Multiple British, Russian, and Turkoman commands worked badly. In short, the situation, financial, political, and military, was unpromising and likely to worsen. Little real strength was available to stop a determined attack, and the flanks could be turned easily. There were only two simple choices: more troops, more guns, more money—or retreat.

[40] Malleson telegrams to CGSI, 30 and 31 December 1918, 1, 3, and 5 January 1919, viceroy (Army Dept.) telegrams to SSI, 24 and 31 December 1918, with minutes, *War Diary,* Persia, 49-50; Teague Jones report, note 31, chapter 3; Ellis, *British Intervention,* pp. 129-30.

[41] IDCE, 7 January and 8 February 1919, *L/P&S/*10/807 (and Eastern Committee of 18 December 1918, *Curzon Papers,* F/11/8, for prior discussion); GOC Constantinople telegram to WO, 6 January, *WO* 106/60; GOC Constantinople telegram to WO and SSI telegram to viceroy (Army Dept.), 8 January, viceroy telegram to SSI, 10 January, GOC Constantinople telegrams to Malleson, 14 January, and to Thompson, Baku, 15 January 1919, *War Diary,* Persia, 50.

Malleson thought safe disengagement required a preliminary forward sweep to the Oxus, but Milne disagreed even with that; his considered recommendation was withdrawal, even from Krasnovodsk. People would suffer, notably the Turkomans; but the only other possible reason for staying was British prestige. Even the 30,000 to 40,000 Austro-German prisoners of war Malleson had reported in the area were no more than some 8000, and no military threat (Milne did not record his opinion of Malleson's intelligence information). In sum, the balance was all in favor of pulling out. Should Britain stay, however, and he, Milne, command, he wished to choose his own subordinates—in other words, Malleson must be sacked.[42]

Milne's recommendations were not universally popular. Kidston, concerned with the general anti-Bolshevik crusade, noted, with a touch of sarcasm, "Until it is realized that the old war is dead & done with & the new war of order against chaos & of open popular Govt. against Govt. by secret committee has begun, even in Germany, withdrawal is the obvious course." In Paris, the military section of the British delegation turned to Milne's alternative choice; wishful thinking about Bolshevik weakness made them prefer to send the four Indian battalions, cavalry regiment, and artillery battery Milne had specified, even though he had said such forces were only the first immediate necessity if Britain were to remain.[43]

The decision was left to the interdepartmental committee. Curzon, reviewing Milne's dispatch in a meeting on 8 February, was concerned that Milne had made no formal recommendation, although his preference was quite obvious, and, more alarming, that withdrawal was to include Krasnovodsk, which Curzon had not thought would be necessary. The deciding vote was cast by Major-General Radcliffe for the War Office. Britain should withdraw, even if this meant the loss of some prestige. Disowning the officers in Paris as unrepresentative of the views of the Chief of the Imperial General Staff, Radcliffe, obviously influenced by Milne's report, cited two main reasons for this reversal of opinion. First, the prospect of a friendly and stable government was nearly nonexistent, particularly since the recent fall of Orenburg to

[42] GOC Constantinople telegram to WO, 3 February 1919, with FO minutes, *FO* 371/4106; Ellis, *British Intervention,* pp. 144-45.

[43] Kidston minute (quoted) on GOC Constantinople telegram to WO, 3 February 1919, *FO* 371/4106; Military Section, British Delegation, 5 February 1919, 591/1/8, *FO* 608/179.

the Bolsheviks meant that direct Moscow-Tashkent communications were now open. Second, if Britain did come to a real test of strength with the Bolsheviks, operations in Malleson's area would be in front of Britain's wire, so to speak. Even in the War Office, in other words, there was some limit to India's defense perimeter. Finally, Radcliffe made one of the few direct connections between the Caucasus and Central Asian situations when he pointed out that if the decision was taken on merit to withdraw from the Caucasus, it would be awkward, to say the least, if troops had to stay on there simply to safeguard Malleson's eventual withdrawal from the other side of the Caspian. The committee decided to propose Malleson's withdrawal to the government of India—even though India was no longer in direct charge of Malleson—but added that, should Malleson fall back on the Persian line, he would once again come under Indian control.[44]

India, needless to say, had no objection to withdrawal; the orders for evacuation, including Krasnovodsk, now went out. Malleson could only ask for enough time to ensure the success of this delicate operation, but he promised to be in Persia by the end of March. India had achieved one goal at least on the Persian-Central Asian frontier and it now asked to be relieved both of longstanding financial responsibility for Persian operations and of intelligence-gathering in Central Asia. By 1 April, Malleson was in Meshed, with orders only to keep northeastern Persia free of Bolsheviks; even two officers left in Ashkhabad for intelligence purposes were promptly ordered out by Milne in Constantinople. A few rifles went to the amir of Bukhara; considerably more supplies were left in Turkoman hands (2300 rifles, for example); still more were turned over to the Ashkhabad Russians (5500 rifles, 3.5 million rounds of ammunition) in the hopes that they would fight on—but the Central Asian expedition was over. India estimated the cost of the entire operation at £70,000, not including the normal cost of maintaining the troops involved; the bulk of this sum had gone to subsidize the Ashkhabad government.[45]

It is difficult to see after the passage of half a century what the foray

[44] IDCE, 8 February, *L/P&S*/10/807; SSI telegram to viceroy, 9 February 1919, *FO* 371/4106. Maj.-Gen. Percy de B. Radcliffe was DMO.

[45] Viceroy (Army Dept.) telegrams to SSI, 11 February and 15 and 28 March, WO telegram to GOC Constantinople, 13 February, Malleson telegram to GOC Constantinople, 17 February and 26 April, SSI telegram to

into Russian Central Asia had accomplished. Certainly Anglo-Russian relations were adversely affected by Malleson's combat with the Bolsheviks, even though the fighting was accidental in the sense that Malleson had not been sent to the Trans-Caspian railway for that purpose. Whether the threat to Persia and Afghanistan, so glibly offered as a replacement for Turko-German aspirations, was a legitimate fear is a moot question. Turkoman resistance and Soviet logistical problems at that time might well have kept the situation open at least during Malleson's stay beyond the Persian frontier. One point was clear, however: it now behooved Britain to consolidate its Persian position without delay. Persia was inadequate recompense for those who shared ". . . the dreams of going on to shoot the cloudy tiger of Turkestan in the reed-beds of the Oxus, and to eat the famed melons of Charjui . . .," as one participant put it, but it was an alternative.[46]

COX AND PERSIA

The task of securing British interests in Persia fell to Sir Percy Cox, chargé d'affaires and special commissioner, whose replacement of Sir Charles Marling in Teheran preceded the Turkish armistice by weeks only. Cox had been sent to achieve an understanding with the recently installed government of Vossuq ed-Dowleh; but already he had succumbed to serious doubts about his assignment. Any treaty, he reported, would have to recognize Persian independence, for that was Persia's main objective. Yet such a concession would bring little return, for the addition of Persia to the victorious Allied coalition was meaningless, while any consequent increase in the power of the Cossack Brigade or other military force would not be to Britain's advantage.[47]

Opinion at home was not so easily changed. Cecil in the Foreign

---

viceroy (Army Dept.), 14 February, *War Diary,* Persia, 51-53; IO to Treasury, 20 February 1919, *FO* 371/3885, on costs (India paid half the Meshed expenses). Ellis, *British Intervention,* p. 154, remarks that a camel-train of rifles, with two Indian NCO's, went to Bukhara in February. The Krasnovodsk perimeter and defenses are described in Ranald MacDonell and Marcus Macaulay, *A History of the 4th Prince of Wales' Own Gurkha Rifles, 1857-1937* (Edinburgh, 1940), I, pp. 375-81 (the 2/4 Gurkhas were the main garrison force here).

[46] Blacker, *On Secret Patrol,* p. 156.

[47] Cox telegram to FO, 1 October 1918, *FO* 371/3262.

Office and Shuckburgh in the India Office both supported an alliance; it would of course include a British pledge to protect Persian integrity and independence, but Britain was already doing the job without making a formal pledge, and larger subsidies, although costly, would regularize Britain's position and provide greater security against anti-British intrigues in Teheran. On the other hand, India argued that Britain had an obligation to withdraw once the war was over, for this would strengthen Vossuq ed-Dowleh's hand and would influence American attitudes; the United States had already evidenced interest in Persia. On 1 November 1918 India suggested that confidence and friendliness would be more successful than interference; a liberal policy, including transfer of the South Persian Rifles, was the answer. But the experts in London saw this as too local a view. There was still the danger of Enver Pasha's pan-Islamic dreams, and at the very least the occupation of Baku and control of the confused Caucasian situation would be necessary before any withdrawal from Persia could be contemplated.[48]

Much depended upon Cox's advice. In mid-November, his conclusions became quite clear. While he did not favor the immediate conclusion of a treaty along the lines previously discussed, he did not suggest withdrawal either: to the contrary, the answer was to say frankly (particularly to the Americans) that Britain wanted a year or two of mandatory responsibility to reform Persia from the ground upwards. It would be tragic, in fact, if extremist agitation, which would arise at the slightest opportunity, resulted in premature evacuation and the sacrifice of all of Britain's effort on the Kermanshah-Enzeli road. Cox was an extremely able man, with a successful career in the Persian Gulf and Iraq behind him, but his training and associations, particularly in Persia, were part of a now anachronistic tradition. This was a world of open diplomacy, self-determination, and the power of public opinion— but, above all, it was a world where Britain could no longer maintain

---

[48] F.O. minutes, *ibid.;* IO minutes on same telegram, *L/P&S/*10/734; Col. Kisch, WO, note, 1 November, with Kidston and Toynbee minutes, *FO* 371/3262; viceroy telegram to SSI, 1 November 1918, *FO* 371/3263. The United States had been involved in prewar reform attempts (and therefore international diplomacy) in Persia: see W. Morgan Shuster, *The Strangling of Persia . . .* (N.Y., 1912), and for a rather later British account which also treats problems of financial reform, J.M. Balfour, *Recent Happenings in Persia* (Edinburgh, 1922).

her former imperial splendor in the face of these pressures and the terrible "wastage" in lives and treasure of World War I. In the period just after the war Cox was hardly alone in being able to write, "It is glorious to feel in such a strong position everywhere, with a strong Govt. and the nation solid behind it. How one must rejoice to have lived in this generation!" But Cox was born in 1864, and his generation was not that of post-1918; how wrong was his estimate of the Persian situation would only become clear in the months to come.[49]

In one respect, however, Cox's policy resulted from the new situation following the war, which some strategists found so attractive. While Russia was in flux, it was desirable that Britain hold Baku and the Caspian; if this was not possible, then at least Britain could keep a mandate for the Baghdad-Enzeli line of communications, and to Cox, as to many, mandate was simply a new name for protectorate. Cox's proposal to that effect brought strong reactions, but mainly from India, despite the regard in which Cox was held by the Foreign Department in Delhi and by the viceroy himself. A mandate would contradict repeated assurances on Persian neutrality, drain Indian military and financial resources, and worst of all do little for Persia save further weaken her political situation and thus lead to ultimate withdrawal. Even in the India Office, opinion was uncertain; a year, wrote Shuckburgh, was a short time for Persian regeneration. Costs would be high, troops would be necessary, and Britain would face the certain protests of both Persian democrats and Persian nationalists (not necessarily the same thing), and probably general Muslim protests into the bargain—doubtless the matter would have to be thrashed out in the Eastern Committee.[50]

But the Eastern Committee had other preoccupations, and when it did take up Persia it was to wrestle with the puzzle of Persian participation at the peace conference. Persia was neither a declared belligerent nor a proclaimed ally and would not normally be given a seat. On the other hand, there had been fighting on Persian soil, and if the conference were to discuss a mandate for Persia it followed that Persia must be part of the conference. It was even more complex than that, however.

[49] Cox telegrams to FO, 14 November 1918 (2 of date, nos. 970-1), *FO* 371/3263, and private to Curzon (quoted), 13 January 1919, *Curzon Papers,* F/2/2; on Cox see references in note 100, chapter 1.

[50] Viceroy telegram to SSI, 26 November, Shuckburgh minute on Cox telegram no. 970, 14 November 1918, *L/P&S/*10/735.

If Britain proposed that the conference designate a mandatory for Persia, the conference just might appoint some other power. Cox might have replied that even that was preferable to anarchy, although obviously Britain was the best equipped and most likely prospect. The main thing was to guarantee Persia against absorption by any power, including Britain, and get on with the job. If Persia objected, it would be told, very firmly, that ". . . she cannot be allowed to wallow in chaos and corruption as she has in the past 20 years, and must submit to treatment."[51]

Cox's main ally was Curzon. Not only did his view of Persia's importance correspond to Cox's—and Curzon, author of *Persia and the Persian Question,* was a recognized expert on the subject—but also Cox was one of the few subordinates in whom Curzon had faith, dating from his own term as viceroy when Cox was responsible for administering Persian Gulf policy. Britain's interests in the Persian Gulf, her past sacrifices, and now the proposed withdrawal of Malleson from Central Asia all argued for just the sort of detailed attention that Cox asked. All of this Curzon argued in the Eastern Committee meeting of 19 December, but he ran squarely into Montagu's objections. Montagu put it fairly simply: the Indian policy of leaving Persia alone was the one policy which had not been tried, and all others had failed badly. Cecil, too, now leaned in Montagu's direction. Perhaps the answer, he advised, was to treat Persia the way the Americans treated Mexico—tolerate disorder but allow no outside intervention. Even Marling, just returned from Persia, and a believer that Persia would simply rot if nothing was done, had to agree that there was little likelihood of a Persian Bolshevik revolution (unless, of course, the Russian Bolshevik forces invaded Persia).[52]

Curzon was given a wedge, however, by Grant, who spoke with some authority for the views of India from which he had recently returned (to aid in preparation of the peace). Grant would intervene in Persia only where Persians themselves requested it, but still he would inter-

---

[51] Eastern Committee, 21 November, *L/P&S/*10/807; Cox telegram to FO, 27 November, with Toynbee minute, 6 December, *FO* 371/3263; Cox private to Oliphant (quoted), 1 December 1918, *FO* 371/3858.

[52] Eastern Committee, 19 December 1918, *CAB* 27/24 (another copy in *Curzon Papers*); *Persia and the Persian Question,* 2 vol. (London, 1892, reprinted N.Y., 1966); on Curzon's relationship to Persia, see Nicolson, *Curzon,* Ch. V.

vene. That, as Cecil pointed out, was an untenable middle ground between going and staying. To Grant, as to India, withdrawal *in toto* would waste all efforts so far expended, to say nothing of destroying British commercial interests in Persia; a mandate, however, meant too great a commitment of men and resources. No other power could, would, or should take the job. The only solution, therefore, was limited aid to preserve a calm Persia, and the essential preliminary of this was for Britain to get Persia's confidence. Grant reflected in a postmeeting memorandum more articulate than his statement to the committee that there was "a curious kind of patriotism or nationalism which is neither to be bought nor overawed," related, perhaps, to the sort of enthusiasm which sent Bengali political extremists bravely to the gallows. Grant's views give striking indication of how much India was learning from its own problems—and how far behind India lay the fossilized views of Curzon and Cox, for they had learned their Persian policy in another era.[53]

Curzon was uncertain on the Caucasus, perhaps, but he was iron-hard on Persia. On 30 December he characterized Montagu's suggestion of withdrawal as "immoral, feeble, and disastrous" (Montagu, it should be remarked, was absent); it would end a century's work and create a dangerous vacuum. Grant's limited aid was only the present policy, executed "in a more ingratiating way;" it was plausible on paper, perhaps, but in reality it was an unworkable compromise between abandonment and resolution. In Curzon's view the best way was to discuss the situation frankly with Persian delegates to the conference (Persia obviously intended sending them whatever the conference's decision) and to outline the possibilities of aid and advice coupled with reassurances on integrity, the abrogation of the Anglo-Russian Accord of 1907, and the withdrawal of troops as soon as circumstances allowed. Cecil, once again changing his tune and now worried about a possible anti-British coup by the Russian Cossack force under its leader Colonel Starosselski, sided with Curzon and then left the meeting. Cecil's support enabled Curzon to carry the day against lesser mortals such as Grant. "I would now show them that within the velvet glove is the iron hand," said the chairman. "We have never shown it to them all this time. We

---

[53] Grant, IO Memorandum C. 188, 20 December 1918, *FO* 371/3858.

have never had the pluck to say to them, 'You are in our hands absolutely to do as we please.' "[54]

Unfortunately, Britain did not really have the power to do as it
pleased. Montagu had already hinted to the Foreign Office that the
Indian half of funds for Persian expenses would no longer be forthcoming if Indian views were disregarded. The Treasury was similarly
negative about costs, running currently at £2.5 million monthly, which
went mostly for the cordons and the South Persian Rifles. Before the
year was out, Cox had been told to pare spending to the bone. This por-
tent was inauspicious, but no decision on larger policy had yet been
reached. Curzon concluded that the committee agreed with his view.
Montagu later protested that neither he nor Balfour nor the Chief of
the Imperial General Staff had been in attendance to speak for their
respective departments, but nevertheless, without a further meeting,
Cox received an outline of the proposed discussions with Persia written
exactly as Curzon had suggested to the committee.[55]

Cox had not been inactive. In mid-January 1919 he reported that
Vossuq ed-Dowleh and two of his associates in the Persian Cabinet
(termed the Triumvirate) had reached the conclusion that Persia's
only chance was to place herself unreservedly in British hands. At
the moment, however, they were hesitant to declare this openly without some substantial concessions. These would have to include more
than the transfer of the Rifles; as Oliphant, Foreign Office expert on
Persia, put it, probably something tangible like a loan was meant—
India had always been "too utopian."[56]

Curzon, who controlled the Foreign Office during the Paris conference, accepted the suggestion with alacrity, but India, as might be
expected, was suspicious of Cox's proposal. One faction of any given
Persian cabinet was hardly an accurate barometer of Persian opinion.

[54] Eastern Committee, 30 December 1918, *L/P&S/*10/735; Nicolson,
Curzon, pp. 132-34.

[55] FO telegram to Cox, 3 December, IO minutes and IO to FO, 24 December, *L/P&S/*10/735; Keynes note, received in FO 31 December, *FO*
371/3263, discussed in Eastern Committee, note 54, chapter 3; FO telegrams to Cox, 31 December 1918, *FO* 371/3263, and 11 January 1919,
FO 371/3858; Montagu private to Curzon, 6 January 1919, *Curzon Papers,*
F/13/1, partly quoted in Nicolson, *Curzon,* p. 133.

[56] Cox telegram to FO, 13 January, with Oliphant minute, 20 January
1919, *FO* 371/3858.

Vossuq ed-Dowleh in particular had proved a risky ally in the affair of the South Persian Rifles. Finally, India could not be burdened with the sort of aid which any elaborate treaty would undoubtedly require, although Persian financial reform, part of the proposed program, had long been an Indian goal. Cox's plan called for an elaborate network of British advisors to be stationed in Teheran ministries and provincial capitals; this savored to India of the procedure which had led to a protectorate over Egypt, and certainly it would be so viewed by world opinion. India's objectives were not that far from Cox's in principle, but in practice advice would have to be cut to the barest minimum both to be successful in Persian and international contexts and to fit within the scale of financial feasibility as viewed from India.[57]

The very process of negotiation required a continued British presence, or so Cox advised. He wished to maintain the South Persia Rifles, for example, despite general agreement in England and India that the force would cause anarchy in the southern provinces and distract a Persian government which ought to concentrate on reforms. The SPR, which numbered at its height seven battalions of infantry and a squadron of cavalry (8000 men), was finally disbanded by April of 1920. Cox's policy rested, essentially, on military strength. Reduction of the SPR in the south, coupled with London's refusal to sanction two companies for Tabriz (requested by Vossuq ed-Dowleh at Cox's inspiration and much opposed by Milne who was trying to reduce north Persian commitments), undermined Cox's position well before the actual conclusion of a treaty. The Foreign Office argued on Cox's behalf, but all that could be won was a postponement of further reductions.[58]

Cox was finding the going tougher than expected, for the Persian Cabinet put forth rather high intial demands, including parts of Russian Azerbaijan and revision of certain outstanding treaties with other parties, such as the Treaty of Turkmanchai with Russia (1828) which had cost Persia some territory and rights on the Caspian. Cox's friends

[57] FO telegram to Cox, 23 January, *ibid.;* viceroy telegram to SSI, 28 January, *L/P&S*/10/735; SSI telegram to viceroy, 20 February 1919, *L/P&S*/10/461.

[58] Cox's plan is in telegrams to FO, 19 January and 10 February, and GS, WO, memorandum, 5 January, *L/P&S*/10/727 (the fortunes of the SPR may be followed in this file); postponement: FO telegram to Cox, 6 February, FO to WO, 20 February, Cox telegram to FO, 22 February 1919, *FO* 371/3858.

perhaps saw territorial gains as compensation for the unpopularity they expected from a British treaty. Details could not be decided, however, until the problem of the Persian delegation to the conference was settled: the delegation, now in Paris, was proving uncooperative. Its leader, Moshaver ul-Mulk, the Persian foreign minister and no friend of Vossuq ed-Dowleh (who was happy to have him out of Teheran), appeared to have a different vision of Persian policy and was attracting attention from France. Lansing, the American secretary of state, told Balfour that the conference should hear the Persians and that he might well raise the issue of Persia if Britain did not. "Why do we not take the bull by the horns and tell the Americans that Persia is for us covered by what is our equivalent in Asia of the Monroe doctrine: this is *our* preserve!" urged Crowe, and Mallet, who was working on the American delegation, added what was surely in everybody's mind: "The Standard Oil are probably at the back of this . . ." Fortunately, the Persian position was seriously weakened by their exhorbitant claims, which, although not officially presented to the conference, were being discussed in the press: Kurdistan, Azerbaijan, Central Asia, Khiva, Merv—the area outlined was too much for even the most sympathetic friend of Persia.[59]

Meanwhile, by 10 April Cox had reached agreement with his friends on a draft treaty which differed from the final version only in some clauses on future frontier revision. The Triumvirate was prepared to sign—in return for an advance consideration of 500,000 tomans (roughly, £166,000). This advance presented some problems, as Cox

[59] Cox telegram to FO, 25 February, Curzon telegram to Cox, 5 March, Persian memorandum for conference, n.d. [February], *FO* 371/3859; Cox telegram to FO, 18 March, Forbes Adam minute, 20 March, Curzon telegrams for Balfour, 7 and 17 April, latter with Crowe (18 April) and Mallet (n.d.) minutes (quoted), *FO* 608/101; Curzon telegram to Cox, 21 March, Balfour telegram to Curzon, 2 April (on Lansing conversation), *FO* 371/3859; Curzon private to Balfour, 23 May 1919, *Balfour Papers,* Add. Mss. 49734.

Persian claims are discussed in Kazemzadeh, *Struggle,* pp. 266-67; Hovannisian, *Republic,* I, pp. 283-84 (from Armenian standpoint). Nicolson, *Curzon,* p. 135, is probably correct in thinking that the policy of allowing Persia to present her claims without interference would have been much more to British advantage. As it was, the claims were presented, but Britain appeared to want to keep Persia quietly in her own British preserve. See also *The Times,* 23 April 1919, remarking on loss of sympathy.

knew well. If London would not give the sum as an installment of subsidy, an advance from the Anglo-Persian Oil Company, or even as a present, he was willing to pay it as part of the £2 million loan for recovery and reform which would be part of the bargain.[60]

The suggestion was not in Cox's style; he had disdained bribery in much more tragic circumstances during the war, when cash seemed the only possible way to relieve the Turkish siege of Kut al-Amara. It might be argued that he was simply conforming to Persian realities, but in fact the situation had gotten the better of him. Cox, whose forte was mastering situations, had failed in Persia. Oliphant in London was most dubious about this method of buying a signature; the Triumvirate might be promised asylum if there was trouble in the future, but half a million tomans was something else. Shuckburgh was also critical but inclined to think the bribe would be money well spent. Hirtzel took India's view: Triumvirate approval was Triumvirate approval and nothing more. Montagu, however, sided with Shuckburgh: there were risks, but there were more risks in Persian chaos. Thanks to Cox's "skillful diplomacy," there was a good chance now to end anarchy, although of course India could pay no share of the cost. Even that was more encouragement than the Foreign Office had expected.[61]

Formal interdepartmental discussion took place on 7 May. Curzon, as usual, began by reviewing the history of the negotiations, including the "typical Oriental proceedings" in Paris. Cox's draft treaty was admirable, and while it "would result in Persia being to a certain extent in the hands of His Majesty's Government," it would also mean "she would be able to avoid the ignominy of being placed under a mandate"— an alternative which seems, in retrospect, never to have been a realistic possibility. India had persistently opposed the treaty, but the India Office did not support the Indian government. In Curzon's view, it was the duty of the British government ". . . to build up the bastions of India, which had always been and must always be the pivot and focus of British interests in the East," and, implicitly, a duty to do so whether In-

---

[60] Cox telegrams to FO, 9, 10, 11, 19, and 25 April 1919, *FO* 371/3860.
[61] Oliphant minute, 29 April, on Cox telegram of 25 April, viceroy telegram to SSI, 24 April, Cox telegram to FO, 30 April, IO to FO, 3 May, with minutes, *FO* 371/3860; Shuckburgh note, 1 May, Hirtzel minute, 2 May, 2307/19, and IO to Treasury, 3 May 1919, *L/P&S/*10/736. Kut bribery attempt: Busch, *Britain, India, and the Arabs,* pp. 102-3.

dia wished it or not. Montagu, for once, supported Curzon. Deluding himself that, as he later wrote Chelmsford, "the most stable government that Persia has had in my time is anxious to come to an arrangement with us that will ensure their independence and assist them to become stable," he maintained that while he had no wish to force Britain upon Persia, in this case Persia was asking for British aid. If they were to cancel that request, he would then object to furnishing aid. Curzon had no argument with this condition: ". . . he could quite conceive of circumstances in which a state of public feeling might arise in Persia which would result in our asking ourselves whether it was advisable for us to reconsider our policy, and to modify our relations with the Persian Government," a remark which committee members would have done well to keep in mind. The bribe was of course a stumbling point, but, as Curzon put it, "it was well known that a little backsheesh was essential to the completion of negotiations with Orientals." Cox, the committee agreed, would be informed of this discussion, including the objections to the bribe.[62]

And so Cox was told. The agreement was of obvious benefit to Persia; surely there was no need to compensate the ministers responsible, beyond the promise of possible asylum. "If Ministers are so frightened of proposed agreement as to fear expulsion, agreement itself would not rest on very secure foundation . . .," Cox was told officially. Privately, Curzon added that Parliament could never be brought to approve such a payment; the most that could be provided for smoothing the way was £ 20,000 from secret service funds. Curzon thought perhaps the sum might be reduced, and perhaps it might be labeled "education of public opinion" or expenses connected with "initiation of reforms." Whatever it was to be called, Cox was most eager to pay it, not merely because he thought the treaty a substantial achievement but because, as already noted, the British retreat in Central Asia made the Persian situation all the more critical. Malleson was in Meshed in April, and he might yet have to retreat before a Bolshevik attack (if so, Cox hoped he would fall back on Teheran, not the Indian frontier). In May, Merv fell to the Bolsheviks, the Ashkhabad government collapsed, and refugees flooded into Persia. A dangerous situation in the Caucasus also

[62] IDCE, 7 May, *L/P&S*/10/807; Montagu private to Chelmsford, 11 June (quoted), and Chelmsford private to Montagu, 14 May, *Montagu Papers,* D. 523/3 and 8; SSI telegram to viceroy, 9 May 1919, *FO* 371/3860.

worried Cox, and Persian opinion was unlikely to greet with enthusiasm the news that Italy was to be guardian of the Caucasus bastion.[63]

By mid-July, Cox was in final negotiations. The Triumvirate rejected a paltry £20,000 as worse than useless if distributed to win friends for this treaty, although how far such distribution would go was not discussed. The alternatives, as seen by Vossuq ed-Dowleh, were to fight the agreement through on its merits or to pay liberally and thus avoid the struggle altogether. The former course would encounter not only anti-British sentiment but anti-reform interests. Cox agreed and asked for the full sum as soon as the treaty was signed.[64]

At home, Montagu admitted that 10 percent of the recovery loan was a high price but perhaps Cox was right and this was the only way. Montagu had already overridden India and agreed that India would contribute half the £2 million, so approval of the bribe was not so radical a step from the India Office viewpoint. It was nearly too late in any case; Cox was even now working out the final text of supplemental letters on frontiers and the shah's subsidy (conditional on Vossuq ed-Dowleh's remaining in power). Curzon, under such pressure, could only wash his hands of the whole affair in a private telegram to Cox, which took the sort of tone which so often made enemies for Lord Curzon: "You know my intense dislike of this phase of transaction and with this expression of my opinion I must leave you to make the most suitable terms you can."[65]

The agreement was formally signed on 9 August; Cox paid over the 500,000 tomans (£131,147 at the current rate) the same day and received in return an additional document, not published with the treaty series which announced the main transaction to the world—a receipt from the finance minister (one of the Triumvirate) for the first

[63] Curzon telegram (quoted) and private telegram to Cox and Cox private telegram to Curzon, 9 May, and private Curzon-Cox telegrams, 17 May (recorded in minutes; copy not in file), 63991 and 73634/150, *FO 371/3860*; CGSI telegram to DMI, 27 May, Cox telegram to FO, 21 June, CinC India telegram to GOC Baghdad, 27 June 1919, *FO 371/3861*.

[64] Cox telegram to FO, 17 July 1919, *FO 371/3861*.

[65] IO to FO, 25 July, *FO 37/3862*; FO telegram to Cox, 30 May (for previous overriding), *FO 371/3861* (*L/P&S/*10/736 for drafts); Cox telegrams to FO, 27 July (3 of date, nos. 502, 504, and 507); Curzon private telegram to Cox, 30 July 1919 (quoted), *FO 371/3862*.

installment of the loan.[66] "To me this is most odious," wrote Curzon, but the "notable act of State policy," which he had termed the treaty in the 7 May meeting, was made reality by this procedure.[67] On the same day as the formal signature, Curzon circulated a self-congratulatory memorandum to the Cabinet which reviewed the entire history of the treaty negotiations since the end of the war. It was not a protectorate which was established here, he claimed, but an assurance of integrity: the advisors and financial aid which Britain would now provide would put Persia on the way to future stability and self-sufficiency. Persian integrity was indeed specifically pledged; a twenty-year loan of £2 million at 7 percent would pay for reforms; existing treaties would be favorably reconsidered, as would Persian frontiers and claims against belligerents; as a fine gesture, Britain agreed not to claim from Persia the cost of troops sent to defend Persia in the war, and Persia would not claim damages from those same operations.[68]

The Anglo-Persian accord was achieved. It was no small achievement at that, when all the adverse circumstances are considered. It remained to be seen how the paper agreement could be transformed into Persian realities, but first press opinions were generally favorable. In Persia itself, "the only real hostility toward the agreement," Cox wrote privately to Arnold Wilson, his successor in Baghdad, "comes from a few irreconcilable democrats backed by disgruntled politicians and ex-ministers who have backed the wrong horse . . .," coupled with dog-in-the-manger Allies and jealous Russians. "The agreement itself

[66] Imperial Bank of Persia to FO, 14 August 1919, *FO* 371/3862. Agreement text in Hurewitz, *Diplomacy,* II, pp. 64-66, and Great Britain, Parliamentary Papers, "Agreement between His Britannic Majesty's Government and the Persian Government . . .," Cmd. 300 (Persia No. 1, 1919).

[67] Curzon minute on Cox telegram to FO, 15 August 1919, *FO* 371/ 3862. The telegram, but not the minute, is in E.L. Woodward, Rohan Butler, et. al., eds., *Documents on British Foreign Policy, 1919-1939,* First Series (London, 1947-1970), vol. IV, no 721. All documents used in this work are from First Series (vol. I-XVIII) only; normally, further references will not be necessary, as they are provided in the published text. Throughout this work, however, the original documents, not the published series, have been used; where necessary, additional FO volume and document numbers will be added to the note [DBFP IV/721, *FO* 371/3862]. Eastern Committee, 7 May 1919, *L/P&S*/10/807.

[68] Curzon memorandum, 9 August 1919, *DBFP* IV/710; Nicolson, *Curzon,* p. 137.

is so transparently simple & innocuous that the more it is studied the less justification will there be for hostility to it . . ."[69] Cox's province at least had been retained, although Central Asia had gone like a pawn too hastily advanced, and the Caucasus as a result had been jeopardized. Unfortunately, the seemingly safe and secure Persian position was now outflanked by a startling and unexpected invasion of India—incredibly enough, by Afghanistan.

THE AFGHAN WAR

Until the spring of 1919, Afghanistan presented no serious problem for British policy. Operations in Central Asia had been limited, partly to avoid arousing Afghani fears. Afghanistan might still be a center for anti-British agitation in India, directed by extremists who had fled to Kabul, but the only directly Afghani issue London appeared to have in early 1919 was whether to reward Amir Habibullah for his wartime neutrality, perhaps even with the Garter—a suggestion from Britain which India wisely neglected to support. The Foreign Department in India, however, was seriously considering substantial alterations in Britain's Afghani policy. The long-standing restriction upon Afghanistan's relations with third powers had proved unenforceable during the war and would remain so until Britain should take up arms to enforce it. That seemed very unlikely to India, so perhaps the restriction could be dropped as a gesture of goodwill.[70]

Habibullah had made it clear to India in mid-February that he wanted Afghani independence. In particular, he requested either Afghani representation at the peace conference or British sponsorship of a conference declaration of Afghani independence. India assumed that Afghanistan could not be represented but was quite willing to renegotiate outstanding treaties. Grant, in Europe to speak for India on such questions, would go even further and ask the conference for a declaration. It would cost little, would in all probability keep Russia away, and

[69] Cox private to Arnold Wilson, 23 August 1919, *Wilson Papers* (British Museum), Add. Mss. 52455; see also file of press cuttings on treaty, 118229-30/150, *FO* 371/3862.

[70] Montagu private telegram to Chelmsford, 20 January, and Chelmsford private telegram to Montagu, 25 January, *Chelmsford Papers,* E. 264/10; Chelmsford private to Montagu, 12 February 1919, *Montagu Papers,* D. 523/8.

at the same time would soothe the amir, who no doubt had heard that
Persia was sending a delegation and would be upset if he could not.
Shuckburgh was quick to spot the flaw, however: an international
declaration would mean international interest, and that was not desirable. In any case, Shuckburgh prophesied with prescient accuracy, if
Habibullah died and civil war broke out over the succession, Britain
might well have to intervene with troops. Montagu agreed, adding that
the amir could certainly not be allowed to approach the conference,
and so India was told. The Foreign Office was informed, with apologies,
only after the fact.[71]

Just as India was given these instructions, Habibullah was assassi-
nated in Jalalabad on 20 February.[72] A struggle for power, in which
India played little part, now occurred between Amanullah Khan, Habibullah's younger son, whose supporters included most of those interested in reform and modernization, and Habibullah's brother Nas-
rullah Khan, who stood for more conservative policies. Amanullah's
initial control of Kabul and its treasury and garrisons proved conclu-
sive, and within a few days he was consolidating his position as amir.
His aims were modernist and anti-British; his chief desire, apart from
the achievement of power, was full independence for Afghanistan.
The delayed impact of the twentieth century upon Afghanistan—
Young Turk reformism, pan-Islamic dreams, Wilsonian (and Bolshevik)
self-determination—all played a role in the sequence of events which
now followed.

[71] Viceroy telegram to SSI, 12 February, with minutes by Grant and
Shuckburgh (15 February), Montagu (18 February), Shuckburgh (21 February, for Curzon), and Curzon (n.d.), SSI telegram to viceroy, 20 February
1919, L/P&S/10/461.
[72] The following paragraphs are based upon Leon B. Poullada, *Reform
and Rebellion in Afghanistan, 1919-1929* (Ithaca, N.Y., 1973), particularly
Ch. II for an extensive portrait of Amanullah; Adamec, *Afghanistan,* Ch.
VI, and the same author's *Afghanistan's Foreign Affairs to the mid-Twentieth Century* (Tucson, Ariz., 1974), Ch. II-III; Gregorian, *Emergence of
Modern Afghanistan,* pp. 215-31; Kapur, *Soviet Russia and Asia,* pp. 216-
22; L/P&S/10/808; Great Britain, Parliamentary Papers, "Papers Respecting Hostilities with Afghanistan," Cmd. 1183, 1919; Thomas D. Farrell,
"The Founding of the North-West Frontier Militias," *Asian Affairs* 59
(1972): 165-78; India, Army Headquarters, General Staff, *The Third Afghan War, 1919: Official Account* (Calcutta, 1926). The only full-length
treatment of the fighting is Lt.-Gen. G.N. Molesworth, *Afghanistan 1919:
An Account of Operations in the Third Afghan War* (London, 1962).

Foreign adventure is a tempting avenue of national unification, and something of the sort may have been in Amanullah's mind when he directed his attention toward his powerful southern neighbor at a time when Russians of all colors were otherwise occupied and thus unable to interfere. It was after all not Russia but British India which controlled Afghanistani external affairs. India's dilatory tactics in responding to his predecessor's communications may have played a role, but Indian troubles over the Rowlatt Acts, doubtless emphasized and distorted by Indian exiles in Kabul, were far more important. An India believed to be in revolt (which would keep British troops fully occupied) and inhabited by potential Muslim allies was an India which might safely be invaded.

Amanullah's plans were unknown outside Afghanistan; but his general desires were clear from policy pronouncements and certain key appointments, notably that of Mahmud Tarzi as "commissar" of foreign affairs (the title was an erroneous translation of an Afghani honorific, but for some weeks, until the error was corrected, "commissar" meant "Bolshevik" to nervous observers). Tarzi, a remarkable man who had spent years in exile and who was also Amanullah's father-in-law, had strong Young Turk associations and was known through his journal *Siraj-ul-Akhbar* as a leading "Young Afghan" anticolonialist. He therefore was naturally regarded as pro-Turkish and anti-British. Although the accusation has been made that high authorities disregarded intelligence reports on Afghani intentions,[73] the extent of the attack was certainly never anticipated; officials can hardly be blamed for failing to grasp the enormity of Afghani misinformation and misinterpretation of the Indian situation. Shuckburgh, by coincidence writing on the very day fighting began, could only be astonished at Amanullah's pronouncements: ". . . indeed, if they are to be read literally, the Afghan Govt appears to have made something like a declaration of war against us."[74] That is exactly what Amanullah had done. His forces crossed the frontier in strength beginning 3 May and inaugurated two weeks of serious fighting, during which Indian alarm

[73] Molesworth, *Afghanistan, 1919,* p. 37. On Tarzi, Poullada, *Reform and Rebellion,* pp. 40-3, and Vartan Gregorian, "Mahmud Tarzi and *Saraj-ol-Akhbar,*" *Middle East Journal,* 21 (1967): 345-368.

[74] Shuckburgh and Grant minutes, 27 and 28 March, 1709b/19, and viceroy telegram to SSI, 4 May, with Shuckburgh minute (quoted), 5 May 1919, *L/P&S/*10/808.

reached substantial proportions and Indian resources were heavily taxed. But the issue was never in doubt once it became clear that Amanullah did not have the loyalty of all the many Muslim frontier tribes. Experienced in British ability to conjure armies out of thin air, they waited and watched—and thus ensured Amanullah's failure. His own men fought well, if in scattered detachments, and the British forces, totaling an incredible ration strength of 750,000, suffered 1700 casualties at his hands, to say nothing of considerable ill-will from troops on their way home from Iraq to be demobilized who found themselves suddenly diverted to a nasty war on the North-West Frontier. There were several small mutinies among the Frontier militia, and there were internal difficulties in policing the Punjab, but India never had the problems which would have accompanied a widespread tribal rising or Muslim revolution. British prestige was hardly damaged; defeat in the Khyber—for Afghanistan claimed victory there—was more than off-set by total victory in the air when British planes twice bombed Jalalabad and even assaulted Kabul, something Afghanistan hardly expected. By the end of May, Amanullah asked for an armistice; by early June, the war was over.

Officials in India were convinced from the start that Amanullah's folly was due to internal pressures. Lieutenant-Colonel Sir George Roos-Keppel, chief commissioner of the North-West Frontier Province, and the man whose territory was most directly affected, was certain that Tarzi, "the most venomous man in Afghanistan," was particularly responsible. Roos-Keppel was also quick to see the saving fact: no thinking Hindu was going to relish a Muslim Afghani invasion. Sir Michael O'Dwyer, lieutenant-governor of the Punjab, went even further: Hindus and Sikhs would, he predicted, solidly support the government in this crisis—an opinion which rather overlooked Amritsar, but which was not far wrong as it happened. On the other hand, Amanullah's real connection with Muslim India was nonexistent, and even liaison with the tribes was faulty. Chelmsford, the viceroy, concluded that Amanullah himself had not known war was coming until he had ordered the attack, a view which helped explain India's unpreparedness.[75]

---

[75] Roos-Keppel private to Sr. J.L. Maffey, 5 May, and Chelmsford private to Montagu, 7 May, *Montagu Papers,* D. 523/8; Sir Michael O'Dwyer private to Chelmsford, 19 May, and Montagu private telegram to Chelmsford, 5 May, *Chelmsford Papers,* E. 264/22 and 10; Montagu private to

Still, as Roos-Keppel knew well, any outbreak in India near the frontier—in Peshawar, for example—for whatever cause, which resulted in any loss of life, could bring the cooperation for which Amanullah hoped; Muslim tribes would take up arms if Muslims were killed in a way they would not over the bodies of Hindus and Sikhs at Amritsar. But even in the midst of crisis, a beneficial side could be seen: defeat of an actual Afghan invasion would forever end the threat of one that Indian Muslim agitators used in their protest against Turkish peace terms. The Frontier had to be reminded periodically that Britain could still control the area, even after a long European war which had denuded India of troops.[76]

As the outcome became clear, the question arose whether British forces should not press on into Afghanistan. Roos-Keppel in Peshawar advocated going to Kabul, or at least to Jalalabad, to drive the lesson home. The Frontier was Roos-Keppel's life work, and such an opportunity to deal effectively with Afghani intrigue was very tempting. The idea received short shrift from Montagu. The proposed advance might settle the tribes, but it would also mean a long war against Afghanistan, hardly warranted by the minor nature of any yet remaining Afghan menace. Lenient diplomacy might well persuade the amir to friendship with Britain, while the military alternative was likely to reduce Afghanistan to anarchy and open it to a possible Bolshevik takeover.[77]

Advance was Roos-Keppel's idea, not the policy the Indian government preferred. Chelmsford, Grant, now returned from London and shortly to assume control for Afghani negotiations, and Denys Bray, secretary of the Foreign Department, were the three men responsible for Afghanistan policy, and while they had to hear Roos-Keppel out as the man on the spot, they had no intention of recommending his policy. Chelmsford immediately ordered that the amir's request for armistice be granted and informed London after the fact. His news was received

Curzon, 7 May, *Curzon Papers,* F/2/2; see also War Cabinet 563, 6 May 1919, *CAB* 23/10.

[76] Roos-Keppel private to Chelmsford, 13 May, and private to Maffey, 17 May 1919, *Montagu Papers,* D. 523/8.

[77] SSI telegrams to viceroy (Army Dept.), 17 May and 5 August, IO Military Dept. Files, Secret Military Telegrams from India (*L/Mil/3*), vol. 2531 and 2511; Chelmsford private to Montagu, 21 May 1919, *Montagu Papers,* D. 523/8.

with less than enthusiasm; London wanted no war, but neither did they want an independent Indian foreign policy. Very suddenly, Chelmsford found himself defending an armistice which London thought far too lenient.[78]

India's arguments, however, were strong. There was no alternative ruler to Amanullah. "There is really no half-way house between policy of complete subjugation of Afghanistan and policy of attempting to establish really friendly relations and mutual trust"—a philosophy which India had already propounded on Persia, although with less success. The trouble with this argument, said Shuckburgh, was that Amanullah should also be brought to realize the enormity of his crime and the extent of his defeat; a draft telegram to that effect was not sent. Montagu, realizing that the armistice was a *fait accompli,* softened Shuckburgh's rebuke and moved it to a private letter where he focused on the peace terms to be negotiated. These, he advised, should achieve certain British aims, such as the cancellation of long-standing subsidy obligations to the amir or the expulsion of Bolshevik agents.[79]

London increasingly feared Bolshevik aggression toward Afghanistan and Persia. Already in May, the Bolsheviks had toppled the Ashkhabad regime, the remnants of which took refuge in Krasnovodsk, reinforced and given a temporary new lease on life at Milne's discretion. Malleson was ordered to prepare a scheme for withdrawal down the eastern cordon to the railhead in case of Bolshevik attack, or, as now seemed possible, a two-sided assault by both Bolsheviks and Afghanis. Etherton in Kashgar reported that the Bolsheviks were making the most of propaganda opportunities provided by the war, and Malleson had information of Afghani incursions in Persia's Seistan province to his south. His officers, moreover, reported considerable pan-Islamic agitation.[80]

---

[78] Chelmsford private to Montagu, 4 June, *Montagu Papers,* D. 523/8; Chelmsford private telegrams to Montagu, 8 and 13 June, Montagu private telegram to Chelmsford, 11 June, *Chelmsford Papers,* E. 264/10; viceroy telegrams to SSI, 1 and 9 June 1919, *L/P&S/*10/808.

[79] Viceroy telegram to SSI (quoted), 9 June, with Shuckburgh draft of unsent telegram (3168/19), *L/P&S/*10/808; Montagu private to Chelmsford, 11 June 1919, *Montagu Papers,* D. 523/3; Adamec, *Afghanistan,* pp. 120-21.

[80] CGSI telegrams to Malleson, 1 and 23 June, GOC Constantinople telegram to CGSI, 14 June, WO telegram to GOC Constantinople, 11 July,

"Pan-Islamic" had a habit of becoming "Bolshevik" in the minds of many, and it was no accident that the India Office now asked authorities in India whether they thought that enough attention was being devoted to stopping Bolshevik propaganda, particularly that emanating from the new Indian Propaganda Bureau in Moscow. Nothing, however, could be done about Moscow's known intention to aid the Afghanis as soon as through communications were open (the Bolsheviks had not yet secured either the Caspian or Bukhara, and large-scale aid was therefore still impossible). This intention was confirmed by an intercepted Russian communication, a source whose importance increased geometrically with the decline of the Whites and the withdrawal of pro-Allied Russian forces. Listening posts were established for the purpose in Quetta, Meshed, and Constantinople.[81]

The immediate possibility of Malleson's withdrawal was ended by the Afghani armistice, and India's most pressing problem became

---

War Diary, Persia, 55-56; viceroy (Army Dept.) telegram to SSI, 15 June, SSI telegram to viceroy (Army Dept.), 21 June, *L/Mil/*3/2511 and 2531; Etherton, Kashgar, telegram to FSI, 2 June 1919, copy in 131260/2269, *FO* 371/4106.

[81] Viceroy (Army Dept.) telegram to SSI, 15 June, *FO* 371/3861; SSI telegram to viceroy, 18 June, Karakhan, Moscow, telegram to Tashkent Soviet (minister of Foreign Affairs), 12 June, 3558/19, Kashgar SIS report, 15 July 1919, *L/P&S/*10/836 and 886.

The problem of intelligence source material is discussed by Ullman, *Anglo-Soviet Relations,* II, pp. 173-75, and III, Ch. VII. While Ullman's discussion goes beyond the meager information on foreign intelligence available in the standard published works, he has, quite naturally, not encountered the occasional mention in the India Office documents as well. The Indian authorities maintained intercept stations at Quetta and Meshed, and from these stations must have come at least as much basic source material for the cryptographers in the Admiralty's Code and Cypher School as provided by the stations in Europe (including Constantinople). The fact that as much as possible of this sort of source material has been removed from the records considerably handicaps the historian's task; it is difficult to know what the principals knew. The sources which at least mention British activities are Richard Deacon [Donald McCormick], *A History of the British Secret Service* (London, 1969); Sir George Aston, *Secret Service* (London, 1930); John Bulloch, *M.I.5, the Origins and History of the British Counter-Espionage Service* (London, 1963); James, *The Eyes of the Navy;* and Sir Basil Thomson's uninformative memoirs, *The Scene Changes* (London, 1939).

peace negotiations. J.L. Maffey, Chelmford's private secretary, now sent up to the Frontier to be chief political officer with the army, was the principal advisor on this stage of affairs; Roos-Keppel, a noted Afghaniphobe, was left to administer his district but bypassed on Afghanistan policy (on the verge of retirement in any case, he was soon replaced by Grant). Maffey thought the best approach was to negotiate two treaties, or rather one treaty in two separate chapters: the first would settle the frontier by establishing demarcation procedures, stop the subsidy as punishment for Afghani misbehavior, and establish a British agent in Kabul. All other problems would be left for later. After a year or so to quiet the Afghanis and show how necessary British friendship and subsidy were, the amir would doubtless appear as supplicant and a new relationship could be worked out to everyone's mutual advantage. Somewhat modified in detail, the plan was passed to London with Chelmsford's approval, for, as Chelmsford put it privately to Montagu, as a great power dealing with a weak neighbor India could afford to be lenient. The leniency included, in the second stage, some serious restrictions: Afghanistan would have no relations with other powers save through British offices (the perpetuation of the status quo, technically), Indian nationalists in addition to Bolshevik and other foreign agents would be expelled, and there would be no Afghani interference in tribal affairs. It was not "leniency," however, that led to home opposition, but the two-stage procedure, which seemed unnecessary. The clause preserving British control of foreign relations was essential— but that, of course, was what the war had largely been about from the Afghani standpoint.[82]

The India Office Political Department at least gave serious consideration to the proposal. Shuckburgh, in a lengthy memorandum of June, clarified what he thought was the situation. The possibilities were, first, something like a protectorate, with closer control; second, predominant influence without close control, approximating the pre-1919 status quo; third, termination of all special relations and subsidy and complete noninterference in Afghani affairs. The third approach

---

[82] Malleson telegram to CGSI, 10 July, CGSI telegram to Malleson, 13 August, *War Diary,* Persia, 56-57;; Maffey private to Chelmsford, 20 June, *Chelmsford Papers,* E. 264/23; Chelmsford private to Montagu, 26 June, *Montagu Papers,* D. 523/8; viceroy telegram to SSI, 29 June 1919, *L/P&S/*10/808.

presented many superficial advantages, including financial savings, but Afghanistan was a poor country which would eventually be driven to seek aid. In all probability Russia would have its hands full for many years, but Britain still could not tolerate any other power's influence here. On the other hand, India had not inflicted such a defeat on Afghanistan as to gain and enforce a protectorate. The department, therefore, favored preserving the *status quo ante bellum*.[83]

To India, this was simple misconstruction of the facts. The amir would never accept that sort of treaty. Even if he did, a clause governing foreign relations would only be so much paper, for Afghanistan would require her own relations with Russians and other neighbors. The solution was to boycott and isolate the amir temporarily to teach him his dependence upon Britain. Diehards at home might be critical, but it was worth a trial, and Grant, now negotiating with the Afghanis in Rawalpindi, was so instructed. He found the Afghani delegates "touchy as Frenchmen," extremely sensitive to any imagined slight to themselves or Afghani independence, of which they insisted upon every outward demonstration. But the "shadow of external freedom," as Grant called it, meant some hard negotiation, and it was soon no longer clear just who was manipulating whom. Since foreign relations were being left to the second stage, Grant was willing to stipulate that nothing in the way of interference was intended; "unprovoked and wanton aggression" became "circumstances which gave rise to the war," and so on. Chelmsford attempted to prepare Montagu for the sort of treaty Grant and Maffey were negotiating, but it was not easy. London as yet refused to yield control of foreign relations.[84]

"Simple surrender," Hirtzel called it; *The Times,* on the other hand, congratulated India for a statesmanlike act. Chelmsford approved the treaty, and once again had to defend himself for failing to obtain prior approval from London. His excuse was that delay might rupture negotiations; if London really disagreed, the home authorities could always repudiate the viceroy and his advisors. But Montagu had approved the negotiations in general—although fighting the terms—and he had

---

[83] Shuckburgh memorandum (A. 778), 29 June 1919, *L/P&S/*10/808.

[84] Viceroy telegram to SSI, 10 July, *L/P&S/*10/808; Chelmsford private to Montagu, 31 July, *Montagu Papers,* D. 523/9; Grant private to Chelmsford, 1 August, and telegrams to FSI, 5 and 6 August 1919, *Chelmsford Papers,* E. 264/23.

little option but to accept the Treaty of Rawalpindi. There was, after all, the chance that India was right; in any case, it was traditionally difficult for London to overrule India's considered opinion on Afghanistan. Nor was Britain prepared for further fighting if the negotiations broke down. To the contrary, indications that the Bolsheviks were encouraging Afghani war efforts made it all the more desirable to conclude peace now, even via the two-stage process which India had initiated.

Bravin, newly arrived Soviet envoy to Kabul, was particularly blamed for disruptive activities. Malleson did all he could from Meshed to discredit Bravin through secret service channels, and Curzon even suggested that the Afghani delegates be challenged openly on this matter — a shortsighted idea, for the intercepts revealed only Bolshevik intent, not Afghani cooperation. The evidence did indicate, however, a shift of Bolshevik policy from Europe to India and the east, and London suggested an intelligence-gathering mission to Bukhara. Chelmsford remained calm throughout; too soon, he replied, to force the pace by addressing the amir on Bolshevik activity, and a Bukhara mission would be very dangerous since it would compromise the amir of Bukhara with the Bolsheviks. Even Malleson now realized that such missions were too late; all that should be done now was to work for international support (from the Paris conference, for example) for Bukhara.[86]

Montagu, frustrated in every suggestion, could only await developments. That he expected a further round of discussions was clear, however, from his refusal to reward Grant and Maffey with the traditional honors given successful negotiators — for the treaty was, on India's own analysis, only half-done. Chelmsford argued that Montagu's control of foreign relations "was and always would be a scrap of paper"; what was wanted was not paper terms but a friendly neighbor. Perhaps this was a change of traditional Indian policy which dated from the

[85] Hirtzel minute, 9 August, 4651/19, *L/P&S*/10/808; *The Times,* 11 August; Chelmsford private telegram to Montagu, 18 August, *Chelmsford Papers,* E. 264/11; Chelmsford private to Montagu, 20 August 1919, *Montagu Papers,* D. 523/9.

[86] Malleson telegram to CGSI, 15 July, *War Diary,* Persia, 56; Curzon private to Montagu, 15 August, Cox telegram to FO, 19 August, viceroy telegrams to SSI, 25 August and 1 September 1919, *L/P&S*/10/836; Kapur, *Soviet Russia and Asia,* pp. 154-60.

Afghan war forty years earlier—but ". . . the whole world has been blown sky high in the last four!"[87]

The Afghan war was over and peace concluded. The Treaty of Rawalpindi left some question as to whether Afghanistan had not in fact gained its larger objective of independence. Instead of British control, there was a Soviet advisor; instead of Malleson in Merv, there was Malleson in Meshed. Clearly the tide had turned in Central Asia, but at least Britain had treaties of some form with Afghanistan and Persia. There yet remained the problem of the Caucasus, which, no longer dependent upon Trans-Caspia, could be treated on its own merits.

WITHDRAWAL FROM THE CAUCASUS

In March 1919 the Interdepartmental Committee and Cabinet had decided to hold the Caucasus on a temporary basis while preparing plans for withdrawal. It was desirable, however, to find a replacement for the British presence other than Denikin, who should be concentrating his efforts on the anti-Bolshevik struggle. It would be even more desirable if at the same time other problems might be solved, as for example if Italy's claims in Asia Minor could be traded for a mandate in the Caucasus. Although the Allied military leaders had discussed possible Italian occupation here, apparently the first approach to Orlando regarding formal mandatory responsibilities was made by Lloyd George on 21 March. Orlando was worried about Denikin but the prime minister assured him that Denikin had been headed off and, as Hankey recorded, "would not receive any assistance in arms if he penetrated into this country," meaning specifically Georgia. After a night's consideration, the Italians agreed—but without prejudice to Italian claims elsewhere.[88]

The decision galvanized such departments as were informed into action, for at last plans could be prepared for evacuation—and evacuation with a reasonably clear conscience. But few departments were

[87] Grant private to Chelmsford, 31 October, *Chelmsford Papers,* E. 264/23; Chelmsford private to Montagu, 8 October 1919 (quoted), *Montagu Papers,* D. 523/9.

[88] IDCE, 6 March, *L/P&S/*10/807; Toynbee memorandum, ca. 22 March 1919, and Hankey (n.s.) note of same date (quoted), 342/8/4, *FO* 608/83; Roskill, *Hankey,* II, p. 78.

informed, and these only slowly. The first written indication received in the Foreign Office was a file copy of a letter dated 2 April from the Admiralty to the Treasury, which informed the Treasury that expenses for the Caspian fleet would continue only until the Italians took it over or, if they did not, until British troops left the Caucasus. Curzon, who had already heard of this surprising plan, now had not only to complain to Paris but also to explain to Cox in Teheran that the decision had been made in Paris without the slightest consultation with the Foreign Office. Curzon tended to blame the Foreign Office representatives in Paris, but the accusation was unjust; how isolated the entire department was is illustrated by Mallet's request—from Paris—for information on how and when and to what extent the Anglo-Italian transfer would be made. As Mallet explained in private, the delegation, try as it might, rarely got information about Council of Four decisions except through private channels or an occasional War Cabinet or British Empire Delegation paper. Having heard of the Caucasus decision indirectly, he merely assumed that Curzon had been consulted—a thrust which Curzon hardly required to emphasize his own sense of isolation.[89]

Not only was Curzon isolated; he was also convinced that the decision was a mistake, or would be if Italy took on in fact what she had so easily done verbally. There were actually signs that Italy intended to go through with it; before the month was past, Rome was reporting the dispatch of a fifteen-man mission to the Caucasus, and in Paris Sonnino talked with the leading Georgian delegate, leaving the impression that Italy was completely serious (no doubt activated, or so the British military representatives concluded, by the need to employ the Italian army and obtain oil for its navy). In May, however, the situation was dramatically altered when the Italian delegation walked out of the conference and Lloyd George assisted the Greek landing at Smyrna.[90]

The Smyrna decision inevitably affected the Caucasus; Lloyd George was unwilling to reward Italy with one hand while punishing it with the other, and he made it clear to President Wilson and Premier Clemen-

[89] Admiralty to Treasury, 2 April; FO to Admiralty, 4 April, to Mallet, 19 April, and telegram to Cox, 24 April; Mallet private to Graham, 28 April, *FO* 371/3667; Mallet telegram to Curzon, 17 April 1919, *FO* 371/3658.

[90] Erskine (Rome) telegram to FO, 27 April, *FO* 371/3662; Lt.-Col. M. Gribbon, WO, note, 22 April 1919, 347/1/6, *FO* 608/85.

ceau in the Council of Four (Three) that while Italian replacement of British troops had been suggested, and Italy had indicated interest, still nothing formal had been done—a viewpoint which found no opposition, since neither Wilson nor Clemenceau favored the proposal. The central problem now, however, was who should replace the British troops which Lloyd George insisted were coming out in any case. Field Marshal Wilson, also present, and no advocate of Caucasian commitments, found himself arguing that violence and anarchy would be the inevitable result if no replacement were found. Lloyd George could not dispute the point, but his mind was made up: the Caucasian units would at once be moved to Constantinople "in order to have them ready to counter any move by the Italians."[91]

This decision did not upset the authorities in Constantinople. They were already torn by the incompatible pressures of demobilization, policing the Caucasus, and enforcing the Turkish armistice—the last usually had least priority simply because there were not enough troops.[92] Officials in the Caucasus and Caspian, however, insisted some arrangements must be made for the future. Particularly nervous was Commander Norris on the Caspian, for his line of retreat was being cut off. Norris had planes, armored merchant ships, and a dozen motorboats sent by rail from Batum with which to counter the Bolshevik fleet in Astrakhan. As Denikin had advanced in February, British planes from Petrovsk had bombed Grozni, an important rail and oil center, and facilitated Denikin's advance to Kislyar 200 miles south of Astrakhan, but the navy could breathe freely only if Denikin captured the mouth of the Volga, and this he failed to do. At this point, morale wavered, the front stabilized, and Denikin ordered units of the Volunteer Fleet paid off for lack of cash. That fleet included the two most powerful ships in the Caspian, the gunboats *Kars* and *Ardahan*, 14-knot vessels with two 4.7" guns each. Should the Volunteer Fleet, already thought to be infiltrated by Bolshevik propaganda, go over to the other side, the rough balance of naval forces on the Caspian would dramatically alter. Norris' only choices—to destroy his fleet or to hand it over to Denikin—were both unsavory. Denikin could not run the ships he already controlled, and if he could he would be just as likely

---

[91] Council of Four, 5 May 1919, *FRUS,* Paris Conference, V, pp. 463-73.

[92] Gough-Calthorpe telegram to FO, 20 April, and FO telegram to Gough-Calthorpe, 9 May 1919, *FO* 371/3667.

to use the fleet to seize Baku from whoever remained there when Britain left as he would to attack Astrakhan; on the other hand, destruction of the fleet would only demonstrate to Denikin Britain's distrust.[93]

Denikin, however, was the only available candidate for controlling Georgia. That control was necessary the military did not doubt; Georgian leaders, reported Milne, were increasingly "truculent and hostile," and he asked for permission to fire on any who moved north of the demarcation line he had set between Georgia and Denikin (Georgia, it should be pointed out, claimed that some Georgian territory lay north of this line). The Georgian attitude was understandable; they too had heard of the Italian solution. Moreover, clashes with the Georgians were useful for Britain, as they made it easier to overlook a British assurance (made through Admiral Webb at Constantinople in January 1919) that Britain viewed the establishment of a Georgian Republic with sympathy and would work for conference recognition. Although there was some question as to just when and how this pledge had been made, it was not now withdrawn. The pledge was a useful counter in Russian negotiations and remained for Denikin to worry about.[94]

It was all very confusing; the only clarity was Lloyd George's determination to get the troops out. In mid-May the War Office ordered Milne to proceed with the evacuation, whether any Italians arrived or not. The fleet was to be given to Denikin. The Interdepartmental Committee, meeting on 22 May, could only confirm decisions already made, for as Curzon reluctantly agreed, the question of withdrawal was not at issue, but only the method. The only issues remaining were where and when Denikin would assume authority over the fleet and whether Italy might yet take over the area.[95]

When it returned to Paris, Balfour applied pressure on the Italian delegation for a decision, informing it that the British evacuation of Baku would commence on 15 June. There was yet time for the Italians

---

[93] Admiralty Naval Staff, Operations Division, memorandum, ca. 28 March, *ADM* 116/1862; Rear Admiral, Black Sea, telegram to Admiralty, 16 May, Admiralty to FO, 17 May 1919, *FO* 371/3667.

[94] GOC Constantinople telegram to WO, 9 May, with minutes; Balfour to Curzon, 30 May, *FO* 608/88; Webb to FO, 25 April, enclosing Brig.-Gen. W.H. Beech (Tiflis) report, Stevens (Batum) to Curzon, 14 May 1919, *FO* 371/3662.

[95] WO telegram to GOC Constantinople, 14 May, *FO* 371/3667; DMI to FO, 21 May, *FO* 371/3662; IDCE, 22 May 1919, *L/P&S*/10/807.

to agree. Milne was still urging delay of evacuation until the Italians did appear, since otherwise all the expense and time spent on the Caucasus would have been wasted. Another factor favoring delay was Denikin. Told in early June of the planned Italian replacement, he proved most suspicious, insisting that the Caspian fleet be turned over to himself and not to Italy, even though he was not prepared to man the ships for some time. Curzon saw reasonable cause for delay in all these uncertainties, but Churchill was adamant that the decision stand; the army should be out by mid-July, and then it would be "the Italians or chaos or both!"[96]

Orders were already being carried out, beginning with advance units in the Caspian. The RAF's 62 Wing, for example, turned over its dozen DH9A's to Denikin, but planned to leave its Short Seaplanes for the Italians in a nice division of material. Perhaps because the Caspian adventure was a completely detached operation which never affected British seapower, the Admiralty was the most loath to go. There was another reason, as one Admiralty official noted: "We congratulated ourselves that the odium of the scuttle from Odessa and the Crimea fell on the French alone, and within a few weeks we deliberately tarred ourselves with the same brush."[97] The only consolation was that the Italian mission under the Prince of Savoy had reached Baku and Norris had settled turnover details with one Commandant Gramafé of the Italian navy, either in ignorance of the decision to give Denikin the fleet or because Denikin was unable to take charge at once. In any case, the Italian mission was badly out of touch. On 19 June Francesco Nitti became premier; Tittoni, his foreign minister, soon showed clear signs of wishing to back out of the commitment. Balfour, after talking with him in Paris, warned that Britain had better proceed on

[96] Balfour to Curzon, 4 June, enclosing British Delegation, Paris, to Italian Delegation, 26 May, *DBFP* III/229; GHQ, Constantinople, telegrams to WO, 27 May and 4 June (latter from "Denmiss," Ekaterinador), *FO* 371/3667; Churchill private to Curzon, 11 June 1919 (quoted), *Curzon Papers,* F/2/2.

[97] Air Ministry telegram to RAFOS, Malta, 13 June (and other documents in file 15/1/204/1), *AIR* 1/34; Admiralty staff minute (signature illegible) for deputy first sea lord, 28 June (quoted), Proceedings 27 May-2 June, *ADM* 137/1741; resident naval officer, Baku, to senior naval officer, Caspian, 28 June 1919, *Norris Papers,* NOS/4; Lt.-Col. F.J. French, *From Whitehall to the Caspian* (London, [1920]), p. 202.

the assumption that Italy was not going in. "Exactly what I have all along prophesied," noted Curzon; "But then what are we to do?" [98]

The Interdepartmental Committee, meeting on 11 July, now faced the fact of withdrawal with no viable replacement. Last minute proposals abounded for staying on. Malleson suggested from Meshed that perhaps Denikin could put in a substantial force at Krasnovodsk (the one Gurkha battalion there could hardly be expected to hold on for long). Even Malleson changed his tune on cooperation with the Whites when he was relegated to Meshed and threatened from Afghanistan as well. The committee, however, was well aware that Denikin could not take over the fleet, let alone spare such a force. But if Denikin could take Astrakhan there was still a chance, and Krasnovodsk would hold for so long as that chance remained. [99]

In a general way, it was decided that unless Astrakhan had fallen by mid-August, there was little chance that the Caspian could be kept out of Bolshevik hands. The Admiralty orders to Gough-Calthorpe (responsible for Caspian operations when Milne took over the Caucasus) made it very clear that there could be no extension beyond that date, and naval squadron and material should be handed over immediately. This was more than the committee had approved, but there was neither means nor point to protest. The War Office was already altering Denikin's southern demarcation line so as to ensure his entry into Petrovsk as the British moved out. [100]

One bright spot, from Curzon's view, was Milne's suggestion that withdrawal might be partially mitigated by leaving some forces temporarily in Batum until the future of that city and province could be

[98] Curzon telegrams to Balfour, 28 June and 6 July, Rodd telegram to FO, 29 June, *DBFP* III/284-5, 296; R. Graham for Curzon, 2 July (reporting phone call from Gribbon), and Balfour to Curzon, 10 July, enclosing 4 July memorandum, *FO* 371/3668; Vansittart for Crowe, 7 July, 347/1/6, *FO* 608/85; Clark Kerr minute, 8 July, 97179/1015, *FO* 371/3662; Curzon minute (quoted) in Graham note for Curzon, 2 July 1919, *FO* 371/3668; Ullman, *Anglo-Soviet Relations,* II, pp. 229-31; Kazemzadeh, *Struggle,* pp. 227-29.

[99] IDCE, 11 July, *L/P&S*/10/807; CinC India telegram to WO, 8 July 1919, *FO* 371/3662.

[100] Admiralty telegram to CinC Mediterranean, 15 July, with FO minutes, *FO* 371/3668; WO telegram to GOC Constantinople, 17 July 1919, *FO* 371/3663.

agreed. Such forces, including guards for British commissions in Tiflis and Baku, would amount to some four battalions. Curzon moved quickly to support the idea in the Cabinet on 25 July. Batum was too important to give up, just when new civilian advisor was being posted there. Oliver Wardrop was an expert on Georgia and most welcome to a people who knew him well and whose language he spoke. The mission was approved, but Wardrop would find the odds very high against him, for evacuation was to begin, according to the War Office, in August. A decision on Batum was postponed, but Batum alone would not help Wardrop in Tiflis.[101]

The Batum foothold was preserved for complicated reasons. The Foreign Office focused upon past pledges to Georgia and the need to discourage new attention from Denikin in the direction of Georgia. Moreover, added Kidston, summing up the department's arguments, a leftist government consigned to the tender mercies of the Whites might well bring a cry of outrage from British Labour groups. Balfour supported the Batum position for humanitarian reasons; as he put it to Lloyd George, an appalling massacre, particularly of Armenians, would probably follow total withdrawal. One final possibility remained, and Balfour asked for time to explore it: perhaps the United States could be asked to take on the job.[102]

Curzon had little thanks to give Balfour. The foreign secretary offered no real hope by this or any other proposal so late in the day. It was too late for all but Batum—and for Batum, Curzon had only won a stay of execution into the fall, on a month-to-month basis. It was merely a small successful rearguard action in a losing war. Curzon left no doubt in his minutes for the Foreign Office of his own position:

This is not a FO matter. I disapprove of the entire Caucasian

[101] War Cabinet 599, 25 July, 601, 29 July, *CAB* 23/11; GOC Constantinople telegram to WO, 21 July, makes suggestion, *FO* 371/3668; Curzon to Wardrop, 22 July, *DBFP* III/329; with Kidston minute on same, 18 July, 102622/1015, and WO to FO, 24 July 1919, *FO* 371/3662. Sir Harry Luke, *Cities and Men: An Autobiography* (London, 1953), II, p. 100, discusses Wardrop's qualifications; he had written a book on Georgia, *The Kingdom of Georgia* (London, 1888), studied the language, and his sister was a noted translator of Georgian poetry. See also MacDonell, "*. . . And Nothing Long*", p. 308.

[102] WO to FO, 30 July, with Kidston minute, 31 July, *FO* 371/3662;

policy of HMG. The decision to evacuate is a military decision, and was concurred in by Mr. Balfour. Similarly I had no responsibility for the Italian suggestion, and I cannot find a policy now to extricate ourselves from a situation produced by acts of which I never approved.[103]

In reality, Curzon had not quite given up on the Caucasus, but by August of 1919 it was a matter of temporary expedients, small missions, and precarious footholds. British control and influence were ebbing rapidly from the Caucasus, and with the Caucasus, inevitably the Caspian and Trans-Caspian, just as, in a vicious circle, withdrawal there weakened the Caucasian position. Vast territories had been occupied and then forsaken in less than a year after the end of the Turkish war, despite the lack of any serious military defeat in the field. On the other side of the ledger, the Persian treaty was an achievement, and perhaps the Rawalpindi settlement would in time come to be similarly regarded. Only occasionally in this story had the old "Indian bastion" arguments and their counterparts, permanent influence and occupation, appeared— certainly not often enough to justify any thesis that Britain intended permanent possession of these areas. The essential element, of course, has long been clear: Lloyd George's disinclination to continue to interfere in Russian affairs. It was a realistic policy considering the political situation in Britain and the unavailability of resources in the postwar era. Such troops as were available were already too few for the adventurous side of Lloyd George's policy in the Greek occupation of Turkey. It must have seemed to the prime minister, moreover, that support of a loyal and friendly Greek ally in the Aegean and Turkey was less a chimera than some of the wilder schemes for puppet regimes in Merv or Ashkhabad. But another factor, seldom seen in the same light, was India's clear and determined reluctance to engage in adventures, whether Caucasian, Persian, Trans-Caspian, or Afghani—a reluctance that persistently ran ahead of thinking even in the naturally pro-Indian India Office. Had India been inclined to use her resources in such ad-

Balfour private to Lloyd George, 9 August, and Curzon to Lindsay, 11 August 1919, *DBFP* III/364, 366.

[103] Curzon private to Balfour, 12 August, *DBFP* III/367; War Cabinet 612, 12 August, and 617, 19 August, *CAB* 23/11-12; Churchill private to Curzon, 14 August and 10 and 17 September, *Curzon Papers,* F/2/2; Curzon minute, 27 July, on Admiralty to FO, 22 July 1919, *FO* 371/3668.

ventures, Britain's postwar Middle East policy might have been entirely different. Such a hypothesis goes beyond the historian's task, and surely it was never close to a reality. The persistent obstructionism and reluctance, however, is no hypothesis, for India obviously found a campaign on her own North-West Frontier more than taxing.

Lloyd George and the authorities in London interacted with India, at least in part, to produce Britain's Middle East policy. That interaction was disruptive, not supportive, in many areas, including Turkey. The prime minister's need for the Caucasian troops in Turkey was decisive in producing the withdrawal. India, however, had already played a role in Turkey, rather to Lloyd George's distaste, and, having so far succeeded in that country as well as areas to the east, India was just as likely to continue her interest and, indeed, just as likely to focus attention upon Turkey as the prime minister.

IV

Slack Tide: Turkey, 1919-1920

The Greek occupation of Smyrna in May 1919 altered the course of Middle Eastern history. From the very first, it was clear that the Turks would oppose the Greek occupation with every means of resistance, however welcomed it might be by the Greek people of Asia Minor. The first clash, in Smyrna itself, left a hundred dead, and it was only the beginning. Regardless of responsibility for provocation (attributed to the Greeks by some) or for the first shot fired (blamed on the Turks by others), the dead were a heavy burden upon the Greek administration locally and in Athens and, in addition, upon future Allied attempts to conclude a workable settlement with Turkey. All the Greek protestations against references to "massacres" in Parliament, explanations of the incident, promises to punish the guilty, and requests for an impartial commission of inquiry were not going to remove the effects of the landing and its aftermath. For the first time since the armistice of Mudros, sizable Turkish demonstrations took place in Constantinople and other towns; they were anti-Greek obviously and anti-British undoubtedly—but not necessarily anti-Allied, since the French had participated only marginally and Italy was no friend to Greece.[1]

Had the Greeks withdrawn immediately, the incident would have remained merely an incident, but instead the Greek forces pressed on,

---

[1] Webb to Curzon, 22 May, including various documents (see particularly James Morgan, representative of high commissioner, Constantinople, at Smyrna, to high commissioner, Constantinople, 20 May), Turkish GOC, Smyrna, telegram to Ministry of War, Constantinople, 20 May, *FO* 371/4218; Lt.-Col. Ian M. Smith, ACO Smyrna, to high commissioner, Constantinople, 24 May, R. Graham, FO, note, 2 July 1919, *FO* 371/4219. The Turkish government released accounts on the landing and the associated atrocities which were read in the Foreign Office: *Rapports officiels*

less to quell Turkish resistance (for there was not yet any organized opposition) than to deny territory to the Italians. By mid-June, a month after the landings, Gough-Calthorpe reported that the Greeks intended to occupy the railway to Aydin, a maneuver which would undoubtedly bring a clash with the Italians. Venizelos was here interpreting the conference's instructions without making further reference to the Allied leaders. To Curzon, the advance aggravated an already dangerous situation and was particularly frustrating since the conference at last seemed to be making progress toward the preservation for Turkey of some, at least, of its former territories. Nobody in the Foreign Office, he reported to Balfour in Paris, favored the recent decisions (Crowe was an exception, but Crowe was in Paris); he sent no protest—"which I cannot but feel will be useless"—but he did advise that clear limits be placed on the Greek advance.[2]

Even Balfour knew something had to be done. The Turks thought the Greek occupation followed from Greek territorial ambitions, and not the Paris conference's desire for law and order. Gough-Calthorpe advised that the Turks might just accept the *fait accompli* of Greek presence if the occupation could avoid incidents and stay within set territorial limits; but while a Greek zone could be established (always assuming Venizelos would agree), an Italian zone could not, for the Italians were there illegally as far as the conference was concerned. The problem was temporarily resolved when the Greeks halted at Aydin, but ominous reports were being received of a clash of Greek and Italian forces on the coast road twenty-five miles south of the Meander River. The area surrounding Aydin was in serious disorder, and numerous deaths, mainly Muslim, were reported—and protested by Montagu. Venizelos intended staying on in the Meander valley, and Balfour supported the Greek position since it was designed to forestall Italy. Balfour's discussions with the Greek leader in Paris raised another issue: even the conference (specifically the heads of delegations remaining in Paris)

---

reçus des autorités militaires Ottomanes sur l'occupation de Smyrne par les troupes Helléniques (Constantinople, 1919), and Ligue pour la défense des droits des ottomanes, *Atrocités Grecques dans le Vilayet de Smyrne* (Geneva, 1919); copies in 123310 and 129830/70100, *FO* 371/4221.

[2] Balfour telegram to Curzon, 18 June, high commissioner, Constantinople, telegrams to FO, 19 June, and to Balfour, Paris, 24 June, Curzon to Balfour, 20 (quoted) and 26 June 1919, *FO* 371/4218.

was unclear as to whether the Greeks were acting under the orders of the Allied occupation commander or were directly responsible to Paris — if, indeed, they were responsible to anybody other than Venizelos.[3]

Only the Italian delegation had a clear-cut objective now: demarcation of Greek and Italian spheres and general retroactive recognition of the latter. The conference, following Clemenceau's lead, was unwilling to legitimize Italy's military action, and the Italian position remained very awkward. They were in illegal occupation with insufficient forces on the spot and only one, unpalatable, alternative to withdrawal — encouragement of Turkish resistance to the Greeks. In the Italian request lay a last chance for preserving the figment of Allied unity, had the Allies recognized the *fait accompli* and set a limited area for Italian occupation, leaving it to Italy to find, soon enough, that the task was more difficult than it appeared on the surface. No evidence, however, exists that British policymakers gave the request more than cursory consideration. It was not only a question of condoning illegality; Curzon, at least, also wanted to limit Greece in Asia Minor to the originally approved area of Smyrna, and any recognition after the fact of Italian expansion might have dangerous repercussions in the Greek sphere.[4]

Curzon's attempt to limit the Greeks could hardly have been less productive. In Paris, it was clear that Lloyd George intended the Greeks to stay. Philip Kerr, Lloyd George's secretary and as Philhellene as his master, urged that after all the Council of Four, not Venizelos, had initiated the action. The Turks could not govern the area, and if the Greeks had been provocative, what about the Turks, and the Italians? And surely the Greeks should now be allowed to take up a defensible position? Balfour, to whom this pleading was addressed, was not prepared to do battle on this issue except to suggest that a Greco-Italian demarcation line, set by General Allenby's officers, would help ease the tension.[5] Allenby was not in command here, and Balfour's misunder-

[3] High Commissioner, Constantinople, telegram to FO, 1 July, Paris telegrams to high commissioner, Constantinople, 4 and 11 July, *FO* 371/4219; high commissioner, Constantinople, telegrams to FO, 16, 17, 23, and 25 July, Montagu private note to Curzon, 22 July 1919, *FO* 371/4220.

[4] Italian note, 12 July, heads of delegations meetings, 12 and 15 July, *DBFP* I/10-11; Curzon telegrams to Balfour, 12 July 1919, *FO* 371/4219.

[5] Kerr to Balfour, 14 July, enclosed in Crowe to Curzon, 10 November, *FO* 371/4222; Balfour telegram to FO, 16 July, *FO* 371/4219; Venizelos

standing of Milne's sphere shows his inattention. Tittoni, the Italian foreign minister, preferred direct Greco-Italian negotiations, but by mid-June the Allies had agreed on a line roughly along the Meander and had established a commission of inquiry to investigate both Greek and Turkish excesses. The Italian problem was sidestepped by a reservation that demarcation was not the same as recognition of Italy's right to occupy—a rather specious legalism, but the Allies saw no advantage in risking the fall of the Italian government, of which Tittoni warned, and Allied unity was always desirable (although not to the Turks, who obviously had more to gain from continued Greco-Italian conflict).[6]

Balfour's additional suggestion designed to ease the conflict, that the Allied commander (by which he still meant Allenby) should have supervision over Italian and Greek movements, was quickly rejected by Field-Marshal Wilson (via Philip Kerr); Milne was under the War Office and subordinate to neither the conference, Allenby, nor the Allied commander on the European side (Franchet d'Espérey). It was not desirable to raise that question again, and in any case the Greek and Italian maneuvers had no official relationship to British armistice-enforcement operations.[7] For the moment, the matter was dropped, and both Greeks and Italians continued to act under their own independent lines of command.

The complicated interrelationships of Greek, Turk, Italian, and

---

to Clemenceau (president of Peace Conference), 10 July, heads of delegations meeting, 16 July 1919, *DBFP* I/11 (appendix, p. 105) and 12.

The standard biography of Kerr is J.R.M. Butler, *Lord Lothian (Philip Kerr), 1882-1940* (N.Y., 1960).

[6] Balfour telegram to FO, 16 July, note 5, chapter 4; Venizelos-Tittoni agreement is discussed in heads of delegations meeting, 18 July, *DBFP* I/14; Crowe to Curzon, 1 August 1919, *FO* 371/4215; Helmreich, *Paris to Sèvres*, pp. 104-5. A brief review of the policies of Tommaso Tittoni and the other postwar Italian foreign ministers may be found in H. Stuart Hughes, "The Early Diplomacy of Italian Fascism: 1922-1932," Gordon A. Craig and Felix Gilbert, eds., *The Diplomats, 1919-1939* (Princeton, N.J., 1953), pp. 210-33, and Denis Mack Smith, *Italy, a Modern History* (Ann Arbor, Mich., 1959), Ch. 38-39. Commission of inquiry: Smith, *Ionian Vision*, pp. 111-3.

[7] Kerr private to Wilson, 19 and 25 July, Wilson private to Kerr, 21 and 24 July, *WO* 106/1572 (Wilson was promoted to field marshal in July 1919); Morgan, Smyrna, to high commissioner, Constantinople, 21 July 1919, *FO* 371/4220.

British interests had not been resolved, let alone the larger problems of Turkey as a whole—but one conclusion was safe: all other parties tended to blame the British. The Turks blamed them for approving Greek intervention, the Italians blamed them for the same and for failure to recognize Italian interests, and the Greeks now blamed them for tying their hands. However, both Greeks and Italians now rested in their respective areas, and the Turkish authorities could hope that this would remain the case. An end, however temporary, to Greco-Italian expansion and a commission of inquiry gave Turkish authorities in Constantinople some small chance to shore up their authority in the interior, an authority which had been badly, perhaps irreparably, damaged by the Greek landings.[8]

THE RISE OF KEMAL

Viewed from the Turkish perspective, the Greek landing in May was the most but not the only annoying Allied action. As has been seen, the Allies had assumed considerable control over Constantinople, although this was an expected consequence of Turkish defeat. In March 1919, however, the Turks were startled by an Allied demand for the apprehension and detention of several dozen war criminals. The subsequent arrests included many government officials, at least some of whom were criminals in the generally accepted sense. They had been responsible for barbarous atrocities in the treatment of British and Indian prisoners-of-war (many of whom never lived to tell of their experiences) or in the extermination of the Armenian community. The lists also included, however, some men of prominence whose culpability in the direct sense was more questionable, such as Ahmed Amin Bey [Yalman], editor of the newspaper *Vakit,* important intellectual and molder of public opinion; Ahmed Agayev [Ağaoğlu], leading westernizer and writer; and Mehmed Zia [Gokalp], an important nationalist theoretician and writer. Damad Ferid Pasha's government was nominally responsible for arrest and trial of the accused but found it con-

---

[8] Morgan, Smyrna, to high commissioner, Constantinople, 30 July, Wilson private note to unidentified recipient, 6 August, 113414/70100, *FO* 371/4220; heads of delegations, 5 and 6 August 1919, *DBFP,* I/28-29.

venient to ask Britain to take charge of (and therefore responsibility for) the prisoners; most were therefore interned on Malta.[9]

Removal of the prisoners coincided with the Smyrna landings, and the French protested that they had not been consulted. The protest was disregarded, and British authorities continued to work from a growing list. It started with a joint Armenian-Greek card file of 6000-7000 names, but others were now added for failure to comply with the armistice, insolence to British officers, and so on. Where a particular case was questionable, "general principles" were applied, meaning that anyone the Ferid Pasha government wished to see out of the country soon was under arrest or had gone underground.[10] Neither those held prisoner nor those forced to flee were particularly enamored of the experience, for which again Britain took full blame. Reaction to the Greek landings was strong, but it should not be used to conceal reaction to the arrest of political leaders. The two events, combined with fears of a future Armenian state and other postwar changes, ensured that from May-June of 1919 Turkish resistance became a visible feature of the Middle Eastern situation.

Already in March the Turkish administrators were reportedly distributing arms to irregular Turkish units for opposing any closer occupation of the interior. In May the Turkish War Ministry had dispatched Mustafa Kemal Pasha, already a well-known general, to the interior as inspector-general of troops in eastern Anatolia. If the British authorities were informed of this posting in advance, no particular

[9] Lists of the arrested may be found in DMI to FO, 26 March (a list of roughly 100 whose arrest was demanded, about half of whom were Germans), high commissioner, Constantinople, to Balfour, 22 March and 9 April (listing those arrested), Webb to Balfour, 7 April, *FO* 371/4173, and high commissioner, Constantinople, to Balfour, 30 May 1919 (on deportations), *FO* 371/4174. See also, for careers of some of those arrested, Niyazi Berkes, *The Development of Secularism in Turkey* (Montreal, 1964), pp. 349, 464-65; Dankwart A. Rustow, "The Army and the Founding of the Turkish Republic," *World Politics* 11 (1959): 531; Halidé Edib, *The Turkish Ordeal . . .* (N.Y., 1928), pp. 36, 59, 343; Schlicklin, *Angora,* pp. 126-28. The Malta camp is discussed in Mackenzie, *Greek Memories,* p. 295.

[10] High commissioner, Constantinople, to Balfour, 30 May and 1 August, and (de Robeck now) to Curzon, 21 September; various documents included in GOC Constantinople to WO, 1 June 1919, refer to French complaint, all *FO* 371/4174.

notice was taken of it. By the first week of June, however, Admiral Gough-Calthorpe was already requesting Kemal's recall for stirring up trouble. The Turkish authorities were officially willing to cooperate, but Kemal was not. A British captain was still able to talk to him in Samsun on 2 June, but even at that time Kemal was sending out a stream of telegrams designed to encourage resistance to the Greeks—and to the friends of the Greeks.[11]

Kemal's road to national leadership, which began in Samsun in May (in later years Kemal would refer to his landing on 19 May as his birthday), has been well presented elsewhere, and there is no need to retrace that story except to remark that while the events which followed were not unknown to the British authorities, there was very little which could be done to alter their course. Kemal's important connection with Kiazim Karabekir Pasha, commander of the remnants of the Caucasian army now based in Erzerum, could not be forestalled any more than could his subsequent congress of Turkish leaders at Sivas (August 1919). Kidston could still write in late June, "I know nothing of Mustapha Kemal . . ." in response to puzzling reports, but some of Kemal's friends were known—such as Rauf Bey, who has signed the armistice— and the High Commission in Constantinople was convinced that the movement was masterminded from the War Ministry in the capital.

[11.] Lt. J.S. Perring (Samsun), 23 March, Capt. L.H. Hurst (Samsun), 24 March and 12 June, reports (58428/521); high commissioner, Constantinople, to Turkish Minister of Foreign Affairs, 8 June, *FO* 371/ 4157-58; Webb to Curzon, 21 May, includes a clipping from the *Moniteur Oriental* on Kemal's appointment; *FO* 371/4191. There is no evidence to support the contention that the British officials in some way were responsible for Kemal's appointment or for his subsequent success, although suggestions to the contrary were born out of Admiral Bristol's strong Anglophobia: "Indications here that may be truth that British are secretly supporting Mustapha Kemal movement," is one example of the unsupported assertions of which he was capable; Bristol telegram to American Peace Mission, Paris, 29 September 1919, *Bristol Papers,* box 27.

Kemal's rise is discussed in Lord Kinross, *Ataturk: A Biography of Mustafa Kemal . . .* (N.Y., 1965), particularly Ch. 19; Hovannisian, *Republic,* I, pp. 423-43; Robinson, *First Turkish Republic,* Ch. 2; Lewis, *Emergence of Modern Turkey,* Ch. 8; all of these works have extensive bibliographies. See also A.A. Cruickshank, "The Young Turk Challenge in Postwar Turkey," *Middle East Journal* 22 (1968): 17-28; and *A Speech Delivered by Ghazi Mustapha Kemal, President of the Turkish Republic, October, 1927* (Leipzig, 1929).

When in June British reinforcements could not disembark at Samsun because the local Turkish commander threatened oppostion and when the grand vizier reported that Kemal had answered recall with resignation, the situation had become alarming. Allied officers in the interior still underestimated Kemal's success—not surprising, given the substantial difficulties he faced at the outset; one report concluded, for example, that ". . . the whole movement appears to have had little success and for the most part not much interest is taken." Any tendency to belittle the movement was offset, however, by the willingness the Constantinople government showed in using Kemal as a sword to dangle over Britain's head: Constantinople could hardly be expected to bring Kemal to heel if the Greeks were going to persist in such actions as the occupation of Aydin.[12]

This deviousness was counterproductive, for it led to the easy conclusion that the Turkish government, or at least the more ardent Young Turk members still in it, was behind Kemal's movement and did have the capacity to control him. "The Turkish Government and the National Defense Organization," as Kemal's movement was now known, "are to all intents and purposes one and the same thing today," wrote one of Gough-Calthorpe's staff. Between Ferid Pasha and Kemal was an unbridgeable gap, but this report shows the attitude adopted by British authorities in Constantinople. Formally, of course, Kemal had severed his connection with the official government, and, as Gough-Calthorpe had to admit, that government's powers in central Anatolia were virtually extinct by mid-summer; still, the movement was more than spontaneous and received encouragement through Young Turk or-

[12] High commissioner, Constantinople, telegram to FO, 23 June, with Kidston minute (quoted), 24 June, *FO* 371/4277; high commissioner, Constantinople, telegram to FO, 8 July, and Webb private to R. Graham, FO, 28 June, *FO* 371/4219. Samsun incident: high commissioner, Constantinople, telegram to FO, 9 July, Lt. Col. Ian Smith report, 13 July, on talk with Rafet Bey (then GOC, III Corps, Samsun), FO to WO, 17 July, DMI to FO, 29 July, and Perring, Samsun, report, 5 July (quoted) 1919, *FO* 371/4158. A different account is in Edib, *Ordeal,* p. 47, claiming that the troops were landed with the idea in mind of breaking up the Sivas conference. Kemal's birthday: Kinross, *Ataturk,* p. 185n. Kiazim Kiarbekir is described in Lt.-Col. A. Rawlinson, *Adventures in the Near East, 1918-1922* (N.Y., 1924), pp. 173-74; his memoirs have been published as *Istiklal Harbimiz* ["Our War of Independence"] (Istanbul, 1960). Rauf Bey: see Arnold J. Toynbee, *Acquaintances* (London, 1967), pp. 230-39.

ganizational support. In this sense, a few well-judged arrests and dismissals might help, but fear of Greek, Italian, and Armenian aggression was the true cause of Kemal's success to date.[13]

A further problem was the Turkish government's request to hold elections for the Chamber of Deputies. This request was difficult to oppose, since it was in harmony with Wilsonian principles—to say nothing of the formal Turkish constitution—but more important, Kemal could always hold elections of his own in the interior. Gough-Calthorpe had no delusions about Ferid Pasha's dim prospects. As he warned Curzon by telegram, "I think you should take into consideration possibility of events taking such a turn as would result in establishment of an independent and probably intensely fanatical and anti-European Government in Asia Minor rejecting authority of Constantinople and sovereignty of Sultan." Ferid Pasha was cooperative enough, but many of his subordinates were not; in fact, it had taken the grand vizier five days of internal struggle just to get Kemal's recall order accepted. Removal of the Greeks by diplomacy might have improved his position, but instead the Greeks assumed more and more control of the Smyrna district, the general effect being, as Milne reported after a personal visit in early August, "a hopeless state of growing anarchy." It was for this reason, in part, that Ferid Pasha requested and Gough-Calthorpe recommended the transfer of responsibility for the "criminals," for both wished to see the current government survive.[14]

Gough-Calthorpe could do nothing about the Greeks, since his hands were tied by orders from Paris. The result was an inescapable vicious circle: Greek presence brought Turkish opposition; opposition meant unrest, particularly where there were Christian minorities but no Allied occupation; unrest brought new fears on all sides, further requests to the Turkish authorities to cease and desist, and therefore further demonstration of the inability of those same authorities to affect events in the interior; such weakness, finally, only strengthened the Kemalist move-

[13] High commissioner, Constantinople, telegrams to FO, 23 and 27 July, *FO* 371/4227, and letter to Curzon, 30 July, enclosing report by Commander C. Heathcote-Smith, 24 July 1919 (quoted), *FO* 371/4158.

[14] High commissioner, Constantinople, telegrams to Curzon, 27 (quoted) July and 1 and 2 August, and letters of 31 July and 5 August 1919, *FO* 371/4227; GOC Constantinople telegram to WO, 11 August (quoted), enclosed in WO to FO, 21 August 1919, *FO* 371/4220.

ment and organized resistance. Even when Ferid Pasha replied that he was able to send men to a particular district, permission was denied on the grounds that any given unit might go over to Kemal once out of the hands of the Constantinople authorities.[15]

Decisions of this sort weakened Ferid Pasha, but the High Commission was not as alarmed as it might have been. The grand vizier had managed to temporize sufficiently on elections (they would be held, but the Chamber of Deputies could not meet for some months), and there was now the prospect of delimitation of the Greek sphere. Finally, if the government fell for any reason (in addition to political complications, it was also bankrupt, or nearly so), the probable successors, Tevfiq Pasha or Izzet Pasha, were regarded as acceptable alternatives. Such complacency is surprising, but it is perhaps to be explained by the very misleading reports that Kemal's most recent conference, at Erzerum (23 July-7 August 1919), had fallen flat and ended by favoring an American or a British mandate for Turkey on the one condition that the mandate include all Turkey. When Admiral Mark Bristol, the American representative in Constantinople, warned the Constantinople government that if massacres of Christians did not stop, the "secure sovereignty" promised Turkey in the Fourteen Points might be withdrawn, British authorities were only annoyed that Bristol had acted independently. They wished he had not given the document to Ferid Pasha but had published it so that Kemal would learn of it—the whole point being, and it is an important point, that despite the irritating independence of Kemal and his supporters, Britain and Paris still believed that they had the upper hand if it came to a trial of strength.[16]

This impression was inaccurate, as Lieutenant-Colonel A. Rawlinson could have said. Responsible for enforcing the armistice in eastern Turkey and Erzerum, Rawlinson was finding it most difficult to track down military equipment, particularly valuable and portable items like machine guns. The Caucasian Army had retreated with its weapons, which therefore should have been in the area. Rawlinson spent two hours with Kemal at Erzerum on the last day of the conference, and

[15] Webb to Curzon, 17 August, *FO* 371/4221, and 23 August 1919, *FO* 371/4158.

[16] Capt. Perring (Samsun) report, 29 July, Webb telegrams to FO, 22 (on Perring report) and 23 (on Bristol, with FO minutes) August, and letter, 30 August (enclosing Erzerum manifesto), *FO* 371/4158; Webb to Curzon, 27 August 1919, *FO* 371/4227.

as a result had no doubts about Kemal's intentions. He was also convinced that the Kemalist and Bolshevik movements were indistinguishable, although Kemal disclaimed any Bolshevik connection, but it was a bit early for his superiors to make that association so easily. Rawlinson was to suffer a lengthy stretch of imprisonment at Kemal's hands, but his report reached the Foreign Office by September, providing Kidston and others with food for thought.[17]

Meanwhile in August Gough-Calthorpe handed over his command and the attached High Commissionership to Vice-Admiral Sir John M. de Robeck. Although de Robeck had a fresh viewpoint, he was under no illusions. By mid-September, he was warning that Ferid Pasha and Milne both agreed that a grave crisis existed. Only the fact that British troops still occupied the railway prevented Kemal's growing forces in the east from assisting the irregulars confronting the Greeks in the west. Even at that, Milne was already pulling his forward units out of Samsun and closing the rail line from Eskishehir to Ankara in order to avoid a clash. If the troops along the remaining rail lines, together with the Italians at Konya and the Indian units at Afyonkarahisar and Eskishehir, were also withdrawn, it would mean the end of remaining British prestige and influence and a serious reduction in Constantinople's food supplies.[18]

Milne needed orders; the War Office asked the Foreign Office, and the Foreign Office asked what did the War Office suggest? If Britain wished to enforce any future treaty with Turkey, she could not withdraw; if she stayed, a clash with Kemal was likely so long as the Greeks and Italians stayed, and probably even if they did not. The worst danger was that British troops might have to stay on to fight the Turks on behalf of the Greeks, a prospect which Lloyd George surely had not considered when he supported the Greek landings; the prime minister was

[17] DMI to FO, 4 September, enclosing Rawlinson report (undated), 126001/521, *FO* 371/4158; GOC Constantinople to Bridges, 20 October 1919, 167965/521, *FO* 371/4161, however, notes that in all other areas save Erzerum Milne, at least, was satisfied with the collection of arms.

[18] High commissioner, Constantinople (Gough-Calthorpe), telegram to FO, 31 July, *FO* 608/108; and (de Robeck) 13 and 18 September, and GOC Constantinople telegram to WO, 17 September 1919, *FO* 371/4158-59. There is no biography of either Gough-Calthorpe or de Robeck, but see, for the latter, Admiral Sir William James, *Admiral Sir William Fisher* (London, 1943), especially p. 85; Fisher was de Robeck's chief of staff.

too often closeted with his friend Venizelos for dispassionate realism to overcome the persuasiveness of their mutual reassurances. Kidston in the Foreign Office, for one, advocated an extreme solution: inviting Kemal to London to discuss terms. "I am not at all sure that we shall not find ourselves compelled to do something of the kind in the end, especially if we have to abandon the railway to him . . .". This was impossible without Lloyd George's unlikely approval, but the Constantinople government could try the direct approach, and Ferid Pasha himself appeared ready to go to Kemal or at least to send a high-ranking representative.[19]

In early October, lack of British support and the hothouse political atmosphere of Constantinople proved Ferid Pasha's undoing, and rather to London's surprise he was replaced by Ali Riza Pasha, an aging soldier loyal to the throne. Meanwhile the War Office, without instructions and faced with growing nationalist pressure, had to take protective measures. Churchill, well aware of the troop shortages and eager to avoid Turkish entanglements, even suggested withdrawal all the way to the Dardanelles. Milne considered such drastic measures unnecessary at the moment, for he had enough troops to hold Eshishehir and Afyonkarahisar. He preferred to withdraw all British troops beyond Izmit and turn over the railway to the Constantinople government's troops if this was possible. The British troops stayed, but Milne was ordered not to use his forces to support the civilian administration of Constantinople. If staying on meant open hostilities against Kemal, he was to withdraw.[20]

Somewhat after the fact, Churchill circulated a memorandum inspired by Milne's request for instructions. Kemal's "patriotic organization" offered only risks if Britain continued a policy which might lead to confrontation. Such a clash would increase pan-Islamic sympathies,

[19] Lloyd George-Venizelos talks, 5 September (Henqueville, Normandy) and 31 October (10 Downing St.), *Lloyd George Papers,* F/92/12/4-5; Kidston minute, 22 September (quoted), 13070/521, *FO* 371/4158; high commissioner, Constantinople, telegrams to FO, 23 and 30 September 1919, *FO* 371/4159.

[20] High commissioner, Constantinople, telegram to FO, 30 September, with FO minutes; WO telegrams to GOC Constantinople, 24 September and 2 October, and GOC Constantinople telegram to WO, 29 September, Webb to Curzon, 10 October 1919, *FO* 371/4159; Ryan, *Dragoman,* p. 141.

perhaps allied with Bolshevism, engender more Arab unrest, and probably mean more Armenian massacres. Withdrawal, on the other hand, would avoid all this and yet not commit Britain to any one policy. Prestige might be lost, but (an argument which would be heard more than once) how much more prestige would be lost if Britain withdrew under Turkish threats. That reoccupation would be most difficult and would also commit Britain to a policy was not mentioned. The answer, said Curzon, was an early peace treaty.[21] But a treaty still seemed no nearer at hand.

PARIS AND KEMAL

The signature of the Treaty of Versailles on 28 June 1919 and the departure of President Wilson for the United States was not the end of the Paris peace conference. The formal treaty-making machinery remained in being, with the Council of Four replaced by a Council of Heads of Delegations. Lloyd George remained a few hours away in London, and Clemenceau was on the scene as continuing president of the conference. Delay would naturally occur if American participation were involved, but this was less important with respect to Turkey than Germany, for the United States was never at war with Turkey and an American signature was not strictly necessary on any Turkish peace. It remained for the other Allies to work out mutually acceptable terms, although there was still hope that the Americans would finally accept some mandatory responsibility for Turkey. For that reason, and because of the continuing problem of Greco-Italian claims in western Turkey, the conference temporized under Clemenceau's direction. All that was done was to send a commission of British, French, and Italian representatives to gather evidence on atrocities, and then the commission's report was shelved in the end, since no Greeks had been admitted and Venizelos's claim of trial without defense was accepted as valid. In the meantime, conference policy, by default, was to wait, both for some American decision and for the report on Middle East opinion from the solely American King-Crane Commission which had been sent out to assess the local situation and was now in Constantinople. Although every indication from Washington showed the

---

[21] Churchill memorandum, 9 October 1919, with Kidston (13 October) and Curzon (undated) minutes, 139550/521, *FO* 371/4159.

Americans unlikely to accept a mandate, the British Cabinet, at least, continued to hope.[22]

Foreign Office experts in Paris went on producing treaty drafts, for it was their job to persevere in the nearly hopeless attempt to achieve Allied unanimity. The revised draft of mid-August, based upon those made the previous spring, outlined mandates for the entire Ottoman Empire, including separate mandatory areas for Constantinople and the Straits and for Anatolia. The new draft was Montagu's first look at a proposed Turkish treaty. India and the India Office had not been consulted, even informally, in either London or Paris, on its preparation, although Montagu had participated in the general preconference discussions about the future of the Ottoman Empire. This failure is comprehensible only when the notorious compartmentalization of the Paris delegation is recalled; it does not detract, however, from the efficacy of Montagu's own intervention at higher levels on India's behalf. "I never remember seeing this Treaty with Turkey before," wrote Montagu on the draft; the Foreign Office had said it was only a draft, but this was taken as an indication that they were about to press for its final adoption. The Indian delegation had simply not been consulted, said Hirtzel; "I think we ought to claim a voice." Montagu soon did exactly that to Curzon: "I may say for your private information that I cannot convince myself that the Indian delegation at the Peace Conference has ever been seriously treated as they were promised they should be, for they have had no opportunity of influencing the decisions about the territories they are interested in," meaning really that the decision had gone against his own ideas.[23]

Montagu was not only making a general protest; he was also opposed to details, particularly on the future of Turkey and the Straits,

[22] Venizelos to Clemenceau, 19 July, 22 August, 28 September, *FRUS, Paris Conference,* VII, pp. 249-50, VIII, pp. 476-77; heads of delegations, 20 August, 30 September, and 16 October, *DBFP* I/38, 68, II/11; Lindsay telegram to FO, 16 August, *DBFP* IV/485; War Cabinet 618-19, 19-20 August 1919, *CAB* 23/12. On the King-Crane Commission, see Harry N. Howard, *The King-Crane Commission . . .* (Beirut, 1963).

[23] Paris Delegation to Curzon, 5 July, *FO* 371/4231; IO to FO, August draft, unsent, Montagu note for Hirtzel (quoted), 19 August, FO to Balfour, 18 August, with Hirtzel minute (quoted) for Montagu, 3 September, Shuckburgh draft letter, 24 July, Montagu private to Curzon, 28 August (quoted), and official version, IO to FO, 14 October 1919, *L/P&S/*10/851.

where the draft to his mind did not correspond to Lloyd George's pledge, and on the hypocrisy and "nonsense" of a Jewish community in Palestine. The point at issue, however, was Turkey, and Montagu's viewpoint was clear as he explained to Hirtzel: ". . . I can never be a party to any Treaty that makes any country other than Turkey responsible for the peace, order and good government of Turkey, and the sooner my view on that point is communicated to the authorities that [be] the better." Specifically, he wanted no reference made to the religious position of the Shaikh al-Islam, normally head of the Muslim judicial process in the Ottoman Empire; no mandatory for Turkey—which should have a treaty similar to Persia; Constantinople to remain Turkish; and any Armenian solution to include participation by the non-Armenian population. All this was spelled out in Montagu's letter to Curzon.

> Is it absolutely impossible to convince you of the necessity for keeping our pledges? Are you unmoved by the united evidence which comes from India without exception that a form of peace such as you contemplate (in which you said at the Cabinet you were thinking of India) is likely to be disastrous to India in present circumstances? If so, it is no use wasting your time and patience by pursuing the subject.

The secretary insisted throughout the discussion that Lloyd George had given his word on Constantinople. That this view was strenuously opposed by both his chief political advisors in the India Office, Shuckburgh and Hirtzel, made little difference; both, like many others, accepted Lloyd George's argument that the "pledge" was no more than a temporarily valid offer to the Turks of certain terms which had been refused at the time. The expediency of giving Constantinople back to the Turks was a debatable issue, but no question of principle arose. Montagu, however, had made his position clear weeks before; the pledge ". . . was made to the world and did not promise special terms to one enemy but gave an assurance that nationality was to be respected in Turkey as elsewhere."[24]

[24] Montagu note for Hirtzel (quoted), 19 August, note 23, chapter 4; Shuckburgh minute, 31 July, on Muslim representations, with Hirtzel, Montagu (quoted) undated minutes, 4216/19, *L/P&S*/10/796; Montagu

Lengthy Cabinet discussions of the Turkish problem (19-20 August) resulted in no alteration of the draft sufficient to please Montagu, although he did emerge convinced that the majority of his Cabinet colleagues shared his viewpoint. Lloyd George's interpretation, however, was decisive, and Montagu was alarmed to find that Curzon, who advocated expelling the Turk from Constantinople, would have the responsibility for further negotiations at Paris; it made little difference that Curzon happened to share Montagu's view on Smyrna. Curzon, however, had had little more to say on the draft treaty than Montagu, for with the exception of details on the Arabian peninsula it was the work of the Middle Eastern political section in Paris (Toynbee, Mallet, Forbes Adam, among others), without consultation with the Foreign Office: "a bad and dangerous arrangement," Curzon called it, but there was little he could do.[25]

In the light of such interdepartmental confusion, it was unlikely that a British draft agreeable to all parties was possible. Until an American answer was forthcoming, a decision was not immediately urgent. But the favorable American decision, expected in August, promised in September, and virtually guaranteed for October, in reality became less and less likely, and at least provisional agreement on the garrisoning of Turkey was necesary. The conference could not continue indefinitely, as Lloyd George pointed out to the French. Since Britain faced serious pressures which inclined policy toward an accommodation

---

private to Lloyd George, 20 August, *Lloyd George Papers,* F/40/2/59; Jones, *Whitehall Diary,* pp. 92-93; *The Times,* 10 September 1919, includes a collective letter warning Lloyd George of Muslim sympathies signed by Aubrey Herbert, Lord Islington, and others. Montagu, although a Jew himself, was a leading opponent of Zionism, and particularly the repercussions of "Balfour's unfortunate letter" (private to Curzon, 28 August, note 23, chapter 4). He himself, ironically, was the target of anti-Semitism on occasion; see Eugene F. Irschick, *Politics and Social Conflict in South India . . .* (Berkeley, Calif., 1969), pp. 145-46, for an example.

[25] War Cabinet 618-19, 19-20 August, *CAB* 23/12; Montagu private to Lloyd George, 20 August and 8 September, *Lloyd George Papers,* F/40/2/ 59-60; Paris delegation to FO, 26 August 1919, with H.W. Young and Curzon (quoted) minutes, 121884/100141, *FO* 371/4231; on the Arab chapter, see Busch, *Britain, India, and the Arabs,* Ch. 6. The lack of consultation with the FO was typical, not exceptional; as Harold Nicolson put it (diary entry, 17 April 1919, *Peacemaking, 1919,* p. 314), "We never tell them what is happening and we never answer any of their letters."

with France on the Middle East, and since the French had made a proposal for the occupation of Cilicia, the way was clear for a partial readjustment. The French plan would ostensibly establish a controlling force in Armenia and eastern Turkey and thereby ameliorate the worsening conditions there. It called for 12,000 of Franchet d'Espérey's forces from Mersin and Alexandretta on the Mediterranean to move by land to Armenia. The idea of such a force marching more than 500 miles from Alexandretta to Erzerum through hostile enemy territory was absurd, and therefore it was concluded that the French had some ulterior motive—perhaps even wished to threaten the British military position, although that reaction was soon disregarded. Britain said it would only support the plan if the troops moved by sea, in which case the stores accumulated in the Caucasus would be handed to them.[26]

The scheme was difficult to fathom, unless the French concluded that they could solve the Turkish question through the forceful creation of "Greater Armenia." But Britain had no interest in such a creation now, particularly if implemented by France; some Foreign Office advisors had already concluded that the real solution lay in a unified Turkey and that any extended French occupation in Cilicia would only make matters more difficult—particularly in getting the Greeks and Italians out. Lloyd George did not share this concern. In the interests of his Caucasian policy (one possible substitute for Britain in that area had always been France) and to solve the bitter Anglo-French quarrel over Syria's future, he was willing, as always, to disregard Foreign Office advice. An Anglo-French agreement in September, besides promising Syria to France, designated Cilicia a French sphere of operations as part of the Syrian command. French forces in the area became the Armée francaise du Levant, and its commander Haut-commisaire de la .République francaise en Syrie et en Cilicie, a recognition of the nature of the trade: in exchange for Syria, France had yielded its claims to Mosul and Kurdistan, and therefore suddenly had far less interest in Greater Armenia.[27]

[26] Heads of delegations, 29 August, *FRUS,* Paris, VIII, p. 11, and 15 September, *DBFP* I/46 and 57; FO telegram to Balfour, 2 September, *DBFP* IV/503; Paris delegation, Military section, telegram to CIGS, 2 September, Graham note for Curzon, 1 August, and Curzon telegram to private secretary, 8 September, FO 371/3668; War Cabinet 621, 2 September 1919, *CAB* 23/12; Helmreich, *Paris to Sèvres,* Ch. VIII-IX.

[27] Hardinge minute on Vansittart memorandum, 5 September, 132926/

French occupation of Cilicia made a unified Turkey very unlikely, but still some settlement was necessary. By the end of October, the Paris delegation was reaching the conclusion that the Americans were probably out of the running. The Greeks, Italians, and French would continue to hold their respective areas in some form, and therefore the largest remaining question was Constantinople and the Straits, although there was also Armenia. In the Straits, since no single power appeared willing to take the job, the only recourse was some sort of international administration, presumably under the League. Various options were still available for the location of the sultan and the government, but only within this framework, or so at least Forbes Adam reported privately to Sir Andrew Ryan, chief dragoman in Constantinople. Solution of detailed questions, however, was "largely dependent on the weight finally pulled by Montagu & the India Office & Indian Muslims."[28]

Crowe in Paris was having very similar thoughts; as the most outspoken advocate of partition, his concern over Indian interference indicates the effectiveness of that pressure.[29] But Crowe was an optimist regarding Allied ability to impose whatever solution they desired upon Kemal. Such an attitude was growing rarer daily. De Robeck, for example, was convinced that conference disregard of the Smyrna investigation (which in general condemned both Greeks and the conference decision which put them there) was having a deplorable effect. Allowing the Greeks to remain in Aydin also stood to Britain's dis-

---

50535, *FO* 371/4215; Balfour note, 13 September, 384/1/1, *FO* 608/106; heads of delegations, 15 September 1919, *DBFP* I/57; Roskill, *Hankey,* II, pp. 114-15; Du Véou, *La Passion de la Cilicie,* p. 81, gives titles.

[28] Forbes Adam (Paris) private to Ryan, 29 October (quoted), Ryan private to Forbes Adam, 26 November, *Ryan Papers* (Public Record Office, *FO* 800/240); Forbes Adam private to Kidston, 8 December 1919, 162140/521, *FO* 371/4161. Ryan's memoirs are *The Last of the Dragomans;* he was the sort of figure regarded by many as an *éminence grise.* As Halidé Edib put it (*Ordeal,* p. 17), he was ". . . the man who had been directing the British policy in Turkey for years."

[29] Crowe private to Kidston, 17 November, *DBFP* IV/596 (". . . but of course there remains the question raised by the attitude of Indian Moslems and the India Office."); see also Hardinge private to Hohler (Constantinople), 15 December 1919, expressing a similar concern, *Hardinge Papers* (Cambridge University Library), 1919, II.

credit, for Britain was not unjustly regarded as Greece's best friend in Turkey. The Council tried to stress the temporary nature of Greek occupation, as part of the Allied occupation, but this view had little visible effect on the Turks and only irritated Venizelos—temporary occupation was not what he had in mind at all.[30]

The plain fact was that the Kemalist movement was growing daily and now had complete control over the interior. Kemal knew of the Caucasian withdrawal, the abandonment of Samsun and other coastal towns, and the pullback along the railway, and all were encouraging signs. The congress in Sivas in September was a further step, for its demands upon Allies and sultan alike and its clear claim to all Anatolia east of Afyonkarahisar reinforced Kemal's strength. As Webb wrote privately to de Robeck, if a stiff treaty were really to be imposed, God help the Christian minority left in Turkey; "the country which is entursted with the Mandate will be able to start in on a nice little war all over again." The one hope, the secret mission from the Constantinople government to Kemal, had ended in failure as a result of Kemal's suspicions and Constantinople's unwillingness to submit to him.[31]

By November the Constantinople regime's credit both materially and figuratively had slipped disastrously. The currency was in a state of collapse, and de Robeck had already advised that without a substantial loan the total breakdown of administration could be expected. The Treasury quickly took exception to a loan, for the only possible security was control of income in some area of Turkey, and such responsibility was hardly desirable under the circumstances. The city government in the capital was also faltering from basic insolvency aggravated by a tragic influx of refugees (and no place to which to send them) and inter-Allied disagreement on many administrative matters. De Robeck concluded that these problems might have to be alleviated by actual formal

[30] High commissioner, Constantinople, to Curzon, 28 October, *FO* 371/4222; and telegrams to FO, 12 and 19 November, *FO* 371/4223; heads of delegations, 10, 11, and 12 November, *DBFP* II/18-20; Lloyd George-Venizelos meeting, 31 October, *Lloyd George Papers,* F/92/12/5; Venizelos private to Crowe, 20 November 1919, 156260/70100, *FO* 371/4223.

[31] Webb private to de Robeck, 11 October, *De Robeck Papers* (Churchill College, Cambridge), 6/24; GHQ, Constantinople, telegram to WO, 18 October, *FO* 371/4159; high commissioner, Constantinople, to Curzon, 28 October and 16 November 1919, *FO* 371/4160.

Allied occupation, and Milne, finding the War Ministry increasingly uncooperative and disclaiming all responsibility for troop movements in the interior toward Greek positions, probably would have agreed.[32]

Formal, declared occupation of the city was one possibility. Another was the hope that a treaty of specified terms, agreed by the Turks, might yet undermine support for the nationalist movement. This came nearer realization, at least, from the aspect of the essential preliminary Allied agreement, when in mid-December France took the initiative and offered a solution which led to intense discussion in late 1919 and early 1920. Such an overture was encouraging to those observers who already feared a separate Franco-Kemalist agreement, since it was doubtless fostered by growing Franco-Turkish disagreement over Cilicia.[33] There existed a third course of action for Britain: the British presence in Iraq offered the chance of backing yet another minority element in Turkey— the Kurds.

KURDISTAN

Kurdistan, normally, is taken to be the mountainous region of southeastern Turkey, northern and northeastern Iraq, and northwestern Persia. In British usage at the time, however, the term meant the Turkish vilayets of Van, Diyarbakir, and Mosul, roughly to a northern line of Erivan-Erzerum-Erzincan-Marash. Persian Kurdistan was a special problem. To the Kurds themselves, Kurdistan was where there were Kurds in any number, and where there were, this hardy mountaineer people could be both problem and opportunity depending upon one's viewpoint. The British in Iraq, having occupied Mosul at the moment of armistice and being very concerned over the future Iraqi frontier, were to find them both.[34]

[32] On finance, see especially high commissioner, Constantinople, telegram to FO, 20 September, Treasury to FO, 1 October, and other documents in file *FO* 371/4140; high commissioner, Constantinople, to Curzon, 10 and 11 November, *FO* 371/4160, and GOC Constantinople to high commissioner, Constantinople, 11 December 1919, *FO* 371/4161.

[33] Derby private to Curzon, 11 December, *Curzon Papers,* F/6/2; high commissioner, Constantinople, to Curzon, 12 December 1919, *DBFP,* IV/399.

[34] Great Britain, Foreign Office, Historical Section, *Armenia and Kurdistan,* p. 1; see also War Office, General Staff (Palestine), Intelligence,

The Iraqi administration was familiar with the Kurds well before Mosul was occupied, and Sir Percy Cox had stopped off in Paris in June 1918 for a talk with Sherif (Cherif) Pasha, self-proclaimed Kurdish leader and member of an important tribe of southern Kurdistan, but one who had not been in his homeland since childhood. "Beau Cherif," as he was called by one expert—"a Stambouli Pasha" to Toynbee—was more familiar with Paris than Kurdistan, but he might still be useful. The pasha urged that Britain take on at least the southern districts, an idea already in the air through the influence of Mark Sykes, as one way to facilitate the simultaneous development of Armenia to the north, since a British-controlled Kurdistan could be a helpful friendly neighbor. But any plans for Kurdistan had to await a peace treaty and solution of the more immediate problem that the Sykes-Picot Agreement had assigned the vilayet of Mosul, and thus much of Kurdistan, to France. For these reasons, only a temporary-appearing military administration was established here, and not the more elaborate structure that had developed in Basra and Baghdad.[35]

Kurdistan and the Kurds (Mt. Carmel, Palestine, [1920]). Useful works by participants include C.J. Edmonds, *Kurds, Turks and Arabs, 1919-1925* (London, 1957); W.R. Hay, *Two Years in Kurdistan . . . 1918-1920* (London, 1921); [Iraq], *Diary of Maj. E.W. Noel . . . on special Duty in Kurdistan . . . 1919* (Basrah, 1919; copy in IO Library); Mesopotamia, Office of the Civil Commissioner, *Precis of Affairs in Southern Kurdistan during the Great War* (by E.J. Ross) (Baghdad, 1919); and, from the Persian side, Hassan Arfa, *The Kurds: An Historical and Political Study* (London, 1966). Further detailed information may be found in A.M. Hamilton, *Road Through Kurdistan . . .* (London, 1937), an interesting account of cutting the road from Arbil to the Persian frontier; Humphrey Bowman, *Middle East Window* (London, 1942), pp. 212-29; Derek Kinnane, *The Kurds and Kurdistan* (London, 1964); Thomas Bois, *The Kurds* (Beirut, 1966); and, for British administration, Lt.-Col. Sir Arnold T. Wilson, *Mesopotamia, 1917-1920: A Clash of Loyalties . . .* (Oxford, 1931), Philip Willard Ireland, *'Iraq: A Study in Political Development* (N.Y., 1938), and Busch, *Britain, India, and the Arabs.*

The "Assyrians" (Chaldean Uniates) are discussed in Lt.-Col. R.S. Stafford, *The Tragedy of the Assyrians* (London, 1935); Rev. W.A. Wigram, *The Assyrians and their Neighbours* (London, 1929), *The Assyrian Settlement* (London, 1922), and, with Sir Edgar T.A. Wigram, *The Cradle of Mankind: Life in Eastern Kurdistan* 2nd ed. (London, 1922); and Harry Charles Luke, *Mosul and Its Minorities* (London, 1925).

[35] Cox memorandum, 3 June, 2614/18, *L/P&S/*10/745; Cox (Mar-

Source: Sherif Pasha, "Memorandum on the Claims of the Kurd People," (1919).

Such was official policy. But Kurdistan was sufficiently remote and difficult to attract those imperial servants who always managed to appear on a troubled frontier to play an independent and important role. While there were many such in Kurdistan, one was outstanding. He was Major E.W. Noel, sent in November 1918 to advise and control the Sulaimaniyah district and its chief personality, Shaikh Mahmud of the Barzinji Kurds. Mahmud was appointed governor of the district by the British administration and with the help of advisors such as Noel extended his authority wherever possible over neighboring chiefs and districts. Noel had already amassed substantial experience in the Gulf and Persia, but he was to have his problems with Mahmud; so, too, was his successor, Major E.B. Soane (despite the experiences reported in his prewar book *Through Mesopotamia and Kurdistan in Disguise*), when Noel was given a roving commission for the whole of Kurdistan. Kurdistan was a most difficult puzzle, in other words, but Noel's first reception in Sulaimaniyah was a warm one, and he soon built support for his own favored solution, a Kurdish state under British protection. This solution was also supported by deputations of Kurds from Baghdad; in fact, so rapidly did the movement develop, according to Noel, that in late November 1918 he advised that if Britain's policy was not to organize the Kurds, a declaration to that effect should be made at once to head off a *fait accompli*.[36]

---

seilles) private to Sykes, 4 June, and Toynbee memorandum, 22 July, 104697/25434, *FO* 371/3398; FO to IO, 2 November, and SSI telegram to commissioner, Baghdad, 5 November 1918, *L/P&S/*10/781.

Sherif Pasha: Toynbee note, 18 January, 375/1/2, *FO* 608/97; T. Hohler private to C. Kerr, 7 September ("beau Cherif"), *FO* 371/4237; autobiographical statement in Cherif Pasha to British Delegation, 24 March 1919, *FO* 371/4215; Arfa, *Kurds,* p. 112.

[36] Commissioner, Baghdad, telegrams to IO, 16 November (with Hirtzel minute, 19 November), 27 November, and 4 December 1918, *L/P&S/*10/781; Arfa, *Kurds,* pp. 111-12; Hay, *Two Years in Kurdistan,* pp. 192-93; Edmonds, *Kurds, Turks and Arabs,* pp. 29-30. Soane's book (London, 1st ed. 1912; 2nd ed. 1926) includes a biographical note by A.T. Wilson in the 2nd edition; see also Diary of Lt.-Col. H.L. Scott (1919), *CAB* 45/99 (Historical Section papers) on Soane's role in the revolt. On Noel, aside from *Diary* (note 34, chapter 4), see Mesopotamia, Office of Civil Commissioner, *Note on the Kurdish Situation by Major E.W.C. Noel* (Baghdad, 1919). There is no useful study of this adventurous individual, who served also in Persia (where he was a prisoner of the Jangalis) and the Caucasus; but see Gould, *Jewel in the Lotus,* pp. 111-12, for a characterization.

Serious consideration had to be given the scheme, but there were obstacles. French claims were one, but the Kurds themselves were another. While at least the southernmost Kurds (Mahmud's sphere) appeared to want British protection and inclusion in an Iraqi state, they did not want inclusion in an *Arab* Iraqi state, and Britain, according to some, had promised such a state to the Arabs. Nor did all Kurds see Mahmud as the best possible leader; nor did the northernmost Kurds show any desire to participate; nor could areas pledged to Persian integrity or Armenian aspirations be included. Finally, Sherif Pasha, the other claimant, might not prove acceptable, particularly since he proposed Kurdish participation in some future Turkish state and wished to go to Constantinople to rally the substantial Kurdish population there. This proposal, even assuming the desirability of keeping Kurds with Turks, would be supporting a separatist movement essentially hostile to the current Turkish government and therefore against accepted British policy.[37]

It was another complicated problem, no more susceptible to isolated solution than Armenia or Constantinople and the Straits. It can be understood why at the end of the year the Eastern Committee fell back on a federation of the southern Kurds. This idea was proposed by Arnold Wilson from Baghdad, supported by the India Office, and justified on the basis of self-determination. For the rest, it was necessary to await conference action, and Sherif Pasha was on hand to make sure the Kurds got a hearing. Meanwhile, however, Kurdish activity had become organized in Constantinople under the leadership of Seyyid Abdülkadir, president of the Council of State and member of the old and powerful Bedr Khan family which made its headquarters in Jazirat ibn 'Umar (Cizre) near the Turko-Persian frontier. Abdülkadir headed a Kurdish Committee which petitioned Gough-Calthorpe with large claims, although the focus was more in the northern, "Armenian" districts than the southern area of Mosul and Sulaimaniyah. With important relatives and contacts in Cairo and elsewhere in the Middle East, another serious contender had entered the field.[38]

[37] Commissioner, Baghdad, telegram to FO, 7 December, Shuckburgh memorandum (B. 303), 14 December, SSI telegram to commissioner, Baghdad, 19 December, *L/P&S/*10/781; IO to FO, 4 December, G. Kidston minute, 20 December 1918, 204219/25434, *FO* 371/3398.

[38] Eastern Committee, 26 December 1918, *CAB* 27/24; high commissioner, Constantinople, to Balfour, 5 January 1919, *FO* 371/3657;

The future of Kurdistan progressed very little in Paris. The conference could produce no solution for Turkey or Armenia or Iraq—and therefore none for Kurdistan either. Conference delay aggravated the situation, for Kurdish leaders who heard of the various proposals began to doubt Allied intentions. Unrest began to spread, flowing in part from across the Persian frontier where a local Kurdish leader in the Lake Urmia area by the name of Simko, Aga of the Shekak Kurds, was at war primarily against the Persian central government and his local Assyrian Christian neighbors. At the time of the conference, the French had not yet given way on Mosul and therefore were unlikely to approve a Kurdish state such as Sykes proposed. Arnold Wilson, fearful disorder would spread and apparently hopeful that an agreement with France was in process, sent Noel into the French section a hundred miles beyond Mosul to occupy Jazirat ibn 'Umar and Urfa. Order soon seemed very necessary: a political officer was killed in a Kurdish outbreak in Zakho in April, and in May Mahmud led a larger revolt against British authority, driven by his own ambition and an impression of growing British control. He disagreed violently with Soane and was particularly galled by checks upon his ability to influence neighboring

---

General Cherif Pasha, *Memorandum on the Claims of the Kurd People* (Paris, 1919), and *Mémoire présenté . . . à Monsieur le President du Conseil Suprême de la Conference de la Paix* (Paris, [1919]), copies in *L/P&S/* 10/745; Toynbee memorandum, 18 January 1919, note 35, chapter 4. Kurdish activities in Constantinople, in addition, are discussed in Webb to Curzon, 21 May 1919, *FO* 371/4191; Basile Nikitine, *Les Kurdes: étude sociologique et historique* (Paris, 1956), p. 196; Pech, *Les Alliés et la Turquie,* pp. 15, 94-95.

Sayyid Abdülkadir's family's power had come to a virtual end in the mid-nineteenth century with the establishment of effective Turkish power in the Jazirat ibn 'Umar area; most of the family had proceeded to Constantinople, where some entered state service. Participation in a 1905 plot brought the exile of many to North Africa. The leader of one family branch, Sureya Bey, had held a government post near Smyrna after the Young Turk revolution (1908) but had moved to Cairo after the Balkan Wars and was in contact with the British administration there; Bedr Khan brothers to Lloyd George (petition of three family members, dated Cairo, 30 March 1919), with Kidston minute, 17 April, 59486/3050, *FO* 371/4191; Iraq, Civil Commissioner, *Personalities in Kurdistan* (Baghdad, 1919), 137430/ 3050, *FO* 371/4192.

tribes. The result was serious fighting during which Britain temporarily lost control of Sulaimaniyah.[39]

There were many local reasons for revolt, but it was natural to con-nect Mahmud's rising with Kurdish leaders in Constantinople, and these leaders in turn with Young Turk officials who were obstructing British policy at every opportunity. Finally there was the whole revolutionary association of pan-Islamicists, nationalists, and Bolsheviks. Such as-sociations were vague at best, and Gough-Calthorpe and his staff had trouble distinguishing friendly from hostile Kurds even in Constanti-nople. The only clarity was the need to restore order, and plans were laid to extend the Iraqi rail system to Mosul and bomb the guilty vil-lages.[40] But what next?

Arnold Wilson, in London in mid-April for an interdepartmental meeting, saw Sherif Pasha and the Bedr Khan claimants as remote and irrelevant. Local disturbances would continue, as he saw it, so long as there was no control. Wilson was no advocate of a Kurdish amirate—in fact he criticized Noel's excess of zeal and overly successful culti-

[39] Cox (Teheran) telegram to SSI, 31 January, FO 371/3858; Curzon to Derby, 12 March, FO 371/4179; DMI to FO (Sykes proposal), 27 Jan-uary, GOC Baghdad telegrams to DMI, 28 March, with Kidston minute, 7 April, and to SSI, 7 April (2 of date); GHQ, Cairo, telegram to GHQ, Baghdad, 7 April, FO 371/4191; commissioner, Baghdad, telegram to delegation, Paris, 12 March 1919, L/P&S/10/818; Edmonds, Kurds, Turks and Arabs, pp. 29-31; Arfa, Kurds, pp. 113-14; Stafford, Assyrians, pp. 28-45; Wigram and Wigram, Cradle of Mankind, pp. 359-91; Frederick G. Coan, Yesterdays in Persia and Kurdistan (Claremont, Calif., 1939), pp. 266-69; Noel Buxton, Travels and Reflections (London, 1929), pp. 28-32. Simko had been responsible for the murder of the Assyrian patri-arch (or "Mar Shimun") in 1911. The works referred to in note 34, chapter 4, outline the history of this tragic people and their wartime tribulations. Much additional information is available in the archives of Randall David-son, archbishop of Canterbury, Assyrian file, 1921-22 (Lambeth Palace, London, to the librarian of which the author is indebted). The Archbishopric sponsored charitable and educational work among the Assyrians and was well informed of events in this area through regular correspondence from field workers such as Rev. W.A. Wigram. This interest—and representa-tions made on its behalf—had to be kept in mind by the FO in formulating any policy toward Kurdistan. For a representative sample, see archbishop of Canterbury to Curzon, 17 October 1919, FO 800/151.

[40] Commissioner, Baghdad, telegrams to SSI, 7, 9, 15, 16, and 20 April, FO to Army Council, 15 April, DMI to FO, 23 April 1919, FO 371/4191.

vation of Kurdish aspirations. Wilson was given what he asked as administrator of Iraq: permission to proceed on the assumption that Mosul would be part of the future Arab state. Beyond the vilayet boundaries, however, there would exist only a fringe of autonomous states with British advisors. Committee members knew this would not satisfy Kurdish spokesmen for unity, but they knew also that satisfaction of wider Kurdish aspirations would always be at the cost of Armenia, a point which made Kurdish cooperation with anti-Armenian Turks far more than a remote possibility. It had occurred in the past; Noel reported from Nusaybin, in fact, that the Kurds feared British punishment for their wartime cooperation in anti-Armenian persecutions, and therefore he suggested a general amnesty as a conciliatory gesture. But too conciliatory a Kurdish policy was an anti-Armenian policy and, by encouraging separatism, an anti-Constantinople policy. Noel was allowed only to make private assurances to calm the fears he had reported.[41]

Kurdish problems could not be resolved in a purely Iraqi framework, obviously—but the need for consultation with Constantinople only made Wilson's task in Baghdad more difficult. The same could be said about the Greek landings, for Muslims tended to equate support of Greek Christians with support of Armenian Christians, and the Kurds at least were Muslims. Wilson agreed with Noel on this point; their concern to quiet Kurdish fears tended to overshadow any sympathy they may have felt for the Armenians. It was disquieting to the India Office to read Wilson's opinion that the best Armenian solution was to give the vilayets of Erzerum and Trebizond to the Armenians and the remaining four of the six eastern provinces to the Kurds, who according to Noel's information were thicker on the ground in those areas. Wilson was the man on the spot, however, and his authority to administer Kurdistan was not reduced.[42]

The correctness of this decision was demonstrated when at the end

[41] IDCE, 17 April, *Curzon Papers,* F/11/8; high commissioner, Constantinople, telegrams to FO, 22 April (on Abdülkadir's interview with Ryan) and 2 May (with Kidston minute, 6 May); commissioner, Baghdad, telegrams to SSI, 26 and 29 April, FO telegram to high commissioner, Constantinople, 14 May 1919, *FO* 371/4191.

[42] Commissioner, Baghdad, telegrams to SSI, 12 May and 13 June, DMI to FO, 15 May, FO to DMI, 30 May, Webb telegram to FO, 21 May, Kidston memorandum, 24 May, with Curzon minute, 26 May, *FO* 371/

of June Mahmud's rising was controlled and the Kurdish leader taken prisoner. This victory would have been more satisfying if Britain had not put Mahmud into office in the first place and if the military authorities had not urged permanent occupation of the Sulaimaniyah Valley at a time when the main desire was to reduce, not increase, such expenditures and commitments. But at least one obstacle to a settlement was removed, and when Noel arrived in Constantinople in early July to consult on behalf of Wilson and Gough-Calthorpe and the Kurdish leaders, there seemed every prospect of a happy result. With Mahmud out of the running Noel and Gough-Calthorpe agreed that some member of the Bedr Khan family would be the Kurdish leader, and members of the family were given permission to travel to Kurdistan. The only dangers now appeared to be either Kemalist hostility or a larger pro-Armenian decision from Paris, which would force the Kurds to side with Kemal. Conference hestitation, however, was as prevalent as ever; there was even less prospect of an American mandate for Armenia in the summer of 1919 than in the spring, and nobody else wanted it. Even the Paris delegation was inclined to organize Kurdistan along the lines Noel and Arnold Wilson advocated.[43]

Opposition to such increased responsibilities now centered mainly in the India Office's general aversion to this sort of Middle Eastern policy, although even the India Office realized there was little choice at the moment, and in the Constantinople high commissioner's concern for the future of Armenia. Their opposition was not decreased by Noel's tactless references to "Armenian vindictiveness and religious fanaticism." But a larger Armenian state faced obstacles as well. Above all after the destruction of the Armenians during the war, there were simply too few of them. Then, too, as Hirtzel pointed out, the Ar-

---

4191; IO copies and drafts, and FO to IO, 29 May, with Shuckburgh minute, 31 May, and SSI telegram to commissioner, Baghdad, 5 June 1919, *L/P&S/*10/781.

[43] Commissioner, Baghdad, telegrams to SSI, 23 June and 23 August and army council to FO, 4 July, *FO* 371/4191-92; Scott Diary, *CAB* 45/99; high commissioner, Constantinople, telegram to Curzon, 10 July, Hohler (political officer, High Commission, Constantinople) private to Sir J. Tilley (FO), 21 July, and private to Clark Kerr, 27 August, *DBFP* IV/451, 464, 498; Hirtzel private to A.T. Wilson, 16 July 1919, *A.T. Wilson Papers,* Add. Mss. 52455; E. Forbes Adam note, 29 July 1919, with Vansittart (30 July) and Crowe (31 July) minutes, 365/1/1, *FO* 608/95.

menian question was also the Kurdish question now, and Iraq was directly involved. The world demanded an Armenian state, but if such a state were carved on large lines it would deny the Kurds self-determination. Should the Kurds be blamed for their unwillingness to submit to minority Armenian authority? Some Armenian leaders would have shouted "yes," if only on account of Kurdish participation in earlier Armenian massacres; Crowe's attitude smacked of that expressed by French Turkophile writer Pierre Loti: *"s'il n'y avait pas eu des Arméniens, il n'y aurait pas eu de massacres d'Arméniens."* Still, Noel was at least correct in concluding that vindictiveness was scanty foundation for a viable state. The Eastern Committee was perplexed once again, and, for the moment, the decision taken in Constantinople to send the Bedr Khans to tour the Kurdish areas and assess the situation was the sum total of policy.[44]

The committee was generally pessimistic, however, particularly about the more immediate situation in Iraq. Several members felt that enlarged military occupation and extension of the railway to Kirkuk, as was now advocated, would only create for Iraq its own problematic North-West Frontier Province. Even Curzon saw no need to hold Sulaimaniyah—but, typically, he and the India Office were at odds, for rather reluctantly Montagu and Shuckburgh supported Arnold Wilson's plea for security. Pessimism was understandable, given the fact that the Kurds ended the war asking for British protection but now seemed like hostile tribes in need of suppression. Perhaps, Baghdad was asked, the best solution was to withdraw and leave the Kurds to their own devices? That, Wilson quickly replied, would only require a stronger force to keep watch on the frontier. It was a temporary question only, resulting from war misery and a desire to test Britain's strength; no government, he argued, could govern without a basis of force in these times. For the moment, Wilson was not overrruled.[45]

The initiative thus lay with Noel and his Bedr Khan candidates,

[44] Webb telegram to FO, 19 August, *DBFP* IV/492; commissioner, Baghdad, telegram to SSI, 3 August, including Noel telegram of 2 August text (quoted), Hirtzel note, 17 August, *FO* 371/4192; L.D. Wakeley to H.W. Young, 8 September, with Vansittart minute, 365/1/1, *FO* 608/95; IDCE secretary note, September 1919, 5004/19, *L/P&S*/10/781. Loti's remark is quoted in Driault, *Histoire diplomatique . . .,* V, p. 377.

[45] IDCE, 20 August and 2 September, and Political Department, IO, memorandum (B. 322), 27 August, *L/P&S*/10/781; SSI telegram to com-

now touring Kurdistan. Unfortunately the delegates assembled at Kemal's Sivas congress were inclined to regard Noel's activities as deliberately hostile and British policy as designed to bring Kurds in on the
Greek side; even if this assessment was in error, the prospect of adding
four Turkish vilayets to Iraq could never be regarded with favor. Once
more, there were complications; the French were having trouble with
the Arabs in Syria and with Kemal in Cilicia, and rumors of an Arab-
Kemalist alliance had already turned up. Such rumors seriously alarmed
Britain's Arabists who, like T.E. Lawrence, felt that "allowing Noel to
flirt with Kurds," who "have no corporate feeling and no capacity for
autonomy or nationality," only drove Kemal to intrigue with the Arabs.
In any case, Kemal ordered Noel's arrest, and Noel was forced to leave
the area under the protection of his Kurdish friends. He could not return without policy support—but policy had just taken another turn
when Britain handed over Syria and Cilicia to France.[46]

Noel's fertile mind had produced a new plan which required the
creation of three zones under mandatory supervision (but Turkish
sovereignty): Armenian, Kurdish, and mixed Armenian-Kurdish par-
tipcation. Such a solution implied Armenian-Kurdish cooperation,
not an entirely impossible proposal at least among the leaders of the
respective peoples who could be found in Paris. It also implied that
some power would assume mandatory responsibility, and Noel, home
for consultation in November 1919, soon found this unlikely. His new
response, therefore, was for Britain to clear out altogether and leave
the Kurds to defend themselves against the Turks; the discussion,

---

missioner, Baghdad, 22 August, commissioner, Baghdad, telegrams to SSI,
23 and 29 August 1919, *FO* 371/4192.

[46] High commissioner (de Robeck), Constantinople, telegram to FO, 7
September, *FO* 371/4159; SSI telegram to viceroy, 23 September, *Chelmsford Papers,* E. 264/11; T.E. Lawrence memorandum (undated; received
in FO 15 September), with C. Harmsworth minute on origins of note (requested by Harmsworth), 129405/129405, *FO* 371/4236; high commissioner, Constantinople, telegrams to FO, 16 and 19 September, commissioner, Baghdad, telegrams to SSI, 20 September, *FO* 371/4192, and
29 September, with text of Noel (Aleppo) telegram to commissioner, Baghdad, 23 September, Crowe to Curzon, 12 October 1919, *FO* 371/4193.
Admiral Bristol, it should be added, viewed all this as preliminary to a
British takeover of Kurdistan which came in response to American backing
of the Armenians; Bristol telegrams to American Mission, Paris, 29 September and 4 October 1919, *Bristol Papers,* box 27.

however, focused on Iraqi frontiers, and Noel disagreed with both Arnold Wilson and the committee: his Kurdistan would require such districts as Sulaimaniyah for survival. To Noel, division of Kurdistan was acceptable only if there was strong mandatory supervision.[47]

Wilson in Baghdad was now asked if he saw any alternative to Noel's proposal of a Kurdish entity which must include all Kurds and which therefore would have a frontier coinciding as closely as possible with Arab-Kurdish ethnological lines. But Wilson by now showed much more interest in a viable northern frontier for Iraq, which would necessarily include some Kurdish areas. The rest would preferably be organized in a fringe of autonomous areas as earlier planned. He saw no real Kurdish movement; and even if there were, the Kurds left alone would not necessarily be either strong or pro-British. The committee wished not to restore Turkish administration to the northern areas, but to Wilson it was there now and would be most difficult to dislodge. Noel's Kurdistan, therefore, was a chimera, while Wilson's Iraq was a going concern. It was hardly likely that the committee would jeopardize Iraqi security and stability to set Noel's much-criticized plan in motion. On the other hand, Wilson was inclined to claim too much for Iraq just as Noel did for Kurdistan, and the India Office finally arrived at a compromise: Sulaimaniyah would be the base of a British-supervised satellite Kurdish entity, but the area beyond the Zab Rivers would be autonomous. The southern Kurds, in other words, would be a separate fringe state under the Bedr Khans at Jazirat ibn ʿUmar; the northern Kurds would have to fend for themselves.[48]

A conclusion had been reached, at least for the time being. Greater Kurdistan was no more a reality than Greater Armenia, although the Kurds were still in existence. Noel, aptly termed "a Kurdish Col. Lawrence," had done his best for his proteges, but his enthusiasm had out-

[47] Commissioner, Baghdad, telegram to SSI, 22 October, *FO* 371/4193; IDCE, 17 November 1919, *L/P&S*/10/807; Noel, *Note on the Kurdish Situation* (Baghdad, 1919), copies in 126299/3050, *FO* 371/4192, and 5374/19, *L/P&S*/10/781.

[48] SSI telegram to commissioner, Baghdad, 22 November, minutes of IO meetings, 27 November and 6 December, commissioner, Baghdad, telegrams to SSI, 27 November and 2 December, *FO* 371/4193; A.T. Wilson private telegram to Hirtzel, 27 November, Hirtzel note for Montagu, 12 December, and IO to FO, 20 December, *L/P&S*/10/781; General Mac-Munn private to Curzon, 9 December 1919, *Curzon Papers,* F/2/2.

run realism, particularly given the puzzling plethora of leadership candidates, obscure tribal rivalries, and Armenian, French, and Persian
involvement.[49]

The Kurdish solution had never really offered the attraction of the
Greek solution as a method of ending the Turkish dilemma. Some more
ardent supporters of Armenian claims might take some encouragement
at this fact, but optimism was not the dominant note as 1919 came to
an end. The only clear conclusion was that a year had passed since the
armistice, and Turkish affairs were vastly more complicated than they
had appeared at Mudros.

ALLIED NEGOTIATIONS

The tendency now was to listen to any plan, even French—and in
early December 1919 France had a proposal to make. Roughly, the
idea was to leave the sultan in Constantinople and to administer the
Straits zone as a sort of Anglo-French condominium behind a Turkish
facade. A similar structure would supervise Turkish railways; another,
with Italian participation, would run the Heraclea coal mines south of
Smyrna. The draft plan, put to Lloyd George on 3 December, included
no solution for Armenia save the assignment of British and French advisors to the Turkish administrators in that area. This proposal was
closely connected to discussions on Palestine, oil pipelines, and Iraq,
to say nothing of the German situation and the proposed guarantee
treaty for France, none of which can be considered here. Nor was it
any accident that the suggestion coincided with the Anglo-French agreement on Syria and Cilicia. Although the scheme bore little resemblance
to the final Turkish treaty, it was an overture and initiated a new round
of serious discussions—really the first since the major leaders had left
Paris.[50]

Lloyd George found the idea of condominium unattractive, and in a
meeting of selected ministers (including Balfour, Curzon, Montagu, and
Churchill) to discuss preparations for forthcoming talks with Clemen-

---

[49] Hohler private to Tilley, 21 July (quoted), *DBFP* IV/464; see also Wilson private telegram to Hirtzel, note 48, chapter 4, and Crowe private to
Kidston, 17 November 1919, *FO* 371/4215.

[50] Allied meeting, 3 December (S-2), *CAB* 23/35; Derby private to Curzon, 11 December 1919, *Curzon Papers,* F/6/2.

ceau, the prime minister indicated his own preference for internationalization of the Straits and Constantinople. The sultan would be left with a Vatican-like enclave as a sop to the Muslim and Indian opinion which was now permanently fixed in his mind. The main opponent to his plan was Montagu, who objected to any division of Turkey and who wanted rather more than a Vatican at Constantinople. Curzon, foreign secretary in Balfour's place since October, once more sided with Montagu on Turkey but with Lloyd George on Constantinople; by the end of 1919, at least the main positions of leading ministers were predictable. Despite demurrers, internationalization and special position for the sultan were the general conclusions of the meeting, subsequently put to France as a counterproposal when the two prime ministers met on 11 December. Lloyd George found Clemenceau pleased with the settlement in Syria and Cilicia, unwilling to touch Armenia, and unconcerned about Constantinople, although he preferred that the sultan stay on. What Clemenceau wanted above all, the prime minister later reported to his colleagues, was to get the Greeks out of Smyrna, perhaps by compensation in Thrace.[51]

Further negotiations on these points followed in London on 22-23 December, on the basis of a new French draft. Curzon and Philippe Berthelot, head of the French Foreign Office and author of the draft, agreed to internationalize the Straits and Constantinople as far into Thrace as the line Enos(Marmora)-Midia (Black Sea), with the coast of Marmora to be under some general League protection. Mosul, the French agreed, would be British, pending satisfactory settlements on oil and Syria. The French proposed a shared Anglo-French responsibility for Kurdistan under Turkish sovereignty. Curzon suggested instead that the inhabitants at some future point determine their own future as one or more states, guaranteed against formal Turkish aggression, but without formal mandatory supervision (south Kurdistan, he indicated, would be treated differently).[52]

[51] Allied meeting, 11 December 1919 (S-5), *CAB* 23/35; See in general on the diplomacy of this period Nicolson, *Curzon,* Ch. IV; Roskill, *Hankey,* II, Ch. V; Earl of Ronaldshay, *The Life of Lord Curzon . . . ,* III (N.Y., 1928), Ch. XII, and Richard D. Challener, "The French Foreign Office: The Era of Philippe Berthelot," in Craig and Gilbert, *The Diplomats,* pp. 40-85, for an overview of French policymaking.

[52] Allied meeting, 22 and 23 (with French note on Kurdistan) December, 1919, *DBFP,* IV/631, 404, and 633-34; also *FO* 371/4239, including an

It was a sweeping and comprehensive settlement, although numerous details, such as Palestinian frontiers, remained to be worked out. What the agreement did not take into account was the strong feeling of Indian Muslims, or so the India Office—and, when it heard of the plan, India—concluded. Montagu had protested the general lines before the late-December negotiations, even to the point of asking that Indian troops be removed from the occupation forces in Turkey (of which, it should be noted, they formed the bulk), since he could no longer guarantee their reliability. Montagu's main concern, as the year closed, was Constantinople; the Turks had lost all their Arab territories, the Straits, and probably Kurdistan: it was vital for world opinion that they at least keep their own capital city. Montagu was well aware of Curzon's opposite view, and when he was informed of the Curzon-Berthelot negotiations (at which the War Office was also represented), he at once protested against the exclusion of the India Office. The conclusions of those discussions he described as "disastrous and incredible," when he actually saw them—particularly so since the last French draft made it clear that they had dropped even the "Vatican" plan only on British representations, and thus the full blame would be Britain's. His only hope now, as he noted on New Year's Day, was that the Cabinet should not approve these conclusions. Privately, to Chelmsford, be even mentioned resignation—for if he, Montagu, should resign over the treaty, the Indian government could better deal with Indian Muslims.[53]

Curzon struck back with a countermemorandum also designed to influence the Cabinet. At last the opportunity had arrived to drive the Turks from Constantinople, particularly now that the French had abandoned Clemenceau's earlier position. Of course there would be some outcry in India, but it would be artificial and ephemeral; such feeling as could be found in India for the caliphate was of recent origin. All

---

English translation of Berthelot's remarks, with marginal FO minutes, not in *DBFP*.

[53] Montagu private to Lloyd George, 13 December, *Lloyd George Papers,* F/40/2/64; Montagu memoranda, 18 December 1919 and 1 January 1920, *FO* 371/4239; Hirtzel note, 24 December, Montagu note to Hirtzel (undated) and private letter to Curzon, 29 December (drafted by Hirtzel) 1919, *L/P&S/*10/781; Montagu private telegram to Chelmsford, 1 January 1920, *Chelmsford Papers,* E. 264/12; Callwell, *Wilson,* II, p. 218, shows that Montagu made the same point to Field Marshal Wilson at a meeting of 30 December 1919.

the experts, including Gough-Calthorpe, de Robeck, many of their staff, and Hardinge, the permanent undersecretary and former viceroy, were agreed. The problem was not going to be Constantinople but taking Smyrna from the Greeks.[54]

On 5 January, a meeting of ministers considered the results of the Anglo-French discussions. Both Montagu and Churchill argued against Turkish dismemberment, and Montagu had heavy artillery to match Curzon's: O'Dwyer in the Punjab, Roos-Keppel on the Frontier, Willingdon in Madras all warned of the effect Turkish partition would have on India. Only officials in Iraq took a hard line, but that was for Iraqi reasons. Bolshevism was moving east, soon it would link with a hostile Kemal, and "we shortly should not have a single friend from Constantinople to China." Leaving the sultan in his palace would not stop this, but it would be one less issue. It was a strong argument, and Lloyd George had already shown response to Indian pressure. Curzon, on the other side, was in an awkward position, for his Anglo-French plan also involved getting the Greeks out of Smyrna, and that ran counter to the prime minister's policy and inclinations alike. Curzon was correct when he answered that leaving the sultan in the capital would not solve the Kemalist problem, but at the time appeasement of the government in Constantinople could normally be expected to undermine support for the Kemalist movement. Lloyd George may also have concluded that giving way to Indian nationalists on Constantinople might bring them to accept the Greeks in Smyrna, thus removing them from the issue and leaving only the Kemalist movement to be dealt with. The War Office had a different view: the sultan would be much easier to control in Constantinople than in Asia Minor. The argument carried over into the larger Cabinet meeting the next day, but the high cards were in Montagu's hand. By a considerable majority, the Cabinet agreed to leave the sultan in Constantinople, strictly limited as to military guard and police escort and separated from Turkey by an international Straits regime. Curzon recorded his strong dissent, but his case was lost.[55]

France, too, was under a certain amount of pressure from Muslim

---

[54] Curzon memorandum, 4 January 1920, *DBFP* IV/646.

[55] Cabinet conference (quoted), 5 January, CAB 1(20), appendix I, CIGS memorandum, 6 January, and Curzon memorandum protesting decision, 7 January 1920 (quoted in Ronaldshay, *Curzon,* III, pp. 270-71), appendix III-IV, *CAB* 23/20. The decision is discussed in Roskill, *Hankey,*

interests, as was clear from Berthelot's next paper, dated 11 January, which added new details. There was now no argument on basic principles: Turkey for the Turks where the Turks were in a majority; no mandates or spheres; no Turkish military presence; absolute freedom of passage of the Straits, to be safeguarded by internationalization; a separate Armenia independent but for League supervision (boundaries to be determined later). Berthelot, aware of strong pro-Armenian sympathy in France, went further than earlier French proposals in suggesting a state based upon Russian Armenia with the addition of Erzerum, Bitlis, and Van. Constantinople also required further discussion; all agreed on keeping the sultan, but would he rule an independent state in European Turkey, or should he still rule all of Turkey (such as was not assigned to someone else) with his European territory reduced accordingly? And what of Smyrna? Berthelot recommended that the Greeks retain only a permanent special position in the town with a free port. Elsewhere the Greeks and Italians would withdraw, and Italy would have a share in the capital and economic development in southern Anatolia.[56]

Soon after this document was in British hands, a meeting of concerned ministers was held at Claridge's Hotel in Paris. Curzon hoped, at least according to Hardinge, that the Cabinet decision would be reversed (and Berthelot's presentation at least gave a hint that the Constantinople question was still open for discussion). Hardinge, however, felt that Montagu had seriously shaken Lloyd George—and Montagu certainly assumed that the Cabinet decision was irrevocable.[57] Montagu was now broadening his attack by criticizing new Foreign Office drafts on the proposed Turkish loss of Adrianople, overly close financial controls, and the Smyrna enclave. Curzon, however, had a powerful ally in Venizelos, who wished to limit the Turkish presence in Europe

---

II, p. 142 (who attributes the change to Montagu's influence); Churchill, *World Crisis,* V, p. 396 (who mistakenly gives 9 January as the critical meeting); and, from the standpoint of the Arab world, Nevakivi, *Britain, France and the Arab Middle East,* Ch. XI.

[56] Berthelot to Lloyd George, 11 January 1920, *FO* 608/272.

[57] Cabinet conference, 11 and 13 January (S-6 and S-8), *CAB* 23/35; Vansittart to Curzon, 12 January and Forbes Adam to Kidston, 13 January, *DBFP* IV/658-59; Hardinge private to V. Chriol, 12 January, *Hardinge Papers,* 1920/1; Montagu private telegram to Chelmsford, 22 January 1920, *Chelmsford Papers,* E. 264/12.

as much as possible. Lloyd George was responsible for soliciting the Greek views (as he doubtless was for keeping Venizelos informed); since the prime minister was also responsible for ordering Curzon and Montagu to write up their various opinions, it is no surprise that the many new position papers produced considerable confusion and some complaint from Montagu that the prime minister—or at least the more vulnerable Curzon—was backsliding on a previously agreed policy.[58]

Shuckburgh might have been remarking upon his own secretary of state when he wrote, ". . . the more we encourage the Indian Mahommedans in their pro-Turkish agitation, the more extravagant their demands grow, & the more inaccurate their statements of fact," and surely Curzon would have agreed. There was indeed agitation in India, but it was Montagu who selected what particular policy points to attack, not the authorities in India. From India came mainly insistence that the problem was urgent and large, and that pan-Islamic agitators were at work raising funds, stirring up Muslim soldiers, and in some cases using Bolshevik arguments, although India had no direct evidence yet of Bolshevik agents at work there. But India did not expect that the treaty as now outlined would lead to any widespread or organized disruption for several reasons, including solidarity shown during the Afghan war and Hindu nationalist distrust of Muslim religious zeal. India's status report makes it clear that Montagu went further than merely representing Delhi's views. It should not be thought, however, that India was not seriously alarmed. A Khilafat (caliphate) conference held in Delhi on 23-24 December, for example, had resulted in a demand—in which Gandhi participated—for boycott as a means of pressuring the government on this issue. A joint Indian National Congress-Muslim League meeting at Amritsar was followed, in late January 1920, by a Muslim deputation to the viceroy led by Shaukat Ali and other "extremists". Provincial governors still agreed that the movement had not really spread to the masses, but it was making dangerous headway.[59]

India and Montagu continued to observe developments closely as

[58] Montagu private to Hankey, 15 January, FO 800/157; Cabinet conference, 15 January (S-9), CAB 23/35; FO drafts dated 15 and 16 January, FO 608/272; Venizelos memorandum, 12 January, in Forbes Adam to Phipps, 19 January, DBFP IV/665, appendix C and E; Montagu private to Lloyd George, 20 January 1920, Lloyd George Papers, F/40/3/2.

[59] Shuckburgh minute, 31 January (quoted), 795/20, viceroy telegram to SSI, 2-3 February (3 parts), L/P&S/10/798; Chelmsford private tele-

the Allies moved on to detailed negotiation in the London conference of mid-February. Lloyd George played host to new leaders in Alexandre Millerand, French premier since January, and Francesco Nitti, Italian premier since the preceding June, both of whom saw little reason to hold out for a punishing treaty for Turkey. It was agreed that the sultan, who would remain in Constantinople, should be so restricted as to be no further menace to Allied interests. Curzon was present to argue his contrary views, but he found little support. The question of limits upon the sultan, however, raised important issues such as the size of the future Turkish army and the boundaries of the internationalized Straits zone. Too small an army could not keep order, said the War Office; nonsense, said Forbes Adam, since the Turkish army more often supervised than suppressed massacres. The Admiralty wanted Gallipoli kept out of Turkish hands, since it was essential for free passage of the Straits. Lloyd George, with conference approval, finally had to set guidelines for the military advisors: viable Straits zone coupled with the minimum possible Allied occupation, including Constantinople only if unavoidable.[60]

For Lloyd George, the main issue was not Constantinople or military strength but Smyrna. France, and to a lesser extent Italy, wished to see the Greeks removed; Italy had already cut its own occupation forces considerably, partly to encourage Greek withdrawal and partly in the realization that the area was likely to cost more to develop than it would ever produce in revenue. It fell to Lloyd George, therefore, to defend his friend Venizelos on all the old grounds. The Greeks had been asked in by the conference and should not be overthrown for the sake of an enemy. Constantinople was concession enough, and so on. One interesting new argument was that Smyrna would serve as a useful bridgehead in case of another war (Gallipoli had proved the cost of acquiring a

gram to Montagu, 4 February, *Montagu Papers,* D. 523/10; H. McPherson, secretary, Home Dept., India, to all local governments, 10 February, and other documents on caliphate conference in file, *Home Political Proc.,* March 1920, 30, part B (National Archives of India); Jones, *Whitehall Diary,* I, p. 103.

[60] Allied conference, 14 February, *DBFP,* VII/6-7; British Naval Section note and General Staff note, 14 January, FO draft and WO to secretary of Cabinet, 12 February (all in 56/56), Lloyd George note, 14 February, WO conference, 16 February 1920, *FO* 371/5103. Helmreich, *Paris to Sèvres,* Ch. XI, discusses the London Conference.

bridgehead in wartime). This argument overlooked the simple fact that the bridgehead itself might be grounds for war. Perhaps the Turks could retain nominal sovereignty, but that was the only concession he would make. The French, however, were concerned above all to retain their dominant prewar financial position in Turkey in any postwar settlement and less worried about the Greeks in Smyrna. Since many issues remained unresolved, the press focused upon the one decision on Constantinople which had been reached. The tendency in some quarters, such as *The Times,* was to regard the decision as a French victory over a previous British position. This interpretation was hardly accurate, and it came as a blow to the India Office, which could no longer claim that it was *their* victory.[61]

It was not a French victory, although the French hoped that the decisions reached would ease their position in Cilicia. At the conference, they maintained a stiff façade, but by early February the armistice had been broken, and broken to serious French disadvantage, in the area of Marash. Available evidence convinced Milne that Kemal was ready for a serious trial of strength, but the French maintained that it was only a bluff; after all, as Berthelot told the conference, France wished no permanent occupation of Cilicia. News was very sketchy, however; observers in Constantinople, Beirut, and Cairo could only repeat optimistic French reports of reinforcements and, by 20 February, the relief of besieged Marash. Clearly, the proposed Armenia could not include a Cilicia dominated by Kemal, and Berthelot claimed that the Armenians themselves admitted this. On this there was agreement, but the future of Erzerum (which the War Office maintained could not be defended by the Armenians) and Batum (which was claimed by Georgia) was referred to a special committee. On 24 February the committee reported on suggested frontiers only to be told that the remaining Armenians in Cilicia were being exterminated in the wake of serious Franco-Kemalist fighting. Any boundaries drawn in London were therefore likely to be unrealistic, and some other solution would be required.[62]

[61] Report, Maj. D. Haskend, 2 February 1920, 144/106, *FO* 371/5132; Allied conference, 16 February, *DBFP* VII/8 (and appended Berthelot note, 16 February); FO telegram to high commissioner, Constantinople, 16 February, *DBFP* XIII/3; *The Times,* 16 February 1920, with Shuckburgh minute, 1082/20, *L/P&S/*10/851.

[62] GOC Constantinople telegrams to WO, 17 and 20 February, Beirut

Special committees were the answer to many detailed questions. Smyrna, European boundaries, and finance were all treated in this fashion once the general decisions had been taken. Smyrna was not particularly difficult once Venizelos, as usual hovering on the fringes, agreed to grant the symbol of Turkish suzerainty if the Greeks kept the substance of control and administration in those areas inhabited by a majority of Greeks. The military authorities also managed to agree on the so-called Chatalja (Çatalca) defense lines (dating from a stand made in the Balkan War of 1912) some twenty miles west of Constantinople as the preferred boundary in Europe. The major stumbling block, therefore, was economic. Both the French and the Italian delegations demanded some compensation which could be displayed to their respective countrymen in defense of the widespread concessions now being prepared for the Turks. Both powers, but above all France (which held by its own reckoning 75 percent of the Ottoman Public Debt), insisted upon this point. Curzon argued that clear demarcation for economic purposes constituted partition, but it made no difference. Nitti soon had in hand a draft tripartite treaty which ultimately took the form of an Allied self-denying ordinance which would be formally recognized by the Turks. Not only general equality was outlined; Cilicia was specifically assigned to France and southwestern and western Turkey (with the exception of the Smyrna enclave) to Italy as a zone of priority of economic concession. Britain would sign, and thus recognize French and Italian zones, but would herself receive no zone.[63]

---

telegram to FO, 17 February, *FO* 371/5041; GHQ, Cairo, telegram to WO, 20 February, CinC Mediterranean telegram to Admiralty, 27 February, high commissioner, Constantinople, telegrams to FO, 29 February, *FO* 371/5042, and 4 February, and to Admiralty, 6 February, *FO* 371/4162, and to FO, 6 February, *DBFP* IV/424; Allied conference, 16 February, *DBFP* VII/10; Hankey to H.W. Malkin, 28 February 1920, enclosing 24 February committee report, *FO* 371/5103. Cilician fighting: Du Véou, *La Passion de la Cilicie;* E. Brémond, *La Cilicie en 1919-1920* (Paris, 1921); Abraham H. Hartunian, *Neither to Laugh nor to Weep* (Boston, 1968) and Stanley E. Kerr, *The Lions of Marash: Personal Experiences with American Near East Relief, 1919-1922* (Albany, N.Y., 1973), giving personal accounts. Major incidents in the fighting included the eighteen-day siege of Marash, and bloody fighting at Aintab, "le Verdun de l'Anatolie" (du Véou, p. 263).

[63] Allied conference, 17, 20, 21, 26, and 28 February 1920, *DBFP* VII/12, 18, 19, 20, 29, 37, 38; Great Britain, Parliamentary Papers, "Tri-

By the end of the month, despite many unsettled details and such large issues as the format of Greek control in Smyrna and the future of Armenia, the main lines of the treaty were established and generally known to the public. The French troubles in Cilicia were now more likely to disrupt the settlement than inter-Allied disagreement, but there seemed no real way of aiding the French. The Cilician and Armenian problems were simply aspects of the whole discouraging situation in interior Turkey. So serious was the general outlook that de Robeck was considering a direct occupation of Constantinople and arrest of the men responsible, for it was still assumed that men in Constantinople were responsible for what happened in the interior.[64] Formal occupation had been discussed before, of course, but this time hypothetical discussion was to become realistic action.

CONSTANTINOPLE OCCUPIED

De Robeck and other Allied representatives in Constantinople had encountered increasing difficulties in their relationships with the Turkish authorities since the fall of Damad Ferid Pasha in October 1919. Ferid Pasha had called for elections before his resignation took place, and late in the year those elections resulted in a largely nationalist body which met in Constantinople (the government refused demands that it meet in the interior) in mid-January. Admiral Webb tended to dismiss its significance as a representative body, but not its significance as an important political pressure complementary to Kemal's military pressure. Milne was finding the Turkish military authorities so uncooperative that he demanded the dismissal of Minister of War Jemal [Cemal] Pasha, formerly a highly placed associate of Enver Pasha and commander of a corps in Palestine. He had been appointed inspector general for the southern area when Kemal was named to the same post for the east, but had returned to Constantinople as minister of war in the Ali Riza Pasha Cabinet formed on 1 October. Milne was convinced

---

partite Agreement between the British Empire, France, and Italy Respecting Anatolia, Signed at Sèvres 10 August 1920," Treaty Series no. 12 (1920), Cmd. 963; Hurewitz, *Diplomacy,* II, pp. 87-89; see also Roskill, *Hankey,* II, p. 147.

[64] High commissioner, Constantinople, telegrams to Admiralty, 27 February, and to FO, 29 February 1920, *FO* 371/5042.

that he and his chief of staff were sending all available material to Kemal. On 20 January the removal of both was accomplished by making a direct demand to the grand vizier; it was one more embittering incident.[65]

Within a week, a major nationalist raid on arms dumps in Gallipoli removed from Allied control some 80,000 rifles and other arms and munitions held under the armistice terms. De Robeck was ordered to remove remaining stocks to Malta or Salonika to keep them out of nationalist hands. The situation appeared increasingly grave to de Robeck and Milne. Such raids were taken into consideration with Cilicia, reported Kemalist-Arab cooperation, and the fact that the Turkish government appeared to be cracking under the pressure of the nationalist assembly and the dismal prospect of an unacceptable peace. Milne wished to recall his Batum troops for greater security; even then, warned de Robeck, if the terms were harsh they would have to be imposed by force—the more so after a government reconstruction of 7-8 February gave every appearance that the Turkish government and the Chamber of Deputies nationalists had reached some agreement. One possible answer, although it carried grave risks, was to unleash the Greeks in Smyrna, for their commander was requesting freedom to go fifteen kilometers beyond the line set by Milne to break up Turkish concentrations opposite the Greek positions. Milne realized it would be most difficult to check further advance, but the War Office gave provisional approval.[66]

For the moment, this approval was a local measure, but Venizelos wished for a major advance not only near Smyrna but also, if Britain occupied Constantinople and the railheads at Scutari across the Bosporus

[65] Webb telegrams to Curzon, 13 and 21 January, high commissioner, Constantinople, telegram to Curzon, 17 January, and FO telegram to high commissioner, Constantinople, 9 January, *FO* 371/4161; GS Intelligence report, 13 January 1920, 177917/521, *FO* 371/4162.

[66] High commissioner, Constantinople, telegrams to FO, 30 January and 6 February, GOC Constantinople telegram to WO, 1 February, and WO telegram to GOC Constantinople, 3 February, *FO* 371/4162; high commissioner, Constantinople, telegrams to Curzon, 10 February, *FO* 371/5041, and 12 ans 13 February, *DBFP* XIII/1 and 2; GOC Constantinople telegram to WO, 8 February, FO to WO, 24 February, WO telegram to GOC Constantinople, 3 March, *FO* 371/5132; Curzon to Venizelos, 24 February 1920, *DBFP* XIII/7; Ryan, *Dragoman,* pp. 141-42; Callwell, *Wilson,* II, pp. 226-28.

and at Pandirma on the Sea of Marmora, to Afyonkarahisar to control all of the railway and compel the Turks to sign the proposed peace—or so Philip Kerr informed the Foreign Office. This sort of hard line was opposed by de Robeck, who preferred a moderate peace coupled with the conciliation of moderate men around the sultan himself. De Robeck's solution would require Turkish possession of Thrace and Smyrna and no doubt Armenia, but he was less inclined to spell out his own suggestions than to warn of the results of a harsh treaty. The peace-makers, however, favored harshness: Lloyd George liked the treaty as it stood, and if formal control of Constantinople was a necessary adjunct to Turkish acceptance, so be it. Millerand, normally willing to coop-erate, found the prospect alarming, for the French had been badly burned in Cilicia and it was easy to visualize more isolated units cut off and more Christians massacred. The resignation of the Constanti-nople government on 3 March worsened the crisis and made occupation all the more likely. On the same day Lloyd George explained to the con-ference the possible need for occupation and other measures to enforce the treaty. Only Churchill was willing to speak out on the fallacy in this argument: maneuvers at Constantinople would not alter the situa-tion in the interior. Lloyd George, however, probably had in mind Veni-zelos's plan to occupy all western Turkey with Greek forces if it became necessary.[67]

Two days later, on 5 March, the French agreed, although with grave forebodings.[68] It was a difficult choice, but an insistent Lloyd George made it clear that Britain was prepared to act alone, even though it preferred Allied cooperation. The alternative, as Curzon summed up in his usual masterful manner, was to alter the treaty and conciliate the moderates, although this would end any hope for Armenia and would reverse all policies so far adopted by the Allies. But how would a strong treaty be enforced? Lloyd George had revealed that Venizelos had six Greek divisions in and about Smyrna and another in Thrace. These forces together with available Allied units made up a total of

[67] High commissioner, Constantinople, telegrams to FO, 29 February and 2 March, *FO* 371/5042, and 5 March, and P. Kerr to R. Campbell, 9 March, *DBFP* XIII/12 and 18; Derby private to Curzon, 5 March, *Curzon Papers,* F/6/3, and private telegram of same date, *FO* 800/157; Allied conference, 3 March 1920, *DBFP* VII/45.

[68] Allied conference, 5 March 1920, *DBFP* VII/50.

160,000 against an estimated 80,000 Turks. And if the Allies were unprepared to use force, they had better begin again and simply ask the Turks what terms they would accept. Paul Cambon, present as French ambassador, recoiled in alarm; occupation of Constantinople with limited forces was one thing, a new war on a vast scale something else. But Lloyd George had a ready reply: he did not mean that these forces would all be unleashed, but only that the Allies could defend themselves if need be; the question at hand was Constantinople.

But what was "occupation" when the Allies were already there? Churchill, who as head of the War Office would have to issue the orders, was particularly interested in the details. Did this mean guards on public buildings, or control of the municipal government, for example? No, was the reply; only those steps would be taken which were necessary for moral effect, not including administration of the entire government. The Turkish War Ministry might be taken over, and—as Venizelos suggested—all orders should require Allied countersignature. The Chamber of Deputies should be dissolved (another Venizelos suggestion). This much could be agreed, and Curzon's draft orders to de Robeck were approved and telegraphed to Constantinople. De Robeck now consulted with his fellow high commissioners and the military commanders on how best to effect the occupation. De Robeck himself saw some utility to occupation, in that it would bring home the situation to the Turks, but it was still no solution to the larger problem of unjustified and unenforceable treaty, for the Admiral regarded the Smyrna and Thracian sections as a device to keep Venizelos in power a few more years. "I confess I am amazed at the apparent light-heartedness with which the Supreme Council seem to contemplate another war," he write privately to Curzon.[69]

But the conference was now only concerned with the details. On the 10th, Lloyd George, Curzon, and Churchill met with Berthelot, Cambon, Scialoja (the new Italian foreign minister), and Venizelos to go over a list proposed by the French and British high commissioners. This included civil administration of the town, arrest of nationalist

---

[69] Curzon telegram to high commissioner, Constantinople, 6 March, *FO* 371/5042; high commissioner, Constantinople, telegrams to FO, 7 and 8 March, and private to Curzon, 9 March 1920 (quoted), *DBFP* XIII/ 14, 15, and 17 (copy of latter also in *Lloyd George Papers,* F/90/1/4); Ronaldshay, *Curzon,* III, p. 272.

leaders, and suppression of the Chamber of Deputies. Some of these points went too far for the Allies, but Venizelos maintained a firm position, and his optimism was the anchor to which were moored the Allied hopes. Only Churchill questioned Venizelos's facts and figures, but so much faith was placed in the Greeks that his opposition was insufficient, particularly since he, like his prime minister, was known to have his own aberrational policies (Russia, in his case). He wanted to withdraw from Turkey and send troops to Russia; Lloyd George would withdraw from Russia and stay on in Turkey. In the end, the only change was to add the Ministry of Posts and Telegraphs to the list of Constantinople buildings to be occupied. De Robeck was of course prepared to carry out these orders, even though the proposed occupation was already being discussed in the Constantinople press because of leaks in London—but he had to warn his superiors that the Turks might then not sign the treaty, or, if they did sign, might not ratify it, or, again, if they did sign and ratify, might not carry it out; in fact, and this was perhaps the least attractive possibility, the government might simply fly to Anatolia and Kemal.[70]

The warning was too late. The War Office was already ordering up scarce troops from Egypt to reinforce Milne, deliberately choosing British soldiers, perhaps believing the India Office about the possible unreliability of Indian units. Milne was issuing formal orders to General F.M. Wilson, the Constantinople garrison commander; Milne's forces were now concentrated in the area of the Straits, Izmit, and the capital, and rather ominously the railway bridges beyond Izmit had been blown up as the last train had pulled into Izmit with the Eskisehir garrison. There were enough troops for the job in hand, however—British and Indian troops, for Allied participation was not a foregone conclusion. The French demanded equality of control in the departments to be occupied, which presumed their cooperation in the occupation, but Italy was hanging back and even suspected of giving aid and comfort to the nationalists. At the last minute, the French pleaded necessary delay, and de Robeck had to anticipate acting quite alone.[71]

[70] Allied conference, 10 March, *DBFP* VII/55-56; Curzon telegram to high commissioner, Constantinople, and high commissioner, Constantinople, telegram to FO, 10 March 1920, with minutes, *FO* 371/5043.

[71] WO telegram to GHQ, Cairo, 10 March, and high commissioner, Constantinople, telegram to FO, 12 March, *FO* 371/5043; WO telegram

No attempt appears to have been made to alter the arrangements.[72] On the early morning of 16 March, British units in the capital supplemented by sailors from the First Battle Squadron took up positions at the War Ministry, the Ministry of Marine, the navy dockyard, the naval base, the Galata Tower, the Ministry of Posts and Telegraphs, and the Central Telephone Exchange, while H.M.S. *Benbow* moved up to Galata Bridge, H.M.S. *Resolution* went to Haidar Pasha, and H.M.S. *Marlborough* moored south of Seraglio point. No significant resistance was offered except at the headquarters of the 10th (Turkish) Division, where two Indian soldiers were killed. Some five to eight Turks died (accounts vary) in another incident, but total casualties were minor

---

to GOC Constantinople, 11 March, *FO* 371/5214; War Diary, Army of the Black Sea, and appendix, especially GOC Constantinople to Lt.-Gen. H. Wilson, 11 March, *WO* 95/4950; GS Intelligence, Constantinople, memorandum, 12 March, *FO* 371/5215; FO telegram to high commissioner, Constantinople, and Curzon to French ambassador, 13 March, *DBFP* XIII/21 and 22; Allied conference, 15 March 1920, *DBFP* VII/60.

[72] The following account is based upon: high commissioner, Constantinople, telegrams to FO, 16 March, *FO* 371/5043, 21 March (2 of date), *FO* 371/5044, letter of 18 March, enclosing Ryan memorandum of 16 March, *FO* 371/5045; Constantinople military report, 23 March, and admiral commanding, First Battle Squadron, to GOC Atlantic Fleet, 23 March, enclosing both captain, *Ramillies,* commanding landing force, to admiral, First Battle Squadron, 17 March, and Brig. Shuttleworth to GOC Constantinople, 16 March, *FO* 371/5046; high commissioner, Constantinople, to Admiralty, 7 April, *FO* 371/5048; and telegram and letter to FO, 20 and 25 March 1920, *FO* 371/5089. Published accounts include Armstrong, *Turkey in Travail,* pp. 110-111; Ryan, *Dragoman,* pp. 142-46; Edib, *Ordeal,* pp. 67-68; Evans, *United States Policy,* pp. 275-77; Azan, *Franchet d'Espérey,* pp. 256-57; Luke, *Cities and Men,* II, pp. 71-73; Philip P. Graves, *Briton and Turk* (London, 1941), p. 200; Waugh, *Turkey Yesterday,* p. 177; Clair Price, *The Rebirth of Turkey* (N.Y., 1923), pp. 170-71; Ahmad Emin Yalman, *Turkey in My Time* (Norman, Okla., 1956), pp. 94-100; Gaston Gaillard, *The Turks and Europe* (London, 1921), pp. 156-59; Harry N. Howard, *The Partition of Turkey: A Diplomatic History 1913-1923* (N.Y., 1966), pp. 256-57; Donald Everett Webster, *The Turkey of Atatürk . . .* (Philadelphia, 1939), pp. 80-86; and Davison, "Turkish Diplomacy," pp. 180-81. Helmreich, *Paris to Sèvres,* pp. 277-83, underestimates the significance of Anglo-French disagreements as a cause of the occupation. One interesting sidelight is Admiral Bristol's complete surprise: Bristol telegrams to secretary of state, 16, 17, and 18 March 1920, *Bristol Papers,* box 28.

indeed, and most of the sailors soon returned to their ships. At 10:00 A.M. on 16 March, Ryan met with the grand vizier to demand, after the fact, that the various offices be turned over and to explain the reasons for the occupation, an explanation which the shocked grand vizier (Salih Pasha) found unintelligible. That night and the following day, suspected nationalist leaders were arrested. A dozen chief figures were taken; many more managed to escape, but among those now sent to Malta were Jemal Pasha and his chief of staff; Rauf Bey [Hüseyin Rauf Orbay], signatory of the armistice, arrested with four other deputies in the Chamber; and Essad Pasha, head of the Red Crescent Society(the equivalent of the Red Cross), who was regarded as a Kemalist agent. Meanwhile, a proclamation in five languages signed by General Wilson was posted in public places: citizens remaining loyal and quiet would not suffer, but those offering resistance could expect trial by military court empowered to pass sentence of death—in effect, a declaration of martial law.

The occupation was quite effective at first sight. The British—for only British had taken part due to French last-minute "delays"—now had control of the key ministries and, although this was not specified, of the city itself. In the Turkish War Ministry, considered the key to Turkish opposition, guards were placed on all rooms, and Brigadier Shuttleworth, in command, saw to it that all but the most urgent (unciphered) work was allowed. Such control would have been more effective had Kemal depended upon the War Ministry, but he did not. The Chamber of Deputies adjourned *sine die*. In April Kemal would call for new elections for a special body to meet in Ankara, so the Allies had simply done Kemal's work for him in disbanding the Constantinople Chamber of Deputies. Kemal's representatives in the capital were under arrest or in flight and a steady clandestine stream of able-bodied Turks into Kemal's territory was underway.

The entire measure was ill-judged when viewed from hindsight, but the easy assurances of Venizelos must be kept in mind. De Robeck, who had warned against occupation, seemed to vindicate Venizelos when he reported that the occupation was exceeding all expectations and that it had been a serious blow to the nationalists while at the same time encouraging the conservatives in the sultan's group. Now was the time, he urged, for a quick conclusion of a peace treaty, in the midst of nationalist disorganization. If the treaty was less drastic than expected, there might be a real chance of Kemalist collapse.

It was good advice, but it overlooked the fact that the occupation was designed to secure Turkish adherence to the treaty as planned, not as revised. Throughout the occupation preparations the conference had continued to work out the details, including borders and status of the Smyrna zone. It appeared to the Turks, moreover, that the occupation presaged the loss of Constantinople despite assurances to the contrary. A proclamation was soon issued which asserted that nationalist attempts to obtain government cooperation had forced the occupation, which was provisional and intended only to strengthen the position of the sultan. Constantinople would still be Turkish, but if disturbances continued, this last promise would be examined—a condition which tended rather to negate the effect of the entire document.[73]

The proclamation was designed to gain time until the treaty was completed, which Curzon did not expect until late April. The final terms depended upon what military requirements were necessary for enforcing the entire treaty; and something of an impasse was reached when the British War Office advised that such force was just not available.[74] But the treaty was not altered accordingly—for that it was too late—and it was ready for presentation in April, essentially in the form it was to take when the final document was signed at Sèvres in August. By August the terms were even further removed from reality, but in late March 1919 the Allies still appeared in a strong position. In the Allied view, Kemal's nationalist movement had been inspired or at least supported by Turkish government authorities as a device to avoid harsh peace terms. British occupation of Constantinople had met this maneuver and formal presentation of the treaty ending the Turkish war would take place before the Turks could initiate any counter-offensive.

---

[73] High commissioner, Constantinople, telegrams to FO, 21 March, *FO* 371/5044, and 25 March, *FO* 371/5045; Smyrna Committee report, 12 March, 1617/106, *FO* 371/5132.

[74] Curzon telegram to high commissioner, Constantinople, 30 March, and GSWO memorandum, 1 April, *DBFP* XIII/35 and 40; P. Kerr to Lloyd George, 7 April 1920, encloses another copy, *Lloyd George Papers,* F/90/1/4.

V

Ebbtide: Turkey, 1920-1921

By the spring of 1920, nearly a year and a half after the Ottoman Empire had been forced out of the war, there was still no treaty of peace, although some slow progress had been made and some basic principles agreed upon. Kemal's movement had proved troublesome, but the Allies' decision to counter it with occupation of the capital is hard to explain, since Allied control over the sultan's government in Constantinople had already proven insufficient to control events in the interior. The lack of both information and understanding and the widely held conviction that Constantinople controlled and directed Kemal must be recalled.

This assumption led to a second: quick agreement on a final treaty and quick signature by the Turkish government would turn chaos into order. When the Allied Supreme Council reconvened at San Remo in April, considerable disagreement and jealousy complicated resolution of the issues held over from February. Armenia, Kurdistan, Straits control, Italy's sphere, or America's participation—the issues were hardly new, but a reading of the minutes shows that the real division was between those who believed that the main lines of the treaty were enforceable and those who did not. Marshal Foch, speaking for the inter-Allied command, fell into the latter group when he presented the impossible requirement of twenty-seven divisions to do the job. Lloyd George, spokesman for protreaty negotiators, challenged this figure as far too high for seizure of the vital parts (Bursa, Konya, Trebizond, and other such centers), possession of which would make Turkey unable to function and force compliance. Foch persisted, with Gallic logic, arguing that unless the Turks were disarmed the treaty was unenforceable, and disarmament was impossible with inadequate forces. Even including Venizelos's Greek divisions, nothing like twenty-seven divisions were available. The diplomats continued to regard the military prognosis as too gloomy, however; there was always the possibility of an Armenian armed force, and enough of Turkey could always be held to force the treaty home without occupying the whole of the country.[1]

Francesco Nitti, Conference host and Italian premiere, did his best to hold out against Lloyd George, but Nitti's statements always sounded pro-Turkish; his pessimism was too easily dismissed as rationalization for Italian jealousy of Greece. Nitti argued against a Greek regime in Smyrna and for a wider Turkish frontier in Thrace (the Enos-Media line rather than the Chatalja lines), but he made no headway. Greece, Lloyd George maintained, could not leave fellow Greeks in Smyrna undefended, and "no one," he added with clear conviction, "believed that Mustafa Kemal would be able to drive the Greeks out of Asia Minor."[2]

Armenia was another vexing issue but could be held over once more pending an expression of American opinion, for President Wilson had not abandoned his interest in the area. The presence of confident Armenian delegates at San Remo, sure of their ability to occupy and hold such areas as might be assigned to them in the future, unwisely detracted from the immediacy of the issue. To the United States, therefore, was left the determination of Armenian boundaries; the Allies hoped, of course, that the Americans would in the end assume full responsibility for the area and thus relieve them of any Armenian burden. Meanwhile, the Allies passed on to the tripartite agreement which recognized the special interests of Italy and France and thus fulfilled long-delayed promises.[3]

Altogether, the San Remo meeting seemed successful. If only inter-Allied agreement had meant Turkish signature, the Allies would have achieved the unachievable.[4] Lloyd George above all was riding the crest

[1] Allied meetings (Supreme Council), 19-26 April, *DBFP* VIII/4-19; P. Kerr to Lloyd George, 7 April 1920, *Lloyd George Papers,* F/90/1/4; Helmreich, *Paris to Sèvres,* Ch. XIII.

[2] Supreme Council, 21 April 1920, *DBFP* VIII/9; Pallis, *Greece's Anatolian Adventure,* pp. 124-39.

[3] Draft annexed to Supreme Council, 23 April, *DBFP* VIII/13. The evidence was strong that there would be no American mandate; Geddes telegram to Curzon, 11 May, *DBFP* XIII/62; secretary of war to secretary of state, 2 June 1920, *FRUS,* 1920, III, pp. 783-85; the Senate rejected President Wilson's appeal in June. See also the report of General Harbord (or which chapter 6, p. 253) "American Military Mission to Armenia," *International Conciliation* (N.Y., 1920), no. 151, pp. 275-312.

[4] Another problem which has not been discussed here and which also

of his Philhellenic wave, convinced that Christian Greece was the ally
of the future in the Mediterranean and trusting in Venizelos's infantry
divisions if another dose of force was required (and to the British fleet
if Greece ever required persuasion in her turn). The voices of opposition had been stifled, and they were not merely Italian. Field-Marshal
Wilson confided his frustration and anger to his diary: the "Frocks"
had again lost their heads over a policy completely out of touch with
reality. "We soldiers," he said thinking of himself and Foch, "think
they are all 'rotters.' " But Lloyd George was used to military opposition,
and Wilson in particular was "a Tory of the most crusted kind"—the
Tories had always been notoriously pro-Turk.[5]

On 11 May Turkish representatives in Paris were handed the treaty
text. It would be three months before they signed the document at
Sèvres, but the basic terms remained essentially the same. In sum, the
Turks and their sultan remained in Constantinople, but the Straits,
permanently opened, would be under an international commission.
Smyrna and adjacent territory (boundaries to be delimited) remained
technically Turkish, but Greece would have responsibility for administration. Within five years a local parliament could request union with
Greece, subject to League plebiscite. Kurdish autonomy and Armenian
independence were recognized, but again the boundaries were left to

---

required agreement was distribution of oil concessions; see Evans, *U.S.
Policy,* pp. 297-300; Busch, *Britain, India, and the Arabs,* p. 387. The
problem is reviewed in Paul C. Helmreich, "Oil and the Negotiation of the
Treaty of Sevres, December 1918-April 1920," *Middle East Forum* (Beirut)
42 (1966): 67-75, concluding that oil played a "surprisingly minor role."

[5] Callwell, *Wilson,* II, p. 235; Lloyd George quoted in Lord Riddell,
Intimate Diary of the Peace Conference and After, 1918-1923 (London,
1933), p. 208. A useful review of Lloyd George's policy and motives toward
Greece is A.E. Montgomery, "Lloyd George and the Greek Question, 1918-
22," in A. J.P. Taylor, ed., *Lloyd George: Twelve Essays* (London, 1971),
pp. 357-84.

One of the murkier aspects of the prime minister's policy is the influence
of the munitions magnate, Sir Basil Zaharoff, who was reasonably close to
Lloyd George, certainly pro-Greek, and undoubtedly influential. Beyond that
point there is little concrete evidence, nor would there likely be in the official records (aside from an occasional vague reference) or, given the
shadowy career of Zaharoff and the reticence of Lloyd George himself, in
the private papers of the prime minister. And yet the enemies of official
policy never doubted his powers; see for example the frustrating pursuit of

the future (the latter to be set by the Americans). Finally, all Arab areas were separated from Turkish rule. Additional financial and other sections completed a comprehensive and elaborate document. The treaty was the most demanding in the territorial sense of all the peace treaties which followed World War I. "I would personally have made a different treaty," Curzon wrote privately to de Robeck; as he saw it, the treaty resulted from unwise promises Lloyd George had made in the previous year to Venizelos. But all things considered, as even Curzon had to admit, Britain had gotten much of what it wanted.[6]

The treaty had yet to be signed by the Turks, however. The terms came as a shock to Constantinople opinion, and the first response was

---

the connection between the two men by Aubrey Herbert in Parliament (*Parl. Deb., H.C.,* 14 and 23 June 1920), discussed in Robert Neumann, *Zaharoff the Armaments King* (London, 1938), pp. 217-18; see also Donald McCormick, *Peddler of Death: The Life and Times of Sir Basil Zaharoff* (N.Y., 1965), Ch. XIV ("The Mirage of a Greek Empire"). A sample of how widespread suspicions were in circles remote from the prime minister (which surely did nothing to smooth policymaking and application) can be found in Commander H. Luke private to de Robeck, 21 February 1921, *De Robeck Papers* (Churchill College, Cambridge), 6/21: Luke, a subordinate of de Robeck's stationed on the west coast of Turkey, went out of his way to explore Zaharoff's early career in Limasol, Cyprus, but, he reported, was unable to uncover anything interesting.

[6] Derby telegram to FO, 11 May, *DBFP* XIII/61; Curzon private to de Robeck, 18 May 1920 (quoted), *Curzon Papers,* F/3/3. The treaty is found in Great Britain, Parliamentary Papers, 1920, "Treaty of Sèvres," Treaty Series No. 11, Cmd. 964; Hurewitz, *Diplomacy,* II, pp. 81-87, gives the main political clauses.

Considerable debate raged on the question of Turkey's future: for example, see the various publications of the Indian Khilafat Delegation listed in the bibliography; William Barry, "Constantinople," *Nineteenth Century and After* 87 (1920): 718-28; Viscount Bryce, "The Settlement of the Near East," *Contemporary Review* 117 (1920): 1-9, and "The Revision of the Turkish Treaty. I. Armenia," *Contemporary Review* 119 (1921): 577-81; Noel Buxton, "The Revision of the Turkish Treaty. III. Thrace," *Contemporary Review* 119 (1921): 586-89; Paxton Hibben, "What the Greek Are Fighting For," *Current History* 14 (1921): 408-15; Andre Mandelstam, "The Turkish Spirit," *The New Europe* 15 (1920): 39-45; Adamantios Polyzoides, "Why the Greeks are Fighting Turkey," *Current History* 14 (1921): 761-66; Sir J. Stavridi, "The Revision of the Turkish Treaty. II. Smyrna," *Contemporary Review* 119 (1921): 581-86; and the many articles of Arnold Toynbee, some of which are listed in the bibliography.

to ask for a delay until July to consider them. The long delay in drawing up the document was rightly taken as evidence of inter-Allied strains, and in Milne's opinion the Turks hoped to persuade the French and Italian governments to modify their stand. Both powers—particularly France—were running into considerable trouble with nationalists in their areas of occupation as Turkish resistance mounted, and their support for the Ottoman request could be taken as evidence that Milne and Constantinople were correct.[7]

The Turkish reply, when it did come, naturally requested considerable modification of the terms. The Allies took only enough time out from German affairs at the Spa conference to return a strong answer with minimal concessions. Ferid Pasha's government was now in a dilemma. As the grand vizier told de Robeck, the treaty would be useless if it could not be imposed upon the population. The temptation to use fear of Kemal as a lever for concessions was almost irresistible; but Ferid Pasha saw the dangers of this approach, for the Allies too easily might come to discount the influence of the official government in Constantinople. The only safe policy for the grand vizier was to sign within the time limit and hope that the British would help restore order in the interior.[8]

Official Turkish signature was only one requirement. The Greco-Italian quarrel on the western coast nearly wrecked the treaty, for it appeared in late July and early August that Greece would not sign until agreement was reached with Italy on a wide range of issues including Albania and the Dodecanese Islands. Greco-Italian hostility impeded progress on the tripartite agreement as well, when in July Britain declined to sign (both France and Britain were reluctant to do so in any case) unless the Greeks were satisfied with the treaty, but Greece waited upon Italy. At last, however, on 10 August, in Paris, the agreements were signed: the Treaty of Sèvres, the Greco-Italian Convention, and

[7] High commissioner, Constantinople, telegram to Curzon, 26 May, GHQ, Constantinople, telegram to WO, 27 May, *FO* 371/5048; GOC Constantinople telegram to WO, 2 June, Derby telegram to FO, 7 June 1920, *FO* 371/5049.

[8] High commissioner, Constantinople, telegram to FO, 10 June, 17 and 22 July, *DBFP* XIII/78, 99, 101; Allied discussion of Turkish reply at Bologne, Allied conference, 21 June, *DBFP* VIII/33; Vansittart to Curzon, 28 June, enclosing Turkish reply, and Curzon telegram to FO (from Spa), 7 July 1920, *FO* 371/5109.

the self-limiting tripartite agreement of Britain, France, and Italy, which was ostensibly designed to avoid the obnoxious prewar international concession-hunting rivalries.[9]

There was scant joy and celebration. All signatories knew that the Sèvres treaty settled very little. Ferid Pasha had already shuffled his government to build a protreaty majority, but de Robeck still felt that the government was collapsing. The high commissioner hoped that Ferid Pasha would last long enough to obtain ratification—one legal hurdle yet to overcome—but he looked more and more like a puppet dancing to an Allied tune. To make matters worse, an Armenian delegate had signed the Sèvres treaty; Curzon, absent from the actual ceremonies, was completely unprepared for this. Signature constituted *de jure* recognition of Armenia, a policy unapproved by the Foreign Office. "I never knew a more ridiculous muddle," Curzon wrote when he found out two weeks after the fact, and it may be taken as an apt summary of the entire process which had produced agreements so far removed from Turkish reality.[10]

The Sèvres treaty was not only unrealistic; it was also achieved only at considerable cost. Already the Turkish government which signed was tainted by its collaboration; already the military authorities had pointed out the virtual impossibility of enforcement. Civilian-military disharmony could be listed, therefore, as one side-effect. Even greater costs, however, could be seen in the British Empire at large, for Turkish policy had become an issue of considerable importance to India. Most important, however, was the increasing determination of the Turkish nationalist movement to resist.

---

[9] The Greco-Italian negotiations may be followed in *DBFP* XIII/104-18; Derby private to Curzon, 11 May and 27 July, and Vansittart private to Curzon, 11 May 1920, explain French attitude, *Curzon Papers,* F/6/3, F/3/3. The tripartite agreement, interestingly enough, was not included in the treaty proper because it was expected that such inclusion would arouse even more Turkish opposition to the whole treaty—if that were possible. Curzon to Buchanan, 12 February 1921, *DBFP* XVII/37.

[10] High commissioner, Constantinople, telegrams to FO, 30 July, *FO* 371/5054, and 1 and 12 August, *DBFP* XIII/110, 121; Vansittart to Curzon, 11 August, Forbes Adam to Tilley, 6 September, with Curzon minute (quoted), 10 September 1920, *FO* 371/5112.

GANDHI AND THE KHILAFAT

The decision to leave the Turks in Constantinople was regarded by Montagu as a personal victory, although he had of course spoken for India. Here too, there were costs. Montagu had at one point contemplated resignation. His enemies were legion, and there was always the possibility that Lloyd George might slide back under the pressure of his British advisors and his Greek friends. For this reason, Montagu made the best case possible in favor of his own participation in San Remo as representative of India. It was just the sort of legalistic case which irked the prime minister, for Montagu made officious references to such things as his appointment as holder of the Great Seal from the monarch. Despite the warning of Bonar Law, Lloyd George's important coalition partner, that Montagu's resignation on this issue would be dangerous, Lloyd George was willing to risk it—or else had correctly concluded that Montagu would not go that far. For the moment, the explanation that India's voice had been heard and that there was no place for further representation from the empire and dominions had to satisfy Montagu, for after all San Remo had made no change in what he had come to see as the most important point of the treaty: Constantinople.[11]

Montagu was to some extent correctly representing widespread feeling among leaders of Indian opinion, both Muslim and Hindu. The Turkish question, generally subsumed under the term "Khilafat," presented a unique opportunity to Indian politicians for Hindu-Muslim cooperation. When the Ali brothers were released from wartime incarceration in late 1919, they proved quite willing to work with Gandhi. In January 1920 the viceroy felt it advisable to receive a substantial Khilafat delegation. In February Shaukat Ali, secretary of the Central Khilafat Committee, embarked on a lengthy Indian tour, and a delegation composed of his brother Mohammad and Sayyid Hussein, editor of the Allahabad *Independent,* left for England, closely observed by the

[11] Montagu private telegrams to Chelmsford, 1 and 22 January, Chelmsford private telegram to Montagu, 3 January, *Chelmsford Papers,* E. 264/12; Montagu private to Chelmsford, 1 April, *Montagu Papers,* D. 523/4; and to Lloyd George, 25 April (quoted in Busch, *Britain, India, and the Arabs,* p. 390); Bonar Law to Lloyd George, 16 and 23 April, *Lloyd George Papers,* F/40/3/5, 31/1/22, 31/11/25; Montagu to Bonar Law, 23 April 1920, *Bonar Law Papers* (Beaverbrook Library), 98/9/28; Waley, *Montagu,* pp. 244-46.

Indian authorities, who were worried about the agitation and even more fearful of some hidden Bolshevik connection. Already indications from Amir Amanullah in Afghanistan showed widespread Central Asian interest in the caliphate question. No immediate trouble was expected, but the signs were ominous.[12]

Nor was agitation confined to Asia. When the delegation reached London, it encountered considerable activity already in progress among several groups. These included, for example, the Islamic Society, working mainly for treaty revision; the Central Islamic Society, turning out pro-Turkish propaganda from a Fleet Street address; the pan-Islamic "Islamic Information Bureau" (not to be confused with another and separate Islamic Bureau, which also had a branch office in Paris); the Anglo-Ottoman Society, established before the war, which included some well-known parliamentary figures such as Aubrey Herbert, Lord Lamington, and J.M. Kenworthy (later Lord Strabogli); and, finally, the important London Indian Association, established in 1913, which was agitating for home rule in India and included among its members such capable men as M.A. Jinnah. The objectives of these groups varied, and there was as much disagreement over funds or personalities as there was cooperation, but collectively they represented a fairly substantial body of opinion capable of reaching both press and Parliament. Several newspapers and journals were produced by the movement itself, notably *The Muslim Outlook,* started in 1919 by the Islamic Information Bureau and sent to all MP's as well as many labor groups and British newspapers. The movement could not be ignored, therefore; it touched and could influence India, Britain, and Turkey itself, either directly by inspiring resistance in Constantinople or Ankara or indirectly by altering the attitudes of those Indian troops who increasingly made up the garrison in Turkey. By the end of 1920 each brigade included one British and three Indian battalions, and this had to be remembered as the army relied more and more on its professional Indian units following

[12] Based upon file *C/J&P*/6/1574 (especially Mohammad Ali to SSI, 12 April); IO memorandum, 10 January (B. 361), viceroy telegram to SSI, 20 January and 2-3 February (3 parts), *L/P&S*/10/798; Chelmsford private to Montagu, 4 February, *Chelmsford Papers,* E. 264/10; *Home Political Proc.,* March 1920, 30, part B.; India, *Histories of the Non-Co-Operation and Khalifat Movements,* pp. 148-49; Niemeijer, *Khilafat,* Ch. IV; Afghani interest in Amanullah to viceroy, 23 February 1920, 3779/139, *FO* 371/5141.

demobilization of drafted men from Britain.[13]

The Khilafat delegation, then, had this background to work with in its meetings with high government officials. The delegation focused specifically upon the caliphate, insisting that the sultan as caliph should continue to control the Arabian holy places of Mecca and Medina and enough territory—hopefully, much of it in the Arab world—to be able to remain a temporal power. Between the delegation's arrival and its meeting with Lloyd George, agitation in India appeared to be reaching a peak as Gandhi called for *hartal*—strike—on 19 March and at the same time urged Indians to renounce government posts and positions (a suggestion which was regarded with considerable suspicion by some Muslims, who saw this as a device to oust Muslims from hard-won government offices). Chelmsford and his advisors concluded that the best reaction would be no reaction, relying on the fact that India's official government sympathy on the Turkish issue would undermine the nationalist agitation. "Shocking weakness," noted Curzon, but the Indian government was worried despite its official unconcern.[14]

[13] Director of intelligence (Scotland House) to FO, 5 March 1920, *FO* 371/5202, and Interdepartmental Committee on Eastern Unrest, meeting, 30 May 1922, review many such organizations' histories, 5795/402, *FO* 371/7790. Samples: Anglo-Ottoman Society to Curzon, 18 February, Islamic Society to FO, 7 March 1920, and many others, file 139/44, *FO* 371/5140. Lt.-Cmd. Hon. J.M. Kenworthy, *Sailors, Statesmen—and Others . . .* (London, 1933), p. 172. On Indian battalions, WO (MO1) note, 6 December 1920, *WO* 106/1434.

[14] Delegation meeting with H.A.L. Fisher (Board of Education, acting for Montagu) and IO officials, 2 March, Shuckburgh note, 16 March, on P. Kerr to Duke (permanent undersecretary, IO), 15 March (asking IO for direction in conduct of meeting), viceroy (Home Dept.) telegrams to SSI, 12 and 17 March, *L/P&S*/10/798; Chelmsford private to Montagu, 17 March, Montagu private to Chelmsford, 23 June, *Montagu Papers,* D.523/ 10 and 4; Curzon minute (quoted) on viceroy telegram to SSI, 12 March 1920, 2505/139, *FO* 371/5141. Niemeijer, *Khilafat,* Ch. V; Theodore Morison, "England and Islam," *Nineteenth Century and After* 86 (1919): 116-22; Arnold J. Toynbee, "The Question of the Caliphate," *Contemporary Review* 117 (1920): 192-96; and "The Indian Moslem Delegation," *The New Europe* 15 (1920): 56-60; Syed Ameer Ali, "The Caliphate and the Islamic Renaissance," *Edinburgh Review* 237 (1923): 180-95; Sir Valentine Chirol, "Islam and Britain," *Foreign Affairs* 1 (1923): 48-58, and "The Downfall of the Khalifate," *Foreign Affairs* 2 (1924): 571-82; Snouck Hurgronje, "Islam and Turkish Nationalism," *Foreign Affairs*

On the 19th Lloyd George met the delegates in order to make sooth-
ing remarks—although it is arguable how quieting the Indians found
the comment that the Turks, like the Germans before them, would
receive justice.[15] The same day, Indian authorities were relieved to see
that Gandhi's *hartal* did not meet expectations, at least the fearful
official expectations. No great rash of resignations followed either.
Despite the feeling that the Khilafat delegation had achieved little,
Khilafat agitation appeared to be dying, while interest in recently proclaimed constitutional reforms was on the increase. Against this im-
proving atmosphere had to be placed the fact that the prime minister
had received a delegation representing a disruptive movement and
headed by a man only recently released from imprisonment for hostile
attitudes. Gandhi, too, indicated that he was under severe pressure to
travel to England. India remained nervous; the movement could still
contaminate the Middle Eastern situation, or, more to the point, the
delicate negotiations with Afghanistan just then going on at Mussoorie.[16]

In particular, announcement of the Turkish terms could bring an
explosion, and to avoid this Chelmsford complicated matters by accom-

---

3 (1924): 61-77; Rev. D.S. Margoliouth, "The Caliphate," *The New
Europe* 14 (1920): 294-300.

[15] Prime minister meeting with delegation, 19 March 1920, and file of
clippings *L/P&S/*10/798. The delegation's activities in England are discussed in *Home Poli. Proc.,* April 1920, 8; M.H. Abbas, *All About the
Khilafat . . .* (Calcutta, [1923]), p. 160; K.K. Aziz, *Britain and Muslim
India . . .* (London, 1963), pp. 108-9; Gopal, *Indian Muslims,* pp. 142-43;
R.C. Majumdar, ed., *Struggle for Freedom . . .,* vol. XI (Bombay, 1969),
pp. 317-18; Colin Forbes Adam, *Life of Lord Lloyd* (London, 1948), p. 142:
Lloyd, governor of Bombay, was asked to lead the delegation; see also Mohammad Ali private to Shaukat Ali, 6 May, enclosed in Chelmsford private
to Montagu, 3 June 1920, *Montagu Papers,* D. 523/10.

[16] Viceroy (Home Dept.) telegrams to SSI, 31 March and 2 and 7 April,
Gandhi telegram to viceroy, 22 April, *L/P&S/*10/798; Chelmsford private
telegram to Montagu, 15 April, and Lord Willingdon (governor of Madras)
private to Chelmsford, 23 April, *Chelmsford Papers,* E. 264/12 and 24;
Willingdon private to Montagu, 20 April 1920, *Willingdon Papers,* F. 93.
Shuckburgh's minute on Gandhi's telegram, when it reached London, is
expressive of the era's attitude: "It is surely no time to give Indian agitators
'joy-rides' to Europe, when war-weary officials and dying Englishwomen
are being held up indefinitely in India." The Mussoorie negotiations are
discussed in Chapter 6, pp. 293-4.

panying publication of the Sèvres terms with an explanation that they were necessary despite the obvious pain they would cause some sections of Muslim opinion—and to those sections he expressed his encouragement and sympathy. Montagu was too busy expressing his disapproval of the treaty as a whole—totally unenforceable, in his opinion—to criticize his viceroy for this maneuver, but even Montagu knew that India would now have to accept the treaty as final; ". . . she cannot be allowed to try and accomplish by threats or agitation what she could not do by argument," he wrote Lord Willingdon in Madras.[17]

No explosion resulted, but by midsummer a peculiar phenomenon on the Afghan frontier demonstrated how alive the issue remained. A number of sadly misguided Muslim peasants, estimated as high as 18-20,000, moved from Sind, the Punjab, and Frontier areas toward Afghanistan, stimulated by Khilafat agitation and encouraged by reports of a warm Afghani welcome. Most of the *muhajirun* ("emigrants") returned impoverished and disillusioned from the frontier, but the Khilafat movement was entering another active phase. A joint Khilafat-Congress program was agreed upon at Allahabad in early June; Gandhi and Shaukat Ali toured the provinces in July. Officials found it hard to separate out Gandhi's new "noncooperation" (a doctrine enunciated in March) from Khilafat agitation, but it was just the conjunction which was so dangerous. In late July an estimated 10,000 people heard "seditious" speeches, as the Khilafat committee rode into the public eye in part on the shoulders of Gandhi's movement. Gandhi's support for the Muslims did not go uncriticized, but to arguments that he was overemphasizing the importance of the caliphal problem for the Indian Muslims, he answered that this was both expedient and a test of friendship in adversity.[18]

The government was increasingly worried, but noninterference on the frontier had been the correct policy. In any case, local muhajirun leaders could not be arrested while the main leaders like the Alis and

---

[17] Viceroy (Home Dept.) telegrams to SSI, 14 May, 19 May, 11 June, and file of clippings, *L/P&S*/10/851 (and *Chelmsford Papers,* E. 264/12); Chelmsford private to Montagu, 19 and 26 May, Montagu private to Curzon and private to Willingdon, 20 May 1920 (latter quoted), *Montagu Papers,* D. 523/10, 4, and 16.

[18] Niemeijer, *Khilafat,* pp. 103-5; India, *Histories of the Non-Co-Operation and Khalifat Movements,* pp. 154-60; Gopal, *Muslim India,* pp. 142-46; Majumdar, *Struggle for Freedom,* pp. 317-19; *C/J&P*/6/1697,

Gandhi remained at liberty. And as Grant, chief commissioner of the North-West Frontier, added, the anti-British flight to Afghanistan might just rid British India of some troublesome fanatics. Mohammad Ali, leader of the London delegation, was currently stopping off in Rome for an audience with the Pope (and, more ominous, talks with leaders of the Italian government). He would soon leave for Paris, so the time was not ripe for the arrest of his brother in India. At least this was Chelmsford's attitude, although not all of his independent-minded subordinates argued with him. The Earl of Ronaldshay, governor of Bengal, was particularly critical in his private letters to Montagu. Lord Lloyd in Bombay was less critical but equally alarmed; Indians, he feared, were likely to make an invidious comparison between the new Indian reforms and the independence Egyptian nationalists appeared to have forced from Britain.[19]

Montagu was aware of these contrary opinions, just as he knew of the nationalist problems in the Middle East. He had little choice but to accept Chelmsford's conclusions, although in passing he felt obliged to note his concern over the association of anti-British extremism and international Bolshevik agitation. In making such a connection, Montagu was for once among the majority in British officialdom. By mid-1920, in fact, an extensive intelligence operation was being created to study just such connections as that between India and Bolshevism. Already during the war a member of the Imperial Indian Police had been assigned to the Directorate of Military Intelligence (MI5) in London for confidential work on enemy-sponsored sedition in India. At the same time, the criminal intelligence director (in 1918 renamed central intelligence director) conducted similar inquiries in India. Immediately after the war a Special Bureau of Information was established to search

---

file 5408; Chelmsford private to Montagu, 11 August, *Montagu Papers,* D. 523/11, gives 20,000; viceroy (Home Dept.) telegram to SSI, 21 August 1920, *Chelmsford Papers,* E. 264/13, 30,000; "muhajirun," it should be mentioned, is the term used for the "emigrants", the companions of Muhammad who accompanied him from Mecca to Medina.

[19] Grant private to Chelmsford, 7 August, *Chelmsford Papers,* E. 264 /25; Buchanan, Rome, telegram to FO, 3 August, Sir B. Thomson, Scotland House, to FO, 18 August, *FO* 371/5142; Earl of Ronaldshay private to Montagu, 23 June and 17 August, G. Lloyd private to Montagu, 27 August, *Montagu Papers,* D. 523/31 and 25; Montagu memorandum for Cabinet, 19 October 1920 (C.P. 2000), *CAB* 24/112.

for Bolshevik activities in India; the bureau remained an independent organization until its absorption by the CID in December 1920. Occasional references in the records to pension and salary problems of seconded officials show that Indian officials were borrowed for "special intelligence duties, with special reference to Eastern affairs" in London.[20]

A problem arose when wartime mail censorship regulations lapsed in August 1919, but India continued to fight sedition through the Rowlatt Acts and through close watch on those individuals considered tinged with Bolshevism. Indian authorities, for all their diligence, were forced to conclude in December 1920, when the Special Bureau was closed, that "inquiries so far made have failed to establish the presence in India of any person who can be described with accuracy as a true Bolshevik agent, despatched from Russia," although no doubt some Indians outside India were in touch with the Bolsheviks. Officials at home simply refused to believe that the conclusion was so safe or simple: Bolshevik-trained Indians were much more to be feared than Russian agents, although "agent" really meant anyone who advocated a policy pursued by any "Bolshevik" anywhere. As Montagu put it to the Cabinet in mid-1921, "we may say definitely that the Soviet Government is using every possible medium to damage Great Britain in India and the East generally, and is making special efforts to co-ordinate many different agencies for a combined effort converging on India."[21]

The year 1920 had thus seen considerable pro-Turkish agitation in India. That agitation may be said to have had considerable effect insofar as it helped to alter the future of Constantinople. India and the India Office were not, of course, solely responsible for that decision, as no one had a viable alternative to suggest. Indian opinion was more than

[20] DMI to IO, 24 July 1916, 2952/16, *C/J&P/6/1450*; Government of India (Home Dept.) to Duke, IO, 2 March 1921, 1954/21, *C/J&P/6/1625*; unsigned note for J.W. Hose (IO), 28 July, Col. V.G.W. Kell (head of MI5) to J.E. Ferard, IO, (quoted) 28 September, SSI telegram to viceroy (Home Dept.), 1 October 1920, 5219, 6607/20, *C/J&P/6/1696*. See chapter 3, note 82.

[21] Viceroy telegrams to SSI, 17 March, 12 April, and 12 October, viceroy in council to SSI (quoted), with minutes, 16 December 1920, D. Bray memorandum, 18 May, and Montagu memorandum for Cabinet, 14 June 1921 (quoted), 2094/21, *L/P&S/10/836*; and unsigned memorandum (by Bray), B. 360, on "Middle East, Turco-Bolshevik Activities," 10 December 1920, 154/154, *FO 371/6342*. See also series of Special Bureau reports, January-November 1920, *L/P&S/10/887*.

negligible, however. Gandhi's cooperation with the Khilafat movement and his initial use of noncooperation as a methodology of activism made the movement all the more potent. The tendency of some to link the movement with Bolshevik agitation only made it appear more threatening and more necessary to appease. Some critics damned the movement as artificial or criminal-led (meaning the Ali brothers); others supported the alternative pro-Greek or anti-Turk (not necessarily the same thing) parties; still others would just not reveal weakness before nonwhite anti-imperialist movements. For all that, however, Turkey was an active issue in Indian agitation, and Indian agitation increased the difficulties of the Turkish question.

The connection was clearly visible to India and the India Office, and although the policy was still watchful noninterference, such a policy did not rule out continued pressure on the Foreign Office and Cabinet to modify the terms of the Sèvres treaty. The justification for such pressure was the hope that concession to Muslim opinion would go far to sever the newly built and fragile connection between Hindu and Muslim.[22] Beyond that objective lay the wider one on which all could agree, despite disagreement on the means to achieve it: to sever the connections which linked Indian and Arab and Egyptian and Bolshevik and Turkish movements into a worldwide revolutionary agitation. In Turkey, however, the immediate problem was the growth of the Turkish nationalist movement, a growth even more directly related to the Sèvres terms than India's Khilafat movement.

THE GREEK OFFENSIVE

Actually there were several Turkeys. One, in Constantinople, appeared to be under firm Allied control, although still nominally independent. Another, in the interior under Kemal, was technically

---

[22] Sir E. MacLagan, Lahore, demiofficial to W.H. Vincent (Home Member of Council), 12 November 1920, For. and Pol. Dept., Secret External files 172-X. In addition to the works listed above, remarks in this section are based on Aga Khan, *The Memoirs of . . .* (London, 1954), pp. 154-58; Moon, *Gandhi,* p. 119; Broomfield, *Elite Conflict,* pp. 145, 155-56; Abbas, *All About the Khilafat,* pp. 336-56; and the following IO files: *C/J&P/ 6/1701* (Hijrat), *C/J&P/6/1669* (Hunter report and agitation), and *C/J&P/6/1644* (prohibition of circulation of ruble currency in India in relation to Bolshevik activities).

subordinate to Constantinople but in reality independent. Then there were Kurds, and Armenians, and brief, meteoric movements near Izmit or in other areas. Finally, there was the Turkey under Greek occupation, subordinate only to Athens. A second problem lay in the meaning of "Allied." Since well before the armistice Allied interrelationship had been bedeviled by squabbles over authority and areas of control, which only worsened after the occupation of Constantinople in March 1920. Despite French and Italian objections, British occupation was translated into British presidencies of the commissions of control posted at the Turkish Ministries of War, Marine, and Posts and Telegraphs. Pending formal settlement of the command issue and allocation of responsibility, local French and Italian commanders were cooperating, but the lack of clear-cut lines of authority could create difficulties in a crisis.

There were other problems as well, some within British ranks. General Milne, for example, defined his position as "General Officer Commanding," and vitriolic correspondence could result from his persistence in accepting orders only from the War Office and neither communicating with nor consulting Admiral de Robeck in his capacity as high commissioner. De Robeck, logically, controlled the Turkish Admiralty, and Milne the War Ministry along with Posts and Telegraphs. Separate fiefs tended to develop; and by June bargaining was taking place as to who would give up just how much authority to the other Allies.[23]

Into this mixture should be added the Greeks, whose representatives in Constantinople (not officially connected to the forces in Smyrna) daily went through an elaborate and offensive, traffic-disrupting, flag-raising ceremony outside the Greek embassy. Complaints of Greek behavior were waved aside (". . . no doubt due to the ineradicable bias against anything and anybody Greek that reigns among our officials at Constantinople," wrote Crowe), but the problem remained. A similar issue arose regarding the Italians, Allies in Constantinople but illegal interlopers in southwestern Anatolia. It was rather miraculous, taken all in all, that any inter-Allied cooperation existed in what was fast becoming an exclusively British venture. That cooperation did survive

[23] Milne private to M. Muller (extract), 11 May (5333/1729), Webb to Curzon, 27 April, FO to Admiralty, 10 June, *FO* 371/5218; and M. Muller memorandum, 14 June 1920, *FO* 371/5219.

was due partly to the artificial life of Constantinople, remote and unreal still, with a floating Allied population that saw considerable mixing on lower levels. More important was common concern with the growing Kemalist movement. The Allies disagreed on how best to deal with it, but between the London conference in early 1920 and the signature of the Sèvres treaty in August there was one shared objective: making the treaty work, even though it might be the best of a bad bargain. Discarding the treaty altogether lay in the future, and it was only then that the Allies would truly fall apart.[24]

Unfortunately, the occupation of the capital, designed to facilitate the general objective, had the opposite effect of forcing an open breach between the Constantinople government and Kemal, which made acceptance of the treaty (as opposed to formal signature) more unlikely. The Constantinople government's position relative to the movement had become increasingly delicate since the Chamber of Deputies elections. Then, a month before the occupation, the Chamber had proclaimed the validity of Kemal's National Pact, reaffirming the necessary unity and independence of the old empire inhabited by an Ottoman (Turkish) Muslim majority (together with security for Constantinople and a plebiscite in western, but not eastern, Thrace). The Ottoman authorities had tried to temporize between the Chamber and the Allies, but the Allies took every attempted delay as evidence of Constantinople-Kemalist cooperation as well as further inspiration to stay on in the capital to break that connection. On the other hand, when the authorities responded to pressure and issued denials of association or decrees condemning the nationalists, they appeared to the Kemalists as puppets only, a view which was confirmed when Ferid Pasha returned to office on 5 April.[25]

Within a short time, Ferid Pasha had made his choice; he requested British aid to support him and the local anti-Kemalist forces of one

[24] Caclamanos to Curzon, 8 April, with Crowe minute, 13 April 1920 (quoted), *FO* 371/5144; Mylès, *La fin de Stamboul*, p. 163 (flag ceremony); Luke. *Cities and Men*, II, pp. 78-89; Sir Robert Graves, *Storm Centers of the Near East: Personal Memories, 1879-1929* (London, 1933), pp. 323-32; Sir Nevile Henderson, *Water under the Bridges* (London, 1945), pp. 100-5.

[25] High commissioner, Constantinople, to Curzon, 12 and 16 November 1919, *FO* 371/4160; and telegrams of 30 March (2 of date) and 3 April 1920, *DBFP* XIII/36-37, 42. National Pact text is in Kinross, *Ataturk*, pp. 571-72, and Hurewitz, *Diplomacy*, II, pp. 74-75.

Ahmad Anzavur, a Circassian whose irregular forces operated between Pandirma and Balikesir and whose position had been regularized in traditional Ottoman style by naming him governor of Balikesir with the rank of pasha. De Robeck and Milne, for once in agreement, approved the request; the Turks were not engaged in civil war. It was clear, however, that cooperation with the British would only reduce Ferid Pasha's prestige within Turkey (and perhaps, it might be added, that of the Allies)—inevitably, because "Allied" still meant "Greek" as well. There seemed scant alternative, however, and with de Robeck's support, official proclamations against the nationalists were again issued, the rump Chamber dissolved (and new elections promised within four months), and permission given to supply the official Turks (regulars being preferred to irregulars) with military equipment conveniently on hand in the remaining dumps of surrendered weapons. The plans came to nothing, however; Anzavur collapsed within a month, and the Constantinople government had very little reliable military force left to oppose Kemal.[26] Meanwhile Kemal had used the opportunity presented by the dissolution of the Chamber to assume its authority for his own Grand National Assembly. His movement was growing, but Britain appeared committed to the losing side in a civil conflict. Milne's discouragement is understandable; in May he concluded that it made no difference whether the Constantinople government signed or not, for the treaty could not be enforced.[27]

The situation was worsening for the French too, and despite the deep-seated Anglo-French rivalry in the Middle East, the British representatives could take no satisfaction from French embroilments. Troubles only weakened French resolve to enforce the treaty. Worse, should

[26] High commissioner, Constantinople, telegrams to FO, 11, 15, and 20 April, Webb telegram to FO, 23 April, *DBFP* XIII/48, 50, 52, 54; GHQ, Constantinople, telegram to WO, 13 April, WO to FO, 17 April, Webb telegram to FO, 20 April, and letter, 22 April (on Anzavur), *FO* 371/5046-47; Webb private to de Robeck, 6 May 1920, *De Robeck Papers,* 6/26, shows at least Webb's discouragement at these events.

[27] WO to FO, 14 May, *FO* 371/5048, and 14 June, enclosing CinC Constantinople telegram to WO, 29 May, *FO* 371/5049; high commissioner, Constantinople, telegram to FO, 17 May 1920, *DBFP* XIII/64. On Kemal's actions, Kinross, *Ataturk,* Ch. 26-27; Robinson, *First Turkish Republic,* pp. 70-72; Webster, *The Turkey of Atatürk,* pp. 83-86; Roderic H. Davison, "Turkish Diplomacy from Mudros to Lausanne," Craig and Gilbert, eds., *The Diplomats,* pp. 172-209.

the French be forced to withdraw, Kemal would be free to turn elsewhere, and in June it became clear that the French did intend withdrawal despite all disclaimers to the contrary. A French representative
"passing through Angora on his way home," as the French explained it,
obtained a twenty-day armistice from Kemal. On the surface it was a
tactical measure to relieve awkward pressure; in fact, it was the first
of a long series of agonizing betrayals (from the British standpoint)
which would come with increasing frequency until the final treaty of
Lausanne in 1923. This particular armistice was likely to result in the
abandonment to Kemal of Cilicia and jeopardy to British positions in
Mosul. If the French in turn used the troops thus freed to press on
against the Amir Faisal in Damascus, Britain's relations with the
Arabs would be strained in another direction.[28]

Milne in Constantinople had more immediate worries, however, as
the government's troops were finding it impossible to hold the Izmit
peninsula and were falling back toward the capital; nationalist forces
held all but the tip of the peninsula and the Dardanelles area to the
southwest. Milne had to report that he did not have sufficient forces
both to repel the nationalists and to keep order in the capital. The choice
as he saw it was plain: either reinforce the British garrison and clear
the Izmit district (according to the still unsigned treaty, part of the
neutral Straits zone) or negotiate with Kemal. The trouble with reinforcement, as the War Office had long been aware, was that it could
lead to a major commitment from which withdrawal might be most
difficult, or, if withdrawal from the Asiatic side was finally necessary
and possible, British prestige would suffer seriously. One further possibility which the War Office urged upon the Foreign Office was to so
pressure the French and Italians that they would at last furnish enough
assistance to make resistance possible. That sort of suggestion, which
said nothing about how to avoid a clash with Kemal, helped very little,

---

[28] Graham, Paris, telegram to FO, 4 June, Allenby telegram to Curzon,
19 June, *DBFP* XIII/75, 265; Derby, Paris, telegram to FO, with Berthelot's explanation, 7 June, and Graham telegram, 15 June 1920, *FO* 371/
5049. Kemal's links with Faisal are discussed in Zeine, *Struggle,* pp. 147-48,
and Elie Kedourie, *England and the Middle East . . .* (London, 1956), p.
170. Throughout these months, the British found their French allies extremely reluctant to provide any details on events in Cilicia; see for example
Derby telegram to FO, 21 June 1920, *FO* 371/5051.

and the Foreign Office continued to find War Office lack of zeal most frustrating.[29]

On 15 June, de Robeck reported that British forces were engaged in active hostilities with the nationalist forces; although Milne considered the nationalist attack desultory, he wanted the added security of the British troops at Batum to reinforce his own positions. Another possible means of dealing with the nationalists was to use the Greeks, for their local commander was anxious to advance in the Aydin area and de Robeck and Milne as anxious to approve the request. The nationalists were in no mood to await quietly the imposition of the peace treaty. The Foreign Office doubted the extent of the crisis, but the Cabinet had already taken up the issue along with an offer of aid from Venizelos. The general policy conclusions were fuzzy, but it is clear that Lloyd George was successful in pressing the Greek case. The Batum force would move to Turkey, the War Office would scrape up whatever other reinforcements might be found in Malta or Palestine, but, above all, the Greeks would be used in whatever way could be worked out on the spot. Britain had no mobile reserves to use in such a crisis, and therefore the exposed ends of long communications lines, such as Batum or Kurdistan or the Persian cordons, would have to be pulled back. None of the withdrawals was undertaken for the moment, but such steps were clearly mandatory if the local commanders reported that they were in danger.[30]

Both Foreign Office and War Office advisors contemplated Greek and British reinforcements with mixed emotions. In particular, since this increasing commitment was in support of the sultan's government, was Britain to take over the administration directly if Ferid Pasha fell? Hardinge, for one, would avoid such a risk by negotiation with Kemal

[29] High commissioner, Constantinople, telegram to Curzon, 10 June, *DBFP* XIII/79; CinC Constantinople telegrams to WO, 14 June (2 of date), and WO to FO, 14 June 1920, including CinC Constantinople telegram to WO of 29 May, *FO* 371/5049.

[30] High commissioner, Constantinople, telegrams to FO, 15 and 16 June (latter with FO minutes, *FO* 371/5050), *DBFP* XIII/83-84; Cabinet 53 (20), 30 September, App. II-III, Conference of Ministers 17 and 18 June, *CAB* 23/22. See, however, Hankey private to Lloyd George, 17 June 1920, *Lloyd George Papers,* F/24/2/38, clearly worried about lack of clarity; Roskill's evaluation in *Hankey,* II, p. 198, differs; Callwell, *Wilson,* II, p. 244.

(a suggestion which the military always seemed to consider was "out of the question"). The basis for negotiation, he advised, should be treaty revision which would include complete evacuation of Asia Minor. If such revision were not begun voluntarily now, "one will be forced on us in a few months' time." As Curzon noted coldly, "The Cabinet favour the alternative policy of a military concentration to hold the Ismid Peninsula and repel Mustapha Kemal." Meanwhile, the military regrouped its forces, unwilling to fight but, if a fight was inevitable, anxious to have the maximum force at hand; and Ferid Pasha's authority dwindled away as rapidly as did his troops before Kemal's forces.[31]

Lloyd George had the matter well in hand. On Sunday, 20 June, he met Millerand at Lympne and outlined the planned Greek movements in Thrace and along the Marmora coast. Kemal had to be given a taste of force: "it was indispensable to show that the Allies meant business," for Kemal now thought he had driven back the British in the Izmit area and forced the French out of Cilicia. Millerand agreed; the Greeks could proceed. After all, French forces were not involved, and a Kemal occupied with the Greeks was a Kemal who could not concentrate on Cilicia and Syria. Foch and Weygand agreed in an inter-Allied meeting at Boulogne the next day, and orders were rapidly dispatched to Greek General Paraskevopoulos. The new spirit of optimism was further reinforced when the Turks at Izmit temporarily retreated after being bombed by seaplanes and shelled by offshore guns.[32]

The sudden Allied unanimity survived only until Millerand, back in Paris and less under Lloyd George's persuasive influence, suggested that while of course cooperation would be complete, confusion would only result from the mingling of forces and areas of responsibility: Britain should be responsible for the Izmit area and the French for the capital

---

[31] High commissioner, Constantinople, telegram, 17 June, with Hardinge and Curzon minutes, undated (quoted), *DBFP* XIII/86; CinC Constantinople telegram to WO, 18 June 1920, *FO* 371/5050. Hardinge's "out of the question" minute, undated, on WO to FO, 14 June, note 29, chapter 5.

[32] Conference at Hythe, 20 June, and Boulogne meeting, 21 June, *DBFP* VIII/26-30 (p. 308 quoted) and 33; Curzon telegram to Derby, 21 June, *DBFP* XIII/87; WO telegram to CinC Constantinople, 18 June, CinC Mediterranean telegram to Admiralty, 21 June, *FO* 371/5050; Bridges, Smyrna, telegram to CinC Constantinople, 23 June 1920, *FO* 371/5051. On the fighting, Armstrong, *Turkey in Travail,* pp. 122-23; Brig. W.E. van Cutsem, "Anatolia, 1920," *Army Quarterly* 92 (1966): 175-85.

city itself. Lloyd George quickly countered with a personal appeal: two commanders would only mean friction, and Constantinople was the essential base for Izmit operations in any case. Surely the French could be magnanimous; it was not a question of prestige, but of stopping the Turks. Paris proved only magnanimous enough to postpone the question, agreeing that unified command was indeed desirable—but on the precedent of Salonika, it should be French.[33]

France was not the only backsliding ally. Count Carlo Sforza, now the Italian foreign minister (1920-21) indicated at the Boulogne meeting that Italy was restless over the planned operations—not unnaturally, since the operations would considerably increase the area of Greek occupation, while Italy was asked to participate for nothing, or at least nothing more. Sforza argued that the Greeks might not succeed, but few expected failure as the Greek forces marched off with considerable spirit and optimism in the direction of Marmora to cut Kemalist communications. Athenian optimism, in fact, was sufficiently high to hope that Kemal would stand, the better to be smashed; if he did not, his prestige would inevitably decline. As for the Italians, their aid was not wanted (they were reportedly negotiating with Kemal in any case). Curzon took the trouble to point out to the Italians at the Spa conference just how much their noncooperation embarrassed the Allies. But there was little he could do to move the Italians from their pro-Kemalist and anti-Greek position, for they continued to be at daggers drawn with their neighbors over a vast range of issues.[34]

The first stage of the Greek advance fulfilled all expectations. On 30 June, Balikesir was taken as one column of Greek troops pushed up the railway from Smyrna toward Alashehir and Ushak (where it stopped), another moved along the northern bank of the Meander

---

[33] Derby telegrams to FO, 23 and 27 June, Curzon telegram to Derby, 25 June, *DBFP* XIII/90, 92, and 96; P. Kerr to R. Campbell, 25 June, *FO* 371/5051; CIGS telegram to CinC Constantinople, 24 June, and CinC Constantinople telegrams to CIGS, 26 June, *FO* 371/5134, and 28 June 1920, *FO* 371/5052.

[34] Granville telegram to FO, 24 June, *FO* 371/5134; high commissioner, Constantinople, telegram to Curzon, 23 June, and FO telegram to Buchanan, 26 June, and letter 10 July, *DBFP* XIII/88, 93, and 98; high commissioner, Constantinople, telegram to FO, 10 July 1920, *FO* 371/5053; see also *DBFP* VIII/47 (Spa conference) and XIII/126-29; Callwell, *Wilson*, II, pp. 251-54.

from Aydin, a third moved from Manisa along the railway to Pandirma, and yet another division was moved by sea to Izmit. British naval units assisted in the occupation of such Marmora towns as Mudanya and Gemlik as the Greeks contemplated a further advance to Bursa. So successful were the operations that the Greek commander now prepared to shift some of his forces to western Thrace in preparation for the occupation of eastern Thrace up to the Sèvres line; it was that area, after all, and not the Marmora coast, which had been promised to Greece. On 8 July, however, Greek forces took Bursa after stubborn resistance—puzzling news, since the Thracian operations were about to begin. Crowe later reported that at Spa Venizelos told him that he had opposed the advance to Bursa as unnecessary, and it was Milne's fault; Milne, Venizelos concluded, was trying to involve the Greeks on the Asian side and thus make it difficult for them to advance in Thrace.[35]

In actuality, there appears to have been a breakdown in the three-way communications between Milne, Venizelos, and the Greek commander. General Bridges, now Milne's liaison with the Greeks, reported that the general plan was first Asian operations, then Thrace, then Asian operations again; Venizelos seems not to have known this. Phase two, in any case, was in progress, for on 26 July Adrianople surrendered to the Greeks. Phase three was now a real possibility, although both Milne and de Robeck advised against it, Milne on the grounds that British military aid would in the end be required to assist an overcommitted Greek army, and de Robeck because any further Greek advance only meant that many more angered nationalists. Such advice really stemmed from "their animus against the Greeks," sneered Crowe; each time the military predicted Greek disaster, and each time they were wrong. Curzon, who had talked at length with Lloyd George and

[35] Bridges, Smyrna, telegrams to WO, 2 and 4 July, high commissioner, Constantinople, telegrams to FO, 5 and 8 (#796) July, WO telegram to CinC Constantinople, 23 June, and CinC Constantinople telegram to WO, 8 July, *FO* 371/5052; high commissioner, Constantinople, telegram to FO, 8 July 1920 (#795), *DBFP* XIII/97. Greek operations: van Cutsem, "Anatolia"; Armstrong, *Turkey in Travail*, pp. 125-28; Toynbee, *Western Question*, pp. 212-31; Pallis; *Greece's Anatolian Adventure*, pp. 62-69; Smith, *Ionian Vision*, pp. 126-8; C.R. Hooper, trans., "The Anatolian Revolt," *Army Quarterly* 12 (1926): 106-19, 323-37; Cyril Falls, "The Greek Anatolian Adventure," *History Today* 16 (1966): 452-58; Col. Bujac, *Les campagnes de l'Armée Hellénique, 1918-1922* (Paris, 1930).

Venizelos at Spa, was more cautious: the Greeks really did not wish to undertake a major campaign in Asia Minor, and according to Venizelos they would only advance on the condition that all necessary equipment and supplies were provided by the Allies, until the Turks signed the treaty.[36]

By early August, the Greek successes were unquestionable. They now occupied substantial sections of western Anatolia, including Bursa, a foothold on the plateau at Ushak, and the entire Marmora coast as far as the Izmit neutral zone. This success and the expiration of the Allied time limit persuaded Ferid Pasha, who had once again shuffled his government, to sign at Sèvres. For the grand vizier, the only alternative was the total destruction of his government and complete submission to Kemal's leadership, and for that he was unprepared. The hope now was that Kemal would bow to reality and accept the treaty in order to bring about a Greek retreat to the territory actually assigned to them. De Robeck urged that a delegation from Ferid Pasha's government should proceed to Ankara to warn Kemal that failure to accept the treaty would mean a further Greek advance and harsher treaty terms, including even the loss of Constantinople.[37]

But time was on Kemal's side. Ferid Pasha's financial straits were so desperate that there were insufficient resources even to meet salary commitments. The only alternative to him, as de Robeck saw it, was a more pronationalist government, which would be unwilling to ratify the treaty. The high commissioner, rather unlike Cox in Persia, knew that there was little point to installing yet another puppet and obtaining a paper ratification. Better, therefore, to support Ferid Pasha and meanwhile hope for the best from a mission to Kemal. The only optimists, at least on the surface, were the Greeks, who promised that if necessary they could advance on Ankara and "liquidate" the opposition— but even Venizelos and General Paraskevopoulos, in talks with General

---

[36] Bridges, Pandirma, telegrams to WO, 14 and 21 July (from Constantinople), CinC Constantinople telegram to WO, 13 July, with Crowe minute, 19 July, FO 371/5052; high commissioner, Constantinople, telegram to FO, 28 July, and FO telegram to high commissioner, Constantinople, 30 July 1920, DBFP XIII/102, 106; Crowe minute, 29 July (quoted), and Curzon minute, 30 July, on telegram of 28 July, FO 371/5053 (these minutes are not given in DBFP).

[37] High commissioner, Constantinople, telegram to FO, 30 July 1920, FO 371/5054.

Bridges in Athens, expressed their conviction that a quick solution was essential whatever happened: the Greek forces, as Kemal knew well, could not sit where they were forever.[38]

A mission to Kemal was imperative, and when Ferid Pasha, knowing it would either be useless or demand his own sacrifice, opposed the plan unless he were first provided with substantial military and financial support, de Robeck concluded that Ferid Pasha should go. The Allies agreed, but a change of government really offered no answer in itself; by mid-October, Lloyd George repeated to the Cabinet Venizelos's opinion that a further advance would be necessary and with it the partition of Turkey well beyond that envisaged in the treaty. On 19 October, Ferid Pasha resigned from "ill health"; his successor, the elderly veteran politician Ahmad Tevfik Pasha [Okday], proved immediately amendable to the mission. Ferid Pasha had been doomed, as de Robeck pointed out, by his logical but erroneous conclusion that if he cooperated with the Allies he would obtain modification of the treaty terms and thus strengthen his position. There were other problems, too. No government could survive, for example, in a financial squeeze described as, "Indispensable monthly expenditure, not less than £ T. [Turkish] 1,400,000. Monthly revenue, less than £ T. 1,000,000, and dwindling. Credit, none. Result, misery."[39]

The problem now was reconciling the proposed mission to Kemal with the proposed renewed Greek advance and at the same time ensuring the survival and cooperation of the Constantinople government. That government was in the same camp as the Allies only by default, it should be remembered; the grand vizier had no more overriding desire to ratify the treaty than Kemal, and when pressed to do so by an Allied collective note in late October he replied that a Chamber would

---

[38] High commissioner, Constantinople, telegram to FO, 10 September, and letter, 28 September, enclosing Ryan note, *DBFP* XIII/136, 144; Bridges, Athens, telegram to WO, 26 September 1920, with FO minutes, *FO* 371/5135.

[39] High commissioner, Constantinople, telegrams to FO, 23 September, 1, 4, and 21 October, Curzon to Derby, 1 October, Venizelos telegram to Lloyd George, 5 October, *DBFP* XIII/142, 147, 149-50, 152, 159 (also minutes in *FO* 371/5055); Cabinet 54 (20), 12 October, *CAB* 23/22; Marquess Imperiali to Curzon, 17 September, *FO* 371/5055; high commissioner, Constantinople, telegram to FO, 19 October, *FO* 371/5056, and letter, 22 October 1920 (quoted), *FO* 371/5057.

have to be elected for the purpose. De Robeck and his colleagues responded that the needed and desired aid, military and financial, would not be forthcoming until ratification, but the Turks remained unimpressed. The mission to Kemal would have to come first, they insisted. It was hard to disagree with the argument that ratification would hopelessly compromise the new government—although there was a hint that substantial Allied concessions, including Greek withdrawal, might bring ratification.[40]

It was difficult to know where to turn. The French, cooperative for once and claiming to be on the offensive in Cilicia, objected to the mission to Kemal: it would turn the Allies into supplicants. The Italians still favored the mission, but then they already were said to have their own representative with Kemal. Finally, the elimination of the Armenian Caucasian republic by the Kemalists and of Wrangel's White forces by the Russian Bolsheviks meant, as London clearly understood, the possibility of much more direct aid and cooperation from the Soviets to Kemal and thus the likely failure of any mission of warning to Kemal, although such a mission was still policy.[41]

These problems were small compared to the significant changes which now occurred in Greece. Venizelos's lengthy absences from Athens had undermined his position there, as did the lack of any apparent result from the recent military successes in Anatolia (and the high taxes to pay for them). In August, after the signature of the treaty, Venizelos was shot by two royalist ex-officers. His wounds were not serious, but the assassination attempt was followed by troublesome antiroyalist outbreaks in Greece. In November, Venizelos, to the surprise of all, was swamped by his opponents in the elections. The sudden death of King Alexander during the preelection campaign complicated matters, for the new royalist government soon called for a plebiscite to pass on the restoration of King Constantine, an old enemy to many

[40] Tilley note, 22 October, 13266/3, *FO* 371/5057; high commissioner, Constantinople, telegrams to FO, 28 October, 8 and 10 November 1920, *DBFP* XIII/166, 172-73.

[41] Lindsay (Paris) telegram to Curzon, 5 November, with Curzon minute, 7 November, high commissioner, Constantinople, telegrams to FO, 10 November, and 22 November (now Rumbold), *DBFP* XIII/169, 174, and 180 (and see Curzon minute, 15 November, p. 177); Crowe note, 11 November, 14218/3 *FO* 371/5057; Derby to FO, 19 October, and de Fleurieu to Tilley, 8 November 1920, *FO* 371/5210.

Allied leaders. To Lloyd George, the effect was immediate; not only was an old friend out of office, but the French, eager to withdraw from the Anatolian imbroglio, used Constantine's hostility, of which they had long been convinced, as justification for a total reversal of Turkish policy. Lloyd George was able to dissuade them temporarily only with the greatest of difficulty.[42]

The implications of the Greek changes were vast, aside from the possible need to interfere in Greece itself if the Allies wished to keep Constantine off the throne. As Lloyd George asked the French, did they wish simply to hand Smyrna and Thrace over to the Turks by abandoning the Greeks? The best, indeed the only feasible, policy would be to preserve detachment and observe Constantine's future policy, for a plebiscite in early December did indeed result in his restoration. The signs were favorable that Constantine intended to continue the same policy in Anatolia. Explanations for this are best left to Greek history, but they include the simple impossibility of a new monarch's renunciation of national claims made so strenuously in the past by his republican predecessors and the need to show that not only Venizelos could win victories. The decision to stay on was a tragic error, but it did help persuade the French to wait and see rather than interfere.[43]

Hope, therefore, was not exhausted. Another encouraging sign was that Constantinople at last dispatched a mission to Kemal under the

[42] Granville telegrams to FO, 15 November (2 of date), and letter, 19 November, Curzon telegram to Granville, 16 November, Derby telegram to FO, 18 November, Curzon telegram to Derby, 19 November, note of Crowe-Cambon conversation, 19 November, and Nicolson memorandum, 20 November 1920, *DBFP* XII/428, 430-31, 434-35, 437-39. On the turn of affairs in Greece, see Smith, *Ionian Vision,* Ch. VII; Dakin, *Unification of Greece,* pp. 228-31: Churchill, *World Crisis,* V, pp. 413-14; Walder, *Chanak,* pp. 84-88. Venizelos's own explanation is in unsigned memorandum by Philip Kerr (to whom he spoke), 27 January 1921, *Lloyd George Papers,* F/90/1/34—adding to the list of causes continued existence of martial law in Greece, perpetual French control in Salonika, and the general "desire for change" predictable after living under one government for a decade.

[43] Curzon telegrams to Granville, 2 and 15 December, Granville telegram to Curzon, 6 December, Nicolson memorandum, 20 December, *DBFP* XII/457, 464, 477, and 488; high commissioner, Constantinople, telegram to FO, 21 November, *DBFP* XIII/178; Allied meetings, 26-27 November and 2 December 1920, *DBFP* VIII/95-97.

leadership of Izzet Pasha, now minister of the Interior. The government, moreover, had promised to ratify the treaty as soon as the mission had explained the details to Kemal, at which point the financial commission would come into effect and the government return to fiscal solvency—at least this was the pious hope. Still, the Allies had always another card to play: treaty modification. That possibility clearly was in the mind of both Allies and British Cabinet officials as the year came to an end. Lloyd George insisted that discussion was premature until both Constantine's policy and the results of the mission to Kemal were clear, but he too had lost enthusiasm for the Greek cause since the fall of Venizelos. Britain was not going to foresake Greece, but if Greek stupidity sacrificed Smyrna to the Turks, that would be the Greeks' own fault. Lloyd George did not yet agree with the French that the higher need now was to sever the Bolshevik-Kemalist connection, and that the Greeks would have to be sacrificed for that end. The policy was still to wait, but the French waited more restlessly.[44]

One other change should be recorded, and it too contributed to hope. Britain had fresh personnel in Constantinople, for in September Lieutenant-General "Tim" Harington replaced Milne as British commander, and he had the complete confidence of both his own men and the higher command in London. Admiral de Robeck still remained Mediterranean commander-in-chief, but his functions as high commissioner had been taken over by Sir Horace Rumbold, a career diplomat, reserved (shy, some said) and solid rather than brilliant, but fully able to handle this difficult post. Harington's appointment in particular led to controversy over the issue of combined higher command. Britain regarded Harington as the Allied commander; the French did not. How relevant the difference was remained to be seen.[45]

[44] High commissioner, Constantinople, to Curzon, 6 December, *DBFP* XIII/189, and Rumbold private to Curzon, 6 December, *Curzon Papers,* F/3/3; Cabinet 70 (20), 13 December, Appendix III, Conference of Ministers, 2 December, *CAB* 23/23; Allied conferences, 3 December 1920, *DBFP* VIII/98-99; Edib, *Turkish Ordeal,* pp. 232-33.

[45] Churchill to Lloyd George, 22 September, *Lloyd George Papers,* F/9/2/43, on his confidence in Harington; Webb to de Robeck, 29 December, *De Robeck Papers,* 6/26; Osborne note, 3 November, *FO* 371/5273; French note to Derby, 6 November, *FO* 371/5275; WO to FO, 31 December 1920 and 12 January, FO to Hardinge, 26 January, and to WO, 14 February 1921, *FO* 371/6482; Callwell, *Wilson,* II, p. 267; Ryan, *Last of the Dragomans,* pp. 150-52. Harington's autobiography is *Tim Harington Looks*

THE LONDON CONFERENCE

The slight hopes the Ankara mission raised proved to be based upon a very weak foundation. A task of a few days lengthened into weeks, and the Constantinople government, well aware that things were not going well (the mission never returned, in fact), was shying away from its ratification pledge. The French were the first to show signs of nerves; in early January the French chargé in London suggested that the Allies should now open direct negotiations with Kemal. Crowe, to whom he gave this message, advised caution; much better to let Kemal take the initiative, as he would inevitably do in order to present a strong front to the Bolsheviks (to Crowe, the Bolshevik-Kemalist link was an unnatural alliance). More practically, Curzon instructed his department to consider possible treaty modifications in detail.[46]

Curzon and the Constantinople government were thinking alike; Rumbold reported that the Turkish authorities assumed, to his mind correctly, that revision was inevitable. To Rumbold, the way out was to use the Greek recall of King Constantine as an excuse for a new and different territorial settlement. Such a reversal would, of course, sacrifice Greece, a useful and "very positive asset in British imperial policy,"

Back (London, 1940); an interesting indication of his character may also be gleaned from his laudatory biography of his former chief in France, *Plumer of Messines* (London, 1935). Neither is very informative on Chanak, for as Harington remarks in *Plumer,* p. 246, "I burnt every document I had the night before I left Constantinople so that I could never write a book." Harington's title, as Armstrong remarks (*Turkey in Travail,* p. 149), was Gilbertian, for his Allied command "consisted in his right to try to persuade his unwilling French and Italian colleagues to act with him."

[46] High commissioner, Constantinople, telegrams to Curzon, 16 December, *FO* 371/5058, and 21 December 1920, *DBFP* XIII/198; Crowe memorandum, 7 January (508/1), and CinC Constantinople telegram to WO, 14 January 1921, *FO* 371/6464. The Bolshevik-Kemalist connection is discussed in Kapur, *Soviet Russia and Asia,* Ch. IV-V, and Richard G. Hovannisian, "Armenia and the Caucasus in the Genesis of the Soviet-Turkish Entente," *International Journal of Middle East Studies* 4 (1973): 129-47, and see chapter 6, note 97. As Harington's telegram shows, there was a persistent tendency to dismiss the importance of reported Russo-Turkish links on the grounds that Russia and Turkey must always be perpetual enemies. Little could be done in any case, and the Special Intelligence Service reports had merely to be filed away without comment.

as Nicolson put it. In Nicolson's own version of a revised treaty, some changes would be made—but Smyrna would still be Greek.[47]

On 20 January Lloyd George attempted to swim against the tide in the Cabinet. His opponents insisted that the full treaty could not be enforced, to which he answered that the Allies could not simply let Kemal tear up the treaty before their very eyes—would Kemal not then demand Thrace as well as Smyrna? The main lines of Sèvres had to be adhered to, particularly in Thrace, although perhaps (it is not clear who made this suggestion) a Turkish governor under League of Nations authority could be conceded for Smyrna. In any case, no Allied mission (as distinct from Constantinople mission) should present Kemal with a gratuitous propaganda victory. The problem was persuading the French and Italians, and Lloyd George and Curzon moved off to Paris to meet Aristide Briand, who had come out of retirement to head the French government once again (1921-22).[48]

Persuasion proved difficult. Briand and Sforza were intent on a settlement, which Sforza insisted would only be achieved by bringing the nationalists directly into the discussions. Curzon wanted to obtain ratification first, and discuss second, but the decision was precisely the reverse. Even in talking first, there were still major problems in dealing with two Turkish governments and an unrecognized King Constantine. Invitation to a conference would confer recognition on both Kemal and Constantine, and it was hard to decide which was the less desirable. As Briand pointed out, there was no guarantee Kemal would accept a conference invitation in any case; he had, after all, pushed back a minor Greek offensive in the Bursa area in January as well as the French and Armenians and British before that. Lloyd George had to accept the idea of a conference, although he made his usual arguments on behalf of the Greeks. Greece, even under Constantine, should not be forced to give up territory as a preliminary to the conference, and with Allied financial aid, after all, they could hold on indefinitely at Smyrna. It was agreed to invite both Greeks and Turks to a con-

[47] CinC Constantinople telegram to WO, 13 January, *FO* 371/6464; Curzon telegram to high commissioner, Constantinople, 13 January, and high commissioner, Constantinople, telegrams to Curzon, 12, 20, and 25 January, Nicolson memorandum, 18 January (quoted), *DBFP* XVII/8, 12, 14, and 18; high commissioner, Constantinople, telegram to FO, 15 January 1921, *FO* 371/6540.

[48] Cabinet 3 (21), 20 January 1921, *CAB* 23/24.

ference in London in February where all would negotiate on the basis of the Sèvres treaty and "such modifications as may have been necessitated by passage of events," as Hardinge, now ambassador in Paris, put it.[49]

Greece accepted with alacrity, expressing surprise that Kemal had been invited. But on the Turkish side, plans began to go awry when Kemal insisted that his Grand National Assembly was the sole voice of Turkey; Britain was aware of the controversy, for British intelligence intercepted Kemal's exchange with Constantinople on the proposed delegation. Some sort of understanding was essential between the two Turkish authorities, as the grand vizier realized, for the Allies had only asked a Turkish government to attend. W.G. Osborne, Foreign Office Middle Eastern expert, was fully convinced that there had been such an understanding all the time: both Kemal and the grand vizier found it useful to have a reluctant delegate with an extreme program paired with an amenable delegate with a moderate program. Still, it was as well to make a gesture to encourage Turkish participation and settlement, and Britain acceded to a French suggestion that some of the Malta prisoners might be allowed to return (again a measure opposed by Curzon, on the grounds that they were either criminals or embittered opponents of the Allies).[50]

Meanwhile the Foreign Office outline of the preconference position, prepared by Nicolson and Osborne, showed that Nicolson at least sensed the wind's direction, for he now would abandon the special sections on Kurdistan and Armenia and modify the Smyrna section so as to include tribute to Turkey. The War Office, as usual, would go much further. The Greeks could not hold Smyrna any more than the Armenians could hold the territory which they claimed. The Mesopotamian revolt of

[49] Allied conference, 25 January, *DBFP* XV/4; Hardinge telegrams to Tyrell, 25 January, and to FO, 26 January (quoted), Nicolson memorandum, 27 January 1921, *DBFP* XVII/19, 20, and 24. The fighting in January is discussed in Toynbee, *Western Question,* p. 232; Walder, *Chanak,* pp. 114-15.

[50] Granville telegrams to FO, 27 and 29 January, high commissioner, Constantinople, to FO, 29 January and 7 February, and telegrams, 31 January and 1 and 6 February, Crowe memorandum, 5 February, Curzon telegram to high commissioner, Constantinople, 11 February, *DBFP* XVII/23, 28-32, 34, 36, and note 3, p. 42, and note 1, p. 54; GHQ Constantinople telegram to WO and high commissioner, Constantinople, telegram to Hardinge, 28 January, *FO* 371/6464; Buchanan telegram to FO, 17 February, with Osborne minute, 18 February 1921, *FO* 371/6465.

1920, the events in Transcaucasia and Persia and Afghanistan and every other part of the Middle East, all were proof of how undesirable a further obligation to defend the indefensible was. Curzon's position as presented to the Cabinet on 18 February included willingness to concede Turkish suzerainty over Kurdistan and recognition that Armenia probably could not be created now. In Smyrna, he suggested, the Greek forces could withdraw leaving only a Christian government with a special gendarmerie which could handle local administration for five years. The general trend of opinion was with Curzon, although Montagu would go even further in concessions in Thrace. Lloyd George, with some weak support from Balfour, was simply unable to persuade his colleagues that Britain should not sacrifice the Greeks of Smyrna to Kemal. The prime minister's discouragement was countered by the assurances of Kalogeropoulos, the Greek prime minister, with whom he talked the same day, that the Greeks would continue to fight on as long as possible rather then give up both Thrace and Smyrna. Lloyd George made it clear, however, that some Greek concession on Smyrna would be essential.[51]

Lloyd George had not yet renounced the Greek cause, and in its defense he reported to Briand that the Greeks did not intend to clear out of Smyrna, although he, Lloyd George, had warned them what their intransigence might cost. Briand wanted to clear them out forcibly if necessary, which Lloyd George said was simply impossible. Briand responded that Greek finances would not be able to maintain the occupation. Lloyd George was more attracted to a different possibility, which had seemed remote since the fall of Venizelos: another Greek advance. Kalogeropoulos maintained that the 120,000 Greek forces in Asia Minor were in position "to scatter the Kemalist forces and to impose the will of the Powers" by advancing to occupy the railway line Adapazari-Eskishehir-Afyonkarahisar which had been evacuated by the Allies and taken over by the Kemalists some months previously.[52]

[51] Osborne-Nicolson memorandum, 17 February, *DBFP* XVII/41; General Staff memorandum, 16 February, 943/21, *L/P&S*/10/852; Cabinet 14 (21), Appendix I, Conference of Ministers, 18 February, *CAB* 23/24; Lloyd George-Kalogeropoulos meeting, 18 February, *DBFP* XV/13; Curzon to Hardinge, 16 February 1921, *FO* 371/6465; the Mesopotamian revolt is treated in Busch, *Britain, India, and the Arabs,* Ch. VIII.

[52] Lloyd George-Briand conference and memorandum by Greek delegation, both 21 February 1921, *DBFP* XV/14 and appendix to 15.

On the first day of the conference (21 February), the late arrival of the Turkish delegation allowed Kalogeropoulos to elaborate upon the plan. His forces, he estimated, were opposed by at most 65,000 Kemalists, some of whom were only forcibly recruited irregulars. In three months, the Greeks could "sweep the country clear of Turks" if necessary—and he did mean the whole of Turkey. Morale was high, conditions were right: the first stage would take Ankara, and the Kemalists would be broken. If necessary, another 200,000 men could be found, and financial backing to match (if Greece were permitted to use her credit freely). It was a striking statement. Only the French, with Cilicia before their eyes, knew better than to dismiss Turkish fighting ability so easily. General Gouraud warned against a campaign which was to extend over 600 kilometers (900 if operations as far as Sivas were contemplated) in a cold and hostile climate against a determined and able enemy fighting on his home ground. Foch, he reminded the conference, had called for twenty-seven divisions to pacify Turkey. With prompting from Lloyd George, however, Colonel Sariyannis, the Greek chief of staff, had enough answers: Bursa, not Smyrna, would be the base of operations, thus halving the distance to Ankara, and so on. In his favor was the fact that the dire predictions before the highly successful Greek offensive of the previous year had proved completely erroneous.[53]

On 23 February it was the Turkish turn. There were actually two delegations, but it was immediately clear that Ahmed Tevfik Pasha, as grand vizier the head of the Constantinople delegation, was deferring to Bekir Sami Bey, Kemal's first foreign minister, an able Circassian in his fifties, who had already traveled to Moscow on Kemal's behalf. Bekir Sami began with a statement of general principles of independence, sovereignty, and national rights which boded ill for preserving the bare bones of Sèvres. Specifically Bekir Sami demanded Turkey's prewar

[53] Allied meetings, 21 February 1921, *DBFP* XV/16-17. The following sources have been used on the London conference: Smith, *Ionian Vision,* pp. 192-7; Ronaldshay, *Curzon,* III, pp. 277-79; Nicolson, *Curzon,* pp. 258-59; Callwell, *Wilson,* II, pp. 280-82; Toynbee, *Western Question,* pp. 93-97; Roskill, *Hankey,* II, p. 221 (which should be compared with Montgomery, "Lloyd George and the Greek Question," 268-74); Davison, "Turkish Diplomacy," 189-92; Ryan, *Last of the Dragomans,* p. 147; Rustow, "The Army," 528-29; Walder, *Chanak,* pp. 116-18; and Edib, *Turkish Ordeal,* pp. 254-55.

frontiers in the east, Smyrna, and Thrace, and he disputed any figures the Allies put forth on non-Turkish populations, declaring that Turkey would welcome any inquiry.[54]

Curzon was alarmed when Thrace was discussed in statistical terms. Conflicting evidence could allow the French and Italians to suggest modification of the treaty in a very undesirable direction. "On the boggy ground of figures we may get stuck in the mud," he advised Lloyd George, and Kalogeropoulos made a similar appeal to justice and the treaty, although he was ready with his own figures. Bekir Sami's appeal for inquiry had been a shrewd ploy, since Greek procrastination on this suggestion, however logical, did not help their general public position.[55]

The time had come for private Allied discussions. Briand urged approval of the Turkish proposal, provided the Turks would agree to abide by the result; if the Greek figures were right, they should welcome such justification of their case. More was at stake, replied Lloyd George, for the Turks had also stated their case on the Straits and Constantinople. What if the investigation did show Greek majorities? Would Kemal accept the results? Unless he did, and in so doing agreed to the remainder of the treaty, Britain could not accept such a solution. Still, the Turks could be asked; it was worth a try.[56]

The next morning, the Greeks and Turks were asked for their answer; the plan had been given to them, and to the press, the evening before. Lloyd George explained that "accepting" the plan and the treaty aside from Smyrna and Thrace did not preclude further discussion of Kurdistan and Armenia. Bekir Sami in reply thanked the Allies for acknowledging the justice of Turkish claims—to Lloyd George's quick objection, he explained that granting an inquiry was as good as admitting the Turkish claims, as the results would show—but the Turks would not bind themselves in advance to any Allied decision on the inquiry's result (which rather belied earlier brave words), nor would they agree not to raise claims on other treaty sections. Pressed, the Turks retreated in good order to reconsider, while, as if at the court of some

[54] Conference, 23-24 February 1921, *DBFP* XV/19-20.

[55] Conference, 24 February, *DBFP* XV/22; Curzon private to Lloyd George, undated (but 24 February 1921), quoted, *Lloyd George Papers,* F/13/3/7.

[56] Conference, 24 February 1921, with appended Curzon draft, *DBFP* XV/22.

ancient Oriental monarch, the emissaries of the Greeks were now brought forward. Kalogeropoulos was in a difficult position. As he explained to the Allies, the Greeks were really only interested in Smyrna and Thrace, and both issues were now raised again. He could not answer without orders from Athens, but he reminded the conference that delay might be fatal to the proposed offensive. That evening the Turks, too, said that the Grand National Assembly would have to be consulted.[57]

Meanwhile, the Allied technical experts discussed Armenia—again with two delegations, one for the Turkish Armenians and one for the Republic of Erivan. Collectively, the Armenians no longer asked for the maximum solution including Cilicia, although they did request a special regime to keep order in that district; basically, they wanted the Allies to stand by Sèvres. As Lord Curzon pointed out, however, there were some small problems. Kemalist forces occupied much of the area concerned and the Republic had negotiated an agreement with Kemal (although the government which had signed had been overthrown the previous week). Finally, the conference still awaited the application of President Wilson's frontier arbitration.[58]

Exit the Armenians; enter the Turks to discuss Armenia and Kurdistan. Bekir Sami challenged any settlement which did not include the Kurds within integral Turkey; that small minority which asked for independence in no way represented true Kurdish feelings, and if this was doubted, a commission of inquiry or plebiscite would be welcomed. If the population so desired, the Turks might accept local autonomy for truly Kurdish districts. Armenia, however, was a different problem. Curzon claimed that the Kemalist-Armenian treaty was invalid since unratified; Bekir Sami was eager to agree—if the same principle were to be applied to Sèvres. Neither party would yield, however, on Armenia: the Allies (meaning Curzon in this case) insisted that Kars, Ardahan, and Alexandropol would have to be part of Armenia; the Turks refused to yield these towns. The only recourse was to postpone the issue, and the conference adjourned to await the formal replies of Athens and Ankara.

[57] Conference, 25 February 1921 (two sessions), *DBFP* XV/24-25.
[58] Conference, 26 February 1921, *DBFP* XV/26, and see note 5, p. 209, and note 9, p. 211; Wilson's arbitration award, dated 22 November 1920 (see map, p. 20) was published on 2 January 1921; *FRUS,* 1920, III, pp. 790-804.

In Athens, the response was anything but favorable. By 1 March the Assembly had passed a resolution stating that any revision of the basic Sèvres provisions was unacceptable. Such a resolution was understandable, but it would be rather awkward if the Turks were now to accept the impartial inquiry while the Greeks had refused. Suppose the inquiry went against the Greeks and they offered resistance, what then? "It will not, I presume, be considered possible to enforce upon an Ally by definite pressure, such as a blockade, the abandonment of a signed treaty for the advantage of an enemy," noted Nicolson in the Foreign Office. Fortunately for the Philhellenes, in the short run at least, the Turks refused to give unconditional acceptance to the commission of inquiry. An intercepted telegram from Kemal to Bekir Sami (forwarded from British intelligence in Constantinople) gave London prior information that Kemal would accept the commission only after Greek withdrawal from the areas concerned and that he would accept no sort of provisional regime for Smyrna.[59]

On 4 March Lloyd George met with Kalogeropoulos. The Greek premier had his position clear by now, and there is evidence to show that the intransigence the Greeks now demonstrated had been encouraged by Lloyd George through his secretary Philip Kerr. At least such was the conclusion Kalogeropoulos and Sariyannis carried away from a preliminary conversation with Kerr before the meeting with Lloyd George, and Kalogeropoulos cabled back to Athens (another intercept) that according to Philip Kerr, "Greece ought to refuse to concur in the decision of the conference." In due course, the Greeks rejected the proposed commission of inquiry. According to the minutes, Lloyd George advised the Greeks to make the best bargain they could. Britain, in any case, could not bail Greece out in a crisis given the lack of Allied cooperation and the changing nature of public opinion. He himself, for example, could conceive of Smyrna under formal Turkish sovereignty but Greek administration with a share of the revenues returned to the Turks. More important, of course, were the private assurances, and Kalogeropoulos would only agree to consult his colleagues in Athens once again.[60]

[59] Granville telegram to FO, 28 February, Crowe memorandum, 2 March, *DBFP* XVII/44-45, 47; Granville telegram to FO, 1 March, with Nicolson (quoted), 2 March, and Crowe minutes, GHQ Constantinople telegram to WO, 2 March, enclosing intercept, 1 March 1921, 2919/1, *FO* 371/6466.

[60] Kalogeropoulos telegram to minister of foreign affairs, Athens, 1

The same day Lloyd George met with the Turks; the main issue was Smyrna. Lloyd George tried out his new idea only to find, as he might have anticipated, that the Turks were unwilling to go beyond the qualified acceptance of an inquiry into population already given. Both parties agreed only that the alternative was for Turks and Greeks to fight it out. Lloyd George asked if the Turks had some other proposal to make. There was none. The meeting adjourned at this impasse, although Lloyd George, in response to Bekir Sami's request, promised to look into the matter of the Malta prisoners.[61]

The Turks had met with Lloyd George at noon. At four, the Greeks were back, along with Briand and Sforza and their advisors. Not more than ten minutes were required for Kalogeropoulos to read a statement repeating Greece's refusal. The Allied leaders spent a fruitless half-hour searching for an alternative, and at 4:40 Bekir Sami reentered, with nothing to add to the official Turkish reply which already had been circulated: the Turks accepted the commission (no demand for prior Greek evacuation was made) provided it was carried out under Allied supervision and control, but no other clauses of the treaty would be accepted in advance. The conference had reached total deadlock, save for a minor agreement to negotiate an exchange of prisoners.[62]

On the 9th, the Allies gathered for a postmortem. Lloyd George reported that so far as he knew, the Greeks now intended to advance, and he did not see how the Allies could stop them. All agreed with that point, but estimates of the Greek capacity for success varied widely. The Allies could only wash their hands of the whole matter and make it clear to the Greeks that any consequences which followed had been brought upon themselves. Lloyd George was not without another suggestion, which he made that evening when it was clear that the separate

---

March 1921, quoted, copy in *Curzon Papers,* F/1/7; the file is labeled in Curzon's handwriting, "the famous Greek intercepts of March 1921 recording secret advice given by Ll.G. to the Greeks during the London Conference of that month."

[61] Lloyd George-Bekir Sami Bey conversation, 4 March 1921, *DBFP* XV/33.

[62] Conference, 4 March 1921, *DBFP* XV/34-35, and note 2, pp. 281-82; R.C. Lindsay note, 7 March, FO telegram to high commissioner, Constantinople, 12 March, *FO* 371/6499; high commissioner, Constantinople, to Curzon, 16 March 1921 and other documents in file 132, *FO* 371/6500, deal with prisoner exchange.

discussions of Curzon and Briand and Sforza with Bekir Sami had all been fruitless. Perhaps, he suggested, the Straits, Constantinople, and the Izmit zone could be returned to the Turks as enough concession to prevent further fighting. The Allies could be satisfied with only a "Gibraltar" at Chanak on the Dardanelles; in return the Turks would accept a zone with limited Greek presence at Smyrna, and Greek forces would remain at Gallipoli.[63]

The morning of the 10th, Lloyd George made the suggestion to Dmitrios Gounaris, Kalogeropoulos's war minister and the power in the government. Gournaris asked for time to study the proposal which had now been fleshed out a bit to suggest that the Greeks would keep the town of Smyrna while the remainder of the sanjak (district) would have a special regime under a Christian governor. The Turks also asked for time, and meanwhile the Allies went on to discuss how the Straits, military, and financial clauses could all be made more palatable to the Turks. But when the Greeks appeared in Curzon's Foreign Office room at 5:15 P.M., their acceptance of the proposal was qualified. They might discuss the military defense of Smyrna, but not the inquiry commission, which they completely rejected. The Turkish response was now critical, but Bekir Sami requested and received time to return to Ankara to discuss the proposal.[64]

The conference adjourned on this note (it would require two weeks for Bekir Sami merely to reach Ankara). Clearly peace had not been achieved, despite steps in that direction; the Greeks stated specifically that they intended to commence military operations toward Ankara within a week. Lloyd George had already told the Turks that since there was no formal armistice nothing could be done to restrain either side. This statement worked to the Greeks' advantage, for it was essential to move rapidly if at all; a renewed Franco-Turkish armistice, negotiated by Briand with Bekir Sami secretly in London on 10 March, was a further spur when its existence became known. Lloyd George's legalistic position was obviously designed to aid the Greeks, but he went rather far in that direction by authorizing discussions between the Greeks and the Treasury regarding the financial guarantees which the Greeks needed badly. Greece, the argument ran, could not be penalized for any steps which it felt necessary to take. Although the prime minister added

[63] Conference, 9 March 1921, *DBFP* XV/48, 51.
[64] Conferences, 10 and 12 March 1921, *DBFP* XV/52-53, 56, 58-59.

that there would not be any formal commitment, obviously he was encouraging the Greek cause. As Kalogeropoulos cabled Athens (yet another intercept): "The British Prime Minister appeared to approve these important measures [of the mobilization by Greece of three new military classes] since he said that nothing must be left to chance because in the event of military operations failing, the Turks will become unmanageable." The news spread quickly. Within three days the Italian ambassador was asking about reports that the British had approved the new Greek mobilization. Crowe denied the report to di Martino, but Curzon noted on Crowe's memorandum, "I am afraid that, with the memory of certain intercepts in my mind, I could not have given the emphatic assurance of Sir E. Crowe."[65]

The Cabinet had yet to meet to consider Britain's position in the coming struggle, despite Lloyd George's obvious prejudice. One question, for example, was the Greek 11th Division which was needed in the campaign but which was currently under British command as part of the Allied occupation force on the Izmit peninsula. It was hard to refuse the request to release the unit, as Lloyd George argued; but how then was Britain to defend Izmit? The War Office, with this question uppermost in mind, had already told Harington not to release the division, and these orders had now to be countermanded. A dividing line was agreed upon in the Izmit peninsula, with the town allotted to the Greeks. No other facilities would be provided them, and the consensus was that Greece should not go on using Constantinople as a base of operations, although that was rather hard to stop. On 23 March the offensive began amid what Athens called high enthusiasm, although Granville, the Philhellene British representative in Athens, found that commodity in scarce supply.[66]

[65] Conference, 16 and 18 March, *DBFP* XV/65, 69, and note 4, p. 448; Kalogeropoulous telegram to minister of foeign affairs, Athens, 19 March 1921, *Curzon Papers,* F/1/7; copy in 3483/1, *FO* 371/6467, with Crowe memorandum and Curzon minute (quoted), 22 March 1921.

[66] Cabinet 14 (21), 22 March, and 15 (21), 24 March, *CAB* 23/24; WO telegram to GOC Constantinople, 22 March, with Osborne minute, 24 March (on talk with DMI who claimed to have received orders from the prime minister via Philip Kerr), *FO* 371/6507; Granville telegram to FO, 23 March, and FO to Greek chargé, 24 March 1921, *DBFP* XVII/67, 71; Callwell, *Wilson,* II, p. 282. The March operations are discussed in Smith, *Ionian Vision,* Ch. X.

Even with Lloyd George's full cooperation, success throughout the London negotiations was remote. No pressure could be applied to Kemal without full Allied participation, and this was never forthcoming—but no pressure could be applied to Greece to give way without British cooperation, and that was not forthcoming either. The prime minister's position was less Philhellene in 1921 than it had been at Paris in 1919 or even in 1920. Allied betrayals, Kemalist successes, Greek politics, Arab repercussions, and opinion at home had all helped dampen his ardor for the cause. He had not yet abandoned Greece, but he was finding his course increasingly lonely as long as both the Foreign and War Offices opposed his policy. One other pressure was working upon Lloyd George: India. Even in the midst of the London conference, Lloyd George had had to deal with yet another Indian delegation, and so seriously did he regard the whole problem of Indian pressure that it emerged in direct discourse with his allies.

THE KHILAFAT DELEGATION

The lengthy delay in the latter months of 1920 in ratifying the peace terms coupled with increasing Khilafat agitation provoked India into sending a series of communications designed to modify the terms, or at least to display India's eagerness for modification. The Khilafat movement, reported India, had spread deep into the lower classes as a result of Gandhi's oratory, and could well spread further—for example, into the rank and file of India's sepoy soldiers. If some solution could be worked out on the continued general authority of the caliph over the world's Muslims, the situation in India might be eased considerably; otherwise further trouble could be expected. Nor had agitation dimmed in England: the friends of Turkey continued to bombard the Foreign Office and Downing Street alike with petitions including signatures of members of Parliament and other prominent people. Loyal Muslims everywhere, insisted India in January, were finding it hard not to succumb to pressures brought upon them to join the movement. Allied refusal to modify the treaty terms could well result in violence; at the least, the difficulties in Persia and Afghanistan could be traced to this cause.[67]

[67] Viceroy telegrams to SSI, 23 November 1920 and 26 January 1921, *L/P&S/*10/852 (with IO minutes); origins in *Home Poli. Proc.,* December

The same view was held by Field Marshal Lord Rawlinson, commander-in-chief in India. As he wrote Churchill, "there is no shadow of
doubt that it will be impossible to stabilize the situation, either amongst
the Mohamedans of India or on the North West Frontier, vis-a-vis Afghanistan, until a really drastic modification in the Treaty with Turkey
has been effected." All eyes, he continued, were directed toward the
London conference, and until an agreeable settlement was forthcoming
there would be no end to the Khilafat agitation and no satisfactory agreement with Afghanistan.[68]

By early February, it was deemed advisable, in the light of the approaching London conference, that two or three unofficial Muslim leaders should visit to represent Indian opinion, mainly as a gesture to that
opinion. The suggestion—emanating from Lord Lloyd in Bombay—
that a high official accompany the mission (Lloyd had Lloyd in mind)
was rejected as implying that the officials who already spoke for India
in London had not done an adequate job. The mission was dispatched
quickly for fear it would arrive too late to see Lloyd George before the
conference made its decision. The main point to be argued concerned
the holy places in the Arabian peninsula; the Indian government hoped
for some positive concession on their subordination to the caliph which
might split an already cracking Muslim-Hindu alliance. Montagu did
his best in and out of the Cabinet to urge concessions in general and in
detail, and the delegation managed to arrive before the conference
adjourned; on 12 March and again on the 24th after the conference
was over, it met with Lloyd George.[69]

1920, 75; Chelmsford private to Montagu, 15 December, enclosing letter
from Sir Stanley Reed, editor of the *Times of India,* 20 November 1920,
Montagu Papers, D. 523/11; examples of petitions: C. Buxton to FO, 22
November 1920, *FO* 371/5142; H.H. Ispahani to prime minister, 3 Jan-
uary 1921, *FO* 371/6549. See also Niemeijer, *Khilafat,* Ch. V; India, Home
Dept., *Histories of the Non-Co-Operation and Khalifat Movements,* pp.
160-81; and D.A. Low, "The Government of India and the First Non-Co-
Operation Movement 1920-1922," *Essays on Gandhian Politics,* ed. R.
Kumar (London, 1971), pp. 298-323.

[68] Rawlinson private to Churchill, 10 February 1921, extract in *Lloyd
George Papers,* F/9/3/7.

[69] Chelmsford private telegrams to Montagu, 6, 15, and 19 February,
Montagu private telegrams to Chelmsford, 7 and 16 February, *Chelmsford Papers,* E. 264/14; Montagu to Churchill, 16 February (passed to
prime minister), and note for Lloyd George, 21 February, *Lloyd George*

No new arguments were made, but Montagu could and did claim that the newly modified Turkish terms showed Indian influence, and indeed were not necessarily yet the maximum Allied concessions. The Indians had certainly affected Lloyd George. After meeting with the Indian delegation on the 12th, he told his conference allies that he had been so impressed with their representations (particularly on the humiliating financial controls) that he had replied "that if the Turkish case had originally been presented with the same ability the original Treaty of Sèvres might have been very different."[70] The contention was arguable, but the remark did show the prime minister's concern—and the utility of Indian pressure as one excuse for modifying the treaty.

India was not satisfied with the new terms. Chelmsford hoped that having gone thus far the peacemakers would now go further. Montagu tried, but found the going difficult with both the prime minister and Curzon, never a close friend in any case, who objected to his constant meddling in foreign affairs.[71] Montagu was justified, however, by the increasing intensity of Khilafat agitation in India. Mohammad Ali, as usual, led in inflammatory speeches; but Lord Reading, Chelms-

---

Papers, F/9/3/21 and F/206/4/13. G. Lloyd private to Montagu, 26 February, *Montagu Papers,* D. 523/26, and Montagu private to Curzon, 28 February, 1196/21, *L/P&S/*10/852; minutes of meeting with delegation, 12 and 24 March 1921, S.-30 and S.-31, *CAB* 23/35; Gaillard, *Turks and Europe,* pp. 126-35.

[70] Montagu private telegram to Chelmsford, 12 March, *Chelmsford Papers,* E. 264/14; conference, 12 March 1921, *DBFP* XV/60, p. 410 quoted.

[71] Chelmsford private to Montagu, 16 March, *Montagu Papers,* D. 523/5, and private telegram, 17 March, *Chelmsford Papers,* E. 264/14; Montagu memorandum for Cabinet (C.P. 2797), 4 April, *FO* 371/6550; Montagu private to Curzon, 11 April, and Curzon private to Montagu, 20 April, *DBFP* XVII, note 1, pp. 134-35; Montagu private to Curzon, 10 June, *Curzon Papers,* F/4/3, and 22 April, and Curzon private to Montagu, 26 April, *FO* 371/6468, and notes on Montagu to Curzon, 23 April, with FO notes and draft answer (not sent as drafted), and Curzon private to Montagu, 29 April 1921, 4882/1, *FO* 371/6469.

The following remarks are based upon India, Home Dept., *Histories of the Non-Co-Operation and Khalifat Movements,* pp. 28-36, 160-76; Niemeijer, *Khilafat,* pp. 132-35; Gopal, *Muslim India,* pp. 148-49; Forbes Adam, *Lord Lloyd,* p. 154; Majumdar, *Struggle,* pp. 360-64; Low, "Government of India"; H. Montgomery Hyde, *Lord Reading . . .* (N.Y., 1967), pp. 331-32; Murray T. Titus, *Islam in India and Pakistan* (Calcutta, 1959),

ford's successor in April, was advised by his subordinates that any arrest of the Ali brothers would lead to major agitation initiated by Gandhi. Considering the possibility of further treaty revisions, Reading wisely decided arrests could wait.[72] At a 14-15 June meeting in Bombay the Congress Working Committee (composed of the principal leaders) resolved not to cooperate with British officials in any way if it came to another British-Kemalist clash of arms. Then in early July the All-India Khilafat Committee declared that it was unlawful for Muslims to remain in British military service. The movement was taking on renewed strength, and although Gandhi apologized for Mohammad Ali's apparently seditious encouragement of violence, it was violence which resulted — although surely less widespread than it would have been without Gandhi's moderating influence. In July and August of 1921, there began a fanatical rising of the Moplahs, a depressed Muslim peasant community of the Malabar coast. The connection between their fanaticism and the political agitation of the Khilafat movement was actually tenuous, but at the time it was another reminder that Khilafat political agitation had dangerous potential.

Gandhi's nonviolent position put the Ali brothers in a dilemma, for as Montagu was shrewd enough to realize either they would have to break with him or adopt nonviolence themselves and thus forfeit much Muslim support. The brothers made the logical choice, given the fact that cooperation with the Congress was at least a marriage of convenience, and continued to preach what the authorities considered sedition, particularly toward police and soldiery. Gandhi appeared now to have lost his zeal for that cause, turning instead to a boycott of foreign-made cloth. The government therefore decided to act and in September 1921 arrested the Ali brothers. By September, however, the Turkish situation had changed so dramatically that its importance to Indian opin-

---

pp. 34-35; Great Britain, Parliamentary Papers, Cmd. 1552, 1921, E. India, "Telegraphic Information, &c., regarding the Moplah Rebellion, 24th August to 6th December, 1921"; Swinson, *Six Minutes,* pp. 163-64; Toynbee, *Western Question,* pp. 24-25; Demetrius Boulger, "The Moplah Warning," *Contemporary Review* 120 (1921): 658-64. Casualties resulting from the six months' disturbances exceeded 2,000, and arrests totalled 40,000.

[72] Mohammad Shafi private to Reading, 30 April 1921, *Reading Papers* (IO Library), E. 238/23.

ion was considerably reduced.[73] The Moplah violence and the growing gap between the Ali brothers' activism and Gandhi's varying forms of "noncooperation" were already working to the advantage of the British authorities who had long sought a wedge which could be used to sunder this "unholy alliance."

While the events of summer and fall 1921 were partly the final postwar involvement of Britain (and Greece) in Turkey, they also had important effects on British policy in the Caucasus, Central Asia, Persia, and Afghanistan. When the renewed Greek offensive began against the Kemalist forces in late March 1921, there were only a few precarious footholds left to Britain outside the Arab world, and even that part of the Middle East was of questionable reliability: all the more reason, perhaps, for Lloyd George's continued association with even a royalist Greece. But his involvement was more cautious, the terms more moderate—and in this change India had had some influence. Nagging Indian complaints and suggestions played a role in the Caucasus and the Caspian as well. In Persia, however, and still more in Afghanistan, India had a major voice in policymaking, and that voice directly challenged and undermined the sudden and gigantic postwar surge of British imperial control in the Middle East.

[73] Reading private to Montagu, 25 August 1921, *Montagu Papers,* D. 523/14.

VI

Ebbtide: The Eastern Marches, 1919-1921

Less than a year after the armistice, the exigencies of Britain's world position had reduced a possible Caucasian bastion to a tenuous foothold. Only Batum was still occupied, and that was under notice of eviction no later than August 1919. Yet British withdrawal was no settlement of the Caucasian problem. To the contrary, the Allied presence had encouraged a false sense of security which freed Caucasian leaders to dispute territorial enclaves and political problems, while they forgot the real dangers outside. The fragile unity forged against the Turkish advance had dissolved and showed no signs of renewal.

All hope of a favorable Caucasus settlement was not forsaken. There was still the Batum foothold, and while the time was hardly auspicious, the Foreign Office at last had a direct channel to Caucasian events through its own representative, Oliver Wardrop. Nor was it totally out of the question that some Allied state might yet assume authority on behalf of order and stability or defense of Armenia; Italy's bubble had burst by midsummer 1919, but there were yet the Americans, or the French, or even, if time and persuasion brought a policy change, Britain herself. Finally, if no direct mandatory could be established, there were still ways of helping the several Caucasian components to preserve their weak hold on life, always depending upon events in Russia.

The best possibility was still the United States. American relief activities were in full swing, and a mission had been sent under Major-General J.G. Harbord to investigate the problems of establishing an Armenian state. But the Americans continued to press Britain to stay on, knowing well that an American mandate was highly unlikely.[1] In

[1] US Peace Mission to State Dept., 3 and 5 July, Lansing telegrams to

mid-August, a meeting at Paris finally demonstrated that no power would do the job. "France could do nothing, Italy could do nothing," said Clemenceau, "Great Britain could do nothing and, for the present, America could do nothing. It remained to be seen whether, as the result of this, any Armenians would remain." The only party eager to take on the Caucasus was Denikin, the one volunteer who was not wanted there.[2]

For a brief moment it looked as if France might be goaded into taking over responsibility for the Caucasus. On 25 August Balfour in Paris took issue with Clemenceau's remark that the French had not even been allowed into Asia Minor. Balfour was seldom aroused, but once aroused was a more than capable opponent. Would France really have sent troops if Britain had not been there? The dry minutes hint of a bitter clash; Clemenceau "would consider the matter," and Balfour "took note of this declaration." Before the week was out Clemenceau had offered his 12,000 troops by rail from the Mediterranean, a proposal which, as has been seen, aroused considerable suspicion and was approved only on the unacceptable condition that the troops move by sea. By the middle of the following month, the proposal was truly dead.[3]

Wardrop, meanwhile, had arrived in Tiflis as British chief commissioner in Transcaucasia, where he received a heart-warming reception from the gratified Georgians followed by appeals for aid and renewed offers of a free port for Britain in Batum (on the unspecified condition, of course, that Britain recognize Georgia's right to the rest of the town). Wardrop's bargaining position was very weak, for he knew that it was highly unlikely that British troops would return. One suggestion he proposed within his first week in Tiflis was formal recognition of the Georgian state. The War Office objected, for recognition would jeo-

---

Davis (ambassador, London), 9, 23, and 26 August, Davis telegrams to Lansing, 12 and 15 August, *FRUS,* 1919, II, pp. 825-27, 828-37; Curzon to Lindsay, 11 and 18 August 1919, *DBFP* III/366, 388. Harbord's mission is discussed in Hovannisian, *Republic,* I, pp. 338-39; Gidney, *Mandate,* pp. 171-77; and his own report, "American Military Mission . . .," (also *FRUS,* 1919, II, pp. 841-89).

[2] Heads of delegations, 11 August, quoted, *DBFP* I/32; War Cabinet 612, 12 August, *CAB* 23/11, and Curzon to Balfour, 12 August 1919, *DBFP* III/367.

[3] Heads of delegations, 25 (quoted) and 29 August and 15 September, *DBFP* I/42, 46, 57; War Cabinet 521, 2 September 1919, *CAB* 23/9.

pardize relations with Denikin, particularly, as Churchill warned Curzon, since an increasingly Bolshevik-minded Georgia seemed likely to
take the offensive against Denikin. The most Churchill would do was
to stay on in Batum until mid-October; recognition or reinforcement
were not possible. Another old suggestion, to provide arms to Armenia,
was revived when the Armenians offered to put their troops under
British officers, but this was equally impossible to a War Office without available staff and conscious that this would only arouse the jealous
spite of Armenia's neighbors.[4]

The chance of prying arms or officers from the War Office was remote, but Curzon, hoping the Cabinet as a whole might be persuaded
to recognize Georgia, questioned his staff on just what responsibilities
recognition would entail. Virtually none, said Kidston. Indeed it would
build Georgian morale; but it would certainly upset Denikin, and,
unless they were given similar recognition, Azerbaijan and Armenia.
Curzon demanded a clear statement on this chaotic situation in which
Britain was anti-Denikin in the Caucasus but pro-Denikin everywhere
else, and pro-Georgia "in so far as she is respectable & orderly" yet
anti-Georgia in so far as she was "Bolshevik & violent." To Churchill,
Curzon was more authoritative; there would be no trouble if Denikin
and his "myrmidons" kept out. As it was, the flames now rising from a
recent revolt against Denikin's occupation in Daghestan, "a rotten little
affair" of a state, were due to just such a cause. Curzon had no handy
solution, but he did have a principle: it was undesirable to restore Russia's authority and its inevitable consequent influence in Persia. Churchill saw Bolshevism as the greater danger. Wardrop was told only that
de jure recognition would prejudice any future settlement, since the
policy would necessarily have to be applied to the entire area. If the states
established some sort of Caucasian federation, and then appealed for
recognition, that would be different, for presumably they would then
have worked out their frontier differences. In the specific case of
Georgia, moreover, some evidence of willingness to cooperate with

[4] Wardrop telegrams to FO, 30 August and 4 September, and FO telegram to Wardrop, 23 September, *DBFP* III/409, 412, 429; Wardrop
telegram to FO, 12 September (#7), and letter, 5 September, WO telegram
to GOC Constantinople, 18 September, *FO* 371/3663; Churchill private to
Curzon, 10 September 1919, *Curzon Papers*, F/2/2. On Wardrop, see
note 101, chapter 3.

Denikin was an essential preliminary to further support.[5]

There was little chance of such cooperation so long as the British military mission with Denikin continued to spur him on against the Caucasus (although little incentive appears to have been necessary) and particularly Georgian socialism, which they saw as yet another pestilential outbreak of Bolshevism. One returned officer expressed surprise to Kidston to find that the Foreign Office policy was not the destruction of these republics; Kidston's interviews with War Office officials produced no change in those attitudes. The higher the rank, the more set in opinion—the War Office, wrote Curzon, would never be satisfied: "anyone who does not bow the knee to Denikin & Kolchak is looked upon as a double dyed traitor."[6]

Georgia's alarm at the White threat had progressed to the point of asking Britain to assume a mandate for the entire country. "Very flattering to us but at the same time inconvenient," said Hardinge in bemused understatement. Unfortunately, it was difficult to know how much Wardrop had prompted this request; he was certainly regarded by the War Office as fanatically committed to his untrustworthy Bolshevik confederates—and he did have a way of giving exaggerated enthusiasm: "I cannot too strongly insist as I have been doing for last two years that nearly all the present misery of world is due to Jewish intrigues," he reflected in one document which suggested handing over the Jews of Daghestan to Denikin's Volunteer Army as a means of ending Daghestan's problems and continued at some length on the "diabolical plot" aimed at the "enslavement of Christendom." This was a sample—which not surprisingly has been omitted from the published documents—of the sort of advice which led Foreign Office officials to agree that his communications were useless. But a warm Armenian reception for Wardrop in Erivan and reports of a movement toward confederation were enough ground for him to continue arguing on behalf of recognition.[7]

---

[5] Curzon minute (quoted), 27 September, on file 131980/1015, private to Churchill (quoted), 2 October, *FO* 371/3663, and telegrams to Wardrop, 2 and 4 October, and Wardrop telegram to FO, 4 October, *DBFP* III/452, 454-55; WO to FO, 7 October 1919, *FO* 371/3979.

[6] G. Kidston note, 9 October, with Kidston minute, 10 October, and Curzon undated minute (quoted), 139216/1015, *FO* 371/3663, and FO to WO, 27 October 1919, *FO* 371/3979.

[7] Wardrop telegram to FO, 14, 19, and 20 (#81 and 85) October, *DBFP*

It was simply that no one knew what to do. The Cabinet agreed that aid to Denikin must stop in the spring and sooner perhaps if he moved on the Caucasus. The Paris conference could do no more: its Caucasian activity amounted to hearing a report from Colonel William N. Haskell, Allied high commissioner to Armenia mainly for relief work, on the emotional rivalries, worthless currencies, numberless refugees (800,000 were being fed in Armenia alone), and vanished political and economic controls. Aside from Batum under the British, the Caucasus was dissolving into anarchy. Some small light was provided by an Armenian-Georgian agreement on a few issues and an extension, really by default, of the Batum occupation pending final conference decision, but the prospects were grim as Curzon summed up the situation in a year's end memorandum.[8]

A typical Curzonian "short historical sketch," beginning with meddieval background ("to go no further back"), demonstrated that Georgians and Armenians had had independent pasts of their own. All three republics, including Azerbaijan, had a genuine desire for continued independence and anti-Bolshevik proclivities, but the Georgians would probably prefer to recognize Lenin, if that meant independence, rather than Denikin, if that meant subjugation. Loss of the Caucasus was a real threat, and Bolshevik control of the railways would open up routes to the Caspian and Turkistan, "seething with Bolshevik and pan-Islamic agitation," and to Persia, "where Great Britain has recently assumed new responsibilities." Britain needed a solution which would treat all of the states equally. It could recognize the states, provided they formed a federation under British or American mandate, although this

---

III/473, 482-84; Hardinge minute on Wardrop telegram of 14 October and Wardrop telegram of 12 October (quoted), *FO* 371/3663; see also WO to FO, 22 October, with Kidston and Tilley minutes interpreting it as asking Wardrop's recall, *FO* 371/3664, and Kidston private to Crowe, 28 November 1919, in his defense, *FO* 371/4215.

[8] Cabinet 1 (19), 4 November, and 8 (19), appendix III, Conference of Ministers, 12 November, *CAB* 23/18; heads of delegations, 14 November, and Clemenceau-Lloyd George discussion, 11 December, *DBFP* II/22, 55; R.M. MacDonell memorandum, 15 November, *FO* 371/3664; IDCE meeting, 18 November, *L/P&S/*10/807; Tilley to de Fleurieau, 26 November 1919, DBFP III/565. See on Haskell, in addition to sources noted in chapter 6, note 1, box 37 of *Bristol Papers,* which includes much correspondence between Bristol and Haskell.

would mean unacceptable new responsibilities for either power; it could abstain from recognition until Denikin's position was clearer, meanwhile urging him not to attack either Georgia or Azerbaijan; or it could recognize the states on a temporary basis subject to a future League of Nations decision on their reincorporation into a federal Russia. Curzon, without making a specific recommendation, seemed to favor this third possibility.[9]

Events now assisted Curzon's policy. Denikin's obvious lack of success made it prudent to consider the repercussions on the Caucasus of his possible collapse. Wardrop, for one, advised that unless Britain was willing to accept Bolshevik control, steps should be taken to reinforce Batum and support Georgia. And as Hardinge put it, at least one reason for not granting recognition—fear that a victorious Denikin might turn upon the republic—was now rapidly dwindling. Recognition might convey some moral support. Curzon promised to take up the question in Paris, but a problem remained regarding Armenian recognition: recognition of what? If only Caucasian Armenia was meant, the Turks would take this to mean victory for their cause, since no Turkish territory would be sacrificed. Turkish, Caucasian, and Russian problems still overlapped too closely. Curzon concluded that recognition would not mean more British responsibility, but anything beyond recognition, like the division of troops Wardrop had asked for, was, as Hardinge had noted, "a huge undertaking which we have neither the troops nor the means to carry out."[10]

In early January, Curzon won agreement from the assembled leaders in Paris that the Council would extend de facto recognition to Georgia and Azerbaijan (leaving Armenia for subsequent consideration in connection with the Turkish treaty). Curzon at once planned an Interdepartmental Committee discussion of staying on in Batum and securing the Caucasus and the Caspian fleet, now in Denikin's hands—for Denikin's setbacks revived ideas of again flying the British White Ensign on the Caspian as the only alternative to scuttling the fleet or leaving it for the Bolsheviks.[11]

[9] Curzon memorandum, 24 December 1919, *FO* 371/6269.
[10] Wardrop telegram to FO, 3 January (#3), *DBFP* III/630; Hardinge minutes on Wardrop telegrams #2 and #3 of 3 January, Peterson-Mac-Donell memorandum, 6 January, on Curzon note of 4 January, with Curzon minute, 6 January 1920, 168836/1015, *FO* 371/3666.
[11] Cabinet 2 (20), 7 January, *CAB* 23/30; Derby (for Curzon) telegram

Curzon's sudden buoyancy was short-lived. On 12 January the committee assembled at the Foreign Office under the nominal chairmanship of Austen Chamberlain, chancellor of the Exchequer. The main protagonists were Hardinge for the Foreign Office and Churchill and Wilson for the War Office (Curzon and Lloyd George remained in Paris). Hardinge had cabled recognition to the two states that morning, and the discussion was therefore on further measures "to stop the Bolshevik onslaught on the Caucasian Republics, Persia, and India." The War Office presented the results of a military study. There were, said Field-Marshal Wilson, three possible defense lines: first, Constantinople-Batum-Baku-Krasnovodsk-Merv, which would require seven divisions; second, Constantinople-Batum-Baku-Enzeli-Teheran-Meshed, sacrificing the Caspian and still requiring seven divisions; and finally, the only real possibility since there were no seven divisions, a line from northern Palestine to Mosul and then to a point some 50-100 miles from Khaniqin on the western road to Meshed (the Meshed force would fall back on Birjand if attacked). Even in this minimum plan, the control of Mosul was uncertain, since there might well be a peace "which would leave the Turk dissatisfied and hostile, the Kurd restless and unquiet, and the Afghan unfriendly."[12]

These were hypothetical lines; the practical issue was Batum. The War Office wished to pull out, now, avoiding another precipitous evacuation like that of the French from Odessa. To support Georgia and Azerbaijan would take two divisions at least, and there were not even two divisions available. Of course, agreed Wilson, loss of the Caspian would be a "first-class disaster" (although he did not contemplate immediate withdrawal from Persia) and would let the Bolsheviks into the Caucasus, but there were no men. "It was his considered opinion that, from a military point of view, the defense of these regions were impracticable"; if the troops were at hand—and they were not—he would rather go to the heart of the issue and use them in an offensive marshalled in Poland for attack on Moscow. "Nothing could have been more disheartening," Hardinge telegraphed privately to his superior; the War Office had not the heart to stop the Bolsheviks, and thus "we shall be throwing up the sponge in Asia and abandoning all our friends to what-

to Hardinge, 10 January 1920, *DBFP* III/635; Ullman, *Anglo-Soviet Relations,* II, pp. 322-24.
    [12] IDCE, 12 January 1920, *FO* 371/3980.

ever fate the Bolsheviks may condemn them," but there seemed no alternative, not even the idea which had quickly crossed his own mind and as quickly been rejected of using Indian troops.[13]

Rather surprisingly, a revived inter-Allied military commission (British, French, and Italian) under Foch's leadership which had been charged with studying the Caucasus had the same day reached different conclusions. While the Bolsheviks could not be stopped on their own ground, certain key passes, including the Caucasus in general, could be blocked, and two divisions would be enough to build a new barrier while the local inhabitants were pulled together to take over responsibility.[14]

Something had to be done to resolve the differences of opinion and arrive at a policy. At the week's end, Churchill, Wilson, and Admiral Beatty were in Paris to confer secretly with Lloyd George and Curzon. All were nervous over loss of the Caspian; none agreed how to prevent it. Curzon would back the Caucasians and take over the fleet, while Churchill regarded desertion of Denikin to associate with worthless allies as utter madness. Field-Marshal Wilson would defend India at the ends of the Mesopotamian and Persian railheads as he had outlined in his memorandum. It was not a case of defending India, said Curzon, but of galvanizing the Caucasus into anti-Bolshevik efforts (he had come a long way from "helping them on their feet"). Lloyd George appeared to lean toward aiding the republics, for it was only giving them what had already been given Poland and the Baltic states, but no immediate decision was reached.[15]

[13] Hardinge private telegram to Curzon, 13 January (quoted), *FO* 608/271, and private letter, 12 January 1920 (also quoted); see also private letter from Paris, 15 January 1921, showing that a year later Hardinge still felt that this decision had been decisive and disastrous; both *Curzon Papers,* F/7/2. Hardinge telegram to Derby, 13 January, and to Wardrop, 15 January 1920, *DBFP* III/640 and 645.

The WO position was based upon the results of a war game, a copy of which (including map) exists in the uncatalogued papers of the military secretary, India Office (India Office Records) (tentatively catalogued by the author as Box I of 1918-20 misc. papers), particularly detailed analysis in WO to Lt.-Gen. Sir A. Cobbe (military secretary, IO), 29 December 1919.

[14] Allied Military Commission, British Section, memorandum, 12 January, appended to Allied conference, 19 January, *DBFP* II/77; also Maj.-Gen. C. Sackville West to Curzon, 13 January 1920, *FO* 608/271.

[15] Conference of Ministers (S.-10), 16 January 1920, *CAB* 23/35; Ullman, *Anglo-Soviet Relations,* II, pp. 330-39.

This was on 16 January. Two days later (the interval having been taken up with hearing requests from Armenian, Georgian, and Azerbaijani spokesmen), Field-Marshal Wilson had prepared estimates of what aid to the republics would cost. Two divisions were the bare minimum, with another in reserve in Constantinople; Kemal, added Churchill, could be expected to attack from the rear. Since Beatty would send no sailors to the Caspian without secure lines of communication, three divisions must be found if the Caspian was really that important. To Churchill, it was not; after all, it was part of a long frontier from the Baltic to Japan and had to be considered in that context. The issue was Russian policy, and if Britain wanted peace, peace should be made. Her friends should not be cut down piecemeal with the likelihood of a disastrous peace in the end in any case. But Beatty knew well that the Caspian could not wait upon Russian events; once control was lost to the Bolsheviks, it could not be regained. He had to have an immediate decision, and he got it: Churchill's argument that stopping the Bolsheviks in the Caspian and the Caucasus "was like using a piece of putty to stop an earthquake" doubtless helped, but it was the impossibility of finding three divisions which was decisive. The navy was not to sail again on the Caspian.[16]

On Monday, 19 January, the Allies gathered at the Quai d'Orsay. The conclusions of the inter-Allied military commission, said Lloyd George, could not be accepted; there were no troops. Curzon led in the Georgian and Azerbaijani spokesmen again, and their united appeals were persuasive in ending the anomalous refusal to recognize Armenia. Lloyd George was also able to obtain qualified military aid for the republics, but the main decision was negative: no three divisions, no Caspian, no Caucasus defense line save what the Caucasians could build themselves with outside aid, the amount to be determined by Foch and Field-Marshal Wilson, neither advocates of Caucasian intervention. The British postmortem left no doubts; it was simply not on, beyond a pious hope of a "pad," as Churchill put it, of a fringe of states to ward off the Bolsheviks as long as possible.[17]

[16] R. Vansittart note, 17 January, *FO* 608/272; Conference of Ministers, 18 January (S.-11), quoted, *CAB* 23/35; Wilson to Curzon, 18 January, *FO* 371/3666, and 11 February 1920, *Curzon Papers,* F/13/9; Ullman, *Anglo-Soviet Relations,* II, pp. 329-37; Callwell, *Wilson,* II, pp. 223-24.

[17] Allied conference, 19 January, *DBFP* II/77; Conference of Ministers, 19 January (S.-12), *CAB* 23/35; Derby telegram to Hardinge, 20 January,

RUSSIA AND THE CAUCASUS

Aid and recognition, but no troops, was a logical decision for the Caucasus but illogical for Russian policy. The Caucasian states would presumably use their aid to fight off the Bolsheviks, but Lloyd George, without making notable use of the Foreign Office, had decided to open the door to trade with Russia. The exchange was not to be mistaken for recognition — Britain's official policy was still no peace until the Soviets had demonstrated a capacity for orderly government and noninterference with their neighbors. On the other hand, the policy could not be war, if only because there were no men. Pragmatic circumstance was thus elevated to general principle, and the Cabinet decided in late January 1920 that the border states would have to make their own decisions on peace or war with Moscow. No encouragement was to be given them which would incur awkward responsibilities for Britain, but such aid as was feasible would be provided, a qualification which at least in spirit negated the larger policy.[18]

Aid implied some means for its provision, and that meant holding on to Batum. Milne needed the troops in Constantinople where the French seemed on the point of deserting the cause, but Curzon pleaded against precipitious withdrawal, so Milne was only given discretion to pull them out when necessary. Wardrop and Curzon both protested; at least, said Curzon, take the time to create some sort of free port under the League. Churchill pledged that the withdrawal would not actually be ordered without further Cabinet approval, but even this seemed a deception, for Milne had given the order to move out. Despite frantic phone calls and appeals, Curzon could only win enough time to ask the Supreme Allied Council to form an inter-Allied force that would control the city until its future could be decided by the conference.[19]

On 25 February Curzon outlined his proposal of international force

---

and Hardinge telegram to Wardrop, 21 January 1920, *DBFP* III/652, 655.

[18] Derby telegram to FO, 22 January, Cabinet Office to FO, 23 January, *FO* 371/4032; Russian Committee (1st meeting), 24 January, *FO* 371/4033; Cabinet 7 (20), 29 January 1920, *CAB* 23/20.

[19] Cabinet conference, 3 February (appendix II to Cabinet 10 (20), 11 February), and Cabinet 11 (20), 18 February, *CAB* 23/20; Wardrop telegram to F.O., 6, 12, and 16 February, and Curzon memorandum for Cabinet (C.P. 594), 9 February, and private telegram to Wardrop, 17 February, *DBFP* XII/496-97, 499, 503, 505; Churchill private to Curzon, 16 Feb-

and free port to Berthelot and Nitti in Paris, being careful to stipulate that the choices were Allies cooperation or British withdrawal. Berthelot promised a French battalion if the British (who had two there at the moment) and Italians both would do the same, to which Nitti gave a very grudging assent. The free port would have to wait, since the Allies were working on the draft treaty clauses for Armenia, which country would also be involved.[20]

Arms aid was something else, for it was of questionable utility. The best safety for Azerbaijan and Georgia lay in an agreement with the Soviets, and the representatives of both states in London asked that Britain use the leverage of her trade negotiations with Russia for just such a purpose. The Foreign Office felt the better answer was to reconsider the decision to send arms (particularly since none had yet been dispatched; a lethargic War Office was still assessing requirements). If arms were sent, they would complicate trade negotiations, and if the states did reach agreement with the Bolsheviks, the arms would have been wasted (or, worse, become Bolshevik property).[21]

The problem soon became irrelevant. Georgia, convinced that Batum must be Georgian if it were not to be British (and above all, that it must never be Armenian), was reported in March to be sending troops into Batum province. The Foreign Office opposed unilateral action, but nobody knew what would be Georgian and what Armenian: the muddle of drafts, angry notes, and cancelled telegrams shows the confusion. It was impossible to expect "cut and dried formulas for a situation which changes every day," remarked Curzon, but the alternative was dangerously close to no policy. Bonar Law put the best face on the matter in Parliament by promising all possible support to the republics if attacked

---

ruary, and H. Wilson private to Curzon, 25 February, *Curzon Papers,* F/3/3; WO telegram to CinC Constantinople, 21 February 1920, *FO* 371/4932; Callwell, *Wilson,* II, pp. 228-29; Ullman, *Anglo-Soviet Relations,* II, pp. 334-37.

[20] Conference, 25 February, *DBFP* VII/27; Hankey note to Malkin (drafting committee), 28 February (C.P. 759), *FO* 371/4932; Curzon telegram to Wardrop, 3 March, and Wardrop telegram to Curzon, 7 March, *DBFP* XII/511, 513. The French battalion soon became a platoon; CinC Constantinople telegram to WO, 13 March 1920, copy in *Curzon Papers,* F/3/3.

[21] Azerbaijani-Georgian delegations to Lloyd George, 6 March, and Osborne note for Tilley, 11 March (1287/1), *FO* 371/4932; Curzon telegram to Wardrop, 15 March, *DBFP* XII/517; WO to FO, 27 March 1920, *FO* 371/4954.

by the Bolsheviks, but at the same time encouraging an equitable Bolshevik-Caucasian settlement. The statement clarified matters very little.[22]

By April the Bolsheviks appeared to be moving on Batum, and it looked ominously as if Bonar Law's pledge might have to be fulfilled. Worse, the French and Italian units showed no signs of appearance; any aid would be British only. If British aid meant British troops, where would they be sent, and against whom? With the Bolsheviks moving south, and the Georgians outside Batum, Milne badly needed some orders. He himself could hold Batum, he reported—but he feared the Bolsheviks and Kemalists might join forces, should the Bolsheviks take the area. De Robeck, still naval commander, was told to stop the Russians if they came by coast, but that was only one possibility in a now collapsing situation. Bitter fighting was in progress between Azerbaijanis and Armenians, for example, without regard for cooperation against the larger threat. On the Black Sea coast, Russian troops pushed into Georgia; on the Caspian, Petrovsk was evacuated and the Russians advancing toward Baku.[23]

The Allies, assembled at San Remo in mid-April, had to consider the issue, although they had little capacity to influence events and many other problems to consider. Thousands of Cossacks were fleeing toward Batum, the navy was shelling their Soviet pursuers, and something had to be done. The War Office told the Foreign Office to assume all responsibility for Batum's defense if it wanted to disregard advice to withdraw, as if the Foreign Office cipher clerks and messengers could suddenly be transformed into Guards battalions. At San Remo, however, remoteness and general conviviality brought easy promises—or rather, repeated promises—from Berthelot and Nitti to send troops. Curzon's report was less trusting this time, and Milne and de Robeck were told

[22] Hardinge note, 11 March, Curzon telegram to Wardrop, 21 March, Stokes memorandum, 21 March, with Curzon minute (quoted), Bonar Law statement, 25 March, Wardrop telegram to Curzon, 1 April, *DBFP* XII/ 521-22, 527, note 2, p. 574, and note 3, p. 583; Hardinge private to Curzon, 22 March 1920, *Curzon Papers,* F/7/3; Roskill, *Naval Policy,* pp. 158-65.

[23] CinC Constantinople telegram to WO, 4 April, high commissioner, Constantinople, to Curzon, 6 April, Admiralty telegram to high commissioner, Constantinople, 8 April, Wardrop telegrams to FO, 3 and 12 April, *DBFP* XII/528-29, 531-32, and 536; WO to FO, 6 and 15 April 1920, *FO* 371/4935.

to continue with their evacuation plans while holding the town. But Milne, faced with possible joint or separate Kemalist and Bolshevik attack just as he was fighting off the Georgians, required two divisions and artillery just to stay on—and no force of that size could be spared from Constantinople. Batum simply could not be held, a fact even more apparent when in April Soviet troops occupied Azerbaijan.[24]

Batum had to be seen in wider perspective. Possession of the port symbolized British influence at the far end of the Black Sea, just as Enzeli, the evacuation of which was also being discussed, was symbolic in relation to the Caspian. With Enzeli gone, northern Persia might succumb, and so on perhaps to the Indian border. Curzon did not argue that Batum's loss would have such consequences, but it was clear that events occurring from the eastern end of the Mediterranean to India were closely interconnected, and the link was the Bolshevik danger. The War Office was inclined to use the same arguments, but in reverse: even if the French and Italians sent help, even if the Bolsheviks held back from Batum in the interests of a trade agreement, in the end it would have to be evacuated; if done now, money and prestige would both be saved. The Cabinet on 5 May once more temporized, permitting the force to stay on while the Allies were again asked for support.[25]

Events in the Caucasus were now moving far too fast for decisions in London to have any serious effect. April and May saw the fall of Baku to the Soviets and serious fighting between Georgians and Bolsheviks only thirty miles outside Tiflis—and that despite a nominal Bolshevik-Georgian peace of early May. Commander H.S. Luke, RNVR, who had replaced a sick Wardrop, reported that Georgia would not last the month. The Caucasus was falling as the Soviets mounted a serious offensive, perhaps in compensation for losses to the Poles further north. The Kemalists, racing the advancing Bolsheviks for prospective Armenian territory, reoccupied three sanjaks near the frontier. Finally,

[24] FO telegram to Curzon, 21 April, Curzon telegram to Hardinge, 23 April, high commissioner, Constantinople, telegram to Curzon, 27 April, Curzon telegram to Wardrop, 27 April, and to Luke, 28 April, and Luke telegram to Curzon, 29 April, *DBFP* XII/542, 544, 546-47, 549-50; Supreme Council (San Remo), 22 April, *DBFP* VIII/10; GHQ Constantinople telegram to WO, 26 April, *FO* 371/4935; Hankey private to Lloyd George, 5 May 1920, *Lloyd George Papers,* F/24/2/30. Azerbaijan's collapse: Kazemzadeh, *Struggle,* Ch. XVIII.

[25] Cabinet 24 (20), 5 May 1920, *CAB* 23/21.

and perhaps worst of all, retreating White forces on the Caspian were pursued by Bolshevik forces which seized Enzeli and allowed the British to leave only with their generous permission. On the basis of these disasters, Churchill, who blamed them in part on the Foreign Office (he himself had urged withdrawal from Enzeli for some time) now proposed substantial withdrawals in Persia and the end of the Batum occupation.

> I do not see that anything we can do now within the present limits of our policy can possibly avert the complete loss of British influence throughout the Caucasus, Trans-Caspia and Persia. If we are not able to resist the Bolsheviks in these areas, it is much better by timely withdrawals to keep out of harm's way and avoid disaster and shameful incidents such as that which has just occurred.[26]

In the Cabinet, on 21 May, Churchill and Wilson had strong supporting arguments to make. Milne had orders to pull out of Batum when necessary; but the Enzeli commander, with similar orders, had been caught: public opinion would not tolerate another such error. Refugees were pouring into Batum and British costs and responsibilities mounting. Curzon, in his uphill struggle to keep the troops in place, could use the fact that the French had at last sent a battalion (Algerian *tirailleurs,* unfortunately, where Europeans had been promised). The Allied council had urged occupation as long as possible, and the situation really had not changed. So long as Batum held, the route to Persia was closed. Curzon's opponents countered that Persia should go her own course and should reach her own agreement with the Russians; Britain's Persian policy was based on a false assessment of British strength in Persia. Indeed, perhaps the forthcoming round of trade negotiations with Russia could be used for some comprehensive agreement. Once

---

[26] Hardinge to Curzon, 11 May, Luke telegram to FO, 17 May, *DBFP* XII/561, 563; Cabinet 27 (20), 12 May, *CAB* 23/21; Luke telegram to FO, 18 May, *FO* 371/4938; Churchill private to Curzon (quoted) and H. Wilson private to Curzon, 20 May 1920, *Curzon Papers,* F/3/3; Luke, *Cities and Men,* II, Ch. XI; MacDonell, *". . . And Nothing Long",* pp. 311-12; and file 1986, *FO* 371/4973, deals with Wardrop's replacement. On arrival of Reds in Baku, see C.E. Bechhofer, *In Denikin's Russia and the Caucasus, 1919-1920 . . .* (London, 1921), pp. 293-324. On Enzeli, see pp. 277-9.

again, deadlock, and once again Milne was to stay on. The Cabinet minutes are not clear on who spoke for these positions, but the debates of the War and Foreign Offices were increasingly bitter on nearly every item of Russian and Asian policy. "It is a great pity," wrote Churchill privately to Curzon, "that we have not been able to develop any common policy between W.O. and F.O."[27]

Churchill meant, of course, that his policy should be adopted. There was no question in his mind about the proper course at Batum, and when Milne warned that the lack of Black Sea shipping capacity meant he needed ten days' notice before evacuation, he was told to collect the ships and give the necessary warnings, although not to proceed with the actual evacuation without further orders. "The W.O. have behaved very badly and have gone behind our backs," wrote Hardinge, for the Foreign Office had protested strenuously; "a wholly indefensible procedure," added Curzon. On 7 June, before the ten days' limit had expired, Curzon in the Cabinet accused the War Office of having exceeded Cabinet instructions. His main point was the telling argument: precipitous withdrawal might undermine the Georgians in their negotiations with the Russians. Because the Soviets needed to focus upon the Poles, Russia might recognize the republics and permit Britain to transfer Batum to Georgia.[28]

Peaceful transfer was at least an honorable way out, and the Soviet-Georgian armistice made it possible. A special representative, Lieutenant-Colonel C.B. Stokes, was now sent to make arrangements with the Georgians and withdraw the Allied troops to Izmit, where they were badly needed. Stokes had no trouble; the Georgians were now acquiring the port they had so long claimed, although they would probably

[27] Cabinet 30 (20), 21 May, *CAB* 23/21; WO to FO, 21 May, and WO telegram to CinC Constantinople, 22 May, *FO* 371/4938; Churchill private to Curzon, 22 May (quoted), and Curzon private to H. Wilson, 23 May 1920, *Curzon Papers,* F/3/3. Derby private to Curzon, 11 May (*Curzon Papers,* F/6/3) and telegram to FO, 11 May (*DBFP* XII/560) refer to the protest against "black" troops.

[28] CinC Constantinople telegram to WO, 30 May, WO to FO, 1 and 7 June, WO telegram to CinC Constantinople, 4 June, with FO minutes (quoted), *FO* 371/4939-40; Luke to FO, 10 June, *FO* 371/4942, and telegram of 9 June, *DBFP* XII/574; Cabinet 33 (20), 7 June, 35 (20), appendix II, conference, 7 June 1920, *CAB* 23/21; the problems of Poland and Russia are discussed in Ullman, *Anglo-Soviet Relations,* III, Ch. I, and Piotr S. Wandycz, *Soviet-Polish Relations, 1917-1921* (Cambridge, Mass., 1969).

have preferred the troops to stay on. On 7 July the Georgians assumed control of the town; by the 9th, the Allied force was gone. The transition was peaceful, and there was no reason, to either Stokes or Luke in Tiflis, why the republics should not still receive encouragement and even aid. Luke had already proposed that the Allies extend de jure—as opposed to de facto—recognition to the Caucasian states. There was very little to work with, however, as Stokes also found when he replaced Luke in October.[29]

In August the Armenian government found it the better part of valor to concede Soviet occupation (on behalf of Azerbaijan) of Karabagh, Zangezur, and Nakhichevan. In September Stokes had to report Turkish incursions into Armenian territory and subsequently a Soviet-Kemalist agreement on the temporary partition of the area—news which brought a firm end to discussions of arms aid to or de jure recognition of Armenia In November, the Turks took Kars, and Batum appeared to be next. The only glimmer of hope in a bad situation was the possibility that Turks and Russians would fall out as always once they had actually made direct contact on a contested frontier. It was sadly ironic that the only Allied action on behalf of the Armenians was presentation to the League of Nations of President Wilson's boundaries for the future Armenia. By now they were hopelessly out of date, since the Turks had already recaptured half the territory and the award was only likely to stimulate their desire for the other half. The League was in no position to take on the burden of Armenia, and the award, wisely and at Foreign Office request, was not generally made public. It should be added, however, that some arms were actually sent, because a bill was presented for their payment. The Georgians took a quarter of the arms as compensation for their transport—little matter since they proved to be Ross rifles the War Office had discarded during the war as useless. Armenia still survived, but only because the Turks turned toward Georgia early in the new year.[30]

[29] Cabinet 35 (20), 11 June, *CAB* 23/21; FO telegram to high commissioner, Constantinople, 11 June, Luke telegrams to FO, 28 June (and minutes) and 11 July, *DBFP* XII/577, 587, 596; Stokes report, 15 July, 9429/1, *FO* 371/4944; Luke private to de Robeck, 13 July 1920, *De Robeck Papers,* 6/26; MacDonell, *". . . And Nothing Long",* p. 297, discusses his impression of Stoke's pro-Muslim bias.

[30] Luke telegram to FO, 11 August, Curzon to Stokes, 21 October, Stokes telegram to FO, 9 November 1920, P. Kerr to FO, 3 January, Stokes

In January 1921 an Allied meeting in Paris considered recognition and aid for the last time. Azerbaijan was gone, but Curzon could still argue on behalf of Georgia and Armenia. The decision was actually taken to extend de jure recognition to Georgia, if that country wished it. It was a simple demonstration of Allied incapacity to alter events in the Caucasus—a gesture only. By the end of February the Russians were in Tiflis; on 19 March the Turkish and Soviet drives met at Batum, where small-scale fighting occurred. Stokes had already left after burning his archives. The details of the subsequent Turkish-Soviet armistice were of little importance; what was important was that fighting had stopped. The final act of the drama was the Turkish treaty, concluded on 13 October 1921 with the three republics, which recognized Turkey's permanent acquisition of Kars and Ardahan and thus spelled the end of the greater Armenian state. The treaty was a clear-cut Turkish victory, but, most important, consolidation in the east meant more Turkish pressure in the west. By the end of 1921 Turkey, not the Caucasus, was the delicate nerve-end.

Stoke's departure in October ended two years' tenuous hold on Batum—residue of briefer, greater ambitions and merely a last beach-head bound to disappear when real pressure was applied. Once gone it could never be recaptured, that much was obvious. But more important was its effect; Curzon had predicted dire results for Persia, while Milne feared a new level of Bolshevik-Kemalist cooperation. In different ways, both Curzon and Milne were all too correct.[31]

---

telegram to FO, 20 January 1921, *DBFP* XII/599, 608, 616, 647, 649-50; Maj. Collins, Tiflis, to WO, 10 August 1920, *FO* 371/4944; Luke telegram to FO, 25 September, *FO* 371/4960; Stokes telegrams to FO, 8 October, *FO* 371/4947, and 3 November, *FO* 371/4962; WO to FO, 26 October, *FO* 371/4961; Stokes private to Curzon, 6 November, *FO* 800/156; Hankey telegrams to Balfour, 26 November and 3 December, *FO* 371/4964; Rumbold to Curzon, 20 December (on Ross rifles), *FO* 371/6265; President Wilson to president, League of Nations, 22 November, and State Dept. to Wallace, 17 December 1920, *FRUS,* 1920, III, pp. 795-804, 808.

[31] Allied conference, 26 January, *DBFP* XV/6; Hardinge telegram to FO, 26 January, *FO* 371/6268; Curzon telegram to Stokes, 11 February, Stokes telegrams to FO, 25 February and 17 March, and letter, 20 April, *DBFP* XII/652, 658, 660, 662; Stokes telegram to FO, 28 February, *FO* 371/6269; CinC Mediterranean telegram to Admiralty, 23 March, *FO* 371/6271; M. Soubatoff, Georgian Legation, to Curzon, 21 November, *FO* 371/6273; high commissioner, Constantinople, to Curzon, 22 November 1921, *FO* 371/6274.

COLLAPSE OF THE PERSIAN POLICY

If the late summer of 1919 began a time of troubles for Britain in the Caucasus, the Anglo-Persian treaty brought a brief era of hope. There were ugly rumors of bribes, and the treaty had its critics, but Cox was able to dismiss the latter as an unrepresentative extremist minority of intriguers motivated by jealousy and sponsored by foreigners, Russian, French, or American. Curzon's first task after the treaty was discouraging a sudden revival of French interest. Paris had announced a special mission to Persia, "almost," as Curzon put it, "in the guise of rival competitors"—for the French had been taken by surprise.[32]

This sort of problem was soluble, presumably. Cox was rather more worried about the Persian reaction to British withdrawal from the Caucasus. The Persians were unenthusiastic at the idea of Italians for neighbors, although they were more worried about Bolsheviks. The Persian foreign minister suggested that perhaps part of Britain's Caspian fleet could be handed over to Persia to police her own coasts. But so long as Denikin was still fighting, this suggestion could not be put into practice, for he would never renounce the privileges, dating from 1828, which made the Caspian a virtual Russian lake. As it happened, the fleet went to Denikin, which Cox considered to be an unnecessary sacrifice of Persia's interests.[33]

Somehow, the hopes of August were dwindling away. The Persians were now taking about formal Majlis (Parliament) approval for the treaty, and even revision to include a specific time limit. Curzon was also finding unexpectedly intense criticism in Rome, in Paris, and in Washington. In defense he outlined his own version of the agreement at

---

[32] Cox telegrams to FO, 13 and 22 August, Curzon to Grahame, 13 August (quoted), Grahame telegram to Curzon, 17 August, *DBFP* IV/ 716-17, 726, 732; Curzon to Lindsay, Washington, 18 August, *FO* 608/ 101; Derby private to Curzon (on French surprise), 27 October 1919, *Curzon Papers,* F/6/2. See also Nicolson, *Curzon,* pp. 137-38; Fatemi, *Diplomatic History of Persia,* p. 25; Lenczowski, *Russia and the West in Iran,* Ch. III; and Ullman, *Anglo-Soviet Relations,* III, Ch. IX.

[33] IO unsigned note, n.d. [August, 1919], 6186/19, *L/P&S*/10/865; Cox telegram to FO, 11 September, *FO* 371/3863; "Denmiss" telegram to WO, 15 September, *FO* 371/3864; Admiralty to FO, 19 October, *FO* 371/ 3865; FO telegram to Cox, 1 November 1919, *DBFP* IV/833. Turkmanchai treaty: Hurewitz, *Diplomacy,* I, pp. 96-102.

a London dinner for the Persian foreign minister, Nosret ed-Dowleh, in September:

> . . . neither I nor my colleagues would have consented to or acquiesced in anything like the creation of a British protectorate over Persia. Those who believe that the British are going as a result of this agreement to settle down in Persia to Anglianise, to Indianise, or to Europeanise it in any sense of the term are grossly mistaken. All we want to do is to give Persia the expert assistance and the financial aid which will enable her to carve out her own fortunes as an independent and still living country.[34]

Critics found it difficult to reconcile such a statement with the continued presence of British troops on the Kasvin-Enzeli road, in Meshed, and on the road to India. Yet those troops were there more to serve as an anti-Bolshevik cordon than to dominate Persia; even the Indian military authorities (not necessarily in agreement with the viceroy or Foreign Department) agreed that the collapse of Denikin and the loss of the Caucasus created a dangerous situation. They advised that the Caspian should be held if possible and Malleson's forces reinforced to whatever level the railhead would support. The viceroy, however, concluded that the intelligence-gathering and morale-boosting function of Malleson's force might better be served by a reformed Persian force which would result from the military advice Britain furnished under the treaty—though of course it would take time. Too much time, in fact: Cox, afraid that if Meshed were abandoned the Bolsheviks would quickly push into Khurasan, wanted to increase Malleson's force to three battalions with cavalry, artillery, and aircraft to match.[35]

There was another reason for keeping British troops on hand. The Cossack force (Persian soldiers in Cossack-style uniforms) was still in being with its (White) Russian officers. The Russians were ostensibly

[34] Cox telegrams to FO, 29 August, 1, 5, and 30 September, and 13 October, Curzon telegram to Grey (Washington), 1 October, Grey telegrams to FO, 10 and 17 October, FO telegram to Cox, 21 October 1919, *DBFP* IV/744, 749, 757, 798, 803, 813, 818, 829; text of speech, quoted, Carlton Hotel, 18 September 1919, 133306/150, *FO* 371/3864.

[35] Viceroy (Army Dept.) telegram to SSI, 10 September, Cox to FO, 12 September, *FO* 371/3863; Malleson telegram to CGSI, 20 September, *L/P&S/*10/886; Treasury memorandum, 11 November 1919, *FO* 371/3865.

allies, but they and their commander, Colonel Starosselski, were as anti-British as the Bolsheviks, embittered by Britain's windfall domination of Persia during Russia's temporary weakness and inability to defend her Persian position. So long as the Persian government was cooperating with the British minister, the Cossack force was untrustworthy, and so long as it was untrustworthy, then Britain had to have sufficient men on hand to deal with it. Persian claims to the Caspian or Azerbaijan made relations with Russians of every color no easier, and their ambitions in Turkish Kurdistan or Britain's long-held Persian Gulf preserve were distinctly embarrassing. Britain, Curzon was forced to tell the Persians, could not support such wide ambitions; but the treaty's only merit for the Persians lay precisely in Britain's apparent support for Persian expansion. The Triumvirate needed some such success for their own survival.[36]

At the end of 1919, however, Persian expansion was academic, for Malleson reported it was the Russians who were planning an invasion. Amanullah of Afghanistan was rumored to be cooperating, an embellishment which India doubted, since he had not had outstanding success in his last war with Britain, and Britain would be involved if Khurasan, the reported target, were actually assaulted. There was also the problem of infiltration from the Caucasus, particularly in the area west of Tabriz, terrorized by Simko and his Kurds, or in Gilan, where the Jangali movement had been suppressed but there was yet a chance of revolt. Possible countermeasures included a cordon from Astara on the Caspian to Ardebil and Tabriz, an advance of the British lines which would incidentally allow repatriation of many refugees now being cared for at British expense.[37]

The Caspian itself might be another place to block Russia, and Cox

[36] Derby telegram to Curzon, 30 September, Cox telegrams to Curzon, 1 and 19 October and 3 November, Curzon to Derby, 25 October, and to Cox, 13 and 28 November and 6 December, and to Persian foreign minister, 19 December 1919, *DBFP* IV/796, 800, 820, 825, 834, 845, 854, 865, and 871. Firuz Kazemzadeh, "The Origin and Early Development of the Persian Cossack Brigade," *American Slavic and East European Review* 15 (1956): 351-56.

[37] Consul general, Meshed, telegram to FSI, 3 November, S.F. Muspratt (G.S. Branch) memorandum, 4 November, viceroy telegram to SSI, 10 November, *L/P&S*/10/886; Cox telegram to FO, 21 November 1919, *DBFP* IV/852.

was now using the treaty as good excuse not to help Denikin with money and ships to reestablish the old Russian control. The navy saw little hope: Cox's policy would alienate Denikin in favor of a Persia which could not conceivably match resources with Russia on the Caspian. Yet Denikin's ships would probably go over to the Soviet side if the Russians sent troops to Enzeli and took Krasnovodsk. Wardrop from Tiflis urged that Britain should reacquire some of the ships if they could not be given to Persia or Azerbaijan, and even India was alarmed, although unable to increase its monetary contribution. But the navy did not wish to participate, the Persians had not the resources (and, if Russian treaties were still valid, was legally barred from the Caspian), and Azerbaijan was too friendly with Kemalist Turkey. There was at least one suggestion that overtures to and recognition of Islamic Azerbaijan might offset the general feeling that Britain had adopted an anti-Muslim policy in Turkey. As Montagu put it unhelpfully to Curzon, "the danger of the Bolsheviks to Persia and to India seems to me to be so largely the fault of the Home Government in their anti-Mohammedan policy that I really don't know how far we shall be able to rely upon Indian troops to assist in any fighting in Persia."[38]

By January 1920 the Admiralty had moved around to the position that it would take over any ships that Denikin would hand over, but not without a secure base at Baku, an impossible qualification, for the War Office was now arguing that only a Palestine-Mosul defense line was feasible. Cox quite naturally protested; Persia was in no position to repel a Bolshevik invasion, and such an invasion after all would be di-

---

[38] Oliphant minute and DNI (Admiralty) memorandum, 1 December, 157899/150, FO to CIGS, 5 December, DMI to Admiralty, 11 December, *FO* 371/3866; Wardrop telegram to FO, 27 December, with Curzon minute, Tilley note, 31 December, with undated Curzon minute, *FO* 371/3666; Maj. C.J Edmonds, Kasvin, memorandum for Cox, 24 December 1919 (from Kasvin records, later placed in custody of Air Ministry), *AIR* 20/565; E.W. Birse, memorandum, 6 January, Cox telegram to FO, 17 January, *DBFP* XIII/364, 367; Montagu private to Curzon, 5 January 1920 (quoted), *Curzon Papers,* F/3/3. Indian finances are discussed in viceroy telegram to SSI, and Cox telegram to FO, 28 December 1919, *L/P&S/* 10/872. In general, India paid for half the nonmilitary expenditures in Persia, and on the military side for Malmiss, while the War Office funded Norperforce, since it was technically part of the Mesopotamian force. The total cost of India's share of nonmilitary expenses alone was nearly £ 1,500,000 for the year September, 1918-October, 1919.

rected against the British and their allies, not the Persians. For that reason Persia was entitled to aid and assistance. The only other solution, which Cox had already successfully proposed in private to the Persian government, was for the Volunteer Fleet to take refuge in Enzeli when the time came. There were serious dangers to this plan: the fleet could turn Bolshevik, or, if it did not, it might be hotly pursued by the Russians.[39]

The plan implied some defenses at Enzeli, but the War Office was not interested. The current Enzeli garrison, a scant three companies, was not enough, and it had orders to fall back if attacked. It would be best to retreat first and thus not suffer the loss of prestige inevitably associated with retreat before the enemy; prestige was badly needed at the moment in the Middle East. If Enzeli had to be held, it would need reinforcements and perhaps a garrison to defend Astara up the coast as well. This would help ensure that the fleet, if it took refuge here, would not turn Bolshevik. But there were no reinforcements to be had, and until some could be found or a workable Anglo-Soviet understanding reached, further trouble in Persia could be expected. It was a vicious circle, all too familiar in coming years to many imperialist powers: hostile agitation was mounted against the imperial power and the local government friendly to it; the agitation weakened the friendly government; continued military presence was required to keep the friendly government in power; military presence led to increased hostile agitation.[40]

The prospect was of further commitment, therefore, and that involved an Indian government already paying far more than it wished for Persian expenses. Authorities in Delhi might agree that influence in Persia and the Caspian was desirable, but it was not essential to India's defense. To Chelmsford, the viceroy, the treaty was unrealistic

[39] Cabinet 2 (20), 7 January, and 4 (20), 14 January, and Financial Committee, 9 February, appendix III, Cab 11 (20), *CAB* 23/20; Derby telegram to FO, 10 January, FO telegram to Derby for Curzon, 13 January, *DBFP* III/635, 640; Cox telegrams to FO, 17 and 29 January, Curzon telegram to Cox, 7 February, *DBFP* XIII/367, 371, 373; Beatty memorandum, 6 January (C.P. 401), *FO* 371/3666; IDCE, 12 January 1920, *L/P&S/* 10/807.

[40] GS, WO, memorandum, 11 February (C.P. 647), FO [Oliphant] memorandum, 18 February, *FO* 371/3868; Cox telegram to FO, 21 February 1920, *DBFP* XIII/375. Ullman, *Anglo-Soviet Relations,* III, p. 360.

in any case and would only stand "so long as it had the support of British bayonets." India had been given no share in the treatymaking; it would accept no share in the enforcement. "We cannot use Indian funds for bolstering up a policy which is of little or no concern to us," he wrote to Montagu. The Malleson force in particular would never be able to resist a serious attack; its watch-and-ward function could be done by the British-officered force outlined in the treaty. Cox again had to take exception, and the local generals commanding respectively the North Persian Force and the Military Commission to Persia agreed with him that withdrawal would be very unfortunate, at the very least jeopardizing the proposed Persian military reforms.[41]

A decision on whether Malleson was to go or stay was essential. On 17 March the Interdepartmental Committee discussed the problem. Curzon, who chaired the meeting, was convinced from the start that both Cox and his own Cabinet colleagues in England were too prone to be pessimistic and to rush in panic to withdraw. Malleson's job, as Curzon saw it, was to man the watchtower, not hold off the Bolsheviks, and here for once he agreed with India. Admittedly nothing could be done on the Caspian, but was the situation really so hopeless? Were ten million Persians to sit quietly by and do nothing, leaving the entire job to Britain? "He was sick of their whining attitude and continual complaints of bad faith . . ." One approach was to stress Persia in the Russian negotiations, and that possibility was mentioned to both Cox and the Persians.[42]

Discussion continued on the Meshed force (Malleson himself had been recalled owing to constant disagreements with the local consul general). On 13 April the Interdepartmental Committee wrestled with

[41] Chelmsford private to Montagu, 12 February (quoted), and Montagu private to Chelmsford, 8 April, *Montagu Papers,* D. 523/10 and 4; viceroy telegrams to SSI, 21 February, *FO* 371/3869, and 19 March, *FO* 371/3870; Cox telegrams to FO, 12 and 16 March 1920, *DBFP* XIII/386 and 388. The generals were, respectively, Maj.-Gen. H.B. Champain, Dunsterville's successor, and Brig.-Gen. W.E.R. Dickson, who had commanded the East Persia Cordon and now was in Teheran as head of the commission to reform the Persian army provided for in the Anglo-Persian treaty (provided, of course, that treaty came into effect).

[42] IDCE, 17 March (quoted), *L/P&S/*10/807; viceroy telegram to SSI, 19 March, *FO* 371/3870; Curzon telegrams to Cox, 22 March and 11 April, and letter, 10 April, *DBFP* XIII/395, 406-7; Cox telegram to FO, 28 March 1920, *FO* 371/3870.

the £6 million annually spent on this force, and in early February a financial committee of the Cabinet decided to withdraw it for reasons of economy. Curzon argued strongly for its retention. India considered its presence an incitement to Bolshevik attack; Curzon thought its withdrawal would encourage them to fill the vacuum, which in turn would cause the entire Anglo-Persian edifice to collapse and the glacis of India to be jeopardized. Curzon's argument thus actually agreed with India's analysis that survival of the treaty depended solely upon British force—but Curzon was now beyond logic on Persia. In any case, said Montagu, India could not share expenses which were military rather than political. In his day, said Curzon scornfully, India had not shied away from Persian responsibilities; Montagu remained unmoved.[43]

Montagu carried on the fight the next day in a private note: the Cabinet decision should be implemented at once, for the actual withdrawal would take five months. Responsibility for any delay would be upon Curzon's head. Responsibility for premature withdrawal would be upon India's, replied Curzon; he had not been present at the Cabinet committee meeting which made the decision, nor could he take the issue to the Cabinet now since he was on the point of leaving England. India objected to paying military expenses, but Malleson's mission was intelligence, and he had not fired a shot since pulling back behind the Persian frontier. "If India disinterests herself in Eastern Persia (to which *she* and not *we* insisted in despatching Malleson's mission), the Foreign Office will feel no disposition to recognize, as they have hitherto done, the predominant interest of India in these regions." But Curzon lost; on 5 May the Cabinet decided firmly to withdraw, and India was so informed.[44]

That left western Persia, where the situation had been deteriorating. On 29 March the Volunteer Fleet had evacuated Petrovsk in the face of the Soviet advance. Arriving at Enzeli on 1 April, the fleet's commander, unwilling to see his dozen-odd ships disarmed and interned at Persian orders, sailed off again to Baku. Unable to reach an understand-

[43] IDCE, 13 April 1920, *FO* 371/3871. Malleson's removal: Montagu private telegram to Chelmsford, 23 December 1919, Chelmsford telegram to Montagu, 7 January, and Dobbs (Simla) private to Chelmsford, 3 April 1920, *Chelmsford Papers,* E. 264/12, 24, and 11.

[44] Montagu private to Curzon, 14 April, and Curzon private to Montagu, 15 April (quoted), *Curzon Papers,* F/3/3; Cabinet 24 (20), 5 May, *CAB* 23/21; SSI telegram to viceroy, 5 May 1920, *FO* 371/3871.

ing with the Azerbaijani leaders there, and realizing that the only alternative to internment was surrender to the Bolsheviks, the fleet had returned and met the terms. Local British officials had agreed with the Persians that simply allowing the Whites to use Enzeli as a base would constitute unwarranted provocation to the Bolsheviks. Unfortunately, the difference between internment and use of a base was too subtle for the Soviets; they wanted the fleet. For the time being, British forces stayed on while a nervous War Office struggled to pull out of the exposed position at Enzeli (and cut the £2 million which it cost annually).[45]

A week after the decision to withdraw from Meshed, Field-Marshal Wilson circulated a memorandum which argued for concentration at Kasvin of outlying forces from Tabriz (where two platoons had been cut off during the retreat to Batum) and Enzeli. Probably the Bolsheviks would then occupy Enzeli, he predicted, but Denikin's collapse made this inevitable, since the new victors in Russia would soon be claiming the old position in Persia. Even if they did not, there was still the threat of several thousand Cossacks. On 17 May the committee, after the usual argument between Curzon (stay) and Montagu (go), decided to issue orders to the local commander similar to those issued to Batum: stay until it was necessary to go—an unnecessary burden of responsibility upon both commanders, as the War Office knew well.[46]

It is doubtful if the orders ever reached Enzeli, for the next day 1500-2000 Soviet troops landed a few miles east of the port and cut the road to Resht and the interior. The Soviet commander, F.F. Raskalnikov, would not allow the few hundred men from the British 36th (Indian) Brigade to evacuate until the ships and material of the Volunteer Fleet and a few guns which had been landed to defend the town were handed over. The Foreign Office could say "I told you so" about insufficient military preparations, but the need was for a viable Middle Eastern policy, not recriminations. Enemies of the government had in the Cau-

[45] Cox telegrams to Curzon, 19 and 26 March, GHQ, Baghdad, telegrams to WO, 9 and 12 April, FO 371/3870; Wardrop telegram to FO, 8 April, GHQ, Baghdad, telegram to WO, 23 April, FO 371/3871; MI2b report, 27 May 1920, with appended report by Sub-Lt. V. Kashinsky, Naval Mission, Crimea, on Caspian, 54661/262, FO 371/5167.

[46] H. Wilson memorandum, enclosing GS memorandum, 13 May (C.P. 647), 197907/150, FO 371/3871; Cox telegram to FO, 14 May, and FO telegram to Cox, 18 May, DBFP XII/425, 433; IDCE, 17 May 1920, Curzon Papers, F/11/8; Ullman, Anglo-Soviet Relations, III, pp. 361-63.

casus and Enzeli a fine weapon for attack. *The Times* spoke of "the Government's spaciously careless attitude towards affairs in the Middle East," notably the "situation of defenceless paralysis" in northern Persia and the "Gallipoli methods" which had been adopted in lighthearted assumption of the responsibilities of the Anglo-Persian treaty. Belatedly, on 21 May, the Cabinet after the usual arguments authorized concentration at Kasvin for subsequent retreat to the railhead in Iraq; a decision on total withdrawal would await the outcome of the Soviet trade negotiations. A week later, the supplemental decision was taken not to reoccupy Enzeli even if, as pledged, the Soviets withdrew once the Volunteer Fleet was in their hands.[47]

In Teheran, repercussions were immediate. Cox faced the sudden demoralization of the Persian Cabinet, but he was earmarked for return to Mesopotamia as high commissioner, and the problem was left for his successor, H.C. Norman, who presented his credentials on 10 June. Four days later Norman reported that Vossuq ed-Dowleh was contemplating resignation, an event of which Cox had already given warning, on grounds of ill health and disagreement with the shah. In reality, the failure of his British friends to defend Enzeli must have been an important factor, but Norman was more concerned for the future. What was needed now was a government which could disarm opposition to the treaty and win Majlis approval, and that Vossuq ed-Dowleh could not do. Anti-British feeling was growing daily, and Britain was steadily drifting into the position Russia formerly occupied—most-hated power. Britain was increasingly associated with the rich and powerful of Persia but unable or unwilling to afford them the protection to which friendship entitled them. London was not keen to dump Vossuq ed-Dowleh, but while London was reflecting, Norman proceeded to bring about a change of ministers.[48]

[47] Cox telegrams to FO, 18 May, *DBFP* XIII/434 (and see Hardinge minute, 20 May, on #433), and 19 May, *FO* 371/3872; Summary of Events in North-West Persia, WO, 21 May, 11/11, *FO* 371/4904; Commander D. Norris to Admiralty, 21 June 1920, 4881/1549, *FO* 371/4921; *The Times,* 20 May 1920; Cabinet 30 (20), 21 May, and appendix I, Conference of Ministers, 28 May 1920, *CAB* 23/21; Ullman, *Anglo-Soviet Relations,* III, pp. 354-70; Callwell, *Wilson,* II, pp. 239-41; Kapur; *Soviet Russia and Asia,* Ch. VI; Lenczowski, *Russia and the West in Iran,* p. 52; Xenia Eudin and Robert C. North, *Soviet Russia and the East, 1920-1927* (Stanford, Calif., 1957), pp. 91-100, and, for Raskalnikov's account, pp. 178-80.

[48] WO to FO, 1 June, *FO* 371/3872; Curzon telegram to Cox, 21 May,

Yet another problem was finance, for the regime's deficit was substantial, and a number of the richest provinces were not under Teheran's control. There was also the matter of the shah's subsidy; the monarch was unwilling to sack Vossuq ed-Dowleh without an assurance that his subsidy would continue. Norman would have given such an assurance, but Lawrence Oliphant, the Foreign Office Persian expert, and Curzon both disagreed. Of the loan of £2 million promised in the treaty, little had been spent a year after signature. This was just as well, for the various advisors had gotten no further than paper plans, and any charges against the loan would have been for the shah's subsidy, Cossack force upkeep, and sundry other charges (and bribes). Once the loan was gone, there was little likelihood of any more cash, and certainly none from India, as the India Office made very clear. No reforms were under way, Malleson's force was being withdrawn and the troops in the west concentrated for a similar move, Vossuq ed-Dowleh had fallen, and the Bolsheviks held Enzeli: even the staunchest Persian friend of Britain had good cause for worry.[49]

Although he had hopes that the new prime minister, Moshir ed-Dowleh, would explain the treaty to the public and push it through the Majlis, both measures which Vossuq ed-Dowleh had avoided, Norman felt that the withdrawal of the Meshed force, still in progress, weakened the government's position badly. Worse, reports in early July that the Soviets had made further landings on the Caspian and proclaimed a Soviet Republic of Gilan with its capital at Resht created near-panic in Teheran. The Cossacks had been sent to block the passes to the north, and Norman asked that the British force in Kasvin also be used to cover Teheran. If the capital fell, British prestige was finished, while aid in its successful defense would have the opposite effect.[50]

The real necessity was an agreement with the Russians. Curzon, at

---

Norman telegrams to FO, 14, 15, 18 (3 of date), 22, and 23 June, and Oliphant memorandum, 14 June, *DBFP* XIII/439, 463-64, 466, 468-70, 479, 484; Norman telegrams to FO, 10 June, *FO* 371/3873, and 24 June, *FO* 371/3874; IDCE, 16 June 1920, *L/P&S*/10/807; Ullman, *Anglo-Soviet Relations,* III, pp. 364-65.

[49] Norman telegram to FO and N. Overy, FO, memorandum, 25 June, *DBFP* XIII/485, 490; FO to IO, 8 June, IO to FO, 15 June, with minutes, *L/P&S*/10/910; details of the various loans, subsidies, and costs may be studied in *L/P&S*/10/872.

[50] Norman telegrams to FO, 26 and 27 June, 3, 4, and 7 July; Curzon

Spa, was able to reach a tentative settlement which forbade military action against Britain (specifically in Persia) as a condition for the resumption of more general trade negotiations. The news was hopeful, although it was difficult to distinguish between the Soviet forces supposedly now withdrawn and the local Persian and Azerbaijani volunteers who stayed on in control of Gilan. Norman and the Foreign Office both urged that the Soviet withdrawal be used as an opportunity to reoccupy the territory between Resht and Kasvin, but, once clear of the area, the War Office was decidedly opposed to reassuming the same old expensive responsibilities, for no purpose which it could see.[51]

To Norman, however, failure to reoccupy only meant the revenues of another province gone. The influence of the Cossack commander appeared to be growing, and the prime minister refused to use any of the loan funds to start army reform until the Majlis accepted the treaty. The Foreign Office argued that nothing in the treaty stipulated that ratification was an essential preliminary to enforcement—indeed, Britain had already implemented the treaty by sending missions and making funds available—but it was no use. Curzon blamed Norman for this change for the worse: "I have only to note that this astounding and lamentable metamorphosis coincided or rather followed upon the arrival of the new British Minister at Teheran."[52]

The fact that the new government now dispatched a mission to Moscow to negotiate directly made the situation no more palatable, but the idea actually dated from Vossuq ed-Dowleh's era. Nor was there any real answer to Norman's argument that only the current government could get Majlis approval. If acceptance was not important, the government could easily be brought down, but a more conservative government would enjoy even less confidence among more progressive Persian elements, and the Majlis still might reject the agreement and

---

telegram to Norman, 1 July, *DBFP* XIII/492-93, 497, 500-2; Montagu private telegram to Chelmsford, 9 July 1920, *Chelmsford Papers,* E. 264/13; Lenczowski, *Russia and the West in Iran,* Ch. III, deals with the Republic.

[51] Curzon (Spa) telegram to FO, 13 July, Norman telegrams to FO, 13 and 18 July, *DBFP* XIII/510-11, 513; GHQ, Baghdad, telegram to WO, 13 July 1920, *FO* 371/4904.

[52] Norman telegrams to FO, 13, 19, and 21 July; Curzon telegram to Norman, 19 July, *DBFP* XIII/511, 514, 516, and note, p. 578; Norman telegram to FO, 13 July 1920 (#486), with Curzon minute, quoted, *FO* 371/4908.

force renegotiation—a suggestion which was anathema to Curzon, whose treaty it was in the first place. To the India Office, merely spectator to the Curzon-Norman exchanges, such hopeful signs as Norman reported were offset by just this fact of Foreign Office hostility to the new government.[53]

Oliphant, in particular, would gladly have accepted a conservative government, particularly when advised by Marling and Cox, two former ministers to Persia, that Norman had little chance now of bringing any minister in who could push the treaty through the Assembly. Oliphant drafted an order to Norman: approval by the Majlis would not be purchased by concession, and the Persians should be pressed to give public confirmation of the treaty. Curzon, for all his anger, replaced this draft with one more critical in tone but milder in purpose: the Majlis should be summoned, although if it disagreed with the treaty British troops would be withdrawn and Persia left to her own devices.[54]

Norman's ability to galvanize the Persian authorities into action was undermined, however, when a substantial part of the four battalions on the Kasvin road were ordered to Iraq to help suppress its Arab revolt. These reductions would have necessitated a retreat from Kasvin to Hamadan, making any military support of the government completely out of the question. As it was, General Champian withdrew the outpost at Manjil, halfway between Kasvin and Resht. Curzon was able to obtain a War Office promise not to withdraw the troops to Hamadan unless the situation at Baghdad was so desperate as to make them indispensable there. Norman was just as worried about Curzon's own orders to himself, however: if Majlis ratification were to be demanded on pain of withdrawal, the new government would fall.[55]

[53] Norman telegrams to FO, 23-24 July, *DBFP* XIII/521-24, and IO minutes on telegram of 24 July 1920, 5721/20, *L/P&S*/10/906.

[54] Curzon telegram to Norman, 31 July, *DBFP* XIII/531; Oliphant draft of this telegram, and other minutes, 2785/82, *FO* 371/4908; Milner private to Curzon, 3 August 1920, *Curzon Papers,* F/3/3.

[55] GOC Baghdad telegram to WO, 3 August, FO telegram to Norman, 7 August, *FO* 371/4905; Norman telegrams to FO, 2, 6, 8, and 9 August, *DBFP* XIII/532, 534, 537-38; IO note, 4 August 1920, 6039/20, *L/P&S*/10/906. Ullman, *Anglo-Soviet Relations,* III, pp. 376-77, using General Ironside's unpublished diary, blames General Champian for panic in the withdrawal from Manjil (an important post for it controlled an essential pass). The withdrawal was no doubt as important as Ullman says, but Champian was surely aware of the likely need for his troops in Iraq.

Curzon needed to use the Majlis as an argument to the Cabinet for staying on until its decision was made, against War Office arguments for immediate withdrawal. He had Cox, temporarily in London, to support him. Cox advised that the 10-13,000 troops then in Persia (at £3.5 million a year) would not need reinforcements once the treaty was ratified, but withdrawal might have dangerous repercussions in the Arabistan oilfields of the south and in Afghanistan to the east. The Cabinet was nervous; the War Office warned that if withdrawal were not ordered now, the forces would have to stay on through the coming winter. Curzon in repeating his former orders to Norman now set a time limit based upon the fact that the longstanding agreement to provide a subsidy to the Persian government would expire in October. If by then the Majlis had accepted the treaty, the subsidy would be renewed—for that long, Britain would wait.[56]

September and October brought not ratification but crisis. The Cossack force, sent to retake Enzeli, suffered a serious reverse at the hands of local Bolsheviks and—if Moscow were to be believed—forces of the independent Azerbaijani Soviet Republic. Defeat of the Cossacks allowed Norman to precipitate a situation in which he and Major-General Sir Edmond ("Tiny") Ironside, commander of Norperforce as of late September and fresh from commanding a successful withdrawal of British forces from northern Russia, brought about the shah's dismissal of Starosselski. His Cossack command functions were temporarily assumed by Brigadier-General W.E.R. Dickson, head of the idle British military commission. The Persian government of the day resigned as a result of this interference.[57]

Curzon, his staff, and the War Office were all finding it impossible to follow a situation in which Norman pleaded for support of the government and then brought about its collapse. But Norman had grasped the chance to assume control of the Cossack force, thus making Britain "practically independent of vagaries of Persian internal politics" and, he claimed, ensuring execution of the treaty. Curzon was most dubious;

[56] Cabinet Financial Committee, 12 August, Cabinet 49 (20), appendix I, *CAB* 23/22; WO to FO, 19 August, *FO* 371/4908, and 26 August, *FO* 371/4909, and telegrams to GOC Baghdad, 1 and 13 September, *FO* 371/4905, and 6 October 1920, *DBFP* XIII/561.

[57] Norman telegram to FO, 29 August, *DBFP* XIII/544; *The Times*, 1 September; WO to FO, 7 November 1920, *FO* 371/4906; Callwell, *Wilson*, II, p. 264.

Norman would have to justify his new policy, adopted on his own responsibility, through success, including Majlis ratification of the treaty. As Curzon told the Cabinet; the new chief minister, Sipahdar-i-Azam, seemed willing to call the Assembly into being eventually, but he would doubtless ask time to prepare the way. The British forces would have to stay on through the winter—and come out, without question, in the spring. In the light of this timetable, Norman was told that the Majlis would have to be called within the month and a decision on the treaty reported by the end of the year.[58]

In the meantime, Curzon felt called upon to defend his policy before the House of Lords (of which he was leader). On 16 November, he outlined the Persian situation in a major policy statement which resounded with typical Curzonian eloquence—but which perhaps reconfirmed the stereotypes already in the minds of his critics. He scornfully dismissed fears of British "wild and reckless adventure and of spread-eagle Imperialism over the wastes of Central Asia," or, even worse, Persian policy as "an act of dementia on my own part, dragging after me a body of reluctant colleagues." The treaty was really conceived in Persia's own interest, not as an infringement upon her independence—and that made his task of trying to explain the delays in ratification and government changes most difficult. But Moshir ed-Dowleh, representing the "Opposition" or "Nationalist Party" preferred to obtain Majlis approval, with which idea Britain acquiesced if it occurred within the remaining four-month life of the subsidy. At the same time, Britain was withdrawing her forces in order to diminish expenses, although this was risky in the light of the Bolshevik threat. The Persian government wished them to stay, in fact, and surely British troops would not be in the process of withdrawal if their intentions were hostile. How then to justify the replacement of Starosselski with Dickson? It was the shah, said Curzon, who had wisely decided to dispense with this anti-British and anti-Persian subordinate. The situation now, therefore, was that a new government was in office, and it had been told that Britain required a decision; it was Persia's choice, to be made in the knowl-

[58] Norman telegrams to Curzon, 27 and 28 (quoted) October and 1 and 5 November, Curzon telegrams to Norman, 29 October and 5 November, *DBFP* XIII/570-71, 573-74, 577; Churchill private to Curzon, 27 October, *Curzon Papers,* F/3/3; Cabinet 59 (20), 3 November, *CAB* 23/23; Norman telegram to FO, 14 November 1920, *FO* 371/4909.

edge that the Kasvin force could not remain beyond the spring.[59]

Again, the speech disarmed no critics. The troops were still there, as were the treaty commitments if the Persians ratified. *The Times* drew upon Curzon's own term "dementia" to characterize expensive distant campaigning at a time when "every dictate of prudence should prompt our instant retirement from Persia to Baghdad, and thence to the sea." Curzon was furious at a *Times* misquote ("helping Persia through" became helping Persia "through troops")—and the paper used a technically correct apology as a vehicle for yet another spirited attack upon him.[60]

Curzon would have been justified if a popular Majlis did ratify, but the signs were to the contrary. The new Persian prime minister was extremely critical of the Triumvirate's malfeasance in office and extremely reluctant to regard the bribe as a legitimate obligation owed Britain. Norman tried to tell him that there were more important questions than recovering the £131,000 from the three culprits, but each "more important" issue—Cossack force, Majlis decision—seemed just as problematic. In desperation, Norman passed home a surprising suggestion that another £100,000 could purchase a friendly Majlis. Norman himself was not enthusiastic, even though the prime minister had suggested it, and Curzon was appalled, but the proposal showed everyone concerned that Norman was floundering.[61]

The concerned included India, quiescent for some time on Persian affairs, but now suddenly moved to say that India would have no part of bribery which in the end could only result in revelations, scandal, and vanished British influence. There was only one acceptable course: modify the treaty enough to make it acceptable, particularly in the financial and military clauses, even, if necessary, letting some neutral country staff the officer corps. Chelmsford took pains in private to be

[59] 16 November speech, print in 11489/82, *FO* 371/4909; on the dismissal of Starosselski, see Ullman, *Anglo-Soviet Relations,* III, pp. 378-82.

[60] *The Times,* 17 November 1920, quoted, and letter on 18th, also quoted.

[61] Norman telegrams to FO, 18 and 25 (3 of date) November, 1 and 2 December, Curzon telegram to Norman, 8 December, *DBFP* XIII/582, 586-88, 592, 594, and 604; Oliphant minute, 30 November, on 12687/82, *FO* 371/4909; Norman telegram to FO, 15 December, *FO* 371/4910; Cox private telegrams to Montagu, 27 December (2 of date) 1920, and Norman private to Cox, 7 January 1921, 91/91, *FO* 371/6421.

certain that India's opinion did not escape Montagu: the whole treaty had been wrong from the start, for Cox and Curzon had focused on efficient government, forgetting the need for public support. Shuckburgh in the India Office remembered that the India Office had initially agreed to the treaty quite against India's advice, but could not accept India's view now: what appeared at first sight to be a moderate middle course was really abandoning Persia to her fate. None of this debate helped win Majlis approval, and a bewildered and concerned Cabinet in London could only be certain that the War Office had withdrawal plans ready for when the snows melted. One draft Foreign Office order to Norman told him to evacuate resident British women and children via Hamadan and to retreat gradually himself to Isfahan where he could organize on the basis of the South Persian Rifles and the Bakhtiari tribesmen. The order was sent on later as a possible plan only, but the general decision to pull out had been taken and was made public. In the House of Commons, Lloyd George said that Britain's work having been done in Persia (just how, he did not specify), "we have had to say to them that we really cannot stay any longer." And, as for ratification, "If the Anglo-Persian Agreement is not ratified, if they do not take steps in that direction, it naturally falls to the ground."[62]

But the Persian government had in mind an easier method of halting the Bolshevik threat: an agreement with Russia. As the year came to a close, Norman reported that Persia had been offered a public nonintervention agreement, abrogating former Russo-Persian treaties and conceding a number of privileges (including equal rights on the Caspian) coupled with a secret agreement allowing Russia the right to intervene in Persia if attacked from that direction. Whatever the terms, Norman warned that the Persians would have to accept them if abandoned and left to themselves—and the Norperforce commander was to have his force in Baghdad by the end of February. The War Office had exceeded its authority in issuing this order, but the question was only one of timing. The Cabinet finally agreed on 4 January 1921 that the force

[62] Viceroy telegram to SSI, 6 December, with Shuckburgh minute, *L/P&S/*10/907; Norman telegrams to FO, 10, 17, 20, and 21 December, G.P. Churchill memorandum, 20 December, Curzon telegram to Norman and WO telegram to GOC Baghdad, 23 December, *DBFP* XIII/607, 613, 615-19; Chelmsford private to Montagu, *Montagu Papers,* D. 523/11; Cabinet 72 (20), 17 December, *CAB* 23/22; *Parl. Deb.,* H.C., 15 December 1920; see also *DBFP* XIII, p. 706, note 7.

should be prepared to move on 1 April. The Soviet offer did give some security that the Russians would not invade Persia so long as the negotiations were in progress, and India, at least, was prepared to gamble on Soviet sincerity.[63]

Meanwhile, the time limit for ratification had expired, but Curzon saw no point in saying so explictly to the Persians; the treaty would remain where it was, in abeyance. Since Norman reported that the Persian prime minister was making only abjectly humble replies to Russia, there seemed no chance of any future ratification. Worse, any prospective British peace treaty with Russia was endangered by the reported Soviet condition that Russia would only conclude a treaty and end its involvement in the Enzeli area if the British pulled out, finally and totally. Norman would even have made that assurance to Moscow, but the Foreign Office dismissed such humility out of hand. Curzon altogether failed to see why panic was necessary—and so Norman was told.[64]

Even the Indian officials found Norman's pessimism too stark. British presence and Russian absence meant by the nature of things British unpopularity and Russian appeal. Overhasty withdrawal from Teheran would be more likely to precipitate the feared collapse than staying on. The best approach was disavowal of the treaty and a return to the old role of "champions of Islam against the Russian Ogre." It was not merely in Persia that India suggested this policy, for its adoption would require dropping the draft Turkish treaty and adopting a more conciliatory attitude in the Afghanistani negotiations then in progress. To Curzon, however, this policy, advocated by Chelmsford and H.R.C. Dobbs, foreign secretary to the government of India, while it had the virtues of consistency, was impertinent: India refused to cooperate in policy for the area, and therefore India should have no voice in making it. "If the Government of India take no interest in Persia,

[63] Norman telegrams to FO, 27 and 31 December 1920, FO to Norman, 3 January 1921, *DBFP* XIII/621, 628, and note, p. 679; Cabinet 82 (20), 31 December 1920, and 1(21), 4 January 1921, *CAB* 23/23-4; GOC Baghdad telegram to WO, 31 December 1920, and Churchill memorandum, 3 January 1921 (C.P. 2407), *FO* 371/6399; Roskill, *Hankey,* II, pp. 202, 210.

[64] Norman telegrams to FO, 8, 9, 13, 15, and 19 January, viceroy telegram to SSI, 10 January, Curzon telegram to Norman, 13 January, and private telegram, 21 January 1921, *DBFP* XIII/640, 642, 643, 647-48, 650, 655, 660.

why are they always lecturing us upon it?" The India Office tended to side with India in this larger question, but the India Office was finding itself consulted by the Foreign Office with considerably less frequency, and that situation was likely to continue until India radically altered its attitude on financial contributions.[65]

Even Sir Percy Cox, now in Baghdad, tended to support India: the treaty he had negotiated was a dead letter now, while a Perso-Soviet treaty would probably reduce Bolshevik activity in Persia. The main thing was not to panic. By summer, if necessary, a base for operations could be established in Isfahan, but a better solution altogether was to negotiate a new and acceptable treaty. Norman must have torn his hair at this suggestion; as he was quick to cable Curzon, the "new" treaty Cox proposed was simply his own proposed modification warmed over, and London had already rejected that idea. There were now three proposals: Cox's treaty revision, Normans assurances to Russia, and India's treaty disavowal in favor of a pro-Islamic stance. Curzon preferred Cox's plan, but, he noted, all three asked that the troops stay on, and where was the money to come from? Even treaty revision was increasingly unlikely, for the Persian government was going through a totally directionless stage. By mid-February, the time limit was up; Norman was told to cease urging Majlis passage. Britain would not denounce or renounce the agreement on her own, but the treaty was quite dead. A bitter Curzon remarked for his staff that, "Personally I will never propose another Agreement with the Persians. Nor unless they came on their knees would I ever consider any application from them, and probably not then. In future we will look after our own interests in Persia not hers."[66]

But Persia was finding her own way out. During the night of 21 February, Cossacks from Kasvin and Hamadan under Colonel Reza Khan moved into Teheran and in a virtually bloodless coup assumed

[65] Viceroy telegrams to SSI, 17 December 1920, with IO minutes, L/P&S/10/908, 22 January (quoted) (also with Curzon minute, FO 371/6400), and 27 January, DBFP XIII/662, 666; Montagu note to Curzon, 23 February 1921, with Curzon minute (quoted), 2524/25, FO 371/6409.

[66] Cox telegram to SSI, 29 January, Norman telegrams to FO, 3 and 11 February, Curzon telegram to Norman, 16 February, DBFP XIII/668, 670, 676, and 678; Curzon minute on Cox telegram, FO 371/6400; Norman telegrams to FO, 12 and 16 February, latter with Curzon minute (quoted), 17 February 1921, FO 371/6401.

control of the government, which was now placed under the leadership of a prominent journalist and nationalist spokesman, Sayyed Zia ed-Din Tabataba'i. The new government was welcomed by all those favoring reform, reported Norman; his own position was rather embarrassing, for so many Persian government changes had been precipitated by British interference that he was automatically assumed to be responsible. Five days later, the Persian-Soviet treaty was signed in Moscow—very much as predicted, except that the secret clause was now part of the published text.[67]

In the light of these developments and the uncertain future, Curzon was unwilling to risk any commitments even though the new government appeared to want aid to reconstruct its armed forces. Despite Norman's warning that this policy would only force the Persians to look elsewhere, Curzon would merely extend the South Persian Rifles subsidy six months. At the end of that time the 7600-man force (all but 350 of which were Persian) would have to be disbanded or incorporated into the Persian armed forces (it was in fact disbanded, since no agreement could be reached with the Persian government). No advisors, no loans—in fact, Persia would be expected to repay all her debts, including the infamous £131,000. Curzon, clearly, had lost his zeal for things Persian. "I cannot maintain Mr. Norman's high level of enthusiasm over each succeeding Persian Ministry," he wrote, "or pretend to be as pleased at the rejection of the Anglo-Persian Agreement as I was at its conclusion."[68]

Actually, the new government wanted no loan; it was itself trying to recover the £131,000 from the Triumvirate, which Curzon now declined to protect from "disgorging the monstrous bribe which they extracted from Sir P. Cox." Under the circumstances, the decision was

[67] Norman telegrams to FO, 17, 21, and 25 February, 3, 12, 18, and 20 March 1921, *DBFP* XIII/679, 681, 683, 688, 695; Leonard Shapiro, ed., *Soviet Treaty Series,* I (Washington, D.C., 1950), pp. 92-94, and Hurewitz, *Diplomacy,* II, pp. 90-94, have Soviet-Persian treaty text.

Ullman, *Anglo-Soviet Relations,* III, pp. 385-86, credits Ironside with putting Reza Khan in a position from which he could rise to power, an account which is based on Ironside's unpublished diary. Although plausible, the account tends rather to underestimate Reza Khan's own ability.

[68] Curzon telegrams to Norman, 14, 16, 17, and 20 March, *DBFP* XIII/696, 698, 700, and 704, and minute on Norman telegram to FO, 18 March, quoted, *FO* 371/6402; FO to Treasury, 23 March 1921, *FO* 371/6421.

wise; the best policy now was noninterference. Norman was told to act with circumspection toward both the government and the new Soviet ambassador. As in the Caucasus, however, Britain had lost much of its capacity to influence events—a role which now fell largely to Reza Khan, the Cossack commander, who stayed in the background (and was seldom mentioned in Norman's reports) until he fell out with the prime minister in May.[69]

Reza Khan had risen from the ranks—and British intrigues to oust the Russian officers had been, ironically enough, the road to his rise. "An honest and capable officer without political aspirations," Norman had written in March, and "an ignorant but astute peasant" in May; but Reza Khan now took on the post of minister of war and turned at once to repression of anti-government forces in several provinces with his 17,000 Cossacks. (This group was three times the size of the old force, so it is clear how he had used the intervening months.) Norman was convinced that Reza Khan's assumption of power had been worked out in conjunction with the jealous Russians, and he predicted that the new minister of war would be no more successful at creating a stable government than his predecessors. This was a satisfying prediction if Norman was right about his Russian associations, but Norman's own favorable attitude toward Zia ed-Din now stood in his disfavor in Teheran, and he had also a new competitor in the game of bazaar politics in the person of Theodore A. Rothstein, Soviet minister to Persia (April 1921-September 1922). Norman was soon complaining that he could not keep pace with Rothstein's expenses and activities, and Reza Khan appeared to be slipping over to the Russian side: the future was grim, so grim in fact, that for some time to come, "the game of Great Britain in Northern Persia is up."[70]

Norman was quite correct. The treaty and the entire policy which it

[69] Norman telegram to FO, 31 March, *DBFP* XIII/705, with Curzon minute, 5 April (quoted), and telegrams to Norman, 9 April, *FO* 371/6402, and 28 April; Norman telegram to FO, 23 April, *FO* 371/6403; IO to FO, 6 May, *FO* 371/6404; military attaché, Teheran, telegram to WO, 15 May 1921, *FO* 371/6405.

[70] Norman to Curzon, 3 March (quoted), *FO* 371/6403, telegram, 5 May (quoted), and letter of same date, *FO* 371/6404, and letter of 5 July 1921 (quoted), *FO* 371/6406; Ullman, *Anglo-Soviet Relations,* III, p. 388. On Rothstein mission, see Lenczowski, *Russia and the West in Iran,* pp. 65-69.

represented had to be called a failure. Cox might say, in reflection, that "I like to think that if I could have been kept on a few months more, things would have shaped different, but God knows," but the times were no longer right for such a treaty relationship, as India had said all along. Chelmsford explained at a meeting of the Central Asian Society that Britain had tried to "schoolmaster" Persia, keeping it as an isolated area which could be managed by a separate policy carried on without reference to developments elsewhere, particularly in India. Norman could always topple governments or whisper in the shah's ear, but never influence opinion enough to get ratification—let alone fulfillment—of the Anglo-Persian treaty. The Foreign Office had to agree: Norman was now recalled (and retired four years later) to be replaced by Sir Percy Loraine, an able professional with prewar experience in Teheran and a distinguished interwar career before him.[71]

The subsequent rise to sole power and royal status of Reza Khan—later Reza Shah—falls beyond the scope of this work. The last months of 1921 and the following year were a time of concern for Persian experts for numerous reasons (including Bolshevik activity centered in Teheran), but Loraine could only be an observer, quietly watching (and, thanks to intercepted telegrams between the Persian government in Teheran and the outlying provinces, listening). Britain could do very little now, even when Reza Shah brought under control the important oil-rich province of Arabistan, whose principal citizen had long been a special friend of Britain's. Britain's "moment" in Persia had passed; it was now, to a lesser extent, a Soviet "moment," but Reza Khan was no man's puppet. Britain's frontier was not on the Caspian or in Meshed, but on the waters of the Persian Gulf, on the Indian frontier, and even, to the extent that influence could be preserved in those countries, in Mesopotamia on the one side and Afghanistan on the other.[72]

Once again, India's objections to policy, and in this case refusal to

[71] Cox private to Curzon, 23 July (quoted), *Curzon Papers,* F/4/3; Central Asian Society dinner, 15 June, reported in *The Times,* 16 June; Loraine appointment discussed in Curzon private telegram to Norman, 7 September, and Norman private telegram to Curzon, 11 September 1921, and other documents in file 9829/34, *FO* 371/6449.

[72] Arabistan is dealt with in *L/P&S/*10/933; Sir Percy mentions the intercepts in a private letter to Curzon, 28 August 1923, *Curzon Papers,* F/6/1; see also Elizabeth Monroe, *Britain's Moment in the Middle East, 1914-1956* (London, 1963), for further general reflections.

cooperate financially, had affected British policy to a considerable degree. And if India's influence was important to Persia, it was—at least traditionally—the dominant influence in policymaking where Afghanistan was concerned.

THE AFGHAN TREATY

The Treaty of Rawalpindi of August 1919, far from settling the problem of India's relationship with Afghanistan, stipulated that Britain would be prepared to receive another delegation for further negotiation only after six months of good behavior in various areas, including frontier tribal relations. The feeling at that time was that the amir would soon realize his dependence upon India. Unfortunately, the Afghanis had other pressures with which to cope, including above all their own tribal relations. The lack of a final settlement tended to invite frontier unrest which could not be controlled from Kabul. In December 1919, for example, minor Indian troubles with frontier tribes—notably Mahsuds and Wazirs—were attributed, although without hard evidence, to Afghani instigation.

As some had predicted, the way in which the Afghani war had been resolved had not adequately convinced the amir and Sardar Mahmud Beg Tarzi, his foreign minister, of their proper role vis-a-vis India, and they seemed to be attempting to harass Britain into cession of various Pashtu-speaking frontier peoples. The amir was generally expansion-minded, and Britain was also concerned that the Russians might buy his loyalty with territorial cession in Central Asia. He seemed to be using British and Russian bogeys alternately to frighten both suitors. The largest danger, as India saw it, was that the amir might be persuaded to join in an attack on Persia, inspired by Soviet intrigue and sympathy over the Turkish peace terms and encouraged by the anti-British revolt in Mesopotamia. Indian military authorities urged that the amir be told at once to expel Bolshevik agitators and cease frontier intrigue, as pledged at Rawalpindi; if he failed to do so, military pressure should be used. Otherwise continued demobilization would make much greater in the spring. With this advice the Foreign Department and the viceroy disagreed, and the disagreement tended to undermine Indian influence in the policy toward Afghanistan.[73]

[73] Viceroy telegram to SSI, 22 December 1919, *FO* 371/4025; IO,

The military advice was rejected, but at least it pointed up the weakness in the Rawalpindi settlement. India had no reliable means of influencing, or even of ascertaining, the course of events in Kabul, and given the general atmosphere of anti-Bolshevik fears, the unknown intrigues of the Russian agent with the amir were more frightening than they might have been if the details were actually known. But certainly the Russians would do all they could to build the amir's own fears of British intentions. Grant, in Peshawar, found it all most irritating. The amir wanted peace; Indian could ill afford war. The answer was direct negotiation: "Why not chuck dignity and settle up with him if we can?" Chelmsford was unwilling to go so far in his letters to Montagu, but India did ask permission to open frank discussions and perhaps even to send a small mission to Kabul with the power to make some concessions in arrears (or renewal) of subsidy, customs duties, representation in London, or the style and dignity of "His Majesty" for the amir, all to counter Bolshevik influence. The idea, as the viceroy explained privately, was to work out some detailed points of misunderstanding. The amir's recent overtures for larger negotiations had to be refused; unless London really needed it, the price of a treaty of alliance would be prohibitively high.[74]

The main concern in London was not Russian-Afghani invasion of any country, but Bolshevik intrigue in Afghanistan and Persia, and here the Foreign, India, and War Offices for once appeared to be in agreement. It was also agreed—with India—that it was not time for a new treaty. The course of Britain's own Russian negotiations and the situation in Central Asia dictated caution. For a brief moment they considered using Enver Pasha, former Young Turk, pan-Islamic leader, and British enemy to make trouble for Russia in Central Asia. Considerable circumspection was maintained in the discussions which were held with Enver Pasha through an intermediary—and there is no evidence that there was ever anything more than verbal support for the

---

Political Dept., memorandum, 14 February 1921, *FO* 371/6747; Poullada, *Reform and Rebellion,* Ch. XI; Adamec, *Afghanistan, 1900-1923,* Ch. VII; Kapur, *Russia and Asia,* pp. 226-39; Eudin and North, *Soviet Russia and Asia,* pp. 103-5.

[74] Grant private to Maffey, 10 (quoted) and 17 January, Maffey private to Grant, 14 January, Chelmsford private telegram to Montagu, 11 January, *Chelmsford Papers,* E. 264/16, 24; viceroy telegram to SSI, 11 January 1920, *L/P&S/*10/810.

activities which eventually led to the Central Asian Basmachi rising. The point is rather that Britain was reluctant to be drawn into Central Asian adventures again; policymakers showed far more relief that the danger of a Soviet or Soviet-Afghani invasion of Persia was past than desire to manipulate Russia's Central Asian problems.[75]

Policy toward Afghanistan was based on this Bolshevik-induced caution. London decided that it was enough to tell the amir that he was not living up to his treaty-imposed obligations to dismiss Bolshevik agents and refrain from tribal interference. Not unnaturally, Amanullah protested: he could not expel innocuous visitors, for example (meaning Indian Bolsheviks and other Indian agitators). Delhi correctly interpreted this answer to mean that the amir would not live up to those obligations without a dose of force, but India had neither the means nor the intention of forcing another war. The only alternative, therefore, despite deep grumbling from London, was moderation—and talk. In March India issued and London approved an invitation to the amir to send a delegation to the hill station of Mussoorie (135 miles northeast of Delhi). It was felt that the amir could be brought to cooperate without having to make any serious concessions; London had already stipulated that any subsidy should only be given as a reward for good behavior (and no "His Majesty," since King George V was strongly opposed to it).[76]

[75] Duke to Montagu (written by Hirtzel), 13 January, on staff meeting of 12th, SSI telegram to viceroy, 15 January, *L/P&S*/10/810; Montagu private to Hankey, 11 January, *CAB* 21/184; Curzon private to Lloyd George, 12 January 1920, *CAB* 1/29; also d'Abernon (Berlin) to Curzon, 16 May 1921, 5978/5978, *FO* 371/6752, on Enver.

On the Basmachis revolt in Ferghana, see Joseph Castagné, *Les Basmatchis* . . . (Paris, 1925), a brief account; Park, *Bolshevism in Turkestan,* pp. 31-54; and Kapur, *Russia and Asia,* pp. 234-35. Enver emerged to assume leadership of the movement in 1921 and was killed the following August; by 1924, the movement had been liquidated.

[76] Grant private to Chelmsford and Amir Amanullah to viceroy, 23 February, and Montagu private telegram to Chelmsford, 16 April, *Chelmsford Papers,* E. 264/24, 12; viceroy telegrams to SSI, 20 February and 12 March (with Shuckburgh note), SSI telegrams to viceroy, 2 March and 16 April, *L/P&S*/10/810; Chelmsford private to Montagu, 4 March, Montagu private to Chelmsford, 8 April 1920, *Montagu Papers,* D. 523/10, 4. The main agitator was Mahendra Pratep, on whose activities in Central Asia and later in the Far East see *L/P&S*/10/898-89.

London had agreed to the whole plan only with reluctance. India was taking the lead out of conviction that secure peace was necessary on the northwest frontier, and that India (and Britain) could no longer dominate Afghanistan in the old nineteenth-century style. To the contrary, India's thinking was defensive: an agreement with the amir might forestall a Soviet-Afghani treaty, reports of which were increasingly frequent as the year 1920 advanced. In London, on the other hand, as J.L. Maffey, Chelmsford's private secretary, reported, the attitude was rather different. Roos-Keppel shared Curzon's attitude (a conviction often held among Old India hands) that the new breed of administrators had less backbone than their predecessors, but Montagu was sympathetic. In fact, Montagu's main fear was not the Bolsheviks but Lord Curzon. "He had evidently been terrorised by an indignant Curzon, a Curzon annoyed *au fond* by the fact that anybody had dared to attempt an Afghan Policy not rooted in Curzon and eager to seize on the most trifling point for a concentrated fire of Curzonian artillery."[77]

In April the Mussoorie discussions began between Dobbs and Tarzi. After breaking off for some days as a result of frontier troubles, the talks continued through late June and July. They covered a vast number of issues, including the caliphate and the whole problem of the Turkish peace, discussion of which contributed not a little to Indian concern over exactly those same issues. Britain refused to grant facilities to an Afghani delegation to make its pro-Muslim case in Paris, since Afghanistan had no *locus standi* to participate in the peace negotiations (having been neither invaded nor at war). Despite their disappointment, the Afghani delegates were quite reasonable, and Dobbs urged that "discussions" be elevated to "negotiations" for a larger treaty which would settle the outstanding issues. Chelmsford supported this proposal to London only after the Mussoorie conference had disbanded in late July, but because the Afghani delegates had had to return to Kabul with some tangible accomplishment to preserve their own personal position, they had already been promised both a subsidy (18 lakhs, or Rs. 18,00,000, per annum, subject to good behavior) and satisfactory settlement of the issues of consular representation, arms import permits, and clear recognition of Afghani independence.[78]

---

[77] Maffey private to Chelmsford, 27 April and 17 May (quoted) 1920, *Chelmsford Papers,* E. 264/16.

[78] Viceroy telegrams to SSI, 13, 15, 19, and 27 June and 24 July, SSI

The course of events now lent urgency to the matter, for India was seriously concerned in the summer by the Hijrat emigrants to the Afghani frontier and by the rising Khilafat agitation. On the other hand, the fall of Bukhara to a Soviet onslaught in September offered a good chance that Kabul would be more worried about Russian than British aggression. The amir might even wish to conclude a defensive military alliance; that would be too dangerous a commitment, but arms and munitions might be possible. When in October the amir requested that a mission proceed to Kabul to conclude a treaty, no clear decision on the desirability of a treaty, let alone its format, had been reached between London and Delhi, and speed was essential.[79]

The advantages India urged were that the very presence in Kabul of the negotiators would counteract the Russians and support the amir (for whom there was no visible substitute at the moment). Refusal to participate, on the other hand, would alienate him and push him into Soviet arms. The risk was that India would come as a suitor, bidding against the Russians, but it was a risk India would take. The Indian case was a strong one: if the policy of London had been followed, said India succumbing to an irresistible "I-told-you-so," and Afghani foreign relations were in Britain's hands, Britain would now have a most embarrassing obligation to defend Afghanistan against a possible Bolshevik onslaught precipitated by that very control.[80]

The arguments were good, but London required to know first whether the amir had signed with the Russians, for if so, and if the treaty included anti-British clauses, negotiations would be useless. Above all

telegram to viceroy, 15 June, *L/P&S/*10/810; Dobbs private to A.N.L. Cater (officiating secretary, Foreign Dept.), 28 June, and private to Chelmsford, 17 and 22 July, *Chelmsford Papers,* E. 264/25; Chelmsford private to Grant, 26 July, *Grant Papers* (IO Library), D. 660/25, and private to Montagu, 22 July, *Montagu Papers,* D. 523/11; Curzon private to Montagu, 27 June, *Curzon Papers,* F/3/3; Chelmsford in Council to SSI, 9 September 1920, enclosed the full report of the Mussoorie proceedings; copy in *FO* 371/5381. These negotiations are dealt with in Adamec, *Afghanistan, 1900-1923,* pp. 148-57. A lakh (or lac) is 100,000, and units are written accordingly: thus "18 lakhs" is 18,00,000.

[79] Grant private to Chelmsford, 15 August, *Grant Papers,* D. 660/25; WO note, 24 September, viceroy telegrams to SSI, 24 September and 15 October, conference notes (at IO), 30 September 1920, *L/P&S/*10/810; Park, *Bolshevism in Turkestan,* pp. 24-49.

[80] Viceroy telegrams to SSI, 15 and 19 October 1920, *L/P&S/*10/810.

the important issue was whether the Soviets would be permitted to establish missions at Ghazni and Kandahar, both dangerously close to the Indian frontier. The amir appeared indeed to have signed; he would not furnish the text but only say that the treaty was not aimed against Britain. India advised accepting this assurance on good faith rather than administering a rebuff, but London strongly disagreed: the text would have to be produced. "The G. of I. have led us on step by step against our will into a position with which nobody here is satisfied," wrote Hirtzel; the mission was far more likely to end in catastrophe than an acceptable treaty, and then India would doubtless urge new and sweeping concessions in order to escape humiliation. "One long series of progressive blunders," said Curzon of India's Afghan negotiations. Montagu, predictably where Curzon was concerned, disagreed, and the differences of opinion were so strong that the issue was forced up to Cabinet level.[81]

In the Cabinet of 6 December opinions were so well balanced that there was no adequate justification to override the considered advice of the government of India. Perhaps Chelmsford's view was shared unknowingly by others: Curzon's policy was in tatters, in Persia surely, in Mesopotamia probably, and there was no reason to suppose his ideas on Afghanistan were any more correct. India was told of the doubts and criticism expressed in the Cabinet but was given reluctant permission to proceed. India then asked to be able to use "His Majesty" as a bargaining counter. Curzon would have nothing to do with it. The whole mission was a mistake, "and I am not therefore qualified to advise upon the plentiful crop of additional mistakes which the initial error is discovered to involve." Grudging acquiescence was won from the king, however, and Dobbs proceeded to Kabul with at least this concession, arriving in the wintery capital on 7 January 1921 with an immense task before him.[82]

[81] SSI telegrams to viceroy, 20 October and (private telegram) 2 December; viceroy telegrams to SSI, 1 and 25 November (latter with Shuckburgh, Roos-Keppel, Cobbe, and Hirtzel—quoted—and Curzon—quoted—minutes), 5 December (private telegram), and 12 December (with Shuckburgh minute, 13 December), L/P&S/10/810; IO Political Dept. Memorandum B. 355, 19 November 1920 (intercepts on Suritz negotiations), L/P&S/10/912.
[82] Cabinet 65 (20), 6 December, CAB 23/23; Chelmsford private to Montagu, 8 December, Montagu Papers, D. 523/11; SSI telegrams to vice-

The price, it soon appeared, would be substantial, for Amanullah clearly intended playing Russia off against Britain; the Russian treaty, he assured Dobbs, was unratified and might remain so if Britain was sufficiently cooperative. Cooperation meant not only the expected statements on independence, a legation in London (an important point, since Kabul's relations with London had always been in the hands of India) and consulates in India, arms aid, and rights for the frontier tribes, but also revision of the Turkish peace. That was clearly impossible, but as it was Dobb's first draft, ready by late February, went too far for London. Montagu, hard pressed by Curzon and others, asked for some clause which might make it possible for the amir to obtain British aid in the conduct of his foreign relations. Chelmsford fought against this instruction, for the amir would not now give up his independence, and the intervention of Soviet diplomacy had lessened Britain's capacity to dictate to him. Chelmsford could acquiesce even in a Soviet subsidy to the amir if used, for example, for the sort of military reorganization which would aid Afghanistan's stability. Britain could no longer forbid Afghani relations with third parties unless she were prepared to outbid Russia at an extremely high cost.[83]

On 3 March the Cabinet again considered the situation, mainly in relation to the wider issue of Russian policy. Dobbs and India gave assurances that the draft treaty included as many of the necessary safeguards as possible; if revelations were forthcoming later of a dangerous Soviet-Afghani relationship, the treaty would simply have to be disavowed. But the India Office and Lord Reading, present at the meeting as Chelmsford's successor-designate, maintained that Britain simply could not sign if the amir had concluded a treaty with Russia which might include anti-British stipulations. Control of foreign policy might be waived, but no treaty could be signed unless the terms of the Russian

---

roy, 8 and 19 December, viceroy telegrams to SSI, 10 and 12 December (latter with Curzon minute, 14 December 1920, quoted), *L/P&S*/10/810.

[83] Viceroy (Army Dept.) telegrams to SSI, 13, 15, 20, and 27 January, 20 and 21 February, and 1 March, SSI telegrams to viceroy, 11 and 19 February, *L/P&S*/10/955; Chelmsford private to Montagu, 1 and 16 March 1921, *Montagu Papers,* D. 523/5. Dobbs's final report on these negotiations, dated 15 February 1922 (copy in 1450/59, *FO* 371/8076) is the most comprehensive source; see also Adamec, *Afghanistan 1900-1923,* pp. 157-66. Soviet-Afghani treaty of 28 February 1921 in Shapiro, *Soviet Treaty Series,* I, pp. 96-97.

agreement were known, nor could the amir collect a subsidy from both powers.[84]

Dobbs, predictably, warned that insistence on this attitude would lead to a rupture in the negotiations, which in any case had not yet formally taken up the issue of the Bolshevik treaty terms. When the issue was raised, Tarzi might be brought to reveal the terms if Britain did not insist on elimination of any clauses on subsidy or arms aid. But in the India Office Dobbs was considered too eager to make concessions; he "seems to survey the whole problem through Afghan spectacles," wrote Roos-Keppel on one of Dobb's telegrams. The Soviet-Afghani negotiations were being conducted at the time in Moscow, and the amir's denial of a firm treaty to Dobbs was flatly contradicted by intercepted radio communications from Moscow to the Soviet representative in Kabul. British Intelligence had provided this information— but not, apparently, to Dobbs.[85]

London therefore continued to insist on disclosure as a test of Afghani good faith, a point more important than a Soviet subsidy or arms aid, as Delhi was told. To approach Moscow directly on this issue seems never to have been regarded with as much favor as working directly upon the amir. After four months of negotiation, however, both London and Dobbs had reached the conclusion that perhaps cash would speak louder than words, and a substantial (40 lakh) subsidy together with a lump sum down payment might yet buy Britain a treaty. It was not simply desperation that urged this suggestion, at least from Dobb's standpoint, for his sympathy for Afghanistan was real (just as that of Cox, say, for Persia was real in its fashion). "One cannot help feeling the pathos of it," Dobbs wrote privately to Reading; "this unhappy, bewildered little State, trying to swim bravely with the rest in the troubled waters of independence, but not knowing how and fiercely suspicious of all help."[86]

[84] Cabinet 10 (21), 3 March, *CAB* 23/24; SSI telegram to viceroy, 4 March 1921, *L/P&S/*10/955.

[85] Viceroy telegrams to SSI, 9, 10 (with Roos-Keppel minute, 14 March, quoted), 15 (2 of date), and 20 March, *L/P&S/*10/955; Chelmsford private to Montagu, 21 March, *Montagu Papers,* D. 523/5; GSI telegram to DMI 19 April 1921, *L/P&S/*10/958.

[86] SSI telegrams to viceroy, 22 March and 15 April, *L/P&S/*10/955; Dobbs private to Reading, 19 April 1921 (quoted), *Reading Papers,* E. 238/23.

The tendency now, however, was to think of the test of strength with Moscow. If the authorities at home would not take up the matter in their negotiations with Russia, India argued, then India had to make the best terms it could with the amir. India believed that Amanullah had worked hard to modify the Soviet treaty, and the only objectionable feature now appeared to be Russian consulates on the frontier. If Britain were to insist on this issue to the amir (and he to the Russians), it, too, would probably be modified by the Soviets in order not to jeopardize their foothold in Kabul. The most important goal was to keep the negotiations alive; in the spring of 1921 India needed an Anglo-Afghani settlement, for Muslim leaders in India had a habit of looking to the amir for possible leadership. The most likely cause of a breach would be refusal to negotiate without full disclosure of, and probably modification of, the Soviet accord. The choices now were three. First, Britain could offer enough cash and arms for Afghanistan to overthrow the Soviet connection and give up foreign policy control to Britain (the "exclusive" treaty). This possibility was more desirable as bringing about a Soviet diplomatic defeat than for strictly Afghani purposes. Second, Britain could adopt the Indian policy of continuing to negotiate the best comprehensive treaty possible. Finally, as a moderate last resort ("pis aller"), Britain could issue a diplomatic statement of agreement settling as many issues as possible but hopefully not involving any subsidy—a suggestion of Dobb's when negotiations appeared to be breaking down. Despite the presence of Chelmsford to argue the Indian case, the Cabinet in early May adopted the first course, failing which the government would, most reluctantly, accept the "pis aller."[87]

Dobbs now had to implement these orders in an increasingly tense atmosphere. The amir was well aware of the events now taking place in Kemalist Turkey, which did not reflect highly on British military strength, just as he was well aware of Soviet pressure. There was a Russian representative in Kabul, and the amir was playing host now to the amir of Bukhara, fled from his capital before the Russians. But Tarzi's position too was awkward. Although the Afghanis were worried about the Russians, they were not in a position to forbid Soviet consulates until it was very clear just how much aid Britain was prepared to provide. Dobbs offered 40 lakhs in subsidy and an immediate grant of

[87] Viceroy telegrams to SSI, 26 April and 5 May, *L/P&S/*10/955; Cabinet 37 (21), 10 May 1921, *CAB* 23/25.

ten more for arms if the Soviet treaty was scrapped, but it was not enough; the Afghanis had no real desire to choose between frying pan and fire and wanted to keep both Russians and British at arm's length. Dobbs and India were more aware of this than London. The authorities at home seriously complicated the whole business by insisting that Britain emerge from the Afghani negotiations with a triumph over Soviet diplomacy.[88]

Any triumph, India knew very well, was not going to be as grand as London envisioned; above all, it was not going to include the control over foreign relations for which London still pined. Amanullah was aware of the recognition accorded Kemal's independence through Turkish agreements with Moscow, Paris, and Rome, and the amir would take no less (indeed, it was a current concern of the Foreign Office that Paris and Rome were even then giving a warm welcome to a traveling Afghani mission). One concession only might buy the amir, and that was control of the frontier tribes—but since a very important objective of the whole process was peace on the frontier, to remove Soviet influence from Afghanistan at that price would be self-defeating. Because of this, and because of Tarzi's evasiveness and the general frustrations of a half-year spent in fruitless negotiation, the India Office came very reluctantly in mid-July to accept the "pis aller" as better than no treaty at all.[89]

Mid-July, however, brought Kemalist successes in Anatolia and a new and more active Soviet representative to Kabul. F.F. Raskalnikov, the Soviet hero of the confrontation with Britain at Enzeli, made even a "pis aller" questionable to Dobbs. India was convinced that the "exclusive" treaty, even in moderate form, would be impossible, and withdrawal of an unsuccessful mission would be a Soviet triumph; the only choice now was the "pis aller," including whatever concessions could be agreed upon, or even a fourth choice: a "gentlemanly" treaty which was nothing more than a mutual pledge of friendship and nonintervention. The Cabinet was not so sure, and, so long as temporary

[88] Viceroy telegrams to SSI, 19 and 31 May, 13, 16, 21 (2) June, SSI telegram to viceroy, 16 June, *L/P&S*/10/955 (also *FO* 371/6750-52); Dobbs telegram to FSI, 17 June 1921, *FO* 371/6741.

[89] Viceroy telegram to SSI, 25 and 28 June and 22 July, SSI telegram to viceroy, 16 July, *L/P&S*/10/955 (see also *FO* 371/6741-42); IO to FO, 6 July, with minutes, *FO* 371/6753; Norman telegram to FO, 9 July 1921, *FO* 371/6742.

Greek successes in Anatolia continued, the government expressed to India its acceptance of the gentlemanly alternative only as a very undesirable last resort to avoid the humiliation of no treaty.[90]

In the last analysis, however, the treaty depended upon the Afghanis, and they had decided upon a moderate gentlemanly agreement. They were willing now to provide the terms of the Russian treaty, because Russia had assured them that Moscow would not at that time demand the projected consulates at Kandahar and Gazni. Since Dobbs and India agreed in recommending signature, the only obstacle appeared to be London's insistence that Afghanistan comply with "full disclosure," meaning disclosure of the suspected secret terms in the Soviet-Afghan treaty. There is no need to review the months of negotiation which followed; suffice it to say that on 3 November a Cabinet weary of Afghanistan finally approved the gentlemanly treaty in principle. On 15 November, after an eleven-hour, grinding session with the amir, during which Dobbs had even ordered up his transport from Peshawar, the last disputed term was settled; the treaty was formally signed on 22 November.[91]

The document stipulated only the establishment of friendly relations; a separate exchange of letters assured Britain that Russia would not be given the opportunity to establish consulates at Jelalabad, Ghazni, or other sensitive spots. Mutual independence; representation for Afghanistan in London and for Britain at Kabul; consulates for Britain at Kandahar and Jalalabad and for Afghanistan at Calcutta, Karachi, and Bombay; Afghan freedom to purchase military equipment; no customs duties for Afghani goods in transit through India—these were the main clauses of the three-year agreement.

Sir Henry Dobbs's task was finished; he had accomplished little for

[90] Viceroy telegrams to SSI, 27, 28, and 30 July and 6 August, SSI telegrams to viceroy, 27 July and 5 August, *L/P&S*/10/955 (and *FO* 371/6742); Cabinet 63 (21), 5 August 1921, *CAB* 23/26; Kapur, *Soviet Russia and Asia*, pp. 226-34.

[91] SSI telegrams to viceroy, 16 August and 2 and 9 September, viceroy telegrams to SSI, 31 August and 6 September, *L/P&S*/10/955; SSI telegrams to viceroy, 12, 13, and 28 October and 3 November, viceroy telegrams to SSI, 1, 10, 17, and 23 October and 1, 10, and 16 November, *L/P&S*/10/960; IO to FO, 15 December, *FO* 371/6750; Cabinet 72 (21), 19 August, 85 (21), 3 November, and 88 (21), 22 November 1921, *CAB* 23/26-27. Text of treaty in Adamec, *Afghanistan 1900-1923*, pp. 183-88.

nearly a year spent at Kabul. During that year, despite disclaimers and protests, first India and then a reluctant London had concluded that British and Indian resources were not sufficient, nor was there real need, to influence events in Afghanistan in a major way. Like Persia, the Bolshevik menace was an important factor in shaping policy toward Afghanistan, although considerably more so in London than in India. Unlike Persia, however, there was neither British military presence nor Bolshevik invasion, and for that reason it was easier for an India increasingly concerned with its internal political problems to view the issues of Turkey, Persia, and Afghanistan from the standpoint of their effect upon those problems rather than as external threats. London, on the other hand, still engaged in anti-Bolshevik activities on a wide scale, was for a long time unwilling to acknowledge the results of the Third Afghani War of 1919. By the treaty of 1921 Afghanistan won recognition of its independence, loser of the war but victor of the final peace.

Throughout the discussions and decisions on the whole frontier from Constantinople to Khyber, from late 1919 into 1922, Soviet interest and activities became an increasingly dominant theme. Britain was so worried it decided to introduce the subject of Bolshevik activity in West Asia directly into the Anglo-Soviet negotiations which occurred during this period.

ANGLO-SOVIET DISCUSSIONS

Anglo-Soviet relations in the immediate postwar era have recently been the focus of substantial scholarly inquiry, thus the following merely offers a summary review of Asia's role in the negotiations between the two powers. In January 1920, it will be recalled, Lloyd George decided to open trade negotiations with the representatives of Soviet cooperatives. The Foreign Office was scarcely involved, in part to avoid formal diplomatic association, more because Lloyd George was not eager to put these negotiations in Foreign Office hands. The Foreign Office participated in the supervisory committee, but the Ministry of Food was given the actual task. The possibility of enlarging the talks was always present, however; in the first serious discussions with L.B.

Krassin, the Russian spokesman, the question of mutual assurances against gratuitous troublemaking was raised.[92]

Curzon was convinced that the Soviets were near economic disaster, and ending Russia's anti-British activities in various corners of the world was a better price to extract for British goods than Russian trade items. Afghanistan was particularly dangerous, for here the Bolsheviks aimed at "the arming and insurrection of the frontier tribes along the entire north-west frontier of India, and the subversion of British dominion there." That India wanted this issue included in the larger negotiation lent weight to Curzon's plea. De Robeck, watching the situation in the Crimea and the Caucasus, was also concerned.[93]

The Cabinet approved, and in late May the whole range of issues along the frontier was raised with Krassin. One obstacle was the continued White connection: Wrangel, for example, despite a decision to give him no more aid, was about to open a Crimean offensive (his retreat at the end of the year ended that hope). More important, there was strong anti-Bolshevik sentiment within the Cabinet and among the Allies that a trade agreement would give the Russian government a new lease on life, so even on that issue British negotiators kept to the narrow path of merely obtaining Russian food stocks for a starving Europe. But the range and complexity of issues were too great to be soluble in a few hours' talk between suspicious and hostile parties. Advances toward Batum, the occupation of Enzeli and Resht (although Russian assurance that they were withdrawing was promising), and aid to the Kemalists were charges countered with Britain's Batum occupation, Caspian swashbuckling, and Persian treaty and occupation. Discussion on these issues were no more fruitful than the larger trade negotiations to which they were appended.[94]

[92] Derby telegram to FO, 22 January, *FO* 371/4032; and private to Curzon, 9 June, *Curzon Papers,* F/6/3; minutes of meeting, 28 May, and Wise to P. Kerr, 5 June 1920, *FO* 371/4035. See especially the three volumes by Richard Ullman, particularly in this case III, pp. 319-25, and 411, for composition of the committee. For other works on the subject, see bibliography.

[93] Curzon memorandum, 27 May, high commissioner, Constantinople, telegram to FO, 7 June, *DBFP* XII/708, 718; Cabinet 33 (20), appendix I, Conference of Ministers, 28 May 1920, *CAB* 23/21; Roskill, *Hankey,* II, pp. 170-71.

[94] Anglo-Russian meeting, 7 June, *DBFP* VIII/25; FO telegram to

Events at the end of 1920 did nothing to alleviate suspicion. On the contrary, the Congress of the Peoples of the East held at Baku in September gave public notice that the Soviets intended to pursue at least propagandistic objectives in Asia.[95] While by November a draft trade agreement was ready for approval, nothing had been done to satisfy Britain's Asian points, and despite Curzon's protests—for Curzon was now in charge of the negotiations—Soviet replies evaded the issue of political assurances. In October Curzon had sent off a lengthy recitation of hostile actions and propaganda, demanding that the Russians live up to their June promise to stop such activity. The Russians believed, however, as Curzon knew from intercepts, that Britain intended to drag out the negotiations until Russia offered a one-sided undertaking in the east. G.V. Chicherin, the Soviet commissar for foreign affairs, countered with the suggestion that a separate conference on political matters follow the trade negotiations. Curzon advised the Cabinet that this plan would undermine Britain's advantage: the Russians wanted the trade agreement, but without paying the necessary price. Once the agreement was signed, the following negotiations would be drawn out and polemical.

> Meanwhile the merry game in the Middle East of intrigue, propaganda, bribery on a colossal scale, military assistance to our enemies, political treaties with persons like the Amir, and a stream of agents pouring into India from every side, will go on while we are discussing exactly what the legal interpretation of propaganda is and what are British interests in Anatolia, or Enzeli, or Turkestan, and whether this or that action of ours in Poland, Roumania or the Ukraine is or is not inimical to Soviet interest.

Curzon did not oppose trade relations, but the Russians should be made to show their good faith first. At the moment, however,

---

Geddes (Washington), 24 June 1920 *DBFP* XII/730; Brinkley, *Volunteer Army,* pp. 251-53; Ullman, *Anglo-Soviet Relations,* III, pp. 106-29.

[95] SIS report XC 5233, 25 October 1920, 13412/345, *FO* 371/5178; Eudin and North, *Soviet Russia and Asia,* pp. 79-84, 165-72 on Baku. Ullman, *Anglo-Soviet Relations,* II, p. 318, correctly notes that almost no attention was paid to this meeting in official British circles; the author has seen nothing in the IO or Indian documents (which Ullman has not used) to contradict his conclusion.

the one objective at which the whole of their policy is and has
been aimed is India, and I firmly believe that the renewed lease
of life which the agreement if concluded will give them, will be
consecrated to no purpose more unswervingly than to the subversion and destruction of the British connection with the
Indian Empire.[96]

The Cabinet agreed that the agreement should draw Soviet attention
to Asian problems once again by stipulating the particular countries
where such activities would be barred. Curzon's arguments had proven
full of fire but weak on evidence, particularly on the Bolshevik-Kemalist
connection. Even his own Foreign Office staff tended to agree with
Lloyd George that the essential ingredient in Russo-Turkish relations
was distrust. Missions had been exchanged, and Military Intelligence
felt that considerable numbers of arms had changed hands, but figures
and proof were impossible to obtain. There was no doubt about Enzeli,
however, and little about Afghanistan where intercepts had informed
Britain of draft clauses in the Soviet-Afghan treaty which would allow
passage of agents and literature and other propagandistic activites. The
amir had rejected these so far, although the future was less certain
(hence, incidentally, the subsequent insistence on full disclosure of that
treaty). The Soviets were engaged in a general diplomatic offensive, it
was clear, motivated by their designs on Armenia, Persia, Iraq, Afghanistan, and India.[97]

There was enough in recorded actions and intercepts to show that
point, so the Cabinet accepted the Asian preamble to the draft treaty.

[96] Curzon's views and participation are reviewed in Curzon memorandum,
14 November 1920 (quoted), 2648/207, *FO* 371/5433.

[97] Cabinet 62 (20), 18 November, *CAB* 23/23; Ullman, *Anglo-Soviet
Relations,* III, p. 420; Roskill, *Hankey,* II, pp. 172-73. On Soviet activities:
SIS report CX. 1205, 25 September, 14638/345, *FO* 371/5178, and FO
to DNI, Admiralty, 17 December, *FO* 371/5172; IO Memoranda B. 355,
19 November, 556/22, *L/P&S*/10/912, and B. 360, "Middle East: Turco-
Bolshevik Activities," 10 December 1920, copy in 154/154, *FO* 371/
6342.

The Soviet-Kemalist connection is discussed in Kapur, *Russia and Asia,*
Ch. IV; Hovannisian, "Armenia and the Caucasus"; Davison, "Turkish
Diplomacy"; the many articles by Gotthard Jäschke, particularly "Der Weg
zur russisch-türkischen Freundschaft im Lichte Moskaus" and "Kom-
munismus und Islam im türkischen Befreiungskriege," *Die Welt des Islams* 20 (1938): 110-34 (and see Chapter 5, note 46).

When Chicherin not unnaturally objected to it, a decision had to be made: adhere to the preamble as drafted, and risk broken negotiations and resulting increase in Soviet activity in Asia, or climb down and accept a diplomatic humiliation of sorts. Neither course was palatable; the decision was to continue to negotiate on the preamble as drafted. After further unproductive telegraphic exchanges, Chicherin in February 1921 proposed mutual pledges of independence and integrity for Persia, Afghanistan, "and the territory of the Turkish National Assembly." "Ludicrous in their absurdity," Curzon characteristically termed 'the proposals; recognition of Kemal, particularly, was a "wholly untenable proposition," so much so, the India Office was told, that the plan was to avoid that entire question in forthcoming negotiations.[98]

In March 1921 the trade agreement was actually signed. The text included mutual self-denying pledges against propagandistic activity. Accompanying the text, however, was a separate letter listing Soviet activities inconsistent with the agreement, the cessation of which was essential "if the good faith of the agreement is to be observed." This letter stressed the activities of Soviet representatives in Kabul and made rather embarrassing use of intercepted information (with the result that this source now substantially diminished in value). Tashkent propaganda activities, Soviet-supported Indian revolutionaries, emissaries intended for India were all specifically listed in preference to the confused Caucasian developments (little point in mentioning them anyway, since Russia had regained that area), Enzeli (where the Soviets seemed to be sitting without intent to advance), or aid to Kemal (no tangible evidence).[99]

The force of these complaints was undermined by the very signature of the agreement, as India was well aware. Chelmsford quickly pointed out that if the Russians were to have both the agreement and Afghanistan activities, Britain's position would be seriously weakened—especially because the amir had delayed negotiations partly to see how the

[98] Curzon private to Lloyd George, 21 December, *Lloyd George Papers,* F/13/1/62; Cabinet 75 (20), 22 December 1920, *CAB* 23/23; Chicherin to Curzon, 9 January, and telegram, 4 February, Jane Degras, ed., *Soviet Documents on Foreign Policy,* I (London, 1951), pp. 226-33; Curzon memorandum, 14 February (quoted), *DBFP* XII/835; FO to IO, 24 February 1921 (quoted), *FO* 371/6853.

[99] Text of agreement, and of Horne to Krassin, 16 March 1921, in Ullman, *Anglo-Soviet Relations,* III, pp. 474-82.

Anglo-Soviet negotiations turned out. India's main fears were for the future of India's relations with Afghanistan, not Bolshevik infiltration in India itself—and India was even then closing down the Special Information Bureau, although assuring London that this meant no relaxation of watchfulness. Denys Bray, the India Office specialist in conspiracies, remained convinced that India simply did not realize the extent of Bolshevik activities, and Montagu's representations of the danger in the Cabinet show that he shared Bray's view.[100]

After a delay of several months, it was time to jog the Soviets again on the essential requisites, clearly stated in the agreement preamble—they should refrain from encouraging Asian anti-British activities, particularly in India and Afghanistan. After hurried last minute redrafting among Foreign Office, India Office, and Downing Street officials, a note was forwarded to Moscow on 7 September 1921 which again catalogued all the breaches of the agreement by the Third International, Soviet-supported Indian revolutionaries in Europe, the Tashkent school for propaganda, the mission to Persia (particularly Rothstein), general encouragement of Kemal. Above all the note decried the attempts to reach an agreement with Afghanistan, the intent of which could only be subversion of India. No formal abrogation of the treaty was announced, but the letter was clear warning that Soviet eastern policy would have to become as quiet as, on reflection, Soviet leaders should realize British policy had become.[101]

"Either unfounded or based on false information and forgeries," responded Moscow. In some cases, the Russians claimed to have ceased a particular activity (for example, connections with Indian revolutionaries), in others to have a completely different motive than assigned by Britain (the consulates in Afghanistan were only for trade and friendly relations). Curzon, convinced of the accuracy of his information, replied to that effect. Not until the following spring did the question become immediate, however, in connection with possible recognition of the Soviet Union. At the Cannes conference in January Curzon had insisted that such recognition could only be granted if Russia

[100] IO to FO, 4 April (enclosing viceroy telegrams to SSI, 24 and 28 March) and 9 April, *FO* 371/6854; Cabinet 13 (21), 14 March, *CAB* 23/24; D. Bray memorandum, 18 May, and Montagu memorandum, 14 June 1921, *L/P&S*/10/886.

[101] Gregory minute, 2 September, 10221/5, and drafts of letter, with minutes and final version to Chicherin, 7 September 1921, *FO* 371/6855.

stopped its Central Asian propaganda. A substantial interdepartmental committee meeting in February to consider political preconditions to recognition agreed that a general self-denying ordinance was essential, but it would have to be limited to generalities: detailed evidence on anything aside from propaganda was lacking. The draft, prepared for the Genoa conference, stipulated that Russia would not aid any movement "which has for its objective the disturbance of the *status quo* in Asia" or interfere in the internal affairs of the non-Russian Asiatic states (Turkey, Iraq, Persia, Afghanistan, Tibet, and China) and in particular would preserve an attitude of strict neutrality in the Greco-Turk struggle.[102]

Curzon was not at Genoa, and he was worried that Lloyd George would be rushed into recognition without insisting on the Asiatic clause. His alarm was only partly justified; Lenin did not appear as expected, but Lloyd George did meet privately with the Russians, and Curzon's representative found it hard to keep in touch with these secret discussions. Nevertheless, the conference group drafting an agreement for presentation to Russia did include the noninterference clause, together with another making reference to possible assistance in settling Anatolian affairs. The Russian response was hostile. Chicherin regarded the status-quo clause as nothing more than an attempt by Britain to defend its own special position and privileges, such as the Persian treaty. Above all, he would not accept the introduction of the Anatolian situation. Britain could not insist, again because information was missing. As one Foreign Office official put it, "We have received continual reports of Russian war material and money being supplied to the Kemalists, but we have no proof that this help has in fact been on a large scale. It seems rather that the Bolsheviks carry out only the minimum of their promises necessary to keep the Kemalists amenable." The agreement was again delayed, largely through other problems such as past debts,

---

[102] Litvinov to Curzon, 27 September (quoted), Degras, *Soviet Documents,* pp. 257-63; Curzon to R.M. Hodgson, Moscow, 2 November 1921, *FO* 371/6856; R. MacDonell note, 7 February, with Forbes Adam, Gregory, and Curzon notes, 1170/646, *FO* 371/8185; report of subcommittee to draft clauses, 28 January, 4327/646, *FO* 371/8190; SSI telegram to viceroy, 12 February (on interdepartmental conference), *L/P&S*/10/912; FO draft, ca. 10 March (quoted), with Maxse minute, 15 March, 2322/646 and 3236/646, *FO* 371/8186-87; Hankey private to Curzon, 3 April 1922, *Curzon Papers,* F/5.

expropriated property, and finally the separate Russo-German agreement at Rapallo.[103]

In the end, however, agreement was the only alternative. Britain could no longer interfere sufficiently to keep the Russians out of any Asian preserve. Even the Central Asian revolt led by Enver Pasha, an opportunity for interference which might have been grasped eagerly in 1918-1919, could not be touched. For a change, India, the India Office, and the Foreign Office all agreed that the area was Russia's, and whatever the temporary dislocation, Russia would return to power there. By late summer 1922 Enver was dead, the movement crushed, and the opportunity had passed. On the other hand, the Bolshevik danger was in no way regarded as diminished. In Mid-August 1922, for example, an Interdepartmental Committee on Eastern Unrest, which included representatives from the Colonial, Foreign, Home, India, and War Offices, with Indian Police, Special Intelligence, and Military Intelligence advisors as well, examined all the evidence again on Turkish, Egyptian, Indian, and pan-Islamic activities. Nationalism was obviously the major cause of the "unrest," aggravated by general postwar conditions—but Bolshevik support and agitation were also clearly linked with the nationalism. Any recent weakening of Soviet encouragement was due to shortage of funds, Russian famine, and other such causes. However, the conclusion of this lengthy report was that while Bolshevism contributed to nationalist agitation, in general most eastern nationalists were anti-Bolshevik. Mutual objectives created contacts and cooperation, but, on the whole, there was "no evidence of any single central organisation directing these intrigues."[104]

The Anglo-Russian controversy continued on a host of issues through 1923, although no further agreement was possible. Indeed, the Turkish peace negotiations at Lausanne complicated the controversy by adding the issue of the Straits passage. In the early summer of 1923, however, Soviet propaganda activities were toned down on orders from Moscow.

[103] Gregory (Genoa) private to M. Lampson, FO, 14 April, *FO* 371/8187, and Curzon private telegram to Gregory, 26 April, Gregory telegram to FO, 29 April, and Schanzer to Chicherin, 3 May, *FO* 371/8189; Litvinov to Curzon, 11 May, Degras, *Soviet Documents,* I, pp. 384-92; R.A. Leeper minute, 18 May (quoted), 6024/646, *FO* 371/8193; FO telegram to Hodgson, 27 July 1922, *FO* 371/8197.

[104] "Report of the Inter-departmental Committee on Eastern Unrest," 17 August 1922 (p. 16 quoted), *FO* 371/7790.

Chicherin gave assurances that this was the case, and he asked only a similar British assurance on aid to the amir of Bukhara and other charges quickly dismissed by the India Office. When Raskalnikov was recalled from Kabul in mid-June and the exiled amir of Bukhara told clearly there would be no British aid, one chapter of Anglo-Russian relations came quietly to an end.[105]

Asia had played a major role in Anglo-Russian negotiations, and not simply through direct British intervention in Central Asia, the Caspian, or the Caucasus. Once the Malleson mission was back in Persia and the Soviet forces held Enzeli, British policy along the Soviet Asian frontier was defensive, attempting to protect such influence as existed in Persia. (Moscow, not unnaturally, had regarded the Anglo-Persian treaty as an offensive maneuver.) Afghanistan was more complicated. Here Britain was in reality trying to preserve Afghani independence from Soviet subversion, but for too long a time too many policymakers thought Britain was trying to keep an influence alive in Afghanistan which it no longer possessed, a point much more quickly realized in Delhi than in London.

By 1923 Britain had retreated far from the furthest reach of the immediate postwar wave. A certain equilibrium had resulted from the alternation of Russian retreat-British advance, Soviet advance-British retreat. Afghanistan was no hostile invader, no British puppet, no Soviet base. Persia was no longer British puppet, nor yet a hostile Soviet base. The Caucasus and Caspian had gone, but then it was the accident of war which had opened them up in the first place. There was no end to Bolshevik sympathy for and cooperation with nationalist movements, of course, but the struggle over Persia, Afghanistan, and the Caucasus was either over or taking on a new character. India had a substantial role in the first two cases—and War Office negativism in the last. One more issue remained to be settled, however, and it now became the focus of attention. In the events now taking place in Anatolia, all these several forces came together: military weakness, Bolshevik sympathy and assistance, and Indian representations.

[105] Great Britain, Parliamentary Papers, "Correspondence between His Majesty's Government and the Soviet Government respecting the Relations between the Two Governments," Russia No. 2 (1923), Cmd. 1869; see also *FO* 371/9368-69.

VII

War's End:
Turkey, 1921-1922

The London conference of early 1921, which offered some hope of a pacific solution in Turkey, had broken down in acrimony as the Greeks, with Lloyd George's backing, prepared to resume fighting. Despite enthusiasm in Athens, however, the Greek diplomatic position was weak. Even Lloyd George found King Constantine far less desirable an ally than his old friend Venizelos, and he faced the opposition of three important departments of state whose influence could not be bypassed forever. Curzon's Foreign Office, thoroughly weakened in policymaking power by Lloyd George's private "garden suburb" staff while Curzon himself was cowed by a leader who always exploited personal weakness, still had advisory responsibilities and was anxious to achieve a general settlement in the Middle East. The War Office abhorred military commitments which were impossible to fulfil, and since Churchill now moved to the Colonial Office, which had charge of the Arab problem, he could add a new department's voice to persistent War Office opposition. Finally, the India Office throughout reported serious political agitation in India which was closely associated with the whole problem of a Turkish peace.

The Allies, too, had indicated total unwillingness to support Lloyd George's Anatolian ventures; in the very midst of the London negotiations, they had concluded agreements with Kemal's representatives. In Italy's document, signed in London on 12 March, the Kemalists promised preference for economic concessions in the area of Italian interest in return for full diplomatic support of Turkish desiderata, meaning full sovereignty over Smyrna and Thrace. The French treaty, concluded the day before, called for a ceasefire and French withdrawal from territory north of the Sèvres frontier. French *amour propre* was served by promises only of economic concessions in the evacuated area and Turkish protection for minorities and charitable activities. Part of the French price, however, was a special regime in the Alexandretta area of its Syrian responsibilities, south of the Sèvres line. Berthelot explained away the agreement as essential for Briand's survival and in no way diminishing France's support for her British ally, but it was clear that only Britain backed the Greeks—and that with grave reservations in some quarters.[1]

Even the staunchest Philhellenes could only give moral support. Greek troops in the Izmit peninsula were of necessity released to the Greek commander, but internal and diplomatic pressures insured that orders went out to stop any other British participation, including aid, supplies, and even medical assistance in Constantinople military hospitals. The prohibition was less damaging than it might have been, because as they advanced the Greeks could requisition abandoned Allied supplies. No opposition could have been offered even had it been desired; Harington's forces were weak, and the bulk of his only possible reinforcement, the Malta garrison, had returned to Britain to help deal with the threatening labor situation at home. The Greeks pushed out in early April in several directions (including the occupation of Afyonkarahisar and requisitioning of French-owned railway stock there), so Harington was ordered to withdraw from Izmit if necessary to keep out of the fighting. Despite the loss of the Greek division, this was not immediately necessary, and Harington's main worry was the French failure to approve joint Allied command on both sides of the Bosporus. Without it, there was no certainty of Allied support in a crisis.[2]

Field-Marshal Wilson's concern was how to avoid such a crisis. Harington, he pointed out to the Cabinet, could not survive pressure upon his defenses if it were timed to coincide with a rising in the city.

[1] Italian agreement: Buchanan (Rome) to Curzon, 19 April, *FO* 371/6573; Buchanan telegrams to FO, 2 and 19 April, and FO telegrams to Buchanan, 15 and 16 April, *DBFP* XVII/81, 108, 114, 120. French agreement: Hardinge to FO, 2 April, *FO* 371/6468, and FO to Hardinge, 19 April, *DBFP* XVII/121. Kemal signed with Moscow on 16 March 1921; Shapiro, *Soviet Treaty Series,* pp. 100-2.

[2] WO telegrams to CinC Constantinople, 24 March, *FO* 371/6507, and 4 April, CinC Constantinople telegram to WO, 6 April, *FO* 371/6508; Cabinet 14 (21), 22 March, 15 (21), 24 March, and 17 (21), 4 April, *CAB* 23/24-25; high commissioner, Constantinople, telegram to FO, 5 April, and FO telegram to high commissioner, Constantinople, 7 April 1921, *DBFP* XVII/88, 93.

The best policy, since there were no reinforcements and little likelihood of a settlement with Kemal, was withdrawal. The decision to pull out became even more urgent when the Greeks suffered a temporary setback in early April and had to return to their starting line to build reinforcements for a further attack; this was regarded as most unlikely in Constantinople. The setback was damaging to chances of Kemalist conciliation; but as Curzon, in the midst of trying (under strong French pressure) to stop private arms sales to the Greeks, pointed out to Lloyd George, it might make the Greeks more reasonable. The Greeks were in fact more inclined to complain that British "neutrality" was blatantly unfair, since the French and Italians were giving aid to Kemal, an assertion which Athens offered to prove.[3]

Curzon, bedridden with persistent back trouble, ignored by Lloyd George, and pressured from all sides, was trapped in a vice: there was no easy middle course between 10 Downing Street and the India Office around the corner. Neutrality in the Foreign Office meant, as Curzon wrote Montagu, that he was "freely belaboured by both parties." Montagu was indeed making good use of the Greek reverses to outline his proposals on financial concessions, Muslim rights in Thrace, and the caliphate, but India's influence was less now that most Indian troops in Turkey had been replaced by British units. Still, Montagu was encouraged enough to report to Reading that the evacuation of Constantinople and certain other concessions were probably assured for the near future.[4]

Meanwhile Allied administrators in Constantinople found it hard to persuade the Turks, locally or in Ankara, of their neutrality, largely because the Greeks still maintained a naval base and mission in Con-

---

[3] CIGS note for secretary of war, 6 April, *FO* 371/6508; high commissioner, Constantinople, to Curzon, 5 April, *FO* 371/6509, FO to Rizo-Rangabé (Greek chargé), 14 April, *FO* 371/6080; high commissioner, Constantinople, telegrams to FO, 7 and 22 April, Hardinge telegram to FO, 20 April, Granville telegram to FO, 22 April, and FO telegram to Hardinge, 28 April, *DBFP* XVII/94, 122, 128-29, 138; Curzon private to Lloyd George, 20 April, *FO* 800/154; Hardinge telegram to FO, 22 April 1921, *FO* 371/6483; Armstrong, *Turkey in Travail,* pp. 145-50; Toynbee, *Western Question,* pp. 233-34.

[4] Montagu private to Curzon, 23 April, with Forbes Adam minute, Curzon private to Montagu, 26 April (quoted), 4882/1, *FO* 371/6469; Montagu private telegram to Reading, 1 May 1921, copy in 5763/1, *FO* 371/6470. Troop replacement is discussed in Shuttleworth, "Turkey," 58.

stantinople. It was easy to miss the fine distinction between a permitted Allied mission and a forbidden base of operations. The high commissioners therefore collectively urged that the Greeks be told to leave, although Athens would regard such a request as decidedly unfriendly.[5]

Some policy more than neutrality was essential if Britain was to be ready in case the Greeks collapsed. As Crowe put it in a memorandum Curzon subsequently used to help frame his Cabinet arguments, Athens must be persuaded that if Thrace was going to be held, Smyrna would have to be abandoned. On the other hand, Britain should help Greece to keep Thrace, for only then would Kemal be reasonable on the Straits or Constantinople. Crowe tended to dismiss or ignore the French, the Italians, and the Soviet-Kemalist connection, but the plan was still feasible. On 31 May the Cabinet heard not only Curzon but also General Harington, who reported on the military situation, including Greek deterioration and Kemalist improvement. He argued that the Greeks might be driven into the sea leaving the tiny Allied force at Constantinople dangerously exposed. Curzon was more concerned that leaving Constantinople would sacrifice all the wartime gains to Kemal (who would probably have the French and Italians at his side). Churchill spoke in a similar vein, for withdrawal would endanger his charges in Palestine and Mesopotamia. Montagu, however, added the truism that Britain would have to come out in the end—better now by peaceful revisionism than later in response to force. Lloyd George could only ask that all concerned write up their positions while a committee reviewed the military dimensions of the problem: "a truly amazing Cabinet," said Henry Wilson.[6]

As some concerned officials knew well, tinkering with Sèvres would not be enough. Turkish nationalist hostility could only be appeased—if it could not be crushed—by the return of Smyrna and autonomy for Thrace at a minimum. Osborne of the Eastern Department, for example, saw only India as a major obstacle in the way of the obvious solution: Smyrna for the Turks, Constantinople for the Greeks ("I

[5] High commissioner, Constantinople, telegrams to FO, 22 April, 4, 9, and 15 May, and FO telegram to high commissioner, Constantinople, 12 May, *DBFP* XVII/128, 149, 161, 164, 166; CinC Constantinople telegram to WO, 27 April 1921, *FO* 371/6511.

[6] Crowe memorandum, 30 May, *DBFP* XVII/201; CinC Constantinople telegram to WO, 26 May, *FO* 371/6514; Cabinet 44 (21) and 45 (21), both 31 May 1921, *CAB* 23/25; Callwell, *Wilson*, II, p. 293, quoted.

hope not," Curzon noted marginally; he would make it European, but not Greek). Under the circumstances such a trade was not possible, but perhaps the Greeks could be bought off with British-held Cyprus? "Please do not make this fantastic suggestion," snapped Curzon, annoyed to find his staff so helpless just when he had to go into the arena again in the Cabinet Committee on the Future of Constantinople.[7]

It was an interesting series of meetings, for Lloyd George, in the chair, faced the combined yet mutually conflicting antagonism of Curzon, Montagu, Churchill, Wilson, Harington, and Worthington-Evans (Churchill's successor at the War Office). The minutes of the first meetings, 1-2 June, demonstrate the confusion, indeed desperation, to which the government had been reduced. Among other last-ditch measures discussed and discarded, for example, was one of dispatching the Aga Khan on a mission of conciliation to Kemal. Field-Marshal Wilson pointed out that Kemal could not be dealt with by holding Constantinople and the Straits any more than Sinn Fein could be dealt with by sitting in occupation of Dublin. Force was simply out of the question, since there was none to use. The real question was whether to stay or go from what was now held, and on this there were differing opinions. If Britain left, the French would only stay on as Kemal's friends, said one (probably Harington); but then the power which stayed would take on all the odium of sole occupying power—to Britain's advantage—said another. Make friends with Kemal; use the loyal Greeks . . . but the extreme solutions had few adherents. Churchill, always to be relied upon for a proposal, suggested offering up the London conference terms with Greek evacuation of Smyrna in addition. The only decision, temporarily, was to talk to Venizelos (who, of course, no longer spoke for Greece). The final verdict was not yet in, and interested parties still were free to make partisan cases.[8]

Venizelos was a shrewd statesman, and he was now trying to obtain a settlement based on the London terms suitably modified. Encouraged

[7] Rattigan, chargé Constantinople, telegram to FO, 1 June, *DBFP* XVII/204, and with Osborne and Curzon (quoted) minutes, *FO* 371/6515; Rattigan private to Crowe, 1 June, *FO* 371/6516.

[8] Cabinet committee on future of Constantinople, 1st-2nd conclusion, 1-2 June 1921, *Lloyd George Papers,* F/206/4; Callwell, *Wilson,* II, p. 294; Walder, *Chanak,* pp. 138-49. Churchill private to Lloyd George and Hankey private to Lloyd George, 2 June 1921, *Lloyd George Papers,* F/9/3/48 and F/25/1/36.

by Venizelos's moderation, Lloyd George pushed his Constantinople committee to the point of considering what would happen if and when the Turks refused the terms: perhaps a Black Sea coastal blockade and arms and cash for the Greeks? The Greeks, meanwhile, were making their own preparations. On 11 June King Constantine and his principal ministers left Athens for Asia Minor; the King was tired and sick, and Gounaris made the real decisions. But the diplomatic forms were still gone through, and Hardinge in Paris sounded Briand on the possibility of approaching Greece to outline possible support if Greece accepted the offered terms and Turkey refused. The French proved willing to talk, and Curzon moved off to Paris with a rare written expression of Lloyd George's views in hand. Curzon should remember, Lloyd George advised, that the War Office had been wrong before in its estimates of Greek weakness and Turkish strength. "The Turk has done no good fighting for over a generation except when led by British or German officers. Kemal's force is not equipped with either." Greece could not be presented with a set of terms which it would have to reject. Even if they did suffer a reverse, it would not end their resistance. Kemal, on the other hand, would only give in if the Greeks won and terms were dictated to him. The best solution would be for the Greeks to oust the Turk from Constantinople while encouraging his advance into the Caucasus. "Drive the Turk to the East. He ought never to have been allowed to come West."[9]

With these generalities in mind, Curzon outlined his own proposals as approved by the Cabinet to Briand and Berthelot on 18-19 June. They included further modification of financial controls, possibly a hint that Turkey would be allowed to expand in the direction of Azerbaijan (it is not clear whether he explained that this was the prime minister's suggestion), and for Smyrna an autonomous province under Turkish sovereignty, but with a Christian governor and a European-officered

[9] Cabinet committee, 3rd conclusions, 9 June, *Lloyd George Papers,* F/206/5; Hirst and Osborne memoranda, 9 June, and Curzon to Hardinge, 14 June, *DBFP* XVII/219-20, 229 (and note p. 245, Lloyd George to Grigg, 13 June); Granville telegram to FO, 11 June, *FO* 371/6517; Churchill private to Curzon, 15 June, and Lloyd George private to Curzon, 16 June 1921 (quoted), *Curzon Papers,* F/4/3; former quoted in Lord Beaverbrook, *The Decline and Fall of Lloyd George* (N.Y., 1963); Callwell, *Wilson,* II, p. 295. On Constantine and Gounaris, Smith, *Ionian Vision,* Ch. VIII and p. 224.

gendarmerie. If Greece now approved these terms, the Turks would be asked; if the Greeks rejected them, then they would have to take their own chances.[10]

The afternoon of the 18th, Briand set out the French view: the British plan was an adequate basis for discussion, but probably Thrace too would have to be autonomous (i.e., not Greek), a suggestion which Curzon found unacceptable, knowing that Athens would not accept mediation if it cost both Smyrna and Thrace. Briand would also renounce prospective rights under the tripartite agreement, but the Italian ambassador, present at the meeting, threw up his hands in horror. In the end, there was no real alternative to the British plan, which would be given to Athens. Curzon even won long-delayed French approval for Harington's general Allied military command. (In exchange France won presidency of the gendarmerie subcommission and secretary-generalship of the financial commission; a later, balancing, post was to be created for Italy.)

Final Cabinet approval was yet required, but when the Cabinet convened on 21 June another idea had surfaced. Harington had reported that a certain ex-Major Henry, traveling to Ankara in search of a mining concession, had returned with the information that Kemal wished to talk directly to Harington. The general supported the idea, provided Kemal came in person to the coast. The Cabinet was reluctant to close any possible means of communication, but the Allied plan called for an approach to the Greeks first. Harington was told to say he would meet Kemal in person, but not to make any specific proposals. More important, the Cabinet approved the draft terms agreed upon in Paris. Some progress had been made, although not all were satisfied (Montagu, for one, would have gone much further in following up the overture from Kemal).[11]

The decision was now up to Greece. Granville in Athens predicted that the Greeks would accept mediation despite confidence in their

[10] Allied meeting, 18-19 June 1921, *DBFP* XV/88.

[11] Rattigan telegram to FO, 20 June, FO telegrams to Buchanan, 22 and 28 June, CinC Constantinople telegram to WO, 20 June, *DBFP* XVII/247, 253, 269, and note 1, pp. 261-62; Cabinet 51 (21) and 52 (21), 21-22 June, *CAB* 23/26; Montagu private to Curzon, 23 June, and H. Wilson private to Curzon, 4 July, *Curzon Papers,* F/4/3; Harington private to de Robeck, 3 July 1921, *De Robeck Papers,* 6/27; Ryan, *Last of the Dragomans,* pp. 156-57.

military machine. Churchill was more prescient in his prediction that the Greeks would refuse: should Britain then sever her connections with the Greeks to protect her own interests? "I am sure the path of courage is the path of safety." But the Hellenic mission, said Rizo-Rangabé, the Greek chargé in London, was "to stand as a bulwark affording security to Europe against dangers from Asia"; in other words, it was "historical necessity" which prompted the Greek refusal — although knowledge of Lloyd George's views certainly helped. But Greece had not yet been seriously defeated, and there was no apparent reason to accept a diplomatic defeat now when military success later might result in a quite different peace.[12]

On 24 June Greece refused. On the 27th the Cabinet, not having had time to absorb the implications and fully caught up with the coal strike which lasted until 1 July, adjourned without a decision. Unfortunately, a decision was vital; the Greeks were even then evacuating their (eastern) portion of the Izmit peninsula, leaving the British position directly open to whatever pressure Kemal might apply. The town of Izmit itself was reported in flames on the 28th, and the Turks were soon in occupation. In considerable alarm, the Cabinet decided on the 29th to remind Harington that any Kemalist encroachment on the British ("neutral") zone of occupation in the Izmit peninsula would be an act of war. Montagu insisted that Curzon should also take diplomatic action at Ankara to avoid a confrontation and make it clear to Kemal's local commander that Britain was only defending her Bosporus position, and not aiding the Greeks — "Otherwise disaster!" as he put it in a note of the same day. Curzon did as he was asked, but Constantinople objected to passing such a warning on while the Turks showed no immediate desire to cross into the British zone.[13]

The question therefore was how to convince Kemal of British neutrality in the new stage of fighting which was so obviously coming. Greek rights as ally in Constantinople were one issue; another was

[12] Granville telegrams to FO, 22 and 25 June, *DBFP* XVII/252, 260; Rizo-Rangabé to Curzon, 23 June (quoted), *FO* 371/6519; Churchill private to Curzon (and to Lloyd George), 25 June (quoted), *Curzon Papers,* F/4/3; Buchanan telegram to FO, 26 June 1921, *FO* 371/6471.

[13] Cabinet 54 (21), 27 June, 55 (21), 29 June, *CAB* 23/26; CinC telegrams to WO, 27 and 28 June, *FO* 371/6520; FO telegram to Rattigan, 30 June and 1 July and Montagu private note to Curzon, 29 June 1921 (quoted), *DBFP* XVII/271, 275.

blockade of Greek access to the Straits, but that would have little effect on the campaign except to ensure that Greek ships could not interfere with Russian aid for Kemal. Military and diplomatic officials in Constantinople agreed that little could be done. This was unfortunate, for the hopeful prospect of direct negotiations with Kemal had been dashed by his apparent insistence that Turkey's full claims to independence be recognized by Britain before any discussions took place, and some way to show good will was very desirable. Kemal, however, was under the impression that the initiative had come from Harington, not himself. It would appear that Major Henry had passed on an inaccurate impression; there was rejoicing in Athens, since the failure to initiate Anglo-Turkish discussions seemed to increase the chance of direct British support.[14]

The support was unlikely, but the prospect of fighting was real enough. British military estimates of Greek fighting capacity varied; officers sent to investigate on the spot found training, equipment, and morale high. The Greeks outnumbered the Turks, but with only a quarter of their 200,000 men in the front lines, the Turks probably outnumbered them there. The Turks were tough fighters, and none of the British observers predicted sweeping Greek victory. Harington went further, for he had no faith at all in the Greek command; Greek plans called for close cooperation among independent subordinate commands in the coming offensive, yet this was a proven Greek weakness. To those who pleaded that British aid would make the difference, the final answer was that the Greeks needed men at the front, not material, and manpower was the one thing which Britain could not provide. Harington was convinced that the Greeks faced defeat, and his concern was to avoid British involvement. To this end he suggested forcing the Greeks out of Constantinople and trying to reach Kemal personally.[15]

---

[14] Rattigan telegrams to FO, 4, 5, and 8 July, Curzon telegram to Rattigan, 8 July, *DBFP* XVII/281, 285, 292-94 (and see note 5, p. 244); CinC Constantinople telegram to WO, 8 July, Montagu note for Cabinet, 15 July (C.P. 3142), *FO* 371/6472; Montagu private to Curzon, 8 July, *Curzon Papers,* F/4/3; Granville telegrams to FO, 11 July (nos. 394-95), Crowe private to Granville, 19 August 1921, *FO* 371/6522.

[15] Worthington-Evans memorandum, 18 July (C.P. 3124), enclosing CinC Constantinople telegram to WO, 18 June 1921, *FO* 371/6521; CinC Constantinople telegrams to CIGS, 13 and 15 July, WO to FO, 15 July 1921, *FO* 371/6523.

London, however, had now a fairly good idea of the terms Kemal would demand. Not only was there his answer to Harington, but also Arnold Toynbee, now a correspondent for the Manchester *Guardian,* had passed a Kemalist statement to the Foreign Office. It asked for the Maritsa River (perhaps the Enos-Midia line) as European frontier; full Turkish sovereignty for Anatolia with perhaps slight territorial concessions to Russian Armenia and to British-held Mesopotamia in Kurdistan (for a share of the oil); the Dardanelles to be garrisoned by the Allies, but not the Bosporus; no financial privileges, although perhaps modified judicial privileges for a decade or so; the Ottoman Public Debt to be paid and to continue on as an institution; no special regimes, no autonomies, and no foreign interference. The Turks would bargain only on the whole.[16] This interesting formulation of July 1921 was far from Sèvres, yet not so far as the Treaty of Lausanne in 1923. The Allies were in no mood for acceptance, however, if only because they could not enforce the terms upon the Greeks. The war, with a new Greek offensive beginning, would have to take its course.

THE GREEK CATASTROPHE

By 19 July the Greeks held Afyonkarahisar and (for the second time) Eskishehir. The population of Athens exploded in mass celebration, which included cheering demonstrations outside the British Legation, and Greek newspapers began to speak of additions to, not modifications of, the Sèvres terms: the road now led to Ankara, not Constantinople. Missed in the enthusiasm was the fact that Kemal's counterattack of 21 July enabled him to disengage and reorganize after what Harington called a "serious but not decisive defeat." It was just as well that Kemal had not been crushed, for there was always the fear of direct Soviet intervention on his behalf, although Harington considered the prospect remote. Lloyd George was more worried that the Allies would interfere by closing the Straits, but that was equally remote so long as he refused to cooperate.[17]

[16] Forbes Adam note, 19 July 1921, enclosing Toynbee memorandum 8417/1, *FO* 371/6473. Toynbee obtained the information from "Rauf Achmet Bey," an associate of Bekir Sami Bey, former Kemalist foreign minister, who had been traveling in Europe to generate pro-Kemalist support.

[17] Granville telegram to FO, 21 July, Rattigan telegram to FO, 24 July,

Through the first weeks of August the Greek advance continued behind the retreating Turks. Lloyd George undoubtedly took pleasure in describing the situation to the House of Commons; for all their preparations over the last months, the Turks could not stand up to the Greeks. Britain, he explained, was standing off as a neutral, prepared when the time came to offer mediation once again. He himself only hoped that the Greeks would not repeat the error of Bulgaria in 1913 (the First Balkan War) and demand too much to make peace possible. Moderation in victory was the watchword, and the Greek government was thinking along the "moderate" lines of an autonomous Constantinople, with the Straits under a joint Anglo-Greek guarantee. All too briefly, Lloyd George shared the Greek moment of victory. "He is delighted with himself at the defeat of the Turks," wrote Montagu privately to Reading. "What foresight he showed! How great is Venizelos! How contemptible are the Military advisors on the General Staff! What brutes the Turks are!"[18]

The euphoria was short-lived. Before August was out, the Greeks were mired in a desperate battle of attrition on the Sakarya River front where the Turks had dug in under Kemal's personal command. After ten days of serious fighting and heavy losses on both sides, the Greeks needed time for rest and reorganization. Their advance had come to an end far short of Ankara and the planned destruction of Kemal's army. Meanwhile, Harington claimed to have foiled a plot by Turkish government officials and officers in Constantinople to precipitate a coup d'etat there or at least to seize stockpiled arms (and eliminate himself). He had taken a very strong line, despite the misgivings of

FO 371/6524; Granville to Curzon, 26 July, CinC Constantinople telegrams to WO, 3 (quoted), 4, and 5 August, FO 371/6525; Allied meeting, Paris, 9-10 August, DBFP XV/93-94; Toynbee, Western Question, pp. 212-18, 235-37; Smith, Ionian Vision, Ch. X; Walder, Chanak, pp. 150-56. L. Worthington-Evans, memorandum, "The Situation in Anatolia, 1st October, 1921," C.P. 5434, 21 October 1921, 11764/143, FO 371/6533, is a useful review of the Greco-Turkish operations of mid-1921 from the WO viewpoint.

[18] Parl. Deb., H.C., 16 August 1921; Granville to FO, 22 August, DBFP XVII/359; Montagu private to Reading, 1 September 1921 (quoted), Montagu Papers, D. 523/13; Maj.-Gen. Sir F. Maurice, "The Crisis as Seen in Constantinople," Contemporary Review 122 (1922): 556-62, deals with the reaction in the Turkish capital.

Allies and British cilivians alike. A number of arrests by the Turkish authorities and a large-scale military display were ordered to preclude repetition of such schemes. As a result, the Allies concluded that the whole affair had been stage-managed to permit Britain to bring up its fleet and march 4000 sailors and marines through the streets.[19]

There was still no feeling in London that the Greeks would be swept from Turkey. Churchill spoke for the general view when he predicted in a Cabinet memorandum of 26 September that the future now would be stalemate as the Greeks retreated to their positions along the north-south railway, destroying the branch line to Ankara behind them. Kemal would not have the resources to press them further, and he would be looking for a way out—for example he might make difficulties in Iraq, where it had already been decided that British troops would have to withdraw. Mosul could only be kept within Iraq, as was now the plan, if there was peace with Turkey: "those who have supported on the one hand the retention of Mosul, and on the other a forward policy on the part of the Greeks, ought really to explain how these policies can be reconciled." It was, he concluded, time for Britain to offer to mediate again, since both sides would be anxious to avoid another bloody campaign. If Greece was unreasonable, blockade the Pireaus; if the Turks, give cash and supplies to the Greeks (a suggestion which overlooked Harington's appreciation that they needed men)—but try to end the fighting. "We seem to have done absolutely nothing during the last three months but watch the progress of this disastrous conflict . . ."[20]

If Britain was to intervene, it must be decided how. Curzon still hoped that negotiation might be possible on the basis of the Paris modifications (i.e., special autonomy for Smyrna). But there was little indication that Kemal would talk, and when Greek delegates turned up in Paris to talk to the French, they proved to be intractable on essentials:

[19] High commissioner, Constantinople, telegram to FO, 5 September, *FO* 371/6528, and letter to Curzon, 7 September, and CinC Constantinople telegrams to WO, 5 and 19 September, *FO* 371/6529; high commissioner, Constantinople, telegrams to FO, 11 and 13 September, and letter, 20 September, *DBFP* XVII/380-81, 387; letter to Curzon 13 September, *FO* 371/6474, and private to Curzon, 4 October, *FO* 800/157. See also Lt. R.S. Dunn (USN) memorandum for Admiral Bristol, 30 September 1921, *Bristol Papers,* box 29, showing doubts in American mission.

[20] Churchill memorandum, 26 September 1921 (C.P. 3328), 11175/143, *FO* 371/6531.

like Venizelos, they would not yield on the essence of Sèvres, certainly not after the high price so recently paid in lives. And yet the War Office estimated that 57,000 Greeks in the lines east of Eskishehir were opposed by 64,000 Turks, while Greek intelligence, supply, and command had all shown glaring weaknesses. Using only Boer War-type guerrilla tactics, the Turks could probably drive their enemies off the railway, and time was on their side. Greece did not have the capacity to achieve a decisive victory.[21]

Allied diplomatic support for Greece, never strong, was weakening in direct ratio to the decline of Greek military strength. Britain seemed unwilling to drop official neutrality; France was not only unwilling to accept Constantine's authority but was also concluding another agreement with Kemal. Henri Franklin-Bouillon, French journalist and politician (in 1917 minister of propaganda) and president of the Chambre Committee on Foreign Affairs, successfully negotiated a wider accord in Ankara signed on 20 October. The London agreement had not been ratified by Kemal's Grand National Assembly for the same reason that Bekir Sami, its Turkish signatory, was sacked: negotiation would proceed on the whole of Turkey's claims, not its parts. The new agreement was essentially a duplicate, for it guaranteed French withdrawal from Cilicia and recognition of a northern Syrian boundary which granted more to the Turks than that of Sèvres. It differed, however, in its greater recognition of Turkish independence; nothing, for example, was said of French economic concessions or participation in such institutions as the gendarmerie. Curzon made the strongest case possible against the agreement to the French ambassador, but the French maintained that nothing in it contradicted France's obligations to her allies, aside from the legalistic matter that a mandatory power could not cede its mandate territory.[22]

Meanwhile, Curzon met with the itinerant Greek delegates, headed by Gournaris. The Greeks kept up the usual facade, but they had little

[21] Forbes Adam memorandum, 1 October, Crowe memorandum, 13 October, Hardinge telegram to FO, 21 October, *DBFP* XVII/405, 407, 417; Hankey private to Curzon (on Grigg-Venizelos discussion), 7 October, *Curzon Papers,* F/4/3; Worthington-Evans memorandum, 21 October 1921, note 17, chapter 7.

[22] Hardinge telegram to FO, 27 October, high commissioner, Constantinople, to FO, 25 October, and telegrams, 1 and 9 November, Curzon to

alternative to placing themselves in British hands. They now agreed, as Curzon explained to the Cabinet on 1 November, to an autonomous Smyrna and a different Thracian frontier—essentially the proposals rejected in June. Allied agreement was the next requirement, but the French leaders had all gone off to the Washington conference, and in any case the Franklin-Bouillon agreement complicated matters. Montagu once more saw the answer in direct negotiations with Ankara, but the Cabinet could no more agree on this than on precisely how to bring the French back to a cooperative attitude. Although not mentioned in the Cabinet conclusions, there was considerable fear that the Franco-Kemalist accord included secret clauses pledging assistance in getting the Greeks out of Anatolia. The agreement might be embarrassing to the local French commander in Constantinople, but Rumbold and Harington knew they could expect little French aid now after this "dishonourable" agreement.[23]

On 10 November the Cabinet studied the French answer to accusa-

---

Hardinge, 3 November, *DBFP* XVII/422-23, 429, 432, 437; Hardinge to FO, 30 October (with text of agreement), *FO* 371/6475; *Daily Telegraph,* 25 October; high commissioner, Constantinople, to FO, 31 October (local French reaction), Hardinge telegram to FO, 7 November, Curzon telegram to Hardinge, 9 November 1921, *FO* 371/6476; Hanotaux to League of Nations Council, 14 January 1922, 940/18, *FO* 371/7872, provided explanation to League of cession of mandated territory. Text of agreement: Hurewitz, *Diplomacy,* II, pp. 97-100; see Du Véou, *Passion,* pp. 303-19, on negotiation and effects; Bekir Sami: see Davison, "Turkish Diplomacy," and Elaine Diana Smith, *Turkey, Origins of the Kemalist Movement . . .* (Washington, D.C., 1959), p. 110.

At approximately the same time, British military authorities were carrying out a rather unsatisfactory exchange of prisoners off the Black Sea coast, which owing to confusion over numbers and circumstances only embittered military feelings against Kemal; Armstrong, *Turkey in Travail,* p. 213 (Armstrong delivered the prisoners held by Britain), and Rawlinson, *Adventures in the Near East,* pp. 335-38 (a prisoner delivered by the Turks).

[23] Cabinet 84 (21), 1 November, *CAB* 23/27; Curzon meeting with Greeks, 27 October, high commissioner, Constantinople, telegram to FO, 10 November (quoted), *DBFP* XVII/425, 439; 10-11th meeting, Allied Control Commission, Constantinople, 8 and 15 November, *WO* 106/1439. Fear of secret clauses: FO Eastern Dept. memorandum, 21 November, 12809/143, *FO* 371/6536, and Hardinge private to Curzon, 30 November 1921, pointing out that there probably were such clauses but that it would be useless to ask the French about them; *Curzon Papers,* F/7/2.

tions of betrayal. Briand claimed to have kept Lloyd George informed of the negotiations all along, an assertion which Lloyd George vehemently denied, but which the Foreign Office by now could neither prove nor disprove. The insoluble question was how to react officially. The old suggestions of unilateral withdrawal, or inviting Kemal to a conference, or sending a representative to Ankara were all revived (although the last was quickly killed since Britain was already complaining about the French having sent their own man). Curzon wished to tax the French with their lack of integrity, but others disagreed—Churchill because the French could exploit the disagreement in such a way as to represent Britain as the Turks' enemy and Montagu, Worthington-Evans, and Lloyd George because it would have little effect. They would simply say to Paris that London took note of the agreement, and that it gave wide liberty of action to Britain.[24]

It seemed best to approach Kemal, particularly since the Greeks had qualified their acceptance of mediation by insisting that the Greek army would still have to guarantee the Smyrna area minorities. However, Rumbold and some Foreign Office specialists thought Kemal might see a direct approach as a declaration of weakness and raise his price. Rumbold was convinced that the most Kemal might do was to attend a conference to work out a settlement; his view was soon confirmed by Ankara's reiteration of its basic position: there would be no modification of complete national sovereignty as stipulated in the National Pact. Despite advice to the contrary, Curzon still believed the Allies should invite Kemal to attend a conference and then make him a joint approach; they could dangle before him the bait of a financial loan and, once the conference had opened, the possible evacuation of Constantinople. The Cabinet had no alternative plans and so accepted Curzon's suggestions.[25]

[24] Cabinet 87 (21), 10 November, *CAB* 23/27; high commissioner, Constantinople, telegram to FO, 13 November, FO telegram to Buchanan, 15 November, Crowe memorandum, 18 November, *DBFP* XVII/442, 444, 447; Churchill to Curzon, 9 November, Harington private to Curzon, 11 November, and Rumbold private to Curzon, 15 November 1921, *Curzon Papers,* F/4/3; Great Britain, Parliamentary Papers, Cmd. 1570 (1922), Turkey, No. 1, "Correspondence between His Majesty's Government and the French Government respecting the Angora Agreement of October 20, 1921."

[25] W.G. Edmonds memorandum, 15 November, 2848/143, *FO* 371/

To work, the new terms must satisfy not only Greeks and Turks but also the Allies. The tripartite treaty would have to go for example, since the Turks would never accept it. Yet Italy would require some concessions; a revised draft of the treaty which avoided all appearance of partition was suggested, and, if that was impossible, perhaps some compensation for Italy elsewhere (Iraqi oil, for example). The biggest issue, however, was how to satisfy Greeks and Turks. The basic draft (prepared for Curzon by Eric Forbes Adam) still left a special regime for Smyrna, now to be under the League and to be run somewhat along the lines of the Saar or Lebanon after the Statute of 1861. The same might be done for Thrace, but Armenia was a hopeless case, except perhaps for a general minority clause. No blame attached to the Allies here; as Osborne put it, "Before a party can be charged with violation of a pledge [to establish the Armenians in Anatolia], it must be established that it is able to fulfil it . . . ." Fortunately this was not typical Foreign Office logic. As for the Straits, the demilitarized zone could be reduced to include basically only Chanak and Gallipoli. Financial and military restrictions would also be eased. Once again, a few more small steps were taken away from Sèvres.[26]

Curzon planned to try these terms out on French and Italian leaders at Paris (and preliminary soundings showed that Briand, suffering pangs of conscience over Franklin-Bouillon, would agree). Then the Allied Supreme Council would approve, for technically revision of a peace treaty was involved. If necessary, Curzon had a further concession in reserve: only three small autonomous zones would be established in Smyrna. If the Greeks refused to accept what the Allies offered, and if there was true Allied agreement, the Allies could then blockade Smyr-

---

6536; Rumbold private telegram to Curzon, FO telegram to Hardinge, and Curzon-Greek meeting, all 19 November, high commissioner, Constantinople, telegram to FO, 22 November, FO telegram to high commissioner, Constantinople, *DBFP* XVII/448-50, 453, 456; Cabinet 88 (21), 22 November, *CAB* 23/27; Curzon private to Hardinge, 28 November, *Curzon Papers*, F/4/5; Harington private to de Robeck, 30 November and 31 December 1921, *De Robeck Papers*, 6/18; Jones, *Whitehall Diary*, I, pp. 178-79.

[26] Forbes Adam memoranda, 6 December, 13375/143, *FO* 371/6536, and 8 December, 13542/1, *FO* 371/6479; Hardinge private to Curzon, 9 December, *Curzon Papers*, F/7/2; Osborne memorandum, 17 December 1921, quoted, 14379/800, *FO* 371/6561.

na. The Cabinet agreed on 21 December. The conference was set for mid-January in Paris, with Curzon, much to his own relief, to handle the British side; Lloyd George, "still as mad for Greece as ever," was capable of personal intervention if present.[27]

Before meeting with the French, Curzon and Lloyd George talked to Gounaris at Cannes on 12 January. The full details of the plan were not spelled out, but Gounaris was realist enough to know that Greece could not force her will on Turkey unassisted; the Greeks might argue, but in the end they would have to give in. Kemal was another matter, and Rumbold felt that he would never accept. Rather ominously, Poincaré, the French premier, appeared to share this view when the Anglo-French talks began on 16 January. The French were not eager for another conference, above all if the plan offered meant the end of the tripartite treaty. Briand seemed of another mind, but France collectively would do no more than think it all over. Poincaré's main concern in thus forcing delay, as Hardinge reported after Curzon left, was to avoid entering further negotiations with Kemal until Curzon had been brought round to concede Turkish sovereignty over the whole of Asia Minor.[28]

There were dangers, too, in going too fast. Immediate Greek evacuation of Smyrna for example, would only make Kemal all the more demanding on other issues. The French would then be eager to leave Constantinople, which Britain could not hold alone; another Greco-Turkish campaign in Thrace (or worse, a Turkish drive toward Mosul) would probably follow. Precipitate withdrawal was in fact what the Greeks now threatened unless financial support was forthcoming. In December the Greeks had been unable to raise a loan on the London money market despite government security, and now the spring campaign season was approaching. Without money, Gounaris told Curzon,

[27] Curzon memorandum, 19 December, 13991/1, *FO* 371/6480; Cabinet 93 (21), 16 December, appendix III, Conference of Ministers, 21 December, *CAB* 23/27; Curzon private to Hardinge, 24 December 1921, quoted, *Curzon Papers,* F/4/5.

[28] Allied meeting, 12 January, *CAB* 23/35; high commissioner, Constantinople, telegram to FO, 15 January, Allied meeting, 16 January, Hardinge to FO, 1 February, and telegram, 3 February, Curzon to Hardinge, 2 February, and Crowe memorandum, 6 February, *DBFP* XVII/506, 508, 516-17, 519, 525; Cabinet 2 (22), 18 January, *CAB* 23/29; Hardinge private to Curzon, 21 January 1922, *Curzon Papers,* F/5.

the Greeks would have to pull back in what amounted to "a complete evacuation of Asia Minor." It might be bluff, and probably was, but London could never be sure. The disadvantages of such a Greek surrender to Kemal almost, but no quite, balanced the advantage of settling with the Turks, a practicable possibility with the Greeks gone. The scales were finally weighted, moreover, by the chance that Athens might not be bluffing and might order withdrawal (local Greek commanders might in turn disobey the order, but that was too great a gamble). But in mid-March when Turkish and Greek delegates appeared in London to talk further, the Greeks were encouraged to resist in talks with Philip Kerr, or so intercepted telegrams to Athens from the Greek delegates showed. Whether or not he had this information—the telegram copy in Curzon's papers shows no date of receipt—Curzon did his best to tell Gounaris that while he had British sympathy he would get no aid. The letter to Gounaris was to reappear later in peculiar circumstances but it was now lost sight of in the rush of events; mounting pressure from India and the India Office for a moderate Turkish settlement had reached a point where Lloyd George felt called upon to demand Montagu's resignation.[29]

KHILAFAT AND THE TURKISH CRISIS

The renewed Greek offensive in midsummer 1921 corresponded with a new high level of tension in India, and the coincidence was only partly accidental. In mid-August, the Indian authorities decided to arrest the Ali brothers for inflammatory speeches at a July Khilafat conference at Karchi. Luckily Gandhi had not attended, for the government did not wish to arrest the Hindu leader as well. The danger was now that Gandhi might court arrest to show sympathy with the Muslim leaders and in so doing patch over the rift which had opened between Muslim and Hindu as a result of the Moplah disturbances. Gandhi's response was mild; Reading reported that the Alis' arrest and sentencing (two

---

[29] A. Ryan memoranda, 9 and 17 February, high commissioner, Constantinople, telegram to FO, 17 February, Lindley telegrams to FO, 19 and 21 February, *DBFP* XVII/526, 531, 533, 536, 539; Gounaris to Curzon, 15 February (quoted), with Osborne minute, 16 February, *FO* 371/7855; Curzon to Gounaris, 6 March, quoted by Lord Birkenhead in *Parl. Deb.,* Lords, 7 December 1922 (see chapter 8, note 31).

years' vigorous internment) had not brought serious difficulties. Gandhi was concentrating on his cloth boycott, and in public statements he had recognized that the Alis had challenged the government and were suffering the requisite response. Gandhi was sincere in his support of the Khilafat movement, but he, too, had been disillusioned by the Moplah response. As Reading put it, all but the most ardent extremists were relieved at the arrest of the Alis.[30]

Gandhi was also open to the argument, however, that by his own disengagement the Muslim leaders bore the full brunt of government persecution. As the weeks passed, his renewed attempt to stand with the movement (for example, in arguing that Indian soldiers should not remain in government pay) was causing trouble. He still played upon the Sèvres terms, disregarding all Indian government publicity on the modifications obtained by their pressure. Reading was soon convinced that Gandhi, too, should be arrested, although no immediate action was taken and Gandhi remained at liberty until the following March.[31]

Gandhi's activities were not the only issue. Sympathizers for Turkey in India were raising a large subscription or loan for Kemal. The India Office was naturally concerned but very wisely took no steps to prevent it on the grounds that this was the best way to quiet the issue. In the end the total subscriptions amounted to under £20,000, but it was an awkward manifestation of pro-Kemalist support, and it showed how accurate were Indian warnings about the danger of Muslim disaffection and the need for treaty revision. But India's statements were all general in nature, for largely propagandistic purposes, and understood as such. Gandhi's noncooperation movement, while a serious problem, was an Indian problem, and it was for the Indian government to deal with it.[32]

---

[30] Reading private to Montagu, 25 August, 15 and 22 September, *Montagu Papers,* D. 523/14; viceroy (Home Dept.) telegram to SSI, 16 September 1921, *C/J&P/6/1763*; on the Moplahs, see chapter 5, note 71, and for the events discussed below, India, Home Dept., *Histories of the Non-Co-Operation and Khalifat Movements,* Ch. V, and Niemeijer, *Khilafat,* Ch. VII.

[31] Reading private to Montagu, 6 October and 3 November 1921, *Montagu Papers,* D. 523/14; Gopal, *Muslim India,* pp. 149-50.

[32] Viceroy telegram to SSI, 9 November; SSI telegram to viceroy, 3 December, *L/P&S/10/852*; IO to FO, 9 December 1921, *FO 371/6345*.

Had India pursued the link of Bolshevik activities with Indian nationalism, ironically, London would have been more interested, but as Montagu complained privately to Reading, India had backed out of European intelligence-gathering commitments just when such activities seemed about to bear fruit. Delhi was unconcerned with Bolshevism, and London was insufficiently concerned with the link between Turkey and Muslim agitation. The India Office continued to insist upon the connections between these various movements and others, from pan-Islam to Persian nationalism. Probably, the Foreign Office was told, activity in places like Karachi was stirred up by agents passing through the corridor of Persia (a point never made by India). India might wish to end its intelligence commitment, but India could not do the job alone anyway, and the time had arrived for a general interdepartmental committee, with field operatives in several areas, to be established on these issues. The Foreign Office was not enthusiastic—there was already a plethora of information sources. Still, the Interdepartmental Committee on Eastern Unrest was established and worked through the spring of 1922.[33]

Montagu's mind was running on a different track from that of his advisors and subordinates in India: the Bolshevik conspiracy added another, deeper dimension to the Kemalist and Khilafat movements. It is hard not to conclude that the constant repetition of this viewpoint inside and outside of the Cabinet had made him appear rather fanatic on the subject—certainly he was a worrisome nuisance on the issue of the Turkish treaty. By the end of 1921 he was clear on his own position: blundering prewar diplomacy had forced the Turk into the enemy camp in the first place, an error which was now being compounded by the severity of Sèvres with consequent effects in India and the Middle East. Turkey had to pay the price of its error, of course, but it was no favor to the Greeks to help them to take on more territory than they could possibly hold. Finally, Britain was pledged by the prime minister's own words of January 1918 and by later elaborations to leave Thrace and Constantinople to the Turks. At the least, he urged in yet another memorandum for the Cabinet, Turkey should have the line Curzon

[33] IO to FO, 9 December 1921, *FO* 371/6345; Montagu private to Reading, 24 November 1921, *Montagu Papers,* D. 523/13; "Interdepartmental Committee on Eastern Unrest," 1st minutes, 15 February, interim report, 24 May, final report, 17 August 1922, *FO* 371/7790, and see chapter 6, especially pp. 302-310.

proposed which ran from the Maritsa River on the Bulgarian frontier to Rodosto on the Sea of Marmora—thus keeping Adrianople, but not Gallipoli. The net result of Montagu's ceaseless bombardment on Turkey and on Indian unrest was that India was in everybody's mind—but so was annoyance at his interference.[34]

By late January 1922 Montagu's concern was substantially increased by Reading's information that the Khilafat conference had defeated a resolution to drop the doctrine of nonviolence only because the timing of the resolution was inexpedient. This, said Montagu, was "one of the gravest challenges with which we have had to deal." The question in his mind was how to bring the crisis home to his colleagues. The possibility of resignation is always before a high Cabinet official—indeed, a letter in *The Times* on 28 January made just that suggestion—but Montagu was not yet ready to destroy his own career, since there was still hope that his views might prevail. He had surely influenced the Foreign Office and the prime minister, as he must have known, but the continued crisis in India required continued pressure in London.[35]

Early March brought another expression of India's views which Montagu had always encouraged. In a telegram Reading again set out the most important Indian desiderata: evacuation of Constantinople, sultan's suzerainty over holy places, the restoration of "Ottoman Thrace" (meaning eastern Thrace), including Adrianople, and Smyrna. As part of its own propaganda effort, the Indian government requested permission to publish the telegram. Montagu circulated the telegram on 3 March; the next day—Saturday—he received another request for publication. That evening, without consulting his Cabinet colleagues, he authorized publication with only a slight change of wording. On Monday the 6th the Cabinet met (Montagu had not expected it to do so, one reason for his permission to publish). Montagu told Curzon about the authorization in private conversation during the meeting, but Curzon, as he later explained in the House of Lords, thought it must be

---

[34] Montagu memoranda for Cabinet, 22 December 1921 and 10 January 1922, (C.P. 3576 and 3602), *FO* 371/7853 and 7938; Montagu private to Curzon, 1 and 12 January, *Curzon Papers,* F/5, and private telegram to Curzon at Cannes, 4 January 1922, *FO* 800/157. Among other points, Montagu urged that Curzon take the Aga Khan along to Cannes as Indian representative.

[35] Montagu private to Reading, 18 and 26 January, *Montagu Papers,* D. 523/13; *The Times,* 28 January 1922.

too late to cancel publication and did nothing in the meeting. Afterwards, he wrote to Montagu what Montagu termed "one of those plaintive, hectoring, bullying, complaining letters which are so familiar to his friends and colleagues . . .". Both Curzon and Chamberlain, who was in the chair, had assumed that Montagu would never give approval without Cabinet permission.[36]

On the 9th Lloyd George returned to work. Having read the telegram that morning, he summoned Montagu and asked for his resignation, which Montagu provided in written form with a justification of his action attached. He requested permission to publish his reasons. Curzon, meanwhile—back in bed again—wrote to Chamberlain also on the 9th to complain of Montagu's action and thus concluded that his own action was influential in obtaining Montagu's resignation. The problem, of course, was that India could not be allowed to express an independent opinion on imperial policy matters. As Curzon said to Chamberlain, if Montagu could pronounce on Turkey, "why not about Ireland or the Isle of Man?" The conference was coming up, but "I decline to go to Paris with my hands tied." Lloyd George agreed, and that same day he expressed his regret to Curzon that the latter's difficult task was complicated by "'Montagu's folly," although he had taken quick action to correct the "unwarranted intervention."[37]

Montagu's folly was note quite done. The evening of the 9th he cabled privately to Reading the news of his resignation, adding that

[36] Account of Montagu's resignation is based upon Waley, *Montagu,* pp. 271-77 (quoting most of the documents mentioned); C.J.C. Street, *Lord Reading* (London, 1928), pp. 228-31; Hyde, *Reading,* pp. 371-74; Nicolson, *Curzon,* pp. 267-68; Ronaldshay, *Curzon,* III, pp. 281-87; Aziz, *Britain and Muslim India,* pp. 98-102; Beaverbrook, *Decline and Fall of Lloyd George,* pp. 154-55; Jones, *Diary,* I, p. 193; Roskill, *Hankey,* II, p. 264; Curzon private to Chamberlain, 9 March (with minute in Curzon's handwriting, "letter from self to A. Chambn. which assisted to bring about resignation of Montagu.") and Chamberlain private to Curzon, 13 March 1922, *Curzon Papers,* F/4/5 and F/5. Montagu's remarks were made in his constituency (Cambridge Liberal Club) 11 March, quoted in Waley, *Montagu,* pp. 273-74; another copy is in Grigg to Lloyd George, 13 March 1922, *Lloyd George Papers,* F/86/1/23.

[37] Lloyd George to Montagu, 9 March, quoted in Waley, *Montagu,* pp. 276-77, and private to Curzon, same date (quoted), original in *Curzon Papers,* F/5; Curzon note of thanks, same date, *Lloyd George Papers,* F/13/3/12; Curzon-Chamberlain exchange noted chapter 7, note 36.

Reading should explain in India that his resignation did not mean Britain rejected India's Turkish desiderata. But Montagu was no longer secretary of state, and his advice was that of a private citizen. Acting quietly, Lloyd George told Worthington-Evans to take over the India Office until a successor was chosen, and the India Office's permanent undersecretary advised India against fulfilling Montagu's request for the time being. Chamberlain and Curzon between them decided (Lloyd George having gone off to Wales) that there would be no parting shot from Montagu, at least in India. Reading was in some difficulty, however; the whole point of publishing the original telegram was that the arrest of Gandhi had at last been set (he was arrested on the 11th and eventually sentenced to six years' imprisonment), and it was strongly desired to disarm critics of the Turkish terms. Since the published telegram had been his, the viceroy thought briefly of resignation, but he had received Montagu's permission to publish, and it was not the time for a viceroy to resign over any issue.[38]

Montagu, barred from official explanations, made an impassioned defense before his Cambridge constituency on the 11th, unfortunately quoting from Curzon's private communications. He justified his actions, then went on to castigate the entire government in which he had long felt uneasy as a result of "the total, complete, absolute disappearance of the doctrine of Cabinet responsibility" under Lloyd George. Not the act of publishing one telegram had brought his resignation, but his hostility to the entire dangerous pro-Greek policy of the prime minister. It fell upon Chamberlain to answer this speech in the Commons on the 13th, but the major speech, which Lloyd George approved in advance, was made by Curzon in the Lords the following day. It was well received by a full and sympathetic audience, reported a biased Edward Grigg to Lloyd George; "Montagu has really got no support anywhere." The debate was not over until Montagu had his day on the 15th, but, overwhelmed by his dismissal, he made a poor showing—sadly, the last of his career.[39]

[38] Montagu private telegrams to viceroy, 9 and 10 March, Duke (permanent undersecretary, IO) private telegrams to viceroy, 11 and 13 March, Lord Privy Seal (Chamberlain) private telegrams to Reading, 14, 15, and 16 March, Reading private telegram to Montagu, 11 March, *Reading Papers,* E. 238/16; *The Times,* 9 March, Grigg note to prime minister, Reading private telegram for prime minister, and draft of Privy Seal private telegram to Reading, all 13 March 1922, *Lloyd George Papers,* F/84/1/22 and F/86/1/25.

[39] Montagu quoted in Waley, *Montagu,* p. 278, and 278-80 on Curzon's

The effect of Montagu's resignation was more noticeable in India than in Britain. Reading reported considerable agitation, and the suggestion was abroad that Montagu had been sacrificed in order to placate the diehards and mark a change in British policy. After the event, however, it appears that Reading was giving vent to some sympathetic emotion, and the reaction, for all Montagu's friends in India, was not overwhelming. By no means all influential Indians regretted his loss; indeed some said that by emphasizing the Khilafat movement Montagu had in a very real sense encouraged it. As Sir C. Sankaran Nair wrote Hardinge, many would not have joined the movement but for him: "it is all nonsense to say that we Hindoos or even the majority of Mahomedans care about the fate of Turkey or Caliph." For every George Lloyd in Bombay who might regret his passing, there was a Hardinge to agree that "he has simply ruined our position in India & everything else . . . . If India is to dictate our policy in Europe the F.O. had better shut up shop," an interesting point made from one former viceroy to another (Curzon). Montagu had many enemies; he was a Jew, and a Liberal, and even his basic claim that Lloyd George had violated Cabinet responsibility carried little weight after he had participated for so many months in such a government. More than one politician, moreover, dismissed the whole incident as a plot against Lloyd George.[40]

In a way, Montagu's resignation, however tragic, was unnecessary:

---

speech; Curzon speech in draft is in Grigg for prime minister, 13 March; Grigg's report (quoted) in note for Lloyd George, 14 March 1922, *Lloyd George Papers,* F/84/1/22 and F/86/1/24.

[40] Reading private telegram to Privy Seal, 14 March, viceroy telegram to SSI, 15 March, *Reading Papers,* E. 238/16; Hardinge private to Curzon, 12 March (quoted), and Sir C. Sankaran Nair private to Hardinge, 11 March (quoted), enclosed in Hardinge private to Curzon, 3 April, *Curzon Papers,* F/7/2 and F/5; Reading private to Lloyd George, 4 May 1922, *Lloyd George Papers,* F/43/2/1. George Lloyd's views: Forbes Adam, *Lord Lloyd,* p. 165. Sir C. Sankaran Nair had been a member of the viceroy's council in India and resigned after Amritsar; see K.P.S. Menon, *C. Sankaran Nair* (New Delhi, 1967).

For appreciations of Montagu and the crisis, see Robert Blake, *Unrepentant Tory: Life and Times of Andrew Bonar Law . . .* (N.Y., 1956), p. 421 (conservatism, Judaism); "India and the Moslem Awakening," *Current History* 16 (1922): 1-9; Sir Valentine Chirol, "Four Years of Lloyd-Georgian Foreign Policy," *Edinburgh Review* 237 (1923): 1-20; Thomas Jones, *Lloyd George* (Cambridge, Mass., 1951), p. 196.

the controversial telegram said nothing new about India's attitude. To that extent, Montagu had blundered, and his political career was ended: in the next election he lost his seat, and in November 1924 he died at the age of 45. Reading realized that Montagu had done his utmost to push the Indian view, and India would appreciate that, but Montagu's resignation and Gandhi's arrest marked a decided change in Indian affairs.[41] The government had done its best on Turkey; on the other hand, the most active Khilafat leaders, both Muslim and Hindu, were in prison, and the movement now entered a serious decline. Indian concern with Turkish peace terms was not over, but the intensity of pressure Montagu exerted was ended. Montagu's resignation may have weakened the Cabinet by raising controversy, but Curzon could proceed to the inter-Allied negotiations knowing that at least one sort of pressure was now diminished.

THE STRUGGLE FOR ARMISTICE

On 9 March Montagu resigned; on the 11th Gandhi was arrested; on the 13th discussion with the Turks began. It was soon clear that the Turks would contemplate no alteration of previously stated demands. Little general progress was made in the first general discussions, although Kemal's foreign minister, Yusuf Kemal Bey, was relatively moderate when the question of general Allied interest in the Straits was raised. But Briton and Turk were as far apart as ever on Armenians or minority protection or whether previous British promises existed concerning Constantinople; the major development was that the Turks told Curzon for the first time officially that they contemplated exchanging populations to settle the problem of the Greeks in Asia Minor, an idea which he dismissed as impracticable considering the numbers involved. Curzon still adhered to his plan of obtaining Allied approval of British plans first, however, and left for Paris with the general backing of the Cabinet.[42]

On the 22nd Curzon put the problem to the Allied leaders; the

[41] Reading private to Peel, 13 July 1922, *Reading Papers,* E. 238/5.

[42] High commissioner, Constantinople, telegrams to Curzon, 5, 17 (quoted), and 27 February; Yusuf-Curzon meetings, 16 and 18 March, *DBFP* XVII/523, 531, 543, 555-56; Cabinet 19 (22), 20 March 1922, *CAB* 23/29.

Greeks (or so he thought) had placed themselves in Allied hands, and the moment was favorable for an offer: first an armistice, then Greek withdrawal in gradual stages over four to eight months, would bring peace. Poincaré was unreceptive, convinced that Kemal would refuse any armistice the Greeks proposed. Special League protections, and commissioners to oversee minority pledges, the French condemned (the next day) as too theoretical. As for Thrace, the French would give Turkey the Enos-Midia line, out of realism.[43]

Curzon at least wished to see honor done on Armenia, but it was impossible to prevail over the "complete indifference amounting almost to open hostility" which he found in Paris.[44] He proposed a formula in the fourth meeting which would set out either Cilicia or the eastern vilayets as an Armenian "national home," with the League assigned the task of making it work. Fine, said Poincaré, as long as it meant no Allied commitments; the Allies had done their best and failed. Curzon, badly battered, emerged with only a vague formula on Armenia and only one lonely victory over Poincaré on Thrace—for the French military advisors had agreed against turning over the whole of Thrace and the Straits to the Turks. The final communique issued to the press on the 27th outlined the result of long negotiation: four months to evacuate, League assistance to be sought on Armenia, a broad demilitarized zone on the Asiatic side of the Straits (with the Allies continuing to hold Gallipoli), the probability of a special regime for Thrace, the Turkish army to be increased from the 50,000 of Sèvres to 85,000, and, in lieu of financial obligations, international commissions to assist in revising the capitulations—more small steps toward Lausanne.[45]

It was now necessary to await a response from Greece and Turkey. Kemal, despite Rumbold's forebodings, accepted the armistice in principle—provided that the Greek evacuation began at once. What Kemal approved, however, was cause for wide-scale hostility in Greece. So long as the Greeks thought that Britain had abandoned them, no Greek government could safely accept the proposals without some secure

---

[43] Allied meetings, 22-26 March 1922, *DBFP* XVII/560-69 (and see notes, pp. 698 and 706).

[44] Hardinge telegram (for Curzon) to FO, 24 March 1922 (quoted), *DBFP* XVII, note, p. 698.

[45] Hardinge (for Curzon) telegram to FO, 26 March 1922, *FO* 371/7858; Great Britain, Parliamentary Papers, "Pronouncement by the Three Powers, 27 March, 1922," Cmd. 1641, Misc. No. 3, 1922.

guarantee for the Asia Minor Christians. But Ankara's qualification was not agreeable either, since the plan called for evacuation after acceptance of the peace. Another problem was the locale of the conference—the original proposal had been Constantinople—but this was the least important issue. The primary task remained the same: an armistice, then acceptance of Allied proposals, and only then a conference.[46]

The signs were unpromising. In mid-April, the Italians gave notice that they were leaving the Meander valley positions, and both Greeks and Turks raced to fill the vacuum. At the same time, Italy, hedging its bets, signed a worthless agreement with the Constantinople government. Once again, London had been caught short, and Kemal had that much more freedom to concentrate against Greek or British positions as widespread as Izmit or Mosul. "In a Russian troika the driver has a certain control," complained Curzon, "but here he is gagged and bandaged on the box while the steeds do precisely what self-interest dictates." As one staff member put it more bluntly, "I have seen many dirty games in my life, but both French and Italians are pretty nearly reaching the limit in Turkey."[47]

Kemal, moreover, continued to demand that armistice, Greek evacuation, and negotiation all be simultaneous, a position the Allies would not accept unless there was absolutely no choice. As Harington saw it, if evacuation were not accompanied by Kemalist demobilization, Kemal could then turn against Iraq with his full forces. The Turks would only agree to discuss procedure at Izmit, a suggestion which France accepted with alacrity, but which the Foreign Office thought was contrary to the larger plan. Finally, in Athens the Greek attitude seemed to be hardening; the British ambassador concluded that the Greeks had some-

[46] Rumbold private to Curzon, 4 April, *Curzon Papers,* F/5; high commissioner, Constantinople, telegrams to FO, 5 and 10 April, FO telegram to Hardinge, 8 April, Lindley telegram to FO, 20 April, Curzon note, 22 April, *DBFP* XVII/583, 588, 590, 601, and note, p. 792; Lindley to Curzon, 6 April 1922, *FO* 371/7862.

[47] Lindley telegram to FO, 15 April, FO telegram to Cheetham, 25 April, Curzon to Italian ambassador, 27 April, *DBFP* XVII/598, 609, 611, CinC Constantinople telegram to WO, 19 April, Lindsay memorandum, 24 April, with Curzon minute (quoted), 24 April; CinC Mediterranean telegram to Admiralty, 3 May, *FO* 371/7862-63; W.G. Tyrrell private to Curzon, 24 April 1922 (quoted), *Curzon Papers,* F/5.

thing up their collective sleeve, perhaps something which would make evacuation more difficult to obtain.[48]

Late spring and early summer of 1922 brought no relief. At Genoa, in late April, all parties jockeyed for position; Curzon, kept away by illness, was afraid that the Greeks would get to Lloyd George again, but the prime minister was kept busy by European problems. In late May Lloyd George was careful in his one (recorded) conversation with Venizelos, still out of office, to make no specific promises beyond possible financial aid if the Turks proved intractable. He warned the Greek leader that the feelings of Muslim subjects of the empire would not permit more. June brought only more inconclusive discussion. Poincaré still wished to meet Kemal at Izmit; both Rumbold and Harington saw this as unlikely to be more than a propaganda victory for Kemal. Commander and high commission agreed that the Paris proposals should be maintained: what had been seen as the extreme limit of concession a few weeks earlier, in other words, was now a position to be defended against further concession.[49]

The Foreign Office was convinced that French policy was to pry more concessions from Britain and to buy time—as Crowe maintained, to provide Kemal enough arms to ensure a Greek defeat. They also feared that Italy might cooperate in that objective, but Italy was much more concerned with some compensation for cancellation of the tripartite agreement. Carlo Schanzer, Italian foreign minister in the first months of 1922, hoped to trade support for Britain for the sort of guarantee Britain had no power to grant. Lloyd George and Balfour (acting for a bedridden Curzon) could only be accommodating in general, even to the point of drafting a general assurance. Without a tangible reward

[48] CinC Constantinople telegram to WO, 28 April, Lindley telegram to FO, 4 May, *FO* 371/7863-64; Hardinge telegram to FO, 1 May, and Curzon to Hardinge, 10 May 1922, *DBFP* XVII/615, 627.

[49] Curzon telegram to Gregory (Genoa), 25 April, and for Lloyd George, 5 May, Gregory telegram (from Lloyd George) for Privy Seal, 4 May, Graham telegram to FO, 4 May, Rumbold telegram to FO, 22 May (2 parts), Hardinge private to Balfour, 8 June, Balfour to Hardinge, 7 June, *DBFP* XVII/608, 620-22, 638-39, 645, and note 6, p. 844; Hardinge private to Curzon, 5 May, Curzon private to Lloyd George, 6 May, *Curzon Papers,* F/7/2, F/13/3/20; note on Venizelos-Lloyd George conversation (House of Commons), 30 May, *Lloyd George Papers,* F/86/2/3; WO to FO, 25 May (enclosing CinC Constantinople telegram to WO, 24 May), and high commissioner, Constantinople, to Balfour, 6 June 1922, *FO* 371/7865-66.

in sight, there was little reason for Italy to cooperate in defense of the Paris proposals, and Schanzer seemed to want to throw up his hands and let the Greeks and Turks fight it out without Allied intervention. By early July there seemed so little prospect of forcing Allied unanimity that Balfour agreed to the Izmit meeting, on condition that the Allies would abide by the Paris proposals, that the meeting be nearer to Constantinople than Izmit (Izmit, after all, was in Kemalist territory), and, finally, that the Greeks be given normal belligerency rights such as that of searching ships (a right so far denied by the Allies). Paris returned an equally, and unacceptably, qualified agreement, so the idea was dead; since Constantinople predicted that Kemal would not accept the qualifications, and Athens said the same of the Greeks, it had little real life in any case.[50]

The more realistic chance was that a new Greek offensive would settle the matter. Once more an intercepted telegram indicated that Lloyd George or Edward Grigg had encouraged the Greeks, although both vehemently denied it. F.O. Lindley in Athens reported that Greece intended resuming its freedom of action, previously placed in British hands. The danger now, therefore, was that the Greeks might seize eastern Thrace or Constantinople. Two Greek divisions in western Thrace had become four, and Harington and Nevile Henderson, Rumbold's temporary replacement in Constantinople, were concerned enough to warn the Greeks away from such an idea. Balfour added his weight by sending the same advice directly to Athens when the Greeks officially asked permission to be allowed to occupy Constantinople. The extent of the threat was never certain, but as Henderson put it, guns could always go off for a variety of causes. In London there was never any serious movement to withdraw from Constantinople under this threat, and the Cabinet on 3 August, somewhat after the fact, approved orders to Harington to resist attack by Turks, Greeks, or both simultaneously.[51]

[50] Hardinge to Balfour, 17 June, and Balfour to Cheetham (Paris), 5 July, *DBFP* XVII/656, 676, and note, pp. 856-57; Allied conversations, 19 June, *FO* 371/7866, and 28 June, and Hardinge to Balfour, 13 July, *FO* 371/7867; Allied conversations, 26 and 29 June and 3 and 6 July, and Schanzer to FO, 27 July 1922, *FO* 371/7799-7800.

[51] Lindley telegram to FO, 23 July, Henderson telegrams to FO, 27, 29, and 30 July, FO telegrams to Cheetham, 27 July, and to high commissioner, Constantinople, 1 August, Bentinck telegrams to FO, 29 and 31 (2 of date)

The threat had one use, for in the debate on summer adjournment of Parliament (4 August), Lloyd George cited keeping the Greeks out of Constantinople as fine proof of Britain's impartiality in holding the ring: "our business is to hold the balance justly and fairly between both parties." Taken overall, the speech was nevertheless solid support for the Greeks. As Lloyd George read the history of the crisis, it was Ankara which had disrupted the London conference: he had certain information that the Greeks would have accepted if the Turks had. Much talk was heard of atrocities, but the balance here was against the Turks in numbers and severity. As for the latest, Paris, proposals, only Kemal's intransigent demand for preliminary evacuation prevented their acceptance—including acceptance by the sultan-caliph in Constantinople. This last remark was obviously designed for Indian opinion, the pressure of which had continued to be substantial despite Montagu's resignation. Finally, Lloyd George took little trouble to glove his threat; his references to Greek inability to wage war with full strength, given Allied occupation of the capital and prevention of search and seizure at sea, meant that if he had his way, and the Turks continued in their current attitudes, these strictures would be removed.[52]

The speech had one other effect, for the French, alarmed that discussions with Kemal might fall through, adopted a more diplomatic attitude; they were willing to accept, as they put it, any reasonable pro-

---

July, high commissioner, Constantinople, telegram to FO, 31 July, *DBFP* XVII/693, 696, 699, 704, 706, 708, 711-14, note, p. 890; Rizo-Rangabé telegram to minister of foreign affairs, Athens, 20 July, Grigg private to Curzon, 10 August ("This intercept simply amazed me. . ."), *Curzon Papers,* F/5, in answer to Curzon private to Grigg, 9 August, *FO* 800/154; Henderson private to Vansittart, 1 August, *FO* 800/157; Cabinet 43 (22), 3 August 1922, *CAB* 23/30.

[52] *Parl. Deb.,* H.C., 4 August (quoted), pp. 1999-2012. Indian pressure, viceroy telegrams to SSI, 22 April and 7 June, *L/P&S/*10/853; IO to FO, 15 May, SSI telegram to viceroy, 22 April, viceroy telegram to SSI, 9 May, *FO* 371/7771; Reading private telegrams to Peel, 30 April and 16 July, and letter, 13 July, *Reading Papers,* E. 238/5 and 16; Foreign and Poli. Dept. (National Archives of India), file 1923/228-x, "Revision of Turkish Peace Terms"; IO to FO, 13 September, enclosing SSI telegrams to viceroy, 4 March and 11 July, and viceroy telegrams to SSI, 9 May and 24 July and 11 September 1922 (C.P. 4186), *FO* 371/7872; Montgomery, "Lloyd George," p. 282, calls this speech the prime minister's last and most dangerous intervention.

posals. Curzon suggested in response that a spot such as Venice should
be chosen for negotiation—and once again the idea of a European conference was alive. French moderation was more than probably encouraged by the fear of having to fight the Greeks in Thrace. Unleash-
ing the Greeks was indeed the one threat Lloyd George had, and it was
one that he flaunted in his Parliamentary remarks. In Athens there was
predictable enthusiasm, for the speech was seen as the first move toward
opening the gates of Constantinople.[53]

Unfortunately for Greek security, the scene of action was to be Asia,
not Europe. Harington knew this well, and once assured that the Greeks
would stay put, he asked permission to move his troops from the
Chatalja lines west of Constantinople to the Asian side. The Allies had
a different view, fearful of the Kemalists in Asia, still fearful of the
Greeks in Europe—but Harington moved half his force across just in
time to witness the opening of a new stage of operations. On 26 August,
a major Turkish attack opened south of Afyonkarahisar. Within a few
days it was clear that the Greeks were not going to hold: the fall of
Afyonkarahisar on the 30th cut the railway and totally disrupted Greek
supply lines.[54] The picture was grim indeed for the outnumbered
Greeks, and September was to be a mouth of nervewracking crisis,
not merely in Athens.

CHANAK

By 2 September Ushak was evacuated, the Greek army was in full
flight, and Athens had decided on complete evacuation, so rapid was
the collapse and ensuing chaos. The disaster came as a total shock—
as much so as the unexpected and substantial Turkish artillery bar-
rages which had opened the campaign. From Smyrna came advice that
the Greeks would not abe able to defend the town: the powers would
have to take whatever defensive measures they found necessary. Rum-

---

[53] Cheetham telegram to FO, 4 August, FO 371/7869; Curzon to Hardinge, 18 August, Rumbold private to Oliphant, 8 August, DBFP, XVII/
737 and note 4, p. 907; and letter to Curzon, 15 August, Bentinck to FO,
10 and 11 August, and telegram, 12 August 1922, FO 371/7871.

[54] CinC Constantinople telegram to WO, 9 August, FO 371/7870;Rum-
bold private to Oliphant, 15 August, CinC Constantinople telegram to WO,
19 August, FO 371/7871; Bentinck telegram to FO, 29 August, DBFP
XVII/745; WO to FO, 30 August 1922, FO 371/7884.

bold was told to work out the details with the military. Harington was confident as usual in the strength of competent British leadership if intervention was desired, but his opinion that the battleships at Smyrna could shore up Greek resistance was a lone voice.[55]

Curzon had now to rise to the occasion, pulled out of bed at 3 A.M. by a Greek request for an armistice. Telegrams soon went out setting in motion a joint Allied appeal to Ankara to negotiate an end to the fighting. Only Rumbold firmly grasped the situation: Greece had collapsed, and Britain had to look to herself. Kemal would only be irritated if Britain seemed once more to be acting on the behalf of Athens, and he would demand the full National Pact, probably including Constantinople. "I do not understand where we are," scribbled Curzon in desperation on one document; Paris and Rome had already been asked, the newspapers assumed that intervention was an accomplished fact—yet Rumbold, who would have to make the communication to Ankara, opposed it. Then there was Lloyd George. Contacted by phone, the prime minister was, as Curzon was told, "hardly convinced that the Greeks were as badly beaten as they made out; he was anxious to avoid all responsibility of advising them to make an armistice in these circumstances . . . ." He thought the situation parallel to the German panic in 1918 which produced more humiliating terms than the situation warranted. The Greeks should make a direct approach to Ankara if they wished.[56]

The Foreign Office was less willing to shed responsibility so cavalierly. In further conversations with Grigg it was argued that such a procedure would really result in worse terms for the Greeks, and there would be odious responsibility if Britain did nothing in response to the Greek request. Lloyd George was not easily budged and would only agree to British association in some possible postarmistice settlement under

[55] CinC Constantinople telegrams to WO, 2 and 3 September, Lamb (Smyrna) telegram to FO and FO telegram to high commissioner, Constantinople, 2 September, Bentinck telegrams to FO, 3 September, *FO* 371/7885; and 2 September (2 of date) 1922, *DBFP* XVII/755-56.

[56] Curzon note for Tyrrell and Lindsay, 3 September, high commissioner, Constantinople, telegrams to FO, 4 September (nos. 373 and 379), Curzon minute, quoted, in 8874/27, Lindsay note for Curzon, 4 September (quoted), on telephone conversation, 8919/27, *FO* 371/7885; Curzon telegrams to high commissioner, Constantinople, 3 September, and to Hardinge, 4 September, and high commissioner, Constantinople, telegram to FO, 4 September (no. 378) 1922, *DBFP* XVIII/2, 4, 6.

League auspices. Foreign Office personnel found the whole discussion most frustrating with both foreign secretary and prime minister in the country, remote from communications.[57]

With or without Allied cooperation, an armistice was essential if a terrible disaster at Smyrna was to be avoided, to say nothing of a confrontation with Kemal when he arrived at the Dardanelles and had the potential power to close off the Straits. In the end Harington and Rumbold—with at least the cooperation of fearful local Allied commanders— sent a message off to Kemal. There was little optimism, however, for the Greek request was not meant to include Thrace and there was only disadvantage to Kemal in agreeing. The greater danger was that Britain would assume untenable responsibility for Smyrna's defense and risk war with Kemal. It was more of a risk than was later taken at Chanak, in fact, for at Smyrna Britain would have stood with Greece and Kemal would have had less patience. Following the advice of Grigg, the main intermediary between prime minister and Foreign Office at the time, to land sailors in Smyrna in the name of local order and world Christianity would have touched off just such a crisis.[58]

On 7 September the Cabinet heard Curzon's explanation of the events to date. Paris had refused to cooperate in intervention unless the Greeks first guaranteed not to move their troops to Thrace and withdrew to the Enos-Midia line, a very unlikely prospect. Lloyd George, in the discussion which followed, revealed his reasons for failing to support Greece now: he was suspicious that Constantine's government had engineered the whole thing to get out of a difficult situation. The Cabinet took refuge in its previous position; whatever the events in Anatolia, Thrace would still be Greek and Gallipoli Allied. The Paris proposals would still be the basis of negotiation, but whatever happened, these two points would be adhered to. Above all, any attempt Kemal made to force the Straits would be met by force. Harington was given

[57] Grigg phone message from Lloyd George for Curzon, 4 September 1922, FO 800/154 (see DBFP XVIII, note 4, pp. 3-4).

[58] High commissioner, Constantinople, telegram to FO, 6 September, Forbes Adam minute, 6 September, 8900/27, FO 371/7885; Lamb (Smyrna) telegram to FO, 8 September, FO 371/7886; CinC Constantinople telegram to WO, 7 September, FO 371/7887; Grigg for Lloyd George, 6 September, Lloyd George Papers, F/86/2/16; Bentinck and high commissioner, Constantinople, telegrams to FO, 6 September 1922, DBFP XVIII/ 10 and 11.

authority to pull back into Constantinople if the Izmit lines were threatened, but the Turks would not be allowed to push further.[59]

The question was not merely academic, since Greek evacuation of the Bursa-Marmora district was likely in the aftermath of the catastrophe at Smyrna. On 9 September the Turks entered that city, and the next several days' events permanently scarred the minds of those who survived. That tragic story has been told many times and need not be repeated here; more important for British policy was a decision Harington made in Constantinople. The morning of the 10th he warned a meeting of Allied high commissioners that Kemal was thinking of occupying the Asiatic side of the Dardanelles, and he asked as a demonstration of Allied solidarity that small French and Italian contingents be dispatched to join the British troops currently in sole occupation of the zone at Chanak. The French and Italian commanders complied; the decision was urgent, but temporary, for all concerned knew that there were not enough troops to hold both Dardanelles and Bosporus along with Constantinople.[60]

On the 11th an important conference was held at Lloyd George's house at Churt in Surrey. The prime minister decided along with his

[59] Cabinet 48 (22), 7 September, *CAB* 23/31; T. Jones to Curzon, 7 September (2 of date), giving Cabinet conclusions, *Lloyd George Papers,* F/26/2/26-27; Peel private to Reading, 7 September 1922, *Reading Papers,* E. 238/5.

[60] CinC Mediterranean telegrams to Admiralty, 9 and 10 September, high commissioner, Constantinople, telegram to FO, 10 September, *FO* 371/7886; CinC Constantinople telegram to WO, 10 September, *FO* 371/7888, and circular to high commissioners, Constantinople, 10 September, *FO* 371/7889; FO telegram to high commissioner, Constantinople, 10 September 1922, *DBFP* XVIII/20.

On Smyrna, see Housepian, *Smyrna Affair;* Beers, *U.S. Navy,* pp. 9-10; Edward Hale Bierstadt, *The Great Betrayal . . .* (London, [1924]), pp. 29-36; George Horton, *The Blight of Asia . . . with the True Story of the Burning of Smyrna* (Indianapolis, 1926), and *Recollections Grave and Gay . . .* (Indianapolis, 1927), by the American consul at Smyrna; Clare Sheridan, *Nuda Veritas* (London, 1927), pp. 279-85; Walder, *Chanak,* pp. 169-77; Smith, *Ionian Vision,* Ch. XIII; Admiral Sir Barry Domville, *By and Large* (London, 1936), pp. 40-66; Edwards, *Grey Diplomatists,* pp. 44ff.; Thomas Woodrooffe, *Naval Odyssey* (London, 1936), pp. 157-75; Lysimachos Oeconomos, *The Martyrdom of Smyrna . . .* (London, 1922); Cmd. Laurence Bernard, "Smyrna and the Dardanelles, 1922," in Brian Tunstall, ed., *The Anatomy of Neptune* (London 1936), 334-352.

minister of war and military commanders (but not Curzon) that Gallipoli was the place to stand, and British troops should withdraw to that
position before Kemal threatened them at Chanak on the Asian side.
"There was no present intention of defending Chanak by land reinforcements," said the conclusions, and both Rumbold and Harington were so
informed. But Harington had already asked Allied cooperation in defending Chanak—thereby exceeding his authority as Curzon saw it—
and at the same time he advised London that British troops alone could
not hold on the Asian side. "If we don't look out the generals will land
us in a first class mess," said Curzon, and he saw to it at least that the
group at Churt focused attention on Chanak long enough to approve
his draft to Rumbold, which went out on the same day.[61]

The Cabinet's policy, Rumbold was told, was to maintain the position in Europe while liquidating the position in Anatolia. Therefore
Chanak would not be held unless, "which is most unlikely," the French
and Italians were prepared to join in its defense. Britain would hold
Gallipoli, with or without the Allies. Harington was therefore given
discretion to evacuate Chanak, although evacuation might be postponed
if French and Italian troops were placed there. Of course that is exactly
what Harington had already asked of the Allies and he was worried
that London might undermine his position. Kemal had been told that
the Allies were united, and "to recede from this position would be fatal,"
for it would then appear that Britain had deliberately tricked her allies
into coming over to Chanak. By Britain, Harington really meant Harington, but in any case his old optimism was at work: "Nationalists will
only threaten and will not attack Allies . . .," he cabled, although the
same telegram added, "Do not let us run away before danger is imminent," which implied that the danger might become so. The Turks
were only awaiting a sign from Britain to become reasonable.[62]

Harington's optimism was infectious. It was a pity, Curzon phoned
the War Office to say, to abandon Chanak and Izmit now that the Al-

[61] Conference of Ministers (quoted), 9207/27, WO telegram to CinC
Constantinople (appendix II), and Curzon minute for Tyrrell (quoted),
9244/27, all 11 September, *FO* 371/7887; Curzon telegram to high commissioner, Constantinople, 11 September 1922, *DBFP* XVIII/21.

[62] WO telegram, note 61, chapter 7; Admiralty telegram to CinC Mediterranean, 11 September, and CinC Constantinople telegram to WO, no.
2248, 4 parts (quoted), 12 September 1922, 9287/27, *FO* 371/7887 (and
see *DBFP* XVIII, note 6, p. 20, and note 4, p. 22).

lies appeared to be cooperating. The War Office agreed. Rumbold was told that "these positions, which as long as they are held by the allies Kemal is not likely to attack, may constitute a useful pawn in negotiations with him." Curzon's prediction was based on Harington's own assessment and nothing more, just as his appreciation of Allied cooperation was based on Harington's request to his local Allied colleagues. A request for cooperation, however, was not the same thing as actual cooperation at all. Harington was the local commander; any general given responsibility to go or stay is always placed in an odious position, for if he goes, critics will say he did so too soon, and if he faces a crisis, he waited too long. But upon Harington falls much of the responsibility for staying at Chanak and thus for the subsequent confrontation.[63]

Mustafa Kemal had now emerged from the fog of Anatolian obscurity. On the 13th he told the British representative at Smyrna that he considered himself "in a state of war with Great Britain." Curzon requested confirmation of this most disquieting news, meanwhile writing and discarding desperate draft appeals for Allied assistance (and defending himself against charges that he earlier had refused to meet with a Kemalist representative, as if that would have made any difference). Fortunately, Kemal was conciliatory; his remark had been unofficial, and there was no war. But neither was there peace, and some formalities would be required. Despite some immediate relief, the situation was still most dangerous, particularly if Paris and Rome disavowed the actions of their local commanders and Kemal tested Britain's declared intention to hold Constantinople and Gallipoli with force.[64]

Rumbold's appreciation of Kemal's intentions was pessimistic, but far worse was Harington's frank report that the French and Italian detachments had not arrived as promised. "I hope to-morrow but there

[63] Oliphant note for Col. Bartholemew, WO, 13 September, 9277/27, FO 371/7887; FO telegram to high commissioner, Constantinople, no. 385, 13 September 1922 (quoted), DBFP XVIII/26.

[64] FO telegram to Hardinge, 11 September, CinC Mediterranean telegram to Admiralty (Lamb for FO, quoted) and high commissioner, Constantinople, telegram to FO, 13 September, FO 371/7887; high commissioner, Constantinople, telegram to FO, FO telegram to Hardinge, and Lamb telegram to high commissioner, Constantinople, all 13 September, DBFP XVIII/23, 25, and note 3, pp. 23-24; draft of letter by Curzon, 12 September 1922 (not sent, in Curzon's handwriting), Curzon Papers, F/9/3.

are excuses daily . . . . It is possible that when it comes to business they may not return compliment of allied unity which I showed over Chatal-ja" when the Greeks threatened to move; Harington was an honest and capable soldier, but he was here sinking in unfathomable diplomatic depths. The afternoon of the 15th the Cabinet heard an explanation from Worthington-Evans: one British battalion at Chanak had actually been joined by a small Italian (but no French) detachment. The Greeks had gone from Smyrna, now partially in smoldering ruins, and were soon to withdraw from Pandirma and Mudanya on the Marmora coast. Obviously, there was no need for any armistice nor a meeting to arrange one.[65]

The point raised now was unsettling at least to Curzon, for Harington and Rumbold agreed that both sides of the Dardanelles were essential for security: it would not be enough to hold Gallipoli. That would require allies, and to Curzon France was the only possibility. But, asked Chamberlain, was Britain to hold the Dardanelles indefinitely? Like Lord Peel, Montagu's successor in the India Office, Chamberlain felt that all this could only be temporary and in any case would have unfortunate repercussions on Mosul or India. Worse still, added Peel, to fight and be beaten. To Lloyd George, however, defeat was an unthinkable word: Britain could not run away from Kemal. Freedom of the Straits and security for Iraq were both of supreme importance, and the

[65] High commissioner, Constantinople, telegram to FO, 15 September, *DBFP* XVIII/27; CinC Constantinople telegram to WO, 14 September (quoted), *FO* 371/7888; Cabinet 49 (22), 15 September 1922, *CAB* 23/31. C.P. Scott, *Political Diaries* (Ithaca, N.Y., 1970), pp. 425-26, records a conversation between Scott and Lloyd George at lunch before the Cabinet; according to Scott, Lloyd George at that time believed that Constantine had engineered the whole retreat.

On the Chanak crisis from the British political standpoint (aside from Walder, *Chanak*), see Beaverbrook, *Decline and Fall*, pp. 159-88; Blake, *UnrepentantTory*, pp. 447-52; Ronaldshay, *Curzon*, III, Ch. XVII-XVIII; Nicolson, *Curzon*, Ch. IX; Churchill, *World Crisis*, V, Ch. XIX; Randolph S. Churchill, *Lord Derby . . .* (N.Y., 1960), pp. 439-40; Birkenhead, *Birkenhead*, II, pp. 176-79; Keith Middlemas and John Barnes, *Baldwin: A Biography* (N.Y., 1970), pp. 112-18; Robert A. Huttenback, *The British Imperial Experience* (N.Y., 1966), pp. 166-67; D.C. Watt, *Personalities and Policies . . .* (South Bend, Indiana, 1965), p. 147; "Australia," "Canada," "New Zealand," "South Africa," *The Round Table* 13 (1923): 183-84, 176-77, 453-56, 199-201.

real problem was only men. Britain would not go to France on her knees. There were other cards to play; Rumania needed the Straits for survival—surely they would pitch in, and with them the other Balkan states. Then there were the Dominions. Curzon warned against placing too much hope on the Balkans, but the decisions were taken: Curzon to Paris, Churchill to ask the Dominions, and requests to be sent off to the Balkans. One thing only was not done: the reserves would not be mobilized. That evening Lloyd George, scornful of Curzon, worked out with Hankey the detailed instructions to all concerned.[66]

The situation now, Curzon reported to Rumbold, was that while all possible men would be brought up from these various sources, the way to safety lay in a new conference to rewrite the basic treaty. Success would depend upon the result of his forthcoming trip to Paris, and meanwhile it was up to Rumbold and Harington. There was little point, however, in keeping a stiff upper lip of this sort to Hardinge, now ambassador in Paris. "But the French and Italians," he wrote privately, enclosing his telegram to Rumbold, "are so profoundly to be distrusted that it is possible at any moment that they may afford [Kemal] an opening by withdrawing their detachments and so to speak letting him in . . .". Lloyd George expected to conjure Balkan armies out of the air—even, after some happy moments at Genoa, to get Italian support at the proposed conference. "He would not of course go. He would send me to fight the battle and to bear the brunt of defeat." Curzon distrusted Italy even more than France, if possible, but Hardinge was to do his best to determine how much the French would hold to the original Paris proposals.[67]

On the 19th Curzon had his answer, from both the French chargé in London and Hardinge in Paris: France preferred to concede the National Pact to Kemal and was even now ordering the French commissioner to withdraw any French forces in the neutral zone at Chanak (in the end, the local commander had sent less than 100 men). The

[66] Lloyd George private to Curzon, 15 September, *Lloyd George Papers,* F/13/3/33; WO telegram to CinC Constantinople, 16 September 1922, and file of telegrams to and from dominions (9774/27 and see C.P. 4200), *FO* 371/7891-92; Riddell, *Diary,* pp. 386-87, reports on Lloyd George's scorn at dinner on the 15th; also Roskill, *Hankey,* II, pp. 283-84.

[67] Curzon private telegram to Rumbold, 16 September, *DBFP* XVIII/32, drafts in 9674/27, *FO* 371/7891; Curzon private to Hardinge, 16 September 1922, quoted, *FO* 800/157.

Dominions had returned a generally unenthusiastic or delaying response, with the sole exception of New Zealand, which offered a battalion. India, fortunately, was not a dominion, and so had no chance to refuse help. As for the Balkan states, the French continued to regard this area as their own diplomatic preserve, not including a Greece with which they utterly refused to cooperate.[68]

Reports of these developments tended to be counteracted by Harington's buoyancy, which stemmed from his confidence in "the knowledge that business is meant by Allies when they speak with one voice and that Mustapha will be taught lesson he wants and shown that solution of this question is by conference and not by bloodshed," he cabled on the 18th (rewritten by the War Office cipher office—but it was the paraphrase which the cabinet read). In another telegram the same day he wrote, "I do not anticipate any bother so long as we show allied determination." The War Office tried to let him down gently: "It will be some days before we shall know what form if any French co-operation will take"; even that was misleading, for French backing was only a hope. Harington remained confident, but even his forcefulness was slipping, for the "one voice" did not exist. By the 19th his conviction that Kemal would do nothing was also shaky: "British policy is going to be tested here at Chanak in my opinion. A withdrawal without fighting would be a signal for an outbreak here which we must avoid and which with present resources we might not be able to cope with."[69]

The only additional resources, however, would have to be British. The French in Constantinople cooperated sufficiently to send a note to Kemal on the 18th to warn him away from the neutral zones, but their order to withdraw still stood. Moreover, Paris had intervened in Bucharest to ensure that the Rumanians withdrew their original indication of support. On the 19th Hardinge taxed Poincaré with his actions, only to be met with a long tirade against British warmongering. "I

[68] Cabinet 50 (22), appendix I-III, Cabinet conferences, 18 (noon and 5 p.m.) and 19 September, *CAB* 23/31; Hardinge telegram to FO, 18 September, *FO* 371/7889, and phone conversation from Paris, 19 September 1922, 9529/27, *FO* 371/7890.

[69] CinC Constantinople telegrams to WO, 18 September, nos. 2304-5, both quoted, WO telegram to CinC Constantinople, 18 September (quoted), with Osborne minute ("How wrong!"), 9655/27, *FO* 371/7891; CinC Constantinople telegram to WO, 19 September (sent 1 A.M., 20 September) 1922, no. 2335, quoted, *FO* 371/7893.

told him flatly that I would not allow him to say that sort of thing to me," reported Hardinge, and Poincaré then calmed down, admitting he was simply worried about Chanak. Withdrawal would only come in full coordination with Harington, but French opinion would not permit lives to be spent on this: an immediate conference was the answer, but Kemal would not come unless assured that he would obtain his territorial demands.[70]

The next day, Curzon met Poincaré in Paris. "I had risen from a bed of sickness in England in a state quite unfit for any prolonged strain," he wrote later, and Poincaré's anger provided more than enough strain. In "a rather lively scene" Poincaré once more repudiated the French high commissioner's action in the Chanak defenses. Only on the conference did they agree. Poincaré worried that Kemal might be pushed by extremist followers into some precipitate action which he did not desire, such as trying to cross the Straits. This possibility he had learned in a conversation with Kemal's representative the day before, he told Curzon. Curzon, however, may have had intercepts which indicated that the same Paris representative was urging Kemal to cross the Straits, or at least assuring him that he would meet no resistance at Chanak. If such advice was offered, perhaps it was because Poincaré had told the Turks there would be no French cooperation in the British plans.[71]

[70] Hardinge telegram to FO, 19 September (quoted), high commissioner, Constantinople, telegram to FO and Sir H. Dering (Bucharest) telegram to FO, 20 September, *DBFP* XVIII/35-36, 39; Dering to Curzon, 19 and 20 September 1922, *FO* 371/7894.

[71] Curzon note, undated, on file cover on Poincaré negotiations, September, quoted, *Curzon Papers,* F/9/3; Curzon telephone message for Cabinet, 20 September (8 P.M., quoted), Hardinge telephone message to FO, 20 September (2 of date) and 21 September, 9624, 9643, 9675-76/27, *FO* 371/7891; Allied conferences, 20 September 1922, *DBFP* XVIII/41-42; Roskill, *Hankey,* II, p. 187.

The intercept, Ferid Pasha telegram to Ministry of Foreign Affairs, Ankara, 20 September 1922, *Lloyd George Papers,* F/209/3 (a file of intercepts which includes American, Italian, Japanese, Turkish, Greek, German, and Russian communications), said, "CHANAK is open to our victorious army and it is possible to believe that even British troops will not be met with"; if an attempt was made to cross the Straits, it would strengthen Loyd George's hand, so therefore it was best to wait. "In my opinion our coming to CHANAK is sufficient threat to force EUROPE to abandon the positions up to the MARITZA boundary." It is probable that Curzon read these cables, but it is not clear when they were received in London.

Curzon could not lose sight of his objective—preconference Allied agreement. Poincaré's statements left no doubt about France's position: the Allies would first have to concede the National Pact terms, and in any case France would not participate militarily on the Asian side of the Straits. The Cabinet in London, with the wind in its sails, disregarded Curzon's reports from Paris; on the early evening of the 20th, out of ignorance, or arrogance, or a false sense of security, or, most likely of all, conviction that an unalterable commitment had been made, it concluded that "apart from its military importance, Chanak had now become a point of great moral significance to the prestige of the Empire," for somehow prestige had come to be measured in a few miles of wire at Chanak. Despite this general resolution, in its next meeting (noon of the 21st) the Cabinet gave full latitude to Curzon in negotiation on the Straits, Constantinople, and other issues, provided only that the Asiatic side would be treated as an integral part of the Dardanelles.[72]

When Curzon met Poincaré on the 22nd such niceties were academic. "Have just returned from meeting of quite unprecedented description," he cabled. Poincaré had exploded when Curzon remarked that if Harington were forced to pull out, the reproach would be against these who abandoned him. Poincaré's anger was to some extent justified, for it was his local high commissioner (Pellé) who had agreed to share in Chanak, not the Paris which had disowned him. To Poincaré, it was Harington's fault for misrepresenting the French and Italian local action as government policy. That Harington's mistake in this regard was logical Poincaré was not prepared to admit. In the end, Poincaré

> lost all command of his temper, and for a quarter of an hour shouted and raved at the top of his voice, putting words into my mouth which I had never uttered, refusing to permit the slightest interruption or correction . . . and behaving like a demented schoolmaster screaming at a guilty school-boy. I have never seen so deplorable or undignified a scene. After enduring this for some time I could stand it no longer and

[72] Cabinet 50 (22), appendix IV and V, Conference of Ministers, 20 September (6:30) 1922, *CAB* 23/31; Churchill's explanation (*World Crisis,* V, pp. 448-49) had too much of the vision of hindsight: "When one knew that a single gesture would immediately restore to them full control of the event, it was surely worth making an effort."

rising, broke up the sitting and left the room. Monsieur Poincaré ultimately came out and made an apology . . . .

But Curzon's account puts himself in the best possible light; as he later
wrote, "on the 3rd day I temporarily broke down . . ." under Poincaré's
badgering.[73] Hardinge, no admirer of Poincaré, had only contempt
for Curzon's collapse; "really the spectacle of Curzon," he wrote later,
"extended in another room, tears pouring down his face and a brandy
bottle by his side, speaking in maudlin tones, was a sight that I shall
not easily forget, as it was so absolutely lacking in dignity and restraint."[74]

The basic disagreement was, above all, over Thrace. Poincaré wanted
to give Kemal the Maritsa frontier and Adrianople immediately. Curzon
would not accept this plan, but neither would Poincaré accept Curzon's
suggestion that Harington and Kemal work out stop lines for the respective military forces pending a conference. The Cabinet, doubtless
aware that the situation was deteriorating along the Straits, could do
little except advise Curzon to hold firm on Thrace while they hurried
reinforcements to Harington. Despite considerable persistence, Curzon
finally had to give way: in the draft communication for Ankara, Kemal
would be asked whether he was ready to negotiate on the basis of Thrace
as far as the Maritsa River (essentially the pre-1914 frontier). For their
part the Turks would have to respect the neutral zones, which would
also become Turkish with suitable demilitarization safeguards.[75]

The danger was that the offer might be too late. Harington reported
on the 24th that Turkish cavalry had pushed into the neutral zone at

[73] Hardinge (from Curzon) telegram to FO (quoted), 22 September,
FO 371/7892; official notes, 22 September sessions, 2 P.M., DBFP XVIII/
48 (minutes show rewritten by Curzon before printed, FO 371/7893);
French official minutes in French Embassy to FO, 5 October 1922, 10908/
27, FO 371/7901; Curzon's later account, quoted, is from covering folder
on Poincaré negotiations, Curzon Papers, F/9/3.

[74] Hardinge's remark is taken from the manuscript draft of his memoirs,
vol. III, p. 122 (South Park, Kent). The author wishes to thank the Dowager
Lady Hardinge of Penshurst for access to this source. A much milder account actually was published; see Lord Hardinge of Penshurst, Old Diplomacy (London, 1947), p. 273.

[75] High commissioner, Constantinople, telegram to FO and Anglo-
French meeting, both 23 September, DBFP XVIII/50-51; Hardinge telegram to FO, 23 September, FO 371/7893; Cabinet 50 (22), 23 September,
CAB 23/31; The Times, 25 September 1922; Hyde, Reading, pp. 377-79.

Chanak (a wired perimeter four miles long, with two battalions on the line and one and a half in reserve). Brigadier Shuttleworth, the local commander (Harington remained in Constantinople; he had still to watch Thrace, Constantinople, and Izmit as well), had warned the Turkish commander that the British would fire if the Turks did not pull back. The Turks had done so for the time being, but there was no assurance that they would not return in force.[76]

On the 26th Curzon reported to the Cabinet on his adventures in Paris. Fearful that Kemal might demand British evacuation before accepting the conference invitation, he advised against pouring more troops into the Chanak position. Here he was overruled, but even Churchill was anxious now. While still breathing fire, he had thought the perimeter was fifteen miles and was shocked to find it only four; the whole point of Chanak was to stop the Turks from dominating the Dardanelles and if they could do so from the hills further back the risk now being run was purposeless. But it was rather too late to alter the plans; the reinforcements would still be sent, and Harington's orders were still to hold on. Knowing the extent of the perimeter and the danger, the reasons now for staying—all references to suitable Straits regime, minority protection, and the like aside—were prestige and bluff. Worse yet, in this bluff Britain had no allies, not even the Dominions, and it was in a weak and limited defense position of little real purpose.[77]

Fortunately Kemalist diplomacy now rose to the occasion. On the 27th the *Daily Telegraph* reprinted an interview with Kemal by a reporter from the Chicago *Tribune* which was read by all concerned Foreign Office officials, including Curzon. Turkey, Kemal was supposed to have said, was prepared to give every reasonable guarantee on the freedom of the Straits if the powers would give equally adequate guarantees on the safety of Marmora and Constantinople. Properly worked out—and Kemal would accept a mixed commission for this task—there need be no Straits fortifications. Christian minorities would be dealt with by population exchange. In fact, the only unacceptable point from the British view was Kemal's claim to Mosul.[78]

[76] CinC Constantinople telegrams to WO, nos. 2415, 2420, 2427, all 24 September 1922, *FO* 371/7895.

[77] Cabinet 51 (22), 26 September 1922, *CAB* 23/31.

[78] *Daily Telegraph,* 27 September 1922; copy in 9873/27, *FO* 371/7893.

The interview was not an official offer, of course, and Cabinet positions had become virtually inflexible. Lloyd George, in a private meeting with some ministers that afternoon and again in a Cabinet meeting that evening, proved as foolish on Chanak as he had been on Greece: "the greatest loss of prestige which could possibly be inflicted upon the British Empire" would result from withdrawal. Not quite, said Churchill; far worse to be driven out by military defeat. But Churchill, too, was concerned that withdrawal would make Britain the world's laughingstock. If Britain was forced out of Izmit, or Constantinople, or Gallipoli, the blame could be placed on Allied treachery; for Chanak, it had only itself to blame.[79]

Kemal was not simply going to let the British remain. His reply to the formal demarche of the Allies, Rumbold reported on the 27th, was that he recognized no neutral zones. He was merely pursuing Greeks, as he put it, and, in passing, referred to Greek use of Constantinople, a reference which prompted Rumbold to initiate the departure of all Greek ships from Constantinople. Chanak, not Constantinople, was the immediate crisis point, however, and Major-General T.O. Marden, now in charge of the growing forces, reported that the Turks were entirely disregarding the neutral zone and pushing up against the British lines. It made little difference, save that of added confusion, that Chanak was not in the "netural zones" outlined to Kemal; those zones had been defined by the presence of Allied occupation and the absence of Greco-Turkish fighting, while London, completely uninformed on the details, assumed that "neutral zones" meant those described in the Treaty of Sèvres. Harington was more concerned about the increasing prospect of a clash than the legal niceties; there were no Greeks in the neutral zone, as he told Kemal. Harington would have gone further and let the Turks into Thrace as far as Maritsa, although this was contrary to the Paris proposals and to orders already issued by London to the military commanders.[80]

[79] Cabinet 52 (22), appendix I, Conference of Ministers, 27 September, 7 P.M. (quoted, see also Cabinet 56 (22), appendix V), *CAB* 23/31; private meeting is in special series, S-65, 27 September 1922, 3 P.M., *CAB* 23/36.

[80] High commissioner, Constantinople, telegrams to FO, 27 September, (nos. 466-68), FO telegrams to high commissioner, Constantinople, 28 September, *DBFP* XVIII/62-64, 69-70; CinC Constantinople telegram to WO, 28 September 1922 (no. 1223), *FO* 371/7896.

The Cabinet met twice on the 28th to consider these reports. The morning meeting wisely considered British objectives: what actually were they at Chanak for? The answer was peace in Turkey (although not to be enforced upon the warring parties); freedom of the Straits (for which force would be used if necessary); and preservation if the alliance with France and Italy (but Britain would stay at Gallipoli with or without allies). If serious fighting developed at Chanak, more reinforcements would be ordered, mobilization decreed, and Parliament summoned from its summer adjournment. No decision was taken on Harington's proposal to let the Greeks into Thrace. That afternoon, the Cabinet held firm to its decisions, although Harington was to be at liberty to withdraw from Constantinople if he needed the troops at Chanak or Gallipoli. Harington's other idea—a personal meeting with Kemal—was vetoed, at least if Harington were unaccompanied. That evening the continued Cabinet muddle resulted in a telegram which did no good at all: "Our policy is to hold Gallipoli at all costs and to hold on to Chanak so long as this can be done without undue military risk."[81]

Harington, in a certain poetic justice, thus had full responsibility for an increasingly dangerous situation. Turkish cavalry were making faces through the wire, he reported, and while Kemal had said that he hoped a satisfactory settlement could be worked out in negotiations at Mudanya, he had also said that he could not now withdraw his troops. Harington hoped the Cabinet would permit him to let the Turks into Thrace as a way to ease the tension, but the Cabinet, meeting now in almost continual session, disapproved the idea on the 29th, for it would require telling the Greeks to pull back beyond the Maritsa and would thus be a further concession to Kemalist pressure. Quite the contrary, a telegram to Harington told him to issue Kemal an ultimatum: the Turks must withdraw from the British perimeter by a specified time or be fired upon. Curzon begged for delay; he had consulted with a spokesman for Kemal who had been most surprised at the extent of the crisis and who had promised to communicate with Kemal. Another factor pro-

---

[81] Cabinet 52 (22), appendix II-IV, 11 A.M., 4 and 7 P.M., 28 September 1922 (appendix IV includes WO telegram to CinC Constantinople, 11 P.M., 28 September, quoted), *CAB* 23/31; Roskill, *Hankey,* II, pp. 289-90, reports on dinner meeting of the 27th of Hankey, Churchill, and Lloyd George.

ducing uncertainty was a coup d'etat in Athens by Venizelist officers pledged to punish those guilty for the Anatolian disaster. Constantine had abdicated and been replaced by George II, a puppet in army hands until his own departure after Venizelos's election victories in December 1923. Curzon asked for twenty-four hours. The request was refused, because, said the military, countermanding the order now would only create chaos.[82]

The Cabinet spent the next day in agonized suspense. Harington had not yet acknowledged the ultimatum order (although the Admiral on the spot had done so). Indeed he and Rumbold appeared still to contemplate meeting Kemal at Mudanya, despite the threatening or even "impossible" situation which General Marden had reported. Harington, it was decided, should demand Turkish withdrawal from the wire as an essential preliminary to any meeting. When the full Cabinet met the evening of Saturday the 30th, some members urged that Harington should be ordered to deliver the ultimatum without awaiting the general's explanation; wisely, the suggestion was rejected, and shortly after midnight Harington's report came in.[83]

Harington noted the Cabinet's decision, but he much preferred to retain freedom of action. There was no serious danger unless the Turks brought up heavy guns and infantry, and in the meantime Marden's eight battalions backed by naval and aerial firepower could hold out. Ankara was even now drawing up a reply to the Allied proposal, and it was the wrong time to jeopardize a peaceful solution. Marden had the authority to take action when necessary, but if Britain fired first, she would appear the aggressor, and Harington would have to use all his

[82] FO telegram to Hardinge, no. 332, 30 September, and to high commissioner, Constantinople, no. 447, 29 September, *DBFP* XVIII/72-73; and letter to high commissioner, Constantinople, 29 September, *FO* 371/7896; CinC Constantinople telegram to WO, no. 2506, 28 September, *FO* 371/7899; Lindley to Curzon, 1 October, *FO* 371/7586 (and for further details on Greek developments, *FO* 371/7586-8); Cabinet 52 (22), appendix V-VI, Cabinet conferences, 11:30 A.M. and 10 P.M., 29 September 1922, *CAB* 23/31.

[83] Cabinet 53 (22), 30 September, 10:30 A.M., Cabinet 56 (22), appendix V, Conference, 30 September, 4 P.M., Cabinet 53 (22), appendix I, conference, 30 September, 7:45 P.M., Cabinet 52 (22), 30 September, 5 P.M., *CAB* 23/31; CinC Constantinople telegram to WO, no. 2538, 30 September 1922 (11:30 P.M., received 12:50 A.M., 1 October), *FO* 371/7899; Roskill, *Hankey,* II, pp. 290-91.

reserves (meaning evacuation of Constantinople). The position *had* been impossible, but the recent arrival of reinforcements and the extension of the perimeter had created a safer position. If Kemal's reply was unsatisfactory, then would be the time for an ultimatum. Harington (and Rumbold and Admiral Brock who agreed with him) had shown considerable wisdom—but it had been Harington's previous report which inspired the ultimatum in the first instance. The Cabinet looked rather foolish, and knew it, particularly when a paraphrased telegram from Harington included the sentence, "It was never dangerous." Marden had been more worried, but the Cabinet was unaware of that fact.[84]

The Cabinet meeting on Sunday morning, 1 October, still was without up-to-date information, but it was clear "without any implication of censure" that the ultimatum had been drawn up "on the basis of information received exclusively from the Constantinople command." The Cabinet might have been more relieved—and more censorious of Harington—had it known then that Kemal had agreed to negotiate at Mudanya. The French claimed credit for this decision; two hard days' negotiation had been necessary, Poincaré claimed, for Franklin-Bouillon to persuade Kemal to talk. The Turks would meet at Mudanya on the 3rd, the discussions to be based on Greek evacuation of Thrace and temporary inter-Allied occupation until the final settlement.[85]

Negotiations up to and including the discussions at Mudanya were complicated, but the main issue was Thrace, as usual. Kemal's negotiator, Ismet Pasha, demanded Turkish occupation as a prerequisite to settlement. After three days' negotiation, with another crisis at hand over just this point, Curzon once more headed for Paris. This time, however, the Cabinet was wavering on Thrace, particularly since Rumbold advised giving in and handing over the civil administration (but not military occupation) to Kemal. In Paris, Poincaré needed no display of

[84] WO to FO, 9 October, *FO* 371/7902, gives figures of garrison: by the 9th of October, eight infantry battalions, one regiment of cavalry totalling some 6000 men; CinC Constantinople telegram to WO, 30 September (quoted), *FO* 371/7899; Marden to Admiral Sir John Kelly (in command of Fleet units), 1 October 1922, *Kelly Papers* (National Maritime Museum), KEL/107.

[85] Cabinet 54 (22), 1 October, 10 A.M. (quoted), and 55 (22), 1 October, 3 P.M., *CAB* 23/31; Hardinge telephone report to FO, no. 494, 1 October 1922, 10276/27, *FO* 371/7897.

anger, for Curzon had little ground upon which to stand. In the end, he got only a face-saving concession: there would be inter-Allied control of Thrace but only for one month. Time again appeared to run out as Kemal's answer was awaited; the Turkish cavalry was reported advancing into the Izmit zone, while the Mudanya negotiations were adjourned and Harington prepared an ultimatum of his own.[86]

In the early hours of 11 October agreement was reached and the Convention of Mudanya signed; so rapidly had events outpaced lethargic official reports that the Foreign Office's first look at the terms was in the *Daily Mail.* Within fifteen days, the Greeks were to be out of eastern Thrace; within thirty days, the whole transfer, including civil administration, would be completed, with an inter-Allied mission to supervise in the interim. Kemal's troops, pending the opening of the conference, would keep out of the neutral zones; these were Gallipoli, Izmit, and Constantinople—but not Chanak.[87]

The immediate crisis was over, although it was by no means the last moment of Anglo-Turkish tension even in the year 1922. Without war, the Allies had abandoned their hold upon Turkey. Chanak would only be held now as a temporary outpost, a fact inspiring the same sort of relief in some as did the withdrawal from Batum and Baku and Enzeli. And yet, it was all unnecessary, a commitment to little purpose, made in London in a heavy fog at least as poisonous as the "fog of war." The situation at Chanak, even the size of the foothold, was as unknown as the reasons for which the decision was made—save to avoid being a "laughingstock." Harington's reports had inspired the ultimatum, but the decision was made in London, in an atmosphere of political crisis (Lloyd George would not finish the month in office) and short-

---

[86] FO telegram to Hardinge, 6 October, *FO* 371/7899; high commissioner, Constantinople, telegrams to FO, 5 October (nos. 512, 514), 6 October (nos. 523-24), and 8 October (nos. 533 and 547), and Anglo-French meeting, 6-7 October, *DBFP* XVIII/91, 93, 96-97, 112-13, 106-8; Cabinet 56-59 (22), 5-7 October, *CAB* 23/31; Hardinge telephone (and telegram) to FO, 7 October, *FO* 371/7900; CinC Constantinople telegrams D. 19 and D. 21, 8 October 1922, *FO* 371/7902.

[87] High commissioner, Constantinople, telegrams to FO (nos. 549-50), 10 October, Crowe memorandum, 12 October, *DBFP* XVIII/117-18, 122; CinC Constantinople telegram to WO, 12 October, *FO* 371/7903; high commissioner, Constantinople, to FO, 12 October 1922, *FO* 371/7905; Walder, *Chanak,* Ch. XVII.

sightedness. The disaster of Smyrna took Britain as much by surprise as the Greeks, for Britain had disregarded all military warning to the contrary. The crucial hour was on Saturday evening, when the order to Harington to deliver the ultimatum nearly forced a war. Some seem to have contemplated resignation if it had come to that—but fortunately it did not.[88]

Britain was thus the last Allied state to acknowledge the realities of Turkish nationalism and withdraw—at far less cost, despite the delay, than Greece, or even France in Cilicia. Chanak was not a crisis toward which British postwar diplomacy inevitably built; it was only one in a series of lessons in reality, faced in Batum, and Teheran, and Kabul, and Baghdad, or even in Amritsar and Delhi and Calcutta. Isolated treatment of Chanak overemphasizes British pigheadedness and magnifies the crisis out of proportion, just as isolated consideration of French policy in Cilicia graces Paris with a wisdom it so lacked in Syria—and freedom to deal at liberty with Damascus was a primary French motive for cutting losses in Anatolia. Chanak could, save for the strategic importance of the Dardanelles, as easily have occurred at Izmit, or Smyrna, or Mosul. It was surely time for Britain to study its whole Middle Eastern policy, but there was too little time for either study or recrimination. A conference was urgently necessary, and at once, or Mosul or Izmit might become a second Chanak, and this time with serious bloodshed.

[88] Sir Arthur S. Boscowan (minister of agriculture) private to Curzon, 2 October, and Lord Peel private to Curzon, 3 October, both indicated that they would have supported Curzon in resignation (and see Curzon's draft letter of resignation, 14 October 1922), *Curzon Papers,* F/1/7 and F/5.

VIII

Aftermath:
Lausanne, 1922-1923

The conference and treaty of Lausanne serve as a major landmark in the recent history of the Middle East. This would be true had the treaty simply recognized nationalist Turkey, but in actuality it did much more. Settlement with Turkey also determined Britain's Asian frontier in the general sense, from Thrace to Iraq, so although other historians have covered the negotiations in detail, some aspects must be reviewed here.

The first problem, chronologically, was to find an acceptable locale for the meeting. The Greeks first made the obvious suggestion that it be held in some neutral spot, and the Foreign Office agreed. Switzerland was the equally obvious choice, but it was not desirable to meet at Geneva, home of the League of Nations. It was hoped the Americans would participate, but the United States was not a member of the League, and there were problems with sending a delegation to Geneva. Lausanne was a pleasant resort city on the direct Orient Express rail line to Constantinople, with many hotels and a moderate climate in winter, and it had been the seat of the Italo-Turkish negotiations of 1912. The second issue was the question of participation. The United States, Russia, and the Balkan states all presented particular problems; since each country should be heard but should not be allowed to intervene on every issue, it was decided that the conference would be composed of states which had been at war with Turkey, although any concerned party would be heard.[1]

---

[1] Lindsay note for Curzon, 11 October, Curzon to Hardinge, 13 October, and memorandum, 26 September, 11084/27, *FO* 371/7903; FO telegram to Hardinge, 12 October, *DBFP* XVIII/121; Cabinet 62A (22), 13 October, *CAB* 23/31; Harvey to secretary of state, 12 October, Hughes telegram to Herrick, 27 October 1922, *FRUS,* 1923, II, pp. 884-85.

There were other organizational problems. India, for example, wished to be represented, but the precedent of Sèvres in 1920, not Paris in 1919, was used: two delegates (signatories) for each country only. Curzon and Rumbold as high commissioner would speak for Britain. France had another proposal which had to be argued down, suggesting that one conference deal with Kemal and Turkey and another, separate meeting treat the Straits (thus only the second would involve Russia and Bulgaria). Discussion on such matters—together with the unavoidable need for each state to prepare its case—tended to delay the meeting. Paris had originally wished to set the first week in November, but Curzon needed time to prepare, and then, as the date approached, he was caught up in a major political crisis.[2]

On 19 October Lloyd George was brought down by his enemies (and some of his friends); on 23 October Bonar Law took on the difficult task of forming a new government and preparing for the general election in mid-November. Curzon was an old opponent of Lloyd George, as well as being a Conservative (Unionist) leader, and although his was not a major role, he did defect from the coalition. Shortly before the crisis, Lloyd George had attempted to keep Curzon aboard the sinking ship, but Curzon, according to his own account (no third party was present), taxed Lloyd George with all his deviousness, the secret meetings, the intercepts: it was clear where Curzon stood. Lloyd George did not fall solely because of Chanak and the failure of his Greco-Turkish policy; Ireland, Russia, Egypt, unemployment, coal strike . . . it is difficult and unnecessary to determine which issue was uppermost in the mind of any one of the plotters. The change meant that Curzon's task at Lausanne was easier to the extent that he need not fear his prime minister was plotting behind his back, but by delaying the conference until the week after the general election, further Kemalist pressure was permitted to build up as the Thracian time limit formulated with such difficulty at Mudanya expired.[3]

[2] Viceroy telegrams to SSI, 3 and 11 September and 2 October (C.P. 4186 and 4263), *FO* 371/7872 and 7901; Poincaré private to Curzon, 14 and 19 October, Curzon private to Poincaré, 18 and 20 October, *FO* 371/7904-5; Peel private telegrams to Reading, 2 and 11 November, Reading private telegram to Peel, 5 November 1922, *Reading Papers,* E. 238/16.

[3] On the crisis, see Curzon's memorandum on the fall of Lloyd George (end of October, 1922), *Curzon Papers,* F/1/7, partially quoted in Kenneth Rose, *Superior Person . . .* (London, 1969), pp. 379-80; Ronaldshay. *Cur-*

On 19 October Kemal's representative, Col. Refet Pasha [Bele], had arrived in Constantinople to a tremendous popular reception. Ostensibly he was there to work out details of the Thracian administration, but he also intended to use his accompanying force of some 130 gendarmes as the nucleus for assuming administrative responsibility for Constantinople as well. Negotiations in the capital were always delicate, and if they broke down war might result irrespective of discussions in Switzerland. Rumbold asked for discretionary powers on when to withdraw if the situation warranted (having been in Berlin in 1914 and Warsaw as the Russians arrived in 1921, he was experienced in diplomatic withdrawals). The appointment of Ismet Pasha, Kemal's negotiator at Mudanya, as foreign minister and the great likelihood of his appearance at Lausanne "portends sabreing," Rumbold reported, for Ismet Pasha had proved a very intractable (and quite deaf) negotiator at Mudanya. Rumbold's respect was fully shared by Harington.[4]

In early November Rumbold's pessimism appeared justified when the Grand National Assembly declared illegal all Constantinople's actions sinee March 1920 (i.e., since the Allied occupation); on the 4th Refet Bey calmly told Harington that the separate Constantinople government was no more, that he had assumed responsibility for telegraph, police, and other administrative functions (he had already done so in Thrace). While Turkey was willing to respect the presence of Allied troops in the various zones, administration was no longer under Allied control. By the 6th the mixed court had been closed, the sanitary control was taken over, Ottoman Public Debt officials had been sent home from the customs, and unilateral increases in customs tariff were ordered. Indignant protests against all this were ignored, and Harington and Rumbold began once again to contemplate military resistance to the obvious Kemalist attempt to squeeze the Allies out.[5]

---

zon, III, pp. 319-20 (and see works cited in chapter 7, note 65); and other standard works on the era.

[4] CinC Constantinople telegram to WO, 20 October, *FO* 371/7905; FO to CO, 26 October, high commissioner, Constantinople, telegram to FO, 26 October, *FO* 371/7906, and 28 October (quoted), and letter, 24 October, *FO* 371/7907; Rumbold private to Oliphant, 28 October, *FO* 800/353; Harington private to Rumbold, n.d. (but October), in Rumbold private to Curzon, 31 October, *Curzon Papers,* F/5; Henderson to FO, 7 December 1922, *FO* 371/7918; David Loch, "Constantinople during the Crisis," *Contemporary Review* 122 (1923): 25-34.

[5] CinC Constantinople telegrams to WO, 2, 3, 4, and 5 November,

Harington now advised that it was time to proclaim a state of siege and disarm the gendarmerie and police. He was aware that this suggestion risked a serious confrontation, but the alternative was to accept another extreme humiliation as the entire administration was taken over before the conference even met. As Rumbold advised, the Turkish delegates would then refuse to discuss issues already settled. Resistance, advised Harington, would still be a "serious business," especially considering he had only three (Guards) battalions in the capital. Fortunately, Harington persuaded Refet Bey to modify some of his measures enough for Harington to withdraw the "state of siege" advice, although the preparations for it would stand. London had already given approval; the Cabinet was once again prepared to evacuate to Gallipoli and Chanak, this time holding the latter only so long as practicable. As usual, there was disagreement in Constantinople; Rumbold was as worried as Harington, reporting that the Kemalists had twice suggested that the Allied forces leave. When their military strength was built up, he predicted, the suggestion would become a demand. Only Harington's assurance, in another change of mind, that he would be able to hold on until the conference met (and, presumably, the pressure moderated) permitted some relaxation in London—but Harington was given the free hand for which he had asked.[6]

Meanwhile, Curzon planned the difficult stages of negotiation with some care. As he explained to the reconstructed Cabinet, first would come the Sèvres issues. Then would follow a wider discussion of the Straits, which would involve nonsignatories of the treaty. The major issues would be Thrace, Mosul, and the capitulations, with the subordinate themes of Russian participation and Indian Khilafat agitation (milder now, but to be feared if the conference broke down) to keep the discussions lively. First, however, Allied cooperation was required,

---

FO 371/7909; high commissioner, Constantinople, telegrams to FO, 6 and 7 (no. 668) November, DBFP XVIII/157-58; Rumbold private to Curzon, 6 November 1922, Curzon Papers, F/16/6.

[6] CinC Constantinople telegrams to WO, 7 November (no. 2932), FO 371/7908, and 8 November (nos. 2941 and 2946), and high commissioner, Constantinople, telegram to FO (no. 669), 7 November, FO 371/7910; and private to Curzon, 6 November, Curzon Papers, F/16/6; Curzon private to Derby, 9 November, and Cavan (CIGS) note for Derby, 10 November, WO 137/5; Cabinet 66 (22), 10 November, and appendix II, WO telegram to CinC Constantinople, 10 November 1922, CAB 23/32.

and Curzon had suggested a preliminary meeting of leaders to Poincaré and the new, unknown Italian leader, Benito Mussolini. He hoped that the Allies would come to London—he had been four times to Paris on this issue—but he had to agree to Paris when Poincaré successfully pleaded a budget debate. Mussolini, similarly fencing for diplomatic points in this, his first major international conference, would meet the other two leaders in Switzerland.[7]

When Curzon met Poincaré on Saturday, the 18th, the French had already agreed to Britain's position on freedom and demilitarization of the Straits, Syrian-Iraqi frontiers, western Thrace, and occupation of Constantinople until the treaty was ratified (Mussolini had suggested evacuation prior to the conference). In a general way, the French also agreed on indemnity and other financial clauses, including confirmation of prewar concessions, a source of later controversy. On the other hand, Poincaré was openly suspicious that Britain might be stealing a march with the sultan. Mehmed VI had found himself rather anachronistic after the Grand National Assembly absorbed his government and Refet Pasha assumed charge of his capital. With Harington's assistance, therefore, on the 17th he quietly left the city with his son and a few companions bound for Malta on a British ship. Far from concocting a devious plot, as Curzon admitted to Poincaré, Britain did not know what to do with him; the India Office had actually protested the action, since it appeared that Britain was unilaterally interfering with the holy caliphate.[8]

The sultan's flight was most revealing, for there was very little reac-

[7] Cabinet 64 (22), 1 November, and 67 (22), 16 November, *CAB* 23/32; FO drafts and notes of late October, *FO* 371/7907 (especially 11785/27); Graham, Rome, telegram to FO, 4 November, with Nicolson minute, 6 November, *FO* 371/7908; Hardinge telegram to FO, 10 November, *FO* 371/7911; Hardinge telegrams to FO, 7 November (no. 572), 10 November, and 15 November (nos. 599-600), FO telegrams to Hardinge (no. 417), 8 November, 11 November, and 13 November (2 of date), and to Graham, 14 November, and Graham telegram to FO, 17 November 1922, *DBFP* XVIII/164, 166, 175, 188-91, 195-96, 201.

[8] Curzon telegram to FO, 18 November, *FO* 371/7914, Allied meeting, 18 November, and Henderson telegram to FO, 17 November, *DBFP* XVIII/204, 198; high commissioner, Constantinople, to Curzon (Lausanne), 20 November, *FO* 371/7962; Henderson to FO, 7 December, *FO* 371/7918; Peel private telegram to Reading, 17 November 1922, *Reading Papers,* E. 238/16.

tion in India. Beyond a doubt the Khilafat movement was dead or nearly so, killed by the estrangement of Hindu and Muslim leaders, the incarceration of leaders from both faiths, and the general self-sufficiency of the Kemalist Turks. Indeed the more modernist of Kemal's sympathizers felt he had every right to deprive the sultan of temporal or even spiritual powers. Kemal was the savior of his Muslim country, and to Kemal, not the sultan, went the admiration of even Muslim Indian nationalist leaders. Indian officials made the mistake of admitting that the issue carried little weight, an admission the Foreign Office received with scorn. "Appalling," said Curzon of the cynicism with which to his mind India had played upon the issue; their attitude "justifies us in not attaching the slightest value to any future representation of the Govt. of India in European politics." India had for too long hammered upon the Foreign Office with the weapon of Muslim feelings, and in so doing had lost a great deal of credibility. As a staff member put it, "We know that whatever we do, and however honest our policy, we will be bitterly assailed by India."[9]

Curzon's meeting with Poincaré was generally amicable despite the issue of the sultanate, and the leaders moved on to Lausanne—only to find from a railway official that they were expected to meet Mussolini for dinner at Territet a few miles beyond Montreux. The Duce wanted the prestige of being met and accompanied to Lausanne by the Allied leaders, although neither he nor Poincaré remained beyond the opening meeting. Mussolini did not appear to be a problem, beyond his strong interest in the Dodecanese Islands; in spite of some strained relationships in the past among the Allies (particularly the "absolutely irreconcilable" natures, as Hardinge put it, of Curzon and Poincaré), it seemed that Curzon could expect reasonable support from his allies. It was primarily the Turks with whom he would have to deal.[10]

[9] Reading private telegram to Peel, 10 November, copy in 12455/27, *FO* 371/7911, with Crowe minute, 11 November: "What a confession! It is worthy of that of the Agha [sic] Khan," and Curzon minute (quoted); second minute (quoted) by Lindsay, 16 November 1922, on 12771/27, *FO* 371/7913.

[10] Curzon telegram (no. 1) to FO, 20 November, *FO* 371/7914; Allied meeting, 19 November, and Curzon telegram to FO, 22 November (no. 13), *DBFP* XVIII/206, 213; Hardinge private to Crowe, 20 November 1922, *FO* 800/386; Hughes, "Italian Diplomacy," pp. 219-20.

LAUSANNE

The Lausanne conference was unique; it was the only postwar conference in which the Allies met the defeated enemy on anything like equal terms. It was also colorful, with delegations from all the major powers, and many of the small, including for flavor one much-discussed woman delegate (from Bulgaria) and one murdered delegate (Voronsky, a Russian observer, was shot dead in the restaurant of a minor hotel in May 1923). Leading diplomats mingled with leading correspondents in flag-decorated hotels of reputable lineage, as the hothouse atmosphere of a resort in winter lent emphasis to the normal surge of whispered rumors inevitably accompanying any such conference. The fact that the French and Turkish delegates both occupied the Lausanne Palace Hotel was enough in itself to cause considerable talk.[11]

The atmosphere of the discussions was more important. From the first opening session on Monday, the 20th, the confrontation took shape: only the president of the Swiss Confederation was scheduled to

[11] On Lausanne and its atmosphere, see Ryan, *Last of the Dragomans,* pp. 174-96; Nicolson, *Curzon,* Ch. X-XI; Ronaldshay, *Curzon,* III, Ch. XX; Blake, *Unrepentant Tory,* pp. 487-90; Davison, "Turkish Diplomacy," 202-7, and "Middle East Nationalism: Lausanne Thirty Years After," *Middle East Journal* 7 (1953): 324-48; Joseph C. Grew, *Turbulant Era,* I (London, 1953), Ch. XVIII-XXI; Waldo H. Heinrichs, *American Ambassador: Joseph C. Grew . . .* (Boston, 1966), pp. 63-93; Henderson, *Water under the Bridges,* pp. 112-21 (on Constantinople during the conference); Richard Washburn Child, *A Diplomat Looks at Europe* (N.Y., 1925), pp. 79-124; Jules Laroche, *Au Quai d'Orsay avec Briand et Poincaré, 1913-1926* (Paris, [1957]), pp. 160-62; Grace Ellison, *An Englishwoman in Angora* (London, [1923]), pp. 193-95, 303, 307; Charles A. Fenton, *The Apprenticeship of Ernest Hemingway . . .* (N.Y., 1954), pp. 187-97; Ludwell Denny, "Up in Curzon's Room," *Nation* 96 (1923): 40-41; Joseph C. Grew, "The Peace Conference of Lausanne, 1922-1923," *Proceedings American Philosophical Society* 98 (1954): 1-10; "The Lausanne Conference," *The Round Table* 13 (1922-23): 342-55; Stephen P. Ladas, *The Exchange of Minorities* (N.Y., 1932); George Slocombe, *The Tumult and the Shouting* (London, 1936), pp. 180-95; Harry J. Psomiades, *The Eastern Question, The Last Phase* (Thessalonika, 1968); Kurt Ziemke, *Die neue Türkei* (Stuttgart, 1930), pp. 181-259; League of Nations, *Greek Refugee Settlement* (Geneva, 1926); and, for the official French account, France, Ministère des affaires étrangeres, *Documents diplomatiques. Conférence de Lausanne,* 2 vols., (Paris, 1923).

make a welcoming speech, but Ismet Pasha managed to make what Curzon called "some very partisan and rather truculent remarks." "With velvet words but steam-roller methods," as American Ambassador Grew put it, Curzon moved to ensure his control of the conference. The three allies had invited the others, and the three allies therefore decided upon procedure: three commissions, each under the presidency of one power, with Britain (Curzon) assuming charge of the all-important Territorial and Military Commission. Ismet Pasha's protests were ignored or discarded, and the conference took up the first major territorial issue: Thrace.[12]

Ismet Pasha's position, outlined on the 23rd, was simple. He claimed all the prewar Thracian territory and demanded a plebiscite for western Thrace. To Curzon's frustration, he backed this position with no satisfactory evidence, and Curzon was adamant in defense of the Maritsa frontier to which the French and Italians had already agreed. No one, in any case, really knew where western Thrace stopped and Greece began, and there could be no plebiscite. The Maritsa frontier with demilitarized zones on both sides survived into the final treaty of Lausanne, with only relatively minor changes (essentially Greek concessions). The boundary was shifted from the eastern shore to the "thalweg" or midchannel of the river and Turkey was given the town of Karagach, a suburb of Adrianople which was important to that town but which lay on the Greek side of the Maritsa. Ismet Pasha fought as strong a rearguard action as possible, but his major artillery, like Britain's once the general Maritsa line was accepted, was not meant for Thrace. Thrace was an opening skirmish, of little real importance to Britain's Asian policy.[13]

---

[12] Curzon telegrams, 20 November (nos. 2 and 6, latter quoted), *DBFP* XVIII/207, 209; FO Record Series 839 includes the files of the British delegation at Lausanne, with most of the original handwritten drafts of Curzon's reports, for he did most of his own secretarial work. Grew, *Turbulent Era,* p. 491, quoted; T.A. Spring Rice to Lindsay, 20 November 1922, *FO* 371/7964, describes procedure; see also official rules in Great Britain, Parliamentary Papers, Turkey No. 1 (1923), Cmd. 1914, "Lausanne Conference on Near Eastern Affairs, 1922-1923 . . ." [hereafter *Lausanne Conf.*] The other commissions were those on Foreigners (second commission, Italian president), and Economic and Financial Clauses (third commission, French president).

[13] Curzon telegrams (nos. 19 and 23) to FO, 23 November, *DBFP* XVIII/

Considerably more important were the Straits. By 28 November, when the Russian delegates arrived, the Turks had already agreed to demilitarized zones. As Curzon saw it, they intended to secure an international guarantee under the guise of neutrality which would protect Constantinople, thus "leaving them absolutely free to prosecute their Turanian policy in Central Asia." The larger problem was how to control passage of the Straits, and the Foreign Office had been at work on this since early October. There were three possible solutions, which Harold Nicolson outlined in a memorandum for Curzon. First, they could restore the prewar rule, closing the Straits to warships and allowing limited commercial passage in peacetime only, but Britain had committed herself to an opposite position, and closure would hardly be fair to allied Rumania (there was much less concern about former enemy Bulgaria). The Turks could still let the Russians out in any case, and overall, closure would "confirm France in her military domination of the continent," since it would prevent British application of seapower in the Black Sea. A second possibility was to bar all warships, but allow commercial passage in peace and war. This was worse than the first possibility, for the Russians could repeat the example of the Russo-Japanese War, when merchant vessels sailed under the commercial flag, and later metamorphosed as warships. A third arrangement, to allow total freedom of passage, as established in the Sèvres treaty, was the only serious one. Basically, there was a deep-rooted strategic question: "the continental, or military system, and the oceanic, or naval system" competed for influence; in this case Britain's navy was pitted against France's continental alliances with such states as Poland and Rumania. Unfortunately, as Nicolson added in a later memorandum, absolute freedom could not be guaranteed, since no occupation forces could be kept, and reduced Allies commitments or some League-supervised organization would probably prove "irksome, expensive and, in the ultimate resort, ineffective."[14]

Free Straits passage thus rested upon military provisions. Foch pro-

---

215, 217, and 26 November (no. 35), *FO* 371/7964; Terr. Comm., 6th session, 25 November 1922, *Lausanne Conf.;* high commissioner, Constantinople, telegram (from Lausanne) to FO, 19 May 1923, *DBFP* XVIII/534, and letter of same date, *FO* 371/9078.

[14] Curzon telegram to FO, 28 November (no. 47, quoted), *DBFP* XVIII/234; Nicolson memoranda, 3 October, 10444/27, *FO* 371/7898, and 15 November 1922 (both quoted), 13027/27, *FO* 371/7915.

posed a scheme which called for demilitarization of the Straits but no Allied occupation. No Turkish forces save the Constantinople garrison would have access to these zones, which would be inspected by a League-sponsored control commission of interested powers. Finally, Turkish military strength in Thrace would be severely limited. Nicolson favored this suggestion, which would stand in the way of systematic fortification—without requiring Allied occupation—and would thus make it easier to "rush the Straits". (Nobody discussed the Straits in 1922 without remembering Gallipoli.) If the proposal did not work, Nicolson would fall back on the League despite resulting problems, placing the Straits under a commissioner and international statute: the main point was not to allow Turkish control. He suggested, therefore, that British policy be first to support the Foch plan, failing which to choose League control, failing which to opt very reluctantly for free commercial passage only and international inspection of such aspects as quarantine and lighting.

Nicolson's position did not go uncriticized by the Admiralty, which felt that his appreciation was based too exclusively on advantages in case of war with Russia and consequent action on the Black Sea. "I would reply," wrote L.S. Amery, the First Lord (1922-24), "that we are not going to war either for or against Russia in our generation, but that we do want to make peace with Turkey now. . . ." Britain's sphere did not lie in the Balkans and Black Sea, but east of Turkey.

> I also feel bound to point out that the whole political case for the military freedom of the Straits is based on the assumption of our unlimited Naval superiority. That was true during the War. But we are now faced with the situation that it will need our utmost financial effort and sacrifice to maintain even a one-Power standard as against Japan or the United States. Under these conditions it is of far more importance to us to discourage the growth and to check the freedom of operation of further naval rivals than to increase our own facilities for naval aggression.

Freedom of the Straits invited Russia to become a naval power on Britain's eastern flank and thus force Turkey into Russia's arms.

> By restoring to Turkey the liberty she desires of defending the narrow channel through her own territory and past her own capital, we shall inevitably estrange her from Russia and be able

to use her as a bulwark both to our naval position in the Mediterranean and to our military position in the whole Middle East.

Therefore, the navy would work for commercial freedom of passage and no more.[15]

With these interesting statements of position, at last linking naval, as opposed to army, realities to the Middle East, Curzon had to begin conference discussion on the subject. His intention was to ask first for the Foch plan. If that failed he would work for unrestricted commercial passage and the passage of warships in time of Turkish neutrality, in return for which he would give the Turks full authority over the Straits, including fortification. The demilitarization which the military advisors (and Nicolson) considered so useful would only give a week's delay to the Turks and then would be useless; however, if his own plan were adopted, the Straits would be fortified but would be closed only in time of Turkish belligerency. Russia would fight furiously against the idea, of course, and even many British would regard Turkish control as renunciation of all war gains, but it was still his favored plan.[16]

On 4 December the territorial commission turned to the Straits for the first time. Ismet left the talking to Chicherin, "attended by a swarm of Myrmidons," as Curzon put it, who claimed to speak for Turkey as well as Russia. He requested unrestricted commercial freedom but passage of only Turkish warships and construction of only Turkish fortifications. Rumania and Bulgaria quickly disagreed; Rumania, friend of the Allies, would allow warships, while Bulgaria, uninterested in warships yet no friend of Turkish control, favored some international Straits regime. Ismet, in response to Curzon's prompting, would only say that the Russian view coincided with that of the Turks. Curzon came away from the meeting in considerable puzzlement, for he had expected Russia to ask for Black Sea neutralization as well—although it is hard to see why, since Black Sea neutralization was unnecessary if Russia obtained closure of the Straits to warships. Ismet's surprising willingness to humiliate himself by simply tagging along on Russian coat-

---

[15] L.S. Amery private to Curzon, 28 November 1922, *Curzon Papers,* F/16/4; P.P. Graves, *The Question of the Straits* (London, 1931); Anderson, *Eastern Question.*

[16] Curzon telegram to FO, 3 December 1922 (no. 68), *DBFP* XVIII/251.

tails also puzzled Curzon, for Chicherin would turn the Black Sea into a Russian lake. The next morning, however, Ismet's strategy was revealed when he sent a junior delegate to tell Curzon in private that Turkey would meet Britain on all points and even break with Russia ". . . if only we would give them Vilayet of Mosul." Curzon was in no position to agree. Mosul was the most difficult of all the specifically Anglo-Turkish issues at Lausanne and Ismet's insistence on connecting it with all the other conference problems made it even more complicated.[17]

Curzon knew well, of course, that Mosul was a major Turkish concern. Ismet Pasha had said so in private conversation the first week at Lausanne and continued at every opportunity to press his interest in the territory and its oil. Curzon had come by December to hope that at least Ismet would give way on territory if he got a share of the oil, but this was not the case: the Turks wanted both.[18] To understand why Curzon would not yield on Mosul, it is necessary to review developments in Iraq and Kurdistan in the months preceding the Lausanne conference.

SOLUTION OF THE KURDISH PUZZLE

At the San Remo conference in 1920, no final settlement for Kurdistan had been reached. The problem of French interest in Mosul was resolved by the offer of a share of Mosul oil. Still unknown, however, were the wishes of the Kurdish people. Considerably more important, finally, was the uncertainty of Britain's own aims. As the draft clauses were being worked out for the Turks, it became clear that there were really three positions. Arnold Wilson in Baghdad argued that the whole of Mosul vilayet was essential for the protection and survival of any state based upon Baghdad. The Foreign Office, on the other hand, was more inclined to withdraw British forces from advanced posts and sponsor an independent or autonomous state, rather like that planned for Armenia. The India Office, taking a middle position once again, argued for a fringe of autonomous enclaves or statelets still under British direc-

[17] Terr. Comm., 9th session, 4 December, *Lausanne Conf.;* Curzon telegrams to FO, 5 and 6 December 1922 (nos. 74 and 80, both quoted), *DBFP* XVIII/255 and 257; Grew, *Turbulent Era,* I, p. 506.

[18] Tyrrell memorandum, 28 November (on conversation with Ismet evening of 27th), 13599/13003, *FO* 371/7965; Curzon telegram to FO, 1 December 1922 (no. 62), *DBFP* XVIII/244.

tion. A fourth possibility, apparently favored by de Robeck, was to leave it all to Turkey as a special district and perhaps incite the Kurds against Kemal—but this appears not to have been discussed seriously. The Foreign Office proposal of withdrawal was open to the criticism (as was de Robeck's) that it would expose both Persia and Iraq militarily, but the India Office, which made this argument, at the same time did not wish to see Britain saddled with the burden of full administration. By the time of San Remo, interdepartmental consideration had suggested that the northern portion of Kurdistan be left to Turkey as an autonomous zone, while the south would be part of the British mandate, free to join either Iraq or Turkey at some later date. But Curzon had gone off to the San Remo Conference without giving this compromise plan final approval. The Sèvres treaty had stipulated that a commission of the three Allied powers would draft a scheme of local autonomy for the predominantly Kurdish areas, with the right of appeal to the League within one year. The southern portion, as planned, was assigned to the British mandate.[19]

In the summer and fall of 1920, however, the Sèvres clauses remained in abeyance while the treaty went unratified and Britain coped with a serious revolt in the Arab districts of Iraq. Direct administration of Mosul by the British continued, although from time to time mention was made of cutting southern Kurdistan off from the rest of Mesopotamia at some future date. Suggestions that the Kurds be used against Kemal were wisely overruled, pending some larger Kurdish request for assistance in the formation of a Kurdish political unit. The request was not forthcoming; there was no demonstrable evidence of a growing Kurdish movement, nor would there be so long as Kurdish leadership remained divided (Simko's activities on the Persian side, for example, continued unabated) and Britain refrained from overt sponsorship and encouragement. Since the British plan—insofar as there was a

[19] SSI telegram to commissioner, Baghdad, 25 March, and minutes, commissioner, Baghdad, telegram to IO, 28 March, Montagu note for Curzon. 8 April, *L/P&S*/10/782; Curzon telegrams to high commissioner, Constantinople, 26 March and 24 April, and high commissioner, Constantinople, telegram to FO, 29 March, *DBFP* XIII/33, 34, 56; IDCE, 13 April, *Curzon Papers,* F/11/8; Hirtzel private to A.T. Wilson, 15 April, *Wilson Papers,* Add. Mss. 52455; Allied meetings (Lloyd George-Millerand, I.C.P. 94A), 18 April, *CAB* 29/85, and 19 April 1920 (San Remo, I.C.P. 97), *DBFP* VIII/5.

plan—was to divide at least north and south Kurdistan, there was little likelihood they would support a united Kurdish movement.[20]

Not until the spring of 1921 was Kurdistan again given serious consideration, this time as part of the resolution of the Iraqi problem at the Cairo conference of 12-30 March. The Hashimite Prince Faisal was offered the kingship of Iraq, but the purely Kurdish districts of southern Kurdistan did not have to remain in an otherwise Arab Iraq; they would be kept under British mandatory supervision until such time as a representative body of Kurdish states should opt for inclusion in Iraq. Continued supervision, however, depended, as did all the Cairo plans, upon reducing British military commitments elsewhere in the Middle East, and this could not be done until northern Iraq and Kurdistan were free of possible Kemalist attacks. In May the Middle East Committee, a new organization established to deal with such problems, considered several ways to achieve this end, including a cession of territory from Kurdistan to the Turks (discarded since Kemal still would demand Mosul), or support of a direct Kurdistan settlement between Kemal and King Faisal. Nothing came of either suggestion, but strong Colonial Office pressure for an arrangement with Kemal was yet another force working upon Curzon for peace.[21]

The post-Cairo months revealed disagreement between Churchill, back in London, and Cox in Baghdad. The latter, realizing the differing levels of development in the several Kurdish areas (principally the divisions of Arbil, Sulaimaniyah, Kirkuk, and Mosul), suggested keeping the administration separate and in, say, three years putting the question directly to the Kurds themselves. Churchill would have preferred immediate establishment of a separate Kurdish regime, but Cox

[20] SSI telegrams to commissioner, Baghdad, 14 June and 15 December, commissioner, Baghdad, telegrams to IO, 17 June and 26 November, *FO* 371/5069; high commissioner, Constantinople, telegram to FO, 28 July, and FO telegram to high commissioner, Constantinople, 31 July, *DBFP* XIII/103, 109; Cabinet 69-77 (20), 13-24 December, *CAB* 23/23; E. Barstow, Tabriz, to Norman, 31 December 1920 (annual report on Azerbaijan and Simko), 3497/3497, *FO* 371/6402; high commissioner, Constantinople (Rumbold), telegrams to FO, 29 December 1920, 1 January 1921, *FO* 371/6436.
[21] Cairo conference report, appendix 10, 4th meeting of political committee, "Kurdistan," 15 March, 8001/533, *FO* 371/6343; M.E.C. 1st minutes, 2 May, 5391/5391, *FO* 371/6344; CO to FO, 5 and 24 May, and FO to CO, 13 and 31 May 1921, *FO* 371/6346.

was the administrator on the spot. The persistant delay, however contributed to unrest in Kurdistan, particularly as it was coupled with the backwash of unrest in neighboring Arab and Anatolian areas. In the summer of 1921 widespread minor disturbances argued in favor of an immediate settlement. Then Simko provided rather a new temptation; he made overtures for British support just as British relations with the central Persian government reached a nadir. Wisely, Britain resisted— there were too many complications, not the least of which was the continuing interest in some quarters (particularly the Archbishopric of Canterbury) in the Christian "Assyrian" community whose deadly enemy Simko had always been.[22]

But the problem would not be put off forever. Faisal, installed as king in 1921, soon asked with some insistence just what was the Kurdistan policy to be? Since no one had yet decided whether the Kurds would remain under the high commissioner in a separate regime or fall under Faisal's authority, it was a hard question to answer. Faisal favored their becoming part of Iraq, not so much to possess a larger state or for strategic reasons, as because a purely Arab Iraq would have had a Shiah Muslim majority, while inclusion of the Kurds would incline the balance toward his own Sunni persuasion. There was also the real problem of defense, however, and since Britain was taking on defense obligations toward the new Iraq, it was a most complex issue.[23]

It was hoped that the Arabs could be made self-sufficient in defense, and there was certainly no intention to assume responsibility against an indeterminate Kemalist threat. On the other hand, until affairs in Turkey were settled, it was not desirable to let Faisal work out the Kurdistan problem with Kemal. Faisal was naturally concerned, and news of the Franco-Kemalist treaty, which altered the Turkish-Syrian frontier in the direction of Iraq, was even more worrying—particularly if a settlement between France and Kemal implied any kind of French

[22] Commissioner, Baghdad, telegrams to CO, 21 June, 5 July, and 26 August, CO telegram to commissioner, Baghdad, 24 June 1921 (and other documents in volume for summer disturbances), *L/P&S/*10/782; on the Assyrians, see *L/P&S/*10/775, and works cited above, chapter 4, notes 34 and 39.

[23] Commissioner, Baghdad, telegrams to CO, 20 and 28 September, Colonial Office records (Public Record Office), *CO* 730/5; and telegram of 25 October, enclosed in Forbes Adam memorandum, 2 November, and M.E.C., 4th minutes, 3 November 1921, *FO* 371/6347.

military aid for the Turks. Faisal was an old enemy of the French, having been driven out of Damascus at gunpoint; he was unlikely to put such an association beyond the realm of possibility.[24]

Negotiation of a satisfactory treaty with Faisal was considerably hampered by this paradoxical situation. Faisal argued that Britain must either fulfill its previous commitment to defend Iraq's frontier or turn the responsibility over to him, in which case he could probably rouse his subjects to stand off the Turkish threat if direct negotiation with Kemal were still prohibited. Doing nothing would probably land the Turks in Mosul in the end. After long and difficult discussion on this and other issues, a compromise treaty was finally concluded on 10 October 1922, which, although it said nothing about Kurdistan, at least seemed to imply that Faisal would be empowered to negotiate with his neighbors. After Chanak and Mudanya, however, Britain had to reconcile Turkish claims to all Kurdistan and Mosul with the integrity of the Iraqi state it had recognized by formal treaty, which included the Mosul vilayet. If Britain should now cede away the northern territories, Faisal would be in an impossible position relative to his own subjects — especially those Baghdadi nationalist leaders who had opposed his British-sponsored candidacy in the first place. Knowing this, Curzon simply could not give way to Ismet's demand for Mosul.[25]

The only alternative, it appeared, was one Cox had suggested and partially implemented: continue to foster a Kurdish movement and thereby develop Kurdish national sentiment in such a way as to push Kemal into an acceptable agreement. The candidate unwisely selected as Kurdish leader was Shaikh Mahmud, already deposed once before for anti-British activities. Mahmud's ambitions had not been diminished by his experience, and from the spring of 1923 onward, his activities,

[24] CO telegrams to commissioner, Baghdad, 11 November and 21 December, Forbes Adam memorandum, 25 November, CO (N.E. Dept.) memorandum, 13 December, Churchill memorandum, 21 December (C.P. 3566) 1921, *FO* 71/6347; Worthington-Evans memorandum, 8 February 1922 (C.P. 3708), *FO* 371/7770.

[25] Commissioner, Baghdad, telegram to CO, 8 February, *FO* 371/7770; CO to FO, 21 February, FO to CO, 27 February, high commissioner, Constantinople, to Curzon, 29 March and 20 June, *FO* 371/7781; commissioner, Baghdad, telegrams to CO, 16 November and 15 December, and CO telegram to Commissioner, Baghdad, 22 December 1922, *FO* 371/7782; treaty is in Hurewitz, *Diplomacy*, II, pp. 111-14.

combined with the general unsettlement, kept Kurdistan seething. Several towns and settlements had to be abandoned, and military operations were mounted against him; the air force came in time to regard Mahmud as "Director of R.A.F. Training" in Iraq. In the end, Mahmud's ambitions for a larger Kurdish state under his personal leadership were frustrated, and in 1924 when the new Iraqi army reoccupied Sulaimaniyah, Mahmud was reduced to guerrilla activities in the hills, although the Kurdish problem was to live on.[26]

Suppression of Mahmud was in the future, however, and the military operations did nothing to reduce Kemal's claims at Lausanne. Kurdistan was not only an important territory of mixed population; there was also oil in the Mosul vilayet. It was soon clear that Mosul's petroleum was an important objective of Ismet Pasha's diplomacy, and at the meetings held to reallocate shares of the old Turkish Petroleum Company Turkey demanded that it participate on the same basis as France and the United States (shares to the latter country having been forced by unrelenting American diplomatic pressure). But when a tentative offer was made to the Turks, they replied they could not answer proposals on oil until the frontiers were settled. Curzon thus faced one more argument for settlement—all the stronger since a new Cabinet committee was in December 1922 discussing whether to withdraw completely from Mosul, or even the whole of Iraq, in response to insoluble problems and the generally undesirable treaty with Faisal. After a close final vote, the Cabinet decided to ratify the Iraqi treaty—a decision which must have relieved Curzon, spending a lonely Christmas in Lausanne.[27]

[26] Loraine, Teheran, telegrams to FO, 8 and 29 November, and commissioner, Baghdad, telegram to CO, 11 November 1922, *FO* 371/7832. Disturbances and Mahmud's career: Edmonds, *Kurds, Turks, and Arabs,* pp. 245-305; Arfa, *Kurds,* pp. 113-16; Capt. R.G. Thurburn, "The Operations in Southern Kurdistan, March-May 1923," *Army Quarterly* 31 (1936): 264-77; Air Chief Marshal Sir Basil Embry, *Mission Completed* (London, 1957), pp. 34-39, quoted.

[27] Admiralty to FO, 28 November, *FO* 371/7784; Curzon telegram to FO (no. 63), 1 December, *DBFP* XVIII/246; FO telegram to Curzon, 9 December, *FO* 371/7785; McNeill private to Curzon, 29 November, Amery private to Curzon, 13 December, and Crowe private to Curzon, 15 December, *Curzon Papers,* F/14/1; Cabinet 69 (22), 7 December, *CAB* 23/32; Cabinet committee on Iraq, conclusions, 8, 11, and 12 December, and FO memorandum, 15 December 1922 *FO* 371/7772; final report, 23 March 1923 (C.P. 167), *FO* 371/9012, copy in *Curzon Papers,* F/14/1,

Curzon had to walk a very narrow tightrope concerning Mosul between persistence in retaining it, which the Cabinet now supported, and breaking up the conference over it, which the Cabinet might repudiate and which might well be a personal defeat. Any such issue could cause a break, for by December all were showing signs of tension induced by the lack of immediate settlement.[28]

THE LAST NEGOTIATIONS

One consideration which Curzon had always to keep in mind was the steady growth of Turkish control on the European side of the Straits. By the first week in December Henderson reported that a stand was necessary if the Allies were to preserve any influence in the capital at all. Since the conference opened, the Turks had taken over passport control, press censorship, and more of posts and telegraphs; the Allies controlled "matters directly affecting the immediate safety of the Allied forces," but that was all. New Turkish measures were expected momentarily, including restrictions upon the Christian population and violation (from the European standpoint) of the capitulatory privileges the Allies claimed. The Turks had already demanded registration of foreign commercial concerns under the Turkish Companies Act of 1914, and compliance would make them Turkish and not foreign firms.[29]

As always the choices were resistance or withdrawal; the former was not practicable without Allied support, and the latter would be humiliating. Bonar Law, unlike Lloyd George, had no intention of standing alone. That being the case, the War Office asked, why leave a small garrison at Constantinople which would tempt, rather than check, Kemal? Even if it were suddenly desirable to administer a dose of force, the force was insufficient. Wishing neither to retreat unilaterally nor to fight unilaterally, Bonar Law went off to France to talk to Poincaré—meanwhile suggesting to Lord Derby, now secretary of war, that Harington be told to so intermix his troops with those of the Allies

---

with "written by C" in Curzon's handwriting. On the Turkish Petroleum Company, see Busch, *Britain, India, and the Arabs,* pp. 303-9, 353.

[28] CO (M.E. Dept.) note on Curzon telegram to FO, 5 December, *Curzon Papers,* F/15/4; Bonar Law private to Curzon, 5 December 1922, *Bonar Law Papers,* 111/12/38.

[29] Henderson telegram to FO, 6 December, *DBFP* XVIII/259, and letter, 7 December 1922 (quoted), *FO* 371/7918.

that Kemal could not attack the one without fighting the other. Derby regarded this order as impossible of fulfillment—and that was as close to a forward step in Constantinople as the Cabinet was willing to go, unless Curzon foresaw a break approaching at Lausanne.[30]

Curzon was still optimistic, despite a Parliamentary attack by his former colleagues for not adequately discouraging Greek resistance at the time of Montagu's resignation. Gounaris could give Curzon no support now—for he and five others had been executed as scapegoats by the new regime in Athens on 28 November.[31] After considerable searching of files, it was clear that Curzon had warned Gounaris, and that he also had circulated his letter to his colleagues, despite their assertions to the contrary in Parliament. It was a temporary episode, soon over, but it naturally worried Curzon who had to remain in Switzerland and let others act on his behalf at home.[32]

On the brighter side, Ismet appeared to have learned wisdom on the Straits, for he agreed to the Allied proposals, provided acceptable formulas could be reached on the defense of Constantinople, entrance of warships into the Black Sea, and the extent of demilitarized zones. Mosul remained deadlocked, and the Turks apparently concluded that it was best to obtain the Straits settlement alone. The new Allied plan to demilitarize both sides of the Dardanelles but to permit the Turks to fortify the southern shore of Marmora was accepted by the Turks but rejected altogether by Chicherin on 18 December. Russia insisted that

[30] Beatty, Admiralty, note, 6 December, *FO* 371/7918; Derby memorandum, 5 December, and private letters to Bonar Law, 5 and 7 December, WO memoranda for Derby, 7 and 8 December, *Derby Papers, WO* 137/5, 10; Cabinet 69 (22), 7 December 1922, *CAB* 23/32.

[31] Smith, *Ionian Vision,* Ch. XIV.

[32] Lindley to FO, 18 November, and telegram, 28 November, Bentinck telegram to FO, 3 December, Curzon telegrams to FO, 1 December (no. 60, for prime minister), and 9 and 10 December (nos. 94 and 101), and FO telegram (from prime minister) to Curzon, 2 December, *DBFP* XVIII, 203, 243, 249, 267, 270, note 4, p. 342, and note 5, p. 342; Osborne memorandum, 13 December, 16657/13, *FO* 371/7588; Vansittart to Curzon, 1 December, and Lindsay note for Curzon, 9 December, *Curzon Papers, F/10/* 5; Curzon private to Bonar Law, 2 and 9 December, *Bonar Law Papers,* 111/12/34 and 44; Vansittart telegram to Tyrrell, 9 December, *FO* 800/154; Hankey to Lloyd George, 21 December 1922, *Lloyd George Papers, F/26/2/30;* Roskill, *Hankey,* II, pp. 324-25; Ronaldshay, *Curzon,* III, pp. 329-31; Blake, *Unrepentant Tory,* p. 477.

all warships be barred. With the Turks and Allies in agreement, the Russians had little chance of prevailing, and only the details remained to be worked out. "Undoubtedly this afternoon's sitting worked a definite break away by Turks from Russian thraldom, which may have larger consequences," cabled Curzon on the 20th, and his buoyancy on this subject carried him through his Christmas dinner, or so reported R.W. Child (an American representative) who shared it with him.[33]

Curzon was inclined to focus on the area of agreement, but many issues remained deadlocked. Even on the Straits, demilitarization was closely related to clauses on Turkish armed forces, and these had yet to be discussed even though the French and Italians had virtually told the Turks that there would be no limitations. Even more serious was the fact that Turkey had the effrontery to ask reparation for damages done by the Allied occupation, particularly by the Greeks at Smyrna, an argument which naturally enraged Venizelos (who once again served as Greek representative, although he did not head the government). Any Greek measures had been merely wartime necessities, and the Greeks had been there at Allied request. And what of Turkish excesses toward the Greek minority? The commission dealing with capitulations and populations was soon deadlocked on such issues (Armenia, predictably, was another), as the Turks continued throughout to object to all capitulations and require vast population exchanges to settle minority problems, including the complete expulsion of all Greeks from Constantinople. The impression made upon the world would be deplorable, said Curzon in a conference session, when it was clear that the Turks would make absolutely no concessions to minorities. His remarks had no visible effect on Ismet Pasha.[34]

Ismet, however, actually had warned Ankara that a break was possible (as usual, a fact revealed by intercepted telegrams), and Curzon

---

[33] Curzon private to Bonar Law, 6 and 20 December, *Bonar Law Papers,* 111/12/41 and 49; Curzon telegrams to FO, 18 and 20 December (latter quoted, text differing slightly from version here), *DBFP* XVIII/282, 284, and *FO* 371/7967; Terr. Comm., 16-18 sessions, 18-20 December 1922, *Lausanne Conf.;* Child, *Diplomat,* p. 112.

[34] Curzon telegrams to FO, 6 December (no. 80), 8 December (no. 92), 10 December (no. 98), 13 December (no. 110), and 14 December (no. 118), *DBFP* XVIII/257, 266, 268, 274, 277; FO telegrams to Curzon, 12 and 15 December, *FO* 371/7966; Terr. Comm., 10-15 sessions, 6, 8 (2 of date), 12, 13, and 14 December 1922, *Lausanne Conf.*

knew that such a possibility did exist. Much of his holiday was spent in drafting a memorandum for Ismet—his plan now was to give the Turks a draft and go over it point by point. But an hour and a half spent with the Turkish diplomat the day after Christmas produced only frustration. Ismet, Curzon complained, "is impervious either to argument, warning or appeal, and can only go on repeating the same catchwords, indulging in the same futile quibbles, and making the same childish complaints. One might just as well argue with the Pyramid of Cheops." Ismet proved to have his own plan: agreement on the Straits, then evacuation of Constantinople, and only then continued negotiation on the other issues. "I do not conceal from the Cabinet," Curzon reported, "that the omens are wholly unfavorable and I can find no solace in any other reflection than that Ismet like all other Turks is doubtless at bottom a true-born son of the bazaars." Despite every concession so far made—demilitarized zones, a share of Mosul oil, abandonment of a planned League of Nations observer for minority clauses, renunciation of much of the Ottoman debt along with many capitulatory privileges— the Turks still held out for their original positions.[35]

Curzon could not afford to give vent to his pessimism in this fashion very long, for Bonar Law was all too likely to give way. He several times urged Curzon that negotiations—particularly over Mosul and oil (Bonar Law would just as soon abandon the area, or trade away the oil)—must not be broken off. Curzon had made a similar suggestion on Mosul in an aberrational moment in early December, but he had recovered his confidence and in Paris over the New Year met Bonar Law at least partly to stiffen the prime minister's resolve. It was now that Curzon justified his appointment as foreign minister, for he found what was probably the only way out of the dilemma of unmodified Turkish demands for a Mosul which Britain could not surrender and yet could not allow to destroy the conference. As Bonar Law put it very clearly in a letter of 8 January, Britain could not fight alone to defend Sèvres or Mosul. "I feel so strongly on both these points that unless something quite unforeseen should change my view, I would not accept responsi-

[35] Curzon telegram to FO, 26 December (no. 154) and letter to Ismet, 26 December, *DBFP* XVIII/293-94; intercepts in CinC Constantinople telegrams to WO, 25 December (nos. 3307 and 3310), *FO* 371/7967; Nicolson memorandum, 27 December, 2/1, *FO* 371/9058; US Mission telegram to State Department, 26 December 1922, *FRUS,* 1923, II, p. 935.

bility for any other policy." The answer which occurred to Curzon was
to separate Mosul from the rest of the treaty for future settlement.
The Turks had to be brought to agree.[36]

The Turks meanwhile had worked upon their own proposal for a
plebiscite in Mosul, if it could not be granted out of hand, and Curzon
had to reject this (the issue being, as he put it, the location of a frontier
and not the allegiance of a people). While drawing up a proposal that
the League of Nations might arbitrate on Mosul, he was horrified to
find that the French delegate had returned from Paris with orders to
give way on every issue to the Turks. Maurice Bompard, now the main
French delegate, told Curzon that Poincaré was seriously worried about
the Greek troops massed on the Maritsa frontier preparatory to marching on the Chatalja lines if the conference dissolved. The French reason was legitimate, although Athens had been warned off any such plan,
but Allied disagreement over the French occupation of the Ruhr had
more probably caused the French change of heart. Although the French
position may not have influenced them, the Turks now rejected any
arbitration of Mosul's frontier; they wanted the entire Mosul vilayet,
which Curzon was not prepared to grant. Curzon made a final appeal to
Ismet, but "I might as well have appealed to the Sphinx of Egypt or
apostrophised the mummy of Tuthankamen," a curious repetition of
the Egyptian image somewhat at odds with Curzon's usual view of the
Turks ("impossible people, who seem to combine the intelligence of
an undeveloped child with the indurated obstinacy of the mule"). Curzon simply replied that he took note of the Turkish arguments, but that
Britain would put up Mosul to the League.[37]

Curzon now saw that the only hope, since the Turks appeared satisfied to stay forever in Lausanne, was to hand over a draft to the Turks

[36] Bonar Law private to Curzon, 21 and 28 December 1922 and 8 January 1923 (latter quoted), Curzon private to Bonar Law, 27 December 1922
and 6 January 1923, *Bonar Law Papers,* 111/12/48, 53-54, 56-57. Curzon's earlier proposal: telegram to FO, 6 December, note 33, chapter 8.
See also Blake, *Unrepentant Tory,* p. 488, and Ronaldshay, *Curzon,* III,
pp. 333-34, which also quote Bonar Law's letter.
[37] Curzon telegrams to FO, 15 January (no. 210, quoted), 21 January
(no. 221), 22 January (no. 222), and 23 January (no. 224, quoted), *DBFP*
XVIII/327, 336, 338, 340, and 23 January (no. 225), *FO* 371/9060; Terr.
Comm., 21-22 sessions, 23 January, *Lausanne Conf.;* Curzon private to
Balfour (Geneva), 25 January 1923, *FO* 371/9061.

on take-it-or-leave-it terms. The whole treaty would be presented, and each commission chairman would explain his own section; the only Mosul reference would say that the issue was going to the League. It was a risky plan, for there was always the danger that the French (and perhaps Italians) would support the Turks in calling his bluff and, depending upon their bitterness over the Ruhr, stay on and conclude a separate treaty. To avoid this Curzon gratuitously reminded Paris of the 1915 mutual Allied pledge not to conclude a separate peace. The draft went to the Allies on the weekend of 27-28 January, and to the Turks formally on Wednesday the 31st, with Curzon scheduled to leave Lausanne no later than 4 February. The Turks showed no signs of nervousness, continuing to argue over each petty detail in the commission on finance; "in this fantastic fog of make-believe and pretence is being spent the last week of my melancholy sojourn at Lausanne," moaned Curzon. Once again, he had quickly to qualify his pessimism and report that the Turks would surely not reject the terms absolutely —for Bonar Law very nearly approved a suggestion from Harington to withdraw to Gallipoli from Constantinople. "Present is not the moment for a display of nervousness or for premature retreat," Curzon cabled Bonar Law, but a nervous prime minister decided against the order only after last-minute consultation with some colleagues at home.[38]

The draft terms, as presented to the Turks, included first the many articles already agreed upon, beginning with the Maritsa frontier (with a 30 kilometer demilitarized zone on both sides) in Thrace. Iraq's frontier would be left to the League Council (a point the Turks had not accepted); the eastern frontiers of Turkey were not considered. The Straits section allowed commercial passage when Turky was at peace, and only very restricted passage of warships (no more than three ships of 10,000 tons maximum each to any one nonlittoral power), but unlimited passage for naval forces of belligerents in time of war when Tur-

[38] Curzon telegrams to FO, 24 January (no. 231, for Cabinet), 27 January (no. 241, quoted), and to prime minister, 29 January (no. 246, quoted), FO telegram to Curzon, 1 February (and see Curzon to Crewe [Paris], 14 February), *DBFP* XVIII/343, 347, 353, 359, 398; Curzon telegram to Crewe, 26 January, *FO* 371/9061; draft telegram to Curzon, 30 January (after Cabinet), *Derby Papers, WO* 137/5; Crewe telegram to FO, 31 January, *FO* 371/9062, and FO to French ambassador, 14 February 1923, *FO* 371/9065.

key was neutral. Fortifications were barred, save for the southern shore of Marmora, and all these provisions were to be overseen by an international commission. The only other military limitations were upon the Constantinople (12,000) and Thracian (8,000) garrisons.[39]

Capitulations were abolished, but a chapter did specify the conditions under which foreigners would reside in Turkey, including special rights to adjudication by national courts of the parties concerned in matters of personal status. For a transition period of five years, a special judicial regime of legal counselors, selected in cooperation with the Permanent Court of International Justice, would help administer the law in respect to foreigners (approving, for example, all warrants for their arrest). A further chapter provided against interference in the working of religious, scholastic, or charitable institutions—all points to which the Turks had already objected. Minority rights were specified in general, with jurists chosen by the League arbitrating disputed cases. There was a general amnesty for political acts committed between 1914 and 1922. Annexed to the draft was a separate Greco-Turkish agreement on the exchange of population, to take effect when both states ratified the larger treaty.

Despite the end of capitulations, however, the section on economic clauses included certain five-year restrictions on customs duty, contracts, and concessions, all subject to review in disputed cases by a mixed arbitration tribunal. Finally, on reparations, Turkey was to pay to the Allies in final settlement of the claims of their nationals arising out of the war a sum of £ T. 15,000,000 in gold (roughly £ 14,250,000 sterling at the time), although Greece and Turkey mutually renounced further reparations claims. The document, six printed pages in its final form, was a considerable retreat from the Treaty of Sèvres—but it was not the treaty which Ismet Pasha was prepared to take back to Ankara.

Ismet asked for time, but Curzon insisted on his schedule. There followed several days of extremely intense diplomatic activity in which both sides made a number of concessions on details (particularly financial clauses) but not on essentials. Ismet could not accept any meaningful residue of foreign control in such matters as military limits in Thrace or juridical privileges. He argued that the points already set-

---

[39] Draft terms, 1178/1, *FO* 371/9062; also *Lausanne Conf.,* pp. 683ff.; Ronaldshay, *Curzon,* III, pp. 339-40.

tled should be separated out and signed—Thracian frontier, Straits, Aegean islands, even later settlement of Mosul. In the last hours of the 3rd, Curzon agreed to suspend his appeal to the League on Mosul for a year to allow direct Anglo-Turkish negotiations and also to set aside the economic clauses for the same period. Two hours before Curzon's train left, Ismet accepted on all issues save the juridical and economic guarantees which impinged upon Turkish independence—and it was on these issues that the conference broke up as Curzon departed at 9:25 P.M. on the Orient Express for Paris (having already delayed the train since 9:00 P.M. waiting to hear the results of Ismet's last session with Bompard). No demonstrable change in the Turkish attitude followed upon his dramatic departure. "Perhaps the most characteristic sequel was that within the next hour Ismet Pasha twice telephoned to find out whether I had really gone. Like a true Turk he thought that he could still catch me before I turned the corner of the street in order to have a final transaction over the price of the carpet." At least the breach had not come over Mosul, and to Curzon, the blame fell upon Ismet, the French, and Italy—but not on Britain.[40]

None of the participants regarded the disagreements, though substantial, as totally irreconcilable, and no armies were now on the march. Ismet lingered for some days in Lausanne, talking to the other delegates in an attempt to reach agreement. The remaining issues were those which interested Britain least—Bonar Law, in fact, was depressed that his foreign minister had struck on trifles. Ismet's view was one of irritated puzzlement (at least according to Admiral Bristol, who traveled home with him on the Orient Express from Venice to Bucharest). The Turks wanted peace (and a separate Turkish-American treaty, which was subsequently concluded), but Ismet had been upset by the sudden introduction of economic terms which he had not studied— and the Allies then demanded immediate signature which forced a rupture. Ismet had to some extent miscalculated also, for as he admitted to Henderson in Constantinople he had not expected Britain to be so

[40] Curzon telegrams to FO, 31 January (nos. 251-52), 2 February (no. 256), and 5 February (unnumbered, quoted), and Bentinck (Lausanne) telegram to FO, 6 February, *DBFP* XVIII/356-57, 360, 370-71; Curzon memorandum, 2 February, 1341/1, *FO* 371/9063; Cabinet 6 (23), 5 February, *CAB* 23/45; Terr. Comm., 24-25 sessions, 31 January and 1 February 1923, *Lausanne Conf.;* Grew, *Turbulent Era*, I, Ch. XIX.

firm on issues of less importance to Britain than to France.[41]

The Foreign Office might conclude optimistically that it was now a matter of final concessions and drafting, but it was not quite that simple. Late in February desultory talks continued in Constantinople. The Allies attempted to limit discussion to the three issues of claims, juridical arrangements, and economic clauses; they introduced a new draft on the juridical arrangement which permitted Turkish nomination of neutral judges from which panels would be selected. This did nothing to alter the basic principle, however, and meanwhile the draft treaty was considered and rejected by the Grand National Assembly. On 8 March Ismet submitted Turkish counterproposals, which led to lengthy discussion on when and where to resume the detailed negotiations that would clearly be necessary. Fortunately, one could regard the Lausanne meeting as having been interrupted, not adjourned, and the easiest procedure was simply to reopen the former conference. This was done in late April.[42]

When the discussions resumed, however, considerable consternation was caused (above all in French financial circles) by a vast concession which the Grand National Assembly had granted to an American, Rear-Admiral Colby Chester. Although the concession eventually came to naught, at the time it looked very much as if the French had been ill-paid for their friendship for the Turks. Another problem, of more direct concern to Britain, was renewed fighting in Kurdistan which involved not only local rebels but Turkish irregulars as well; the situation was reported to have stabilized by the time the conference reopened, however, and Rumbold—now in charge of negotiations while Curzon re-

[41] Bentinck memorandum, 7 February, minutes of informal interdepartmental conference, FO, 8 February, 1599/1, *FO* 371/9065; Henderson telegrams to FO, 9, 12, and 17 February, Curzon telegram to Henderson, 12 February, *DBFP* XVIII/381, 387, 388, 402; Bristol telegram to secretary of state, 15 February 1923, *FRUS,* 1923, II, pp. 969-70 (and see, on the American treaty, signed 6 August, pp. 1148-74); Jones, *Diary,* I, p. 228; Henderson, *Water Under the Bridges,* pp. 114-16.

[42] FO telegram to high commissioner, Constantinople, 20 February, high commissioner, Constantinople, telegrams to FO, 27 and 28 February and 7 March (2 of date), inter-Allied meeting at FO, 27 March, *DBFP* XVIII/406, 421, 427-28, 458, and note 1, p. 572; SIS section to Oliphant, 8 March, 2569/1, *FO* 371/9069; Ismet to Curzon, 8 March, *FO* 371/9070; American Mission telegram to secretary of state, 23 April 1923, *FRUS,* 1923, II, p. 989.

mained in London—was given no real flexibility to negotiate on Mosul.[43]

Rumbold found working with Ismet no easier than Curzon had, despite the fact that the larger issues had to a large extent been resolved. Minor differences, such as Italy's continued possession of the island of Castellerozo, had the capacity to exhaust as much energy as any larger issue had in the first Lausanne session. Juridical and other questions still divided Allies from Turks, and the Allies themselves were divided on whether to reopen the question of reparations. The press rather looked forward to fireworks on the Chester scheme, although the issue was fairly well avoided. Still another vexing problem was when the final Allied evacuation of Constantinople should take place. The only issue, however, on which Rumbold feared that the conference might again dissolve was juridical privilege; it simply could not be harmonized with full Turkish independence. "We are undoubtedly asking for something inconsistent with judicial practice of civilised countries and few people outside Turkey realise cogency of reasons for demanding it," he advised the Foreign Office (the justification, in fact, was that Turkey was not expected to build a "civilized" judicial process for some years).[44]

Nagging last minute issues continued to delay final settlement, although Rumbold tended generally to give way, in part because intercepts showed that delay was weakening Ismet's position. The Grand National Assembly session was postponed until June, then postponed

[43] High commissioner, Constantinople, to FO, 27 March and 10 April, *FO* 371/9149, Henderson to FO, 24 April, *FO* 371/9150; Air O.C. Baghdad, telegram to Air Ministry, 20 March, Devonshire (Sec. Colonies) to prime minister and Cox demiofficial telegram to Devonshire, 22 March, *FO* 371/9004; high commissioner, Constantinople, telegram to FO, 2 May 1923, *DBFP* XVIII/491.

On the concession (over 4000 kilometers of railway line and associated rights), see *The Times,* 3 April 1923; *FRUS,* 1923, I, pp. 1198-1252; "Text of the Chester Concession," *Current History* 18 (1923): 485-89; for the Turkophile views of the Chester family, father and son, see Rear Admiral Colby Chester, "Turkey Reinterpreted," *Current History* 16 (1922): 939-47, and Arthur T. Chester, "Angora and the Turks," *Current History* 17 (1923); 758-64; Mears, *Modern Turkey,* pp. 378-80.

[44] High commissioner, Constantinople, telegrams to FO, 23 April (no. 3), 24 April (no. 6), 4 May (nos. 31 and 33), and 5 May (no. 35), *DBFP* XVIII/477, 478, 496, 498, 500; Ryan private to Henderson, 24 April and 1 May, *FO* 800/240; high commissioner, Constantinople, private to Curzon, 12 May 1923, *Curzon Papers,* F/6/1.

again, as Kemal wrestled with his internal opposition, altering his Defense Association into a political People's Party, ramming through a new treason law, and establishing special tribunals to quiet his critics and opponents—altogether a situation which made Ismet's lack of a diplomatic victory at Lausanne most unsatisfying. Harington, in fact, reported that his intelligence told him that Ismet had been ordered to break off negotiations rather than give in on the last remaining points.[45]

The last delays, through the month of June, were inspired mainly by the French—another bit of irony, so insistent had Paris been on reaching settlement—because of their financial interests in Turkey. The French held over 60 percent of the Ottoman (prewar) public debt and 54 percent of foreign commercial enterprise (compared to 21 percent and 33 percent respectively for Germany and 14 percent and again 14 percent for Britain). Russia's renunciation of outstanding foreign debts had insured that French investors were extremely sensitive toward investments elsewhere, including a Turkey where the Chester Concession boded ill for Franco-Turkish economic association in the future. The Turks, however, were not interested in paying the corrupt debts of the old regime and were convinced at the same time that such funds as were available would be essential for future development. The opposing positions were thus very firm, and the most the French would concede was that the bondholders and concession-holders should work out their differences separately with the Turks, pending which rigorous occupation of Constantinople would continue.[46]

Fortunately, even the French realized that there would be no war to enforce any terms, and the issue was resolved in a "sordid anti-climax" (Henderson's term) of public agreement to disagree in a squabble over money and concessions. Rumbold had played a major role at the end to avoid another breach over an issue of little intrinsic importance in any but a financial and economic context. His own tendency, interestingly,

[45] Rumbold private to Curzon, 2 June, *Curzon Papers,* F/6/1; Henderson telegram to FO, 6 June, *FO* 371/9130, and 24 June, and letter of 25 July, *FO* 371/9131; CinC Constantinople telegram to WO, 10 June 1923, *FO* 371/9082.

[46] Rumbold private to Crowe, 19 June, *FO* 371/9083, and telegrams to FO, 20 June (no. 215), 23 June (no. 220), and 28 June (nos. 232-33, 236), *DBFP* XVIII/626, 632, 639-40, 642; S.D. Waley, Treasury, memorandum, 19 June, *FO* 371/9084; *The Times,* 19 June 1923; percentages from Dept. of Overseas Trade to FO, 13 March 1922, 2803/2803, *FO* 371/7945.

was to credit much of the victory (for by July 1923 signature itself was a victory) to the intercepted telegrams: "the information we obtained at the psychological moments from secret sources was invaluable to us, and put us in the position of a man who is playing Bridge and knows the cards in his adversary's hand."[47]

In essence, the Treaty of Lausanne as finally signed on 24 July (along with a dozen separate instruments) was as agreed in February, except that the only reparations were Turkish gold already in Allied hands. The continued Turkish demand for Greek reparations was paid, in effect, by Greek cession of Dedagatch near Adrianople. The judicial issue was settled by providing merely for notification of arrests of foreigners immediately following the arrest. Only impotent foreign judicial advisors were left and that for only five years. Military limits were noticeable by their absence. Bonds and debts and concessions were all consigned to limbo, for "future settlement."[48]

"None of the Allied Powers will pretend that the treaty which has been concluded is a really satisfactory document from their point of view," Rumbold finally reported to Curzon, "but it is perhaps the best which was obtainable, given the circumstances in which the negotiations necessarily had to be conducted." "We took peace without great honour," said Sir Andrew Ryan later—more reflective a summary than the conclusion of one former prisoner in Turkey: "the blackest, most pitiable and wicked treaty that England ever signed."[49] There would long be disagreement as to whose victory the treaty was: Curzon's, for overcoming the weakness of the British position, of the Allies, and

[47] High commissioner, Constantinople, telegrams to FO, 4 July (no. 249), 17 July (no. 292), 19 July (no. 297), *DBFP* XVIII/653, 677, 680, and 9 July (no. 263), *FO* 371/9086, and private to Oliphant, 18 July (quoted), *FO* 800/353; Henderson private to Ryan, 17 July 1923 (quoted), *FO* 800/240.

[48] For text, see *Lausanne Conf.,* or Hurewitz, *Diplomacy,* II, pp. 119-27; remaining questions are treated in "Handbook to various questions discussed at the Lausanne Conference which were left unsettled or which were the subject of commitments entered into during the Conference but not included in the Treaty and the Instruments signed on July 24, 1923," 109 pp., 10303/1, *FO* 371/9090.

[49] High commissioner, Constantinople, to Curzon, 24 July 1923 (quoted), *FO* 371/9089; Ryan, *Last of the Dragomans,* p. 198 (quoted); Oliver Baldwin, *Six Prisons and Two Revolutions . . .* (London, [1924]), p. 38 (quoted).

even of his own prime minister; Venizelos's, for showing statesmanship in his last-minute cession of Dedagatch; or Ismet Pasha's, for holding out until he got Dedagatch or simply for bringing off "probably the greatest diplomatic victory in history."[50]

In Constantinople, however, there was no doubt, as enthusiastic celebration showed. In Kurdistan there was uncertainty as the Kurds awaited a League decision on Mosul; it was finally awarded to Iraq in 1925 and included the following year rather unwillingly in that state.[51] While Britain prepared its Kurdistan case for the League in the correct expectation that direct negotiation with Ankara would fail, the last immediate problem was a humanitarian one. Before final evacuation the British had to remove nearly 2000 people from Constantinople who had been friends to the Allies and who now sought refuge. By 1 October this was accomplished; the next afternoon, the last date stipulated in the treaty for evacuation, a short military parade was held in which British, French, and Italian detachments formed two sides of a square completed by Turkish troops and foreign diplomats and spectators. A hundred men each from the 2nd Battalion, Grenadier Guards, and 3rd Battalion, Coldstream Guards, together with the combined drums of the Guards brigade and a specially chosen Irish Guards color party (all over six feet tall) formed the British contingent. At 11:30 the Allied commanders arrived on foot, the drums played a final salute, the troops were inspected, and the Allied colors were posted—and the Turkish colors and troops were paraded in their turn, all in a ceremony carefully rehearsed days earlier. At noon, the British troops embarked; that afternoon, General Harington and his staff joined them on the transport *Arabic*—ironically, to steam out of final sight of the rusting but reparable hulk of the German battlecruiser *Goeben,* long a visible reminder of one spark which had helped touch off the Anglo-Turkish war of 1914-23. The *Arabic* moved out into the channel with the battleship H.M.S. *Marlborough* behind, the men manning the tops and the band

[50] Davison, "Turkish Diplomacy," 206-7 (Ismet); Grew, *Turbulent Era,* I, p. 569 (Ismet); Ryan, *Last of the Dragomans,* p. 191 (Venizelos); Nicolson, *Curzon,* Ch. XI ("Lausanne: The Final Triumph"); Gordon A. Craig, "The British Foreign Office from Grey to Austen Chamberlain," in Craig and Gilbert, *The Diplomats,* p. 37 (Curzon over Bonar Law).

[51] Later fortunes of Mosul followed in Howard, *The Partition of Turkey,* pp. 337-40; Stephen H. Longrigg, *'Iraq 1900 to 1950 . . .* (London, 1953), pp. 152-58.

playing an unscheduled "Auld Lang Syne" for friendly Turkish spectators. The ships exchanged a last salute with the flag station at Dolma-
bahch and slipped down into the Sea of Marmora. The war with Turkey
was over, and the troops were going home.[52]

CONCLUSION

Nearly five years of occupation had passed between the armistice
of Mudros and the evacuation of Constantinople. During that time
much had occurred, but above all a defeated and decadent Ottoman Empire had become the victorious new nationalist Turkey; Britain, and the
world, had learned an important lesson in twentieth-century nationalism. The way was now cleared to future friendly relations, despite
some bitter memories; as Henderson put it, none of the Turks who suffered imprisonment on Malta ("the one action of ours since 1918 which
I am absolutely incapable of defending") would soon forget the experience.[53] Mosul and oil, although not the Straits, yet remained to embit-
ter relations for awhile, but Turkey now pursued an independent course,
sufficiently satisfied with Lausanne to avoid extremities of anti-Allied
or anti-British policy.

The occupation of Constantinople and the Straits had served a useful purpose in several ways, facilitating intervention in the Caucasus
and Russia so long as that was desirable and evacuating refugees when
the moment had passed. Once intervention in Russia was over, however, control of the Straits was of far less value—a dead end frontier
with the Bolshevik and Kemalist enemies, leading nowhere and useless
except as listening post and watchtower. Whether the temporary utility
justified the more than £20,000,000 sterling spent on Constantinople's
occupation is another question.[54] By the time of Lausanne, the Turkish
Straits were a naval Khyber Pass, a passage through to hostile territories, to be kept open only in those rare moments of vastly superior
strength. The Admiralty in 1923, like the Indian Army at least as early

[52] Henderson to Curzon, 2 October, *FO* 371/9164; Admiralty to FO, 9
August 1923, *FO* 371/9170; Waugh, *Turkey Yesterday,* pp. 188-89;
Henderson, *Water Under the Bridges,* pp. 123-26; Edwards, *Grey Diplo-
matists,* pp. 78-79.

[53] Henderson private to Oliphant, 3 September 1923, *FO* 800/353.

[54] *Parl. Deb.,* H.C., 11 July 1923.

as 1919, preferred to see reality in defensive, not offensive, operations.

But Caucasian and Caspian operations were always temporary to all but a few individuals, shaped by chance more than by design. With the White effort destroyed, very few felt that a different solution could be enforced upon Russia. But Turkey was a defeated enemy, and withdrawal from occupation and inability to enforce the Treaty of Sèvres required substantial reeducation. To that extent, the events described above served as an object lesson in the nature of the postwar world. Sèvres was the harshest treaty—but it was never put into effect. In a certain sense, Gallipoli in 1915-16 and Chanak in 1922 were campaigns in a larger war to impose Allied—specifically British—desires upon Turkey, Ottoman or Kemalist. Such an interpretation tends to disguise the nature of Kemal's changes in Turkey—but so much has been written on that subject that perhaps such an interpretation is a useful corrective.

Policies pursued toward Armenia and Kurdistan required similar reevaluation. Kurdistan has received considerably more treatment in these pages than Armenia, in part because the literature on Armenia is as vast as that on the Kurds is slender, but also because Britain's ability to alter events was much more theoretical in Armenia. Parts of Kurdistan remained under British control until the very end. From a practical standpoint, the Kurds were more important to Britain, although the Armenians were the focus of massive world attention. It was the tragedy of both peoples that their past and future were so closely interconnected; there can be little question that the connection impeded the settlement of both Armenian and Kurdish problems.

Persia was a similar problem. Britain expanded suddenly to fill a fortuitous vacuum, only to find itself blamed for all foreign imperialism in a time of Persian nationalist recovery. Again, a rather traumatic reeducation was required before the troops could be evacuated from the footholds at Enzeli and Meshed. Tashkent, Merv, Baku, Derbent, Tiflis, Crimea marked only the one highest wave in every tide; the normal high water mark should have been Constantinople, Mosul, and Teheran. Now Britain was reduced to the Arab areas of the Middle East; Egypt, Palestine with its trans-Jordanian satellite, Iraq, and the Persian Gulf. Nationalism produced major problems in the Arab world but there, unlike the Turkish and Persian and Afghani worlds, it was truly "Britain's Moment." Moreover, withdrawal from Persia and Turkey did permit the consolidation in the Arab world of scarce British resources.

Limited resources was not the sole cause for withdrawal. Considerable pressure operated within the British Empire itself to limit Britain's capacity to intervene. The Dominions showed a growing disinclination to be drawn into conflicts of little interest or importance to themselves, as was proven at Chanak. More important to overall Asian policy, however, was the constant nagging of India's spokesmen. The combined pressure of Indian officials and the Indian nationalist movement contributed greatly to the policy of moderation and withdrawal which came to dominate in West and Central Asia.

Turkey was a unique issue in the Indian context, and it may be that Montagu gave unnecessary encouragement to the Indian Khilafat agitation, but the movement was real enough so long as Muslim and Hindu leaders were willing to cooperate in the cause. It was Gandhi's arrest and that of the Ali brothers, together with the estrangement caused by the Moplah troubles and the Afghani war, which reduced Hindu-Muslim cooperation. The victories of Kemal and the deposition first of the sultan and later of the caliph finally killed an already dying movement. The agitation had served several purposes, however, not least of which was to arouse Indian officials to the nationalist danger and the possible use of extra-Indian issues, such as the Turkish peace, to diminish that danger. In this Indian imperial administrators were ahead of opinion in London, which still tended to see the empire and its neighbors through prewar, Curzonian spectacles. To Curzon and others, the Indian attitude was at once too moderate—he would know how to deal with extremists—and too parochial: New Delhi bureaucrats persistently refused to recognize, let alone search out, the connection between the Bolshevik danger and their own immediate problems.

How much Indian agitation served to alter British policy is far less clear-cut. Obviously there was a vast difference between an India which would provide no troops and which urged wide-scale concessions and a hypothetical India which might have urged enforcement of Sèvres and offered up vast sepoy armies. British policy had inevitably to be based upon real resources, and they did not include Indian troops. Lloyd George, of course, regarded Greek evzones as an acceptable alternative —but when the Greek venture collapsed, there were no Indian replacements at hand, only continued Indian pressure. It cannot be concluded that India influenced the prime minister any more than did the warnings of the War Office or the Foreign Office—but when Lloyd George needed an easy scapegoat for withdrawing from his commitment, India was conveniently there.

Finally, the story of British policy in western Asia in the postwar era cannot be divorced from the pattern of Anglo-Russian relations. Russia's collapse had first sent British forces moving forward in an effort to continue the war, then the Soviet recovery led Britain to keep the routes open so as to assist the anti-Bolshevik struggle, and in the end, the Soviets forced a British retreat. The entire frontier, from Batum to Kabul, was, in a sense, Russian ebb, British flood—Russian flood, British ebb.

But Russia was only part of the story—not as big a part as some thought at the time. Kemalist nationalists might sign treaties and accept Soviet military aid and Indian nationalists turn to Moscow for support, but they were nationalists first and Soviet agents—if at all— only a very reluctant second. Moreover, Britain often succumbed to a curiously irresistible temptation of seeing a strong permanent ally in some temporary local Caucasian or Central Asian authority. The fog and mist which shrouded remote and unknown areas, including Ankara, made it all too easy either to overmagnify or to underestimate any given leader.

From the Dardanelles to the Khyber Pass, the events following 1918 took place in a unified whole. No consideration of Britain's Turkish policy, let alone a particular crisis such as Chanak, can approach accuracy unless one also examines events in the neighboring areas, to say nothing of problems at home which have not been considered here. Poincaré's response to British accusations of betrayal at Franklin-Bouillon's treaty with Kemal must be understood, for example, not only in the light of Cilicia and Anglo-French relations with the Arabs in Syria, but also in connection with French surprise and anger at Britain's secretly negotiated treaty with Persia. In a similar way, the Afghan treaty negotiations were influenced by Turkish events, and Persian military policy was complicated by the Kurdish problems in Iraq.

Turkey—Caucasus—Caspian—Persia—Afghanistan—India: the frontier in West Asia was at much a continuous chain of vitally linked segments as any other single international frontier, so long as Britain was involved in each and every portion. The "journey through chaos" of the years between 1918 and 1923 must always pass the milestone of West Asia.

Bibliography

MANUSCRIPT COLLECTIONS

Official Correspondence

Great Britain.
   Commonwealth Relations Office: India Office Records, London.
      Judicial and Public Department, Departmental Papers (C/J&P/6). 1918-1923.
      Military Department, Secret and Confidential Telegrams to and from India (L/Mil/3), War Diaries (uncatalogued), Military Secretary's files and correspondence (uncatalogued), 1918-1923.
      Political Department, Political and Secret Subject files (L/P&S/10), Regular Series files (L/P&S/11), 1913-1923.
   Public Record Office, London.
      Admiralty files, series 1 (Admiralty and Secretariat Papers), 137 (Historical Section, 1914-1918 War Histories), 1918-1923.
      Air Ministry files, series 19 (Private Office), 20 (Unregistered Papers), 1919-1921.
      Cabinet files, series 1 (Committee of Imperial Defence, Misc. Records), 21 (Cabinet registered files), 23-24 (Cabinet minutes and memoranda), 25 (Supreme War Council, 1917-1919), 27 (Cabinet Committees, General Series), 28 (War Cabinet: Allied conferences), 44 (Historical Section, official war histories, military narratives), 45 (Official Histories, Correspondence, and Papers), 1918-1923.
      Colonial Office files, series 730 (Iraq), 732 (Middle East), 1920-1924.
      Foreign Office files, series 371 (post-1905), 608 (Peace Conference), 839 (Lausanne Conference), 1916-1924.
      War Office files, series 32 (Registered papers), 33 (Misc. reports and papers), 95 (War Diaries), 106 (Directorate of Military Operations and Intelligence papers), 158 (Correspondence and papers of military headquarters), 161 (Misc. unregistered papers), 1918-1923.

India.
   National Archives of India, New Delhi.
      Home Department Proceedings. Political files, 1918-1924.
      Foreign Department Proceedings. Secret External and War files, 1917-1920.

Private Correspondence

Beaverbrook Library, London.
  The Papers of the Rt. Hon. Andrew Bonar Law.
  The Papers of David, Earl Lloyd George of Dwyfor.
British Museum, London.
  The Papers of Arthur James Balfour, 1st Earl of Balfour. Add. Mss.
    49683-49962.
  The Papers of Lord Edgar Algernon Robert Cecil, Viscount Cecil of
    Chelwood. Add. Mss. 51071-51204.
  The Papers of Lt.-Col. Sir Arnold Talbot Wilson. Add. Mss. 52455-
    52459.
Cambridge University Library.
  The Papers of Charles, Baron Hardinge of Penshurst.
Churchill College, Cambridge.
  The Papers of Admiral of the Fleet Sir John de Robeck, 1st Baronet.
India Office Library, London.
  The Papers of Frederic John Napier Thesiger, 1st Viscount Chelmsford.
  The Papers of George Nathaniel Curzon, 1st Marquis Curzon of Kedleston.
  The Papers of Sir Arthur Hamilton Grant.
  The Papers of the Hon. Edwin Samuel Montagu.
  The Papers of Rufus Daniel Isaacs, 1st Marquess of Reading.
  The Papers of Freeman Freeman-Thomas, 1st Marquess of Willington.
  The Papers of Lawrence John Lumley Dundas, 2nd Marquis of Zetland
    [to 1929, Earl of Ronaldshay].
King's College, London, Centre for Military Archives.
  The Papers of Maj.-Gen. Sir William R. Marshall.
Lambeth Palace, London.
  The Papers of Rt. Hon. and Most Rev. Randal Thomas Davidson, Arch-
    bishop of Canterbury.
Library of Congress, Washington, D.C.
  The Papers of Admiral Mark Lambert Bristol, USN.
National Maritime Museum, Greenwich.
  The Papers of Admiral Sir William A.H. Kelly.
  The Papers of Admiral David T. Norris.
  The Papers of Admiral of the Fleet Sir John Kelly.
Public Record Office, London.
  The Papers of Arthur James Balfour, 1st Earl of Balfour (*FO* 800).
  The Papers of Lord Edgar Algernon Robert Cecil, Viscount Cecil of
    Chelwood (*FO* 800).
  The Papers of George Nathaniel Curzon, 1st Marquis of Kedleston (*FO*
    800).
  The Papers of Edward George Villiers Stanley, 17th Earl of Derby
    (*WO* 137).
  The Papers of Sir Arthur Nicolson (*FO* 800).
  The Papers of Rt. Hon. Sir Lancelot Oliphant (*FO* 800).
  The Papers of Sir Andrew Ryan (*FO* 800).

PUBLISHED DOCUMENTS

Degras, Jane, ed. *Soviet Documents of Foreign Policy.* Vol. I: 1917-24. London: Oxford University Press, 1951.

Eudin, Xenia Joukoff, and Robert C. North. *Soviet Russia and the East, 1920-1927: A Documentary Survey.* Palo Alto, Calif.: Stanford University Press, 1957.

France.

Ministère des affaires étrangères. *Documents diplomatiques. Conférence de Lausanne.* Paris: Imprimerie Nationale, 1923. 2 vols.

Great Britain.

Committee of Imperial Defence. Historical Section. *History of the Great War Based on Official Documents.*

The Campaign in Mesopotamia, 1914-1918. Compiled by Brig-Gen. F.J. Moberley. London: H.M.S.O., 1923-1927. 4 vols.

Naval Operations. Compiled by Sir Julian S. Corbett. London: Longmans, Green, 1920-1928. 5 vols. in 9.

Foreign Office.

Documents on British Foreign Policy, 1919-1939, ed. by Rohan Butler, J.P.T. Bury, and E.L. Woodward. First series, vols. I-XVIII. London: H.M.S.O., 1947-1972.

Historical Section. *Peace Handbooks.* No. 62, "Armenia and Kurdistan," London: H.M.S.O., 1920.

Parliament. *Parliamentary Debates* and *British and Foreign State Papers.* London: H.M.S.O., 1918-1924.

War Office. General Staff (Palestine). Intelligence. *Kurdistan and the Kurds.* Mt. Carmel, Palestine: G.S. (I), Printing Section, [1920].

Greece.

Greece Before the Peace Congress of 1919: A Memorandum dealing with the Rights of Greece submitted by Eleutherios Venizelos. N.Y.: Oxford University Press (for American-Hellenic Society), 1919.

National Assembly. *Anti-Greek Persecutions in Turkey 1908 to 1921. Statements Submitted to the Third National Assembly in Athens. Sessions 5th, 6th, and 8th April, 1921.* London: G.S. Vellonia, 1921.

Hurewitz, J.C., ed. *Diplomacy in the Near and Middle East: A Documentary Record.* Vol. II: 1914-1956. Princeton, N.J.: D. Van Nostrand, 1956.

India.

Army Headquarters. General Staff.

The Third Afghan War, 1919: Official Account. Calcutta: Central Publications Branch, Government of India, 1926.

Operations in Waziristan, 1919-1920. Calcutta: Superintendent of Government Publications, 1921.

Home Department. *Histories of the Non-Co-Operation and Khalifat Movements,* by P.C. Bamford. Delhi: Government of India Press, 1925.

Iraq.

Office of the Çivil Commissioner.

Diary of Maj. E.M. Noel, C.I.E., D.S.O., on Special Duty in Kurdistan from June 14th, to September 21st, 1919. Basra: Superintendent of Government Press, [1919].

Note on the Kurdish Situation by Major E.W.C. Noel. Baghdad: Government Press, 1919.

Personalities in Kurdistan. Baghdad: Government Press, 1919.

Precis of Affairs in Southern Kurdistan during the Great War. Baghdad: Government Press, 1919.

League of Nations. *Greek Refugee Settlement.* Geneva: League of Nations, 1926.

Ligue pour la défense des droits des ottomanes. *Atrocités Greques dans le Vilayet de Smyrne; documents inédits et témoignages des officiers anglais et francais.* Geneva: Imprimerie nationale, 1919.

Mantoux, Paul, ed. *Paris Peace Conference, 1919. Proceedings of the Council of Four (March 24-April 18).* Geneva: Librairie Droz, 1964.

Mitra, H.N., ed. *Punjab Unrest Before and After.* Calcutta: N.N. Mitter, 1920.

[Mustafa Kemal Pasha, Ataturk]. *A Speech Delivered by Ghazi Mustapha Kemal, President of the Turkish Republic, October, 1927.* Leipzig, K.F. Koehler, 1929.

Paris Peace Conference. *Recueil des actes de la conférence.* Part IV: "Commissions de la conférence," C: "Questions territoriales," 51: "Commission chargée d'étudier les questions territoriales intéressant la Grèce." Paris: Imprimerie nationale, 1923.

Shapiro, Leonard, ed. *Soviet Treaty Series.* Vol. I: 1917-1928. Washington, D.C.: Georgetown University Press, 1950.

Turkey.

Ministry of Foreign Affairs. *Rapports officiels reçus des autorités militaires Ottomanes sur l'occupation de Smyrne par les troupes Helléniques.* Constantinople: Imprimerie Osmanie, 1919.

Ministry of Interior.

Greek Atrocities in Turkey. Constantinople: Ahmed Ihsan, 1921. 2 vols.

La guerre de l'indépendance turque. Ankara, n.p., 1937.

United States.

Department of State.

Papers Relating to the Foreign Relations of the United States. The Paris Peace Conference, 1919. Washington, D.C.: G.P.O. 1942-1947. 13 vols.

Papers Relating to the Foreign Relations of the United States. 1919; vol. II; 1920, vol. III; 1923, vols. II-III. Washington, D.C.: G.P.O. 1934-1938.

Roberts, Thomas D., et al. *Area Handbook for the Republic of Turkey.* Washington, D.C.: G.P.O., 1970.

BIOGRAPHIES AND MEMOIRS

Aga Khan. *The Memoirs of Aga Khan: World Enough and Time.* London: Cassell, 1954.

Alastos, Boris. *Venizelos: Patriot, Statesman, Revolutionary.* London: Percy Lund Humphries, 1942.

Ali, Mohamad and Shaukat. *For India and Islam.* Calcutta: Saraswaty Library, 1922.

Anderson, Nora. *Noel Buxton: A Life.* London: G. Allen & Unwin, 1952.

Andrew of Greece, H.R.H. Prince. *Towards Disaster: The Greek Army in Asia Minor in 1921.* London: John Murray, 1930.

Armstrong, Harold. *Turkey in Travail: The Birth of a New Nation.* London: John Lane the Bodley Head, 1925.

Azan, Général Paul. *Franchet d'Espérey.* Paris, Flamarion, 1949.

Bailey, Lt.-Col. F.M. *Mission to Tashkent.* London: Jonathan Cape, 1946.

Baldwin, Oliver. *Six Prisons and Two Revolutions: Adventures in Trans-Caucasia and Anatolia, 1920-1921.* London: Hodder and Stoughton, [1924].

Balfour, J.M. *Recent Happenings in Persia.* Edinburgh: Blackwood, 1922.

Barker, A.J. *Townshend of Kut: A Biography of Major-General Sir Charles Townshend, K.C.B., D.S.O.* London: Cassell, 1967.

Beaverbrook, Lord. *Men and Power, 1917-1918.* N.Y.: Duell, Sloan, & Pearce, 1956.

Bechhofer, D.E. *In Denikin's Russia and the Caucasus, 1919-1920. Being the Record of a Journey to South Russia, the Crimea, Armenia, Georgia and Baku in 1919 and 1920.* London: Collins, 1921.

Birkenhead, [2nd] Earl of. *Frederick Edwin, Earl of Birkenhead, by his Son.* 2 vols. London: Thornton Butterworth, 1933.

Blacker, L.V.S. *On Secret Patrol in High Asia.* London: John Murray, 1922.

Blake, Robert. *Unrepentant Tory: The Life and Times of Andrew Bonar Law, 1858-1923, Prime Minister of the United Kingdom.* N.Y.: St. Martins, 1956.

Bonarjee, N.B. *Under Two Masters.* Oxford: Oxford University Press, 1970.

Bowman, Humphrey. *Middle-East Window.* London: Longmans, Green, 1942.

Bridges, Lt.-Gen. Sir Tom. *Alarms and Excursions: Reminiscences of a Soldier.* London: Longmans, Green, 1938.

Brun, Capt. A.H. *Troublous Times: Experiences in Bolshevik Russia and Turkestan.* London: Constable, 1931.

Butler, J.R.M. *Lord Lothian (Philip Kerr), 1882-1940.* N.Y.: St. Martin's, 1960.

Buxton, Rt. Hon. Noel. *Travels and Reflections.* London: Allen & Unwin, 1929.

Callwell, Maj.-Gen. Sir C.E., ed. *Field-Marshal Sir Henry Wilson, Bart., G.C.B., D.S.O.; His Life and Diaries.* 2 vols. London: Cassell, 1927.

Catroux, Général. *Deux missions en Moyen-Orient (1919-1922).* Paris: Librairie Plon, 1958.

Chester, S.P. *Life of Venizelos.* London: Constable, 1921.

Child, Richard Washburn. *A Diplomat Looks at Europe.* N.Y.: Duffield, 1925.

Churchill, Randolph S. *Lord Derby: King of Lancashire: The Official Life of Edward, Seventeenth Earl of Derby, 1865-1948.* N.Y.: G.P. Putnam's Sons, 1960.

Coan, Frederick G. *Yesterdays in Persia and Kurdistan.* Claremont, Calif.: Sanders Studio Press, 1939.

Collier, Basil. *Brasshat: A Biography of Field-Marshal Sir Henry Wilson.* London: Secker & Warburg, 1961.

Dickson, Brig.-Gen. W.E.R. *East Persia: A Backwater of the Great War.* London: Edward Arnold, 1924.

Domville, Admiral Sir Barry. *By and Large.* London: Hutchinson, 1936.

Donohoe, Maj. M.H. *With the Persian Expedition.* London: Edward Arnold, 1919.

Dunsterville, Maj.-Gen. L.C. *The Adventures of Dunsterforce.* N.Y.: Longmans, Green, 1920.

————. *Stalky's Reminiscences.* London: Jonathan Cape, 1928.

Dyer, Brig.-Gen. R.E.H. *The Raiders of the Sarhad. Being the Account of a Campaign of Arms and Bluff against the Brigands of the Persian-Baluchi Border during the Great War.* London: H.F. & G. Witherby, 1921.

Edib, Halidé. *The Turkish Ordeal: Being the Further Memoirs of . . .* N.Y.: Century, 1928.

Ellison, Grace. *An Englishwoman in Angora.* London: Hutchinson, [1923].

Embry, Air Chief Marshal Sir Basil. *Mission Completed.* London: Methuen, 1957.

Etherton, Percy Thomas. *In the Heart of Asia.* London: Constable, 1925.

Forbes Adam, Colin. *Life of Lord Lloyd.* London: Macmillan, 1948.

Forbes-Leith, F.A.C. *Checkmate: Fighting Tradition in Central Persia.* London: Harrap, 1927.

French, Lt.-Col. F.J.F. *From Whitehall to the Caspian.* London: Odhams Press, [1920].

Gandhi, Mohandas K. *An Autobiography: The Story of My Experiments with Truth.* Boston: Beacon Press, 1957.

Gates, Caleb Frank. *Not to Me Only.* Princeton, N.J.: Princeton University Press, 1940.

Gibbons, Herbert Adams, *Venizelos.* 2nd ed. Boston: Houghton Mifflin, 1923.

Gould, B.J. *The Jewel in the Lotus: Recollections of an Indian Political.* London: Chatto & Windus, 1957.

Graves, Philip. *The Life of Sir Percy Cox.* London: Hutchinson, 1941.

Graves, Sir Robert. *Storm Centers of the Near East: Personal Memories 1879-1929.* London: Hutchinson, 1933.

Grew, Joseph C. *Turbulent Era: A Diplomatic Record of Forty Years, 1904-1945.* 2 vols. London: Hammond, Hammond & Co., 1953.

Hamilton, A.M. *Road Through Kurdistan: The Narrative of an Engineer in Iraq.* London: Faber & Faber, 1937.

Hardinge of Penshurst, Lord. *Old Diplomacy: The Reminiscences of . . .* London: J. Murray, 1947.

Harington, General Sir Charles. *Plumer of Messines.* London: J. Murray, 1935.

————. *Tim Harington Looks Back.* London: J. Murray, 1940.

Hartunian, Abraham H. *Neither to Laugh nor to Weep: A Memoir of the Armenian Genocide.* Trans. from Armenian by Vartan Hartunian. Boston: Beacon Press, 1968.

Hay, W.R. *Two Years in Kurdistan: Experiences of a Political Officer, 1918-1920.* London: Sidgwick & Jackson, 1921.

Heinrichs, Waldo H., Jr. *American Ambassador: Joseph C. Grew and the Development of the United States Diplomatic Tradition.* Boston: Little, Brown, 1966.

Henderson, Sir Nevile. *Water under the Bridges.* London: Hodder & Stoughton, 1945.

Hibben, Paxton. *Constantine I and the Greek People.* N.Y.: Century, 1920.

Horton, George. *Recollections Grave and Gay: The Story of a Mediterranean Consul.* Indianapolis: Bobbs-Merrill, 1927.

Hyde, H. Montgomery. *Lord Reading: The Life of Rufus Isaacs, First Marquess of Reading.* N.Y.: Farrar, Straus, and Giroux, 1967.

James, Admiral Sir William. *Admiral Sir William Fisher.* London: Macmillan, 1943.

————. *The Eyes of the Navy: A Biographical Study of Admiral Sir Reginald Hall, K.C.M.G., C.B., Ll.D., D.C.L.* London: Methuen, 1955.

Jones, Thomas. *Lloyd George.* Cambridge, Mass.: Harvard University Press, 1951.

————. *Whitehall Diary,* ed. by Keith Middlemas. Vol. I: 1916-1925. London: Oxford University Press, 1969.

Kenworthy, Lt.-Cmd. Hon. J.M. *Sailors,-Statesmen—and Others: An Autobiography.* London: Rich & Cowan, 1933.

Kerr, Stanley E. *The Lions of Marash: Personal Experiences with American Near East Relief, 1919-1922.* Albany, N.Y.: State University of New York Press, 1973.

Kinross, Lord. *Ataturk: A Biography of Mustafa Kemal, Father of Modern Turkey.* N.Y.: William Morrow, 1965.

Laroche, Jules. *Au Quai d'Orsay avec Briand et Poincaré, 1913-1926.* Paris: [1957].

Lloyd George, David. *Memoirs of the Peace Conference.* 2 vols. New Haven, Conn.: Yale University Press, 1939.

————. *War Memoirs.* 2 vols. London: Odhams Press, [1938].

Luke, Sir Harry. *Cities and Men: An Autobiography.* Vol. II: "Aegean, Cyprus, Turkey, Transcaucasia & Palestine (1914-1924)." London: Geoffrey Bles, 1953.

McCormick, Donald. *Peddler of Death: The Life and Times of Sir Basil Zaharoff.* N.Y.: Holt, Rinehart, & Winston, 1965.

MacDonell, Ranald. *". . . and Nothing Long."* London: Constable, 1938.

Mackenzie, Compton. *Aegean Memories.* London: Chatto & Windus, 1940.

————. *First Athenian Memories.* London: Cassell, 1931.

————. *Greek Memories.* London: Chatto & Windus, 1939.

MacMunn, Lt.-Gen. Sir George. *Behind the Scenes in Many Wars: Being the Military Reminiscences of . . .* London: John Murray, 1930.

Marshall, Lt.-Gen. Sir William. *Memories of Four Fronts.* London: E. Benn, 1929.

Mélas, George M. *Ex-King Constantine and the War.* London: Hutchinson, [1920].

Menon, K.P.S. *C. Sankaran Nair.* New Delhi: Government of India, Ministry of Information and Broadcasting, Publications Division, 1967.

Middlemas, Keith, and John Barnes. *Baldwin: A Biography.* N.Y.: Macmillan, 1970.

Moon, Penderel. *Gandhi and Modern India.* N.Y.: W.W. Norton, 1969.

Mufty-Zade, K. Zia Bey. *Speaking of the Turks.* N.Y.: Duffield & Co., 1922.

Murphy, Lt.-Col. C.C.R. *Soldiers of the Prophet.* London: John Hogg, 1921.

Neumann, Robert. *Zaharoff the Armaments King.* London: G. Allen & Unwin, 1938.

Nicolson, Harold. *Curzon: The Last Phase, 1919-1925: A Study in Post-War Diplomacy.* London: Constable, 1934.

————. *Peacemaking 1919.* N.Y.: Grosset & Dunlap, 1965.

Panikkar, K.M. *His Highness the Maharaja of Bikaner: A Biography.* Oxford: Oxford University Press, 1937.

Patrick, Mary Mills. *A Bosporus Adventure: Istanbul (Constantinople) Women's College, 1871-1924.* Stanford, Calif.: Stanford University Press, 1934.

Powell, E. Alexander. *Free-Lance.* London: Harrap, 1938.

Presland, John [Gladys Skelton]. *Deedes Bey: A Study of Sir Wyndham Deedes, 1883-1923.* London: Macmillan, 1942.

Rawlinson, Lt.-Col. A. *Adventures in the Near East, 1918-1922.* N.Y.: Dodd, Mead, 1924.

Repington, Lt.-Col. C. à Court. *The First World War, 1914-1918: Personal Experiences of . . .* 2 vols. London: Constable, 1920.

Riddell, Lord. *Intimate Diary of the Peace Conference and After, 1918-1923.* London: Gollancz, 1933.

Ronaldshay, Earl of. *The Life of Lord Curzon, being the authorized biography of George Nathaniel, Marquess Curzon of Kedleston, K.G.* Vol. III. London: E. Benn, 1928.

Rose, Kenneth, *Superior Person: A Portrait of Curzon and His Circle in Late Victorian England.* London: Weidenfeld & Nicolson, 1969.

Roskill, Stephen. *Hankey, Man of Secrets.* 2 vols. London: Collins, 1970-71.

Ryan, Sir Andrew. *The Last of the Dragomans.* London: Geoffrey Bles, 1951.

Scott, Charles Prestwick. *The Political Diaries of C.P. Scott, 1911-1928.* Ithaca, N.Y.: Cornell University Press, 1970.

Seymour, Charles, ed. *The Intimate Papers of Colonel House.* Vol. IV. Boston: Houghton Mifflin, 1928.

Sheridan, Clare. *Nuda Veritas.* London: Thorton Butterworth, 1927.

Skrine, Sir Clarmont. *World War in Iran.* London: Constable, 1962.

Slocombe, George. *The Tumult and the Shouting: The Memoirs of . . .* London: Heinemann, 1936.

Soane, E.B. *To Mesopotamia and Kurdistan in Disguise with Historical Notices of the Kurdish Tribes and the Chaldeans of Kurdistan.* 2nd ed., London: John Murray, 1926.

Street, C.J.C. *Lord Reading.* London: Geoffrey Bles, 1928.

Swinson, Arthur. *Beyond the Frontiers: The Biography of Colonel F.M. Bailey, Explorer and Special Agent.* London: Hutchinson, 1971.

Sykes, Christopher. *Wassmuss, "The German Lawrence."* London: Longmans, Green, 1936.

Thomson, Sir Basil. *The Scene Changes.* London: Collins, 1939.

Toynbee, Arnold J. *Acquaintances.* London: Oxford University Press, 1967.

Vansittart, Lord. *The Mist Procession.* London: Hutchinson, 1958.

Waley, S.D. *Edwin Montagu: A Memoir and an Account of His Visits to India.* N.Y.: Asia Publishing House, 1964.

Wilson, Lt.-Col. Sir Arnold T. *Mesopotamia, 1917-1920: A Clash of Loyalties. A Personal and Historical Record.* Oxford: Oxford University Press, 1931.

Woodrooffe, Thomas. *Naval Odyssey.* London: Jonathan Cape, 1936.

Yalman, Ahmed Emin. *Turkey in My Time.* Norman, Okla.: University of Oklahoma Presss, 1956.

ARTICLES

Adalia. "The Problem of Asia Minor," *Edinburgh Review* 235 (January 1922): 131-46.

Allen, W.E.D. "Military Operations in Daghestan, 1917-21," *Army Quarterly* 19 (July-October, 1934): 39-53, 246-60.

Ameer, Ali, Syed. "The Caliphate and the Islamic Renaissance," *Edinburgh Review* 237 (January, 1923): 180-95.

"American Military Mission to Armenia," *International Conciliation* no. 151 (June 1920): 275-312.

"Anglo-Indian Troops in Persia, Transcaucasia and Turkestan, 1914-20," *Central Asian Review* 8 (1960): 296-99.

"Australia. III. Turkey," *Round Table* 13 (1922-23): 183-84.

Barry, William. "Constantinople," *Nineteenth Century and After* 87 (April 1920): 718-28.

Boulger, Demetrius. "The Moplah Warning," *Contemporary Review* 120 (November 1921): 658-64.

Bryce, Viscount. "The Revision of the Turkish Treaty. I. Armenia," *Contemporary Review* 119 (May 1921): 577-81.

— — — —. "The Settlement of the Near East," *Contemporary Review* 117 (January 1920): 1-9.

Bryson, Thomas A. "An American Mandate for Armenia: A Link in British Near Eastern Policy," *Armenian Review* 21 (Summer 1968): 23-41.

— — — —. "Mark Lambert Bristol, U.S. Navy, Admiral-Diplomat: His Influence on the Armenian Mandate Question," *Armenian Review* 21 (Winter 1968): 3-22.

Butler, Lt.-Col. P.R. "Grief and Glamour of the Bosporus," *Blackwood's* 209 (February 1921): 203-12.

Buxton, Noel. "The Revision of the Turkish Treaty. III. Thrace," *Contemporary Review* 119 (May 1921): 586-89.

"Canada. III. The Near East Crisis," *Round Table* 13 (1922-23): 176-77.

Carrère d'Encausse, Hélène. "Civil War and New Governments," and "The Fall of the Czarist Empire," in E. Allworth, ed., *Central Asia: A Century of Russian Rule.* N.Y.: Columbia University Press, 1967. Pp. 207-53.

Challener, Richard D. "The French Foreign Office: The Era of Philippe Berthelot," Gordon A. Craig and Felix Gilbert, eds., *The Diplomats, 1919-1939.* Princeton, N.J.: Princeton University Press, 1953. Pp. 49-85.

Chester, Arthur Tremaine. "Angora and the Turks," *Current History* 17 (1923): 758-64.

Chester, Rear Admiral Colby M. "Turkey Reinterpreted," *Current History* 16 (1922): 937-47.

Chirol, Sir Valentine. "Four Years of Lloyd-Georgian Foreign Policy," *Edinburgh Review* 237 (January 1923): 1-20.

— — — —. "Islam and Britain," *Foreign Affairs* 1 (15 March 1923): 48-58.

— — — —. "The Downfall of the Khalifate," *Foreign Affairs* 2 (15 June 1924): 571-82.

Craig, Gordon A. "The British Foreign Office from Grey to Austen Chamberlain," Craig and Gilbert, eds., *The Diplomats, 1919-1939.* Pp. 15-48.

Cruickshank, A.A. "The Young Turk Challenge in Postwar Turkey," *Middle East Journal* 22 (Winter 1968): 17-28.

Daniel, Robert L. "The Armenian Question and American-Turkish Relations, 1914-1927," *Mississippi Valley Historical Review* 46 (September 1959): 252-75.

Davison, Roderic H. "Middle East Nationalism: Lausanne Thirty Years After," *Middle East Journal* 7 (Summer 1953): 324-48.

— — — —. "Turkish Diplomacy from Mudros to Lausanne," in Craig and Gilbert, eds., *The Diplomats, 1919-1939.* Pp. 172-209.

Denny, Ludwell. "Up in Curzon's Room," *The Nation* 116 (10 January 1923): 40-41.

Douglas, Maj.-Gen. J.A. "The Bushire-Shiraz Road, 1918-19," *Journal of Central Asian Society* 10 (1923): 104-22.

Dunsterville, Maj.-Gen. L.C. "Military Mission to North-West Persia, 1918," *Journal of the Central Asian Society* 8 (1921): 79-98.

Dyer, Gwynne. "The Turkish Armistice of 1918," *Middle East Studies* 8 (May-October 1972): 143-78, 316-48.

Ellis, C.H. "Operations in Transcaspia 1918-1919 and the 26 Commissars Case," *St. Antony's Papers, No. 6: Soviet Affairs, No. 2* ed. David Footman. London: Chatto & Windus, 1959. Pp. 129-53.

Falls, Cyril. "The Greek Anatolian Adventure," *History Today* 16 (July 1966): 452-58.

Farrell, Thomas D. "The Founding of the North-West Frontier Militias," *Asian Affairs* 59 (June 1972): 165-78.

Footman, David. "Nestor Makhno," *St. Antony's Papers, No. 6: Soviet Affairs, No. 2* ed. David Footman. Pp. 75-127.

Gauvain, Auguste. "Five Years of French Policy in the Near East," *Foreign Affairs* 3 (15 December 1924): 277-92.

Gounaris, Demetrios. "What Greece Has Won from the Turk," *Current History* 15 (1921-22): 911-14.

Grabill, Joseph L. "Missionary Influence on American Relations with the Near East, 1914-1923," *Muslim World* 58 (1968): 43-56, 141-54.

Gregorian, Vartan. "Mahmud Tarzi and *Saraj-ol-Akhbar:* Ideology of Nationalism in Afghanistan," *Middle East Journal* 21 (Summer 1967): 345-368.

Grew, Joseph C. "The Peace Conference of Lausanne, 1922-1923," *Proceedings of the American Philosophical Society* 98 (February 1954): 1-10.

Helmreich, Paul C. "Oil and the Negotiation of the Treaty of Sevres, December 1918-April 1920," *Middle East Forum* 42 (1966): 67-75.

Hibben, Paxton. "What the Greeks are Fighting for," *Current History* 14 (April-September 1921): 408-15.

Hill, Commander Laurence Bernard, "Smyrna and the Dardanelles, 1922," in Brian Tunstall, ed. *The Anatomy of Neptune.* London: Routledge, 1936. Pp. 334-352.

Hooper, C.R., trans. "The Anatolian Revolt," *Army Quarterly* 12 (1966): 106-19, 323-37.

Hovannisian, Richard G. "Armenia and the Caucasus in the Genesis of the Soviet-Turkish Entente," *International Journal of Middle East Studies* 4 (April 1973): 129-47.

————. "The Allies and Armenia, 1915-18," *Journal of Contemporary History* 3 (January 1968): 145-68.

————. "The Armeno-Azerbaijani Conflict over Mountainous Karabagh, 1918-1919," *The Armenian Review* 24 (Summer 1971): 3-39.

Hughes, H. Stuart, "The Early Diplomacy of Italian Fascism: 1922-1932," in Craig and Gilbert, eds., *The Diplomats, 1919-1939.* Pp. 210-233.

Hurgronje, Snouck, "Islam and Turkish Nationalism," *Foreign Affairs* 3 (15 September 1924): 61-77.

"India and the Moslem Awakening," *Current History* 16 (1922): 1-8.

Jäschke, Gotthard, "Zur Geschichte des türkischen Nationalpakts," *Mitteilungen des Seminars für orientalische Sprachen* 36 (1933): 101-16.

————. "Die türkische-armenische Grenze und der Friedensvertrag von Gümrü (Alexandropol)," *Mitteilungen des Seminars für orientalische Sprachen* 35 (1932): 162-71.

————. "Urkunden I. Der Weg zur russische-türkischen Freundschaft im Lichte Moskaus," *Die Welt des Islams* 20 (1938): 118-34.

Kazemzadeh, Firuz. "The Origin and Early Development of the Persian Cossack Brigade," *American Slavic and East European Review* 15 (October 1956): 351-56.

Khan, Rasheeduddin. "The Peace Settlement, Arab Diplomacy and Anglo-French Power Politics: 1919-1920," *Islamic Culture* 42 (April and July 1968): 57-73, 133-50.

Klieman, Aaron S. "Britain's War Aims in the Middle East in 1915," *Journal of Contemporary History* 3 (July 1968): 237-52.

Knollys, Lt.-Col. D.E. "Military Operations in Transcaspia, 1918-1919," *Journal of the Central Asian Society* 13 (1926): 89-110.

"The Lausanne Conference," *The Round Table* 13 (1922-23): 342-55.

Loch, David H. "Constantinople during the Crisis," *Contemporary Review* 122 (January 1923): 25-34.

Low, D.A. "The Government of India and the First Non-Co-Operation Movement, 1920-1922," in R. Kumar, ed., *Essays on Gandhian Politics: The Rowlatt Satyagraha of 1919.* Oxford: Clarendon Press, 1971. Pp. 298-323.

Malleson, Maj.-Gen. Sir Wilfrid. "The British Military Mission to Turkestan, 1918-1920," *Journal of the Central Asian Society* 9 (1922): 95-110.

Mandelstam, André. "The Turkish Spirit," *The New Europe* 15 (22 April 1920): 39-45.

Margoliouth, D.S. "The Caliphate," *The New Europe* 14 (8 April 1920): 294-300.

Maurice, Maj.-Gen. Sir F. "The Crisis as Seen in Constantinople," *Contemporary Review* 122 (November 1922): 556-62.

Mehotra, S.R. "The Politics Behind the Montagu Declaration of 1917," in C.H. Philips, ed., *Politics and Society in India.* N.Y.: Praeger, 1962. Pp. 71-96.

Mejcher, Helmut. "Oil and British Policy Towards Mesopotamia, 1914-18," *Middle East Studies* 8 (3 October 1972): 377-92.

Montgomery, A.E. "Lloyd George and the Greek Question 1918-22," in A.J.P. Taylor, ed., *Lloyd George: Twelve Essays.* London: Hamish Hamilton, 1971. Pp. 257-84.

Morgan, Gerald. "Myth and Reality in the Great Game," *Asian Affairs* 60 (February 1973): 55-65.

Morison, Theodore. "England and Islam," *Nineteenth Century and After* 86 (July 1919): 116-22.

Nevakivi, Jukka. "Lord Kitchener and the Partition of the Ottoman Empire, 1915-1916," in K. Bourne and D.C. Watt, eds., *Studies in International History: Essays Presented to W. Norton Medlicott, Stevenson Professor of International History in the University of London.* Hamden, Conn.: Archon Books, 1963. Pp. 316-29.

"New Zealand. VII. The Near Eastern War Cloud," *Round Table* 13 (1922-23): 453-56.

Norris, Capt. David. "Caspian Naval Expedition, 1918-1919," *Journal of the Central Asian Society* 10 (1923): 216-40.

"Operations in Persia, 1914-1920," *Central Asian Review* 10 (1962): 85-89.

Owen, H.F. "Organizing for the Rowlatt Satagraha," in Kumar, ed., *Essays on Gandhian Politics.* Pp. 64-92.

Polyzoides, Adamantios T. "Why the Greeks are Fighting Turkey," *Current History* 14 (April-September 1921): 761-66.

Rustow, Dankwart A. "The Army and the Founding of the Turkish Republic," *World Politics* 11 (July 1959): 513-52.

Sarkisyanz, Manuel. "Russian Conquest in Central Asia: Transformation and Acculturation," in Wayne S. Vucinich, ed., *Russia and Asia: Essays on the Influence of Russia on the Asian Peoples.* Stanford, Calif.: Hoover Institution Press, 1972. Pp. 248-88.

Shuttleworth, Col. D.L. "Turkey from the Armistice to the Peace," *Journal of the Asian Society* 11 (1924): 51-67.

Smith, C.J., Jr. "Great Britain and the 1914-1915 Straits Agreement with Russia: The British Promise of November 1914," *American Historical Review* 70 (1965): 1015-34.

"South Africa. I. The Union and the Dardanelles," *Round Table* 13 (1922-23): 199-201.

Stavridi, Sir J.J. "The Revision of the Turkish Treaty. II. Smyrna," *Contemporary Review* 119 (May 1921): 581-86.

Sykes, Brig.-Gen. Sir Percy. "The British Flag on the Caspian: A Side-Show of the Great War," *Foreign Affairs* 2 (15 December 1923): 282-94.

"Text of the Chester Concession," *Current History* 18 (1923): 485-89.

Thurburn, Capt. R.G. "The Operations in Southern Kurdistan, March-May 1923," *Army Quarterly* 31 (January 1936): 264-77.

Tod, Col. J.K. "Operations in Trans-Caspia, 1918-1919," *Army Quarterly* 16 (April-June 1928): 280-303.

————. "The Malleson Mission to Transcaspia in 1918," *Journal of the Central Asian Society* 27 (1940): 45-67.

Townshend, Maj.-Gen. Sir Charles. "Great Britain and the Turks," *Asia* (N.Y.) 22 (December 1922): 949-55.

Toynbee, Arnold J. "Angora and the British Empire in the East," *Contemporary Review* 123 (June 1923): 681-91.

————. "The Draft Treaty with Turkey," *The New Europe* 15 (20 May 1920): 136-38, 162-64.

————. "The Indian Moslem Delegation" *The New Europe* 15 (29 April 1920): 56-60.

————. "The Meaning of the Constantinople Decision," *The New Europe* 14 (19 February 1920): 129-31.

————. "Meeting the Turk Half-Way," *Asia* 22 (August 1923): 577-81.

————. "Mr. Montagu's Pound of Flesh," *The New Europe* 14 (26 February 1920): 145-49.

————. "The Problem of the Straits and Constantinople," *Review of Reviews* 61 (January 1920): 39-43.

————. "The Question of the Caliphate," *Contemporary Review* 117 (February 1920): 192-96.

————. "The Revulsion in Greece," *Contemporary Review* 99 (January 1921): 10-19.

————. "The Truth about Near East Atrocities," *Current History* 18 (July 1923): 544-51.

Van Cutsem, Brig.-Gen. W.E. "Anatolia, 1920," *Army Quarterly* 92 (July 1966): 175-85.

Williams, Aneurin. "Armenia, British Pledges and the Near East," *Contemporary Review* 121 (April 1922): 418-25.

MONOGRAPHS AND SPECIAL WORKS

Abbas, M.H. *All About the Khilafat . . .* Calcutta: R. & R. Choudhury, [1923].

Abbott, G.F. *Greece and the Allies, 1914-1922.* London: Methuen, 1922.

Adamec, Ludwig W. *Afghanistan 1900-1923: A Diplomatic History.* Berkeley, Calif.: University of California Press, 1967.

————. *Afghanistan's Foreign Affairs to the mid-Twentieth Century: Relations with the USSR, Germany, and Britain.* Tucson, Ariz.: University of Arizona Press, 1974.

Ahmad, Feroz. *The Young Turks: The Committee of Union and Progress in Turkish Politics, 1908-1914.* Oxford: Clarendon Press, 1969.

Allen, W.E.D., and Paul Muratoff. *Caucasian Battlefields: A History of the Wars on the Turco-Caucasian Border, 1828-1921.* Cambridge: Cambridge University Press, 1953.

Allworth, Edward, ed. *Central Asia: A Century of Russian Rule.* N.Y.: Columbia University Press, 1967.

Anderson, M.S. *The Eastern Question, 1774-1923: A Study in International Relations.* London: Macmillan, 1966.

Arfa, Hassan. *The Kurds: An Historical and Political Study.* London: Oxford University Press, 1966.

Aston, Sir George. *Secret Service.* London: Faber & Faber, 1930.

Avery, Peter, *Modern Iran.* London: E. Benn, 1965.

Aziz, K.K. *Britain and Muslim India: A Study of British Public Opinion vis-à-vis the Development of Muslim Nationalism in India, 1857-1947.* London: Heinemann, 1963.

Barton, James L. *Story of Near East Relief (1915-1930): An Interpretation.* N.Y.: Macmillan, 1930.

Beaverbrook, Lord. *The Decline and Fall of Lloyd George.* N.Y.: Duell, Sloan and Pearce, 1963.

Beers, Henry P. *U.S. Naval Detachment in Turkish Waters, 1919-1924.* Washington, D.C.: Office of Records Administration, Navy Dept., 1943.

Berkes, Niyazi. *The Development of Secularism in Turkey.* Montreal: McGill University Press, 1964.

Bierstadt, Edward Hale. *The Great Betrayal: A Survey of the Near East Problem.* London: Hutchinson, [1924].

Bois, Thomas. *The Kurds.* Beirut: Khayat's, 1966.

Brémond, E. *La Cilicie en 1919-1920.* Paris: Imprimerie Nationale, 1921.

Brinkley, George A. *The Volunteer Army and Allied Intervention in South Russia, 1917-1921: A Study in the Politics and Diplomacy of the Russian Civil War.* Notre Dame, Ind.: University of Notre Dame Press, 1966.

Broomfield, J.H. *Elite Conflict in a Plural Society: Twentieth-Century Bengal.* Berkeley, Calif.: University of California Press, 1968.

Brown, Judith M. *Gandhi's Rise to Power: Indian Politics 1915-1922.* Cambridge: Cambridge University Press, 1972.

Bujac, Col. *Les Campagnes de l'Armée Hellénique, 1918-1922.* Paris: Charles-Lavauzelle, 1930.

Bulloch, John. *M.I.5: The Origin and History of the British Counter-Espionage Service.* London: Arthur Barker, 1963.

Burne, Lt.-Col. A.H. *Mesopotamia, the Last Phase.* Aldershot: Gale & Polden, 1936.

Busch, Briton Cooper. *Britain, India, and the Arabs, 1914-1921.* Berkeley, Calif.: University of California Press, 1971.

————. *Britain and the Persian Gulf, 1894-1914.* Berkeley, Calif.: University of California Press, 1967.

Castagné, Joseph. *Les Basmatchis: le mouvement nationale des indigènes d'Asie Centrale depuis la Revolution d'octobre 1917 jusqu'en octobre 1924.* Paris: Editions Ernest Leroux, 1925.

Chatterton, E. Keble. *Seas of Adventures: The Story of the Naval Operations in the Mediterranean and Aegean.* London: Hurst & Blackett, 1936.

Chirol, Sir Valentine. *India Old and New.* London: Macmillan, 1921.

Choudhary, Sukhbir. *Indian People Fight for National Liberation (Non-Cooperation, Khilafat and Revivalist Movements) 1920-22.* New Delhi: Srijanee Prakashan, 1972.

Churchill, Rt. Hon. Winston S. *The World Crisis,* V. "The Aftermath." London: Thorton Butterworth, 1929.

Collins, Dorreen. *Aspects of British Politics, 1904-1919.* Oxford: Pergammon Press, 1965.

Cosmetatos, S.P. *The Tragedy of Greece.* London: Kegan, Paul, Trench, Trubner, 1928.

Cosmin, S. [S.P. Cosmetatos]. *Diplomatie et presse dans l'affaire Grecque, 1914-1916.* Paris: Société Mutuelle d'Edition, 1921.

Cumming, Henry H. *Franco-British Rivalry in the Post-War Near East: The Decline of French Influence.* London: Oxford University Press, 1938.

Curzon, George N. *Persia and the Persian Question.* Reprint. N.Y.: Barnes & Noble, 1966.

Dakin, Douglas. *The Unification of Greece, 1770-1923.* N.Y.: St. Martin's, 1972.

Dane, Edmund, *British Campaigns in the Nearer East, 1914-1918, from the Outbreak of War with Turkey to the Armistice.* 2 vols. London: Hodder & Stoughton, 1919.

Daniell, David Scott. *The Royal Hampshire Regiment.* Vol. III (1918-1954).

Aldershot: Gale & Polden, 1955.

Datta, V.N. *Jallianwala Bagh.* Ludhiana: Lyall Book Depot, 1969.

David, Robert. *Le drame ignoré de l'Armée d'Orient: Dardanelles-Serbie-Salonique-Athéne.* Paris: Libairie Plon, 1927.

Deacon, Richard [Donald McCormick]. *A History of the British Secret Service.* London: Frederick Muller, 1969.

Deygas, Capt. F.-J. *L'Armée d'Orient dans la Guerre mondiale (1915-1919).* Paris: Payot, 1932.

Dos Passos, John. *Orient Express.* N.Y.: Jonathan Cape & Harrison Smith, 1922.

Douglas, Rev. J.A. *The Redemption of Saint Sophia: An Historical and Political Account of the Subject.* London: Faith Press, 1919.

Driault, Edouard. *Histoire diplomatique de la Grèce de 1821 a nos jours.* Vol. V: "La Grèce et la Grande Guerre de la révolution turque au Traité de Lausanne (1908-1923)." Paris: Presses Universitaires de France, 1926.

Du Véou, Paul. *La Passion de la Cilicie, 1919-1922.* 2nd ed. Paris: Librairie Orientaliste Paul Geuthner, 1954.

Edmonds, C.J. *Kurds, Turks and Arabs: Politics, Travel and Research in North-Eastern Iraq, 1919-1925.* London: Oxford University Press, 1957.

Edwards, Kenneth. *The Grey Diplomatists.* London: L. Rich & Cowan, 1938.

Ellis, C.H. *The British 'Intervention' in Trans-Caspia, 1918-1919.* Berkeley, Calif.; University of California Press, 1963.

Elston, Roy. *The Traveler's Handbook for Constantinople, Gallipoli and Asia Minor.* London: Thomas Cook, 1923.

Evans, Laurence. *United States Policy and the Partition of Turkey, 1914-1924.* Baltimore: John Hopkins University Press, 1965.

Fatemi, Nasrollah Saifpour. *Diplomatic History of Persia, 1917-1923: Anglo-Russian Power Politics in Iran.* N.Y.: Russell F. Moore, 1952.

Fenton, Charles A. *The Apprenticeship of Ernest Hemingway: The Early Years.* N.Y.: Farrar, Straus, Young, 1954.

Frangulis, A.F. *La Grèce et la crise mondiale.* Paris: Librairie Félix Alcan, 1926.

Gaillard, Gaston. *The Turks and Europe.* London: Thomas Murphy, 1921.

Gehrke, Ulrich. *Persien in der deutschen Orientpolitik während des Ersten Weltkrieges.* 2 vols. Stuttgart: W. Kohlhammer, [1961].

Georges-Gaulis, Berthe. *Angora, Constantinople, Londres: Moustafa Kémal et la politique anglaise en Orient.* Paris: Librairie Armand Colin, 1922.

————. *Le nationalisme turc.* Paris: Librairie Plon, 1922.

————. *La question turque: un page d'histoire turque et d'erreurs européenes, 1919-1931.* Paris: Editions Berger-Levrault, 1931.

Ghose, Akshaya K. *Lord Chelmsford's Viceroyalty.* Madras: Ganesh & Co., [1921].

Gidney, James B. *A Mandate for Armenia.* Kent, Ohio: Kent State University Press, 1967.

Gökalp, Ziya. *The Principles of Turkism.* Trans. Robert Devereaux. Leiden: E.J. Brill, 1968.

Gontaut-Birion, Comte R. de. *Comment la France s'est installée en Syrie (1918-1919).* Paris: Librairie Plon, 1922.

Gopal, Ram. *Indian Muslims: A Political History (1858-1947).* N.Y.: Asia Publishing House, 1959.

Graves, P.P. *The Question of the Straits.* London: E. Benn, 1931.

――――. *Briton and Turk.* London: Hutchinson, 1941.

Gregorian, Vartan. *The Emergence of Modern Afghanistan: Politics of Reform and Modernization, 1880-1946.* Stanford, Calif.: Stanford University Press, 1969.

Hall, William H., ed. *Reconstruction in Turkey: A Series of Reports Compiled for the American Committee of Armenian and Syrian Relief.* N.Y.: American Committee of Armenian and Syrian Relief, 1918.

Hankey, Lord. *The Supreme Control at the Paris Peace Conference, 1919: A Commentary.* London: Allen & Unwin, 1963.

Helmreich, Paul C. *From Paris to Sèvres: The Partition of the Ottoman Empire at the Peace Conference of 1919-1920.* Columbus, Ohio: Ohio State University Press, 1974.

Horton, George. *The Blight of Asia: An Account of the Systematic Extermination of Christian Populations by Mohammedans and of the Culpability of Certain Great Powers: with the True Story of the Burning of Smryna.* Indianapolis: Bobbs-Merrill, 1926.

Hovannisian, Richard G. *Armenia on the Road to Independence, 1918.* Berkeley, Calif.: University of California Press, 1967.

――――. *The Republic of Armenia.* Vol. I: "The First Year, 1918-1919." Berkeley, Calif.: University of California Press, 1971.

Howard, Harry N. *The King-Crane Commission: An American Inquiry in the Middle East.* Beirut: Khayat's, 1963.

――――. *The Partition of Turkey: A Diplomatic History, 1913-1923.* N.Y.: Howard Fertig, 1966 (reprint of 1931 ed.).

Housepian, Marjorie. *The Smyrna Affair.* N.Y.: Harcourt, Brace, Jovanovich, 1971.

Huttenback, Robert A. *The British Imperial Experience.* N.Y.: Harper & Row, 1966.

Indian Khalifat Delegation. *Atrocities Committed in Smyrna.* London: Indian Khalifat Delegation [I.K.D.], 1920.

――――. *India's Verdict on Turkish Treaty.* London: I.K.D., 1920.

――――. *Justice to Islam and Turkey.* London: I.K.D., 1920.

――――. *A People's Right to Live.* London: I.K.D., 1920.

――――. *The Prime Minister and the Indian Khalifat Delegation.* London: I.K.D., 1920.

――――. *The Secretary of State for India and the Indian Khalifat Delegation.* London: I.K.D., 1920.

――――. *The Turkish Settlement and the Muslim and Indian Attitude.* London: I.K.D., 1920.

Ireland, Philip Willard. *'Iraq: A Study in Political Development.* N.Y.:

Macmillan, 1938.

Irschick, Eugene F. *Politics and Social Conflict in South India: The Non-Brahman Movement and Tamil Separatism, 1916-1929.* Berkeley, Calif.: University of California Press, 1969.

Johnson, Clarence Richard, ed. *Constantinople Today, or the Pathfinder Survey of Constantinople: A Study in Oriental Social Life.* N.Y.: Macmillan, 1922.

Kapur, Harish. *Soviet Russia and Asia, 1917-1927: A Study of Soviet Policy Towards Turkey, Iran and Afghanistan.* London: Michael Joseph, 1966.

Kazemzadeh, Firuz. *Russia and Britain in Persia, 1864-1914: A Study in Imperialism.* New Haven, Conn.: Yale University Press, 1968.

––––. *The Struggle for Transcaucasia (1917-1921).* N.Y.: Philosophical Library, 1951.

Kedourie, Elie. *England and the Middle East: The Destruction of the Ottoman Empire, 1914-1921.* London: Bowes & Bowes, 1956.

Kenez, Peter. *Civil War in South Russia, 1918: The First Year of the Volunteer Army.* Berkeley, Calif.: University of California Press, 1971.

Kinnane, Derek. *The Kurds and Kurdistan.* London: Oxford University Press, 1964.

Klieman, Aaron S. *Foundations of British Policy in the Arab World: The Cairo Conference of 1921.* Baltimore: Johns Hopkins University Press, 1970.

Kumar, R., ed. *Essays on Gandhian Politics: The Rowlatt Satyagraha of 1919.* Oxford: Clarendon Press, 1971.

La Chenais, P.-G. *Les Peuples de Transcaucasie pendant la guerre et devant la paix.* Paris: Editions Bossard, 1921.

Ladas, Stephen P. *The Exchange of Minorities: Bulgaria, Greece, and Turkey.* N.Y.: Macmillan, 1932.

Lang, David Marshall. *A Modern History of Georgia.* London: Weidenfeld & Nicolson, 1962.

Larcher, Commandant M. *La guerre turque dans la guerre mondiale.* Paris: Etienne Chiron, 1926.

Lawson, J.C. *Tales of Aegean Intrigue.* London: Edward Arnold, 1931.

Lewis, Bernard. *The Emergence of Modern Turkey.* 2nd ed., N.Y.: Oxford University Press, 1968.

Longrigg, Stephen Hemsley. *Iraq 1900 to 1950: A Political Social and Economic History.* London: Oxford University Press, 2nd ed., 1956.

Luckett, Richard. *The White Generals: An Account of the White Movement and Russian Civil War.* N.Y.: Viking Press, 1971.

Luke, Harry Charles. *Mosul and Its Minorities.* London: Martin Hopkinson, 1925.

MacDonell, Ranald, and Marcus Macaulay. *A History of the 4th Prince of Wales's Own Gurkha Rifles, 1857-1937.* 2 vols. Edinburgh: Blackwood, 1940.

Mack Smith, Dennis. *Italy: A Modern History.* 2nd ed. Ann Arbor, Mich.: University of Michigan Press, 1969.

Majumdar, R.C., ed. *Struggle for Freedom (History and Culture of the Indian People)*. Bombay: Bharatiya Vidya Ghava, 1969.

Marder, Arthur J. *From the Dreadnought to Scapa Flow*. Vol. II: 1914-1916, and Vol. V: 1918-1919. London: Oxford University Press, 1965, 1970.

Marston, F.S. *The Peace Conference of 1919: Organization and Procedure*. London: Oxford University Press, 1944.

Martin, Laurence W. *Peace Without Victory: Woodrow Wilson and the British Liberals*. New Haven, Conn.: Yale University Press, 1958.

Marty, Andre. *The Epic of the Black Sea*. London: Modern Books, [1940].

Maurice, Sir Frederick. *The Armistices of 1918*. London: Oxford University Press, 1943.

Mayer, Arno J. *Politics and Diplomacy of Peacemaking: Containment and Counter-revolution at Versailles, 1918-1919*. N.Y.: Knopf, 1967.

Mears, Eliot Grinnell. *Modern Turkey: A Political-Economic Interpretation, 1908-1923*. N.Y.: Macmillan, 1924.

Miroshnikov, L.I. *Iran in World War I*. Moscow: Oriental Literature Publishing House, 1963.

Mitra, H.N., ed. *Punjab Unrest Before and After*. Calcutta: N.N. Hitter, 1920.

Molesworth, Lt.-Gen. G.N. *Afghanistan 1919: An Account of Operations in the Third Afghan War*. London: Asia Publishing House, 1962.

Monroe, Elizabeth. *Britain's Moment in the Middle East, 1914-1956*. London: Methuen, 1965.

Mylès, Henri. *La fin de Stamboul. Le décor. Les survivances. Les fantomes humains. Les condres*. Paris: Editions E. Sansot, 1921.

Nash, Gerald D. *United States Oil Policy, 1890-1914: Business and Government in Twentieth Century America*. Pittsburgh: University of Pittsburgh Press, 1968.

Nevakivi, Jukka. *Britain, France, and the Arab Middle East, 1914-1920*. London: University of London, Athlone Press, 1969.

Niemeijer, A.C. *The Khilafat Movement in India, 1919-1924*. The Hague: Martinus Nijhoff, 1972.

Nikitine, Basile. *Les Kurdes: étude sociologique et historique*. Paris: Imprimerie nationale, 1956.

Oeconomos, Lysimachos. *The Martyrdom of Smyrna and Eastern Christendom: A File of Overwhelming Evidence, denouncing the Misdeeds of the Turks in Asia Minor and Showing their responsibility for the Horrors of Smyrna*. London: Allen & Unwin, 1922.

Paillarès, Michel. *Le Kémalisme devant les alliés*. Constantinople: Edition du 'Bosphore,' 1922.

Pallis, A.A. *Greece's Anatolian Venture—and After: A Survey of the Diplomatic and Political Aspects of the Greek Expedition to Asia Minor (1915-1922)*. London: Methuen & Co., 1937.

Palmer, Alan. *The Gardeners of Salonika*. London: Andre Deutsch, 1965.

Park, Alexander G. *Bolshevism in Turkestan 1917-1927*. N.Y.: Columbia University Press, 1957.

Paz, Maurice. *Les Révoltes de la Mer Noire.* Paris: Librairie du Travail, 1921.

Pech, Edgar. *Les Alliés et la Turquie.* Paris: Les presses universitaires de France, 1925.

Pernot, Maurice. *La question turque.* Paris: Bernard Grasset, 1923.

Pierce, Richard A. *Russian Central Asia, 1867-1917: A Study in Colonial Rule.* Berkeley, Calif.: University of California Press, 1960.

Poullada, Leon B. *Reform and Rebellion in Afghanistan, 1919-1929: King Amanullah's Failure to Modernize a Tribal Society.* Ithaca, N.Y.: Cornell University Press, 1973.

Price, Clair. *The Rebirth of Turkey.* N.Y.: Thomas Seltzer, 1923.

Psomiades, Harry J. *The Eastern Question: The Last Phase. A Study in Greek-Turkish Diplomacy.* Thessalonika: Institute for Balkan Studies, 1968.

Redan, Pierre. *La Cilicia et la problème ottoman.* Paris: Gauthier-Villars, 1921.

Reshetar, John S., Jr. *The Ukranian Revolution, 1917-1920: A Study in Nationalism.* Princeton, N.J.: Princeton University Press, 1952.

Robinson, Richard D. *The First Turkish Republic: A Case Study in National Development.* Cambridge, Mass.: Harvard University Press, 1965.

Roskill, Stephen. *Naval Policy Between the Wars.* Vol. I: 1919-1929. N.Y.: Walker & Co., 1968.

Rudin, Harry R. *Armistice 1918.* New Haven, Conn.: Yale University Press, 1944.

Sacher, Howard M. *The Emergence of the Middle East, 1914-1924.* N.Y.: Knopf, 1969.

Schlicklin, Jean. *Angora . . . L'Aube de la Turquie nouvelle (1919-1922).* Paris: Berger-Levrault, 1922.

Seaman, L.D.B. *Post-Victorian Britain, 1902-1951.* London: Methuen, 1967.

Shuster, W. Morgan. *The Strangling of Persia: Story of the European Diplomacy and Oriental Intrigue that Resulted in the Denationalization of 12 Million Mohammedans. A Personal Narrative.* N.Y.: Century Co., 1912.

Silverlight, John. *The Victor's Dilemma: Allied Intervention in the Russian Civil War.* London: Barrie & Jenkins, 1970.

Smith, C. Jay, Jr. *The Russian Struggle for Power, 1914-1917: A Study of Russian Foreign Policy During the First World War.* N.Y.: Philosophical Library, 1956.

Smith, Elaine Diana. *Turkey: Origins of the Kemalist Movement and the Government of the Grand National Assembly (1919-1923).* Washington, D.C.: privately printed, 1959.

Smith, Michael Llewellyn. *Ionian Vision: Greece in Asia Minor, 1919-1922.* N.Y.: St. Martin's, 1973.

Sousa, Nasim. *The Capitualtory Régime of Turkey: Its History, Origin, and Nature.* Baltimore: Johns Hopkins, 1933.

Stafford, Lt.-Col. R.S. *The Tragedy of the Assyrians.* London: Allen &

Unwin, 1935.

Suny, Ronald Grigor. *The Baku Communce, 1917-1918: Class and Nationality in the Russian Revolution.* Princeton, N.Y.: Princeton University Press, 1972.

Swettenham, John. *Allied Intervention in Russia, 1918-1919, and the Part Played by Canada.* London: Allen & Unwin, 1967.

Swinson, Arthur. *Six Minutes to Sunset: The Story of General Dyer and the Amritsar Affair.* London: Peter Davies, 1964.

Sykes, Brig.-Gen. Sir Percy. *A History of Persia.* 3rd ed. 2 vols. London: Macmillan & Co., 1930.

Taylor, A.J.P., ed. *Lloyd George: Twelve Essays.* London: Hamish Hamilton, 1971.

Thompson, John M. *Russia, Bolshevism, and the Versailles Peace.* Princeton, N.J.: Princeton University Press, 1966.

Thomson, Sir Basil. *The Allied Secret Service in Greece.* London: Hutchinson, 1931.

Titus, Murray T. *Islam in India and Pakistan: A Religious History of Islam in India and Pakistan.* 2nd ed. Calcutta: Y.M.C.A. Publishing House, 1959.

Toynbee, Arnold J. *The Western Question in Greece and Turkey: A Study in the Contact of Civilisations.* 2nd ed., London: Constable, 1923.

Trask, Roger R. *The United States Response to Turkish Nationalism and Reform, 1914-1939.* Minneapolis: University of Minnesota Press, 1971.

Trumpener, Ulrich. *Germany and the Ottoman Empire, 1914-1918.* Princeton, N.J.: Princeton University Press, 1968.

Ullman, Richard H. *Anglo-Soviet Relations, 1917-1921.* 3 vols. Princeton, N.J.: Princeton University Press, 1961-1972.

Vaidyanath, R. *The Formation of the Soviet Central Asian Republics: A Study in Soviet Nationalities Policy, 1917-1936.* New Delhi: People's Publishing House, 1967.

Waler, David. *The Chanak Affair.* London: Hutchinson, 1969.

Wandycz, Piotr S. *Soviet-Polish Relations, 1917-1921.* Cambridge, Mass.: Harvard University Press, 1969.

Wardrop, John Oliver. *The Kingdom of Georgia.* London: Samson & Low, 1888.

Watt, D.C. *Personalities and Policies: Studies in the Formulation of British Foreign Policy in the Twentieth Century.* South Bend, Ind.: University of Notre Dame Press, 1965.

Watt, Richard M. *The Kings Depart: The Tragedy of Germany: Versailles and the German Revolution.* N.Y.: Simon & Schuster, 1968.

Waugh, Sir Telford. *Turkey Yesterday, To-Day and Tomorrow.* London: Chapman & Hall, 1930.

Weber, Frank G. *Eagles on the Crescent: Germany, Austria, and the Diplomacy of the Turkish Alliance, 1914-1918.* Ithaca, N.Y.: Cornell University Press, 1970.

Webster, Donald Everett. *The Turkey of Atatürk: Social Process in the Turkish Reformation.* Philadelphia: American Academy of Political and

Social Science, 1939.

Wheeler-Bennett, John W. *Brest-Litovsk: The Forgotten Peace, March 1918.* London: Macmillan, 1938.

Wigram, Rev. W.A. *The Assyrians and their Neighbours.* London: G. Bell, 1929.

————. *The Assyrian Settlement.* London: S.P.C.K., 1922.

————, and Sir Edgar T.A. Wigram. *The Cradle of Mankind: Life in Eastern Kurdistan.* 2nd ed. London: A. & C. Black, 1922.

[Yalman], Ahmad Emin. *Turkey in the World War.* New Haven, Conn.: Yale University Press, 1930.

Zarevand [Zaven and Vartouhie Nalbandian]. *United Independent Turania: Aims and Designs of the Turks.* Trans. from Armenian by V.N. Dadrian. Leiden: E.J. Brill, 1971.

Zeine, Zeine N. *The Struggle for Arab Independence: Western Diplomacy and the Rise and Fall of Faisal's Kingdom in Syria.* Beirut: Khayat's, 1960.

Zenkovsky, Serge A. *Pan-Turkism and Islam in Russia.* Cambridge, Mass.: Harvard University Press, 1960.

Ziemke, Kurt. *Die neue Türkei: Politische Entwicklung, 1914-1929.* Stuttgart: Deutsche Verlags-Anstalt, 1930.

Index

Busch, Briton Cooper.
    Mudros to Lausanne : Britain's frontier in West Asia, 1918-
1923 / Briton Cooper Busch. — Albany : State University of
New York Press, 1976.

    430 p., [7] leaves of plates : maps ; 22 cm.

    Bibliography: p. [393]-414.
    Includes index.
    ISBN 0-87395-265-0

    1. Great Britain—Foreign relations—Near East.   2. Near East—Foreign re-
lations—Great Britain.   3. Near East—History—20th century.   I. Title.

DS63.2.G7B86   327.41'056   76-21641
                                                        MARC

Library of Congress   76